THE COYOTE CHRONICLES

A CHRONOLOGICAL HISTORY OF CALIFORNIA STATE UNIVERSITY, SAN BERNARDINO,

1960-2010

by

Michael Burgess

THE BORGO PRESS

An Imprint of Wildside Press LLC

MMX

Copyright © 2010 by Michael Burgess

All rights reserved.
No part of this book may be reproduced in any form
without the expressed written consent of the author
and the publisher.

www.wildsidebooks.com

FIRST EDITION

CONTENTS

Selected Bibliography 6

Introduction, by President Albert K. Karnig 7

Preface, by Retired Provost Louis A. Fernández 8

Acknowledgments 9

How to Use This Book 10

Abbreviations 11

Building Abbreviations 13

Key Dates 15

Building Openings and Renamings 17

In the Beginning: 1955-1962 19

The Administration of John M. Pfau: 1962-1982 23

The Interim Administration of Gerald M. Scherba:
    1982 170

The Administration of Anthony H. Evans: 1982-1997 175

The Administration of Albert K. Karnig: 1997-DATE 336

Major Campus Administrators 474

Afterword: Of the Making of Books 506

About the Author 508

Index 509

DEDICATION

To John M. Pfau,

Whose vision of the University
Has become a concrete reality;

and

To the memory of my dear friend,

J. C. Robinson
(1940-1998)

Now a part of history himself.

SELECTED BIBLIOGRAPHY

Administrative Council Minutes, 1975-Jul. 1984, Oct. 1995-Jun. 1997, Jan. 1998-DATE (the other dates appear lost).
Alumni Assoc. newsletters and magazines: *Panorama*, Jan. 1980-Jan. 1984, Feb. 1985-Spring 1991/92; *Cal State San Bernardino Magazine*, Fall 1992/93-Fall/Winter 2006/07 (Spring 1995/96 not published), *CSUSB Magazine* (Winter 2008-DATE).
Bulletin, Jan. 12, 1966-Feb.11, 2000 (not issued Sept. 17, 1999-Jan. 28, 2000).
Campus Archives (located in the John M. Pfau Library).
Campus newspapers: *Communique*, Nov. 9, 1965-Oct. 21, 1966; *Pawprint*, May 9, 1967-Nov. 23, 1983 (missing Oct. 28, 1966-Oct. 1967); *Cal State Chronicle*, Jan. 12, 1984-DATE.
Campus yearbooks: *T Tauri* (1967), *Casabo* (1968).
McAfee, Ward M. *In Search of Community: A History of California State University, San Bernardino*. San Bernardino, CA: California State University, San Bernardino, 1990.
Media and news releases (unpublished archive, John M. Pfau Library, CSUSB), 1966-84, 1986-DATE.
Newspaper clippings (unpublished archive, John M. Pfau Library, CSUSB), 1962-81, 1983, 1985-2005 (1969 & 1978 incomplete, missing Jul.-Dec. 1996).
San Bernardino Sun, 1962-DATE.
Schroeder, Peter. *Forty Years of English at CSUSB*. San Bernardino, CA: California State University, San Bernardino, 2006.

INTRODUCTION

by President Albert K. Karnig

A few weeks ago, the author of this history reminded me that I had just passed my 13th anniversary at Cal State San Bernardino. It doesn't seem possible more than a decade has elapsed since my arrival on campus—and yet as I page through this book, I realize that my time as custodian of this august educational institution represents just over a fourth of its history—13 years out of 48.

And what a history it's been, filled with drama, development, and heroes of all kinds! The men and women who built this university initially envisioned it as a liberal arts college—the so-called Dartmouth of the West. The academic standards they set were high, the student body and class size small. In order to graduate, those first Cal State students had to pass a foreign-language exam, and to take large numbers of general education classes.

But such a model proved impractical for a modern state university, and when enrollment began to plateau or even decline in the early 1970s, changes had to be made. The curriculum was modified, and the stage was set for the continued rapid growth of the campus.

At each stage of its development, CSUSB—and its administrators, faculty, and staff—have demonstrated a capacity for change. As the local community has changed, as the needs of the students have changed, we too have changed, adjusting our mission statement, goals, and curriculum development. The present school year marks another milestone (among so very many) in our history, with the offering of our very first engineering degree.

And who knows what the future will bring? I can hardly wait to see the marvelous new developments that Cal State will experience in the future. More programs, more buildings, more opportunities—all of these are certain. And so too is the legacy of CSUSB in fulfilling the educational needs of the diverse people of the Inland Empire.

PREFACE

by Emeritus Provost Louis A. Fernández

This is my final year at Cal State San Bernardino [written in 2009]. I came here from New Orleans in the summer of 1991 as Dean of the School of Natural Sciences, and later had the good fortune to be named VP of Academic Affairs and Provost.

These years have gone very quickly. During that time I've seen the campus double in size, and I've had the opportunity to work with tremendously talented colleagues at every level. So many things have happened, in fact, that it's hard to focus on just one or two. In paging through this chronological history of the University, I'm reminded of the many good times and the bad, of the major events and the minor, and of all the individuals who have appeared on this campus, thereby contributing to the enjoyment and education of students and faculty alike.

One is almost overwhelmed by the details—and the rush of memories that they bring. And while the parts and pieces of this book are interesting in and of themselves, it's the complete picture that they form that's important in the end: that of an actively developing and growing education institution moving into the twenty-first century.

I'm proud of my own contributions to CSUSB, while being all too aware that my efforts have been bolstered and made more effective by so many others on campus. I'll miss Cal State San Bernardino, where I've spent almost half of my professional life, but I'll treasure this history—and my many memories.

Ave utque vale.

ACKNOWLEDGMENTS

This book builds on the work of other individuals, particularly those of my friends and colleagues, Ward M. McAfee, whose pioneering work, *In Search of Community: A History of California State University, San Bernardino*, was published in 1989; and Peter R. Schroeder, whose delightful memoir, *Forty Years of English at CSUSB*, appeared in 2006.

I relied heavily on runs of the *(Friday) Bulletin* (published from 1966-2000) for source material, plus the student newspaper, the Campus Archives housed in the John M. Pfau Library, the *San Bernardino Sun*, newspaper clippings and releases, and the campus yearbooks. I also sifted through the memories of many early administrators and faculty, especially CSUSB Presidents John M. Pfau, Anthony H. Evans, and Albert K. Karnig, who were very accommodating and supportive.

Thanks also to William Aguilar, Sarah Baker, Lou Fernández, Cynthia Flores, Paul Garrity, Paul Johnson, Sandra Kamusikiri, Laurel Lilienthal, Maria Lootens, Trish McGuckian, Ross Moran, Karen Newman, Ken Phillips, Johnnie Ralph, Frank Rincón, Sid Robinson, Sam Romero, Sam Sarmiento, Kent Schofield, Jimmy Urata, Dale West, Joselyn Yap—and to all the others who answered my pesky little questions. Your help is much appreciated.

—Michael Burgess

HOW TO USE THIS BOOK

To locate a specific person, please consult the alphabetical index at the end of this book. The tables of administrators can help determine which individual held a specific office at a particular time, but the user should note that the titles of such offices have changed frequently over the years. When I say that a person is "named" to a particular position, I'm indicating that the date listed is when that individual actually assumed office, not when he or she was appointed. All cities, towns, and places listed without other attribution are assumed to be located within the state of California.

ABBREVIATIONS

Act.—Acting
AR—Alder Room, Commons
Arena—James and Arianthi Coussoulis Arena
ASB—Associated Student Body
ASI—Associated Students, Inc.
Assoc.—Associate/Association
Asst.—Assistant
Ave.—Avenue
Barnes Theatre—Ronald E. Barnes Theatre
Blvd.—Boulevard
Brown Hall—Jack H. Brown Hall
CAB—College Advisory Board
Calif.—California
CCU—Cross Cultural Center, Santos Manuel Student Union
Chair—Chairman/Chairwoman/Chairperson
Co.—Company
Coll.—College
Corp.—Corporation
CSC—California State College
CSCSB—California State College (at) San Bernardino
CSU—California State University (System)
CSUC—California State University and Colleges System
CSUSB—California State University, San Bernardino
CVC—Coachella Valley Center/Coachella Valley Campus
Dept.—Department
Dir.—Director
Dist.—Dist.
Div.—Division
Dr.—Drive
Emer.—Emerita/Emeritus
EOP—Educational Opportunity Program
ER—Eucalyptus Room, Commons
Exec.—Executive
FTE—Full-time equivalent (students)

Fullerton Art Museum—Robert V. Fullerton Art Museum
Gov.—Governor
Int.—Interim
L.A.—Los Angeles
LC—Lower Commons, Commons
LCP—Lower Commons Plaza/Patio, Commons
Lect.—Lecturer
Libn.—Librarian
Lt. Gov.—Lieutenant Governor
NSF—NSF
OA—Oliphant Auditorium, Palm Desert Campus
Off.—Office/Officer
OR—Oak Room, Commons
PDC—Palm Desert Campus
Perm.—Permanent
Pfau Library or Library—John M. Pfau Library
PiR—Pine Room, Commons
Pkwy.—Parkway
PL—John M. Pfau Library
PR—Panorama Room, Commons
Pres.—President
Prof.—Professor
Rep.—Representative
RH—Recital Hall, Performing Arts
SA—Seymour and Mignon Schweitzer Auditorium, Art Museum
S.B.—San Bernardino
Sen.—Senator
Soc.—Society
SR—Sycamore Room, Commons
SRFC—Student Recreation and Fitness Center
St.—Street
Sum.—Summer
SUC—(Santos Manuel) Student Union Courtyard
SUEC—(Santos Manuel) Student Union Events Center
SUMP—(Santos Manuel) Student Union Multipurpose Room
SUP—(Santos Manuel) Student Union Patio
SUT—Santos Manuel Student Union Theater
UAB—University Advisory Board
UC—Upper Commons/University of California
Univ.—University
VP—Vice President
WP—Wylie's Pub, Commons
WRI—Water Resources Institute

BUILDING ABBREVIATION CODES

AD—Administration
AF—Auto Fleet Services
AG—Animal Greenhouse (later AH—Animal House)
AH—Animal House/Vivarium
AS—Administrative Services
AV—Arrowhead Village Housing
BI—Biological Sciences
BK—Coyote Bookstore
C—Cafeteria Building (later CH—Chaparral Hall)
CA—Creative Arts (later PA—Performing Arts)
CC—Children's Center
CE—College of Education
CH—Chaparral Hall
CO—Commons
CS—Chemical Sciences
DD—University Center for Development Disabilities
ES—Environmental Health and Safety
FA—Fine Arts (later VA—Visual Arts)
FB—Foundation Building
FM—Facilities Management
FO—Faculty Office Building
FS—Facilities Services Storage
GF—Geology Lab
HA—HVAC Central Plant (originally Heating & Air Conditioning)
HC—Student Health Center
HP—Health and Physical Education/Coussoulis Arena
HS—Palm Desert Health Sciences Building, Palm Desert Campus
HU—Humanities Classroom (later CH—Chaparral Hall)
IC—Information Centers (#1—University Pkwy., #2—Coyote Dr.)
IWC—Indian Wells Center for Educational Excellence, PDC
IWT—Indian Wells Theater, Palm Desert Campus
JB—Jack H. Brown Hall
LC—Library-Classroom Building (later PL—John M. Pfau Library)

OT—Foundation Building Addition (Office of Technology Transfer)
PA—Performing Arts/Theatre/Recital Hall
PE—Physical Education
PK—Parking Structure (#1—West; #2—East)
PL—John M. Pfau Library
PP—Physical Plant (later PW—Plant/Central Warehouse)
PS—Physical Sciences
PW—Plant/Central Warehouse
RA—Residence Halls (later SV—Serrano Village Housing
RF—Student Recreation and Fitness Center
RG—Mary Stuart Rogers Gateway Building, Palm Desert Campus
S—Student Services (later SS, later SH—Sierra Hall)
SB—Social and Behavioral Sciences
SH—Sierra Hall
SS—Student Services (later SH—Sierra Hall)
SU—(Santos Manuel) Student Union
SV—Serrano Village Housing—BD (Badger), JS (Joshua), MJ (Mojave), MR (Morongo), SD (Shandin), SM (San Manuel), TR (Tokay), WA (Waterman)
T—Trailers (later TA/TC/TK/TO)
TA—Temporary Academic Modular Buildings
TC—Temporary Classrooms
TK—Temporary Kinesiology Annex
TO—Temporary Offices
UH—University Hall
UP—University Police
UV—University Village Housing
VA—Visual Arts Building (later CH—Chaparral Hall)
VA—Visual Arts Center/Robert V. Fullerton Art Museum
YC—Yasuda Center for Extended Learning

Campus parking lots—A, B, B Annex, Bio, C, D, E, F, G, H. L, M. **Palm Desert Campus lots**—A, B.

Named campus streets—Ash Dr., Athletics Dr., Berger Circle Dr. (PDC), Campus Dr. (Piedmont Dr. on early maps, but never actually used), Cook St. (PDC), Coyote Dr., East Campus Circle, Education Lane, Fairview Dr., Frank Sinatra Dr. (PDC), Little Mountain Dr. (originally Western Ave.), Museum Dr., North Campus Circle, Northpark Blvd. (originally North Park Circle Dr.), Serrano Village Dr., Sierra Dr., Thermo Dr., University Pkwy. (originally State College Pkwy., originally State St.), West Campus Circle.

KEY DATES

29 APR. 1960. Calif. Gov. Edmund G. "Pat" Brown Sr. signs into law Senate Bill 4, authorizing the creation of **San Bernardino-Riverside State College** (its first official name).

7 FEB. 1962. John M. Pfau takes office as first President of San Bernardino-Riverside State Coll.

8 FEB. 1963. The CSC Board of Trustees selects the S.B. site for the campus, renaming it **California State College at San Bernardino**.

1 DEC. 1964. Groundbreaking is held for the 3 initial buildings to be erected on 13 acres at the site for CSC in San Bernardino.

16 AUG. 1965. The first 3 campus buildings are occupied.

5 OCT. 1965. Classes begin for the first term on campus.

10 JUN. 1967. The first Commencement is held, with CSC Chancellor Dumke giving the keynote address for the initial 59 graduates.

25 JUL. 1968. The CSC Board of Trustees renames the campus **California State College, San Bernardino**.

22 JAN. 1971. Pres. Pfau appoints the first department chairs.

22 SEPT. 1972. The academic "Divisions" are renamed "Schools," their "Chairmen" becoming "Deans."

16 JUN. 1973. The campus awards its first M.A. degree.

24 NOV. 1980. The Panorama Fire burns several campus buildings.

13 FEB. 1981. Robert M. O'Brien is the 1st Outstanding Professor.

31 Jul. 1982. Gerald M. "Gerry" Scherba, VP for Academic Affairs, is named VP in Charge of CSCSB, replacing Pres. Pfau.

1 Nov. 1982. Anthony H. Evans takes office as 2nd President of CSC, San Bernardino, replacing VP in Charge Scherba.

23 Jul. 1984. The Calif. Postsecondary Education Commission renames the campus **California State University, San Bernardino**.

22 Sept. 1984. The campus plays in its first NCAA athletic contest.

1 Sept. 1989. The campus abandons the Ruml Plan, shifting from 5 unit credits granted per course to 4.

16 Aug. 1997. Albert K. Karnig takes office as 3rd President of CSU, San Bernardino, replacing Pres. Evans.

2 Nov. 1998. The academic "Schools" are renamed "Colleges."

16 Jun. 2001. W. Benson Harer receives the 1st honorary doctorate.

11 Oct. 2001. Coachella Valley Campus is renamed the Palm Desert Campus of CSU, San Bernardino.

8 Dec. 2001. The first Winter Commencement is held in the Arena.

17 Jun. 2002. The first building at the permanent Palm Desert Campus site in Palm Desert is occupied.

25 Oct. 2003. The Old Fire burns several campus buildings.

1 Sept. 2007. The campus begins offering its 1st doctoral degree.

BUILDING OPENINGS AND RENAMINGS

NOTE: The dates listed are the earliest known dates of occupancy by any campus tenant, or the dedication date, if no other date is known.

16 AUG. 1965. Administration, Library (later Student Services and Sierra Hall), and Cafeteria (later Fine Arts, Visual Arts, Humanities Classroom, and Chaparral Hall).
28 SEPT. 1967. Physical Science(s).
15 OCT. 1967. Biological Science(s).
5 JAN. 1968. Central Heating and Air Conditioning Facility.
11 OCT. 1968. Physical Education Building and old Gymnasium.
18 FEB. 1969. Physical Plant and Corporation Yard.
18 JAN. 1971. Library-Classroom (later John M. Pfau Library).
12 JUN. 1971. The ex-Library Building is renamed Student Services.
25 SEPT. 1972. Commons Building and Residence Halls (Serrano Village): No. 1 (Tokay), No. 2 (Arrowhead, later San Manuel), No. 3 (Joshua), No. 4 (Mojave), No. 5 (Morongo), No. 6 (Waterman), No. 7 (Badger), No. 8 (Shandin). The Cafeteria Building is renamed Fine Arts.
3 May 1974. Warehouse Receiving and Mail Building/Campus Stores.
4 JUN. 1977. Creative Arts (later Performing Arts) and Theatre.
19 SEPT. 1977. College Bookstore.
19 JAN. 1978. Student Union.
25 JUN. 1979. Student Health Center.
1 SEPT. 1980. The Fine Arts Building is renamed Visual Arts.
7 JAN. 1981. Child Care Center/Children's Center.
26 MAY 1982. Library-Classroom is renamed John M. Pfau Library.
7 FEB. 1985. College Bookstore is renamed Coyote Bookstore.
17 AUG. 1987. Faculty Office Building.
15 NOV. 1991. Foundation Building.
10 DEC. 1991. University Hall.
21 SEPT. 1993. Jack H. Brown Hall.
DEC. 1993. The Student Services Building is renamed Sierra Hall (between Dec. 3-Dec. 17).

17 JAN. 1994. Parking and Information Building.
21 JUL. 1994. John M. Pfau Library Addition.
26 SEPT. 1995. Health and Physical Education Complex and the James and Arianthi Coussoulis Arena.
23 OCT. 1995. Yasuda Center for Extended Education.
10 OCT. 1996. Visual Arts Center and Robert V. Fullerton Art Museum. The old Visual Arts Building is renamed the Humanities Classroom Building.
2 FEB. 1998. The Humanities Classroom Building is renamed Chaparral Hall.
1 JUL. 1999. University Police Building.
27 MAR. 2000. Creative Arts Building is renamed Performing Arts.
3 JUL. 2000. Facilities Management Building.
17 JUN. 2002. Mary Stuart Rogers Gateway Building at Palm Desert Campus.
10 SEPT. 2002. Social and Behavioral Sciences Building.
17 SEPT. 2002. Arrowhead Village Housing.
14 MAY 2003. The Student Union is renamed the Santos Manuel Student Union.
19 SEPT. 2004. University Village Housing.
29 NOV. 2004. Indian Wells Center for Educational Excellence and Indian Wells Theater at Palm Desert Campus.
5 JUL. 2005. The Office of Technology Transfer and Commercialization Building.
18 JAN. 2006. Chemical Sciences Building.
3 APR. 2007. Student Recreation and Fitness Center.
14 AUG. 2008. Palm Desert Health Sciences Building at Palm Desert Campus.
25 SEPT. 2008. College of Education Building.

IN THE BEGINNING

1955 - 6 FEBRUARY 1962

Senate Bill No. 4, Chapter 64, Statutes of the 1960 First Extraordinary Session of the California Legislature, provides that:

Section 1. Article 11 (commencing at Section 25201) is added to Chapter 13 of the Division 18 of the Education Code to read:

Article 11. State College for San Bernardino and Riverside Counties.

> 25201. There is hereby established a state college, to be located in San Bernardino County, to be known as the San Bernardino-Riverside State College.
>
> 25202. The provisions of Sections 23601 to 23607, inclusive, Sections 23651 to 23958, inclusive, Sections 24051 to 24703, inclusive, and Sections 24951 to 24954, inclusive, and all other laws pertaining to state colleges are applicable to the San Bernardino-Riverside State College.

29 April 1960

1955

UNKNOWN DATE. A study committee of the Calif. State Legislature concludes that there is a need for a State College serving the San Bernardino-Riverside area.

1959

UNKNOWN DATE. Calif. State Sen. Stanford C. Shaw states that he sees an excellent chance for the passage of a bill in the 60th session of the State Legislature, creating a state college to service the San Bernardino-Riverside area. "We are going to have a State College in the near future," he states, "and it apparently will start as a two-level institution, due to limited funds. My bill specifically provides that a state college shall be located in San Bernardino County."

5 JAN. 1959. Edmund G. "Pat" Brown takes office as 32nd Governor of California, replacing Goodwin J. Knight.

11 MAY 1959. Raymond H. Gregory takes office as 23rd Mayor of San Bernardino, replacing Elmer D. Kremer.

1960

29 APR. 1960. Gov. Brown signs a bill into law creating a State Master Plan for Education. He had called the State Legislature into special session to consider a report that he had commissioned on reorganizing California's system of higher education. The legislation puts the existing state colleges into an organized, partially self-governing structure called the California State Colleges System, headed by a Chancellor and a Board of Trustees. The original report had also recommended creating 2 new state colleges, the institutions later called CSU, San Bernardino and CSU, Dominguez Hills. Gov. Brown also signs into law Senate Bill 4, co-sponsored by State Sens. Stanford C. Shaw (D-Ontario) and Nelson S. Dilworth (R-Hemet), authorizing the creation of 2 new state colleges, including **San Bernardino-Riverside State College** (its official name), as part of the implementation of the report recommending a new State Master Plan for Education. The $600,000 appropriation that would have been used to begin construction of the new institution is stripped from the bill at the last minute, leaving the question of funding to the next fiscal year.

> **Stanford Clare "Stan" Shaw** was born 25 Apr. 1913 in Illinois, the son of Ralph E. and Alice G. Shaw. He moved with his parents to California, and grew up at Ontario, Calif. He attended Stanford Univ., and received his law degree from Loyola Univ. in 1945. After a brief private practice, he was appointed Justice of the Peace for Etiwanda Township in 1947. He lost an election as a Democrat for the Calif. State Assembly in 1948, but served 2 terms from 1951-56, and then in the State Senate from 1959-63, representing the 36th Dist. He died at Newberry Springs in San Bernardino Co. on 8 May 1993, just after his 80th birthday. His will provided for the creation of a scholarship at Cal State in his name.
>
> * * * * * * *
>
> **Nelson Smith Dilworth** was born 27 Jun. 1890 at East Palatine, OH, the son of Albert and Margaretta Dilworth. He served in the Assembly from 1936-44, and in the State Senate from 1944-60, representing the 37th Dist. He died at Hemet on 21 Jun. 1965.

1961

UNKNOWN DATE. The Calif. Legislature appropriates funds for the purchase of a site for San Bernardino-Riverside State College.

8 MAY 1961. Donald G. "Bud" Mauldin takes office as S.B. Mayor, replacing Raymond H. Gregory.

1 SEPT. 1961. Buell G. Gallagher is named first Chancellor of the CSC System, and Glenn S. Dumke is named Vice Chancellor.

1962

19 JAN. 1962. The CSC Board of Trustees selects John M. Pfau, Chair of the Social Sciences Div. at Sonoma State Coll., as the first President of San Bernardino-Riverside State College. He continues working at Sonoma until the end of Fall term there.

Senate Resolution No. 58, relative to the state college to be established in the San Bernardino-Riverside vicinity, is as follows:

WHEREAS, The Master Plan for Higher Education in California, which was submitted to the Legislature at the 1960 Regular Session recommends that a state college be established in the San Bernardino-Riverside vicinity, to be in full operation by 1965; and

WHEREAS, The enactment of Senate Bill No. 4 of the 1960 First Extraordinary Session will effect the establishment of this sorely needed institution of higher education and will serve to authorize the commencement of the several undertakings which will be required to make its planned availability in 1965 a reality; and

WHEREAS, The complexities involved in selecting and acquiring an appropriate site are such that these steps are ordinarily completed only after a period of from one to three years; and

WHEREAS, In view of the rapid rise in land values, which is prevalent throughout California as a whole and is particularly pronounced in the southern areas of the state, it is especially important that actions to select and acquire an appropriate site be commenced at the earliest possible time to the end that substantial savings in cost be realized through early acquisition;

NOW, THEREFORE, BE IT RESOLVED BY THE SENATE OF THE STATE OF CALIFORNIA, That the Director of Education is directed to undertake immediately all action necessary to the preparation of specifications and all of the other necessary steps appropriate for the early acquisition of a site for the state college proposed for the San Bernardino-Riverside vicinity, and that the Public Works Board is similarly directed to commence at once upon its several duties in connection therewith to carry the proceedings toward such acquisition to as near the point of consummation as is permissible under the provisions made by the Legislature in this respect; and

BE IT FURTHER RESOLVED, That the Secretary of the Senate is directed to transmit copies of this resolution to the Director of Education and to the Public Works Board.

THE ADMINISTRATION OF

JOHN M. PFAU

7 FEBRUARY 1962 - 30 JULY 1982

ABOUT JOHN M. PFAU

JOHN MARTIN PFAU was born 28 Apr. 1918 at Gakovo (also spelled Gakova or Gakowa), then part of the Voyvodina Region of the Austro-Hungarian Empire, later part of Yugoslavia, and now part of northwestern Serbia. He came to the United States with his parents, Anton and Anne Pfau, in 1921, settling in Chicago, Illinois. He earned his A.B. degree in American history from the Univ. of Chicago in 1947, his A.M. there in 1948, and his Ph.D. in 1951. He married Antreen McDonnell in 1942, and has 2 daughters, Madelaine and Ellen.

Dr. Pfau accepted a position in 1951 at Chicago Teacher's College (later Northeastern Illinois State Univ.), and quickly advanced to the position of Dean. He became Chair of the Dept. of Social Sciences and Prof. of History at Chico State College in 1959, taking a similar position as one of the founding faculty at Sonoma State College in the Fall of 1961. He was named President of California State College at San Bernardino in Jan. 1962, and served over 20 years, retiring in Jul. 1982. He and his wife currently live in Northern California.

His philosophy of education is highlighted in his inaugural speech, in which he said: "A college education may encompass many things, but primarily it must be an intellectual experience. If we do not provide for the student an atmosphere which arouses his intellectual curiosity and stimulates his mind, we have missed the mark.... That portion of the curriculum devoted to specialization must be constructed around the principle that nothing is more constant in modern life than change.... When one considers that the typical member of the first graduating class of this college will still be earning a livelihood in the year 2010, the need for adaptability becomes evident."

1962 (continued)

7 FEB. 1962. John M. Pfau takes office as the first President of San Bernardino-Riverside State College, being the first campus president selected by the new CSC Board of Trustees. His charge includes selecting a planning staff, finding a set of offices to act as the administrative center for the new institution, and beginning the hiring of administrators, faculty, and staff, as well as construction of the physical campus. He operates initially out of the Inglewood offices of the Chancellor of the CSC System at 2930 W. Imperial Highway.

12 FEB. 1962. Pres. Pfau makes his first appearance in San Bernardino, Calif., giving a speech before the 5th Annual Meeting of the Arrowhead United Fund (chaired by attorney Robert V. Fullerton, for whom the campus art museum is later named). There he outlines his vision of a liberal arts college servicing the Inland Empire.

14 FEB. 1962. Buell G. Gallagher, 1st Chancellor of the CSC System, abruptly resigns after just 5 months in office; Vice Chancellor Glenn S. Dumke assumes executive powers until a replacement is hired.

13 MAR. 1962. Pres. Pfau states in an appearance before the Riverside Co. Board of Trade that the CSC Board of Trustees has approved the new State College as a "maximum size" campus, requiring a site of at least 320 acres to house 20,000 students.

5 APR. 1962. Pres. Pfau distributes "Bulletin #1," the first issue of a newsletter relating to the development of the College. In it he mentions the appointment of Kenneth Phillips as Executive Dean, effective July 1, and notes the impending appointments of George L. McMichael, Robert G. Fisk, and Gerald M. Scherba.

6 APR. 1962. Glenn S. Dumke, Vice Chancellor of the CSC System, is named 2nd Chancellor by the CSC Board of Trustees.

28 APR. 1962. Pres. Pfau meets with several members of his planning staff at Chico.

5 JUN. 1962. An old house at 532 N. Mountain View in S.B. is razed, creating a site for the building of the College Planning Office Building; construction begins immediately on the new complex. State Proposition 3, a bond issue that would have provided construction money for the new State College, is defeated at the polls.

1 JUL. 1962. The College Planning Office opens for business in a building constructed during June by Arrowhead Building Corp. and developers Warner W. Hodgdon and Charles Racoosin north of the corner of Fifth and Mt. View at 532 N. Mountain View St. The structure, which includes 11 offices, a library, secretarial anterooms, and a conference room, is occupied by Friday, July 6. Leonard B. Farwell is named first Business Manager and the campus's first employee. Joyce Drayton is named Secretary to the President, the campus's first full-time clerical employee. Robert G. Fisk is named first Dean of Students. Kenneth Phillips is named first Exec. Dean. The first general secretary is Marjorie Sue Wallace, a student at UC Riverside.

12 JUL. 1962. A screening committee of the CSC Board of Trustees reduces the number of possible sites for the new state college from 26 to 5: Pellisier Ranch, at Center St. and Riverside Ave. in San Bernardino Co. on the Riverside Co. line, a mile west of I-215, adjoining the Santa Ana River (350 acres); Cooley Ranch, just southeast of the junction of I-10 and I-215 in Colton (325 acres); Morrow, on Pepper Dr. and Randall Ave. and adjoining Morrow Field airport ½ mile north of I-10 in Colton, Rialto, and San Bernardino (340 acres); Rialto, north of Foothill Blvd. on Linden Ave. in the City of Rialto (380 or 310 or 690 acres); and San Bernardino, in San Bernardino Co. north of the San Bernardino Airport, a mile east of I-15E (now I-215) and northwest of the San Bernardino City boundary (460 acres, of which 360 are level).

16 JUL. 1962. George L. McMichael is named first Dean of Faculty (initially called Dean of Instruction).

19 JUL. 1962. A group of CSC Trustees tours the 5 proposed sites for the new state college with Pres. Pfau.

1 AUG. 1962. Mary Helen Lybarger is named Secretary to the Exec. Dean.

1 SEPT. 1962. Gerald M. Scherba is named first Chairman of the Natural Sciences Div.

5 OCT. 1962. The Board of Directors of the S.B. Chamber of Commerce adopts a resolution supporting the efforts of S.B. Mayor Mauldin to secure the location of the new state college in S.B.

7 NOV. 1962. Calif. voters approve Proposition 1-A (the replacement for Proposition 3—see 5 June), providing $3,215,000 for development of the new state college, including $1 million for site acquisition, $985,000 for site development, $330,000 for master planning and working drawings, $800,000 to erect the first 3 buildings, and $100,000 for the first phase of library construction.

16 NOV. 1962. The S.B. Valley Coll. Board of Trustees, at the behest of Pres. H. J. Sheffield, adopts a resolution recommending that the new state college only be allowed to enroll juniors and seniors, reserving freshmen and sophomores to SBVC.

21 NOV. 1962. The Riverside Chamber of Commerce passes a resolution opposing the selection of S.B. as a college site, instead championing the Pellisier Ranch or Cooley Ranch sites.

20 DEC. 1962. Pres. Pfau states that the College site selection hearing before the CSC Board of Trustees has been postponed, likely delaying the campus opening from Sept. 1964 to Sept. 1965.

24 DEC. 1962. The S.B. Co. Board of Supervisors passes a resolution urging "full speed ahead" in the selection of a campus site.

1963

25 JAN. 1963. Albert C. Martin and Assocs. submits a study of the 5 proposed sites for the new college to the CSC Board of Trustees.

30 JAN. 1963. The S.B. Co. Board of Supervisors temporarily rezones the unincorporated areas around the 5 state college sites for residential use only.

4 FEB. 1963. The S.B. City Council passes Resolution #6641, stating: "That, upon selection of the San Bernardino site [by the Board of Trustees], the City will, in cooperation with the Board of Trustees, prepare and adopt a master plan for land use and development of all lands within the college zone of influence; that prior to the adoption of said master plan, an emergency ordinance will be adopted, restricting immediate land development to single family residential use." It also offers to donate 160 acres of land to the college, and extend all municipal services gratis to the campus. Gov. Brown proposes that $250,000 be set aside in the 1963/64 State budget to provide development money for the new campus, including $100,000 for plans and site development and $150,000 for the purchase of library books; he also recommends a further allocation of $207,849 for College operating expenses.

6 FEB. 1963. The S.B. City Board of Water Commissioners and the Valley Water Dist. state that they will "do everything legally possible and within [their] power to furnish and provide an adequate water supply" for the proposed college.

7 FEB. 1963. A public hearing is held before the CSC Board of Trustees to discuss the selection of a site for the proposed state college, with a 16-man delegation from S.B. attending, led by S.B. Mayor Mauldin, Chair of the Citizens Committee W. R. "Bob" Holcomb, and S.B. Chamber of Commerce Pres. Harold Zenz. Also present are Pres. Pfau, Dean McMichael, and Dean Phillips.

8 FEB. 1963. The CSC Board of Trustees, meeting in San Jose, selects the permanent site for San Bernardino-Riverside State College, comprising 590 (later cut to 429) acres on and near Badger Hill (also called Mt. McPherson) on the northwestern edge of the City of S.B. between the S.B. Airport and the S.B. Mountains; and renames the campus **California State College at San Bernardino**. The S.B. site is the least expensive of the 5 alternatives, costing $625,000; the land owners are the Harriet Munn estate; Marjorie M. Adams and Harriet S. Farley; Shandin Hills Development Co.; and Ryland M. Thomason, Mr. and Mrs. Newton E. Anderson, Mr. and Mrs. Eldon G. McPharlin, and Mr. and Mrs. William J. Connors. Pres. Pfau announces that the new campus will also build a basic library collection for the new South Bay Coll. in the Los Angeles area, in addition to its own; and that the first classes will be offered in Sept. 1965.

9 FEB. 1963. S.B. Mayor Mauldin tells the *San Bernardino Sun* that "I think this [the selection of S.B. as the college site] is the finest thing that has ever happened to San Bernardino. It can now hold its head high and feel proud of being the leading city of the Inland Empire. I feel the esthetics of this campus will make it one of the most attractive colleges anywhere." Pres. Pfau says: "I think the site selected is a very beautiful site and offers great potential."

12 FEB. 1963. The S.B. City Council approves a resolution to begin the lengthy annexation process for the S.B. Co. land where the new state college is located.

11 MAR. 1963. Dean Phillips states, in a letter to Pres. Pfau, Dean Fisk, Business Manager Farwell, and Chairman Scherba, that "Professional curriculum facilities need not be located as centrally on campus as are facilities for the Liberal Arts and Sciences and the Library. Furthermore, it is unlikely that such professional facilities will draw as much interest from the community. Therefore, they need not be as accessible to the community as other campus facilities."

1 APR. 1963. Arthur E. Nelson is named first College Librarian (at age 35, the youngest ever appointed in the Cal State System), initially operating out of the Campus Administration Building on Mountain View Ave.

8 APR. 1963. Frances Ríos is hired as the first Library employee.

3 MAY 1963. The S.B. City Council agrees to spend up to $10,000 to develop a planning and study zone of the area surrounding the new state college. The S.B. Co. Board of Supervisors approves a similar amount on 6 May.

15 MAY 1963. James W. Jones, Publisher of the *Rialto Record*, files an injunctive action lawsuit in Los Angeles Co. Superior Court against the CSC Board of Trustees, the City of S.B., and the State Public Works Board, seeking to block construction of the campus at the S.B. site, alleging that "certain trustees and certain of the public officials" who approved the site had "personal interests, direct or indirect, which were in conflict with their duties as public servants." He also states that S.B. City officials had promised to make gifts of land to the college that they had no authority or power to do, that the Trustees were given a false impression of the cost estimates for site preparation, and that the site is situated on the San Andreas Fault, has no adequate water supply, and has limited access to highways.

27 MAY 1963. Everett Grubb, General Manager of the Western Municipal Water Dist., states that a lawsuit filed by the City of Riverside, if successful, would severely limit the well water that S.B. could tap to supply the new state college.

3 JUN. 1963. Albert C. Martin and Assocs. submits a map to the CSC Board of Trustees delineating the parcels that need to be acquired by the Board to complete the acquisition of the new campus site for CSCSB: 195 acres in the northeast from McPharlin at a cost of $2,000 per acre, or $390,000 total, less a gift of $80,000; 160 acres in the west and northwest from Munn at a cost of $2,500 per acre, or $400,000 total, less a gift of $280,000; 65 acres in the south from Thomason at a cost of $3,000 per acre, or $195,000 total; 9 acres in the southwest from San Bernardino Co. (transferred without cost); for a grand total of 429 acres (346 acres level, 83 acres on Badger Hill) at a cost of $985,000, less $360,000 in gifts, for a final acquisition price of $625,000.

30 JUN. 1963. Robert R. Roberts, Assoc. Prof. of History at San Jose State College, is named first Chair of the Social Sciences Div.

SUM. 1963. Ellena Brothers of Cucamonga harvest 50 acres of its champagne vineyards on the CSCSB site for the last time; remnants of the vines continue to be visible on campus through the late 1970s.

1 JUL. 1963. James E. Segesta is named Head of Technical Services, being the first librarian to join the Cal State faculty—and thus the first faculty member who is not also an administrator.

12 JUL. 1963. Chancellor Dumke proposes a $21,800,000 budget for the 5-year construction of the initial buildings on campus. The CSC Board of Trustees adopts a resolution to purchase the land at the S.B. site for CSCSB:

California State College Board of Trustees' Resolution for California State College at San Bernardino:

RESOLVED, By the Trustees of the California State Colleges that the Trustees approve and, pursuant to Government Code Section 13854.1, recommend for acquisition by the State Public Works Board, as the permanent location for the California State College at San Bernardino, the site known as the "San Bernardino site" as delineated on the map (College Site Boundary Map) dated June 3, 1963 prepared by A. C. Martin and Associates, such approval and recommendation being subject only to the consummation of agreements satisfactory to the Chancellor, with the City of San Bernardino and such other parties as may be appropriate, for:

Acquisition of rights-of-way and construction of roadways for the following roadways as shown on the map dated June 3, 1963 prepared by A. C. Martin and Associates:

> North Park Circle Drive, from Riverside North-Piedmont Drive to Western Avenue; North Park from Western Avenue to Electric Avenue; Western Avenue from Kendall Drive to Badger Hill; and State Street from the Barstow Freeway to North Park Circle Drive; and

1. Availability of an adequate supply of water for said College.

And be it

RESOLVED further, That the Chancellor is authorized to cooperate with the State Public Works Board and the Property Acquisitions Division of the State Department of Finance in connection with the acquisition of said site.

RESOLVED further, That the Trustees acknowledge the offer of certain of the property owners to make cash gifts aggregating $280,000 in trust for the endowment of scholarships, public lectureships, student union facilities and similar programs of said College, and declare that it is the desire of the Trustees that such gifts be accepted in trust and devoted to such purpose, and be it

RESOLVED further, That the Trustees express their gratitude and warm appreciation for the cooperation and support of the City Council of the City of San Bernardino, the Board of Supervisors of the County of San Bernardino, the Steering Committee for the State College, the property owners and others who have subscribed gifts to complement the program of said College, and to the many other citizens, community groups and governmental entities who are supporting and assisting in the establishment of said College.

31 JUL. 1963. James H. Urata is named first Building Program Coordinator (later Building Coordinator).

1 AUG. 1963. The campus rents a warehouse at 731 S. Lugo St. in San Bernardino as the initial Library Building, with Coll. Libn. Arthur E. Nelson being charged with building two 50,000-volume collections, one for CSC at San Bernardino, and one for the "South Bay Campus" (later CSU, Dominguez Hills), the creation of which was authorized at the same time as CSCSB.

15 AUG. 1963. Assemblyman John P. Quimby, State Public Works Dir. John Erreca, State Finance Dir. Hale Champion, State Facilities Planner for the State Colleges Harry Harmon, and State Sen. Luther E. Gibson visit the CSCSB site.

1 SEPT. 1963. Seismologist Charles F. Richter is quoted in the *Ontario Daily Report* as recommending thorough soil testing of the proposed site for the new state college before construction. On Sept. 12, he is quoted in the *Rialto Record* as stating: "If there are other sites available out there, I'd say it would be better to build it [the campus] elsewhere."

5 SEPT. 1963. Pres. Pfau recommends, and the CSC Board of Trustees ultimately approves, a 3-3 quarter system for CSCSB, with students taking 3 courses each term (the so-called "Dartmouth Plan"), with most classes being offered either as large lecture or small discussion groups, eschewing the conventional classroom size of 30-50 students—and with an increased assignment of outside independent reading, lab work, and written papers.

30 SEPT. 1963. The S.B. City Council passes a resolution stating that it will supply the new State College campus with 1,142 acre-feet of water, charging the same rate it assesses other government users.

13 OCT. 1963. The CSC Board of Trustees hires LeRoy Crandall Associates to conduct soil tests of the CSCSB site.

14 & 21 OCT. 1963. The proposed master plan for the new CSCSB campus is discussed by joint meetings of the S.B. City Council and the S.B. Co. Supervisors.

17 DEC. 1963. The State Coordinating Council for Higher Education rejects the idea that the new campus be restricted to junior and senior students, as had been proposed by S.B. Valley College.

20 DEC. 1963. The state rejects the proposal by S.B. Valley Coll. that the CSCSB be restricted to junior and senior students.

22 DEC. 1963. Dean Phillips tells the *Riverside Press-Enterprise* that the College Planning Staff is preparing a master plan that includes a curriculum based on the ideas of Beardsley Ruml and Donald H. Morrison (as expressed in their book, *Memo to a College Trustee* [1959]), using a quarter instead of semester system on a five-credit-for-four plan, in which "reduced attendance in class is compensated for by assignment of increased outside written work, as well as increased independent reading and laboratory work." The key to this system is requiring that 22% of a student's classes be held in large lectures, plus restricting "an unnecessary proliferation of [small] courses," with the focus on general liberal arts classes that all students would have to take in order to graduate. The Chancellor's Office ultimately sees the Ruml Plan as saving operating costs if generally implemented, and approves it at CSCSB on a test basis.

1964

2 JAN. 1964. The State of Calif. pays $2,500 to the S.B. City School Dist. for a 1-acre plot located on the state college site, whose ownership was uncovered in a title search. The land had been donated to the Fairview School Dist. in 1888 to build and operate a 1-room schoolhouse, which was abandoned in 1899. The Fairview School Dist. was then taken over by the Arrowhead School Dist., which in turn was absorbed by the S.B. City School Dist. in 1924. The 1-room school site later becomes the subject of an archeological excavation by the campus (see 24 Jul. 1986).

23 JAN. 1964. The Committee on Educational Policy of the CSC Board of Trustees issues a mission statement for the new campus: "It is the purpose of The California State College at San Bernardino to provide opportunities for education in the finest tradition of the liberal arts and sciences. The College is committed to the proposition that while education may have many valuable purposes, it should be fundamentally an intellectual enterprise. Thus, the academic program of the College is designed to encourage intellectual growth, excellence in the basic skills of educated men, and ample exposure to the liberal arts and sciences." The Committee also approves the use of large lecture classes on the new campus.

27 JAN. 1964. The State Public Works Board approves the selection of the S.B. site for the new state college, ratifying agreements with the City of S.B. to provide water and access roads. This resolves all remaining disputes over the choice save the federal lawsuit filed by James W. Jones; however, Jones is quoted in the *Ontario Daily Report* as saying that he will let his suit "die a natural death." In August, Los Angeles Superior Court dismisses Jones's lawsuit with prejudice (meaning it cannot be refiled), thus removing the last legal impediment to building the college.

30 JAN. 1964. The S.B. City Council holds a special meeting to ratify an agreement with S.B. Co. for a joint planning study of the new State College site by Albert C. Martin and Associates.

23 APR. 1964. S.B. Co. begins legal proceedings to donate the 9-acre Kendall Park area to the College.

18 MAY 1964. Albert C. Martin & Associates presents the first of 2 reports on the economic impact of CSCSB to the S.B. City Council.

1 JUN. 1964. H. Stephen Prouty Jr. is named Dir. of Admissions and Records. Robert R. Roberts receives a $1,000 grant from the American Philosophical Soc. to do research on Rev. Washington Gladden.

30 JUN. 1964. Gov. Brown cuts $150,000 from the 1964/65 state budget that would have funded additional library books at CSCSB.

1 JUL. 1964. The campus leases offices in the Skinner Building on Arrowhead Ave. in S.B. to house the Admissions Off.

30 JUL. 1964. The CSC Board of Trustees requests $5,900,000 from the State Legislature for the construction of the initial buildings and physical plant at CSCSB. The State buys 195 acres of land comprising the northeast corner of the CSCSB site from Harriet S. Farley and Marjorie M. Adams at a cost of $311,000.

UNK. AUG. 1964. The campus issues its first *College Catalogue* (dated 1965/66). Claire Cantlay is named Secretary to the Dir. of Admissions.

3 AUG. 1964. The S.B. City Council annexes 1,340 acres on the northwest edge of S.B., including the CSCSB site, zoning it R1 (single-family residential); the Local Agency Formation Commission gives its approval on 26 Aug.

1 SEPT. 1964 (?). Ralph H. Petrucci is named first Chair of the Chemistry Dept.

21 SEPT. 1964. The State purchases the final 50 acres of land comprising the original 429-acre site for CSCSB.

1 OCT. 1964. C. Michael O'Gara is named first Chair of the Physical Education Dept. and Prof. of Physical Education. Herbert E. Brown is named first Dir. of the Physical Plant.

13 OCT. 1964. The State Off. of Architecture and Construction calls for bids on the construction of the first 3 buildings on campus.

14 & 21 OCT. 1964. The S.B. City Planning Commission and the S.B. Co. Planning Commission hold joint public hearings at S.B. City Hall to discuss the proposed San Bernardino State College Area General Plan.

13 NOV. 1964. J. D. Diffenbaugh Inc. receives a $1,138,430 contract to construct the 3 initial buildings at CSCSB, plus a parking lot.

16 NOV. 1964. The S.B. Co. Board of Supervisors and S.B. City Council conduct a joint meeting to approve the State College Master Plan on 16 Nov., and the City on 23 Nov.

1 DEC. 1964. Groundbreaking is held for the 3 initial 1-story buildings to be erected on 13 acres at the western edge of the CSCSB site: a 21,000-square-foot Administration Building; a 19,500-square-foot Library-Classroom Building; and a 15,300-square foot Science and Activity-Cafeteria Building. The complex also includes a 285-car parking lot located between the buildings and Northpark Blvd., plus walkways, a drainage system, lighting, and utilities. Present at the ceremony are Pres. Pfau, S.B. Mayor Mauldin, S.B. Co. Supervisor Paul J. Young, and contractor J. D. Diffenbaugh.

1965

7 JAN. 1965. The Social Lites, a local African-American women's social and civic organization, becomes the first group to establish a scholarship fund at CSCSB, donating $1,000, which is later augmented.

12 JAN. 1965. The campus begins distributing enrollment applications for the Fall 1965 term.

21 JAN. 1965. The CSC Board of Trustees approves the CSCSB master development plan.

25 JAN. 1965. Gov. Brown proposes a $6.6 million budget for 1965/66 to support the development of Cal State: $1 million in operating expenses, plus $5.6 million to fund construction of a Biological Science Building, a

Physical Education Building, a swimming pool, a Central Heating and Air Conditioning Plant, and support equipment, plus general site development.

15 FEB. 1965. Michael R. Abernathy becomes the first student to apply for admittance to CSCSB.

3 MAR. 1965. The CSC Board of Trustees approves the plans for a Physical Science Building at CSCSB.

24 MAR. 1965. Robert R. Roberts tells the Downtown Democratic Club in S.B. that the college will pioneer a new educational approach—the Ruml Plan—that will require more individual study time by students and less time in the classroom.

28 MAR. 1965. The Library receives a gift of 1,000 technical and scientific journals from Aerospace Corp., S.B. Operations.

3 MAY 1965. The *San Bernardino Sun* publishes an article stating that, contrary to the administration's expectations, half of the faculty being hired for CSCSB consists of junior professors straight out of graduate school.

10 MAY 1965. Al C. Ballard takes office as S.B. Mayor, replacing Donald G. Mauldin.

11 MAY 1965. The campus and S.B. City close off the dirt roads leading to Badger Canyon.

24 MAY 1965. The S.B. Co. Board of Supervisors renames State St. from Cajon Blvd. to the Barstow Freeway (later I-215), and thence to the campus, as State College Pkwy.

17 JUN. 1965. Construction workers go on strike, thereby delaying completion of State College Pkwy. from the freeway to the campus, and of North Park Circle Dr. along the southern campus boundary.

21 JUN. 1965. Pres. Pfau states in the *San Bernardino Sun* that the new campus will not develop intercollegiate sports.

7 JUL. 1965. The exit sign at the Barstow Freeway (now I-215) and State College Pkwy. is changed to reflect the 24 May name change from State St.

20 JUL. 1965. Ex-Rep. Harry R. Sheppard donates his collection of government documents to the Library.

1 AUG. 1965. Robert H. Ross is named Chair of the Humanities Div.

15 AUG. 1965. Kenton L. Monroe is named first Assoc. Dean of Counseling. The campus accepts the 3 initial buildings at CSCSB.

16 AUG. 1965. Administrative offices move from temporary quarters near Mountain View and 5th Streets to the Administration Building on the permanent campus site in northern S.B., and the Library begins moving its collection from its Lugo St. warehouse to what is now called Sierra Hall. This can be regarded as the official occupation date for the new campus.

31 AUG. 1965. Kenneth Phillips, Exec. Dean, resigns to become the founding Pres. of Metropolitan State College in Denver, Colorado.

1 SEPT. 1965. Dr. Samuel M. Plaut is named first Dir. of the Student Health Center, and Vivian McEachern the first registered nurse.

20 SEPT. 1965. *The San Bernardino Daily Sun and Evening Telegram* publishes a 48-page supplement, "San Bernardino's New State College," which includes a map of the surrounding area, a map of the campus showing its master development plan (projected through the year 2000), articles, and photographs of the new facility, stating: Academic standards at the new college will be high. A degree earned at [CSCSB] will command respect."

26 SEPT. 1965. Joseph K. Thomas, Campus Planning Official for the CSC System, is named Exec. Dean, replacing Kenneth Phillips.

27 SEPT. 1965. Orientation meetings begin on campus for the initial 273 students (193 FTES) planning to attend CSCSB, including 90 FTES freshmen and 103 juniors (sophomores and seniors were not enrolled until Sept. 1966). Classes are offered on the 5-for-4 credit hour "Ruml Plan," which also provides for additional annual augmentations to the Library materials budget, and the guarantee of single-member faculty offices. The Plan is facilitated by breaking the school year into quarters, and by dispensing with a departmental structure. At the beginning of CSCSB's first school year, its Administrators include: John M. Pfau, Pres.; George L. McMichael, Dean of Faculty; Robert H. Ross, Chair of the Humanities Div.; Gerald M. Scherba, Chair of the Natural Sciences Div.; Robert R. Roberts, Chair of the Social Sciences Div.; C. Michael O'Gara, Chair of the Physical Education Dept.; Joseph K. Thomas, Exec. Dean; Robert G. Fisk, Dean of Students; Arthur E. Nelson, Coll. Libn.; H. Stephen Prouty, Dir. of Admissions and Records; Leonard B. Farwell, Business Manager. 29 faculty and 61 staff are hired for the first term. The first-year operating budget is $1,060,000. The campus initially offers majors in English, French, Spanish, History, Political Science, Mathematics, and Biology. To graduate, students must take half of their units in general education courses, demonstrate proficiency in English as well as a foreign language, participate in a college-wide reading program, and pass a comprehensive exam.

1 OCT. 1965. The CSC Board of Trustees appoints the first Coll. Advisory Board: Earl "Tiny" Wilson, Exec. Secretary of the Central Labor Council, AFL-CIO, of San Bernardino, Vice Chair of the Redevelopment Agency of the City of S.B., and a Dir. of the S.B. Co. Fair; Wilma (Mrs. Don H.) Goodcell, wife of the Dir. of Public Service for The Sun Co.; Leslie I. Harris, Pres. and General Manager of The Harris Co.; James A. Guthrie, Editor Emer. of *The San Bernardino Sun-Telegram*; Leroy Hansberger, Pres. of Tri-City Concrete Co. and VP of the Regional Economic Development Council; and Hayes Hertford, Riverside citrus grower and Pres. of the Board of Directors of Gage Canal Co.; Dr. Henry W. Holder, a physician at Patton State Hospital, is added on 14 Oct. The Library receives a gift of 850 journals from Aerospace Corp.

5 OCT. 1965. Classes begin for the first term on campus.

12 OCT. 1965. CSC Chancellor Dumke proposes a 2nd-year operating budget of $1,700,000 for CSCSB.

20 OCT. 1965. CSC Chancellor Dumke and aides visit the campus; he praises the new college for its "significant pioneering in curriculum planning…. I think this will develop into one of the leading institutions in the state."

21 OCT. 1965. Dean Fisk calls the first meeting of the Student Organization Committee (SOC), precursor to the Associated Student Body (ASB); Richard J. Bennecke is elected first Chair.

25 OCT. 1965. Pres. Pfau speaks before the Redlands Democratic Club to discuss the development of the new campus.

9 NOV. 1965. *Communique*, the first newspaper of the Cal State student body, appears as a mimeographed publication.

17 NOV. 1965. Retired Army Col. Herbert E. Brown, new Dir. of the Physical Plant, receives the Legion of Merit from Pres. Lyndon B. Johnson, honoring his service with the Army Corps of Engineers.

19 NOV. 1965. The campus hosts its first student dance.

30 NOV. 1965. A ribbon-cutting ceremony on the Devils Canyon Channel Bridge marks the official opening of State College Pkwy. (later University

Pkwy.), a $180,000, 4-lane reworking of the old, unsurfaced State St. and Devils Canyon Rd. linking CSC at San Bernardino to the Barstow Freeway (then Federal Highway 395, later Interstate 15E [1972], now Interstate 215). Attendees include S.B. Mayor Ballard and S.B. Co. Supervisor Paul J. Young.

1 DEC. 1965. *Facts Shoppers' Guide* (a supplement of the *Redlands Daily Facts*) notes that the yet-to-be-constructed Library Building will be the "theme building" erected at the very center of campus, denoting the centrality of intellectual curiosity and exploration.

8 DEC. 1965. The Library acquires a "Ducostat" machine; photocopies are 10¢ per page.

1966

12 JAN. 1966. The *CSCS Bulletin* (sometimes called *The Friday Bulletin*) begins publication. This weekly newsletter is a primary source for news and information for the early years of the Cal State campus. The periodical becomes *The Bulletin* with its Jan. 24 issue, and continues to be issued in physical form through Feb. 11, 2000.

17 JAN. 1966. A Santa Ana windstorm impacts the campus.

19 JAN. 1966. The CSC Board of Trustees approves schematics for the construction of the $4.4 million Library-Classroom Building.

25 JAN. 1966. ASB conducts campus-wide elections for the first time, ratifying the School Constitution, and choosing Richard J. Bennecke as Pres., John Kirwan at VP, Paul Leithner as Treasurer, Mark Mollet as Junior Class Pres., and Terry Nicholson as Freshman Class Pres. The students also pick the college mascot, the golden condor (chosen over badgers, Saint Bernard dogs, and Sumerians), plus school colors of brown and gold. 183 students vote out of a class of 236. In a runoff election held on Jan. 27, Sandra Bergstrand is elected Secretary.

27 JAN. 1966. The campus receives a $600 gift from the Social Lites Club to add to its scholarship fund.

28 JAN. 1966. A framed copy of the new School Constitution is presented to Pres. Pfau, with the attendance of S.B. City Mayor Ballard and City Councilmen Alan Guhin and Robert D. Henley.

31 JAN. 1966. Robert L. West is named Prof. of Education and first Chair of the Education Dept.; this position is the precursor to the Dean of the Coll. of Education.

9 FEB. 1966. The campus awards a contract for the construction of the Physical Education Building and Gymnasium

15 FEB. 1966. The students adopt a $6.50-per-quarter fee to support ASB activities by a one-vote margin (104-50) over the ⅔ required.

19 FEB. 1966. The campus receives a $250 gift from the S.B. Junior Women's Club to support the Student Loan Fund.

22 FEB. 1966. Entomologist Mir S. Mulla speaks on "Pesticides—Their Wildlife Relationships."

24 FEB. 1966. Forsberg and Gregory receive a $1,500,000 contract to construct the Biological Science Building.

28 FEB. 1966. The campus begins planting 800 trees, shrubs, and grass around the 3 original buildings, including evergreen pears, black alders, olive, camphor, eucalyptus, and a loquat.

4 MAR. 1966. The campus shows the first film in its Foreign Film Series, *Ikiru*.

10 MAR. 1966. The Drama and Music Depts. co-sponsor a one-time presentation of Eugène Ionesco's *The Bald Soprano* in C-116.

15 MAR. 1966. J. Putnam Henck Co. receives a $1,501,346 contract to construct the Physical Science Building. The campus announces that 4 new majors—Chemistry, Sociology, Business Administration, and Psychology—will be offered in 1966/67.

18 MAR. 1966. Russell J. DeRemer receives a NSF fellowship at Texas A & M Univ. for summer 1966.

24 MAR. 1966. The Coll. Library receives a $210 gift from the S.B. Dist. 21 Women's Clubs to purchase books.

25 MAR. 1966. Groundbreaking is held for the Biological Science and Physical Science Buildings, with the attendance of S.B. Mayor Ballard, City Councilman Alan Guhin, architects Wendell Mounce and Whiting Thompson, CSC Chief Facilities Planner Harry Harmon, CSC Dean of Academic Planning Ellis E. McCune, and contractor J. Putnam Henck.

29 MAR. 1966. Peter T. Marcy, Asst. Prof. of History, is named Assoc. Dean for Academic Administration and Dir. of Summer Session. C. Michael O'Gara (Physical Education), Fernando Peñalosa (Sociology), and Alexander D. Sokoloff (Zoology), are promoted to full Professor, effective

Sept. 1966, being the first members of the CSCSB faculty to be advanced in rank.

1 APR. 1966. Historian John G. A. Pocock speaks in C-116 on "Political Time: A Dimension of Political Theory."

5 APR. 1966. The students vote for a 2nd time on a school mascot and colors, choosing the St. Bernard dog, and brown and light blue.

14 APR. 1966. The campus creates the State College Faculty Wives booster group, which conducts its first event, a Spring Dinner at the Rancho Verde Country Club, on this date.

1 MAY 1966. R. Joy Robertson is named Purchasing Officer.

2 MAY 1966. The campus receives a $365,110 grant from the Higher Education Facilities Act to help construct the Physical Education Building and Gymnasium.

4 MAY 1966. John M. Pfau is inaugurated as first Pres. of CSC at San Bernardino on the Mall between the 3 original buildings. Attendees include: CSC Chancellor Dumke, who installs the new executive; Lt. Gov. Glenn M. Anderson; Alan Simpson, Pres. of Vassar College, who provides the keynote address, "A Livable Environment"; Rev. John Ryan, who provides the invocation; Ralph Bradshaw, Pres. of Riverside City College; State Sen. Gordon Cologne; David Bieber, Pres. of La Sierra College; and CSC Trustees Charles Luckman and Herman H. Ridder. The March Air Force Base Band provides the processional and recessional music. That evening, Gov. Brown speaks at a black-tie dinner in the Empire Room at the National Orange Show in S.B. to honor newly inaugurated CSCSB Pres. John M. Pfau, and states that the state's investment in the campus has gone "to insure that all able and willing young Californians shall not be denied the benefits of quality education"; ex-S.B. Mayor and State Sen. James E. Cunningham, now a Judge of the S.B. Co. Superior Court, presides over the ceremony. The S.B. City Council and the S.B. Co. Board of Supervisors each contribute $3,000 to support the event.

5 MAY 1966. The Calif. State Legislature adopts a joint resolution congratulating the new campus, co-sponsored in the Assembly by Stewart Hinckley and John P. Quimby, and in the Senate by Eugene G. Nisbet and Gordon Cologne. The resolution reads in part: "The California State Colleges are dedicated to educating the youth of California in order they may better cope with the complexities of modern society; and.... The California State College at San Bernardino was created to fulfill the expanding educational needs of the State of California and...meet the growing educational requirements of the counties of San Bernardino and Riverside. This state college at San Bernardino has been extremely fortunate in having Dr. John Pfau as its first president, for it has been in large part due to his outstanding ability, reputation, and energy that this college has acquired its gifted and distinguished faculty."

6-7 & 13-14 MAY 1966. The campus hosts the 1st drama produced on campus, Jean-Paul Sartre's *No Exit*; to commemorate the first school of acting created in ancient China (the so-called "Young Folk of the Pear Garden"), the production group is named "The Players of the Pear Garden" by Ronald E. Barnes, Assoc. Prof. of Drama.

12 MAY 1966. The campus receives an $808,916 grant from the Higher Education Facilities Act to help construct the Physical Science Building.

15 MAY 1966. The College holds its 1st all-campus cookout at Wildwood Park on the corner of Waterman Ave. and 40th St.

17 MAY 1966. Poet James Dickey, the 1st writer to appear on campus, reads from his work in C-116.

24 MAY 1966. Historian Van L. Perkins speaks on "American Affluence: Basis for Greatness or Prelude to Decline?"

25 MAY 1966. The Coll. Library holds an open house for 130 librarians from Riverside and San Bernardino Counties.

26 MAY 1966. The campus receives a $761,000 grant from the U.S. Higher Education Facilities Act to help build the Biological Science Building.

30 MAY 1966. The State College Faculty Wives elect Arie L. Marcy, wife of Peter T. Marcy, as their 1st President.

1 JUN. 1966. Doyle J. Stansel is named Dir. of Placement and Financial Aid.

5 JUN. 1966. Pres. Pfau is presented with a scroll by the Board of the Directors of the S.B. Chamber of Commerce honoring him for his "outstanding leadership in higher education."

11 JUN. 1966. A student dance is held at the Mission Inn in Riverside, CA, featuring music by the Lamplighters. The campus's first yearbook, *T Tauri*, is published.

23 JUN. 1966. The campus receives a $7,999 grant from the U.S. government to purchase audiovisual equipment and to begin development of a closed-circuit TV system.

15 JUL. 1966. James E. Segesta, Technical Services Libn. and the 1st faculty member not also an administrator on campus (1963-66), resigns; he later becomes a librarian at CSU, Bakersfield.

23 AUG. 1966. James Alan Guthrie, a member of the first CAB, dies at age 77.

31 AUG. 1966. George L. McMichael, Dean of Faculty, returns to the ranks as Prof. of English. Robert G. Fisk, Dean of Students, returns to the ranks as Prof. of Education.

1 SEPT. 1966. Gerald M. Scherba, Chair of the Div. of Natural Sciences, is named Act. Dean of Academic Affairs, replacing George L. McMichael. Kenton L. Monroe, Assoc. Dean of Counseling, is named Dean of Students, replacing Robert G. Fisk. Ralph H. Petrucci is named Act. Chair of the Div. of Natural Sciences, replacing Gerald M. Scherba. Jesse Hiraoka is named Act. Chair of the Humanities Div., replacing Robert H. Ross. G. William Hume is named Assoc. Dean of Activities and Housing.

27 SEPT. 1966. The campus receives a gift of ties from Southern Pacific Railroad to mark off spaces in the temporary parking lot.

1 OCT. 1966. Pres. Pfau sponsors a reception for returning students, which is followed by a dance for students and their guests on the Mall in front of the Library, with music by The Other Guys.

7 OCT. 1966. The Library receives a gift of the Freedom Shrine from the Downtown Exchange Club of S.B., with reproductions of the major documents relating to the founding of the United States.

14 OCT. 1966. A student editorial in *Communique* protests the required campus Reading Program.

21 OCT. 1966. The final issue (Vol. 2, No. 4) of *Communique* is published. The name of the campus newspaper changes to *The Pawprint* with the next issue, reflecting the new campus mascot.

21 OCT. 1966. Clifford Langley receives a contract to construct the Physical Plant-Grounds Equipment Storage Building.

19 DEC. 1966. The campus announces that majors in Physics, Music, and Art will be offered in Fall 1967.

21 DEC. 1966. The campus awards contracts of $801,459 to J. Putnam Henck, Hansen Plumbing and Heating Co., and Mark Cox Electric to construct a utility tunnel connecting the Air Conditioning Plant with the 2 science buildings under construction.

1967

2 JAN. 1967. Ronald W. Reagan takes office as Governor of California, replacing Edmund G. "Pat" Brown Sr.

6 JAN. 1967. The campus receives approval for new B.A. degrees in physics, art, and music, beginning with 1967/68.

10 JAN. 1967. Soprano Marie Gibson performs at 2 noon concerts.

12 JAN. 1967. Pres. Pfau addresses a faculty meeting to announce a temporary freeze in enrollment in the CSC System, and a reduction in faculty recruitment.

27 JAN. 1967. Jesse Hiraoka, Act. Chair of the Humanities Div., is named permanent Chair.

10 FEB. 1967. Joyce Drayton, the campus's first full-time clerical employee (1962-67), resigns.

17 FEB. 1967. State Sen. Gordon Cologne and Assemblyman John P. Quimby speak on the Cafeteria Patio, presenting arguments for and against the idea of tuition being charged in the CSC System.

20 FEB. 1967. The campus opens a Saturday information booth for visitors, staffed from 11 A.M. to 3 P.M.

3 MAR. 1967. The Motor Enthusiasts Club holds a "Gimmick Rallye: Lost I" in the campus parking lot. Doris Ward, first Secretary in President's Off. (1963-67), resigns.

7 MAR. 1967. The campus receives a $100 gift for the Student Loan Fund from Del Rosa Grange Number 711.

17 MAR. 1967. Leo Kreter performs "How About a Sonata with Lunch?" in the Cafeteria.

18 MAR. 1967. Chella Dean Moore, campus booster, dies at age 77.

31 MAR. 1967. The first CSCSB chapter of the Calif. State Employees Assoc. (CSEA) is formed by Fred Cordova. Lucas G. Lawrence is named first Dir. of Audio-Visual Services.

11 Apr. 1967. George W. Strem speaks in C-110 on "Three Aspects of Agnostic Ethics."

14 Apr. 1967. The campus forms a College Union Committee to develop plans for a Student Union building. The campus establishes a Dean's List to honor full-time students with grade points above 3.5.

19 Apr. 1967. Fred Waters speaks in L-117 on "Matrix Algebra."

21 Apr. 1967. The campus receives a $14,000 grant from the U.S. Dept. of Health, Education, and Welfare to support the EOP.

27 Apr. 1967. The campus receives a $12,600 grant from NSF to support an In-Service Institute in Chemistry for teachers of science in local high schools.

28 Apr. 1967. Folksinger Sam Hinton performs on the Cafeteria Patio.

3 May 1967. V. Merriline Smith speaks in L-117 on "Symmetry."

9 May 1967. The first issue of *The Pawprint* printed through an offset process appears; the newspaper's name is suggested by Rosemarie Gonzáles to reflect the College mascot.

12 May 1967. Peter T. Marcy, Dir. of Summer Session and Assoc. Dean for Academic Administration, resigns, and is partially replaced by Robert L. West as Dir. of Summer Session. Coast State Builders receives a $1,115,000 contract to build the Gymnasium and Swimming Pool.

19 May 1967. 300 students and faculty conduct a "Bitch-in" to protest a CSCSB requirement that they pass a comprehensive exam in order to graduate; the exam is abolished 2 years later. A faculty member states: "Such a gathering shows there is life in the school."

20 May 1967. Erin Rollins is crowned Casabo Queen of CSCSB at the Casabo Dance.

22 May 1967. At the first organization meeting of the new CSEA Chapter of CSCSB, Fred Cordova is elected Chair. The chapter is given the designation "Badger Hill No. 184" in July.

24 May 1967. Aletha Lorber is named Senior Woman of the Year at the Theta Psi Omega (ΘΨΩ) Installation Banquet. U.S. Secretary of the Navy Paul B. Fay Jr. speaks in C-116 on "John F. Kennedy." CSCSB receives a matching $6,200 grant from NSF to purchase electronic calculators.

25 May 1967. The campus creates The Alumni Assoc., with 6 former students meeting in the Library Building.

27 May 1967. Zeta Pi (ZΠ), the CSCSB chapter of the Spanish Honor Soc., Sigma Delta Pi (ΣΔΠ), is installed on campus.

1 Jun. 1967. The S.B. Chamber of Commerce honors 7 graduating seniors from the first class at a lunch at the Holiday Inn, with James K. Guthrie, Publisher of the *San Bernardino Sun-Telegram*, giving the keynote address, honoring: Geraldine Ruth Brame, Charlene Kaye DeBranch, Aletha Lorber, Claudia Peterson, Carl Sundin, Clemens Tarter, and Dorothy Wissler.

6 Jun. 1967. Groundbreaking is held for the Physical Education Building, with Physical Education Dept. Chair C. Michael O'Gara digging the first hole with his golf club.

9 Jun. 1967. Joyce Hauber is named Manager of the Cafeteria, replacing Laurie Howard.

10 Jun. 1967. The 1st Commencement is held at 5:30 PM on the Mall between the 3 original buildings, with CSC Chancellor Dumke giving the keynote address, "Frontiersmen in Higher Education," before an audience of 750. The initial graduating class at Cal State consists of 59 students, with 5 receiving honors: Geraldine Ruth Brame, Charlene Kaye DeBranch, Aletha Lorber, Claudia Peterson, and Dorothy Wissler.

15 Jun. 1967. R. O. Boyette Co. receives a $5,843 contract to landscape the area behind the Administration Building.

19 Jun. 1967. The campus offers its first "Summer Session" classes.

7 Jul. 1967. Pres. Pfau is named to the State Accreditation Committee of the State Board of Education.

14 Jul. 1967. The campus receives a $1,622,426 grant from the U.S. Dept. of Health, Education, and Welfare to help build the Library-Classroom Building scheduled for completion in Sept. 1969.

21 Jul. 1967. Gerald M. Scherba is elected Pres. of the S.B. Co. Museum Assoc.

28 Jul. 1967. Frances Ríos, Secretary to the Coll. Libn. (1963-67), resigns.

1 Aug. 1967. John M. Hatton is named Assoc. Dean of Counseling and

Testing.

4 AUG. 1967. Triangle Construction Co. receives a contract from S.B. City to construct a two-lane section of Western Ave. from Kendall Dr. to Northpark Blvd., and extend Northpark Blvd. from its new intersection at Western Ave. to the main entrance of the campus at State College Pkwy., and thence north to the campus parking lot and the levee marking the northern boundary of the College. Work on the new roads begins on Aug. 10.

18 AUG. 1967. The campus receives approval to offer a B.A. degree in Drama, effective with the 1968/69 school year.

1 SEPT. 1967. James H. McKone is named Publications Manager. James T. Freeman is named Dir. of Institutional Studies. Ralph H. Petrucci, Act. Chair of the Natural Sciences Div., is named permanent Chair.

5 SEPT. 1967. The campus bus stop is moved to an area southwest of the Library adjoining the parking lot.

11 SEPT. 1967. Frank Mardis Amy, who had graduated in June, is killed in an automobile accident at age 32, becoming the first Cal State alumnus to die.

15 SEPT. 1967. 20 faculty members occupy their offices in the new Physical Science Building, thereby marking its opening.

18 SEPT. 1967. The 2nd campus yearbook, *Casabo*, is published in a 100-copy print run under the editorship of Linda Luetcke and Cheryl Porter. A sculpture by Richard Manchester Hetrick, "The Dynamism of an Atom," is unveiled in the Physical Science Building courtyard.

19 SEPT. 1967. The annual convocation is held in PS-10.

20 SEPT. 1967. Bud Hutchinson, Exec. Secretary of the College Council of the American Federation of Teachers, AFL-CIO, states at a meeting of the CSC Board of Trustees that a system-wide faculty strike will be called unless the Trustees allow faculty collective bargaining. Kenneth Phillips, ex-Exec. Dean and first Pres. of Metropolitan State College in Denver, is honored with a luncheon.

28 SEPT. 1967. The Physical Science Building opens for business, thanks to last-minute work by campus personnel.

5 OCT. 1967. Enrollment exceeds 1,000 students for the first time, with 1,002 registered (850 full-time equivalent [FTES]), a 67% increase over

1966. The campus parking lots, whose capacity is only 730 vehicles, are overwhelmed by the unexpected surge.

7 OCT. 1967. Folksinger Clabe Hangan performs at the Activities Day celebrations.

10 OCT. 1967. Carl Dolmetsch and the Dolmetsch-Schoenfeld Ensemble perform in PS-10.

15 OCT. 1967. The Biological Science Building opens for business.

16 OCT. 1967. Dorothy Strack is named Manager of the CSCSB Cafeteria, replacing Joyce Hauber.

19 OCT. 1967. Alexander D. Sokoloff receives a $32,200 grant from NSF to support the transfer of his tribolium beetle stock center from UC Berkeley to CSCSB. Psychiatrists Duke Fisher and J. Thomas Ungerleider speak on "LSD and Young People."

20 OCT. 1967. A handful of students picket on the campus mall, calling for an end to the Vietnam War.

25 OCT. 1967. The Alumni Assoc. conducts its first public meeting; 58 alumni (graduates of the class of 1967) are polled by mail to elect the first officers of the group, with Richard J. Bennecke being named Pres., Peter Shapiro VP, Aletha Lorber Secretary, and Dorothy Wissler Treasurer.

26 OCT. 1967. *The Underdog*, an underground newspaper edited by George Anderson Jr., debuts on campus. The CSC Board of Trustees rejects a proposal to allow collective bargaining for faculty.

7 NOV. 1967. S.B. Mayor Ballard speaks in PS-10. A forum is held to discuss the possibility of intercollegiate athletics.

14 NOV. 1967. Pianist Dottie Ogle Nix performs in PS-10.

15 NOV. 1967. The campus hosts the first of a series of Philosophy Forums featuring a panel of faculty members.

17 NOV. 1967. Jean Atterbury is named Cafeteria Manager, replacing Dorothy Strack. The campus receives permission to offer a B.A. degree in Philosophy, beginning Fall 1968.

21 NOV. 1967. Thomas F. Evans speaks in PS-122 on "The Systems Approach to Community Development."

1 DEC. 1967. C. Carl Johnson Jr. is named first Chief of Campus Security, and is asked to organize a campus police force. The campus hosts a workshop on the National Defense Education Act.

5 DEC. 1967. The first officers of the campus chapter of CSEA are installed: Fred Cordova, Pres.; Dale Lohmuller, First VP; Leo Kreter, Second VP; Birdene Lewis, Exec. Secretary; Joanna Funner, Recording Secretary; John E. Fredricks, Treasurer. Tran Van Dinh, ex-Washington Bureau Chief for the *Saigon Post* and ex-Act. Vietnamese Ambassador to the United States, speaks in PS-10 on "The Third Way to Peace in Vietnam"

8 DEC. 1967. René F. Dennemeyer (Mathematics) and C. Michael O'Gara (Physical Education) are awarded tenure, effective Sept. 1968. George L. McMichael, Robert A. Smith, and Edward M. White are awarded sabbatical leaves for 1968/69.

13 DEC. 1967. The campus experiences its coldest weather to date, including a 1-inch snowfall.

16 DEC. 1967. The campus wins a first-place trophy from the Rialto Jaycees in the Civic Organization Div. of the annual Jaycees' Christmas Parade for a float entitled, "All I Want for Christmas."

31 DEC. 1967. Mary Helen Lybarger, Secretary to the Exec. Dean (1962-67), resigns.

1968

5 JAN. 1968. The Central Heating and Air Conditioning Facility in the new Physical Plant Building is completed at a cost of $898,800. The Biological Science Building hosts its first classes.

14 JAN. 1968. The campus begins offering weekly, hour-long guided tours conducted by students at 3:00 P.M. each Sunday.

16 JAN. 1968. Actor Anthony Zerbe reads from the works of poet e. e. cummings in PS-10. J. Putnam Henck Inc. receives a $145,264 contract to landscape the 2 science buildings.

18 JAN. 1968. The campus receives a $14,044 grant from the Federal Work Study Program.

30 JAN. 1968. Pianist Marie E. Astor performs in PS-10.

1 FEB. 1968. Lloyd G. Ingles narrates his African wildlife film, *East of the Mountains of the Moon*, in PS-10.

3 FEB. 1968. The campus holds its 1st Science Day on the Mall, with 300 attendees and a presentation by Lloyd G. Ingles.

4-24 FEB. 1968. The campus unveils its first formal art exhibit in BI-101 (the new Art Gallery), featuring paintings and drawings by William L. Haney and his wife, Carol Schille.

9 FEB. 1968. The campus establishes a rotating display of faculty publications on the first floor of the Physical Science Building.

14 FEB. 1968. Fred Cordova takes office as first Pres. of the Badger Hill Chapter of the Calif. State Employees Assoc.

19 FEB. 1968. Richard J. Bennecke, first Associated Student Pres., is named Act. Activities Advisor, replacing John Humphries.

20 FEB. 1968. Historian A. L. Rowse speaks in PS-10 on "The Historian and Shakespeare." The S.B. Valley Alumnae Chapter of Pi Lambda Theta sponsors a panel on "Progress and Developments in the Field of Teacher Education," with dinner in the cafeteria.

22 FEB. 1968. The campus installs a speaker's platform next to the flagpole beside the Administration Building, which is now termed the "Free Speech Area."

26 FEB.-1 MAR. 1968. The campus offers its 2nd extension course, a weeklong course on Literary Study in the Secondary Schools. The first extension course, a NSF course for chemistry teachers, had previously been offered at an unknown date. All further extension courses are postponed until the Faculty Senate has a chance to develop formal extension policies.

29 FEB. 1968. The students celebrate "Leap Day" by racing frogs on the Mall—the winner is Erin Rollins's "Mark 4." The campus produces its first TV program on a one-inch videotape recorder, showing students Carmen Molina and Nancy De Lozier speaking Spanish and German.

1 MAR. 1968. A "temporary" unpaved parking lot with 200 spaces opens northeast of the Biological Science Building—it's still in use in 2009!

4 MAR. 1968. The campus begins landscaping the area near the new science buildings, the animal house, and the greenhouse.

7 MAR. 1968. Ex-British M.P. and *Newsweek* editor Eldon W. Griffiths speaks in PS-10 on "A New Concept of World Order."

8 MAR. 1968. Alfred S. Egge is named Coordinator of the Dept. of Biology. Peter R. Hammond of the U.S. Naval Weapons Center speaks in PS-10 on "Charge-Transfer Interactions and Electron Affinity Measurement of Electronegative Materials."

13 MAR. 1968. Geologist Robert Renolds speaks in the Cafeteria to the Faculty Wives on the "Prehistory of San Bernardino County."

15 MAR. 1968. The Interim Committee of the Staff Council becomes a Working Committee, with Dale Lohmuller as Temporary Chair.

19-21 MAR. 1968. The campus hosts the 12th Annual Inland Science Fair, drawing some 200 high school and junior high participants and 2,000 visitors to the 389 exhibits.

21 MAR. 1968. Ward Ritchie of Ward Ritchie Press and Jake Zeitlin of Zeitlin & VerBrugge Bookstore speak at the Book Collectors' Club meeting in the Cafeteria.

22 MAR. 1968. Arlo D. Harris receives a $1,000 NSF summer fellowship grant.

26 MAR. 1968. CSC Chancellor Glenn S. Dumke visits the campus.

28 MAR. 1968. American Asphalt Paving Co. receives a $62,300 contract to extend the main campus parking lot east along Northpark Blvd., adding 321 additional parking spaces. A group of students conduct a free speech rally.

29 MAR. 1968. Arthur E. Nelson is named to the Advisory Board of the Univ. of Southern California's School of Library Science (until 1971). *The Pawprint* increases its size to tabloid format.

2 APR. 1968. Roy Slade speaks in PS-10 on "British Art Today." The State Public Works Board approves construction of the Library-Classroom Building.

5 APR. 1968. Campus offices and classes close for an hour to commemorate the assassination of Dr. Martin Luther King.

8 APR. 1968. Rep. John V. Tunney speaks on the Mall on "Student Power."

9 APR. 1968. Willard Wilcox speaks in PS-10 on "South Asia in America's Strategy: The Next Decade."

10 APR. 1968. Soprano MaryLou Ham performs in PS-10.

12 APR. 1968. The campus installs its first speed bump on the road leading to the Science Parking Lot, drawing so many complaints that it is quickly replaced. The Physical Plant begins building a temporary access road from Northpark Blvd. to the athletic facilities. The campus now employs 209 individuals.

16 APR. 1968. Rep. Jerry L. Pettis speaks to students and faculty about his opposition to the Civil Rights Bill. Guitarist Jim Owen and flamenco dancer Arlene Acuña perform in PS-10.

19 APR. 1968. Theater organist Gaylord Carter provides musical accompaniment for 8 short silent films shown in PS-10.

22-26 APR. 1968. The CSCSB chapter of Students for a Democratic Soc. conducts a series of workshops on the Vietnam War.

23 APR. 1968. Poet Kenneth Rexroth reads from his work in PS-10.

26 APR. 1968. *Los Angeles Times* Science Editor Irving S. Bengelsdorf speaks in PS-10 on "Communications and the Future," as part of a 2-day lecture series, "Scientists Look to the 21st Century," marking the official opening of the Biological and Physical Science Buildings. Emma Bormann, mother of Prof. Jorun B. Johns, completes an oil painting of the inauguration of Pres. Pfau; in 2009 it is displayed in PL-4005-A in the Pfau Library. Cal State student (Anna) Marchand Archuletta is named "Miss Redlands."

27 APR. 1968. Entomologist Robert L. Metcalf speaks in PS-10 on "The Challenges of Applied Biology." Geochemist Harrison Brown speaks on "Research and Man's Future." Both participate in a panel in PS-10 on "Science and General Education."

5 MAY 1968. A Cinco de Mayo cookout attracts 400 attendees.

10 MAY 1968. George L. McMichael becomes the first faculty member to receive a Fulbright Fellowship, studying in Greece during 1968/69. The campus is named as one of "51 Alternatives to the Multiversity" in the May issue of *Mademoiselle*: "The course offerings are rich and varied, including a senior seminar in 'Utopia: The Idle Dream?'"

23 MAY 1968. B-C Construction receives a $147,975 contract to build the Corporation Yard on the northwest edge of campus.

1 JUN. 1968. The first issue of *Panorama*, the official publication of the Alumni Assoc., is published.

8 JUN. 1968. The 2nd Commencement is held on the Mall, with 103 students eligible to receive degrees; Arleigh Williams, Dean of Students at the Univ. of Calif., Berkeley, delivers the keynote address, "Carved on a Stone," and the 15th Air Force Band provides music.

18 JUN. 1968. James I. Barnes Construction Co. receives a contract for $4,281,000 to build the new Library-Classroom Building at the center of campus. "We will have one of the finest libraries in Southern California," Dean Thomas says.

25 JUN. 1968. Michael Mazur speaks in PS-10 on "Spatial Envelopes."

28 JUN. 1968. The Library receives a $6,130 grant from the U.S. Dept. of Health, Education, and Welfare to purchase books.

30 JUN. 1968. G. William Hume, Assoc. Dean of Activities and Housing, resigns. John Humphries, Activities Advisor, resigns.

1 JUL. 1968. Russell J. DeRemer, Asst. Prof. of Physics, is named Assoc. Dean of Activities and Housing, replacing G. William Hume. Alumnus Richard J. Bennecke is named Activities Advisor, replacing John Humphries.

9-10 JUL. 1968. Staff members approve a constitution for a proposed Staff Council.

12 JUL. 1968. The College's Standard Teaching Credential Program receives accreditation from the State Board of Education. Dorman/Munselle Associates are named consulting master plan architects for CSCSB, replacing A. C. Martin Associates (1963-68).

25 JUL. 1968. The CSC Board of Trustees renames the campus **California State College, San Bernardino**.

1 AUG. 1968. Mary A. Dye, Barbara J. Snell, Jody Evans, Lyn Young, Charles E. Byrd, John A. Cervantes, and Jesse C. Rowe are elected as the first members of the Staff Council.

27 AUG. 1968. Groundbreaking is held for the new Library-Classroom Building. The Library receives a gift from Dr. and Mrs. S. Paul A. Joosten of a 126-volume set of the Nürnberg war crimes trials transcripts. Construction begins on the 10,830-square foot Corporate Yard and Physical Plant Building at the north edge of campus.

1 SEPT. 1968. Gerald M. Scherba, Dean of Academic Affairs, is named VP of Academic Affairs, being the first of that rank at CSCSB. Edna L.

Steinman is named Dir. of College Publications, replacing James H. McKone, who is named Dir. of College Relations. James D. Thomas is named Assoc. Dean for Academic Administration, replacing Peter T. Marcy. Lawrence E. Johnson is named 1st Financial Aid Director. The campus begins an experimental admissions program. Richard W. Graves is named first Chair of the newly established Dept. of Business Administration, thus establishing a 6th academic division for the campus. The campus makes its Reading Program voluntary, effective with Fall term.

2 SEPT. 1968. The campus receives a $73,710 grant from the National Defense Student Loan Program, with the College providing an additional 10% in matching funds.

6 SEPT. 1968. Jody Evans is elected first Chair of the Staff Council.

12 SEPT. 1968. Construction begins on the Library-Classroom Building at the exact center of campus.

16 SEPT. 1968. Gerald T. Sullivan Co. receives an $82,820 contract to landscape the Gymnasium-Swimming Pool complex.

19 SEPT. 1968. The annual convocation is held.

22-24 SEPT. 1968. The campus conducts an overnight "Live-In Orientation" for students at the Forest Home Conference Center.

28 SEPT. 1968. The campus hosts a Yearbook Workshop for 200 local high school students.

11 OCT. 1968. The 36,000-square-foot Physical Education Building is completed at a cost of $1,200,000. It includes a 1,450-seat gymnasium, 1 regulation and 2 practice basketball courts, an activity room, classrooms, faculty and staff offices, a locker room, and an external 75-x-45-foot swimming pool with depths ranging to 13 feet.

17 OCT. 1968. CSCSB is named one of the top 50 colleges in academic standing in the United States.

18 OCT. 1968. Paul Melmed speaks in PS-10 on "The Problems of Teaching Language Arts to the Culturally Disadvantaged."

23 OCT. 1968. Artist James Strombotne conducts a slide-lecture program on his paintings in PS-10.

25 OCT. 1968. Northpark Blvd. is expanded from 2 to 4 lanes along the northwest edge of the campus, with a median strip and curbs.

28-29 OCT. 1968. A student referendum to increase student fees to finance a Student Union Building fails to attain the ⅔ margin required, with 53% voting in favor (229-205).

31 OCT. 1968. The campus opens a College Information Center at the Home of Neighborly Service at 839 N. Mount Vernon Ave.

5 NOV. 1968. Ex-Hungarian Prime Minister Ferenc Nagy speaks in PS-10 on "The Fight of the Intellectuals for Freedom in East-Central Europe."

15 NOV. 1968. Zeigler Construction Co. receives a $22,387 contract to remodel several science laboratories.

21 NOV. 1968. The campus hosts a discussion in the Student Lounge on the possible student evaluation of professors.

22 NOV. 1968. The campus organizes a CSCSB Speakers Bureau to coordinate requests for off-campus speakers.

1 DEC. 1968. C. Carl Johnson, Dir. of Campus Police, resigns.

2 DEC. 1968. CSCSB alumnus Walter S. Kadyk is named Dir. of College Police, replacing C. Carl Johnson.

12 DEC. 1968. Arlo D. Harris accepts an exchange position at the Univ. of Nottingham in England in 1969/70. The campus hosts a conference for local college counselors.

13 DEC. 1968. S.B. City begins landscaping the median strip of State College Pkwy. from Kendall Dr. to Northpark Blvd.

1969

7 JAN. 1969. The campus begins offering a course on "The Negro Novel" taught by Robert A. Lee.

8 JAN. 1969. The campus receives a $10,700 federal grant to support the education of police officers.

9 JAN. 1969. Anti-draft activist Terrence Cannon speaks to a group of students and faculty.

14 JAN. 1969. The Science Parking Lot floods in heavy rains.

17 JAN. 1969. Cartoon voiceover artist and TV writer Daws Butler speaks in PS-10 on his work.

20 JAN. 1969. San Francisco Mime Troupe performs in PS-10.

20-21, 23 JAN. 1969. The campus hosts 3 convocations to discuss student unrest in the CSC System, with classes scheduled between 11 AM-1 PM being cancelled. 250 students participate in a dialogue with a 6-member panel—CSC Asst. Vice-Chancellor Tom McGraff, Pres. Pfau, and faculty members Edward M. White, Robert R. Roberts, Kent M. Schofield, and Ronald E. Barnes.

22 JAN. 1969. The campus conducts a workshop devoted to computer-assisted instruction, with James Finn, Head of the Dept. of Instructional Technology at the Univ. of Southern California, giving the keynote address.

24 JAN. 1969. The Biological Science Building is named one of the top 15 college buildings in the country by *College and University Business*, and is also honored in the Apr. 1969 issue of *American School & University Magazine*. The masthead of the *Friday Bulletin* is changed to reflect the campus's new name—California State College, San Bernardino *Bulletin*—with a design by James R. Gooch.

25-26 JAN. 1969. A winter storm floods the open foundation of the Library-Classroom Building, delaying the completion timetable for that building by at least 2 weeks, and also the construction of the Physical Plant Shops and Offices by 2 weeks.

28 JAN. 1969. Tenor Val Stuart and soprano Lila Stuart perform in PS-10.

31 JAN. 1969. Library employees form a Library Staff Assoc., with Libn. Rosemary T. Ward being elected first Pres. The Alumni Assoc. is granted tax-exempt status by the Internal Revenue Service.

5 FEB. 1969. Turkish Ambassador to the U.N. Nuri Eren speaks in PS-10 on "Why Is America Misunderstood in the World?"

7 FEB. 1969. American Asphalt Paving Co. receives a contract for $106,000 to add 600 spaces to the east side of the main parking lot. The campus receives a $400 gift from the Social Lites Club of San Bernardino to fund scholarships.

8 FEB. 1969. Singer Clabe Hangan performs in the Student Lounge.

14 FEB. 1969. The campus celebrates the St. Valentine's Day Massacre with readings in PS-122 by faculty, students, and staff; students decorate the Biological Science Building with a large orange-and-yellow plastic daisy.

17-24 FEB. 1969. The faculty votes 40-26 to support a resolution adopted by the Academic Senate of the CSC on May 24, 1968 expressing a lack of confidence in CSC Chancellor Glenn S. Dumke and asking him to resign; the system-wide margin is 3,395-1,850.

18 FEB. 1969. The Physical Plant and Corporate Yard is accepted by the campus, and the stores, maintenance, ground keeping, data processing, College Police, and accounting offices begin moving into the new facility on Feb. 25.

19 FEB. 1969. Mathematician Bernard R. Gelbaum speaks in BI-101 on "Logic Decidability Theorems and Computers."

26 FEB. 1969. Albert Elsen, scheduled to speak in PS-10 on "Picasso as a Sculptor," is forced to cancel due to a storm; the heavy rains damage the homes of several staff members.

28 FEB. 1969. The Music Dept. presents its first faculty recital in PS-10, featuring oboist Charles Gower and pianist Michael Andrews.

7 MAR. 1969. The campus opens a footpath to the Physical Plant.

13 MAR. 1969. 150 students march to urge the administration to hire Sarojam K. Mankau as a tenure-track faculty member—she was!

14 MAR. 1969. The campus forms a Committee on Ethnic Studies Program, comprising 5 faculty and 2 administrators. Cal State student Anna Marchand Archuletta is named Queen of the 54th Annual National Orange Show.

24 MAR. 1969. Pres. Pfau announces that he has accepted the recommendation of the Faculty Senate that the Comprehensive Exam requirement for graduation for most departments be dropped.

31 MAR. 1969. Gov. Reagan declares a day of mourning for ex-Pres. Eisenhower's death, thereby closing the campus.

4 APR. 1969. The soothsayers' prediction that all of California west of the San Andreas Fault would fall into the sea during a giant earthquake on this date fails—alas!—to materialize. Construction begins on a parking lot at the corner of State College Pkwy. and Northpark Blvd. S.B. City Councilman Robert Henley visits the campus.

11 APR. 1969. The campus receives a $2,400 gift from the estate of Leon S. Heseman and the Riverside Foundation to fund 4 $600 scholarships.

12 APR. 1969. The 2nd Annual Science Day for local high school students, scheduled for this date, is postponed until Nov.

15 APR. 1969. Sculptor Ross Drago speaks in PS-10 on "Explanations of Experiments in Art and Technique."

18 APR. 1969. Cal State history major Elviretta Emmarose "Rose" Crist dies of rheumatoid arthritis at age 21.

20-26 APR. 1969. The Library sponsors the first of a series of student book collection contests.

21 APR. 1969. The campus unveils 6 experimental college courses, the so-called Community University, to be conducted through the last week in May.

22 APR. 1969. Roy C. Barnett Co. receives a $289,000 contract to landscape the west side of the campus, in, around, and behind the cluster of 3 original buildings, including the creation of a small outdoor amphitheater. Philosopher Michael Scriven speaks in PS-10 on "The Obligation to Revolution."

27 APR. 1969. The Library celebrates the acquisition of its 100,000th book, *Decisive Battles of the U.S.A*, by J. F. C. Fuller, part of a gift of 200 volumes from local historian Burr Belden.

5 MAY 1969. Psychologist Halmuth H. Schaefer speaks in PS-10 on "Behavioral Modification." Alan F. Guttmacher, Pres. of Planned Parenthood-World Population, speaks in PS-10 on the "The World Population Problem: How It Affects You."

7 MAY 1969. Chemist Kenneth N. Trueblood speaks in PS-10 on "Symmetry in Nature and in Man's World."

10 MAY 1969. Guy Carawan performs in the Cafeteria Lounge.

14 MAY 1969. Art historian Albert Elsen speaks in PS-10 on "Picasso as a Sculptor."

16 MAY 1969. H. Stephen Prouty Jr., Dir. of Admissions and Records, is named Assoc. Dean for Admissions and Records. Doyle J. Stansel, Dir. of Placement and Financial Aid, is named Assoc. Dean for Placement and Financial Aid.

20 MAY 1969. Biologist Donald E. Rounds speaks in BI-101 on "The Biological Effects of Laser Energy."

25 MAY 1969. The campus hosts its first "Homecoming," a barbecue cook-off for Cal State alumni.

1 JUN. 1969. The first volume of *The Prickly Pear*, the campus literary magazine, is published. The Alumni Assoc. holds its first "Welcome Home" event, with 15 alums attending.

3 JUN. 1969. Alfred Finley Moore, an astronomer at the Smithsonian Institute, dies in San Bernardino at age 81; half ($185,415) of his estate is left to CSCSB to establish the Alfred F. and Chella D. Moore Scholarship Fund. Biologist John Randall speaks in BI-101 on "Application of Liquid Scintillation Counting to the Life Sciences," and also on "Activation Analysis as a General Research Tool."

6 JUN. 1969. The campus receives approval from the Chancellor's Off. to begin offering a major in Economics in 1969/70.

9 JUN. 1969. The Faculty Senate approves an Ethnic Studies Program to be offered beginning with 1969/70.

13 JUN. 1969. The 3rd Commencement is held in the new Gymnasium, with 185 students (including 27 who started in 1965) eligible for degrees; Louis H. Heilbron, ex-Chair (1960-63) of the CSC Board of Trustees, provides the keynote address, "There Once Was a College at Camelot." A student group publishes *The Unicorn Horn*, providing informal student evaluations of faculty teaching.

27 JUN. 1969. The Library receives a $5,431 grant from the U.S. Dept. of Health, Education, and Welfare to purchase materials.

1 JUL. 1969. Lawrence E. Johnson, Dir. of Financial Aid, is named Dir. of the Experimental Admissions Program.

7 JUL. 1969. Gilbert R. Rangel is named Financial Aid Coordinator, replacing Lawrence E. Johnson.

21 JUL. 1969. The campus closes after Pres. Richard M. Nixon proclaims a "Day of Participation" for the first Moon landing.

25 JUL. 1969. The College announces that it is limiting enrollment for the first time, having achieved its maximum capacity of 1,800 students. The Campus Police move to the Heating and Air Conditioning Facility, along with the *Pawprint* and the ASB offices.

5 AUG. 1969. Hemisphere Constructors receives a $668,450 contract to build the Library-Classroom Building utility tunnel. Several campus construction projects, including the Library-Classroom Building, parking lot, and landscaping, are delayed by labor strikes of the Operating Engineers' and Plumbers' unions.

29 AUG. 1969. Fontana Paving Inc. receives a $14,954 contract to repave the Science Parking Lot.

31 AUG. 1969. Jesse Hiraoka, Chair of the Humanities Div. (1966-69), returns to the ranks as Prof. of French. James T. Freeman, Dir. of Institutional Research, resigns.

1 SEPT. 1969. Robert D. Picker is named first Dean of Instruction. Ronald E. Barnes Jr. is named Act. Chair of the Humanities Div., replacing Jesse Hiraoka. Fred Roach is named first Dean of Continuing Education, replacing Robert L. West, Dir. of Extension. L. Theron Pace is named the first Housing Coordinator. Robert A. Schwabe is named Dir. of Institutional Research, replacing James T. Freeman. The campus hires its first full-time African-American faculty, Vernon O. Leviege and Leonard S. Mbogua.

9 SEPT. 1969. The campus hosts a 9-day EOP orientation program, with 40 minority students attending.

10 SEPT. 1969. Joseph Jerz, Coll. Personnel Off. (1965-69), resigns.

12 SEPT. 1969. Alexander D. Sokoloff receives a $35,000 grant from NSF to study tribolium flour beetles.

15 SEPT. 1969. Gladys M. Hubbard is named Placement Advisor. James H. McKone, Dir. of College Relations, is granted a year's leave to become a novelist in Texas.

19 SEPT. 1969. 3 trailers are installed behind the old Library Building to accommodate offices for the Dean of Students, Assoc. Dean of Placement and Financial Aid, the Financial Aid Coordinator, Placement Advisor, Assoc. Dean of Activities and Housing, Housing Coordinator, and EOP Dir.

19-21 SEPT. 1969. The campus offers a live-in orientation for 150 new students at Camp Arbolado in Barton Flats, with Dr. Stephen B. Lawrence giving a microlab demonstration.

22 SEPT. 1969. The annual convocation is held in PS-10.

26 SEPT. 1969. CSC Chancellor Glenn S. Dumke issues Executive Order 79-70, reaffirming a system policy that "Dismissal by an individual faculty member of his classes as a demonstration in support of a particular social or political movement shall be considered a violation of professional ethics and a failure or refusal to perform the normal and responsible duties of the position, and Presidents shall institute formal disciplinary actions in such cases."

29 SEPT. 1969. A 616-space parking lot opens next to the original campus lot, with a temporary access road connecting it to State College Pkwy. The College Information Center, located at the front counter of the Admissions Off., opens for business.

3 OCT. 1969. Richard S. Saylor announces plans to form a campus orchestra. The campus sponsors a food truck to provide snacks for evening students and staff from Monday to Thursday.

7 OCT. 1969. Myrlie Beasley Evers-Williams, widow of slain civil rights leader Medgar Evers, speaks in PS-10 on "Black Protest."

15 OCT. 1969. The ASB sponsors a Vietnam War moratorium, with workshops and rap sessions aimed at discussing the situation in Southeast Asia, and 200 individuals participating.

16 OCT. 1969. Hartman Construction Co. receives a $105,277 contract to remodel parts of the Biological Science Building.

17 OCT. 1969. The Gospel Five perform in PS-10.

22 OCT. 1969. William Harwood conducts a fencing workshop in the Physical Education Activities Room.

28 OCT. 1969. Lou Smith, Pres. of Operation Bootstrap, speaks in PS-10.

6 NOV. 1969. The Dept. of Business Administration forms a Board of Counselors comprised of local business and professional leaders: Robert C. Fess (Chair), Walter K. Deacon, Palm Springs City Manager Frank Aleshire, Robert M. Young, Allen B. Gresham, Verne F. Potter Jr., Harold C. Harris Jr., John J. Butler, and G. David Ackley.

7-9 NOV. 1969. A 2nd student moratorium on the Vietnam War is conducted at Perris Hill Park in San Bernardino, the S.B. Co. Courthouse, and in the city of San Francisco.

8 NOV. 1969. Eric Burdon, The Middle Earth, and The Youngbloods perform in the Gymnasium.

13-14 NOV. 1969. An accreditation team from the Western Assoc. of Schools and Colleges (WASC) visits the campus to evaluate its curriculum, led by Franklin P. Rolfe of UCLA; a team from the Calif. Dept. of Education, led by Olaf Tegner of Pepperdine Coll., visits the campus to evaluate its teacher credential and intern programs.

17 NOV. 1969. Oscar C. Jackson, Jr. is named College Personnel Officer, replacing Joseph Jerz.

25 NOV. 1969. Geraldine Rickman, Pres. of COPE Foundation, speaks in PS-10 on "Black Is the Color of Progress."

30 NOV. 1969. The campus hosts a meeting in C-116 and C-117 of the National Soc. for the Preservation of Tent, Folk, and Repertoire Theatre, with actors Paul Brinegar and Anne B. Davis, and James V. Davis, owner of the Schaffner Players.

1 DEC. 1969. James D. Thomas, Assoc. Dean of Academic Administration, is named Dean of Academic Administration.

5 DEC. 1969. The campus announces an expansion of its Extension Program to include courses responsive to the needs of the community. The TV wiring of PS-10 is completed.

6 DEC. 1969. Milton Blander, T. P. Onak, and William D. Clark speak to a conference of local chemistry teachers.

8 DEC. 1969. Assemblymen John P. Quimby and C. Jerry Lewis and State Sen. William E. Coombs tour the campus.

10 DEC. 1969. Clarinetist Ellis Potter and pianist Dennis Dockstader perform in C-104.

12 DEC. 1969. The campus receives a $10,495 grant from NSF to promote science education.

14 DEC. 1969. Pat Quanstrom wins $700 on the TV show, *Let's Make a Deal*, the program being broadcast on Jan. 8, 1970.

1970

1 JAN. 1970. The CSC institutes a common admissions program for all 19 campuses. The campus installs swing gates to the Science Parking Lot, with plastic cards required to gain access, plus the display of special parking decals.

5 JAN. 1970. The campus begins offering extension courses for the first time in 11 towns: San Bernardino, Banning, Beaumont, Barstow, Colton,

Corona, Fontana, Little Rock, Palm Desert, Redlands, Rialto, and Victorville. A coin-operated gate is installed in the parking lot north of the bus stop shelter; the fee is 25¢ per day.

7 JAN. 1970. Violinist Karen Phillips performs in C-104.

9 JAN. 1970. The campus receives a $400 gift from the Faculty Wives to fund scholarships.

10 JAN. 1970. The newly organized unofficial basketball team plays S.B. Valley College in its first intercollegiate game.

12 JAN. 1970. The College's new Art Gallery, under the supervision of Roger P. Lintault, opens in PS-22 with an exhibition of sculptures by CSCSB students.

14 JAN. 1970. State Dept. official Thomas P. Shoesmith speaks in BI-101 on "Continuity and Change in U.S. Policy in Asia."

15 JAN. 1970. Rep. George E. Brown speaks on campus to announce his candidacy for the U.S. Senate.

16 JAN. 1970. The campus announces 3 new extension classes in Feb. in Palm Desert, the start of an effort that will eventually lead to the Palm Desert Campus.

20 JAN. 1970. Writer Norman V. Petersen speaks in PS-10 on "The Ethic of a Free Technology."

23 JAN. 1970. The Library publishes a 41-page booklet, *Black and Brown Bibliography: History: A Selected List of Books Relating to the History of Afro-Americans and Mexican-Americans*, edited by Mary Jo Meade, delineating titles of interest to the study of the history of African-Americans and Hispanic-Americans.

6 FEB. 1970. The Western Assoc. of Schools and Colleges (WASC) reaccredits CSCSB for 5 years. Paul Gendrop presents a slide-lecture in PS-10 on "The Grandeur of Mexico."

10 FEB. 1970. State Sen. John L. Harmer speaks in PS-10. G. Donald Chakerian speaks in BI-101 on "Unsolved Problems in Elementary Geometry," and in BI-101 on "Sets of Constant Width."

17 FEB. 1970. Irving S. Bengelsdorf, Science Editor of the *Los Angeles Times*, speaks in PS-10 on "Spaceship Earth: Population, Poverty, and Pollution."

20 FEB. 1970. An $110,000 HEW research grant, "Facilitation of Cognitive Development Among Children with Learning Deficits," is transferred from Michigan State Univ. to the CSCSB Foundation to establish a Human Learning Center in San Bernardino to train retarded children under the direction of Rosaria Bulgarella, wife of Prof. Dominic Bulgarella. The play *Spoon River Anthology* by Charles Aidman begins a 5-night run in the Little Theater, with every show sold out.

26 FEB. 1970. Dave Tunno speaks in PE-129 to the Business Management Club. Poet Bill Knott reads from his work in PS-10.

27 FEB. 1970. The Class of 1969 donates a sign, "CSC California State College, San Bernardino," to be erected at the Main Entrance. Rossetti Construction Co. receives a $32,420 contract to convert several classrooms to laboratories in the Physical Science Building.

1 MAR. 1970. Arthur Gage, Campus Budget Officer, resigns.

2 MAR. 1970. Jim G. Martínez is named Campus Budget Officer, replacing Arthur Gage.

4 MAR. 1970. The campus receives a second $3,000 grant from the Riverside Foundation to establish 5 $600 scholarships to honor the late Leon S. Heseman.

4-5 MAR. 1970. The students again vote on a fee to construct a Student Union; the tally fails to attain the ⅔ majority needed (296-234).

5 MAR. 1970. Poet Bill Knott reads from his work in PS-10.

8 MAR. 1970. Writer Ray Bradbury speaks in PS-10 on "The Space Age: A Creative Challenge."

11 MAR. 1970. Students from the Sherman Institute in Riverside perform Indian tribal dances in the Free Speech Area.

13 MAR. 1970. The Chancellor's Off. approves new majors in Anthropology and Social Sciences, effective with 1970/71.

15 MAR. 1970. College Police Sergeant Mickey Carns captures an armed robbery suspect after a high-speed chase on Kendall Dr.

20 MAR. 1970. The campus expands its extension offerings to Banning, Barstow, Beaumont, Big Bear, Blythe, Corona, Little Rock, Ontario, Perris, Redlands, Rialto, Riverside, San Bernardino, Victorville, and Twenty-Nine Palms.

3 APR. 1970. Sandy Kime is named Cafeteria Manager, replacing Jean Atterbury. The New Minds performs the folk musical *Tell It Like It Is* in PS-10.

16 APR. 1970. Gordon E. Stanton receives a $12,021 grant from NSF to provide an in-service institute for 30 high school social studies teachers. Dr. Gwen Auxier speaks in PS-10 on "California's Abortion Law."

17 APR. 1970. The De Anza College Chorale performs in PS-10 under the direction of Royal Stanton. The campus leases a $120,000 IBM 360-20 computer.

19 APR. 1970. The campus observes Earth Day for the first time.

21 APR. 1970. The Illegitimate Theater acting troupe from the Palo Alto Cabaret Theatre performs in PS-10.

22 APR. 1970. Writer Edison P. McDaniels speaks on the Mall.

24 APR. 1970. The Library publishes a 2nd 22-page booklet, *Black and Brown Bibliography: Literature, Art, Music, Theatre: A Selected List of Books Relating to the Culture of Afro-Americans and Mexican-Americans*, edited by Mary Jo Meade. Zoologist Wilbur W. Mayhew speaks in PS-10 on "Population, Pollution, Poverty, and Peace." Folksinger Sally Thomas performs in the Cafeteria.

29 APR. 1970. Naturalist Sherwin Carlquist speaks on "Evolution of the Hawaiian Islands."

1 MAY 1970. The rock group "1" performs in PS-10.

2 MAY 1970. The campus hosts a conference, "Crisis in Public School Finance," in PS-10, with speakers Assemblyman Victor Veysey, Erick L. Lindman, Charles A. Briscoe, Allan Smith, Delbert Lobb, George Caldwell, Ray Berry, Harvey Irwin, Paul Zintgraff, Edward V. Moreno, Kenneth Bailey, Chester Gilpin, Gordon H. Winton, James L. Ferguson, Ray Kniss, and Laird Roddick.

5 MAY 1970. The campus hosts a symposium, "The Chicano in a White Society," in PS-10, with speakers Ricardo Ontiveros, Raúl Loya, Rev. Manuel Guillén, Enrique Ramírez, and Burt Corona.

6 MAY 1970. Gov. Reagan closes all CSC campuses from May 7-10 in reaction to the massacre of student protestors at Kent State Univ. CSCSB students conduct a series of meetings during the rest of the day, and call a strike on May 7-8. The campus flag is lowered to half-mast.

11 MAY 1970. *The Pawprint* publishes a "Statement of Concern" over the events at Kent State and in the war in Southeast Asia, signed by 300 faculty, students, and staff.

13 MAY 1970. Sociologist Robert A. Nisbet speaks in PS-10 on "The Academic Community and Its Enemies."

14 MAY 1970. The campus hosts a public meeting in the Cafeteria to allow students to express their concerns over recent events.

15 MAY 1970. The Chancellor's Off. approves a new B.A. degree in Humanities, effective with 1970/71. 8 students are inaugurated into the new CSCSB chapter of the national French honor society, Phi Delta Phi (ΦΔΦ).

18 MAY 1970. The campus hosts a symposium, "Abortion: Ethical Considerations," sponsored by Zero Population Growth, with speakers Rabbi Hillel Cohn, Rev. Robert Perry, Rev. Leo Petit, and Dr. Gwen Auxier.

19 MAY 1970. Chemist Edward L. King speaks in BI-101 on "Ions in Mixed Solvents."

21 MAY 1970. Pres. Pfau calls a meeting of administrators and faculty to discuss demands by African-American students to increase campus minority representation and opportunities.

29 MAY 1970. Pres. Pfau accepts a Faculty Senate report recommending the formation of academic departments within the College divisions, beginning 1970/71.

5 JUN. 1970. Joyce Allen is named Senior Woman of the Year by Theta Psi Omega.

13 JUN. 1970. The 4th Commencement is held in the Gymnasium, with 280 graduates eligible for degrees; O. Meredith Wilson, Dir. of the Center for Advanced Study in the Behavioral Sciences at Stanford Univ., gives the keynote address, with music provided by the Antelope Valley Concert Band. The campus awards its first B.A. [sic] degree in Physics.

26 JUN. 1970. Folksingers Keith McNeil and Rusty McNeil perform in PS-10 as the inaugural event in the "Summer Chautauqua" series. A fire burns 115 acres on Wiggins Hill near the campus.

29 JUN. 1970. The Library publishes a 3rd 19-page booklet, *Black and Brown Bibliography: Philosophy, Social Sciences, Political Science, Education: A Selected List of Books Relating to the Culture of Afro-Americans* *and Mexican-Americans*, edited by Mary Jo Meade.

1 JUL. 1970. Lucas G. Lawrence, Dir. of Audio-Visual Services, resigns. Student Assistant pay rates increase to $1.84 per hour.

10 JUL. 1970. Philosopher John R. Searle speaks in PS-10 on "Social Unrest and Its Backlash as Reflected in the College Community."

14 JUL. 1970. The CSC Board of Trustees establishes new grievance procedures for Cal State faculty.

16 JUL. 1970. The campus and 4 other S.B. Co. colleges receive a $52,500 grant from the U.S. Dept. of Justice to provide financial aid to students interested in a law enforcement career.

17 JUL. 1970. The College's Teacher Credential Program is accredited by the State Dept. of Education. The Faculty Wives award their first scholarship to Dianna Pelletier (later a campus employee).

22 JUL. 1970. Rep. Jerry L. Pettis announces that the campus has received a $400,000 loan guarantee from the U.S. Dept. of Health, Education, and Welfare to help build the Commons Building, with the balance needed ($1,250,000) being provided from State funds.

24 JUL. 1970. The German-language film, *Recht auf Gewissen*, based on the life of Nikolai E. Khokhlov, shows on West German TV, with actor Heinrich Schweiger playing Khokhlov.

31 JUL. 1970. 19 high school students receive certificates for completing the 6-week Operation Second Chance course.

1 AUG. 1970. Cal State student Paul Michael Amberg dies in a truck accident on guard duty at Ford Ord at age 22.

3-7 AUG. 1970. The campus hosts an In-Service Institute in Sociology for local high school teachers.

7 AUG. 1970. The Chancellor's Off. approves new options in Mexican-American Studies and Black Studies for the B.A. degree in History and Sociology. Rep. Jerry L. Pettis announces that the campus has received loan guarantees of $53,900 and $30,300 from the U.S. Dept. of Health, Education, and Welfare to help construct the residential housing complex.

11 AUG. 1970. The Viking Construction Co. receives a $2,192,724 contract to construct the Residence Halls complex.

14 AUG. 1970. Cal State student Doreen Ann Brown dies in an automobile accident on I-10 in Colton at age 26. Work on the $668,450 campus utility tunnel is completed by Hemisphere Constructors. Robert F. Gentry, Asst. Dean of Students (1968-70), resigns. Harvey Wichman, David Squire, and Clifford T. Paynton receive an $84,856 grant from the Calif. Council of Criminal Justice to help rehabilitate narcotics parolees.

18 AUG. 1970. Cal State student David L. Randolph, ex-Asst. Dir. of the EOP, drowns in Lake Elsinore at age 31.

21 AUG. 1970. Physical plant craftsmen begin building a $20,000 art facility on the south side of the Cafeteria Building, housing labs and a kiln for ceramics, wood sculpture, and metalworking.

30 AUG. 1970. CSC Chancellor Glenn S. Dumke announces a major overhaul in student disciplinary proceedings for the system.

31 AUG. 1970. Ronald E. Barnes, Act. Chair of the Div. of Humanities, returns to the ranks as Prof. of Drama.

1 SEPT. 1970. P. Richard Switzer is named Chair of the Div. of Humanities, replacing Ronald E. Barnes. Robert A. Senour is named Dir. of Audio-Visual Services, replacing Lucas G. Lawrence. Kate Wilson is named Activities Advisor. George A. Meneses is named Asst. Dir. of the Educational Opportunity Program. Edward J. Carlson is named Coordinator and Act. Chairman of the Dept. of Administration, replacing Richard W. Graves. Parking fees increase to $9 per quarter. Ann and Harvey Wichman, Esther and Elliott R. Barkan, and Nikolai E. Khokhlov begin an informal effort to create a campus carpool; they eventually persuade over 400 individuals to join the program. The campus begins offering Ethnic Studies options in History and Sociology.

11 SEPT. 1970. *Psychedelic Shack—America and the Home Front*, a soul-rock musical created and directed by Gray Kirkwood, is performed by the S.B. West Side Youths in the Gymnasium.

18-20 SEPT. 1970. The campus hosts an orientation retreat at Camp Arbolado near Barton Flats in the S.B. Mountains to allow 160 students to meet with 15 faculty and administrators.

21 SEPT. 1970. The annual convocation is held in PS-10.

26-27 SEPT. 1970. The campus provides a resting place in the Gymnasium for 450 fire fighters working a blaze in the Lytle Creek area.

28 SEPT. 1970. The campus offers 57 extension classes in Palm Desert,

Indio, Palm Springs, Twenty-Nine Palms, Eagle Mountain, Riverside, Hemet, Blythe, Colton, Corona, San Bernardino, Fontana, Hesperia, Littlerock, Perris, Redlands, Rialto, and Victorville. This represents a huge expansion of the Continuing Education program.

30 SEPT. 1970. Rep. Jerry L. Pettis announces that the campus has received a $152,258 grant from the federal government to fund student loan programs.

2 OCT. 1970. The campus institutes telephone service for the Evening Program Off.

7 OCT. 1970. A 50-acre brush fire burns in Devil Canyon north of the campus. Roy C. Barnett Co. receives a $69,800 contract to provide walkways, external lighting, and an access road to the loading dock for the new Library-Classroom Building.

8 OCT. 1970. Pres. Pfau speaks at a breakfast meeting of the Colton Chamber of Commerce about proposed building plans at CSCSB.

9 OCT. 1970. CSC Chancellor Glenn S. Dumke approves new grievance procedures for all Cal State faculty, as mandated by the CSC Board of Trustees on Jul. 14, to "provide fairness, peer judgment, and prompt disposition of cases with the State College System." These authorize the establishment of committees of senior tenured faculty on each campus "to consider and make recommendations in faculty complaints in the areas of retention, promotion, and tenure, taking the form of peer group hearings." S.B. City and the State agree to share the $50,000 cost for the installation of a traffic signal at the corner of Kendall Dr. and State College Pkwy.

14 OCT. 1970. Deputy State Superintendent of Public Instruction Wilson Riles speaks in the Free Speech Area.

15 OCT. 1970. The campus hosts its first Parents Night in PS-10. Richard Romo, Peace and Freedom Party candidate for Governor, speaks in the Free Speech Area.

16 OCT. 1970. The Free Speech Area is moved to "The Green" north of the old Library building.

23 OCT. 1970. A referendum to add a student representative to the Faculty Senate fails by 3 votes.

24 OCT. 1970. Teatro Urbano premieres a Chicano play, *Dark Root of a Scream*, in PS-10. The campus hosts a conference, "Adolescence in Crisis," in PS-10, with Michael Peck and Paul Pretzel, co-directors of the

L.A. Suicide Center, leading the discussion.

30 OCT. 1970. The campus organizes a local chapter of Sigma Xi (ΣΞ), the national scientific research honorary society.

31 OCT. 1970. The campus hosts the People's Fair and Folk Fest in the Quad, with a Folk Fest Hootenanny in C-117 featuring Tundra.

1 NOV. 1970. The phone number dialing requirement in the San Bernardino area, including Cal State, changes from 5 to 7 digits, making the campus number prefix "887."

2 NOV. 1970. Work begins on the Residence Halls complex.

3 NOV. 1970. Leta M. Adler is named Prof. of Sociology, becoming the first woman full professor on the CSCSB faculty. The campus holds a staff convocation in PS-10.

4 NOV. 1970. Labor activist Diane Feeley speaks in PS-10 on "Strategy for Women's Liberation." Baritone James Farhinger and pianist Dave Elson perform a "Song Recital."

5 NOV. 1970. The campus co-hosts (with schools in Riverside and San Bernardino Cos.) a conference at the S.B. Holiday Inn on "The Principal's Role in Conflict Management," with Robert Stout giving the keynote address, and H. Darwyne Vickers, Lorne Bargman, Donald Wheeler, W. Paul Whaley, and Donald Baer participating.

10 NOV. 1970. The campus hosts a panel, "Who's Come a Long Way, Baby?" in PS-202.

11 NOV. 1970. Pres. Pfau, interviewed in *The Pawprint*, again states that he will not consider an intercollegiate sports program. The Music Dept. organizes a Choral Soc.

12 NOV. 1970. Psychologist Loh Seng Tsai speaks in PS-202 on "Animal Intelligence, Aggression, Peace, and Cooperation."

14 NOV. 1970. The campus hosts a conference, "The Changing World of Women," in PS-10, with speakers Elizabeth Cless, S.B. Co. Supervisor Nancy Smith, Theresa Philler, Mary Sánchez, Frances Grice, Helen Fenton, Alma Murray, *El Chicano* Editor Marta Macías McQueen, and Catherine Arnott.

19 NOV. 1970. The campus hosts a program, "Why Women's Studies?" in PS-10, with Barbara Kessel as keynote speaker. The Circle K Club of

CSC, San Bernardino receives its charter from Circle K International, being the first national service organization to be chartered at CSCSB.

23-25 NOV. 1970. The campus hosts an International Festival to celebrate the 25th anniversary of the founding of the United Nations, featuring an exhibit of Oriental art from the collection of Ingrid Ahl, a program of Indian music by Ashish Khan, Zakir Hussain, Pranesh Khan, T. Viswanathan, and T. Ranganathan, films from Latin America and Africa, and a panel discussing international education.

25 NOV. 1970. Israeli Consul-General for L.A. Benjamin Abileah speaks in PS-22 on "The Current Political Situation in the Middle East." Students Maxie N. Gossett and John B. Thwing create a Spiro T. Agnew Fan Club on campus.

30 NOV. 1970. Gov. Reagan announces a projected budget deficit of $100 million, with major cuts to be made in all state agencies.

3 DEC. 1970. The Calif. Retired Teachers Assoc. establishes a $500 revolving scholarship fund to provide emergency assistance to upper-division and graduate students.

8 DEC. 1970. MEChA sponsors a Testimonial Performance by the Teatro Tecato for its late Dir. Freddie Veruman.

11 DEC. 1970. Alexander D. Sokoloff receives an $113,319 grant from the National Advisory Environmental Control Council of the U.S. Public Health Service to study tribolium beetles.

1971

2 JAN. 1971. The campus begins offering extension classes on a semester basis to accommodate local teachers. Robert A. Schwabe, Dir. of Institutional Research, is also named Supervisor of the Data Processing and Computer Center.

4 JAN. 1971. The Art Facility, a $20,000, 33-x-80-ft. concrete block building constructed by the campus adjacent to the south side of the Cafeteria Building, opens for business.

12 JAN. 1971. P and A Construction Co. receives a $1,325,000 contract to build the Cafeteria Building (now the Commons). Mary Jane Shoultz speaks in PS-122 on "Family-Caused Failure."

14 JAN. 1970. *The Pawprint* returns to a smaller page size.

15 JAN. 1971. John E. Hafstrom, Chair of the Dept. of Mathematics, is named Act. Chair of the Natural Sciences Div., replacing Ralph H. Petrucci, who goes on sabbatical leave for Winter and Spring terms. The Library announces a reciprocal borrowing agreement for faculty and students with the Univ. of Redlands. The rock groups The Weather Cocks, Rocky Mountain News, and Extreme Flash perform on The Green.

18 JAN. 1971. The campus begins occupying the Library-Classroom Building when the Language Lab moves into the LC basement.

19 JAN. 1971. Madelyn Reel speaks in PS-10 on "Women's Liberation and the Third World Woman."

22 JAN. 1971. Pres. Pfau announces a reorganization of Academic Affairs, appointing the first campus department chairs for History (Robert R. Roberts), Political Science (Brij B. Khare), Sociology (Clifford T. Paynton), Art (Robert R. Harrison), Drama (Ronald E. Barnes), English (Edward M. White), Foreign Languages (Joe F. Bas), Music (Richard S. Saylor), Philosophy (Leslie Van Marter), Biology (Alfred S. Egge), Chemistry (James D. Crum), Mathematics (Denis R. Lichtman), Physics (C. Fred Kellers), and Physical Education (C. Michael O'Gara). The first 3 departments become part of the Social Sciences Div., the next 6 become part of Humanities, and the next 4 become part of Natural Sciences, with the P.E. Dept. standing alone for administrative purposes. The courtyard in the west wing of the Administration Building is outfitted with tables and benches to provide a tranquil spot for lunches or breaks. W. R. "Bob" Holcomb, candidate for S.B. Mayor, speaks on The Green.

26 JAN. 1971. Roy C. Barnett Co. receives a $133,780 contract to landscape the area around the Library-Classroom Building.

30-31 JAN. 1971. The campus hosts an Institute in Bilingual Communication Skills coordinated by Sergio D. Elizondo.

2 FEB. 1971. The campus hosts a panel discussion in PS-10 on "The Rights of Prisoners," with Anthony Kemp, Don Dibble, David Flint (Chair), and Vernon O. Leviege.

5 FEB. 1971. The campus adopts standardized abbreviations to identify its buildings: A (Administration), AG (Animal-Greenhouse), BI (Biological Sciences), C (Cafeteria), CO (Commons), HA (Heating and Air Conditioning), LC (Library-Classroom), PE (Physical Education), PP (Physical Plant), PS (Physical Sciences), RA (Residence Halls), S (Student Services), T (Trailers). The campus receives a $13,200 grant from the U.S. Dept. of Housing and Urban Development to help construct the Commons Building.

7 FEB. 1971. Violinist Endre Granat, pianist Charles Fierro, and cellist Nathaniel Rosen perform chamber music in PS-10.

16 FEB. 1971. The Interactors of San Bernardino perform the play *Black, White, and Mrs. Green* in PS-10.

17 FEB. 1971. Opera soprano Lorna Castaneda performs in C-104. The U.S. Dept. of Housing and Urban Development issues $325,000 in bonds to support construction of the Commons Building.

19 FEB. 1971. Problems with the heating and air-conditioning system in the new Library-Classroom Building, and the delivery of incorrect carpeting, force a delay in occupancy until June for the Library portion of the structure. The campus hosts an "Indian Day" with the Native American Students Alliance, including lectures by Arthur Hill, Jerry Hill, Dan Bombarry, Jack Allen, Harvey Wells, and Lehman Brightman (speaking on "American Indian Problems"), and dances by the Sherman Indian High School Dancers, the American Indian Tribal Dancers, and the American Drum Feather Club. The rock groups New Decade and Allis Chalmers perform on The Green. The group Monterey Pop performs in PS-10. Elliott R. Barkan and Nikolai E. Khokhlov are interviewed on ABC Radio about their computerized carpool system, the first of its kind in the U.S. Bonham Richardson receives a grant from the American Philosophical Soc. to study for 3 months in Trinidad.

22 FEB. 1971. Poet Michael Dennis Browne reads from his work in the Little Gym. Fanny R. Shaftel speaks in the Little Gym on "Role Playing for Social Values."

25 FEB. 1971. Mathematician Leonard Tornheim speaks in BI-101 on "Linear Programming."

26 FEB. 1971. The campus receives approval to offer a B.A. degree in Geography beginning with 1971/72. Strong Santa Ana winds impact the campus.

27 FEB. 1971. The Music Dept. sponsors a High School Day for local students.

1 MAR. 1971. The student government adopts a resolution opposing Gov. Reagan's proposed cuts in the EOP budget. S.B. Co. approves lower parking violation fines for the campus, from $2-$10.

3 MAR. 1971. Raquel Montenegro, Assoc. Dir. of Project MAESTRO, speaks in PS-10 on "The Chicana—Past, Present, and Future."

5 Mar. 1971. Bruce Golden and Robert A. Lee receive National Endowment for the Humanities fellowships, with Golden scheduled to study 16th- and 17th-century drama in England during 1971/72.

7 Mar. 1971. Circle K and Theta Psi Omega (ΘΨΩ) sponsor a benefit fashion show, "In Like a Lion," on the Cafeteria Patio, to fund a scholarship in memory of Cal State student Rose Crist.

11 Mar. 1971. The CSC System faculty adopt a statement of professional responsibilities, based in part on the American Assoc. of University Professors' statement of ethics. Ex-astronaut Brian O'Leary speaks in PS-10 on "The Exploration of the Planets."

12 Mar. 1971. Robert A. Lee receives a Fulbright-Hayes award to lecture at Hacettepe Univ., Ankara, Turkey, during 1971/72.

13 Mar. 1971. Cal State senior Bernice Marie Gramlich is chosen Miss San Bernardino 1971.

15 Mar. 1971. Construction begins on the Commons Building.

18 Mar. 1971. Cal State students Jimmy Perry, Larry Culberson, and Rosalyn Jacquett embark on a 2-week trip to Nairobi, Africa.

31 Mar. 1971. Guitarist, lutenist, and singer Donna Curry performs Renaissance music in C-104.

1 Apr. 1971. George A. Meneses, Asst. Dir. of the EOP Program, is named Asst. Dean of Students, replacing Robert F. Gentry.

2 Apr. 1971. The campus installs bicycle stands at 3 locations. Grade school chemistry teacher (a student at CSCSB), George Danchuk, and 6th-grade students George Bonton and Edward Gonzáles, are burned when their experiment explodes outdoors on campus.

5 Apr. 1971. Pacific Van and Storage receives a $2,772 contract to move the old Library to the new one. MEChA sponsors a panel in PS-122 featuring drug addicts from Patton State Hospital. Kate Wilson, Activities Advisor, is named Financial Aid Advisor.

7 Apr. 1971. The campus hosts a careers conference on nursing, "Advancement Through Education," in PS-10, with Sister Eugene Teresa, Betty Jacobson, Dorothy Martin, Robert Murphy, and Christine Sisley. Psychiatrist C. R. Schweitzer speaks in PS-202 on "Clinical Social Work."

8 Apr. 1971. The campus begins a trial program of Student Evaluation of

Teaching Effectiveness (SETE).

13 APR. 1971. The Data Processing Center moves to the Library-Classroom Building basement, with operations resuming on Apr. 16.

14 APR. 1971. Pianist Lily Pan-Diehl and violinist Alfred Walters perform in C-104. Ceramic artist Susan Petersen speaks in PS-10 on the Japanese potter Hamada.

15 APR. 1971. Critic Melvin J. Friedman speaks in S-145 on "William Styron and the Politics of Urgency."

16 APR. 1971. Frederick H. Damaske receives a grant from NSF to participate in its Summer Institute in Mass Political Communication.

19 APR. 1971. The 55-piece Oakland Symphony Youth Orchestra, under the direction of Denis de Coteau, performs on the Mall with classical guitarist Rey de la Torre in a moving rendition of Joaquín Rodrigo's *Concierto de Aranjuez*.

20 APR. 1971. Bruce Halstead, Dir. of the World Life Research Institute, speaks in PS-10 on "Ocean Suicide."

21 APR. 1971. The UCR Madrigal Singers perform in C-104. The campus hosts an Earth Day panel moderated by Elliott R. Barkan, with John Palmer, Leroy Simmons, J. R. Gomen, and Tom Chinn participating.

22 APR. 1971. Students pass a 3rd referendum for a fee supporting construction of a Student Union Building, by a vote of 661-461, allowing the issuance of $912,000 in bonds.

23 APR. 1971. The campus receives an $11,516 grant from NSF to conduct an in-service institute for social science teachers.

28 APR. 1971. The Dept. of Chemistry is accredited by the American Chemical Soc.

30 APR. 1971. Harvey Wichman is named first Chair of the Psychology Dept.

1 MAY 1971. The campus hosts a conference on "Computer Carpooling" in PS-10, with Joseph V. Behar, Robert Schwitzgebel, Al Maleson, Ronald Loveridge, and Dallas Holmes participating.

3 MAY 1971. Classes are offered for the first time on the 2nd floor of the Library-Classroom Building.

5 MAY 1971. Chicano activist Oscar Acosta speaks in PS-10 on "The Chicano in the Court." The Teatro Aztlán of San Gorgonio High School performs *Actos de la Vida* in PS-10.

7 MAY 1971. Joseph K. Thomas, Exec. Dean, is named VP for Administration.

10 MAY 1971. W. R. "Bob" Holcomb, an early supporter of the campus, takes office as S.B. Mayor, replacing Al C. Ballard. Ann Singer speaks in PS-122 on "Psycho-Biological Differences Between Men and Women."

11 MAY 1971. Attorney Dennis Powell speaks in PS-10 on "With Liberty and Justice for All."

14 MAY 1971. The campus receives a $12,500 grant from the Calif. Coordinating Council for Higher Education, and a $3,920 grant from IBM to support the EOP Program. The campus hosts the Spring Conference of the South Asia Colloquium of Southern California, with Renée Renouf speaking in LC-267 on "Cultural Show and Tell," Raghuvan Iyer speaking on The Green on "Some Thoughts on Asia," and Paul Wallace speaking at a dinner meeting at The Castaway Restaurant.

17 MAY 1971. S.B. City awards a contract to construct a traffic signal at Kendall Dr. and State College Pkwy.

18 MAY 1971. A fire caused by the spontaneous combustion of a pile of rags soaked with paint destroys a storage shed belonging to Viking Construction Co., contractor for the CSCSB Residence Halls, causing $50,000 in damage to redwood siding and electrical panels.

19 MAY 1971. Oboist Charles Gower Price and harpsichordist Rachel Jupe perform in C-104. The campus co-sponsors with the World Affairs Council of Inland Southern Calif. a dinner at the Orange Show for Israeli Ambassador to the United States and General Yitzhak Rabin, who speaks on "The Middle East Conflict."

26 MAY 1971. Hemisphere Constructors receives a $449,500 contract to construct utility lines and tunnels connecting the Commons Building to the Air Conditioning Plant.

27 MAY 1971. Psychologist Marie B. Edwards speaks in PS-10 on "The Challenge of Being Single."

28 MAY 1971. Sergio D. Elizondo receives a post-doctoral fellowship to study at the Colegio de México during the summer. Michael Burgess is named Co-Editor of Newcastle Publishing Co., Inc.

3 Jun. 1971. Ruth "Dee" Simpson speaks in BI-101 on "Archeological Investigations at the Calico Hills Site."

4 Jun. 1971. Cal State senior Harvey Friedman directs a play, *Lunchtime*, in the Little Theatre. Poets Donald Justice and Charles Wright read from their work in LC-27.

6 Jun. 1971. Pres. Pfau is a guest on the program *Inland Youth Forum* at radio station KBON.

7 Jun. 1971. Harpsichordist Rachel Jupe performs in C-104.

9 Jun. 1971. The campus receives a $2,000 grant from International Business Machines Corp. to help fund the EOP Program.

11 Jun. 1971. The campus accepts the Library-Classroom Building.

12 Jun. 1971. The 5th Commencement is held in the Gymnasium, with ex-Sen. Thomas H. Kuchel (1953-69) giving the keynote address; 425 students are eligible to receive degrees.

12-20 Jun. 1971. The Library moves its 150,000-volume collection into the new, 5-story Library-Classroom Building, opening again for business on Monday, Jun. 21. The Library occupies the 1st, 3rd, and 4th floors of the structure, and part of the basement, with the Data Processing Center, Language Lab, Education Dept., and Audio-Visual Dept. sharing the basement, the Humanities Div. (including classrooms and faculty offices) occupying the 2nd floor; additional faculty offices are later constructed by campus personnel on the 5th floor. This is the first library in the CSC System to be completely carpeted, and the 2nd largest building designed for human occupancy in S.B. Co. (the largest is the Loma Linda Univ. Hospital). The old Library Building is renamed the Student Services Building, and the structure is remodeled during the summer months to accommodate Admissions, Financial Aid, and EOP.

1 Jul. 1971. The campus Accounting Dept. converts to an automatic data processing system. John E. Fredricks, College Accounting Officer, is named Asst. Business Manager. Bernard Higuera is named College Accounting Officer, replacing John E. Fredricks.

2 Jul. 1971. The campus designates a number of parking spaces for carpool vehicles only.

8 Jul. 1971. The local chapter of the Calif. State Employees Assoc. votes by a 3-to-1 margin to authorize a strike (it never happens).

9 JUL. 1971. Czech pantomimist Antonin Hodek performs "A Touch of the Silent" in PS-10.

15 JUL. 1971. Victor Valley College and CSCSB agree to offer 3rd-year college courses at VVC in 1971/72. The play *The Rainmaker* by J. Richard Nash begins a 6-night run, with TV actor Paul Brinegar in the leading role.

16 JUL. 1971. Historian and organist William G. "Doc" Blanchard performs in PS-10, providing live music for the silent screen classic, *Our Hospitality*, starring Buster Keaton.

28 JUL. 1971. The campus receives a $71,071 grant from the College Work-Study Program.

1 AUG. 1971. Jo Ann Von Wald is named Admissions Officer.

2-11 AUG. 1971. The campus hosts an extension anthropology class taught by Larry Stucki at the Havasupai Indian Reservation at the Grand Canyon in Arizona.

24 AUG. 1971. The campus receives a $3,120 grant from the Law Enforcement Education Program, and a $140,272 grant to fund Federal Higher Education student loans.

29 AUG. 1971. Pres. Pfau appears for a 2nd time as guest on the program *Inland Youth Forum* on radio station KBON.

31 AUG. 1971. Robert R. Roberts, Chair of the Social Sciences Div., returns to the ranks as Prof. of History. Robert D. Picker, Dean of Academic Planning, resigns.

FALL TERM 1971. The Cal State System implements a Common Admissions Program, with students filing one application form that lists 4 choices of CSC campuses in order of preference. Student fees increase from $200 to $1,110 a year.

1 SEPT. 1971. Ward M. McAfee is named Chair of the Social Sciences Div., replacing Robert R. Roberts. Lee H. Kalbus is named Act. Dean of Academic Planning, replacing Robert D. Picker. Edward J. Carlson, Act. Chairman of the Dept. of Administration, is named Chairman. The campus begins offering a teaching credential program.

17 SEPT. 1971. The traffic signal at the corner of Kendall Dr. and State College Pkwy. is completed at a cost of $32,316. George A. Meneses, Asst. Dean of Students, resigns.

21 Sept. 1971. The annual convocation is held.

24 Sept. 1971. Alexander D. Sokoloff receives a $20,000 grant from NSF for tribolium research. John H. Craig receives a $7,500 grant from the Petroleum Research Fund to research the nature of bonding in carbon compounds. The campus installs closed-circuit TV monitors at 3 locations to provide up-to-the-minute information on closed classes. The campus opens a vending machine snack area in S-145.

1 Oct. 1971. The pop group Allis Chalmers performs in the Pool Area. Library overdue fees are raised by the Chancellor's Off. to 15¢ per day. Carl P. Wagoner is named Assoc. Dean of Academic Planning, partially replacing George A. Meneses, Asst. Dean of Students.

11 Oct. 1971. South Indian violinist Lalgudi G. Jayaraman and flautist N. Ramani perform with other Carnatic musicians in PS-10.

15 Oct. 1971. CSCSB receives an $185,415 bequest from the estate of Alfred F. Moore (an astronomer who died in 1969) to establish the Alfred F. and Chella D. Moore Scholarship Fund. The campus hosts a YWCA Conference on Racism.

19 Oct. 1971. The Black Student Union accuses the campus of not supporting the Dir. of the EOP Program.

20 Oct. 1971. Pianist Lee Stern performs in C-104.

22 Oct. 1971. The campus receives approval to offer a Teaching Credential in Early Childhood Education. Walter S. Kadyk, Dir. of College Police, is also named Emergency Planning Coordinator.

28 Oct. 1971. Attorney John Kennedy speaks in PS-10 on "The Law and You."

1 Nov. 1971. Rev. Theophane A. Mathias, S.J., speaks in PS-10 on "Christianity and Hinduism."

2 Nov. 1971. Psychologist Reginald Jones speaks in LC-27 on "Black Education and Black Psychology."

3 Nov. 1971. Geophysicist Douglas G. Fox speaks in PS-10 on "Environmental Problems," also in BI-101 on "Turbulence in Geophysics and What We Can Do About It."

5 Nov. 1971. The Learning Laboratory opens in the LC basement.

10 Nov. 1971. Trumpeter Lawrence Johansen and harpsichordist Judith Johansen perform in C-104.

11 Nov. 1971. The Administrative Council adopts a policy stating that dogs on campus must be constrained by a leash.

12 Nov. 1971. The Faculty Senate creates a new standing Committee on Computer Affairs. The Library sponsors its first major exhibit in its main display case on the first floor—the annual traveling exhibit of the Chicago Book Clinic of the 57 Top Honor Books of the 1971 design competition.

19 Nov. 1971. In response to declining enrollments, Assoc. Dean DeRemer circulates a memo to administrators, delineating the results of a survey of 200 students who had left the college without graduating—their reasons include: the foreign language requirement, too many general education requirements, a restricted number of majors, and not enough night classes.

20 Nov. 1971. The campus hosts the Calif. Continuing Education Assoc. Conference in PS-10, with speakers William J. Atkins, Peter Marin, Mitchell L. Voydat, John Gathings, Susan A. Stark, Robert E. Botts, Paul L. Riggins, Raymond Choinière, and George E. Magnuson.

29 Nov. 1971. Gov. Reagan signs a bill renaming the CSC System as the California State University and Colleges, and beginning the conversion of individual campus names to "State Universities."

3 Dec. 1971. S.B. Mayor Holcomb speaks in PS-10 on "Politics by Default." Educator George Lucas speaks in LC-27 on "Employment Opportunities in the San Bernardino-Riverside Areas for Teachers."

4 Dec. 1971. The campus hosts the annual conference of the Inland Empire Council for the Social Studies, "Effective Thinking in the Social Studies," in LC-500, with speaker Todd Clark, and participants James Randles, Andrew Smith, James Reardon, Julia Coleman, and Lenel Shuck.

6 Dec. 1971. Mary Ann Cisar, Assoc. Prof. of Political Science (1965-71), dies in San Bernardino of a cerebral hemorrhage at age 39, being the first CSCSB faculty member to die in service; a Mary Cisar Memorial Fund is established in her name. Gerhard Friedrich, CSC Dean of Academic Planning, meets with faculty in LC-27.

8 Dec. 1971. The campus receives an $8,841 grant from NSF.

9 Dec. 1971. Leslie Irving Harris, a local businessman and a founding member of CAB (1965-1971), dies in San Bernardino at age 77.

14 DEC. 1971. Folksinger Esteban Ramón performs in PS-10.

1972

1 JAN. 1972. John F. "Jack" McDonnell is named Asst. to the Dean of Academic Administration.

6 JAN. 1972. Nigerian scholar Ucecukwu C. Ogike begins teaching an upper-division English course in Black Literature.

14 JAN. 1972. The gospel folksingers Good News Singers perform the musical, *Show Me*, in PS-10. Robert A. Blackey, Assoc. Prof. of History, is named first Relations-with-Schools Officer.

17 JAN. 1972. Attorney Al Sanders speaks in PS-10 on "The Campus and the Police."

19 JAN. 1972. Pres. Pfau commits the campus to an affirmative action program "to achieve an appropriate representation among all groups. This program will be designed to broaden our efforts to recruit, train, and promote minority members and women. This is both a moral and a legal obligation."

20 JAN. 1972. The campus hosts a philosophy forum, "Why Revolution?" in LC-241.

22-23 JAN. 1972. Faculty and administrators meet at Monte Corona Conference Center in Twin Peaks to discuss campus development, and to examine possible changes in the curriculum and graduation requirements that will increase enrollment.

25 JAN. 1972. As a direct result of the Monte Corona Conference, the Faculty Senate unanimously recommends that the foreign language requirement for graduation be dropped; Pres. Pfau approves the measure on Jan. 27, with effect from Mar. 27.

27 JAN. 1972. The Inland Empire Library Tech Teachers meet on campus to discuss "What's Wrong with Our Library Tech Programs?" Physicist Darrell J. Drickey speaks in LC-241 on "Americans at Serpukhov: An Experiment in American-Russian Collaboration."

29 JAN. 1972. The campus receives a $700 grant from Standard Oil Co. of Calif. to plant 200 trees along State College Pkwy., with the participation of S.B. Fifth Ward Councilman Lionel Hudson, S.B. Mayor Holcomb, John McGuire of Standard Oil Co., Gordon Burgess of Southern Calif. Edison Co., and Gerald W. Stoops, Chair of the Natural Beauty Program.

31 Jan. 1972. Rosemary T. Ward, Curriculum Libn. (1966-72), resigns. Cal State student Scott Marvin Taylor dies in San Bernardino at age 22.

4 Feb. 1972. Pres. Pfau appoints an Ad-Hoc Committee to Review the Academic Goals and Programs of the College, under the chairmanship of Alfred S. Egge; the Committee interviews individuals and groups regarding the campus's General Education Program.

8 Feb. 1972. 200 students, part of a group called SUFFER (Students United for Furthering Educational Rights), march on campus to demand equal representation on the Task Force formed to review the General Studies Program.

11 Feb. 1972. The campus installs 2 emergency phones at opposite ends of the main parking lot. The campus receives an $8,611 grant from NSF to conduct an in-service Institute for Sociology and Social Studies for high school teachers, under the direction of Gordon E. Stanton. Folksingers Bill Carlson and Greg Durio perform in S-100.

15 Feb. 1972. An editorial in *The Pawprint* states that "The dream is ending: the 'Swarthmore of the West' is dead."

16 Feb. 1972. The campus hosts the first of a series of public forums in LC-27 to discuss academic goals and programs. Statistician Jerzy Neyman speaks in LC-27 on "Mechanisms Leading to Cancer," and in BI-101 on "The Evaluation of Galaxies."

18 Feb. 1972. Sociologist Jack D. Douglas speaks in PS-10 on "Crime and Justice in American Society."

23 Feb. 1972. Robert L. Schwitzgebel speaks in LC-27 on "Psychologists as a Travel Agent: Designing Good Life Trip."

24 Feb. 1972. Charity James speaks in LC-500 on "Young Lives at Stake: A Reappraisal of Secondary Schools." Poet Marvin Bell reads from his work in PS-10. Norman P. Roadarmel speaks in PS-122 on "What's Happening in Asia."

28 Feb. 1972. Anita Viksne speaks in LC-27 on "History and Romance of Diamonds—Their Origin, Traditions, Use, and History."

29 Feb. 1972. The Task Force on Academic Goals and Programs submits its first recommendations to Pres. Pfau and the Faculty Senate, suggesting that the number of required general studies courses for graduation be significantly reduced, and the number of optional courses increased, with small classes being retained.

1 MAR. 1972. Louis Bluth speaks in PS-122 on "Eckankar: Ancient Science of Soul Travel."

3 MAR. 1972. John M. Pfau is honored on his 10th anniversary as Pres. of CSCSB with a luncheon at Arrowhead Country Club, with 50 attendees, including ex-Exec. Dean Kenneth Phillips.

7 MAR. 1972. Rabbi Norman Feldheym speaks in LC-241 on "A Little Anarchy Now and Then."

10 MAR. 1972. Renowned geneticist Theodosius Dobzhansky speaks in LC-27 on "Genetic Diversity and Human Equality."

20 MAR. 1972. Pres. Pfau approves an M.A. degree in Elementary Education, beginning with 1972/73. This is the first master's program to be offered by the campus.

23-24 MAR. 1972. The campus hosts the 16th Annual Inland Science Fair in the Gymnasium, with 229 students participating.

24 MAR. 1972. Cal State alumnus Theodore "Ted" Krug is named Financial Aid Advisor.

27 MAR. 1972. Dr. Edward Dainko speaks in PS-10 on "Kidney Transplants."

28 MAR. 1972. The campus begins constructing an ecology pond 50 feet in diameter and several feet deep, plus with a redwood bridge, near the olive grove on the north edge of CSCSB.

1 APR. 1972. George L. McMichael, Prof. of English and ex-Dean of Faculty (1962-66), resigns to become Dean of Arts, Letters, and Social Sciences at CSC, Hayward. The campus hosts a foreign film festival through Jun. 2, showing 17 films from 8 countries.

3 APR. 1972. For the first time, the campus begins making regular college courses available through its Extension Program.

3-7 APR. 1972. The campus hosts a week-long open house to celebrate the grand opening of the Residence Halls.

4 APR. 1972. Frank E. Stranges speaks in PS-10 on "Why You Should Believe in UFO's." The CSUC Board of Trustees designates 13 state colleges as "state universities," effective Jun. 1, and establishes the criteria for other institutions in the system to apply for university status at a future date.

8 APR. 1972. Science writer Irving Bengelsdorf speaks in PS-10 on "The Energy Crisis" as part of the Math-Science Day event.

14 APR. 1972. Ray Huerta speaks in PS-202 on "Farm Workers Union."

15 APR. 1972. The campus hosts a seminar in "Multiethnic Education" in LC-27, with James Deslonde giving the keynote address.

17 APR. 1972. The last visible power pole is removed from campus.

19 APR. 1972. Lora Moorehead speaks in LC-500 on "Black Control of the Black Community."

21 APR. 1972. Satirist Mort Sahl and folksinger Alicia Cory perform in the Gymnasium. *College Courses*, a cookbook edited by Antreen Pfau and Barbara Robinson, is published by the CSCSB Faculty Wives, with proceeds going to support scholarships.

24 APR. 1972. George E. Brown speaks in LC-500.

26 APR. 1972. The UCR Madrigal Singers perform in C-104.

27 APR. 1972. The campus hosts a conference in LC-500 for local high school counselors.

28 APR. 1972. The campus receives a $50,537 grant from Title I of the U.S. Higher Education Act to broaden educational and career counseling opportunities for residents of San Bernardino and Riverside Counties, with an additional $45,619 being provided by CSCSB and local community colleges and agencies. The Chancellor's Off. approves a new M.A. Degree in Elementary Education to be offered in 1972/73. State Sen. William E. Coombs speaks in LC-500.

29 APR. 1972. The campus hosts an art fair in the Commons that attracts 700 local children.

30 APR. 1972. *The San Bernardino Sun-Telegram* publishes a front-page article, "Cal State S.B.—Bright Promise Gone Awry?" by Carl Yetzer, alleging that CSCSB "is in trouble—trouble serious enough to hamper its effectiveness for some time to come," pointing to an over-elite curriculum, low enrollment, lack of development of the surrounding community, and failure to reach out to community colleges. The essay ignores changes recently proposed by Pres. Pfau, as well as the low enrollments being experienced at the time by most Calif. colleges.

1 MAY 1972. Filmmaker Andrew Águilar speaks in PS-10 on "The Mexican-American and the Media," and shows 3 of his films.

3 MAY 1972. Olga Rodríguez speaks in PS-10 on "The Chicana Liberation."

4 MAY 1972. The campus hosts a conference for local college counselors in LC-500 to acquaint them with the numerous changes in the University curricula being introduced during 1972/73.

5 MAY 1972. The Task Force on Academic [or Educational] Goals and Programs submits its report on reducing General Education requirements for graduation to Pres. Pfau and the Faculty Senate.

8 MAY 1972. The State Coordinating Council for Higher Education approves changing the names of 13 of the 19 campuses in the CSUC System from "colleges" to "universities."

12 MAY 1972. A new electronic music studio opens in the Cafeteria Building.

13 MAY 1972. Selma S. "Jerry" Keller, Libn. (1966-72), resigns.

14 MAY 1972. The newly formed Chamber Orchestra of CSC, San Bernardino debuts in PS-10.

19 MAY 1972. Educator Nathan Hare speaks on The Green on "The Black Liberation Struggle and Education," as part of the campus's "Black Solidarity Day." The rock group Earth, Wind, and Fire performs on The Green.

22 MAY 1972. The Calif. State Legislature's Joint Committee on the Master Plan for Education meets in LC-500 to evaluate how CSCSB and the local community colleges are interacting. Pres. Pfau testifies before a special subcommittee of the Joint Committee on the Master Plan for Higher Education of the State Legislature concerning enrollment problems and community issues facing the campus; area residents, students, faculty, and alumni also speak, some of them charging that the campus has failed to meet local needs, and that the broad general education requirement has become an impediment to enrollment growth. One student states: "Transfer students from community colleges are faced with loss of units and so much ambiguity in the evaluation of transcripts that it is often impossible to determine what courses are actually needed and which classes here are equivalent to those at the community colleges."

23 MAY 1972. The Faculty Senate approves the General Education Program recommended by the President's Task Force, reducing the number of general education units required to graduate from 90 to 70, effective Fall 1972; this represented the last major change from the academic program established when CSCSB first opened in 1965, and began shifting the campus towards a career-oriented curriculum. Ex-U.S. Sen. Ernest Gruening speaks on The Green in support of Sen. George McGovern for President.

26 MAY 1972. Political impressionist David Frye performs in the Gymnasium with the Mill Creek County Folk Group.

31 MAY 1972. An original children's drama, *Reingold*, by graduate student Joan Newmannis, is presented in the Little Theatre.

2 JUN. 1972. Antiwar activist David Harris speaks on the Mall on the "Air War Initiative."

3 JUN. 1972. The Alpha Kappa Psi (AKΨ) business fraternity grants a charter to the newly-formed Cal State chapter, Iota Omicron (IO) at an installation dinner; its initiation ceremony occurs on Dec. 2, with S.B. City Councilman and alumnus Tony Campos giving the keynote address. Sociology students and faculty receive tentative approval to form the Pi Iota (ΠΙ) chapter of Alpha Kappa Delta (AKΔ), the national honorary sociological fraternity; formal approval is received on Nov. 17. The campus hosts its 2nd Annual High School Theatre Workshop.

6 JUN. 1972. The campus opens an Electronic Music Studio with a synthesizer built by Donald Buchla of Oakland.

9 JUN. 1972. The campus receives a $401,520 grant from the Higher Education Act. The campus begins accepting credit cards for payment of student fees.

10 JUN. 1972. The 6th Commencement is held in the Gymnasium, with Paul D. Saltman, Provost of Revelle College at UC San Diego, giving the keynote speech; 550 students are eligible for degrees.

15 JUN. 1972. The campus establishes an Inland Empire Management Center under the Directorship of Edward J. Carlson, Chair of the Dept. of Administration.

29 JUN. 1972. Moulder Brothers receives a $90,840 contract to landscape the area around the Commons Building. Robert R. Harrison, Prof. of Art and Chair of the Art Dept. (1965-72), is named the first Emer. Prof. at CSCSB upon his retirement. The campus establishes a toll-free phone number (825-3833) for Redlands and Riverside.

30 Jun. 1972. The State Board of Education accredits 3 campus teaching credential programs.

7 Jul. 1972. Theologian John B. Cobb speaks in PS-10 on "The Theology of Ecology."

13 Jul. 1972. The campus denies a rumor in the *San Bernardino Sun* that it is selling some of its undeveloped land.

16 Aug. 1972. The campus receives approval to offer a B.A. degree in Administration, effective with Fall 1972.

17 Aug. 1972. American Asphalt Paving Co. receives a $149,330 contract to construct a 390-space parking lot near the new residence halls.

25 Aug. 1972. Cal State student Brian R. Collins dies at Barstow at age 29.

28 Aug. 1972. CSUC Chancellor Glenn S. Dumke announces the first mutual-use library agreement within the Cal State System, giving students and faculty at 6 Southern California campuses, including CSCSB, access to each other's collections.

31 Aug. 1972. Lee H. Kalbus, Act. Dean of Academic Planning, returns to the ranks as Chair and Prof. of the Chemistry Dept. Carl P. Wagoner, Assoc. Dean of Academic Planning, returns to the ranks as Asst. Prof. of Sociology. Robert A. Blackey, Relations-with-Schools Officer, returns to the ranks as Prof. of History.

1 Sept. 1972. Ralph H. Petrucci, Chair of the Div. of Natural Sciences, is named Dean of Academic Planning, replacing Lee H. Kalbus. James D. Crum, Chair of the Chemistry Dept., is named Chair of the Natural Sciences Div., replacing Ralph H. Petrucci. Kent M. Schofield is named Assoc. Dean of Academic Planning, replacing Carl P. Wagoner. Michael M. Rose is named Relations-with-Schools Officer, replacing Robert A. Blackey. H. Arthur "Hal" Hoverland is named Chair of the Dept. of Administration, replacing Edward J. Carlson. Arthur E. Nelson, Coll. Librarian, is named Library Dir. The campus begins offering a master's degree in Elementary Education, and a B.A. degree in Social Sciences through Coll. of the Desert in Palm Desert.

11 Sept. 1972. The annual convocation is held.

15 Sept. 1972. Jesse Hiraoka, Prof. of French and ex-Chair of the Div. of Humanities (1966-69), resigns. Tom M. Rivera is named Assoc. Dean of Students for the EOP. The campus unveils a new entrance on the east side of the Student Services Building. The campus appoints an advisory committee of nursing and health experts to help develop B.S. degrees in Nursing and Health Science.

21 SEPT. 1972. The Chancellor's Off. announces a program to develop self-paced learning and academic achievement evaluation projects, including grants of $9,965 to Kenneth A. Mantei and $32,000 to Ralph H. Petrucci.

22 SEPT. 1972. The Chancellor's Off. approves renaming the 4 academic divisions as follows: School of Humanities, School of Education, School of Natural Sciences, and School of Social Sciences, with the Chairs of each Division becoming "Deans." Louis C. Hodnett, Prof. of Sociology and Ethnic Studies Coordinator; Vernon O. "Ollie" Leviege, Coordinator of Ethnic Studies and Assoc. Prof. of Sociology; and Lawrence E. "Larry" Johnson, Dir. of the EOP, resign to protest alleged racism on campus; they are quickly joined by Clyde E. DeBerry, Lect. of Psychology; and Harvey M. Johnson, Lect. of Sociology. Johnson had stated in a Jun. 1971 letter to Assemblyman Willie Brown that: "I think this college will have to find other ways of staffing or recruiting qualified staff in lieu of the Ph.D. equivalency. Qualification is the equivalency of which I am speaking. I think of experience in terms of the law of supply and demand. Again, I feel that the college has made very little effort in dealing with this specific problem." The resignations were prompted by Leviege's request for a leave with pay to work on a Ph.D. degree out of state—a request that was denied by Pres. Pfau because Leviege had failed to meet the requirement under state law that he complete 6 years of service before a paid leave could be granted.

25 SEPT. 1972. The 8 buildings comprising the new Residence Halls, collectively called Serrano Village, begin accepting their first students; they include No. 1 (Tokay), No. 2 (Arrowhead, later San Manuel), No. 3 (Joshua), No. 4 (Mojave), No. 5 (Morongo), No. 6 (Waterman), No. 7 (Badger), and No. 8 (Shandin). The Commons Building opens for business, offering students, faculty, and staff a 600-seat, 2-level structure for dining and entertaining. The former Cafeteria Building is renamed the Fine Arts Building.

27 SEPT. 1972. Van C. Andrews, Associate Student Body Pres. since May, and Alice Turner, Student Affairs Committee member, resign to protest alleged racism on campus; Andrews is automatically succeeded by ASB VP Bruce Prescott.

28 SEPT. 1972. The Chancellor's Off. approves an option in History for the new M.A. in Education degree.

29 SEPT. 1972. Stella T. Clark is named Assoc. Dean of Academic Administration. A temporary parking lot is graded for the use of dorm students until a permanent lot is constructed. State Assemblyman John P. Quimby and S.B. County Supervisor Nancy E. Smith meet with campus administrators, the African-American faculty who had recently resigned, and members of the local African-American community, in an attempt to resolve the conflict. Many speakers suggest that Pres. Pfau should "bend the rules" and grant exceptions to African-American faculty to meet the requirements for retention, promotion, and tenure.

30 SEPT. 1972. The campus hosts the Fall Conference of the Inland Empire Chapter of the Southern Calif. Assoc. for the Education of Young Children, with Assemblyman C. Jerry Lewis speaking on "New Policies: The Legislative View of Needs in Child-Care." Assemblyman John P. Quimby phones CSU Chancellor Dumke, seeking some compromise in the growing racial confrontation between African-American faculty and the campus administration; Dumke responds by saying that "There were specific legal prohibitions against granting [Leviege's] leave [request to work on his Ph.D. degree], and that President Pfau was right in denying this request." Vernon O. Leviege then files a complaint with the U.S. Equal Employment Opportunity Commission (EEOC), which drags on for nine years, until it is finally dismissed on Apr. 9, 1981.

2 OCT. 1972. The Administrative Council approves a 24-hour campus phone number.

5 OCT. 1972. Cal State Biology major Charles Eugene Hill dies in Redlands at age 24.

6 OCT. 1972. The Chancellor's Off. approves an option in English for the M.A. degree in Education.

13 OCT. 1972. The President's Task Force to Review Educational Goals and Programs submits its final 85-page report, *The Changing College*, to Pres. Pfau.

16 OCT. 1972. The Administrative Council approves the installation of a Library telecopier that will provide direct contact with other libraries on a leased line. The Black Student Union meets with Pres. Pfau to demand the rehiring of the African-American faculty who resigned in Sept.—they are not reinstated.

19 OCT. 1972. D. Gaye Perry is named Asst. Dean of Students, replacing George A. Meneses, becoming the first woman dean on campus.

20 OCT. 1972. The Campus Police announces the availability of a 24-hour-per-day, 7-day-per week telephone hotline (887-6311). The Library becomes a founding member of the Inland Empire Coll. Library Cooperative, the others being Calif. Baptist College, Loma Linda Univ. (Loma Linda and Riverside campuses), Univ. of Calif., Riverside, and Univ. of Redlands.

25 OCT. 1972. Hal P. Shawlee of the Union Oil Co. speaks to 104 local high school students and teachers in the Commons.

26 OCT. 1972. Lionila López Saenz speaks in PS-10 on "Women's Rights in Federal Government, Careers, and the Constitution."

27-28 OCT. 1972. The campus hosts the inaugural meeting of the Southwest Soc. for Eighteenth Century Studies, with harpsichordist Janice Eastman, and speakers Robert W. Quinn, Craig Walton, Mary Elizabeth Green, James R. Groves, J. Douglas Canfield, and Charles R. Ritcheson.

31 OCT. 1972. Jeanette M. Bernthaler, Libn. and Head of Public Services (1968-72), resigns.

2 NOV. 1972. Cal State students Robert Tadeo Okura (age 22), Frank Clayton (age 21), and Randall Lloyd Shriner (age 25) are killed on I-15 near Barstow when their sports car plunges over an embankment; the campus flag is lowered to half-mast in their honor.

5 NOV. 1972. Harpsichordist Lynn Watts and soprano Linda Knowles perform in PS-10.

8-10 NOV. 1972. The campus hosts a tax conference in LC-500.

10 NOV. 1972. The Lower Commons is named "Mother Bear's" in a student contest; the appellation doesn't stick. The new M.A. degree program in Education, to be offered Winter 1973, begins enrolling students. The reggae band Zendik performs in Mother Bear's. Activist Chukia Lawton speaks in LC-27 on "The Gary Lawton Case."

17 NOV. 1972. Michael Burgess sells 2 reference books to Gale Research: *Cumulative Paperback Index, 1939-59* and *Science Fiction and Fantasy Literature*. The Coll. Library acquires 3 chess sets, 3 checkers sets, 2 domino sets, and a Scrabble game that can be checked out by students.

18 NOV. 1972. The campus hosts 130 high school students for "Issues '72," featuring an address by Assemblyman John P. Quimby, and a simulated U.S. Senate; Jim Kelch chairs the event; this is the first of a series of programs designed to introduce local high school students to the College.

1 DEC. 1972. The atrium in the Student Services Building is remodeled to provide a covered skylight over a lunch and snack area serviced by vending machines. Ron Bowers is named Cafeteria Manager, replacing Dean Stack.

3 DEC. 1972. Moulder Brothers completes the landscaping around the Commons Building.

6 DEC. 1972. The College's new Art Gallery is dedicated in the Fine Arts Building in the space formerly occupied by the Cafeteria, with Don Woodford being named Gallery Dir. The first exhibit features a collection of contemporary paintings by 14 artists from L.A. galleries. French writer Juliette Minces speaks in LC-500 on "May, 1968 in France: The Myth of the Revolution."

7 DEC. 1972. Attorney John R. Van de Water conducts a management seminar in LC; this is the inaugural event sponsored by the new Inland Empire Management Center.

8 DEC. 1972. S.B. City begins widening State College Pkwy. from 2 to 3 lanes between Northpark Blvd. and Kendall Dr., including a median strip with curbs, automatic sprinklers, and grass.

15 DEC. 1972. At the suggestion of Michael Burgess, the Library purchases 500 paperbacks for recreational reading, to be featured on display racks located on each floor.

1973

5 JAN. 1973. The Chancellor's Off. approves a new B.S. degree in Physics, beginning with 1973/74. Robert A. Lee is named first Assoc. Dean for Academic Affairs. The New Program Development and Evaluation Div. of the Chancellor's Off. funds a $40,000 pilot project to provide freshman English equivalency testing, with Edward M. White as Program Dir. and Chief Reader.

12 JAN. 1973. The campus receives approval from the Chancellor's Off. to offer a "Special Major" B.A. degree beginning in 1973/74. The campus announces that it will establish a College Learning Skills Center, effective with Spring Quarter. The campus begins using a new recruitment slogan, "Learning is not a sink-or-swim proposition at Cal State, San Bernardino," emphasizing its new emphasis on providing tutorial services to struggling students.

19 JAN. 1973. The campus begins building an Information Kiosk at the Main Entrance.

26 Jan. 1973. The Christian music singer Greg Laurie performs with the Maranatha Singers in Mother Bear's. The rock group Bones performs in Mother Bear's. The campus receives gifts of a $500 student loan and $250 scholarship from the Calif. Retired Teachers Assoc.

29 Jan. 1973. Chess master John Hall presents a 3-sided exhibition of his skills in PS-10.

31 Jan. 1973. Kundalini master Yogi Bhajan speaks in PS-10.

1 Feb. 1973. Jesse D. Moses is named Dir. of Supportive Services for the EOP.

2-3 Feb. 1973. Hypnotist Ormond McGill performs in UC.

9 Feb. 1973. The campus receives a $19,460 grant from the U.S. Dept. of Education to purchase audiovisual equipment.

12 Feb. 1973. Barry Romo, National Chair of Vietnam Veterans Against the War, speaks in LC-500 about his Christmas trip with Joan Baez to Hanoi, North Vietnam.

14 Feb. 1973. Shandin Hills Junior High Choir performs in FA-104.

15 Feb. 1973. Bernard Higuera, Accounting Officer, resigns.

16 Feb. 1973. The campus receives approval from the Chancellor's Off. to offer an Ethnic Studies Option for the B.A. degree in Social Studies, beginning in 1973/74. The satirical group The Credibility Gap and singer Penny Nichols perform in LC.

18 Feb. 1973. Betty Jackson conducts an opera workshop in PS-10.

22 Feb. 1973. Mathematician Joseph M. Martin speaks in BI-101 on "What Is a Knot?" and also on "Wild Spheres."

22-23 Feb. 1973. The campus hosts the Black Cultural Festival, attracting 500 local high school students to campus; among the participants are soul singer Billy Paul and the Cal State Northridge Dance Troupe, who perform in the Gymnasium on Feb. 22.

23 Feb. 1973. The campus receives approval from the Chancellor's Off. to offer a B.S. degree in Biology beginning in 1973/74. The Library installs a dollar bill changer on the first floor.

25 Feb. 1973. The campus co-hosts with S.B. Valley College a special show and buffet, "Come to the Cabaret," in LC-500.

27 FEB. 1973. Janie Block of the National Organization of Women speaks in LC.

27-28 FEB. 1973. Greg McArthur speaks in BI-101 and in PS-201 (on Feb. 28) on transcendental meditation.

1 MAR. 1973. The campus changes its official workweek to begin on Sunday Midnight and conclude the following Sunday Midnight. Donald E. Sapronetti is named Accounting Officer, replacing Bernard Higuera (1971-73). Rabbi Norman Feldheym speaks in LC-241 on "Freedom and Love."

2 MAR. 1973. Serrano Village Parking Lot D opens, providing 393 new parking spaces adjacent to Northpark Blvd.

2-4 MAR. 1973. Hollywood actors Al Molinaro, Leo V. Matranga, and Eleanor Lee perform in FA-117 in 3 one-act plays, *Box and Cox*, *Rosalind*, and *The Stronger*.

5 MAR. 1973. Linguist James C. Bostain speaks at the World Affairs Council Dinner in the Commons on "Communicating Across Cultural Barriers."

8 MAR. 1973. Craig Walton speaks in LC-241 on "Freedom and Power."

16 MAR. 1973. The Dallas-based Alpha-Omega Players of the Repertory Theater of America perform Mark Twain's *The Diary of Adam and Eve* and Samuel Beckett's *The Endgame* in PS-10.

17-21 MAR. 1973. The campus hosts the 17th Annual Inland Science Fair.

22 MAR. 1973. The S.B. Co. Superintendent of Schools holds a workshop for 100 local school principals.

24-25 & 31 MAR.-1 APR. 1973. The campus hosts the 36th Annual San Bernardino Tennis Championships.

28 MAR. 1973. Retired Air Force Lt. Col. Frank(lin) D(aniel) Campbell Jr. (1915-1982), publishes an article, "Skinny-Dipping in the Fountain of Youth" in the Mar. 1973 issue of *Air Force Magazine*, about his experiences as a student at CSCSB. He later writes a book, *John D. MacDonald and the Colorful World of Travis McGee* (Borgo Press, 1977).

30 MAR. 1973. Carl P. Wagoner is named Act. Assoc. Dean of Academic Planning, replacing Kent M. Schofield, who goes on sabbatical. Bruce

Golden receives a Folger Fellowship to study at the Folger Library in Washington, DC, during Jul.-Aug.

4 APR. 1973. Actress Jane Fonda is scheduled to speak in the Gymnasium on medical aid to Indochina, but her appearance is canceled.

5 APR. 1973. José López speaks on "The Chicano and Education" during the campus celebration of "El Día de Educación en Aztlán."

6 APR. 1973. Cal State students Noreen White, David Wheaton, Roland Swanson, and Vernon Stauble are named Outstanding College Athletes of America. Folksingers Bill Carlson and Greg Durio perform on LCP.

11 APR. 1973. Gladys M. Hubbard, ex-Placement Advisor (1969-72), dies of cancer at age 61. Psychologist Gilbert Brighouse speaks in the Commons on "Leadership and Communication."

12 APR. 1973. The campus hosts a day-long choral festival and clinic for local schools in LC-500, with well-known choral director Howard Swan giving the evaluations.

15 APR. 1973. The Music Dept. offers an "Olde English Renaissance Banquet" in the Commons, the first rendition of what later becomes the annual Renaissance Banquet, with period dancing and scenes from the Shakespeare play, *Macbeth*, in addition to a dinner of roast beef, Queen Elizabeth Strawberry Trifle, and other delicacies.

19 APR. 1973. Folksingers The Hendersons, Nathan-Elaine, and Chevy perform in the Gymnasium.

20 APR. 1973. The campus forms the Leslie I. Harris String Quartet, named in honor of the late campus booster.

23-27 APR. 1973. The campus hosts "Women's Week," featuring talks by psychologists Harvey Karmen and Anita Lampel, writer Mary Jane Shoultz, attorney Karen Kaplowitz, artists Ruth Iskin and Arlene Raven, and printmaker Noel Quinn.

24 APR. 1973. Sociologist Herbert Blumer speaks in LC-500 on "Critical Assessment of Current Sociological Points of View."

26 APR. 1973. Rep. Jerry L. Pettis speaks in LC-500 on "Social Legislation in Contemporary America."

27 APR. 1973. Blues singer Kajsa Ohman performs on LCP.

3 May 1973. The campus hosts "State College Day," with high school and community college students participating in a series of special programs, including a noon rock concert; the success of this event leads the campus to develop a series of "Career Days." MEChA (Movimiento Estudiantil Chicano de Aztlán) holds a Cinco de Mayo fiesta, with Ramón Navarro of Escuela de la Raza Unida giving the keynote speech, plus a performance by Ballet Folklórica de Blythe, and a Mexican musical concert, *Suavecito*.

6 May 1973. Musicians from CSC Dominguez Hills perform in PS-10 under the direction of Marshall Bialosky.

14 May 1973. Groundbreaking is held for the play yard of the new Child Care Center; trailers are moved to the site during the summer and converted into modular classrooms for child care use.

14-15 May 1973. The campus hosts the Asian Conference of Southern California, featuring a keynote address by Claude Buss, Kabuki dancers, an Asian dinner, an Indonesian Concert, and talks by Seymour Scheinberg, Melvin Gortov, V. More, Sidney Klein, Paul Lingren, David Lawrence, and Suresht Bald.

21 May 1973. Torma Ettinger, Vice Counsel for Information for the Israeli Counsel General's Off., speaks in LC-500 on "Israel's Role in the Middle East."

23 May 1973. The Leslie I. Harris String Quartet, with violinists Armen Turadian and Clyda Yedinak, violist Victoria Shapiro, and cellist Catherine Graff, debuts in PS-10. The campus hosts "Language Day" for foreign-language students in 55 local high schools.

25 May 1973. Indian bass bamboo flautist G. S. Sachdev performs with Zakir Hussain in PS-10.

2 Jun. 1973. Photojournalist Chuck Scott speaks before the Art Journalism Seminar. The campus hosts a High School Theatre Workshop in the Little Theatre, with actor Paul Brinegar present.

6 Jun. 1973. Harpsichordist Dennis Dockstader performs in FA-104. George S. Odiorne speaks on "Management by Objectives."

7 Jun. 1973. Michael R. Brown, Libn. (1970-73), resigns.

9 Jun. 1973. George A. Weiny visits the Pacific island of Truk to train local divers in salvaging 100 Japanese warships sunk there during World War II.

16 JUN. 1973. The 7th Commencement is held in the Gymnasium, with James G. Bond, Pres. of CSU Sacramento, giving the keynote address, "Excellence Revisited," and actor Ben Omar attending. 677 students are eligible to receive bachelor's degrees. The campus also awards its first-ever M.A. degrees (in Elementary Education); the first person to complete the degree requirements is Liston Caldwell, a principal in Big Bear and Angeles Oaks; the others are: Pete Carrasco Sr., Daniel Carrasco (his brother), Susan Orrock, Ruby Rubio, and Constance Wallace. The campus awards its first B.S. degree in Chemistry to Kenneth Thomson.

29 JUN. 1973. The Chancellor's Off. approves a new B.A. degree in Liberal Studies, beginning in 1973/74.

6 JUL. 1973. V.P. Joseph K. Thomas issues a letter to all faculty and staff, stating that the campus must begin conserving energy, the first time this issue has been officially addressed. Thermostats around the College are raised during the summer months, and lowered during the winter.

11 JUL. 1973. The CSUC Board of Trustees approves a new master plan for the campus, establishing a projected enrollment peak of 12,000 FTE students. The plan also anticipates erecting an Administration Building by 1980—it has yet to be realized in 2009.

12 JUL. 1973. Cal State student Jeanie Nelson is named Miss Ontario Motor Speedway for 1973-74.

13 JUL. 1973. The Chancellor's Off. approves new B.A. degrees in Environmental Studies and Child Development for 1973/74. The campus denies a report that it will sell some of its land.

20 JUL. 1973. The campus receives a $24,231 grant from the U.S. Dept. of Health, Education, and Welfare to implement a veterans' instruction program. BBC interviews Nikolai E. Khokhlov on the psychological factors affecting totalitarian regimes.

1 SEPT. 1973. Robert G. Fisk, Prof. of Education and ex-Dean of Students (1962-73), retires. Jesse D. Moses, Dir. of Supportive Services for the EOP, is named Placement Officer. Rudolph A. Johnson Jr. is named Dir. of Supportive Services for the EOP, replacing Jesse D. Moses, who is named Placement Officer. A number of laboratory facilities, classrooms, and storage areas in the BI and PS buildings are transferred to the rapidly growing Dept. of Psychology.

12 SEPT. 1973. The annual convocation is held.

14 SEPT. 1973. The Chancellor's Off. approves a new B.A. degree in

Criminal Justice, effective with 1973/74. Lorraine Smith is named the campus's first "live-in activities adviser" at Serrano Village. Michael Burgess's 2nd book, *Cumulative Paperback Index, 1939-1959*, is published by Gale Research Co.

21 SEPT. 1973. Actor, director, and playwright Harry Cauley is named Artist-in-Residence for the Fall term. The campus opens a swimming pool for the use of Serrano Village students.

22 SEPT. 1973. Gloria E. A. Toote, Asst. Secretary of the U.S. Dept. of Housing and Urban Development, speaks at a housing seminar on campus, with S.B. Mayor Holcomb, S.B. Co. Board of Supervisors Chair Nancy E. Smith, and Housing Coalition Chair Valerie Pope.

25-26 SEPT. 1973. The campus hosts a Management Center Conference, "Management by Goals and Results," conducted by John R. Van de Water.

28 SEPT. 1973. The Chancellor's Off. approves new M.A. degrees in Psychology and Administration, effective with 1973/74.

5 OCT. 1973. The campus receives a $64,000 grant from the U.S. Off. of Education to establish an Upward Bound Program, with Gilbert B. Lara being named first Dir. Alexander D. Sokoloff receives a $5,000 grant from NSF and $103,000 from the U.S. Army Research Center to support tribolium research.

9 OCT. 1973. In response to a 13% student increase, marking the end to the first CSCSB enrollment crisis, Pres. Pfau is quoted in the *San Bernardino Sun* as saying: "College enrollments have leveled off nationally, but San Bernardino continues to grow."

10 OCT. 1973. The Sheikh Chinna Maulana troupe performs Indian music in PS-10.

11 OCT. 1973. The gospel rock group Psalm 150 performs on LCP.

12 OCT. 1973. The campus begins offering a pilot External Degree Program in Elementary Education at the Coll. of the Desert in the Coachella Valley, representing the start of a program that later leads to the establishment of the Palm Desert Campus of CSUSB. Art dealer Jack Glenn speaks in the Art Gallery.

13 OCT. 1973. The campus hosts a conference on junior high school students, "Meeting the Fears of the In-Between Years," in LC-500, with Don McNassor giving the keynote address.

14 Oct. 1973. A 4-acre brush fire erupts on Wiggins Hill at the intersection of State College Pkwy. and Kendall Dr. The campus adds a covered tram seating 24 persons to its Sunday tours.

15 Oct. 1973. Stephen Rosenberg speaks in PS-10 on "Local Health Depts."

19 Oct. 1973. Kent M. Schofield, Assoc. Dean of Academic Planning, assumes the additional post of Evening Services Coordinator.

22 Oct. 1973. John Morey, Dir. of Admissions, resigns.

23 Oct. 1973. Paul Douglas speaks in LC-27 on "The Commune in Nineteenth-Century America."

24 Oct. 1973. State Sen. Mervyn M. Dymally speaks in LC-500 on "Issues in 1974." Actress Jane Fonda speaks in the Gymnasium on "Political Prisoners in Saigon."

27 Oct. 1973. The campus hosts the National Boys AAU Cross County Championships.

30 Oct. 1973. Joseph J. Chouinard, Music Libn. (1970-73), resigns to take a post at SUNY, Buffalo. State Sen. W. Craig Biddle speaks in PS-122 on "Reapportionment and Air Pollution." The campus hosts a conference on "Recent Trends in Education" in LC-500.

31 Oct. 1973. Richard Roberts and Gene Zdunowski speak in PS-10 on "Organization and Functions of Community Health Services."

1 Nov. 1973. The campus hosts a Career Planning Day, with 500 local high school seniors attending; participants include S.B. Co. Board of Supervisors Chair Nancy E. Smith. The campus opens an Evening Service Center in LC-226 to serve night students.

7 Nov. 1973. The campus hosts the annual recognition dinner of the Industry-Education Council of San Bernardino and Riverside Counties in UC, with ex-Dean Kenneth Phillips giving the keynote address. State Dir. of the Dept. of Motor Vehicles Herman Sillias speaks in LC-500.

9 Nov. 1973. Michael Burgess signs a contract with Arno Press to edit a 65-book reprint series of books on science fiction. James L. Robinson is named Ethnic Studies Coordinator.

10 Nov. 1973. The campus hosts a Conference on Strengthening Family Life, with Herbert A. Otto, Chair of the National Center for the Exploration of Human Potential, giving the keynote address. The campus celebrates the Molière Tricentenary with a lecture by Thomas Braga on "*Alceste* and the Critics," a musical performance, and the presentation of 2 Molière plays with actor Harry Cauley.

12 NOV. 1973. Leonard Lightborne speaks in PS-10 on "Law and Public Health."

14 NOV. 1973. Norman Sillas speaks in LC-500 on current politics. Siegfried Centerwall speaks in PS-10 on "Child Health Services."

15 NOV. 1973. The Inland Empire Management Center sponsors a seminar and workshop, "Strategies for Personal Growth and Managerial Effectiveness," in LC-500 under the leadership of Robert D. Rutherford. Harold Chandler speaks in LC-241 on "A Bushman's Holiday in the Land Down Under." The campus hosts "French Students' Day" for local high school students, including musical and dramatic performances and slides of 17th-century art.

20 NOV. 1973. Criminologist Gilbert Geis speaks on "Hypes, Hippies, and Hypocrites" in LC-500.

21 NOV. 1973. George B. Smith Jr. speaks on "Disease Control Services" in PS-10.

25 NOV. 1973. Jack Arthur Sullivan Jr., Instructor in Sociology and Dir. of the Victor Valley Coll. Human Services Center, dies of a heart attack at Hesperia at age 43.

30 NOV. 1973. The Calif. State Board of Nursing Education and Nursing Registration approves the campus's curriculum for Nursing, effective Jan. 1974.

1 DEC. 1973. The Library signs a reciprocal borrowing agreement for with S.B. Valley College and Crafton Hills College.

7 DEC. 1973. Florence A. Mote is named Asst. Dean of Academic Administration. The Bethelaires perform an Otis Skillings musical, *Love*, in PS-10.

10 DEC. 1973. The campus shuts down its air-conditioning systems to save energy, restarting them on 20 Apr. 1974.

14 DEC. 1973. Nikolai E. Khokhlov is the subject of a cover story in the British magazine, *Radio Times*.

1974

7 JAN. 1974. The Coll. Library reduces operating hours to save energy. The campus begins offering a minor in Recreation.

8 JAN. 1974. Leonard Edmonson speaks in the Art Gallery.

9 JAN. 1974. John F. "Jack" McDonnell, Asst. Prof. of Administration, is named Dir. of the Inland Empire Management Center.

11 JAN. 1974. The campus opens a Minority Information Center, with Mike Duran as Dir.

16 JAN. 1974. Pianists Steve Prutsman and Brian Gould perform in FA-104.

18 JAN. 1974. The campus establishes a Recycling Center for newspapers and aluminum cans on the road leading to the Biological Science Building and Physical Plant. The campus receives authorization to offer a School Counseling Option for the M.A. degree in Education.

23 JAN. 1974. The CSUC System adopts a system-wide policy on nondiscrimination and affirmative action. James D. Thomas, Dean of Academic Administration, is named Chair of an Ad Hoc Committee to Develop an Affirmative Action Plan at CSCSB.

24 JAN. 1974. Tom Proctor speaks in LC-500 on "Bioenergy."

25 JAN. 1974. The campus receives a $4,800 grant from NSF. Michael White, Walter Lacey, Bobby Hutcherson, and Bobby Humphrey perform in the Gymnasium at the "Jazz Explosion."

1 FEB. 1974. Richard T. Ackley is named Assoc. Dean of Academic Administration. Florence Weiser is named Asst. Dean of Academic Administration. The campus installs cable TV in the residence halls.

3 FEB. 1974. The campus begins its celebration of "Renaissance Month" with a reception and dinner in the Commons on Feb. 3 for Serena de Bellis, owner of the Frank de Bellis collection of Renaissance books and manuscripts, who speaks on "Mirrors and Gateways: A Collector's View."

6 FEB. 1974. The Library receives a gift of Calif. case law histories from ex-attorneys Homer M. Bail and E. John Eriksson.

7 FEB. 1974. The BBC airs a film on the KGB, including a segment interviewing Nikolai E. Khokhlov.

8-10 FEB. 1974. The Travelers Co. of Hollywood performs in the campus production of Niccolò Machiavelli's play, *Mandragola*, featuring actors Britt Leach, Charlotte Douglas, Leo V. Matranga, John Smalley, Peter Mamakos, Kayce Barron, and James Matranga. "Songs Between Acts," performed during the intermission, features singer Ann Alexander and guitarist Thomas Barnett.

10 FEB. 1974. Fredi Chiappelli speaks in FA-104 on Niccolò Machiavelli's play, *Mandragola*.

14 FEB. 1974. The campus hosts Black Career Day for local high school students in the Gymnasium and LC-500.

19 FEB. 1974. Peter F. Drucker conducts a management seminar in LC-500. Jeff Beane speaks in PS-224 on "Gay Prisoner's Program."

24 FEB. 1974. The campus hosts a medieval-style banquet to close the celebration of "Renaissance Month."

27 FEB. 1974. Pianist James Spaights performs in FA-104.

28 FEB. 1974. S.B. City Attorney Ralph Prince speaks in LC-500 on "San Bernardino's Crime Problem."

4-8 MAR. 1974. The campus hosts a series of noon talks, "Take a Look in the Mirror," on career planning for women, with speakers Tina Floan, Cecelia Hyman, Gina Martin, and Pat Bozzi.

6 MAR. 1974. Mathematician John R. Reay speaks on "How to Take a Walk on a Graph" and "How to Color on the Sphere, Doughnut, and Other Surfaces" in BI-129.

7 MAR. 1974. The campus hosts a faculty forum on "Civil Disobedience" in PL-241.

15 MAR. 1974. The rock band Bielfelt und Greis performs in PS-10.

20-23 MAR. 1974. The Cal State Concert Choir, making its first concert tour, performs in Palm Desert, Apple Valley, Victorville, Barstow, Needles, and Lake Havasu City.

25-26 MAR. 1974. The campus hosts the 18th Annual Inland Science Fair in the Gymnasium.

1 APR. 1974. The campus begins offering housing for married students in the residence halls.

3 APR. 1974. Chemist Henry Eyring speaks in LC-500 on "The Degenerative Diseases of Aging" and on "Local and General Anesthesia." Pianist Martha Novak Clinkscale and violinist David Ambroson perform in FA-104.

5 APR. 1974. The campus receives approval to offer an M.A. degree with a Special Major, effective 1974/75.

6 APR. 1974. Margaret J. Lenz is named Pres. of the Board of Directors of the YWCA.

9 APR. 1974. F. F. Liu receives a $3,500 grant from Research Corp. of New York under the Cottrell Research Grants Program to study the decay properties of Particle K.

12 APR. 1974. Rock groups Toad, Bickham, and Davey and the Corvettes perform in the Gymnasium.

16-21 APR. 1974. Cal State students participate for the first time in the annual Model United Nations Program in New York City, representing the country of Kuwait.

17 APR. 1974. The campus hosts an education and careers conference, "La Fiesta de Educación y Carreras en Aztlán," in the Gymnasium and in LC-500 for 400 local Chicano students, with H. Frank Domínguez giving the keynote address. The dance group Escuela de la Raza Unida performs in the Commons.

19 APR. 1974. Jack E. Acker is named Admissions Officer.

23 APR. 1974. Bruce Anderson performs 18 different percussion instruments in PS-10, including Pyrenees cowbells and glockenspiel. The campus receives a 3rd $500 grant from the Calif. Retired Teachers Assoc. to provide emergency loans to teaching students.

24 APR. 1974. The campus hosts a Creative Writing Conference for high school students in S.B. and Riverside Cos. in LC, with W. Ross Winterowd giving the keynote address, "Literature as Rhetoric."

25 APR. 1974. Behavioral scientist Frederick L. Herzberg conducts a management seminar, "Managing and Motivating Members of the Organization," in LC-500.

26 APR. 1974. The Nursing Program receives accreditation from the Calif. State Board of Nursing Education and Nursing Registration. The campus announces that summer session classes will only meet 4 days a week (Monday-Thursday) in order to save energy.

30 APR. 1974. Avraham Shifrin speaks in LC-500 on his experience as a Russian Jew.

1 MAY 1974. Choral director Roger Wagner acts as guest conductor during a music clinic for 750 local high school students. The campus hosts a Chicanos for Law scholarship luncheon on LCP. Cal State grad student Martin A. Smith dies while bicycling at age 29.

3 MAY 1974. The Warehouse Receiving and Mail Building, including the Campus Stores Receiving Dept., opens for business; the structure was built by Physical Plant personnel.

5 MAY 1974. Betty Jackson conducts an opera workshop in PS-10.

6-8 MAY 1974. The campus hosts a series of noon forums in LC on the energy crisis, featuring George Williamson on "Gasoline Shortage: Real or Imaginary?," Ken Huskey on "Other Sources of Energy for the Future," and Courtney S. Buse on "Energy Crisis 1980?"

8 MAY 1974. The music faculty and music teachers from the S.B. Unified School Dist. present a "Career Night in Music" for local high school students in LC-500.

9 MAY 1974. Poet John Anderson reads from his work in LC-500. Lawrence S. Hill speaks in PS-122 on "Life Goals," and repeats his talk the next day. Morris Knight speaks in PS-202 on "Where Are We Now and Where Are We Going in Gay Liberation?"

10 MAY 1974. Jackie A. Green, Library Asst. (1963-74), retires. Rev. Richard Nash speaks in PS-224 on "The Unfinished Challenge of Gay Liberation."

16 MAY 1974. Tony Gneck gives a karate demonstration in LC-500.

17 MAY 1974. State Superintendent of Public Instruction Wilson Riles speaks at the Annual Media Luncheon in the Commons.

19 MAY 1974. Soprano Juanita Phillipsen performs in PS-10.

24 MAY 1974. The Chancellor's Off. approves a 2nd external degree program, to be offered by CSCSB in the Barstow-Victorville Area beginning

1975/76.

29 MAY 1974. Spencer Kagan speaks in PS-224 on "A Novel Behavioral Choice Point: A Method for Understanding Anglo American, Chicano, and Mexican Children and Their Parents."

1 JUN. 1974. The campus hosts its 4th Annual Drama Workshop for local high school students in the Little Theatre, with the participation of TV drama critic Chuck Walsh and Paul Little.

5 JUN. 1974. Representatives of the American Veterans Movement speak on the "National Veterans Crisis."

9 JUN. 1974. Clarinetist Edward Casem performs with the Leslie I. Harris String Quartet in PS-10.

13 JUN. 1974. John Fisher, Custodian (1969-74), dies in San Bernardino at age 51.

15 JUN. 1974. The 8th Commencement is held for the first time on the lawn south of the Gymnasium Building, with 46 students eligible for master's degrees, and almost 640 for bachelor's degrees. For the first time, the ceremony does not feature a keynote speaker, and is conducted in the morning. The campus awards its first M.A. degrees in Elementary Education earned in the Coachella Valley, and its first master's degrees in Administration and Psychology.

19 JUN. 1974. Summer session begins, with all classes being conducted for the first time on a 4-day-per week schedule.

21 JUN. 1974. Rep. Jerry L. Pettis announces that the campus has received a $72,729 grant from the Federal College Work-Study Program to support 151 students.

29 JUN. 1974. A student ignites a piece of solid rocket propellant in Waterman House, burning himself and causing damage to his room.

30 JUN. 1974. Fred Roach, Dean of Continuing Education, resigns to become Editor and Publisher of the *Terry Tribune* in Montana.

9 JUL. 1974. William T. Eason receives a $149,339 contract to remodel the Student Services Building (the old Library).

12 JUL. 1974. The Chancellor's Off. approves a B.S. degree in Nursing and an M.S. degree in Biology, to be offered in 1974/75.

14 JUL. 1974. Rep. Jerry L. Pettis announces that the campus has received a $29,543 grant from the Federal Law Enforcement Assistance Administration to support law enforcement students.

19 JUL. 1974. Sharon Ward is elected Dir. of Region XII of the Calif. State Employees Assoc.

22 JUL. 1974. CSUC Trustee Jeanette Richie visits the campus.

23 JUL. 1974. State Sens. Walter Stiern and Ruben S. Ayala, Assemblyman C. Jerry Lewis, S.B. Co. Supervisor Nancy E. Smith, S.B. City Councilman Edward Wheeler, and S.B. Mayor Holcomb visit the campus.

11 AUG. 1974. The Youth Symphony String Quartet from the San Bernardino Youth Symphony Orchestra debuts in PS-10.

29 AUG. 1974. Herbert E. Brown, Dir. of the Physical Plant (1964-74), retires. James T. Weir, Campus Police (1965-74), retires. Cal State Psychology junior Lanse Palmer Curtis dies at age 27. The College Faculty Wives Club establishes a perpetual scholarship fund with an initial contribution of $2,132.

30 AUG. 1974. Ex-U.S. Navy Lt. Commander Andre A. Maurel is named Chief of Plant Operations, replacing Herbert E. Brown, Dir. of the Physical Plant.

31 AUG. 1974. Robert L. West, Dean of the School of Education, returns to the ranks as Prof. of Education. Ward M. McAfee, Dean of the School of Social Sciences, returns to the ranks as Prof. of History.

1 SEPT. 1974. Ronald G. Petrie is named Dean of the School of Education, replacing Robert L. West. Freeman J. Wright is named Dean of the School of Social Sciences, replacing Ward M. McAfee. Stephen A. Bowles is named Dean of Continuing Education, replacing Fred Roach, and becoming the youngest Dean in the Cal State System. H. Arthur "Hal" Hoverland, Chair of the Dept. of Administration (1972-74), is named the first Dean of the School of Administration, the 5th major academic division on campus. Walter S. Hawkins is named Dir. of the Upward Bound Program.

5 SEPT. 1974. The Redevelopment Agency of San Bernardino announces that it will construct a $200,000 amphitheater across from the campus at the base of Wiggins Hill as part of the city's Bicentennial celebration; the structure is never built.

16 SEPT. 1974. The annual convocation is held.

22-23 SEPT. 1974. The campus hosts a 2-day orientation for new students, "How to Survive College."

24 SEPT. 1974. The campus begins offering an external B.A. degree in Social Science with classes meeting in Barstow.

1 OCT. 1974. Fred Cordova appears with sportscaster Chick Hern on the TV program, *Bowling for Dollars*.

3 OCT. 1974. Rep. Jerry L. Pettis announces that the campus has been awarded a $4,034 grant from the U.S. Dept. of Health, Education, and Welfare to support nursing education.

16 OCT. 1974. State Sen. Ruben S. Ayala speaks in LC-500.

21 OCT. 1974. Rep. Jerry L. Pettis speaks in LC-27. State Sen. W. Craig Biddle speaks in LC-500.

24 OCT. 1974. The campus hosts a Conference on Electoral Reform, with Rep. George E. Brown Jr. speaking in LC-27, and also later that day in LC-500 with Sen. Joseph R. Biden, ex-Rep. John R. Schmidhauser, ex-State Sen. William E. Coombs, 1972 Libertarian Presidential candidate John Hospers, 1972 American Independent Party Presidential candidate and ex-Rep. John G. Schmitz, State Controller Houston I. Flournoy, L.A. City Attorney Burt Pines, and S.B. Co. Board of Supervisors Chair Nancy E. Smith, among others, at a seminar focusing on reform in the campaign and election process. The campus signs a contract with the S.B. Co. Board of Supervisors to allow use of County Medical Center facilities by CSCSB's nursing students.

25 OCT. 1974. The campus receives approval from the Chancellor's Off. to offer a pilot external B.A. degree program in Social Sciences in the Barstow area.

26 OCT. 1974. The campus hosts a Conference on the Junior High-Middle School in PS-500, with speakers Newton Metfessel, Don Glines, Lorne Bargmann, Robert Beal, Ethel Graber, Peggy Harding, Horace Jackson, Matt Bogatin, and Shirley Boring.

31 OCT. 1974. Assemblyman C. Jerry Lewis speaks in LC-500.

1 NOV. 1974. The Admissions and Records Off. is placed under the Student Services Div. The Library joins 20 local university libraries in the Inland Empire Academic Library Cooperative (IEALC), with member institutions sharing their resources with faculty and students. The campus awards its first 10-year service pins to James H. Urata, Leonard B. Farwell, Corky Moffett, Geraldine Jones, Frances A. Ekaitis, Linda R. Evans, Claire Cantlay, and Mary Williams.

2 NOV. 1974. Pianist William A. "Andy" Sollars performs in PS-10. The campus holds a reception to honor "Twelve Contemporary Chicano Artistas" featured in an Art Gallery exhibition, including René Yáñez, Armando Cabrera, Gilberto Luján, Leonard Castellanos, Esteban Villa, Juan Orozco, Ruday Cuellar, José Montoya, Alvado López, George Beltrán, Armando Cid, and Joe Moran.

11 NOV. 1974. Jerome Resnick speaks in LC on "Psychological Science and Society: Ethical Dilemma."

13 NOV. 1974. Sergio Martínez speaks in PS-122 on "A Comparative Study Between the Chicano and Anglo Cultures Using the Semantic Differential Technique."

16 NOV. 1974. The campus and S.B. Valley Coll. co-sponsor a conference on "Early Childhood Development" at SBVC.

19 NOV. 1974. The campus hosts a conference on "Crisis Intervention," conducted in LC-500 by the Tri-Counties Chapter of the Calif. Probation, Parole, and Correctional Assoc.

20 NOV. 1974. The gospel rock group Sonrise performs on LCP. David Warren speaks in PS-122 on "Perceptual Factors in Reading Acquisition."

21 NOV. 1974. National badminton singles champions Stan Hales and Diane Hales conduct a demonstration in the Gymnasium.

22 NOV. 1974. Actor Alan Hewitt speaks in LC-27. The campus receives approval from the Chancellor's Off. to offer a B.S. degree in Health Science, effective with 1974/75.

27 NOV. 1974. The CSUC Board of Trustees adopts a merit pay plan for faculty members. Susan Gillig, Information Officer, the British Consulate General in L.A., speaks to the International Club.

3 DEC. 1974. Mafia informer William R. Geraway speaks in LC-500 on "Re-establishment of Capital Punishment and Reform of the California Prison System." The campus receives approval to offer a B.A. degree in Health Science, effective with 1974/75.

6 DEC. 1974. The campus announces that painter Nicholas Krushenick will serve as a Visiting Artist during Winter Quarter 1975.

8 DEC. 1974. High Santa Ana winds break a window in the Coll. Library, and topple several trees on campus.

13 DEC. 1974. Richard T. Ackley receives a $300 annual grant from the National Strategy Information Center.

16 DEC. 1974. The campus Foundation receives a $4,696 grant from S.B. City to buy equipment for a children's day care center.

18 DEC. 1974. Wallace T. Cleaves receives a 2-year post-doctoral research fellowship from the National Institute of Mental Health, to conduct research on sensor-motor integration in infants and young children at the Univ. of Minnesota Institute of Child Development.

1975

1 JAN. 1975. Lee H. Kalbus, Chair of the Dept. of Chemistry, is named the first Assoc. Dean of Academic Planning for Graduate Studies, being replaced as Dept. Chair by Kenneth A. Mantei. Walter O. Zoecklein is named Dir. of the new Center for Professional Development.

6 JAN. 1975. Edmund G. "Jerry" Brown Jr. takes office as Governor of California, replacing Ronald W. Reagan.

10 JAN. 1975. The campus receives a $447 gift from the Faculty Wives Club to add to their $2,000 scholarship fund.

14 JAN.-6 MAR. 1975. The campus offers its first televised course for credit (on ethnic minorities) on Channel 24 in San Bernardino (KVCR) and Channel 62 in Riverside.

15 JAN. 1975. Literary critic Robert Cromise speaks in LC-500.

16 JAN. 1975. Defense attorney Paul Steinman speaks before a seminar on rape and self-protection.

17 JAN. 1975. Irish folksingers Bielfelt & Greis perform in PS-10.

19 JAN. 1975. The Chamber Players of CSU Northridge, directed by Lawrence Christianson, perform Igor Stravinsky's *L'Histoire du Soldat* in PS-10.

23 JAN. 1975. The campus hosts a symposium on "Northern Ireland: Where the Heart Turns," in LC.

31 JAN. 1975. The campus hosts an exhibition basketball game in the

Gymnasium between the Cal State All-Stars and the Los Angeles Police Revolver and Athletic Club.

31 JAN.-1 FEB. 1975. The campus hosts the S.B. Co. Music Educators Assoc. Mid-Winter Conference in the Commons and Fine Arts Buildings.

1 FEB. 1975. Cal State student Sarah Ramírez is named Miss San Bernardino 1975.

10-16 FEB. 1975. The campus hosts a series of activities to celebrate Black History Week.

12 FEB. 1975. Bob McKenzie Jr. speaks in LC-500 on "Efficient City Government."

14 FEB. 1975. Rep. Jerry Lyle Pettis, a campus booster, is killed in a light plane crash at Banning at age 58.

17 FEB. 1975. Norris Gregory and John D. Hobbs speak in LC. The campus observes Black Renaissance Week (through Feb. 21).

18 FEB. 1975. Artist Nicholas Krushenick speaks in PS-10 on "The Pulse of the 21st Century."

20 FEB. 1975. James H. Urata speaks at the Kiwanis Club in San Bernardino about his experiences in a Japanese-American internment camp during World War II. The rock group Love Train Ltd. performs on LCP. Ralph Thomlinson speaks in LC-500 on "Experiencing Culture Shock in Population Research: Thailand and Morocco." Psychobiologist James McGaugh speaks in PS-224 on "The Effects of Drugs and Electrical Stimulation of the Brain on the Memory-Storage Process."

21 FEB. 1975. High Santa Ana winds break a $1,500 window in the Coll. Library; workmen must brace north-facing windows on the 5th and 1st floors to protect them from further damage. The jazz group The Traveler performs on LCP. Retired Air Force Lt. Col. Frank T. Slaton is named first Manager of Data Processing Services.

24-25 FEB. 1975. A referendum on student fee assessments is held throughout the CSUC System, with CSCSB students voting to retain their previous fee schedule.

25 FEB. 1975. Historian Carl Degler speaks in PS-10 on "What Is Women's History?"

5 MAR. 1975. Ernest F. García is re-elected a Trustee of the Rialto City

Unified School Dist. Board, John M. Hatton is elected a Trustee of the S.B. City Unified School Dist., and Michael Rose a Trustee of the Banning Unified School Dist.

6 MAR. 1975. Abstract painter Robert Kabak speaks in FA-104 on "The Necessity for Art."

7 MAR. 1975. George E. Slusser receives a Fulbright-Hays Fellowship to study at the Univ. of Paris at Nanterre in 1975/76. The campus is designated a "Servicemen's Opportunity College" by the Dept. of Defense and the Carnegie Corp.

10 MAR. 1975. Glass sculptor Harvey Littleton speaks about his work in LC-500.

11 MAR. 1975. The campus receives a $1,000 grant from Kaiser Steel's Manufacturing Division to help support the EOP Program.

13 MAR. 1975. The campus hosts a High School Choral Festival in LC-500, with some 800 students attending.

17 MAR. 1975. The campus receives permission to offer an Administrative Services Credential, beginning with Spring 1975.

27 MAR. 1975. Gilbert B. Lara, Dir. of the Upward Bound Program, resigns.

29 MAR. 1975. Edward M. Hay, Supervising Night Custodian (1968-74), dies at age 47.

31 MAR. 1975. The campus abandons its telephone switchboard and implements a new Centrex system, allowing direct dialing for the first time; all campus numbers now begin with "887-".

1 APR. 1975. Artist Pamela Weir-Quiton speaks in FA-104.

2 APR. 1975. Cal State Fine Arts student Mavis A. John dies in Redlands at age 48; the student art show is dedicated to her memory.

5 APR. 1975. Elizabeth McLellan speaks on campus at the annual Southeast Dist. Conference meeting of the American Assoc. of University Women.

9 APR. 1975. Michael H. Armacost of the U.S. State Dept. speaks in LC and in LC-211 on "Asian Security."

10 Apr. 1975. Ernest F. García is elected Pres. of the Rialto City Unified School Dist. Board of Trustees.

10-11 Apr. 1975. The Calif. Folklore Soc. holds its 23rd Annual Meeting in LC-500.

14 Apr. 1975. Physicist and Walt Disney consultant Julius Sumner Miller, "Professor Wonderful," speaks in PS-10 on "Some Dramatic Demonstrations in Physics Together with Some Enchanting Questions for Enquiring Minds." The campus receives an $112,803 grant from the U.S. Off. of Education to support student loans.

16 Apr. 1975. Tony Casas speaks in PS-500 on "What Is Going on in Prisons?"

17 Apr. 1975. Nick Pokrajac Inc. receives a $2,639,000 contract to construct the Creative Arts Building, but later withdraws its bid, claiming a "$200,000" error; the campus is forced to scale back building plans during a 2nd round of bidding.

18 Apr. 1975. The CSUC Board of Trustees Committee on Educational Policy meets in C-104, including W. O. Weissich, Winifred H. Lancaster, Frank P. Adams, Richard A. García, Claudia H. Hampton, Mary Jean Pew, and Karl L. Wente.

22 Apr. 1975. Philosopher John A. Hutchison speaks in LC-241 on "Freedom, from Free Will to Politics."

25 Apr. 1975. Folk guitarist Clabe Hangan performs on LCP.

27 Apr. 1975. Harpsichordist David Hatt performs in PS-10.

29 Apr. 1975. The campus celebrates its 10th anniversary with a luncheon in the Commons for 175 faculty, students, and guests, including ex-State Sen. Stanford C. Shaw, S.B. Co. Supervisor Nancy E. Smith, and S.B. Mayor Holcomb. Pres. Pfau states that the campus should "take the lead" in revitalizing general education for the student. Harvard Univ. historian Frank Freidel gives a keynote speech in LC-500 on "Is the New Deal Relevant in the Crisis of 1975?" Groundbreaking is held for the new Creative Arts Building.

30 Apr. 1975. Rudolph A. Johnson Jr., Dir. of Supportive Services for the EOP Program, resigns. James Malone speaks in LC-211 on "Recent Arms Control Initiatives in the Field of Strategic Arms Control Talks and Mutual and Balanced Force Reductions in the NATO-Warsaw Pact Areas."

1 MAY 1975. Victor Construction Co. receives a $168,900 contract to construct the new Main Entrance to campus at the corner of State College Pkwy. and Northpark Blvd. The project includes a divided road from State College Pkwy. to the campus perimeter road, a new entrance and exit to the main parking lot, overhead street lighting, and landscaping of the median and both sides of the road.

3-4 MAY 1975. Radio personality Dr. Demento and the Roto Rooter Good Time Christmas Band perform during the "Fireball '75" spring festival in the Gymnasium.

5-6 MAY 1975. The campus celebrates Cinco de Mayo with a "Fiesta de la Revolución" under the sponsorship of MEChA, including performances by Teatro Cultural de Colton, and a lecture by Emilio Benavides of CSC Los Angeles.

6 MAY 1975. Robert Hunt speaks in LC-241 on "The Reasonableness of Suicide."

7 MAY 1975. Newspaper columnist William Greenburg speaks in PS-10 on the local smog problem. *San Bernardino Sun* columnists Pat Sheeran and Ed Mauel participate in a Conference on Creative Writing for local high school students in LC-500.

8 MAY 1975. Barbara Jacob, Deputy Dir. of the European Community Information Service, speaks in LC-8.

14 MAY 1975. Army Col. Carl F. Bernard speaks in LC-211 on the "Soviet Military Threat, Tactical Nuclear Weapons, and the Need to Restructure NATO Ground Forces."

14-15 MAY 1975. The campus hosts the 3rd Biennial Asian Studies Conference, including an Asian dinner, classical dances from India and Tibet, films, and lectures; participants include ex-Indian Minister of Health S. Chandrasekhar, and dancers Sujata and Asoka.

16 MAY 1975. The campus hosts its Annual Inland Area Personnel Management Assoc. Seminar, with State Sen. Robert B. Presley speaking on "Labor Relations '76." In an article in the *Riverside Press-Enterprise*, Rich Zeiger predicts that CSCSB will eventually reach a total enrollment of 4,000-4,500, instead of the 20,000 originally projected—just slightly off the mark! The campus receives a $750 gift from the Calif. Retired Teachers Assoc. to add to its scholarship and student loan fund.

29 MAY 1975. The CSUC Board of Trustees approves a measure to permit the sale of beer on Cal State campuses.

31 May 1975. The campus hosts its 5th Annual Theatre Workshop for local high school students in the Little Theatre.

1 Jun. 1975. A. Harry Bliss speaks in BI-124 on "Organization and Functions of Environmental Health and Safety in Private Section and Their Relationship to Regulatory Agencies."

4 Jun. 1975. The campus receives a $1,200 gift from MEChA to fund 6 $200 scholarships for Chicano students.

5 Jun. 1975. Rudolfo Álvarez, ex-Dir. of the UCLA Chicano Studies Center, speaks in LC-500 on "The Mexican-American in Sociology."

7 Jun. 1975. The Public Employees Coordinating Council of San Bernardino-Riverside Counties sponsors a dinner and panel in the Commons on collective bargaining, with State Sen. Robert B. Presley and Assemblymen William McVittie and Walter Ingalls.

10 Jun. 1975. In a 2nd round of bidding, Nick Pokrajac Inc. receives a $2,597,094 contract to construct the Creative Arts Building.

14 Jun. 1975. The 9th Commencement is held on the South Gymnasium Lawn, with 643 bachelor's and 117 master's candidates being awarded, with the participation of Mrs. William E. Leonard.

20 Jun. 1975. James H. Urata is named to the S.B. City Water Commission. Robert Logsdon is named to the Central City Advisory Board.

23 Jun. 1975. Construction begins on the Main Entrance to campus.

27 Jun. 1975. Walter Otto Zoecklein, Assoc. Prof. of Philosophy (1969-75) and a retired Commander in the U.S. Navy, dies in Loma Linda of cancer at age 57.

4 Jul. 1975. Pichai Sereerojyn becomes the first Cal State student to earn a Certificate in International Relations.

8 Jul. 1975. Harry Snow speaks in LC-500 on "Backpacking."

17 Jul. 1975. Rep. Shirley N. Pettis announces that the campus has received a $3,317 grant from the U.S. Dept. of Health, Education, and Welfare to support nursing education.

22 Jul. 1975. Sen. Alan Cranston and Rep. Shirley N. Pettis announce that the campus has received a $25,842 grant from the federal government to support services for Vietnam veteran students.

24 JUL. 1975. Ronald G. Petrie, Dean of the School of Education, resigns to take a similar position at Portland State Univ.

31 JUL. 1975. Rep. Shirley N. Pettis announces that the campus has received an $8,004 grant from the Law Enforcement Assistance Administration to support law enforcement students.

6 AUG. 1975. Walter S. Hawkins, Dir. of the EOP, is named Dir. of Supportive Services for the EOP.

7 AUG. 1975. Walter S. Kadyk, Dir. of College Police, resigns.

8 AUG. 1975. Michael A. Gómez, Police Sergeant, is named Dir. of College Police, replacing Walter S. Kadyk. The campus receives a $206,800 grant from the federal Teacher Corps, with matching grants of $74,000 each to the S.B. City Schools and the Rialto City Schools, to fund a teacher improvement program.

11-14 AUG. 1975. Actress Marte Boyle Slout conducts a summer acting workshop together with her husband, William L. Slout.

19 AUG. 1975. Shirley C. Booe, Library Asst. (1968-75), retires.

21 AUG. 1975. The Chancellor's Off. approves a new B.A. degree in Vocational Education, effective 1975/96.

24 AUG. 1975. The Frank E. Scully Piano Trio, named for a local music teacher who died in 1974, debuts in PS-10.

31 AUG. 1975. Freeman J. Wright, Dean of the School of Social Sciences, resigns to accept a position as Deputy Commissioner for Academic Affairs in the Montana Univ. System. Jesse D. Moses, Placement Officer, resigns.

1 SEPT. 1975. Ward M. McAfee is named Act. Dean of the School of Social Sciences, replacing Freeman J. Wright. Michael Preston is named Dir. of the Upward Board Program, replacing Walter S. Hawkins. Florence A. Mote is named Act. Dean of the School of Education, replacing Ronald G. Petrie; she is the first woman Dean to head a school at Cal State, and was the first woman faculty member on campus to become a tenured full professor. Construction begins on the Creative Arts Building.

7 SEPT. 1975. Violinist Diane Byington and pianist Denise Tallman perform with the San Bernardino Youth Symphony in PS-10.

15 SEPT. 1975. The annual convocation is held.

18 SEPT. 1975. Kutania People sponsors a campus conference, "Living for the City," with 100 local African-American students present.

25 SEPT. 1975. The campus unveils its new Main Entrance at the corner of State College Pkwy. and Northpark Blvd. A brush fire burns for 24 hours in the S.B. Mountains behind the campus. The Coll. Library opens its south entrance to the public for the first time.

26 SEPT. 1975. The Chancellor's Off. approves new Master of Public Administration and Master of Business Administration degrees, effective with 1975/76. Stuart R. Ellins receives a $3,500 grant from the L.A. Co. Agricultural Commissioner to supervise a coyote taste aversion project in the Antelope Valley.

5 OCT. 1975. The Dept. of Motor Vehicles office in S.B. unveils a set of murals created by Prof. Joseph Moran and 5 of his students.

10 OCT. 1975. The campus receives a $56,100 grant from the State for the creation of a bilingual cross-cultural teacher-training program under the directorship of Ernest F. García. Michael Burgess forms his own publishing company, The Borgo Press (1975-1999), to publish academic books in history and literature; many of the initial publications are written by CSCSB faculty; joining him in Oct. 1976 is his new wife, Mary A. Burgess. Cheryl A. Weese is named Admissions Officer.

11 OCT. 1975. The campus hosts "Child in the Middle Years," a conference for junior high and middle school educators, with Ned S. Hubbell giving the keynote address, "Communicating the Curriculum to Parents."

11-12 OCT. 1975. The campus hosts a chess tournament in LC sponsored by Woodpushers Anonymous and the S.B. Chess Club.

22-23 OCT. 1975. Norman Polmar, American Editor of *Jane's Fighting Ships*, speaks in LC-500 on the "Soviet-American Naval Balance," and also appears at the World Affairs Council dinner in the Commons.

24 OCT. 1975. Poet Jonathan Griffin speaks in PS-10 on "Poetry Today." Elgar Hutto of the RCA Co. speaks in LC-500 on "Eldridge Johnson and the Victor Talking Machine Company." Cal State grad student Alberto Porras Campos dies of a heart attack at age 44.

29 OCT. 1975. The campus hosts the 18th Annual Recognition Banquet of the San Bernardino-Riverside Counties Industry-Education Council, with Arthur W. Smith Jr. giving the keynote address.

6 NOV. 1975. The S.B. Co. Heart Assoc. sponsors a campus symposium on the effect of diet on heart disease.

10 NOV. 1975. Playwright Oliver Hailey speaks in LC-500 on the campus presentation of his play, *For the Use of the Hall*. Cal State student William Carroll Racobs dies at Hesperia at age 27.

13 NOV. 1975. Geographer George F. Carter speaks in LC-500 on "Pleistocene Man in North America."

14 NOV. 1975. The campus installs an anemometer on top of the Student Services Building, thereby completing the University's first Weather Station (most of which is located near the Olive Grove at the north end of campus). Nick Pokrajac Inc. receives a $147,357 contract to construct the utility services for the Creative Arts Building.

15 NOV. 1975. Pianist Michael Tacchia performs in PS-10.

18 NOV. 1975. Philosopher Richard Wasserstrom speaks in LC-500 on "Some Moral Problems of Punishment." Poet James McMichael reads from his work in LC.

19 NOV. 1975. Oceanographers Jean-Michel Cousteau and Richard Murphy speak in PS-10 on "Project Ocean Search—Wuvulu."

23 NOV. 1975. Construction begins on the Creative Arts Building. The campus introduces the Cal State Jazz Ensemble.

25 NOV. 1975. The CSUC Board of Trustees approves the relocation of the sites for the Student Health Center to an area northeast of the Commons Building, and for the Security-Storage Facility to an area adjacent to the Heating and Air Conditioning Building.

28 NOV. 1975. James G. Rogers is named Dir. of the Inland Empire Management Center.

5 DEC. 1975. Alexander D. Sokoloff receives an $11,000 grant from the Army Research Off. to continue his tribolium research.

9 DEC. 1975. CSUC Chancellor Glenn S. Dumke authorizes campus police officers in the Cal State System to carry firearms.

12 DEC. 1975. Cal State Nursing student Kazuko Shibasaki French dies of a heart attack at age 39.

29 DEC. 1975. Prof. George A. Weiny is seriously injured in an automobile accident on I-15 near Escondido that also kills his 14-year-old son,

Arden G. Weiny.

1976

9 JAN. 1976. Robert D. Blake, Pres. of Scientific Methods Inc., conducts a management institute in LC-500.

14 JAN. 1976. The CSCSB Inter-Organization Council and the Veterans Club sponsor an open forum on campus policies in C-104. Robert D. Blake, Pres. of Scientific Methods Inc., speaks in LC-500 on the "Managerial Grid Concept."

16 JAN. 1976. The campus unveils an octagonal Information Kiosk at the new Main Entrance, designed by Robert F. Lohnes and built by the Physical Plant. The bands Fire and Ice and Sixth Finger Funk perform at a student dance at the S.B. Convention Center.

21 JAN. 1976. Pianists Jack Behrens and Sonja Behrens, clarinetist Diane Bryan, and singer Irene Gubrud perform in FA-104.

22 JAN. 1976. Philosopher Frederick Olafson speaks in LC-241 on "Textbooks and People: Some Reflections on the Humanities."

23 JAN. 1976. The campus implements PIMS, a centralized personnel and payroll system.

26 JAN. 1976. Jet Propulsion Lab physicist William J. Kaufmann III speaks in PS-10 on "Black Holes and the Theory of Relativity."

30 JAN. 1976. The campus receives a $12,388 grant from the CSUC Chancellor's Off. to establish the Desert Studies Center on a 40-acre site in the Mojave Desert at Soda Springs (formerly Zzyzx Mineral Springs), to be operated by a consortium of 7 CSUC campuses with the U.S. Bureau of Land Management. Dalton D. Harrington, who helped secure the grant, is named first Project Dir. The campus receives a $600 gift from the Faculty Wives, to honor the memory of Mary Alyce Smith, wife of Prof. Robert A. Smith, who died on 16 Jan. 1976.

3-4 FEB. 1976. Psychologist Robert Perloff speaks in LC-500 on "Program Evaluation," and also conducts a seminar there.

6 FEB. 1976. The Computer Center installs a Digital Equipment Corp. PDP 11/45 computer that will support 8 simultaneous users on terminals in 4 campus buildings.

6-7 FEB. 1976. The campus hosts a seminar on "Child Abuse," with Anita

Lampel, Thomas Moore, and Alayne Yates.

9 FEB. 1976. Julius Sumner Miller, "Professor Wonderful," speaks in PS-10 on "History of Science—A Philatelist's View."

13 FEB. 1976. The campus receives a $6,675 matching grant from the Calif. Dept. of Education to help establish a Child Development Center near the University. The campus begins numbering the lanes in the main parking lot.

19 FEB. 1976. The first student-directed campus play, *A Gap in Generations*, begins its run, with Johnny W. Pipkin at the helm.

23 FEB. 1976. Assemblyman C. Jerry Lewis introduces a resolution, ACR 157, to authorize construction of an $871,000 Student Health Center at CSCSB, to be financed from a CSUC special health facilities fund.

24 FEB. 1976. Comedian Tim McMullen performs in CO-104.

25 FEB. 1976. Paul Zall speaks in LC-500 on "Ben Franklin and the Comic Spirit."

26 FEB. 1976. The campus hosts a Festival of the Arts and Humanities in LC-500, featuring a concert by the 65-member Concert Choir and Kellogg Chamber Singers, and artist David King speaking on "The Role of the Visual Arts in Contemporary Society."

27 FEB. 1976. The campus receives a $3,707 grant from the National Endowment for the Humanities to evaluate its classes in the humanities. Edward J. Erler receives a $3,200 grant from the Earhart Foundation.

29 FEB. 1976. Dr. Samuel M. Plaut, first Medical Dir. of the Student Health Center (1965-76), retires.

1 MAR. 1976. Dr. Ross L. Ballard is named Medical Dir. of the Student Health Center, replacing Dr. Samuel M. Plaut.

3 MAR. 1976. Richard P. Barthol conducts an Institute on "Communications in Business Relationship."

5 MAR. 1976. The campus hosts a workshop in LC-500 on the Health Planning and Resources Act. The School of Administration creates its first 2 new academic departments, Public Administration (with James J. Finley as Chair) and Business Admi1nistration (with John F. "Jack" McDonnell as Chair).

11 Mar. 1976. Tony Allward speaks in CO-104.

17 Mar. 1976. The Rainbow Players perform *Noah and the Ark '76: A Musical Elixir* on LCP.

29 Mar. 1976. The CSCSB Child Care Center, with the support of a $6,675 grant from the Calif. Dept. of Education, opens on the campus of Kendall Elementary School at 4951 State St. in S.B.

1 Apr. 1976. Stephen A. Langhammerer donates 900 classical '78 RMP records to the Music Dept.

3 Apr. 1976. The S.B. Co. Heart Assoc. sponsors a cardiac and respiratory auscultation symposium, under the direction of Dr. Carl L. Cook Jr. and Dr. Phillip Gold.

6 Apr. 1976. Artist Gary Beydler speaks in FA-104 on his work. Hope Werness speaks in FA-109 on "Van Gogh's Chairs."

7 Apr. 1976. The Inland Empire Management Center sponsors a workshop on "Setting and Realizing Individual Career Goals."

8-9 Apr. 1976. Cal State student David Hatt becomes the first piano soloist to play Erik Satie's "Vexations" (a one-page, 180-note piece repeated 840 times) within the 18-hour, 40-minute timeline set by the composer—he plays continuously (with only a few 3-second breaks) for 17 hours and 51 minutes. This is followed by a 16-hour presentation of Richard Wagner's "Ring" Cycle of 4 operas in the home of Prof. Richard S. Saylor.

15 Apr. 1976. Cal State alumna Pam Zmolek becomes the first female police officer on campus. The band Caldera performs on LCP.

21 Apr. 1976. Folksinger Karla Bonoff performs on LCP. John Medved speaks in LC-500 on "Attack on Zionism—How to Fight Back." Cal State grad student Barbara Evelyn Hahn dies at age 51.

22 Apr. 1976. Historian John Caughey speaks in LC-500 on "Two Hundred Years Ago in Southern California."

23 Apr. 1976. Claire Cantlay, Secretary, P.E. and Recreation, retires.

24 Apr. 1976. Bruce Golden signs his new book, *The Beach Boys: Southern California Pastoral*, at D.J. Books in S.B.

27 Apr. 1976. Dr. Snootful's Medicine Show performs in LC.

28 APR. 1976. Psychologist Hector Myers speaks in LC on "Mental Health Issues and the Culturally Different Client."

29 APR. 1976. Donald R. Smith speaks in BI-129 on "Optimal Controls of Rockets and Vibrating Beads by Elementary Methods." The magician Mr. Deception performs in LC. A construction worker falls off the roof of a campus building.

30 APR. 1976. Alexander D. Sokoloff receives an $11,000 grant from the U.S. Army Research Center to study tribolium beetles.

5 MAY 1976. Retired Navy Rear Admiral W. N. Dietzen Jr. speaks in LC-5. Charles Kegley speaks in LC-241 on "God Is Not Dead, but Theology Is Dying." John Hubacher speaks in PS-10 on "Kirlian Photography." As part of the campus's Cinco de Mayo celebration, the groups Mariachi de Valley de Indio, Folklórico el Instituto de Bellas Artes, and Ballet Folk-lórico ITZ perform on LCP, writer Ron Arias and Dir. of the Instituto del Pueblo Evelina Alacón Cruz speak on LCP, the group Salsa Brava performs in the Gymnasium, and Colton Mayor Abe Beltrán speaks in LC-500 to MEChA students. Victorville City Manager James L. Cox speaks on campus.

7 MAY 1976. Joel Sheinfield speaks in PS-10 on "Israeli Kibbutz." The Library receives a gift from Jim Ritchey of the complete World War II issues of the *Los Angeles Times*.

7-13 MAY 1976. The 1938 Surrealist Exhibition in Paris, France, is recreated in the CSCSB Gallery by the Art 426 class.

10 MAY 1976. Judith Van Baron, Dir. of the Bronx Museum of the Arts, speaks in FA-109 on "Super Realism."

11 MAY 1976. The campus holds its first Social Sciences Field Day on "The Quality of Life in the Year 2000."

12 MAY 1976. Over 350 local high school students participate in the annual Foreign Language Field Day.

14 MAY 1976. The campus receives approval from the CSUC Chancellor's Off. to offer a new B.A. degree in Human Services, effective with 1976/77.

15 MAY 1976. As part of Spring Fling '76, the campus hosts its first lizard race north of the Physical Education Building.

17 MAY 1976. S.B. Dist. Attorney James Cramer speaks on campus.

18 May 1976. The new CSCSB Child Care Center is officially dedicated at Kendall Elementary School in San Bernardino.

19 May 1976. Elliot W. Eisner speaks in LC-500 on "The Impact of Achievement Testing on the Quality of Education." S.B. Mayor Holcomb speaks on campus.

20 May 1976. Comic singer Tim McMullen performs on LCP.

21 May 1976. Moshe Rubenstein speaks in LC-500 on "Patterns of Problem Solving."

23 May 1976. The campus hosts a Bicentennial "Sunday Afternoon in the Park," with performances by the Barstow College Band, Coll. of the Desert Band, and Riverside Concert Band.

24 May 1976. Jan Mrozinski speaks in PS-122 on "Recent Direction in U.S. Ceramics." Riverside Co. Supervisor Norton Younglove speaks on campus.

25 May 1976. Poet Diane Wakoski reads from her work in LC-500.

26 May 1976. Larry Agran, Dir. of the History of Cancer Control Project at UCLA, speaks in BI-101 on "Cancer-Producing Substances in the Environment."

27 May 1976. Sociologists Elizabeth Nelson and Edward Nelson speak in LC-500 on "Work Alienation and Role Salience."

28 May 1976. Floyd Williams speaks in LC-500 on "An Economic Analysis of Earthquake Prediction."

31 May 1976. Fred Dixon, Campus Guard (1965-76), retires.

1-2 Jun. 1976. The campus hosts a Women's Day Celebration, featuring wiccan Z. Budapest speaking in LC on "Women's Religion and Goddess Worship," Joan Robins and Rosa Montez speaking in LC, poet Dell Fitzgerald-Richards reading from her work in LC, Susan Berk speaking in LC on "Women's Legal Rights," and The New Miss Alice Stone Ladies Soc. Orchestra performing on LCP. Joe Wallock speaks in LC-500 on "The Accounting Profession."

2 Jun. 1976. Philosopher Efraim Shmueli speaks in LC-500 on "The Moral and Political Significance of the Emergence of Israel." Oceanographer Don Walsh speaks in LC-5 on "The Navy, National Ocean Policy, and the Uses of Ocean Space."

3 JUN. 1976. Magician Mr. Deception performs in LC. Grant Carter speaks in LC-500.

4 JUN. 1976. Dean H. Arthur "Hal" Hoverland is named "Faculty Member of the Year" by students of the School of Administration at an awards' banquet held at the Arrowhead Country Club, with Assemblyman C. Jerry Lewis attending. The CSUC Chancellor's Off. relocates to its new headquarters building in Long Beach.

7 JUN. 1976. State Sen. Ruben S. Ayala speaks on campus.

12 JUN. 1976. The 10th Commencement is held on the South Gymnasium Lawn, with nearly 900 students eligible to receive degrees, including the first M.S. degree in Biology, the first M.S. in Nursing, and the first Master's of Business Administration (M.B.A.).

14 JUN. 1976. Art Prof. Joseph Moran and 5 of his students begin painting a 40-foot-long mural depicting the history of San Bernardino in the S.B. City Hall.

25 JUN. 1976. The campus receives approval to offer an M.S. degree in Psychology, effective with 1976/77. *College Courses II*, a campus cookbook compiled by Antreen Pfau and Kyla DeRemer, is published by the Cal State Faculty Wives; an autograph party is held on Jul. 6 in President's Conference Room. The campus receives a $12,061 grant from the Chancellor's New Program Development Off. for "Modules for Teaching and Reinforcing Counseling Skills," to be managed by Lloyd Campbell and Robert A. Senour.

29 JUN. 1976. Nick Pokrajac Inc. receives a $627,726 contract to construct the Student Union Building.

10 JUL. 1976. Margaret J. "Peggy" Lenz receives a $12,078 grant from the U.S. Bureau of Land Management to develop, prepare, and package 100 multimedia secondary level teaching units for an environmental education program.

31 JUL. 1976. Wilma Morris, Asst. Secretary in President's Off. (1966-76), retires.

1 AUG. 1976. Paul Esposito Jr. is named Placement Officer, replacing Jesse D. Moses.

4 AUG. 1976. The Bank of America underwrites $500,000 in bonds to construct the Student Union Building.

19 AUG. 1976. 5 Bicentennial murals painted by Art Prof. Joe Moran and 5 Cal State students are dedicated at S.B. City Hall.

20 AUG. 1976. The campus receives a $56,100 grant from the Calif. Dept. of Education to continue the Bilingual Bicultural Teacher Training Program, under Ernest F. García. Kathy Pezdek receives a $10,000 grant from the Spencer Foundation to research semantic integration. Claire Cantlay, Secretary to the Dir. of Admissions and also in the Physical Education Dept. (1964-76), retires.

26 AUG. 1976. The Calif. State Assembly approves ACR 157, a resolution introduced by Assemblyman C. Jerry Lewis to allow the construction of a Student Health Center on campus.

31 AUG. 1976. Florence A. Mote, Act. Dean of the School of Education, returns to the ranks as Prof. of Education. Kent M. Schofield, Assoc. Dean of Academic Planning, returns to the ranks as Prof. of History.

1 SEPT. 1976. Nathan C. Kravetz is named Dean of the School of Education, replacing Florence A. Mote. Ward M. McAfee, Act. Dean of the School of Social Sciences, is named permanent Dean. Catherine Colby Gannon is named Assoc. Dean of Academic Planning, replacing Kent M. Schofield. L. Theron Pace, College Housing Coordinator (1969-76), is named an EOP Researcher and a Placement Counselor. The Library occupies part of the 5th floor, displacing faculty offices there with the Curriculum Library. The campus begins offering a credential in women's studies, and a B.A. degree in Human Services. The campus inaugurates its "Open College" to allow admission of new students (those who fail to qualify for admission to the main program) through the Office of Continuing Education, thereby providing them a possible "back door" into CSCSB.

10 SEPT. 1976. Stuart R. Ellins receives a $4,500 grant to study coyote behavior; his research ultimately leads to the establishment of the Coyote Research Laboratory. The annual convocation is held.

17 SEPT. 1976. The campus receives a 2-year $152,902 grant from the U.S. Off. of Education to continue funding for the Teachers Corps. The campus announces a new 11-course certificate program in Women's Studies.

24 SEPT. 1976. Nikolai Khokhlov is interviewed by the Canadian Broadcasting Corp.

29 SEPT. 1976. Groundbreaking is held for the new Student Union Building, with the $860,576 cost being raised from student fees and the sale of revenue bonds.

16 & 23 OCT. 1976. The campus hosts a conference in PS-10 on "Diabetics."

17 OCT. 1976. The campus hosts its 2nd Annual Legislative Forum, with the participation of State Sens. Ruben S. Ayala, Robert B. Presley, Walter W. Stiern, and John Stull, and Assemblymen C. Jerry Lewis, Larry Chimbole, Walter Ingalls, Tom Suitt, Terry Goggin, William McVittie, and John Briggs.

20 OCT. 1976. Leon F. Litwack conducts a multimedia presentation of the history of the 1930s and 1960s in the Gymnasium.

22 OCT. 1976. The campus approves a new certificate program in Paralegal Studies. Alexander D. Sokoloff receives a $96,000 grant from the U.S. Army Research Off. to research tribolium beetles.

27 OCT. 1976. Drs. Gordon Rick, Elmer Kelln, James Nethery, Ralph J. Thomson, and Roland Zimmerman conduct a seminar on oral cancer for dentists and physicians in the Commons.

28 OCT. 1976. The campus hosts its 4th Annual Career Day, with speakers Sherry Johnson, Ailien Mentemeier, Rob Tonsberg, Chuck Kozel, Hector Rousseau, Larry Luxton, Rosemary McClure of the *San Bernardino Sun-Telegram*, Don Blair, René Jacober, and Leon Kedding.

29 OCT. 1976. Dalton D. Harrington, Dir. of the CSUC Desert Studies Center, is also elected Chair of the Board.

3 NOV. 1976. The campus hosts the Annual Banquet of the Industry Education Council.

5 NOV. 1976. The campus opens the Center for New Directions under the direction of Cheryl A. Weese to provide free counseling services for students, and to encourage housewives to attend CSCSB.

11 NOV. 1976. Sylvia Woodburne of the Inland Manpower Assoc. speaks in LC-266 on "Jobs for Women." The national business fraternity Alpha Kappa Psi initiates its first 3 women members into the San Bernardino Chapter.

12 NOV. 1976. The campus receives approval from the State Commission on Teacher Preparation and Licensing to begin offering an Early Childhood Specialist Credential Program.

18 NOV. 1976. A. L. Basham speaks in PS-10 on "Indian Thought and the West" and also on "Asia and Medieval Europe." The campus hosts 80 local educators for a Symposium on Bilingual/Bicultural Education, with Robert A. Cervantes and Edward A. DeAvila as keynote speakers.

21 Nov. 1976. Ernest F. García is burned over 15% of his body while working in his garage.

22 Nov. 1976. Gloria Macías, Publisher of *El Chicano*, speaks in LC-266 on "Careers for Minority Women."

24 Nov. 1976. Dawnell Foskey, Dir. of the Woodridge School, speaks in LC-266 on "How to Run Your Own Business."

3 Dec. 1976. The Library purchases 1,410 rare books from the estate of Henrietta Heltzel (who died in 1974).

4 Dec. 1976. Philosopher Charles King speaks in BI-129.

10 Dec. 1976. Richard J. Bennecke announces his candidacy for the office of S.B. Mayor, challenging incumbent W. R. "Bob" Holcomb; he eventually loses.

28 Dec. 1976. Cal State alumnus Robert R. Southworth dies in San Bernardino at age 70; at his graduation in 1975, he was then the oldest CSCSB student ever to receive a degree.

31 Dec. 1976. Frank D. Campbell, Library Clerical Asst. (1975-76), retires.

1977

1 Jan. 1977. Calif. State Senate Bill 1588 becomes law, allowing CSUC faculty and staff to examine their own personnel records.

7 Jan. 1977. Craig E. Henderson is named Housing Coordinator, replacing L. Theron Pace.

12 Jan. 1977. Carl C. Pfeiffer, scheduled to speak on campus on Jan. 20, suffers a heart attack and postpones his appearance.

14 Jan. 1977. The campus receives a $75,000 gift from S.B. Co. to use its federal community development funds to construct a Child Care Center.

19 Jan. 1977. Psychologist Gary Evans speaks in LC-500 on "Personal Space and Crowding."

24 Jan. 1977. The campus expands its child care program to cover infants and toddlers aged 3 months to 2 years.

4 FEB. 1977. In response to the energy crisis, CSUC Chancellor Dumke directs that building temperatures throughout the system be maintained at 65° (winter) and 76° (summer).

10 FEB. 1977. Philosopher William Jacobs speaks in LC-241 on "Plato on Legal Rights and the Art of Ruling."

11 FEB. 1977. The campus trampoline team performs in the Central City Mall. The campus receives an $110,000 grant from the Federal Public Works Program for repairs and maintenance.

16 FEB. 1977. Accountant Donald A. Driftmier speaks in LC-500. Drury Sherrod speaks in LC-500 on "Physical and Cognitive Environments—Where Is Reality?"

18 FEB. 1977. The campus receives a $6,000 gift from architect Jay Dewey Harnish to construct a reflecting fountain pool in the courtyard of the new Creative Arts Building. The campus hosts its annual Science Day, with astronaut Col. Edwin E. "Buzz" Aldrin Jr. speaking in the Gymnasium on "Space Frontiers—Past, Present, and Future," Marshall Johnson speaking on "Research Systems Aboard the Viking I and II Probes"; and Steven P. Loer in LC-500 on "Biology Experiments Aboard the Viking I and II Probes." Moon rocks are displayed in LC-500.

22 FEB. 1977. Lois J. Carson, Jewel Shelton, and Anne Rhodes speak in the Cafeteria as part of the Black Women in America program for Black History Week.

23 FEB. 1977. The gospel groups Biblical Gospel Singers and Donald Roberts & Co. perform in PS-10.

24 FEB. 1977. Australian economist Richard Staveley speaks in LC-500 on "Keynes and the Classical Economists."

28 FEB. 1977. George J. Hock, Custodian (1969-77), retires.

4 MAR. 1977. Painter Jim Rosen speaks on his work in FA-104.

7 MAR. 1977. Statistician Nancy Sue Johnson speaks in BI-129 on "A Non-Parametric Approach to Categorical Data."

8 MAR. 1977. Ward M. McAfee is elected to the Wrightwood Elementary School Dist. Board; Tom M. Rivera is elected to the Colton Unified School Dist. Board.

9 MAR. 1977. Sociologist Thomas Scheff speaks in the C-104 on "Labeling Madness." U.S. Navy Capt. James W. Kehoe Jr. speaks in LC-5 on "U.S. and Soviet Warships."

11 MAR. 1977. Tim Tucker is named Veteran's Affairs Coordinator, replacing Hank White.

14 MAR. 1977. Psychologists W. T. Plant and Mara Southern speak in LC-500 on "Much Ado About Little."

16 MAR. 1977. The CSCSB Infant Care Center, located at College Dale Baptist Church, holds an open house.

17 MAR. 1977. Howard C. Edmiston Co. receives a $141,930 contract to construct the 5,000-sq.-ft. College Bookstore Building.

23-25 MAR. 1977. The campus hosts a Band and Orchestra festival for 2,500 local high and junior high school students.

31 MAR. 1977. James C. Pierson receives a National Endowment for the Humanities fellowship to study at the Univ. of Florida.

8 APR. 1977. Loren H. Filbeck receives a National Endowment for the Humanities award to study at the Univ. of Illinois at Urbana. Richard H. Rowland receives a grant from the Kennan Institute for Advanced Russian Studies of the Woodrow Wilson Center for Scholars to study at the Smithsonian Institution. Cal State alumnus and retired Library Clerical Asst. Frank D. Campbell Jr. publishes his first book, *John D. MacDonald and the Colorful World of Travis McGee* (Borgo Press).

12 APR. 1977. Poet Marvin Bell reads from his work in LC-500. A copy of *Among the Valiant* by the late Raúl Marín is presented to the Coll. Library by his widow, Ramona T. Marín, in a ceremony in the Library attended by Mary Ornelas, Pete Hernández, Hiram Díaz, Frank Gutiérrez, Filiberto H. Rivera, and Aurora Sánchez.

13 APR. 1977. Paleoanthropologist F. Clark Howell speaks in PS-10 on "Unraveling the Distant Human Past."

15 APR. 1977. Lois McAfee receives a $1,190 grant from the U.S. Environmental Protection Agency to chair a forum on air quality and regional economics, "As We Live and Breathe." Pres. Pfau is named to a 4-year term on the Calif. Council for the Humanities in Public Policy.

17 APR. 1977. Florence Alida Blades Mote, Prof. of Education, ex-Act. Dean of the School of Education, the first woman dean on campus, and the first woman tenured full Prof. (1967-77), dies in Victor Valley at age 64 of a stroke suffered on Apr. 9.

28 APR. 1977. Daniel Rosenthal speaks in PS-10 on "Humanities and Science: A Dual Approach to Problem Solving."

29 APR. 1977. The campus receives a $10,000 grant from NSF to conduct a "Women in Science" Career Workshop, under the direction of Florence Weiser. Poets Larry Miller and Carla Coldiron read from their work in PS-10.

30 APR. 1977. James Reed, Lead Groundsworker (1970-77), retires. The campus hosts a conference, "Reading Is Everyone's Concern," in LC-500, with Mary Ann Gatheral giving the keynote address.

4 MAY 1977. Psychologist Leah Light speaks in LC-500 on "Memory for Faces." Philosopher Gerald A. Press speaks in LC-241 on "Rhetoric, Philosophy, and the Educated Man."

5 MAY 1977. Eluid Martínez, Ricardo Mendoza, and Gloria Macías Harrison of *El Chicano* speak in the Gymnasium as part of the Cinco de Mayo celebration. The teatro group Los Terrones, mariachi band Los Luceros, and dance group Ballet Folklórico Teotihuacán perform on LCP.

6 MAY 1977. The campus assigns new building ID codes to the Bookstore (BK), Creative Arts (CA), Health Center (HC), and Student Union (SU). ASB Pres. Kevin Gallagher is elected Chair of the CSUC Student Body Presidents Assoc.

9 MAY 1977. Norwegian Army Maj. Gen. Björn Egge speaks in LC-500 on "NATO and the Warsaw Pact." Gerald M. Scherba is named to the Commission on Extended Education.

11 MAY 1977. Psychologist Joe Martínez speaks in LC-500 on "Neurobiology of Memory."

17 MAY 1977. The Coll. Library celebrates the acquisition of its 250,000th volume, *Deathbird Stories*, by acclaimed writer and futurist, Harlan Ellison, who speaks in LC-500 on "Revealed at Last: What Killed the Dinosaur, and You Don't Look So Terrific Yourself," and who is also fêted at a luncheon in LC. Bernice Biggs speaks in LC-500 on "Experiential Learning." Oliver Johnson speaks in LC-241 on "Three Concepts of Justice."

18 MAY 1977. CSUC Chancellor Glenn S. Dumke visits the campus.

25 MAY 1977. Philosopher William Sacksteder speaks in LC on "Mixed

Drama: Tragedy, Comedy, or Whatever."

26 May 1977. Nancy Mann of Rockwell International Science Center speaks in BI-129 on "Using Statistical Methods of Reliability Analysis to Model the World."

27 May 1977. Albert Blair, Equipment Technician (1970-77), retires.

31 May 1977. Lester Leathers, Custodian (1971-77), retires. In compliance with the Calif. Indoor Clean Air Act, the campus establishes a non-smoking area in the Commons, effective Fall 1977.

2 Jun. 1977. Malcolm W. Klein speaks in PS-10 on "The Problem of Juvenile Gang Delinquency."

3 Jun. 1977. The College Chamber Orchestra receives a national award from the American Soc. of Composers, Authors, and Publishers (ASCAP) for "Adventuresome Programming of Contemporary Music."

4 Jun. 1977. The campus hosts an all-day Drama Workshop for local high school students in the Fine Arts Building, with the participation of Stuart Campbell, Colin Cameron, and Bruce Bilson.

4-5 Jun. 1977. The opera *Four Saints in Three Acts*, by Virgil Thomson and Gertrude Stein, becomes the first production presented in the new Recital Hall of the Creative Arts Building.

7 Jun. 1977. The campus conducts an Open House for the new Creative Arts Building.

13 Jun. 1977. Ex-Cal State student Sondra Theodore is featured as the "Miss July" centerfold in the Jul. 1977 issue of *Playboy*.

14 Jun. 1977. Flautist Candice Mitchell and clarinetist Allan Reisert perform in RH.

15 Jun. 1977. Robert McKenna conducts a workshop for medical personnel who deal with cancer patients in LC-500.

16 Jun. 1977. The campus receives a $20,000 grant from the National Endowment for the Humanities to establish a new Writing Center in cooperation with the Univ. of California.

17 Jun. 1977. Pianists Bethany Ulmer and Sherri Moore perform in PS-10.

18 Jun. 1977. The 11th Commencement is held on the South Gymnasium Lawn, with 633 students eligible for bachelor's degrees and 182 for master's degrees, including the first Master of Public Administration and Bachelor of Vocational Education degrees.

19 Jun. 1977. The Music and Theatre Arts Depts. begin occupying the new Creative Arts Building. Cal State student Richard "Dickie" Salas is shot and killed at age 26.

24 Jun. 1977. The campus receives a $211,727 grant from the U.S. Dept. of Health, Education, and Welfare to fund a Bilingual Teachers Corps training project.

25 Jun. 1977. Cal State student Connie Lee Haugen, Miss San Bernardino County, is named Miss California 1977 at Santa Cruz.

Sum. 1977. Retirements: Charles V. Hartung, Assoc. Prof. of English (1969-77); C. Michael O'Gara, Prof. of Physical Education and Recreation and Chair of the Dept. of Physical Education (1964-77).

11 Jul. 1977. The College approves new B.A. degrees in Liberal Studies and Social Sciences in collaboration with the Coll. of the Desert, effective with 1977/78.

14-30 Jul. 1977. *Tonight in Samarkand* by Jacques Deval and Lorenzo Semple Jr. is the last of 43 productions staged between 1966-77 in the Little Theatre of the Fine Arts Building.

15 Jul. 1977. The campus receives a $125,000 grant from the CSUC System to build a storm drain along Northpark Blvd.

25 Jul. 1977. Construction begins on a Campus Mall connecting the Library, the Student Union, and the Creative Arts Buildings, with Roy C. Barnett Landscaping receiving the $83,700 contract.

8 Aug. 1977. The Bureau of Land Management local Dist. office holds a public meeting in LC-500 to discuss a proposed plan for the Cadiz Valley-Danby Lake area.

22-29 Aug. & 1-9 Sept. 1977. The Library installs an electronic security system, closing its doors to erect the alarm panels and insert metal targets in each book volume.

1 Sept. 1977. The School of Social Sciences is renamed the School of Social and Behavioral Sciences; the Drama Dept. is renamed the Theatre Arts Dept. The campus adopts a grading point system for grades awarded in between the standard A, B, C, D, and F.

10 SEPT. 1977. Cal State student Connie Lee Haugen, Miss California 1977, competes in the televised Miss America Pageant at Atlantic City, New Jersey, where she reaches the semi-finals, placing among the top 10 candidates.

15 SEPT. 1977. K. L. Neff Construction receives an $855,200 contract to build the 11,000-sq.-ft. Student Health Center building.

16 SEPT. 1977. Alethea J. "Lea" Prenzlow, Secretary to the Library Dir. (1966-77), retires.

19 SEPT. 1977. The new College Bookstore opens for business. The new Campus Mall is completed in time for the start of classes. The annual convocation is held.

6 OCT. 1977. The Mixed Motion Dance Co. performs in the Theatre.

11 OCT. 1977. The Faculty Senate approves a constitutional amendment allowing a student representative to serve as a voting member of the Senate for the first time.

13 OCT. 1977. Mime Mark Wenzel and alumna belly dancer Carolee Kent perform in the open-air Greek Theatre.

14 OCT. 1977. Pianist Leonard Pennario performs in RH of the Creative Arts Building as the first artist in "The President's Premiere" series of gala events inaugurating the facility.

19 OCT. 1977. Pianist Althea Mitchell Waites performs in RH.

21-22 OCT. 1977. The campus hosts a workshop in the Commons on "The Roles of Women in Science," with endocrinologist Estelle R. Ramey giving the keynote address, "Society and Male/Female Roles."

29 OCT. 1977. State Sens. Ruben S. Ayala and Robert B. Presley, and Assemblymen C. Jerry Lewis, William McVittie, and Tom Suitt speak before the 3rd Legislative Forum, with Austin Sylvester chairing the proceedings.

1 NOV. 1977. John Chesney is named Dir. of the Upward Bound Program, replacing Michael Preston.

4 NOV. 1977. The campus hosts a panel and dinner in the Commons on media rights, with Jim Johnson of Walnut Properties Inc., Jim Foy of KNBC, Ed Keller of the S.B. Bar Assoc., Bill Honeysett, Publisher of the

San Bernardino Sun-Telegram, and Ned Pia of the *Riverside Press-Enterprise*.

7 NOV. 1977. The campus approves a policy to allow retired CSCSB personnel to use its recreational and library facilities at no charge.

9 NOV. 1977. The CSU Fullerton Wind Ensemble performs in RH.

10 NOV. 1977. D. J. Stine Co. receives a $364,000 contract to install a storm drain along Northpark Blvd. from the main entrance to the flood control channel. The campus presents its first dramatic production in the Theatre, Anton Chekhov's *The Sea Gull*, with performances continuing through Nov. 19.

17 NOV. 1977. The campus states: "Cal State, San Bernardino [now] leads all of her system campuses in the California State University and Colleges System in percentage increase in actual student enrollment, and ranks second in full-time-equivalent student percentages." This represents a major step in the College's 5-year effort to alter its curriculum to career-oriented offerings, and to increase its outreach to the local community.

16 NOV. 1977. Accountant Shirley Loreman speaks in PS-10.

18 NOV. 1977. The Chancellor's Off. approves an M.A. degree in Education to be offered in Hemet and Palm Springs. Psychologist Stephen E. Berger speaks in LC-500 on "Sex Role Discrimination on Intellectual Functioning of Black and White Women."

19 NOV. 1977. Ina Souez, star of the Glyndebourne Opera, speaks and conducts a master class in RH. Alex Bannatyne conducts a one-day workshop on Learning Disabilities with Special Emphasis on Reading Remediation in BI-101.

22 NOV. 1977. Neville Johns Spencer, Assoc. Prof. of Mathematics (1968-77), dies in Colton of an immunological reaction at age 37.

23 NOV. 1977. Pianist Michael Tacchia and cellist Michele Brosseau perform in RH.

26 NOV. 1977. The campus hosts the Women's National AAU Cross-Country Championship.

30 NOV. 1977. Craig Stubblebine and Howard Sherman debate in PS-120 on "Is Capitalism Good for Human Beings?"

2 DEC. 1977. The campus receives $100,000 from the CSUC System to complete the funding of the new Student Health Center.

6 DEC. 1977. Assemblyman C. Jerry Lewis and State Sen. Robert B. Presley speak in PS-122 and LC-500 on "What Is the Difference Between a Democrat and a Republican?"

8 DEC. 1977. Philosopher Bernd Magnus speaks in LC-241 on "Nietzsche's Mitigated Skepticism."

9 DEC. 1977. The campus receives approval to offer an M.A. degree in Education with a Bilingual/Cross-Cultural Option in Spring 1978. In his annual Christmas message to faculty and staff, Pres. Pfau states: "1977 was a very good year for the College. We opened the new Creative Arts Building and the Bookstore Building, and saw the Student Union completed. Recently we received approval to proceed with construction of the Student Health Center. Our student enrollment showed a substantial increase, and our new academic programs continued to grow and develop. In looking ahead to the coming year, we hope that the College will continue the steady progress in all areas which has marked its development from the beginning."

11 DEC. 1977. Pianist and alumnus Michael Tacchia performs with the S.B. Chamber Orchestra in RH.

25 DEC. 1977. Cal State Psychology freshman Julie Renée Richards dies at age 19 from injuries suffered in a truck accident.

1978

1 JAN. 1978. The campus's affirmative action practices, applications, and conditions are extended to include disabled persons. Laura Gómez is named Outreach Counselor.

5 JAN. 1978. Construction begins on the Student Health Center south of the Library-Classroom Building.

6 JAN. 1978. The new campus bus stop at the Main Entrance opens for business, and old bus stop near Student Services is closed and demolished. Shirley Koeller receives a fellowship to attend the Economics Education Institute for College and Univ. Social Studies Educators at Purdue Univ.

6-8 & 13-15 JAN. 1978. *A Glass of Water*, a play by Eugène Scribe, newly translated by Dean of Humanities P. Richard Switzer, directed by stage and TV actor Leo V. Matranga, and starring the Los Angeles-based Travelers' Co., is presented in the Theatre.

8 Jan. 1978. Harpsichordist Phyllis Benson performs in RH. Cal State Psychology senior Vernon Frank Rowell dies at age 55.

11 Jan. 1978. Psychologist Leah Light speaks in LC-500.

13 Jan. 1978. The campus receives approval to offer a Special Education Specialist Credential: Learning Handicapped, beginning with Winter 1978. The campus receives a $565 gift from the Faculty Wives to augment their scholarship fund to $4,693.

16 Jan. 1978. The campus authorizes the creation of an all-weather campus map at the Information Kiosk.

18 Jan. 1978. L.A. Lakers forward Tom Abernathy and Asst. Coach Stan Alback conduct a basketball clinic in the Gymnasium. William D. Gean organizes the first faculty philosophy seminar, on "John Rawls's *Theory of Justice*," in LC-241. Pianist Richard Collins performs in RH.

19 Jan. 1978. The campus officially accepts the Student Union Building, after a delay of 4 months.

25 Jan. 1978. The CSUC Board of Trustees authorizes the Chancellor to establish an Instructionally Related Activities Fee for all campuses, beginning Sept. 1978.

30 Jan. 1978. Anthropologist Brian M. Fagan speaks in RH on Egyptian King Tutankhamun.

1 Feb. 1978. The 15,000-square-foot Student Union Building opens when the office of the Student Union Coordinator, Richard J. Bennecke, is occupied. The facility includes a multi-purpose room that can be used for dances, lectures, and films, student government offices, the school newspaper office, a "noisy room" with 2 billiard tables, pinball machine, ping pong tables, a vending machine room and snack bar, and a lounge with a fireplace and outdoor patio. Psychologist Susan Haviland speaks in LC-500 on "The Role of Given and New Information on Comprehension of Sentences."

3 Feb. 1978. Philosopher Ann Garry speaks in LC-241 on "Pornography and Respect for Women."

6 Feb. 1978. Historian Robert Hine narrates a presentation in PS-10 on "Los Banditos Chicanos: The Social Bandit in California."

11 Feb. 1978. Karl Nobuyuki, Exec. Dir. of the Japanese American Citizens League, speaks in the Commons.

13 FEB. 1978. Pharmacologist Carl C. Pfeiffer speaks in LC-500 on "Trace Elements in Psychosis and Nutritional Disease"; he had originally been scheduled to speak on Jan. 20, 1977. Psychologist Ramon Rhine speaks in LC-500 on "Order or Chaos in Moving Troops of Free-Ranging Baboons."

14 FEB. 1978. S.B. Co. Supervisor James L. Mayfield speaks in LC-5 on "Local Politics."

15 FEB. 1978. Educator Donald Cheek speaks in LC-500 on "A Cross-Cultural Approach to Assertive Training." Psychologist Ovid Tzeng speaks in LC-500 on "Memory and Comprehension."

16 FEB. 1978. A ribbon-cutting ceremony marks the dedication of the new Student Union Building, with ex-ASB Pres. and Student Union Coordinator Richard J. Bennecke cutting the tape, and bluegrass band Bodie Mountain Express providing the music.

22 FEB. 1978. Psychologist Donald Rumelhart speaks in LC-500.

1 MAR. 1978. Barbara Jasper speaks in SU on "Child Abuse: Its Characteristics and Protective Services." Gerontologist David Walsh speaks in LC-500 on "Effects of Aging on Memory." The campus hosts a jazz festival clinic for local high school students in RH.

2 MAR. 1978. The New York theatre group Voices performs *Journey into Blackness* in SU.

2-4 & 7-11 MAR. 1978. *The Houdini Deception*, a mystery drama penned by seniors Paul DeMeo and Danny Bilson, debuts in the Theatre, with the 2 playwrights starring in the lead roles of Sherlock Holmes and Harry Houdini. Campus reception for the play is enthusiastic. DeMeo and Bilson later become successful Hollywood TV, film, and game writers.

3 MAR. 1978. The campus issues its first Emergency Plan booklet.

7 MAR. 1978. Psychologist Joellen Hartley speaks in LC-500 on "The Effects of Alcohol on the Memory."

12 MAR. 1978. James K. Guthrie serves as guest conductor of the Chamber Orchestra in RH.

13 MAR. 1978. Psychologist Gary Evans speaks in LC-500 on "Cognitive Mapping: Environmental Comprehension."

24 MAR. 1978. George John Hock, retired Custodian (1969-77), dies of cancer at age 62.

31 MAR. 1978. Gov. Brown appoints ASB Pres. Kevin Gallagher to the Board of Trustees of the CSUC. Bondiman-McCain receives a $106,000 contract to complete the campus drainage system. J. D. Stine Co. receives a $26,000 contract to grade the mall area between the Student Union and Creative Arts buildings.

4-6 APR. 1978. The campus hosts a Band and Orchestra Festival in the Creative Arts Building, with 2,500 local students attending.

6 APR. 1978. The Faculty Development Center sponsors a debate, "Should the E.R.A. Be Ratified?," in LC-500, with Mary Smith, Pres. of the Calif. National Organization of Women, and Eagle Forum members Rita Miller and Sharon Gabler.

11 APR. 1978. Mathematician Phillip Krausher speaks in BI-129 on "Graph Theory: Local Connectedness and Hamiltonian Cycles." Skin diver Jack McKenney speaks in SU on "From California to Cayman."

12 APR. 1978. Attorney and alumnus René Jacober speaks in SU as part of a "Career Conversation" program.

13 APR. 1978. Everett W. Hesse speaks in LC-500 on "The Spanish Comedia as Popular Culture."

14 APR. 1978. Arthur A. Moorefield receives a $2,500 fellowship from the National Endowment for the Humanities to do research in central Europe on Johannes Galliculus.

18 APR. 1978. Frederick Williams speaks in LC-500 on "Sex Role Stereotyping and Television."

20 APR. 1978. Donald Helinski speaks in the Gymnasium and in PS-10 on "Recombinant DNA—Genetic Engineering." Electronic synthesizer group Haynes and Ramey performs in SU. Peggy Harvey speaks in SU.

22 APR. 1978. The campus hosts a Children's Festival in SUMP, with magician Ron Bonneau and drama group The Pick-Up Players performing.

23 APR. 1978. Ex-Metropolitan Opera baritone Robert McFerrin performs in RH.

24 APR. 1978. Mathematician Gloria Olive speaks in BI-129 on "What Is a b-Transform?" Avigdor Haselkorn speaks in LC-5 on "Soviet Collective Security Systems."

25 APR. 1978. Susan Futterman, Manager of Children's Programs for the ABC TV network, speaks in LC-500 on "Children and Television—a View from Both Sides of the Issues."

26 APR. 1978. Oceanographer Don Walsh speaks in LC-5 on "Ocean Policy and the Law of the Sea."

27 APR. 1978. Surendra Suri speaks in SU on "Shared Values in America and India." The campus hosts a Creative Writing Conference for local high school students in LC-500.

28 APR. 1978. The State Commission for Teacher Preparation and Licensing grants the campus the authority to process all teaching credentials locally. The campus receives a $13,600 grant from NSF for the "Development of a Microcomputer Laboratory in a Certificate Program."

1 MAY 1978. The campus is granted authority by the Chancellor's Off. to make final decisions on the classification and reclassification of employees. William Anderson, Refrigerator Mechanic (1970-78), dies in S.B. at age 47.

3 MAY 1978. Pianist Tamas Ungar performs in RH. Criminologist Simon Dinitz speaks in PS-10 on "Dangerous Criminals: Who Are They and What Can We Do About Them."

4 MAY 1978. The campus celebrates Cinco de Mayo with performances by theatre group Escuela de la Raza Unida, the band Brown Society, and guitarist Andrés Bustamante, and speeches by Rev. Gustavo Benson, Ernest F. García, Ámparo Holguín, and Armando Navarro.

5 MAY 1978. Mathematician Paul Halmos speaks in BI-101 on "A Mathematical Problem Sampler."

12 MAY 1978. The Chancellor's Off. approves a new B.A. degree in American Studies, to be offered beginning 1978/79.

17 MAY 1978. Psychologist Robert Singer speaks in LC-500 on "Violence in Television." The Colton High School Wind Ensemble performs with the Cal State Wind Ensemble in RH.

19 MAY 1978. The campus receives a $235,479 grant from the National Endowment for the Humanities to improve student writing. Bruce Golden receives a National Endowment for the Humanities Fellowship to study at UC Berkeley.

20 MAY 1978. The campus hosts a one-day seminar in LC on the history of San Bernardino.

22 MAY 1978. The Riverside City College Wind Ensemble performs with the Cal State Wind Ensemble in RH.

25 MAY 1978. The campus hosts a debate in LC-500 on the Jarvis-Gann Initiative (Proposition 13), with George Gibbs, J. Cordell Robinson, S.B. Co. Supervisor James L. Mayfield, and Fontana City Manager Jack Ratelle, and Carol F. Goss as moderator. Philosopher James Bogen speaks on "An Empirical Refutation of Skepticism."

31 MAY 1978. Gerald I. Gordon and Mark Lipsey speak in LC-241 on "The Public Role of Community Mental Health Agencies in Combating Juvenile Delinquency."

3 JUN. 1978. The campus hosts its 8th Annual Theatre Workshop for local high school students in the Theatre.

4 JUN. 1978. Kathleen Lucille Goedeck, Physical Plant Custodian (1975-78), dies at age 35.

8 & 10 JUN. 1978. The Music Dept. presents its first full-length opera in RH, Wolfgang Mozart's *Cosi fan tutte*.

10 JUN. 1978. The Spanish Club sponsors a program of Hispanic performances in the Theatre, including poetry read by Karen Claussen, dancing by the Ballet Folklórico, songs by Gena Baca and Silvia Silva, and a play directed by María Carmona and Enrique Martínez.

17 JUN. 1978. The 12th Commencement is held on the South Gymnasium Lawn, with more than 600 bachelor's and 200 master's degrees being offered. The campus publishes its first yearbook since 1967, and only its 3rd in history.

23 JUN. 1978. The Chancellor's Off. extends the pilot period for another year for the M.A. in Education with Elementary Option and M.A. in Education with Counseling Option in the Coachella Valley.

29 JUN. 1978. The S.B. Business and Professional Women's Club establishes a scholarship honoring Nancy E. Smith, ex-Chair of the S.B. Co. Board of Supervisors (1956-76).

7 JUL. 1978. M. Jeanne Hogenson is named Act. Dir. of Activities.

18 JUL. 1978. R. Joy Robertson, Business Services Officer (1966-78), retires.

19 JUL. 1978. Janice L. "Jan" Lemmond, Purchasing Agent, is named Support Services Officer, replacing R. Joy Robertson. Mary A. Burgess is named Purchasing Agent, replacing Janice L. Lemmond.

26 JUL. 1978. The campus receives a $6,000 gift from the Friends of Nancy E. Smith Committee to establish a scholarship in her name.

31 JUL. 1978. Russell J. DeRemer, Assoc. Dean of Activities and Housing and Assoc. Prof. of Physics (1965-78), takes a position as Dean of Students at Whitman College; his position is abolished. Doris Scott, Secretary in Activities and Housing (1967-78), retires.

17 AUG. 1978. Bernhardt L. Mortensen, Assoc. Prof. of Sociology (1968-78), retires.

27 AUG. 1978. Peter M. Briscoe, first Library Bibliographer (1973-78), takes a position as Chief Collection Development Officer and Head of Special Collections at UC, Riverside.

30 AUG. 1978. Buell Gordon Gallagher, first Chancellor of the CSC System (1961-62), dies in New York City at age 74.

8 SEPT. 1978. The campus is designated a member of the Servicemen's Opportunity Colleges by the American Assoc. of State Colleges and Universities. Gloria A. Cowen and Jill Kasen receive a $30,000 grant from the National Institute of Education for the project, "The Letter of Recommendation: A Key to Women's Career Equity in Academia."

11 SEPT. 1978. The annual convocation is held.

21 SEPT. 1978. The Child Care Center is renamed the Children's Center.

23 SEPT. 1978. The campus hosts the Cal State Student Presidents Assoc. Conference in SU.

27 SEPT. 1978. The CSUC Board of Trustees adopts system-wide standards governing the student evaluation of teaching.

29 SEPT. 1978. The campus receives a $14,000 grant from the U.S. Dept. of Justice Law Enforcement Assistance Administration to train law enforcement personnel.

1 OCT. 1978. Esraj player Sri Chinmoy performs in RH.

5 OCT. 1978. J. D. Stine Co. receives an $180,000 contract to construct a 350-space parking lot between the campus Main Entrance and the residence halls.

6 OCT. 1978. The campus receives a $99,000 grant from the U.S. Off. of Public Works to complete the landscaping of the Campus Mall, and to construct additional turfed playing fields.

10 OCT. 1978. Charles R. McPherson, Building Services Engineer (1976-78), dies of a heart attack at age 64.

19 OCT. 1978. The campus receives approval from the national headquarters of the Honor Soc. of Phi Kappa Phi (ΦKΦ) to establish local Chapter 215 at CSCSB. The Music Dept. acquires a Schlicker pipe organ, to be installed in the Creative Arts Building.

20 OCT. 1978. Joseph Herrbach, Custodian, retires.

27 OCT. 1978. The Chancellor's Off. approves a new B.A. degree in Liberal Studies with an Emphasis in Bilingual/Cross-Cultural Studies, to be offered through the Coll. of the Desert beginning Winter 1979. Cal State Social Sciences graduate student George Patrick Bigley dies of a heart attack in Riverside at age 43.

28 OCT. 1978. The campus hosts the *Sun-Telegram* 10K Run, with 659 participants.

30 OCT.-13 NOV. 1978. The campus hosts a series of seminars on Government Public Relations, with speakers Al Bruton, Rep. George E. Brown, Elaine Marable, and John E. Husing.

1 NOV. 1978. The Native Sons of the Golden West dedicate an historical marker commemorating Old Devil Canyon Road on State College Pkwy. between Kendall Dr. and Northpark Blvd., with Gerald Doyle giving the historical background. Pianist Althea Mitchell Waites performs in RH. Sociologist Leon Sheleff speaks in SS-171 on "Born to Oppression: The Young as a Deprived Minority."

8-9 NOV. 1978. Cal State students vote to change the name of their government organization from the Associated Student Body (ASB) to the Associated Students, Incorporated (ASI).

27 NOV. 1978. Musician Fred Fox of the L.A. Philharmonic Orchestra presents a clinic for brass players in RH.

28 NOV. 1978. Sociologist G. William Domhoff speaks in LC-500 on "State and Ruling Class in Corporate America."

29 Nov. 1978. Gov. Brown suggests to the CSUC Board of Trustees that CSCSB be combined with UC Riverside—it didn't happen!

30 Nov. 1978. Sally Watson, Accountant (1965-78), retires.

21 Dec. 1978. The campus establishes the Center on Economic Education, under the direction of R. James Charkins.

29 Dec. 1978. Lucy E. Hauer, Library Asst. (1967-78), retires.

31 Dec. 1978. Andre A. Maurel, Chief of Plant Operations (1965-78), retires. Dorothy Stuart, Dir. of the Children's Center, resigns.

1979

1 Jan. 1979. James H. Urata, Building Coordinator, is named Dir. of the Physical Plant, replacing Andre A. Maurel. Teresa Lantz is named Act. Dir. of the Children's Center, replacing Dorothy Stuart. Calif. State Senate Bill 130 takes effect, raising the mandatory retirement age for state employees from 67 to 70.

10 Jan. 1979. Organist Robert L. Tusler performs in RH.

18 Jan. 1979. The campus hosts a seminar on Vandalism, Burglary, and Arson for local educators.

24 Jan. 1979. Margaret Shelton performs in RH.

29 Jan. 1979. The campus removes the gate arm from the parking lot near the Student Services Building, instead installing a parking decal dispenser at a cost of 25¢ per day.

30 Jan. 1979. Art Seidenbaum, Book Editor of the *Los Angeles Times*, speaks in RH on "Ethics and Sin in Southern California."

31 Jan. 1979. The UCLA Woodwind Quintet performs in RH.

1 Feb. 1979. The Dept. of Physical Education and Recreation, previously an autonomous unit in Academic Affairs, is placed for administrative purposes under the School of Natural Sciences. Medical historian Robert P. Hudson speaks in PS-10 on "The Right to Live and the Right to Die," and also on "Lessons Learned from Legionnaire's Disease."

7-9 Feb. 1979. Composer Vincent Persichetti speaks on "Current Trends in Music," and conducts the Cal State Choir and Wind Ensemble in RH.

8 FEB. 1979. L.A. Lakers guard Norm Nixon, forward Don Ford, and Asst. Coach Stan Alback conduct a basketball clinic in the Gymnasium.

14 FEB. 1979. William R. Van Cleave speaks in LC-5 on "SALT II." Felix Nigro speaks on "Civil Service Reform Act of 1978."

16 FEB. 1979. The campus hosts a "Blacks in the Arts" festival, featuring a fashion show by designer Leon Childress, a talk by actress Abbey Lincoln on "The Black Artist," and a play, *Taking Care of Business*, presented by the Miklac Players from USC and produced by award-winning director Michael Rayson.

20 FEB. 1979. Psychologist William Banks speaks in LC-500 on "Spatial Memory."

21 FEB. 1979. Sociologist Norman Friedman speaks in LC-241 on "Success, Failure on the Hollywood Scene: A Sociological Analysis." Pianist Katherine Whitescarver performs in RH.

23 FEB. 1979. Paul J. Johnson receives a $10,000 grant from the National Endowment for the Humanities to attend the International Hobbes Tercentenary Congress at Univ. of Colorado. The campus hosts a Solo and Ensemble Festival in RH for high school students.

28 FEB. 1979. Jazz trumpeter Greg Adams of Tower of Power performs in RH.

1 MAR. 1979. Max A. "Marty" Bloomberg is named Asst. Library Dir.

2 MAR. 1979. The campus installs 6 emergency telephones at strategic locations around the University.

14 MAR. 1979. Woodworker and furniture designer Morris Shepherd speaks about his work in FA-104.

16 MAR. 1979. The campus receives a $34,000 grant from the Chino Basin Metropolitan Water Dist. for dairy waste research, supplementing a previous grant of $63,858.

23 MAR. 1979. Larry Montáñez, Mail Room Supervisor (1969-79), resigns.

27 MAR. 1979. The campus hosts a workshop, "Women in Science," at Victor Valley Coll.

2 APR. 1979. The campus and the Redlands School Dist. receive a 5-year,

$70,404 grant from the U.S. Off. of Education to support Teacher Corps projects. Artist and social historian T. J. Clark speaks in SUMP on "Conceptual Art."

3-5 APR. 1979. The campus hosts its 3rd annual Band and Orchestra Festival, with some 2,500 local students attending.

5 APR. 1979. The campus hosts a Symposium on Outdoor Sculpture in The Gallery, featuring Aldo Casanova, George Herms, Roger P. Lintault, and critic Susanne Muchnic, with Poppy Sullivan, Dir., Cal State Art Gallery, acting as moderator.

6 APR. 1979. The campus receives a $10,507 grant from NSF to conduct a seminar in economic education for elementary school teachers. William D. Gean receives a $2,500 grant from the National Endowment for the Humanities to complete a book entitled *The Concept of Emotion*.

9 APR. 1979. The College Police begin providing an escort service for students, faculty, and staff.

11 APR. 1979. The Collegium Musicum of the Univ. of Calif., Riverside performs in RH.

18 APR. 1979. Richard Falzalore speaks in SU on "Entry Level Positions in the Health Sciences." The experimental music ensemble Harkins and Larson perform in RH.

21-22 APR. 1979. William J. Kaufmann III conducts a 2-day lecture on "Black Holes, Quarks, and Quasars"

26 APR. 1979. Writer C. Brooks Peters speaks in PS-10 on "Inside Hitler's Germany: A War Correspondent's Experiences."

28 APR. 1979. The campus and the Federal Teacher Corps co-sponsor its 3rd Annual Reading Conference. The campus hosts a seminar on History of the Blues.

1 MAY 1979. William D. Gean, A. Vivien Bull, and Fred Keene are named Danforth Associates. A forum to celebrate Cinco de Mayo, "The Chicano: Now and the Future," is held in SUMP, with guest speakers Rev. Gustavo Benson, Ana Nieto-Gómez, and Armando Navarro. John Reseck Jr. speaks on "Underwater Spear-Fishing and Conservation Today."

2 MAY 1979. The campus hosts a Choral Festival in RH for local high school students.

2-5 MAY 1979. *Sleeping with the Enemy*, a play by ex-CSCSB Dramatist-in-Residence Harry Cauley, starring William L. Slout and his wife, actress Marte Boyle, begins its West Coast premiere.

3 MAY 1979. The band Mariachi Cocula and the dance group Ballet Folklórico de San Bernardino perform on LCP.

4 MAY 1979. Lalo Guerrero, composer and lyricist for *Zoot Suit*, speaks in SUMP, following a performance of the play, *Las Dos Caras del Patroncito*. The campus receives a $5,000 award from the Western Electric Fund for a program for aspiring women executives, with Margaret K. Gibbs, the instructor who created the course, receiving $1,000. J. Cordell Robinson receives a Humanities Summer Faculty Seminar Award from the National Endowment for the Humanities to study at the Univ. of Texas, Austin.

5 MAY 1979. A float designed and manned by Cal State students, "Sí Se Puede con Educación," wins first prize in the San Bernardino Cinco de Mayo Parade.

8 MAY 1979. The campus hosts a Career Marketplace in SU.

12 MAY 1979. Anthropologist Woodrow W. Clark speaks to a seminar in LC-500 on "Violence in the Public Schools." The campus hosts a seminar in PS-10 on "Perspectives on Gay Rights," with speakers Susan McGrievy, Rob Jurina, and Duncan Donovan.

14 MAY 1979. Writer and performance artist John White speaks in The Gallery of the Fine Arts Building. The campus hosts the Creative Writing Conference in LC-500.

16 MAY 1979. Social ecologist Gilbert Geis speaks in PS-10 on "Respectable Crime and Respectable Criminals: White-Collar Crime."

19 MAY 1979. The Lung Assoc. of San Bernardino, Inyo, and Mono Counties sponsors a 10 kilometer run on campus.

22 MAY 1979. James T. Weir, retired Police Officer (1965-74), dies at age 61; in Aug. 1965 he was one of the first members of the Campus Police.

23 MAY 1979. Allan Metcalf speaks in LC-241 on "California Dialects." Cal State student John Reece Harris dies in San Bernardino at age 20.

30 MAY 1979. Painter Joe Fay speaks in SUMP on "The Contemporary Los Angeles Art World." Richard West speaks in SUMP on "Those Who Fought—Those Who Didn't: A Statistical Profile." Helen A. Holt, Library Clerical Asst. (1979), resigns. Pianist Althea Mitchell Waites, clarinetist

Phillip Rehfeldt, and flautist Karlin Eby perform in RH.

31 May 1979. Well-known humorist Richard Armour speaks in RH on "A Satirist at Work."

2 Jun. 1979. The campus hosts a conference on "The Prevention of Crimes Against People" in PS-10. The Jun. 2 issue of the magazine *Art Week* features a full-page illustrated review of the campus's outdoor sculpture display.

16 Jun. 1979. The 13th Commencement is held on the South Gymnasium Lawn, with 865 students eligible to receive diplomas. Helen Alice Holt, ex-Library Clerical Asst. (1979), dies at age 63, 2 weeks after resigning.

20 Jun. 1979. TV reporter Dan Rather interviews Prof. Nikolai E. Khokhlov on campus for the CBS program, *60 Minutes*.

21 Jun. 1979. The Staff Council holds its final meeting; having been founded in 1968, the organization is disbanded due to the advent of collective bargaining in the CSUC System. The final members include: Fred Cordova (2-time Chair), Colleen F. Artrup, Joseph Bell, Jo Ann Von Wald, Mary A. Burgess, Linda Thorvaldson, Charles W. Dulaney, Sue Ellis, Frank Lootens, and Janice Williams.

25 Jun. 1979. The Student Health Center opens for business.

Sum. 1979. Retirements: René F. Dennemeyer, Prof. of Mathematics (1966-79); John E. Hafstrom, Prof. of Mathematics (1965-79).

1 Jul. 1979. The Calif. Higher Education Employer-Employee Relations Act (HEERA) takes effect, authorizing the election of a faculty bargaining agent for the CSUC System.

3 Jul. 1979. The S.B. City Planning Commission approves a 158-unit condominium complex, "University Meadows," on Northpark Blvd. east of State College Pkwy.

6 Jul. 1979. The Chancellor's Off. approves an Option in Vocational Education for the M.A. degree in Education, effective with 1979/80.

16 Jul. 1979. A new 350-space parking lot east of the main entrance opens for business.

31 Jul. 1979. Stanley Ziegler, Equipment Technician (1969-79), retires.

1 Aug. 1979. Joseph R. Sartor, Tractor Operator (1965-79), retires.

31 Aug. 1979. Robert A. Lee, Assoc. Dean for Academic Affairs, returns to the ranks as Prof. of English. Nathan C. Kravetz, Dean of the School of Education, returns to the ranks as Prof. of Education. P. Richard Switzer, Dean of the School of Humanities, returns to the ranks as Prof. of French.

1 Sept. 1979. J. Cordell Robinson, Assoc. Prof. of History, is named Assoc. Dean for Academic Affairs, replacing Robert A. Lee. Ernest F. García, Coordinator of Bilingual Education, is named Dean of the School of Education, replacing Nathan C. Kravetz. Irving H. Buchen is named Dean of the School of Humanities, replacing P. Richard Switzer. Mary Ongaro is named Dir. of the Children's Center, replacing Teresa Lantz. L. Theron Pace is named Dir. of Disabled Student Services. Parking fees increase from $10 per quarter to $12, to $4 per month for faculty and staff, and daily parking rates to 50¢. Joseph Richard Sartor, retired Tractor Operator (1965-79), dies in Fontana at age 60, a month after retiring.

10 Sept. 1979. The annual convocation is held.

11 Sept. 1979. Eason Construction Inc. receives a $218,500 contract to remodel the Fine Arts Building, to include art studios and other facilities, an expanded Art Gallery, and faculty offices.

21 Sept. 1979. The Commons sets aside a dining room (CO-219) exclusively for faculty and staff use.

25 Sept. 1979. H. M. "Hank" Plotkin speaks in LC-224 on "Starting and Running a Small Business."

28 Sept. 1979. Demetrios "Jim" Arabatzis, Bookstore Manager (1965-79), resigns to manage a restaurant in Hemet. Sherrie R. Bartell is named a CSUC Administrative Fellow.

8 Oct. 1979. The Computer Center is moved administratively from Institutional Research to the Off. of Academic Administration. State Sen. Alan Robbins speaks in LC-500 on "Busing."

9 Oct. 1979. S.B. City Councilman Ralph Hernández speaks in PS-122 on "Local Elections and the Ballot."

17 Oct. 1979. Clarinetist Phillip Rehfeldt and Barney Childs perform "new music" in RH.

25 Oct. 1979. Economist James Earley speaks in LC-500 on "The Causes and Cures of Inflation."

28 Oct. 1979. Chicago chamber ensemble Trio dell'Arte performs in RH.

The San Bernardino Sun sponsors a 10-kilometer run on campus.

29 OCT. 1979. The campus hosts a seminar on "The Role of Education in the Acculturation of the Black Family" in SUMP.

30 OCT. 1979. Political scientist Heinz Eulau speaks in LC-5 and again in LC-500 on "The Politics of Representation."

31 OCT. 1979. Ex-British diplomat Raymond Hutchings speaks in PS-10 on "How Efficient Is the Soviet Economy?" and also on "Soviet Arms to the Third World: Patterns and Implications."

1 NOV. 1979. LeRoy A. Weber is named Bookstore Manager, replacing Demetrios "Jim" Arabatzis.

1-2 NOV. 1979. Howard Schwartz conducts a 2-day seminar in LC-500 on "New Laws Affecting Employee Relationships."

2 NOV. 1979. The campus receives a $79,385 grant from the U.S. Dept. of Education to continue the Bilingual Teacher Corps Project.

3 NOV. 1979. Assemblyman William R. "Bill" Leonard speaks in PS-10 about Senate Bill 666.

9 NOV. 1979. Arthur M. Butler, Police Sergeant, is also named Environmental Health and Safety Officer.

13 NOV. 1979. Eugene I. Bender speaks in LC-241 on "Self-Help Research: A Neglected Area of Social Research."

14 NOV. 1979. Poet James Tate reads from his work in LC. Sergeant Paul Curry and Detective Peggy Williams of the S.B. Co. Sheriff's Office, and Jackie Dewar of the S.B. Rape Crisis and Assault Services Program, speak in SUMP on "Rape Awareness and Prevention."

17 NOV. 1979. Pianist Juan Emanuel Silva Hidalgo performs in RH.

25 NOV. 1979. Theodore C. "Ted" White, Building Services Engineer (1969-79), dies in Fontana of liver failure at age 55.

2 DEC. 1979. Soprano Jolene Schwandt and her group perform in UC.

10 DEC. 1979. Dean Wright is named Bookstore Manager, replacing LeRoy A. Weber.

31 DEC. 1979. Retirements: Woodrow Wilson, Supervising Groundsworker; Raoul Monzon, Groundsworker.

1980

4 JAN. 1980. The campus receives a $94,136 grant from the U.S. Dept. of Health, Education, and Welfare to participate in a joint health project with Chico State College and CSU, Northridge. This is the 2nd year of a grant that initially awarded $156,453. The first professionally designed issue of the Alumni Assoc. magazine, *Panorama*, is published under the editorship of Edna L. Steinman.

6 JAN. 1980. Cal State student James C. Van Mouwerik dies in a train accident in Sweden at age 22.

8 JAN. 1980. The lowest contractor's bid for construction of the Child Care Center comes in 27% over budget, and the campus is forced to rebid the contract.

9 JAN. 1980. Heavy rains on this day, Jan. 14, Jan. 29, and Feb. 16 overflow the Harrison Canyon flood control basin, inundating Hampshire Ave. in S.B. with mud; on Feb. 10, 20 Cal State students and administrators volunteer to help clear away some of the debris. The Corona-Norco School Board approves an agreement with CSCSB to offer teacher education courses in Corona.

10 JAN.-7 FEB. 1980. Woodpushers Anonymous sponsors a 5-week chess tournament in SU.

11 JAN. 1980. Kathy Pezdek is named Dir. of the Faculty Development Center.

14 JAN. 1980. The campus hosts a reception to open the remodeled and expanded Art Gallery, with the first exhibit featuring a selection of new works by the College faculty.

15 JAN. 1980. William Clarence "Bill" Agnew, Bookstore Book Buyer (1970-80), dies in San Bernardino at age 50.

16 JAN. 1980. The Nursing Program is accredited for 6 years by the National League for Nursing.

23 JAN. 1980. Activist Gloria Allred, ex-Rep. Shirley N. Pettis, and Judge Dana Harvey of the Fontana Municipal Court speak in SU as part of the Women in Government Conference.

27 JAN. 1980. Gilbert L. Blount and the Univ. of Southern California's

American Early Music Consort perform in RH.

29-30 JAN. 1980. The campus hosts a backgammon tournament in SU.

30 JAN. 1980. The campus is ordered by the state to cease offering of extension classes in Las Vegas.

1-2 FEB. 1980. The campus hosts the 2nd Annual Special Education Conference, "Whose Kid Am I, Anyway," featuring Frank Siccone, Maryl Bannatyne, Robert Mosby, and Lee Kochenderfer as speakers.

5 FEB. 1980. The campus receives approval to offer an M.A. degree in English Composition, beginning with 1980/81. Psychologist John Gillis speaks in PS-500 on "Successful Therapeutic Techniques in Psychotherapy."

8 FEB. 1980. R. James Charkins receives a $19,957 grant from NSF to provide economics education for schoolteachers. Stage and screen actor Danny Scarborough performs his show, "Something Called Freedom," in PS-10.

12 FEB. 1980. Social worker Don Gumbleton speaks in SU on "The Place of Sexual Therapy in Our Lives."

13 FEB. 1980. Trumpeter Mike Vax conducts a jazz clinic and concert for 300 local high school students in RH.

19 FEB. 1980. Harry Templeton and the S.B. Community Choir perform gospel music in SUMP as part of "Black History Week."

20 FEB. 1980. Art historian Gert Schiff speaks in SUMP on "The Triptychs of Max Beckmann." Melvin G. Hawkins hosts a panel in SUMP on "Housing, Education, and Employment for Blacks in the Inland Empire," featuring Barnett Grier, Robbin Hawkins, and Michael Teer.

21 FEB. 1980. The Shades of Black theatre group performs an original 3-act play, *The Organizer*, in SU. The campus hosts a community forum, "The Inland Empire in 1980 and the Coming Decade," in RH. The CSCSB Faculty Wives donates $875 to its campus scholarship fund.

22 FEB. 1980. The campus hosts a Solo and Ensemble Festival for local high school students.

27 FEB. 1980. UC Riverside's Collegium Musicum performs in RH.

28 FEB.-1 MAR. & 4-8 MAR. 1980. *The Robber Bridegroom* by Alfred

Uhry and Robert Waldman becomes the first musical drama staged at CSCSB.

4 MAR. 1980. Psychologist Beverly Birns speaks in PS-10 on "The Changing Concept of Motherhood." K. L. Neff Construction Co. receives a $170,500 contract to construct the Child Care Center.

7 MAR. 1980. The campus hosts a workshop in SU on "Agent Orange," with speakers Joseph S. Goldman, Venita L. Carver, Tom Niehoff, Rowland Fisher, Frank Terry, and William Pavano.

22 MAR. 1980. James Joseph Finley, Prof. of Administration and Ex-Chair of the Dept. of Public Administration (1973-80), dies in San Bernardino of cancer at age 61.

23 MAR. 1980. The campus hosts a 10-kilometer "Run for Fun" sponsored by the Southern Cal Road Runners.

24-26 MAR. 1980. The campus hosts the Third World Counselors Conference.

25 MAR. & 2 APR. 1980. The campus hosts its annual Band and Orchestra Festival, featuring 25 local school bands.

2-7 APR. 1980. The CSCSB Chamber Singers perform at the Collegiate Choral Festival in Mexico City, winning a bronze medallion.

3 APR.-1 MAY 1980. Woodpushers Anonymous, the campus chess club, sponsors a 5-week tournament in SU.

8 APR. 1980. The *Pawprint* reduces its physical height by an inch.

9 APR. 1980. Soprano Gwendolyn Lytle and pianist Althea Mitchell Waites perform in RH.

11 APR. 1980. Barbara Nolte, Dir. of the College Relations Off. and Editor of 650 weekly issues of the campus newsletter, *The Bulletin* (1966-80), retires; the responsibilities of her office are redistributed among other campus units.

15 APR. 1980. Welsh philosopher D. Z. Phillips speaks in LC-500 on "Magic and Education," and in LC-241 on "Wittgenstein's Full Stop." CSCSB is one of 6 CSUC campuses participating in a program for Student Affirmative Action designed to increase the number of underrepresented ethnic groups in higher education.

18 APR. 1980. Cora Lee "Corky" Moffett, Secretary to the Dean of Students (1964-80), retires.

19 APR. 1980. The campus hosts the first Southern California Black Student Union Conference, moderated by KNXT-TV broadcaster Truman Jacques.

22 APR. 1980. A time capsule buried in 1967 by the first graduating class near the flagpole of the Administration Building is opened. The campus celebrates the 10th anniversary of Earth Day in SUMP, with Chuck Bell speaking on "An Energy Outlook for San Bernardino County," Ike Eastvold on "Countdown for the California Desert," and Larry LaPre on "1980—The Year of the Coast."

23 APR. 1980. The campus hosts a Choral Festival for 500 local high school students.

25 APR. 1980. John Westrick, Plant Operations, retires. The campus airs its first TV commercial (produced by the Audio-Visual Dept.) on local stations KSCI (Channel 18) and KVCR (Channel 24.

26 APR. 1980. The campus hosts a reading conference, "Competencies in the '80s."

26 APR.-10 JUN. 1980. The campus hosts a major exhibit of 19th-century symbolist art in The Gallery, featuring works by Pablo Picasso, Odilon Redon, and Vincent Gauguin.

27 APR. 1980. The campus celebrates its 15th anniversary with an open house featuring an academic brunch, glassblowing, tours, art and science demonstrations, a children's fair, vocal and instrumental musical performances, drama productions, folk dancing, special library exhibits, a 5-kilometer family run, and a presentation of the play *Typists* by the Schisgal Touring Theatre Group. Robert E. Botts, Lois J. Carson, Deborah Daniel (Tharaldson), James F. Penman, and Glenn G. Rymer receive the first Distinguished Alumni Awards during a special recognition brunch in the Commons. Roma Sill wins the pie baking contest with her pecan pie. An article in the *San Bernardino Sun* pessimistically states, "College officials would like the public to drop by and participate, but they're worried that people won't know where to find the campus. For today, 15 years after the doors opened, the College is still not generally regarded as an integral part of the community"—and further suggests that the school will remain isolated until it introduces intercollegiate athletics. However, the open house is generally regarded as a great success, and marks the beginning of a campaign by CSCSB to better reach out to the local community.

30 APR. 1980. The Faculty Wind Quintet/Sextet of the Univ. of Redlands performs in RH.

1 MAY 1980. The Colton High School Wind Ensemble and Agoura High School Wind Ensemble perform in RH.

5 MAY 1980. The campus celebrates Cinco de Mayo with performances on LCP by the band Mariachi Cocula and dance group Folklórico Lindo. Art historian Henri Dorra speaks in SUMP on "Redon and the Unconscious."

6 MAY 1980. French scholar Georges Lubin speaks in LC-500 on "George Sand: The Rights of Women and Politics." Religious historian James M. Robinson speaks in RH on "Orthodoxy and Heresy in Early Christianity."

9 MAY 1980. Groundbreaking is held for the new Children's Center, with architect Jack Causey and S.B. Co. Supervisor Robert Hammock participating. The Coll. Library receives grants from the Calif. Real Estate Endowment ($10,000) and the U.S. Dept. of Health, Education, and Welfare ($1,900) to purchase books. Arlo D. Harris is invited by the Sudanese government to teach at the Univ. of Khartoum during the summer. Cal State student and Riverside Co. Deputy Sheriff Glenn Bolasky is shot twice while pursuing bank robbers in Lytle Canyon; he later recovers.

9-10 MAY 1980. The campus hosts its 1st annual Renaissance Banquet in the Commons, with the Chamber Singers providing the musical program, "Festivo Musica Transalpina," and a full-dressed roast pig being served.

10 MAY 1980. The Cal State Faculty Wives vote to change the name of their organization to the Cal State Associates, and to expand their membership to include faculty and staff.

12 MAY 1980. El Teatro de la Esperanza de Santa Barbara performs the play *La Victima* in SUMP.

14 MAY 1980. Sociologist LaMar T. Empey speaks in PS-10 on "The End of Childhood and Juvenile Justice." Bruce W. MacDonald conducts a seminar in LC-500 on "Soviet-American Relations and SALT II."

15 MAY 1980. Science writer Irving Bengelsdorf speaks in PS-10 on "Where Are We? What Are We? The Majesty of the Physical Universe." The remodeling of the Fine Arts Building nears completion.

18 MAY 1980. TV newscaster Connie Chung speaks in RH on "Current Trends in Television News," being the first of a series of "celebrity speakers" designed to bring more visitors to campus; an overflow crowd greets her appearance.

21 May 1980. The Community College Chorus of Victor Valley College performs in RH.

22 May 1980. Contractor Jack Stines begins construction of a new campus Playing Field, including softball diamonds, football fields, and soccer fields. Robert Solomon speaks in LC-241 on "Jealousy."

28 May 1980. Renée Hubert speaks in SUMP on "Baudelaire, Rimbaud, and the Prose Poem."

29 May 1980. The Rolling Stars play the Cal State All Stars in a game of wheelchair basketball in the Gymnasium.

29-31 May & 3-7 Jun. 1980. The campus hosts the American premiere of the 1859 French comedy, *She Loves Me! She Said So!* by Eugène Scribe, newly translated by Helene W. Koon.

31 May 1980. Frank Warren, Chief of Custodial Services (1965-80), retires.

5 Jun. 1980. John C. Overton, Night Supervisor (1978-80), is named Chief of Custodial Services, replacing Frank Warren.

6 Jun. 1980. Dean Wright, Bookstore Manager (1979-80), resigns.

13 Jun. 1980. The campus hosts a program on "Agent Orange" in LC-500, featuring Venita L. Carver, Joseph S. Goldman, Robert H. Sulnick, Frank Terry, and Robert Stafford.

14 Jun. 1980. The 14th Commencement is held on the South Gymnasium Lawn, with 880 students eligible to receive degrees. Linda D. Miller, Libn. (1974-80), resigns.

27 Jun. 1980. Staff retirements: Anthony "Tony" Britto, Supervisor of Campus Stores (1966-80); Anton Gorkowski, Custodian; Fred Cordova, the first campus Plumber and founder of the CSCSB CSEA Chapter (1965-80); Betty J. Gregory, Physical Education Equipment Attendant (1967-80).

Sum. 1980. Retirements: Robert L. West, Dean of the Coll. of Education and Prof. of Education (1966-80); Margaret K. Gibbs, Prof. of Administration (1975-80); Harold A. "Jim" Jambor, Lect. in Sociology (1975-80).

5 Jul. 1980. The campus hosts a 5th Anniversary Banquet for the Executive Women International in UC.

11 JUL. 1980. Carol Dunlap is named Bookstore Manager, replacing Dean Wright. The campus receives a $171,440 grant from the U.S. Dept. of Education to fund the Upward Bound Program.

2 AUG. 1980. The campus records its first instance of unauthorized hacking into its mainframe computer.

1 SEPT. 1980. The Fine Arts Building is renamed the Visual Arts Building (VA), although the external building sign is not replaced until Mar. 1981. The Dept. of Special Services is renamed the Dept. of Educational Support Services, under the direction of Assoc. Dean Tom M. Rivera. The campus begins offering night courses leading to an M.A. degree in Psychology.

4 SEPT. 1980. The Commission for Teacher Preparation and Licensing approves new credentials in School Psychologist Services and Special Education Specialist: Severely Handicapped.

5 SEPT. 1980. Faculty members begin moving into the newly remodeled Visual Arts Building.

12 SEPT. 1980. The campus receives an $84,117 grant to continue its Core Student Affirmative Action Program for another year.

15 SEPT. 1980. The annual convocation is held.

19 SEPT. 1980. The campus receives a 4-year, $500,000 grant from the U.S. Dept. of Education to provide support services for students with academic difficulties, under the coordination of Jean Peacock. The campus reaches maximum capacity in its residence halls (416 students) for the first time. J. Cordell Robinson, Assoc. Dean for Academic Affairs, is named Assoc. VP for Academic Affairs.

1 OCT. 1980. Violinist Irina Tseitlin and pianist Yuri Lotakov perform in RH, the first in a year-long subscription concert series.

2 OCT. 1980. The rock band ICE performs in SUMP.

3 OCT. 1980. Helene W. Koon is named Act. Dean of the School of Humanities, while Dean Irving H. Buchen recuperates from heart surgery. The campus receives a $61,050 grant from the State Dept. of Education to help fund its Bilingual Teachers Corps Program.

8 OCT. 1980. Philip F. Straling, Bishop of the S.B. Diocese of the Catholic Church, speaks in SUMP on "Morality in Contemporary Life." The campus signs an agreement with Control Data Corp. to install the then-largest computer dedicated for instruction and administration at an academic institution.

10 OCT. 1980. Edward C. Teyber, Asst. Prof. of Psychology, is named Dir. of the Community Counseling Center.

13 OCT. 1980. Rep. George E. Brown speaks in SUMP.

13 OCT.-24 NOV. 1980. The Art Gallery mounts a major exhibition of the works of Gaston Lachaise.

15 OCT. 1980. The campus proposes establishing an Army Reserve Officers Training Corps (ROTC) center on campus.

16 OCT. 1980. State Sen. Robert B. Presley speaks in SUMP.

17 OCT. 1980. The campus receives a $13,720 grant from the U.S. Dept. of Health, Education, and Welfare to support Nursing.

23 OCT. 1980. The Inland Brass Quintet performs in RH.

27 OCT. 1980. William David Gean, Assoc. Prof. of Philosophy and Chair of the Philosophy Dept. (1976-80), dies at Fontana at age 44 of a heart attack suffered while jogging.

29 OCT. 1980. Rep. C. Jerry Lewis speaks in SUMP. British philosopher Frances Berenson speaks in LC-241 on "Understanding Persons and Literature."

30 OCT. 1980. Trumpeter Larry Johansen performs in RH. Assemblyman William R. "Bill" Leonard speaks in SUMP.

4 NOV. 1980. Marine biologist Don Walsh speaks in LC-5 on "Law of the Sea and America's Ocean Policy."

5 NOV. 1980. CSUC Chancellor Glenn S. Dumke implements a major restructuring of the general education requirements for students in the Cal State System.

7 NOV. 1980. The campus announces that it will participate in the CSUC's Outstanding Professor of the Year Award program for the first time. The campus installs a computer terminal in Badger Hall.

8 NOV. 1980. The campus hosts 5- and 10-kilometer races sponsored by the *San Bernardino Sun*.

11 NOV. 1980. The campus announces that its conservation program has cut energy usage 11.92% in one year, saving $79,029.

13 NOV. 1980. U.S. Air Force Major General Jack L. Watkins speaks in SUMP on "The Essence of National Defense."

14 NOV. 1980. The classical group Musick's Recreation performs in RH. The campus adds horseshoe pits to its recreational facilities.

15 NOV. 1980. Santa Ana winds destroy 4 trees. The campus hosts its 3rd Annual Women in Management Conference in LC.

18 NOV. 1980. Abstract artist Karl Benjamin speaks in VA-110 on "Insights into an Artist's Development."

20 NOV. 1980. UCR's Collegium Musicum performs in RH. Helene W. Koon, Act. Dean of the School of Humanities, returns to the ranks as Prof. of English.

21 NOV. 1980. Irving H. Buchen resumes his position as Dean of Humanities.

24 NOV. 1980. The arson-generated Panorama Fire destroys 284 homes in the northwestern section of S.B., aided by high Santa Ana winds. The fire burns up to the perimeter of the campus and sweeps by it on its way to Devore, engulfing the Shipping and Receiving Building and one cooling tower on the Heating and Air Conditioning Building, damaging a 2nd cooling tower, and burning 6 electric carts, tools, and office supplies. The campus is evacuated at 1:45 P.M. The cost of replacing the lost structures and materials is estimated at $554,800. Many faculty, staff, and students lose their homes, among them: Dianne Briley, Alice Coble, Carolyn Duffy, Gordon Eckstrom, Sue Ellis, John M. Hatton, Dorothy Johnson, Lee H. Kalbus, John Lawson, Heather Levy, C. Michael O'Gara, Ralph H. Petrucci, Michele Profant, and Sandra J. Warren. A fund established by Pres. Pfau to aid the victims eventually totals $3,000. John M. Hatton wins $60,000 on the NBC TV game show, *Blockbusters*, unaware that his house had burnt while the 5 shows were being taped.

25 NOV. 1980. The campus is closed in order to evaluate damage to its infrastructure from the Panorama Fire.

26 NOV. 1980. Classes resume their normal schedules.

27 NOV. 1980. Gov. Brown tours the fire-damaged campus and northwestern part of S.B., stating that it looks "like a war zone."

1 DEC. 1980. Assemblyman William R. "Bill" Leonard introduces an emergency appropriations measure in the State Legislature to help replace the buildings and supplies destroyed by the Panorama Fire.

9 DEC. 1980. Peter R. Schroeder and Eugene Garver receive National Endowment for the Humanities Fellowships for 1981/82.

23 DEC. 1980. Brij B. Khare meets with Indian Prime Minister Indira Gandhi at New Delhi.

1981

2 JAN. 1981. *The Bulletin* adopts a new masthead.

7 JAN. 1981. The Children's Center opens for business, enrolling 70 offspring of Cal State students each term, and providing both childcare and preschool instruction. Edna L. Steinman is named Woman of the Year by the S.B. Chamber of Commerce.

14 JAN. 1981. Soprano Devy Buchen performs in RH.

18 JAN. 1981. Conductor Frederick Fennell conducts a clinic for 60 high school and college band and orchestra directors.

19 JAN. 1981. Historian Kenneth D. Barkin speaks in LC-500 on "German National Socialism: Its Origins and Reign of Power."

30 JAN. 1981. The campus receives a $7,331 grant from the Chancellor's Off. to expand its Adult College Opportunity Program.

6 FEB. 1981. Kathy Pezdek receives a $122,000 grant from the National Institute for Education to study children's TV viewing habits. The campus installs a speed bump near the Children's Center.

13 FEB. 1981. Robert M. O'Brien is named Outstanding Professor for 1980/81, the first time that CSCSB has participated in the Board of Trustees' Outstanding Professor Awards.

16 FEB. 1981. The First Baptist Loveland Church of Fontana Choir performs in RH, as part of Black History Week. State Sen. Ruben S. Ayala speaks in LC-5 and in LC-244. Cal State Business Administration student Geraldine Elizabeth Pethoud dies in an automobile accident at age 53. Jenifer Pollak speaks on "Retail Marketing."

18 FEB. 1981. The Trio dell'Arte performs in RH. The Black Student Union performs "Variations" in SU.

19 FEB. 1981. Robert Godinez speaks to 90 counselors from local high schools.

20 FEB. 1981. Danny Scarborough performs his one-man show, "Something Called Freedom," in RH.

21-22 FEB. 1981. The worst Santa Ana winds ever to hit the campus destroy 3 windows and a glass door in SU, rip gutters off the SU roof, topple numerous trees, and deposit an inch of dirt in the Heating and Air Conditioning Plant.

23 FEB. 1981. Gerald Prince speaks in LC-241 on "Narrativity; or, What Makes a Good Story."

25 FEB. 1981. F. M. Thomas Air Conditioning receives a contract for $120,300 to rebuild the cooling tower destroyed in the Heating and Air Conditioning plant by the Panorama Fire in Nov., and to repair a 2nd tower. Trombonist Ashley Alexander performs with the Jazz Ensemble and Dixieland Band in RH. Psychologist Drury Sherrod speaks in PS-122 on "Illusions of Self." An arson fire damages Waterman House dormitory.

26 FEB. 1981. Cal State Criminal Justice student Abdul Mutakabbir Zakariyya is shot and killed in San Bernardino at age 30.

3 MAR. 1981. David Morse speaks in SUMP on "Marketing Through Merchandise Marts and the History of the California Mart."

4 MAR. 1981. Poet Robert Hass reads from his work in SUMP.

11 MAR. 1981. G. William Domhoff speaks in SUMP on "Who Rules in America: Have We Learned Anything New Lately?"

13 MAR. 1981. Nikolai E. Khokhlov is interviewed by David Brinkley for the NBC TV program, *David Brinkley's Magazine*, talking about his research on parapsychology. The San Diego State Univ. Balinese Gamelan ensemble performs in RH.

17 MAR. 1981. Actors Walter Matthau and Jack Lemmon and director Billy Wilder visit the campus to film a scene from the motion picture *Buddy Buddy*, with the Student Health Center being transformed into "The Zuckerbrot [Sex] Clinic." Artist Arie Galles speaks in VA-110 on "Reflective Color Construction."

19 MAR. 1981. Brian Mudd speaks in PS-10 on "Biological Basis for Air Pollution Toxicity; or, How Bad Is Smog?"

20 Mar. 1981. The Visual Arts Building sign is unveiled.

24-27 Mar. 1981. The campus hosts the Southern Calif. High School Band and Orchestra Festival in RH.

29 Mar. 1981. Stuart R. Ellins is interviewed on the syndicated TV program, *Agriculture U.S.A.*, airing locally on KNBC, on his research developing taste aversion in coyotes to domestic livestock.

31 Mar. 1981. Melvin E. Artrup, Supervising Custodian, retires.

3 Apr. 1981. Kenneth Aldrich speaks in RH on "Court Entertainment in the 17th and 18th Centuries." The campus establishes an Army Reserve Officers Training Corps (ROTC) Center, after a vote approving the program by the Faculty Senate.

6 Apr. 1981. South Indian singer Gowri Kuppuswamy performs in RH, accompanied by Ramnad Raghavan on a mridangam (a barrel drum). Dr. John Charles Wilcox, ex-physician in the Student Health Center (1972-75), dies of a heart attack at age 71.

10 Apr. 1981. The campus receives a $1,000 grant from the Chancellor's Off. to produce a newsletter for teachers of writing. Michael Burgess's book, *Science Fiction and Fantasy Literature*, is named an Outstanding Academic Book of 1980-81 by *Choice Magazine*.

15 Apr. 1981. Calif. Secretary of State March Fong Eu speaks in RH. Robert J. Rubel speaks in PS-10 on "School Violence."

17 Apr. 1981. Elizabeth Thiessen, Asst. Manager of the Commons, is named Dir. of Operations, replacing Bill Fennell. A 2nd arson fire damages Waterman House dorm.

21 Apr. 1981. The French horn/tuba duo, Solid Brass (Froydis Ree Wekre and Roger Bobo), performs in RH with pianist Zita Carno.

22 Apr. 1981. Phyllis Bennis of the U.S. Committee in Solidarity with the People of El Salvador speaks about the civil war there.

24 Apr. 1981. Robert G. Stein is named to a 5-year term as a Danforth Associate for the Danforth Foundation. A ribbon-cutting ceremony marks the dedication of the Children's Center. Dr. Ross L. Ballard, Dir. of the Student Health Center, is named Dir. of Student Health Services.

25 APR. 1981. The campus hosts its 5th annual Reading Conference, "Changing Dimensions in Reading," with Brenda U. Beal giving the keynote speech, and Harry Singer giving a memorial address honoring the late Prof. Florence A. Mote. Cal State student Cindy-Lea Whale is named Miss Fontana 1981.

26 APR. 1981. The campus hosts its 2nd Annual Open House in conjunction with the Southern Calif. Health Fair Expo '81, attracting more than 2,000 visitors to campus.

28 APR. 1981. An arson fire damages Waterman House dormitory, the 3rd such blaze in a period of 3 months, injuring 5 students who are forced to jump from their 2nd-story windows; the residence hall is closed for repairs for the rest of the academic year.

29 APR. 1981. The S.B. Valley College MEChA performs the Latino musical, *Noches de Aztlán*, in the Commons.

30 APR. 1981. Oscar C. Jackson, College Personnel Officer (1969-81), resigns.

1 MAY 1981. Sandra Lyn "Sandi" Jensen is named College Personnel Officer, replacing Oscar C. Jackson.

6 MAY 1981. The Victor Valley Community Choir, High Desert Symphony, and Cal State Concert Choir perform Joseph Haydn's *The Creation* in RH.

8 MAY 1981. The campus hosts a seminar on Agent Orange in LC-500, with panelists Albert Branscomb and Robert H. Sulnick.

14 MAY 1981. *60 Minutes* TV pundit Andy Rooney speaks before an overflow crowd in RH on "The Truth as a Last Resort."

15 MAY 1981. The Heating and Air Conditioning Plant is restored with the repair of the cooling tower damaged by the Panorama Fire.

20 MAY 1981. The Music Dept. and The Riverside Opera Assoc. perform 2 one-act Gilbert and Sullivan operettas, *Cox and Box* and *The Zoo*, in RH.

23 MAY 1981. El Teatro de la Esperanza performs the Chicano play, *The Octopus*, in RH. Pres. Pfau returns from a 3-week trip to Taiwan, China, and Japan, where he sought to inaugurate discussions on faculty-student exchanges between CSCSB and other campuses.

26 MAY 1981. Sculptor John Gillen speaks in VA-110 on "Site-Oriented

Sculpture."

28 MAY 1981. The East L.A. artist group, Asco, performs "Living Chicano Art: Discussion and Performance" in VA-109.

29 MAY 1981. The Beer Garden patio on the southwest end of the SU opens for business.

30 MAY 1981. The UCLA Wind Ensemble performs in RH. Cal State alumnus and pilot Melvin Dwight Cooper dies in the crash of a Loma Linda Univ. Medical Center helicopter in San Timoteo Canyon near Beaumont at age 34. The campus hosts its 11th Annual High School Theatre Workshop in the Theatre for local students.

31 MAY 1981. The Collegiate Chorus debuts in RH.

6 JUN. 1981. The film *Andromedan!*, the first campus-generated film production, premieres in RH, produced by O. P. Hadlock, scored by Philip West, plus special effects and acting by 18 faculty, staff, and students, among them William L. Slout and Amanda Sue Rudisill.

11 JUN. 1981. Bob Field Construction Co. receives a $92,146 contract to rebuild the Shipping and Receiving Warehouse, which was destroyed in the Panorama Fire in Nov. 1980.

13 JUN. 1981. The 15th Commencement is held on the South Gymnasium Lawn, with 950 students eligible to receive degrees; CSUC Trustee Wallace Albertson forms part of the platform party, together with Rabbi Hillel Cohn.

16 JUN. 1981. Stephen A. Bowles, Dean of Continuing Education, returns to the ranks as Prof. of Psychology.

17 JUN. 1981. Sherrie R. Bartell is named Act. Dean of Continuing Education, replacing Stephen A. Bowles.

22 JUN. 1981. The Administration Building closes for the summer while a new roof is installed, under a $325,051 contract awarded to San-Val Air Conditioning.

24 JUN. 1981. Tom M. Rivera, Assoc. Dean of Educational Support Services and a member of the Colton Joint Unified School Dist. Board of Education, is rushed to the hospital with Guillain-Barre Syndrome, and goes on emergency medical leave.

7 JUL. 1981. CSUC Chancellor Glenn S. Dumke announces his retirement, effective in 1982.

24 JUL. 1981. Marsha Liss receives a $12,017 grant from the National Institute of Mental Health for her project, "The Justification of Aggression by Prosocial Models."

10 AUG. 1981. The Computer Center installs a CYBER 170 Series 700 $1,200,000 computer, expanding the college's computing power by 108 times.

21 AUG. 1981. The campus dedicates a grove of flowering plum trees donated by Tachikawa, Japan, near the Creative Arts Building.

1 SEPT. 1981. Walter S. Hawkins is named Act. Assoc. Dean of Educational Support Services, replacing Tom M. Rivera. Employee parking fees increase from $4 per month to $5. The campus completes a conversion of its outside lighting from mercury vapor to high pressure sodium lamps. The Children's Center is placed administratively under the Assoc. Dean of Students. The campus begins offering certificates in Social Work and Educational Technology.

8-11 SEPT. 1981. The Administration Building is reoccupied following a summer reroofing project.

14 SEPT. 1981. The annual convocation is held. Waterman Hall reopens for occupancy after being repaired during the summer.

18 SEPT. 1981. Cecelia O. Torres, Library Asst. (1974-81), resigns to take a position in Media Services. Bill Fennell returns as Commons Manager, replacing Elizabeth Thiessen.

25 SEPT. 1981. The campus receives $130,870 as the 2nd part of a 4-year grant to support the SAIL Program.

28 SEPT. 1981. The Sequoia String Quartet performs in RH.

2 OCT. 1981. The campus installs solar panels to heat the Serrano Village swimming pool. The Off. of Extended Education begins an American Culture and Language Program designed to bring foreign students to campus.

4 OCT. 1981. William Hugh Wilson, local attorney and a member of the Foundation Board for 11 years, dies at age 66; he helped secure a 1971 $185,415 bequest from Alfred F. and Chella D. Moore.

8 OCT. 1981. Lee I. Porter is named Dean of Continuing Education, replacing Sherrie R. Bartell.

10 OCT. 1981. Harpsichordist Joyce Lindorff performs in SU. 7

13 OCT. 1981. Tubist L. Keating Johnson performs in RH.

15 OCT. 1981. CSUC Chancellor Glenn S. Dumke, responding to the state budget crisis, issues an executive order freezing all personnel transactions and purchasing through Nov. 18.

16 OCT. 1981. The campus and the Calif. School Counselors Assoc. host the CSUC Southern Calif. High School Counselor Conference, with 350 attendees.

23 OCT. 1981. The campus receives a $4,305 grant from the Chancellor's Fund to study innovation and improvement in education. The Art Dept. receives a $2,420 grant from the Calif. Arts Council to support several exhibitions. The campus establishes a New Student Services Off.

25 OCT. 1981. Actor and director John Houseman speaks on LCP on "From The Mercury Theatre to *The Paper Chase*."

28 OCT. 1981. Soprano Maurita Phillips-Thornburgh performs in RH.

30 OCT. 1981. Mary A. Burgess, Purchasing Agent (1975-81), resigns. Scott James, Duplicating (1969-81), retires.

31 OCT. 1981. Santa Ana winds damage newly installed solar panels on the roof of the Housing Off.

2 NOV. 1981. Blind pianist Janne Irvine Newman performs in RH.

4 NOV. 1981. Artist Judith Simonian speaks on her work in VA-110.

5 NOV. 1981. Michael A. Gómez, Dir. of the Dept. of Public Safety (1975-81), resigns. The Riverside Concert Band performs in RH. In response to the budget crisis, Chancellor Dumke imposes a $46 surcharge on all CSUC students, effective with Winter term, and also orders $5 million in systemwide cuts (with CSCSB's share being $93,000), plus a hiring, promotion, and purchasing freeze. Student fees increase to $98.25 per quarter.

6 NOV. 1981. Arthur M. Butler, Police Sergeant (1971-81) and Asst. Dir. (1975-81), is named Act. Dir. of the Dept. of Public Safety, replacing Michael A. Gómez.

7 NOV. 1981. Pianist Rena Zagha debuts in RH. Film and TV actor D'Urville Martin speaks in the Commons to the Upward Bound Recognition Dinner.

11 NOV. 1981. Guitarist William Stanford performs in RH.

13 NOV. 1981. Michael D. Rasmussen, Chief Engineer of Heating and Air Conditioning Services (1967-81), retires.

14 NOV. 1981. LeRoy A. Wilke is named Act. Chief Engineer of Heating and Air Conditioning Services, replacing Michael D. Rasmussen.

16 NOV. 1981. Rep. George E. Brown speaks in SUMP on "World Peace, the Arms Race, and Hunger," as part of "Peace Week."

18 NOV. 1981. Wayne King speaks in SUMP on "World Hunger." The CSUC Board of Trustees doubles student fees, effective with Fall 1982, from $261 to $477 per year.

19 NOV. 1981. Barbara A. Gutek speaks in PS-122 on "Sexual Harassment on the Job."

22 NOV. 1981. The Victor Valley College Singers and Community College Chorus joins Cal State's Concert Choir and Chamber Singers in performing holiday music in RH.

4 DEC. 1981. The School of Education and the S.B. City Unified School Dist. begin a cooperative schools venture. As part of the program, CSCSB student teachers and professors begin teaching at 2 elementary schools, Arrowhead and Parkside, while teachers from these schools lead sessions in School of Education classes. In addition, 5th and 6th graders begin visiting microcomputer labs on campus to learn basic computer skills.

11 DEC. 1981. LeRoy A. Wilke, Act. Chief Engineer of Heating and Air Conditioning Services, is named permanent Chief Engineer. Pam J. Stewart becomes the first woman Police Sergeant at CSCSB.

12-13 DEC. 1981. Psychiatrist William H. Holloway presents a workshop, "Transactional Analysis: What It Is and What It Isn't."

25 DEC. 1981. F(rederick) Eugene Mueller, Lect. in Education (1973-81) and retired Superintendent of Schools for the S.B. School Dist. (1950-70), dies in San Bernardino at age 77.

30 DEC. 1981. The Housing Off. opens for business in a new structure at the end of the Residence Hall quad area.

1982

UNK. 1982. Interstate 15E, the nearest freeway to the campus, is renamed Interstate 215.

1 JAN. 1982. The California State University and Colleges system is renamed the California State University system, beginning a series of name changes that result in new designations for the individual campuses over the next few years.

6-9 JAN. 1982. *Next Time for Real*, an original play by ex-dramatist-in-residence Harry Cauley, premieres at Cal State.

11 JAN. 1982. Pres. John M. Pfau announces that he will retire at the end of the academic year; in response, CSU Chancellor Dumke states that "President Pfau's impending retirement will be viewed with regret throughout the California State University system. Not only is Dr. Pfau the president with the greatest longevity on our 19 campuses, but his wise counsel over the years has helped to shape decisions in my office for the betterment of all higher education. As founding president of CSC San Bernardino, Dr. Pfau exercised an opportunity that comes only to a few in higher education, and has followed it through to an important legacy. Starting with no staff, no faculty, no students, and not even land for a campus, he has overseen the birth and development of an institution with inestimable worth in the Southern California Inland Empire."

13 JAN. 1982. Pianist Father Nicolas Reveles performs in RH.

14 JAN. 1982. The Music from Oberlin Trio performs in RH.

15 JAN. 1982. Cal State Associates add $753 to their scholarship fund.

18 JAN. 1982. Lydia Savala speaks in LC-500 on "How to Handle an IRS Audit." Henry C. Metternich speaks in LC-241 on "German Genesis: Problem of Creating a Nation."

18-19 JAN. 1982. The CSU Committee on the Future visits the campus, meeting with members of the campus community concerning the future of the Cal State system.

19 JAN. 1982. David Wise speaks in SUMP on "An Overview of the Information Processing Field."

20 JAN. 1982. Electronic violinist Akar performs in RH.

21 Jan. 1982. Chuck Painter speaks in LC on "A Day in the Life of a Stockbroker."

22 Jan. 1982. Frederick A. Newton is named Outstanding Professor for 1981/82.

24 Jan. 1982. The Inland Brass Quintet performs in RH.

25 Jan. 1982. Alumna belly dancer Carolee "Sah-ra" Kent performs in SUMP. Students form a new Islamic Club.

26 Jan. 1982. Campus police arrest 3 non-students on campus for grand theft auto.

29 Jan. 1982. The State adopts a pilot program developed by Cal State graduate student Richard Piercy to help make state parks more accessible to people with disabilities.

8 Feb. 1982. Alumnus David Hoover speaks in BI-129 about his mathematical work.

10 Feb. 1982. The Five Centuries Ensemble performs in RH. Paul O. Straubinger speaks in LC-241 on "Images of Austria."

12 Feb. 1982. The German band The Barons performs in SU.

13 Feb. 1982. The campus hosts the Sonic Art Show in the Art Gallery, featuring visual works with sound.

17 Feb. 1982. John Snortum speaks in CA-186 on "Drunk Driving in Scandinavia and the United States."

18 Feb. 1982. Roderick Sykes of St. Elmo Village speaks in SUMP. Cal State Business Administration student Dean Wilton Pelt dies at age 27. Michael Tacchia performs in RH.

19 Feb. 1982. The Affirmative Action Program receives an $11,488 grant from the Chancellor's Off. The campus hosts the 2nd Annual Band Directors Clinic in RH, with H. Robert Reynolds acting as Clinician.

20 Feb. 1982. Michael Teer, Pres. of the Inland Area Urban League, speaks as part of Black History Week in LC on "We've Come So Far…Yet Have So Far to Go."

21 Feb. 1982. Cal State Accounting student Arturs Studans dies at age 40.

1 MAR. 1982. Arthur M. Butler, Act. Dir. of Public Safety, is named permanent Dir.

2 & 4 MAR. 1982. The National Shakespeare Co. performs William Shakespeare's plays, *The Tempest* (2 Mar.) and *The Taming of the Shrew* (4 Mar.) in RH.

5 MAR. 1982. Mary Ongaro, Dir. of the Children's Center, resigns.

6 MAR. 1982. The campus hosts its 6th Annual Reading Conference, "Reading and Writing: The Literature Connection," with Jacque Wuertenberg giving the keynote address.

7 MAR. 1982. The Chamber Orchestra debuts in RH.

9 MAR. 1982. Jules-Pierre Mondolini, Asst. Cultural Attaché at the French Consulate in L.A., speaks in LC-500 on "Careers for Students of French."

12 MAR. 1982. John H. Rodríguez, Asst. Undersecretary for the U.S. Dept. of Education, speaks in LC-500 on "Current Happenings in Education from the Washington Point of View."

17 MAR. 1982. Artist Don Sorenson speaks on his work in VA-110.

19 MAR. 1982. Max A. "Marty" Bloomberg, Asst. Library Dir., is named Assoc. Library Dir.

20 MAR. 1982. The campus hosts an all-day "Conference on the Use of Computer, Media, and Library Resources in the Classroom."

2 APR. 1982. Pamela I. Dortch is named Dir. of the Children's Center, replacing Mary Ongaro. John M. Hatton wins $60,000 for a 2nd time on the NBC game show, *Blockbusters*.

8 APR. 1982. Pianist Betty Oberacker performs in RH.

12 APR. 1982. Hans-Bernhard Moeller speaks in LC-500 on "Central European Exiles and the American Cinema."

14 APR. 1982. Koto player Yoko Ito Gates performs in RH. Dave Lumian speaks in SUMP on "Nuclear Arms."

15 APR. 1982. Harpsichordist Carl Dominik performs in RH.

16 APR. 1982. The ensemble Nightspore performs in RH.

19 APR. 1982. Alumna Yolanda T. Moses is named Act. Dean of the School of Arts at Calif. State Polytechnic University, Pomona.

22 APR. 1982. Primate communication expert Roger S. Fouts speaks in PS-10 on "Chimpanzees, Communication, and Controversy." Pianist Janne Irving performs in RH, and again in UC on Apr. 24.

23 APR. 1982. The campus hosts 150 students from 8 high schools in an all-day Model Congress. The campus hosts the Reduce, Reuse, and Recycle Conference in PS-122.

29 APR. 1982. San Diego State Univ. Faculty Trio performs in RH.

30 APR. 1982. The campus holds a retirement dinner in the Commons for VP Joseph K. Thomas, with ex-Exec. Dean Kenneth Phillips acting as Master of Ceremonies.

1 MAY 1982. The campus hosts a conference, "Special Education in Crisis," in LC-500, with Assemblywoman Marian Bergeson giving the keynote address, "The Future of Special Education."

3 MAY 1982. The Veterans Affairs Off. sponsors a conference, "Cambodia Today, Vietnam Yesterday," in SUMP, with featured speakers Richard Diez and Thomas Wulbrecht.

4 MAY 1982. Harold W. Rood speaks in SUMP on "The Strategic Position of the United States."

5 MAY 1982. The campus celebrates Cinco de Mayo with dancers from La Escuela de la Raza performing on LCP.

6 MAY 1982. Flautist Jayne Close performs in RH.

11 MAY 1982. The 2nd election for union representation of the CSU faculty results in 6,473 votes for the United Professors of Calif. (UPC), 6,454 votes for the Congress of Faculty Assocs. (CFA), with some 500 votes being challenged by the parties involved. The first election in Feb. had resulted in both organizations tying at 42%, plus 16% wanting no representation. After a review of the challenged ballots, CFA is declared the official faculty bargaining representative.

17 MAY 1982. S.B. City begins improving State College Pkwy. from Kendall Dr. to the I-15E freeway, having awarded a $187,264 contract to Angel's Construction Co. to add gutters, curbs, an irrigation system, pine trees, and grass to the median strip, plus the addition of sprinklers, pine trees, and grass to the median strip and one side of the Pkwy. from Kendall

Dr. to Northpark Blvd, with work being completed on June 17.

19 MAY 1982. Sarnoff A. Mednick speaks in SUMP on "Biological Factors in Antisocial Behavior."

26 MAY 1982. The Coll. Library is renamed the John M. Pfau Library by the CSU Board of Trustees to honor the retiring President, the first building on campus to be named for an individual.

2 JUN. 1982. Writer Vicki Hearne reads from her work in LC-241.

4 JUN. 1982. The campus holds a retirement dinner in the Commons for Pres. John M. Pfau; included among the 410 guests are retiring CSU Chancellor Dumke, CSU Trustee Blanche C. Bersch, and 6 of the CSU presidents, with ex-*San Bernardino Sun-Telegram* Publisher James K. Guthrie serving as Master of Ceremonies. A portrait of Pres. Pfau by Maxine Olson is unveiled, to be displayed in the PL.

7 JUN. 1982. Jo Eleanor Elliott, Dir., Div. of Nursing, U.S. Public Health Service, speaks in SUMP on "The Nursing Climate for the Recent Graduate," and in RH on "Trends and Issues in Nursing."

9 JUN. 1982. Jean S. Felton speaks in PS-10 on "Health and the Work Environment in the Arts." The Cajon High School Wind Ensemble performs with the Collegiate Chorus in RH.

17 JUN. 1982. The campus holds a reception for retiring Pres. Pfau on the first floor of the Pfau Library, where the President's official portrait, painted by Maxine Olson, is put on permanent display.

18 JUN. 1982. Joseph K. Thomas, Prof. of Education and Exec. Dean and VP for Administration (1965-82), retires.

19 JUN. 1982. The 16th Commencement is held on the South Gymnasium Lawn. James H. Urata, Dir. of Plant Operations, is named Act. Exec. Dean, replacing Joseph K. Thomas.

25 JUN. 1982. Rasmussen Construction receives a $14,062 contract to remodel the Financial Aid Off. in the Student Services Building. Edward J. Erler receives a $6,128 grant from the Institute for Educational Affairs to work on a project, "Supreme Court and equal Protection: A Case Study in the Failure of Judicial Statesmanship."

30 JUN. 1982. Alice K. Wilson, Assoc. Libn. and Curriculum Libn. (1969-82), retires.

Sum. 1982. Robert A. Smith, Prof. of History (1965-82), retires, becoming one of the first campus participants in the Faculty Early Retirement Program (FERP).

2 Jul. 1982. Steven R. Wagner receives a $50,000 grant from the Calif. Dept. of Education to train psychologists and educators in 2nd language and psychological assessment at Cuernavaca, México.

6 Jul. 1982. The campus adopts a policy of allowing Emeritus faculty to park free at the University.

14 Jul. 1982. The presidential search to replace Pres. John M. Pfau collapses when 2 of the 3 finalists—Joseph D. Olander and David G. Brown—withdraw, leaving only Judith A. Sturnick; the choice of a replacement is postponed until Sept. CSU Chancellor Glenn S. Dumke names Gerald M. Scherba, VP for Academic Affairs, as VP in Charge of CSC, San Bernardino, effective with Pfau's retirement. The campus receives a $29,800 grant from Kurzweil Computer Products to install a reading machine that converts printed material into high quality English speech for the visually impaired.

23 Jul. 1982. The campus holds an informal fête in the Administration Building Lobby honoring John M. Pfau on his last day at work.

26 Jul. 1982. Walter Neal Danz, Plant Operations, dies at age 45.

30 Jul. 1982. John M. Pfau, Prof. of History and President of the University (1962-82), retires, being the longest-serving president in the Cal State System at the time of his retirement. The Presidential Selection Advisory Committee is recalled by the CSU Board of Trustees, in order to generate a new pool of candidates for the position of President of CSCSB, the first search having failed.

THE INTERIM ADMINISTRATION OF
GERALD M. SCHERBA
31 JULY 1982 - 31 OCTOBER, 1982

ABOUT GERALD M. SCHERBA

GERALD MARRON "GERRY" SCHERBA was born Feb. 9, 1927 at Chicago, Illinois. He married Coral Matthews on Dec. 14, 1951 in Chicago, and had 3 children: Coral Elise, Rachel, and Julia Ann. He obtained his B.S. in Biology at the Univ. of Chicago in 1950, his M.S. there in 1952, and his Ph.D. there in 1955, specializing in animal biology and behavior. He joined the American Academy of Arts and Sciences in 1957, and served with NSF from 1962-64. He died on Feb. 5, 2001 of congestive heart failure.

VP Scherba was an Assoc. Prof. of Biology at Chico State College from 1955-62. In 1962 he accepted a position at Cal State San Bernardino as Prof. of Biology and Chair of the Natural Sciences Div. He was instrumental in helping to plan the Biological and Physical Science Buildings on campus, and in establishing the initial curriculum for the Natural Sciences departments. In 1966 he was named Dean of Academic Affairs; in 1968 he was promoted to VP of Academic Affairs, remaining in that position through the Summer of 1984. He then took a year's leave of absence, but was appointed the 3rd Dir. of the CSU Desert Studies Center east of Baker, Calif. in 1985, serving in that role until his retirement in 1991.

His impact on the early development of CSU, San Bernardino, was 2nd only to that of Pres. John M. Pfau, with whom he worked very closely. After Pres. Pfau's retirement in 1982, Gerry Scherba served as Act. Chief Executive of the campus (with the title of VP in Charge) for 3 months, until a new President could be hired. It was typical of the man's inherent modesty that he sought no particular credit for this service: he did what was expected of him, and he made the transition to the new administration easy and problem-free.

1982 (continued)

31 JUL. 1982. Gerald M. "Gerry" Scherba, VP for Academic Affairs, takes office as VP in Charge of CSC, San Bernardino, replacing Pres. Pfau.

13 AUG. 1982. The Off. of Continuing Education receives a $3,000 grant from the Academy of Continuing Education to enhance teachers' skills in the classroom. Hour Glass and Mirror Inc. receives a $3,800 contract to install reinforcement beams for the windows in the Commons Building.

25 AUG. 1982. Donald Gordon Mauldin, ex-S.B. Mayor (1961-65), dies in Orange Co. at age 55; he served as chief executive when the site for the new State College was being chosen, and had lobbied unceasingly to bring the campus to San Bernardino.

27 AUG. 1982. The campus approves a new program in Adapted Physical Education for teachers. Cal State senior Shari Mills is named Collective Bargaining Dir. for the Calif. State Student Assoc.

28 AUG. 1982. The campus hosts the Pacific Championship Tournament of the Southern Calif. Polynesian (Tongan) Rugby Council, with over 1,000 attendees.

31 AUG. 1982. Glenn S. Dumke, Chancellor of the CSU System (1962-82), retires to become Pres. of the Institute for Contemporary Studies.

1 SEPT. 1982. W. Ann Reynolds is named Chancellor of the CSU System, replacing Glenn S. Dumke. Michael Burgess publishes his 25th book, *The Paperback Price Guide No. 2* (with Kevin Hancer).

2 SEPT. 1982. Jim Delamar of the U.S. Secret Service conducts a seminar in LC on recognizing counterfeit money.

3 SEPT. 1982. The campus changes the 2-letter designation for the John M. Pfau Library from "LC" to "PL," reflecting its new name, and completes the remodeling of the Financial Aid Off. Cal State Political Science senior Angela Lavin is named to the CSU System-Wide Advisory Committee on the Student Services Fee.

10 SEPT. 1982. Richard T. Ackley receives a $300 grant from the National

Strategic Information Center.

14 SEPT. 1982. Anthony H. Evans, Provost and VP for Academic Affairs and ex-Act. Pres. of Eastern Michigan Univ., is named the 2nd President of CSC, San Bernardino. However, he is unable to assume his duties until Nov.

15 SEPT. 1982. The Commons reopens for business with a remodeled west wing. Parking in the Science Lot is restricted to faculty and staff only, even during off hours. Retired Pres. John M. Pfau is named President Emeritus by the CSU Board of Trustees.

17 SEPT. 1982. Pres.-elect Evans attends a faculty reception in the Commons. Colleen F. Artrup, Custodian (1973-82), retires.

1 OCT. 1982. The Chancellor's Off. approves a new B.S. degree in Physical Education, to be offered in Winter 1983. Cal State Economics senior Susan Paull is named to the CSU Committee on Academic Planning and Program Review.

3 OCT. 1982. Verna Reynolds hosts a reception on the first floor of the Pfau Library in conjunction with an exhibition of the personal papers and memorabilia of her late husband, Harry Reynolds, known as "Mr. Democrat" in S.B. Co. politics.

8 OCT. 1982. Pres.-elect Evans appears on campus to chair an Administrative Council Meeting.

10 OCT. 1982. Harpsichordist Phyllis Benson and organist Raymond Boese perform in RH.

13 OCT. 1982. The campus hosts a seminar on crime prevention, "Lady Beware," in SUMP, with Shirley Eastman and Laura Lewein speaking.

14 OCT. 1982. Leonard B. Farwell, Business Manager, becomes the first campus employee honored for 20 years of service. Actor Ken Richters conducts a workshop in SUMP.

15 OCT. 1982. Actor Ken Richters performs his one-man show, "Mark Twain on Tour," in RH.

17 OCT. 1982. Alfred Severin Egge, Prof. of Biology (1966-82), dies of brain cancer at Houston, Texas, at age 49.

22 OCT. 1982. The campus receives a $330,500 grant from the National Institute of Education to support college writing programs.

25 Oct. 1982. Writer Tom Hauser speaks in SU on his book, *Missing*.

27 Oct. 1982. The chamber ensemble Musical Offering performs in RH, with guest soprano Maurita Thornburgh.

28 Oct. 1982. Rep. George E. Brown speaks in SU on "The Environment and Reaganomics."

29 Oct. 1982. The Chancellor's Off. approves an M.A. degree in Criminal Justice, to be offered with 1983/84, and a B.A. degree in Computer Science, to be offered Winter 1983. The Firebird Theatre Co. performs The Grimm Brothers' *The Fisherman and His Wife* in the Kabuki style in RH.

31 Oct. 1982. Gerald M. Scherba, VP in Charge of CSCSB, returns to his position as VP of Academic Affairs.

THE ADMINISTRATION OF

ANTHONY H. EVANS

1 NOVEMBER 1982 - 15 AUGUST 1997

ABOUT ANTHONY H. EVANS

ANTHONY HOWARD EVANS was born Sept. 24, 1936 in Clay Co., Arkansas, the son of William Raymond Evans and Thelma Fay Crews. He married Lois Fay Kirkham on 29 Aug. 1959. He earned B.A. at East Texas Baptist College in 1959, his M.A. at the Univ. of Hawaii in 1961, and his Ph.D. in History at the Univ. of Calif., Berkeley in 1966.

He served as a program officer for the Peace Corps at Seoul, South Korea, from 1970-72; as chief program planning officer for the Peace Corps at Washington, DC, from 1972-73, and as Dir. of the Planning Off. there from 1973-75; he also served as Act. Dir. of the Peace Corps. In 1975 he was named Asst. to the Pres. of Eastern Michigan Univ., becoming Exec. VP there in 1976, and Provost and VP for Academic Affairs in 1979; he served as Act. Pres. of Eastern Michigan Univ. from 1978-79.

Pres. Evans outlined his philosophy of education at a special convocation held on 12 Jan. 1983, stating: "May I share with you my one dream for the College? That dream is to help the College reach its natural potential as a regional university noted for its service throughout the Inland Empire. To achieve this distinction is bigger than one person, and can be accomplished only by the effective mobilization of the entire campus community. This goal did not originate with me, but was the mandate for the College's creation years ago. That unchanging mission is still our purpose for existence: to build a College that is unmistakably regional in its outreach. In my judgment, that is our primary mission."

1982 (continued)

1 Nov. 1982. Anthony H. Evans takes office as the 2nd President of CSC, San Bernardino, replacing Gerald M. Scherba, VP in Charge.

3 Nov. 1982. Don Walsh, Dir. of the Institute for Marine and Coast Studies, speaks in PL-297 on "Implications for the U.S. in Not Signing the Law of the Sea Treaty."

7 Nov. 1982. The Inland Brass Quintet performs in RH.

10 Nov. 1982. Seismologist Ralph Turner speaks in RH on "The Human Response to the Earthquake Threat."

11 Nov. 1982. The campus hosts the conference, "Voluntarism and the American Way of Life," in SUMP, with speakers Walter Berns, Mark Blitz, Richard Stevens, Gary McDowell, and James Williams. The Riverside Concert Band performs in RH.

12 Nov. 1982. Photographer Gillian Brown speaks about her work in VA-110.

13 Nov. 1982. Cal State senior Art Major Angelikia DeJong dies in a hit-and-run automobile accident at age 48.

13-14 Nov. 1982. The campus hosts a meeting of the Calif. State Student Assoc.

15 Nov. 1982. Indian singer Salem S. Jayalakshmi performs in RH.

17 Nov. 1982. Photographer Michael Hughes speaks about his work in VA-110.

19 Nov. 1982. Betty Fogg, Senior Secretary in Academic Administration (1969-82), retires.

21 Nov. 1982. The Cal State Concert Choir and the College Singers from Victor Valley College perform selections from Handel's *Messiah* in RH.

23 Nov. 1982. Edwin M. Epstein speaks in PL-500.

1 DEC. 1982. Ann Bermingham speaks in VA-110 on "Terra Cognita: The Victorian Suburban Landscape."

2 DEC. 1982. The campus hosts a reception in LC to honor Pres. Anthony H. Evans and Mrs. Lois Evans.

3 DEC. 1982. The Teatro de los Puppets mime and puppet group performs *¡Viva Olympia!* in RH.

11-12 DEC. 1982. The campus co-hosts (with the Colton Youth Soccer Club) the Dist. Five Commissioners Cup in Soccer, with some 35 teams and 600 players appearing.

17 DEC. 1982. Meredith Morrow, Administrative Aide in the School of Humanities (1971-82), retires. To save energy, Pres. Evans directs that temperatures within campus buildings will be maintained between 65° - 78°.

27 DEC. 1982. The campus establishes a $5,000 scholarship in honor of S.B. attorney William H. Wilson, who died on 4 Oct. 1981.

29 DEC. 1982. Cal State student John Anthony Rivera dies at age 23 in a fall from a 700-foot cliff while cross-country skiing near the Aerial Tramway in Palm Springs.

31 DEC. 1982. Elton N. Thompson, Prof. of Education (1968-82), retires.

1983

1 JAN. 1983. Field Cablevision in Redlands and Liberty Cable in San Bernardino begin broadcasting campus-related news on their cable channels. Calif. Senate Bill 1458 takes effect, adding a faculty representative to the CSU Board of Trustees, from names suggested by the Statewide Academic Senate. Gilbert Sánchez is named Coordinator of the Student Affirmative Action Program.

2 JAN. 1983. Joan Dornemann conducts an opera master class in RH, as part of the Italian Opera Theatre Festival.

3 JAN. 1983. George Deukmejian takes office as Governor of California, replacing Edmund G. "Jerry" Brown Jr.

5 JAN. 1983. Chancellor Reynolds freezes hiring in the CSU System.

8 JAN. 1983. World Music from San Diego State performs in RH.

9 JAN. 1983. Mezzo-soprano Elizabeth Mannion and pianist John Perry perform in RH. Kenton L. Monroe, Dean of Students (1966-83), returns to the ranks as Prof. of Psychology.

10 JAN. 1983. John M. Hatton is named Act. Dean of Students, replacing Kenton L. Monroe. Opera star Elizabeth Mannion conducts a master class in RH.

12 JAN. 1983. At the annual convocation in RH, Pres. Evans outlines his plans for campus development: "…To help the College reach its natural potential as a regional university. This goal did not originate with me, but was the mandate for the College's creation years ago. That unchanging mission is still our purpose for existence: to build a college that is unmistakably regional in its outreach. That is our primary mission…. We exist only to meet educational needs." He notes 4 areas where the campus needs to improve: community relations, admissions outreach, curriculum development, and campus vitality. "We must create partnerships with communities throughout our service areas," he says, including increasing the number of off-campus programs in other regions. "At this moment, the Coachella Valley and the Barstow areas are regions not being well served by this College or any other 4-year institution." In admissions, the campus needs to bring more prospective students to campus, identify target populations, and develop specific programs and strategies to reach these groups. In its curriculum, the College needs to diversify its program to include more practical, career-oriented majors, and to work toward making campus life more vital. "We need more spirit, more verve, more character," he notes. "We have a far too limited curriculum for the 1980s. …Many students in our region are going to other colleges because of those institutions' perceived program strengths in areas such as engineering, technology and the applied sciences…. The public perception, especially among many high school counselors, is that our programs are limited and less career-oriented than at several competitor institutions. This is a problem requiring immediate attention…. I look forward to learning why we have not already launched practical programs such as journalism, communications, speech, industrial arts, and still other applied sciences." In summation, he asks the 600 campus employees to recruit one new student each during the following year, help retain at least one student who needs assistance, and participate in one additional community activity. "Until the College has distinguished itself in community service, we cannot expect the region to reciprocate in its support for the College. I believe that we must initiate this process, because we cannot expect the community to come to us. Numerous community leaders have urged me…to shorten the distance between the campus and the community." His remarks, combined with an almost simultaneous change in 1983 in the state rules governing off-campus programs (which prior to this time had to be completely self-sufficient, but now could be state-supported), mark the start of long-term campus efforts to build a satellite campus in the Coachella Valley.

16-23 JAN. 1983. 38 vocalists from around the country perform 3 operas by Handel—*Rodelinda, Giulio Cesare,* and *Acis and Galatea*—with guest conductors Michael Recchiuti and Fiora Contino, and introductions by opera historian Martha Novak Clinkscale.

17 JAN. 1983. Pres. Evans creates a 12-person Special Task Force to investigate the possibility of intercollegiate athletics at the College. Tom M. Rivera returns to his post as Assoc. Dean of Educational Support Services, replacing Walter S. Hawkins.

21 JAN. 1983. Frances F. Berdan is named Outstanding Professor for 1982/83. The Californians Quartet performs in RH.

22 JAN. 1983. Cal State Political Science senior Guadalupe Martín Meléndez dies at age 33.

26 JAN. 1983. Poet Adrienne Rich reads from her work in RH.

28 JAN. 1983. The Dept. of Public Safety is moved administratively under Act. Exec. Dean James H. Urata.

1 FEB. 1983. The Shalom Club plants 5 redwood saplings near Serrano Village to celebrate the Jewish holiday Tu b'Shevat.

5 FEB. 1983. James D. Weinrich speaks in LC on "Evolution and Homosexuality."

9-10 FEB. 1983. Tenor Paul Sperry performs in RH, and also conducts a master class there (Feb. 10).

11 FEB. 1983. S.B. City Councilman Gordon Quiel visits CSCSB.

13 FEB. 1983. The Cal State San Bernardino Wind Ensemble and the Univ. of Redlands Wind Symphony perform in RH. Cal State student Kelly C. Preston dies in Palm Springs at age 22.

14 FEB. 1983. The Shades of Black acting troupe perform the plays *A Cold Day in Hell* and *'Justments* in RH. Pianist Althea Waites speaks about Margaret Bonds and performs her works in RH.

15 FEB. 1983. Rev. Billy G. Williams portrays Rev. Martin Luther King Jr. and S.B. City Councilman John D. Hobbs speaks in RH, as part of Black History Week. Denise Benton and Elva Williams perform in SUMP.

16 FEB. 1983. The D.J. group R.B. Conclusive Inc. performs in SUMP. The Center for General Education sponsors a forum with Pres. Evans in LC to discuss the general education program at the College.

17 FEB. 1983. The Calif. Public Employee Relations Board certifies The Calif. Faculty Assoc. as winning a system-wide runoff election with the United Professors of Calif. by 39 votes (6,580-6,541), thus becoming the official bargaining unit representative for Faculty Unit 3. The campus receives a $125,636 grant from the U.S. Dept. of Education to fund the Student Assistance in Learning (SAIL) Program. The campus hosts a reception in LC for French Commercial Attaché M. Dellaguardia, Austrian Press Attaché Ulf Bacher, and Mexican Consul Emerenciano Rodríguez, who discuss careers for foreign language majors.

18 FEB. 1983. Disabled Performers in Television and Films perform in RH, with deaf mime artist Bronisław "Miko" Machalski and actress Victoria Ann Lewis. Campus news is now being shown on cable networks Group W in San Bernardino and Fontana, and Buena Vista Cable in Colton. The campus hosts a community reception in LC honoring Pres. Evans.

20 FEB. 1983. The campus hosts a Gospel Concert in RH, with Ed Jenkins serving as M.C.

21 FEB. 1983. Speed bumps are installed in the main parking lot; after complaints are made about their height, the bumps are rebuilt. The campus rejoins the American Council on Education.

23 FEB. 1983. Violinist Carol Cheek performs in RH.

25 FEB. 1983. The campus relocates its Weather Station to an empty field north of the science buildings, with all monitoring equipment now being centralized at one site.

26 FEB. 1983. The campus hosts the conference, "New Directions in Special Education," with Louis Barber giving the keynote address, "New Directions in Special Education: Federal, State, and Local."

27 FEB. 1983. Jazz trumpeter Larry Ford performs in RH.

28 FEB. 1983. CSU Chancellor Reynolds visits the campus for the first time, and says that CSCSB is "a beautiful rosebud that needs to open and unfold." The college has an "unrealized potential" for growth, she says, and despite the current budget shortfall and enrollment issues, has never been considered for closure. "You have a dramatically attractive campus. It has developed conservatively and with basically sound principles. You recognize quite well the potential in the immense geographic region that lies outside the immediate San Bernardino environs." She urges the campus to "seize...possibilities for enrollment development."

1 MAR. 1983. Pres. Evans is interviewed on Barstow radio station KIOT.

4 MAR. 1983. Sherod M. Santos wins the 4th annual Delmore Schwartz Memorial Poetry Award from New York Univ., receiving $1,000 at a ceremony in New York City on Mar. 9.

5 MAR. 1983. The campus hosts its 7th Annual Reading Conference, "Literacy in the '80s: Reading, Writing, and Technology," with Alvin Granowsky giving the keynote address.

7 MAR. 1983. The campus bans smoking for "formal meetings" and class sessions, and restricts smoking to designated areas.

9 MAR. 1983. The campus publishes its first environmental studies report, containing data recorded by the Weather Station from 1976-81, including annual rainfall, wind velocity and direction, temperature, humidity level, and barometric pressure. The Steed Woodwind Quintet performs in RH. The campus receives a $4,000 gift from the Western Assoc. of Food Chains to fund 4 $1,000 scholarships for students in Business Administration.

11 MAR. 1983. B. Jill Buroker receives a $2,700 grant from the National Endowment for the Humanities to conduct research on philosopher Immanuel Kant. The Imagination Players perform in the Theatre. The campus conducts a pageant in SUMP to choose male models to use in a calendar.

12 MAR. 1983. The campus hosts the 13th Annual High School Theatre Workshop in the Theatre.

17 MAR. 1983. The Education Chapter of the Alumni Assoc. holds a reception in LC to honor Pres. and Mrs. Evans.

25 MAR. 1983. Frances F. Berdan is named an Outstanding Professor for the CSU System, the first CSCSB faculty member to achieve that goal, receiving a $1,000 award. Mime artist Judi Garratt performs in RH.

29 MAR. 1983. Rep. George E. Brown speaks in PL-500 on "Federal Funding Sources" as part of a grants seminar.

30 MAR. 1983. Venner Farley speaks in LC on "Power and Politics in Nursing."

1 APR. 1983. The Pfau Library begins offering on-line database searches in DIALOG, with students paying a fee to offset the partially subsidized cost of the service. The campus moves its daily parking permit dispenser from the Science Lot to the Main Entrance adjacent to the Information Booth.

4 APR. 1983. The campus begins granting Certificates of Attendance to families of deceased students, and mentioning such individuals at graduation ceremonies.

6 APR. 1983. Renée Firestone speaks in RH on "The Holocaust: Auschwitz, a Personal Remembrance."

8 APR. 1983. The *San Bernardino Sun* publishes an essay criticizing the campus, saying it "…is not what you'd call fully integrated into the social fabric of the Inland Empire. When's the last conversation you had with a neighbor about the county's only four-year public institute of higher learning…? If CSCSB were a television personality, its 'Q' rating would be zero."

11 APR. 1983. The UCLA Cappella Choir performs in RH. The campus approves an official seal, to be embedded in the bronze mace that will be created for the May 17 installation of Pres. Evans.

13 APR. 1983. Ward Schincke speaks in PS-10 on "The Regional War in Central America."

15 APR. 1983. The Children's Opera Factory performs Engelbert Humperdinck's *Hansel and Gretel* in RH. The campus co-sponsors a conference on "Migrant Education."

16 APR. 1983. William Goff speaks on "Techniques on Observing Variable Stars." Cal State Art Major Virginia R. Merritt dies in Redlands at age 49.

17 APR. 1983. Marvin Donald Frost, Assoc. Prof. of Geography (1976-83), dies of a heat stroke and heart attack at age 43 while doing research in the jungles of Belize; his body is found on Apr. 21.

18 APR. 1983. U.S. Sen. Daniel Inouye speaks in RH on "Nursing and the National Political Arena."

20 APR. 1983. The Kronos Quartet performs in RH.

21 APR. 1983. The campus hosts a High School Counselors' Conference.

22 APR. 1983. The campus begins implementing a system-wide management information system, Integrated Business System (IBS), to facilitate required financial reporting to government agencies and to standardize CSU's financial records. Dr. James R. Savage is named Act. Medical Dir. of the Student Health Center, replacing Dr. Ross L. Ballard, who goes on leave.

22-24 APR. 1983. The campus hosts a Microtechnology for Everyone Festival in the Gymnasium, with performances by puppeteers Jack Cox and Becky Johnston.

23 APR. 1983. The South Coast Repertory performs *Bits and Bytes* in RH.

24 APR. 1983. The *San Bernardino Sun* publishes an article on the campus debate over the possibility of adding intercollegiate athletics. Ex-Pres. Pfau refuses a request to comment. One faculty member is quoted as saying: "I think the faculty as a whole has a strong feeling about the scale of the school. We can walk across campus and personally greet most students. This isn't Long Beach or San Diego or Fullerton. With our scale comes a comfort that I think might be at risk" [if athletics are inaugurated]. However, the same piece quotes University of Redlands Pres. Douglas R. Moore as saying: "We think it [Redlands' NCAA Division III athletics program] is worth it. There are many things learned from the discipline and sacrifice and training that goes into the higher level of competition that goes with intercollegiate athletics."

25 APR. 1983. Francesca Bero speaks in PL-500 on "Special Education Programs for the Disabled in Japan." Esteban Soriano, Coordinator of Student Affirmative Action in the Chancellor's Off., visits the campus.

27 APR. 1983. The campus holds a forum in SUMP on the possibility of instituting an intercollegiate athletic program, with Ward M. McAfee, head of the Special Task Force, serving as Chair. Chilean exile Kemy Oyarsun speaks in PS-10. Economist Jim Devine speaks in PS-10 on "A Socialist Response to Reaganomics."

28 APR. 1983. The campus holds a memorial service for Prof. Marvin D. Frost near the campus Weather Station that he developed.

30 APR. 1983. Alvin Poussaint speaks at an NAACP scholarship fundraising dinner held in the Commons.

3 MAY 1983. The body of Cal State alumnus Raymond Richard "Monie" Vásquez (age 40) is found on Kendall Dr. near the corner of State College Pkwy.; his killer is arrested on campus.

4 MAY 1983. Chuck Sohner and Ben Dobbs speak in PS-10 on "The Democratic Left and Politics in the 1980s." Pianist Althea Waites performs in RH.

6 MAY 1983. Richard W. Griffiths and Robert G. Stein receive a $75,000 grant from the Calif. Mathematics Project of the Univ. of California to help teachers improve their competency in mathematics. Pres. Evans approves the establishment of a Dept. of Criminal Justice, effective with 1983/84.

11 MAY 1983. Poets Mark Strand and Charles Wright read from their work in RH.

13 MAY 1983. Psychotherapist Albert Ellis conducts a seminar on "Rational-Emotive Therapy" (RET) in RH. Ronald Pendleton and Alvin M. Wolf receive a $2,438 grant from the Calif. Dept. of Transportation to conduct a workshop on time management.

14 MAY 1983. The campus hosts a Conference on Women's Health in the Commons.

17 MAY 1983. Dr. Anthony H. Evans is inaugurated in the Gymnasium as 2nd President of CSC, San Bernardino, with CSU Chancellor Reynolds investing the President with his office. Michigan Supreme Court Justice James H. Brickley, ex-Pres. of Eastern Michigan Univ. and ex-Lt. Gov. of Michigan, gives the keynote address on "Battling Mediocrity in Education." Cal State Art Major Mark Petherbridge designs the bronze mace that is used in the ceremony, and alumnus Howard Dexter creates a 40-foot canvas mural depicting the campus logo. Other attendees include: CSU Trustees Lynne Myers, Wallace Albertson, Blanche C. Bersch, Claudia H. Hampton, and Robert K. Kully, and ex-ASI Presidents Richard J. Bennecke, Barry B. Thompson, Judith A. Jones, Timothy Hamre, Pauline Barbour, and Kathryn Fortner. The campus holds a reception in the Commons for the new President. In his remarks, Pres. Evans states that his hope is that the College will have "the will to do and the soul to dare [quoting Sir Walter Scott]. I have been left a very rich legacy. I accepted the presidency because I wanted to become associated with a college that was still developing and expanding its mission. I sensed that this area was destined for much future growth and economic expansion, but I did not anticipate that the San Bernardino-Riverside area was to become not only the fastest growing area in California, but in the entire nation." Milo Lenz, ex-Painter (retired 1979), dies of a heart attack in San Bernardino at age 66.

18 MAY 1983. Ellie Cohen speaks in PS-10 on "First Strike Weapons: Is Nuclear War Winnable?" Alan Crafton speaks in SUMP on "Computers for the Blind."

19 May 1983. Thomas S. Schrock speaks in SUMP on "The Fate of Constitutionalism in Hobbes' *Leviathan*."

24 May 1983. Shirley Eastman speaks on "Defensive Living" in the Commons, as part of Crime Prevention Week.

26 May 1983. The Chamber Choir of Fort Hays State Univ. performs in RH.

27 May 1983. Cal State English grad student Thomas Jay Cummins dies at age 50.

3 Jun. 1983. Pres. Evans approves the establishment of the Dept. of Computer Science, effective with 1983/84. Sherod M. Santos receives a Guggenheim Fellowship for 1983/84. Marvin R. Newman, Plant Operations, becomes the first campus employee to receive the Governor's State Employee Safety Award.

7 Jun. 1983. By a vote of 11-1, the Task Force on Intercollegiate Athletics recommends to Pres. Evans that the campus begin participating in NCAA Division III intercollegiate athletics in Fall 1984.

10 Jun. 1983. Loralee MacPike is chosen to participate in the CSU Administrative Fellows Program for 1983/84.

12 Jun. 1983. The Alumni Chorus premieres in RH.

17-24 Jun. 1983. Offices in the Student Services Building are vacated to allow the structure to be reroofed during the summer.

18 Jun. 1983. The 17th Commencement is held on the South Gymnasium Lawn, with Ralph H. Petrucci giving the keynote address; some 950 students are eligible to receive degrees.

24 Jun. 1983. The campus receives approval to offer an M.A. degree in National Security Studies, beginning with 1983/84. The campus receives an $187,185 grant from the U.S. Dept. of Education to fund the Upward Bound Program.

27 Jun. 1983. CSCSB joins the Riverside Chamber of Commerce.

30 Jun. 1983. Retirements: Charles W. Dulaney, Maintenance Mechanic (1972-83); Dorothy Johnson, Prof. of Nursing and ex-Chair of the Dept. of Nursing (1976-83); Willie Ruth Kelly, Housing Maintenance (1975-83).

1 Jul. 1983. The campus receives a $500 grant from the Union Pacific Foundation to support graduate students in Business. Gov. Deukmejian orders a freeze in purchasing and hiring in state agencies, and although the CSU is not legally bound to comply, Chancellor Reynolds issues an executive order extending her previous freeze of Jan. 5 through Jul. 31.

5 Jul. 1983. William L. Marsh, Plant Operations (1967-83), retires.

11 Jul. 1983. Cal State Natural Science student Seyed Hamid Gharavi is murdered with his family in Upland at age 23.

15 Jul. 1983. Elliott R. Barkan is named a Fulbright Lecturer, to teach in India in 1983/84.

16 Jul. 1983. Charles Wilborn "Chuck" Dulaney, retired Maintenance Mechanic, Serrano Village (1972-83), dies at age 65, a few weeks after retiring.

22 Jul. 1983. The School of Education offices relocate to the 5th floor of the Pfau Library Building.

29 Jul. 1983. The campus, together with 8 other campuses in the Cal State and UC systems, receives a $618,000 grant from the Calif. Mathematics Project. The campus receives a $32,000 gift of a mini-computer from the Digital Equipment Corp.

2 Aug. 1983. Dr. Ross L. Ballard, Dir. of the Student Health Center (1975-83), retires, and is replaced by Dr. James R. Savage as Act. Dir.

5 Aug. 1983. The campus receives a $124,000 grant from the U.S. Dept. of Education to support a 3-year bilingual education program. A sign stating "Welcome to California State College, San Bernardino," designed by Robert F. Lohnes, is erected at the corner of Kendall Dr. and State College Pkwy.

7 Aug. 1983. A thunderstorm floods part of the Student Services Building during a reroofing project that leaves it unprotected.

8 Aug. 1983. Rep. George E. Brown holds a Congressional hearing in PS-10 on "Technology, Employment, and Future Growth."

12 Aug. 1983. Dorothea Hino, Secretary, Plant Operations, retires.

13 Aug. 1983. Dorothy J. McCarthy, Library Asst. (1978-83), retires.

14 Aug. 1983. Virginia McKenzie, Secretary, Music and Theatre Arts

(1971-83), retires.

15 AUG. 1983. Michael W. Anderson is named Exec. Dean for College Relations, replacing James H. Urata, who is named Dir. of Administrative Affairs, in addition to his previous responsibilities as Dir. of Plant Operations. Retirements: Richard Belser, Lead Grounds Worker (1974-83); Frances A. Ekaitis, Library Asst. (1963-83); James Kelly, Instructional Support Technician (1966-83); Beatrice Lee, Clerical Asst. (1973-83); Mary Newman, Graphic Artist, Audio-Visual Services (1969-83); Marion Piel, Senior Accounting Clerk (1972-83); Margaret Richards, Library Asst. (1966-83); Dorothy Wiley, Library Clerical Asst. (1962-64, 1978-83).

16 AUG. 1983. The CSU Board of Trustees ratifies the first collective bargaining agreement in the history of the CSU System with the Calif. Faculty Assoc. (CFA).

17 AUG. 1983. An unprecedented summer cloudburst, the most intense rainfall ever recorded in San Bernardino, inundates parts of 5 campus buildings with depths as much as 12 inches: Administration, Creative Arts, Biological Science, Library, and Student Services. Newly arrived Exec. Dean Michael W. Anderson falls during mop-up operations and cracks a bone in his right wrist.

31 AUG. 1983. Ralph H. Petrucci, Dean of Academic Planning, returns to the ranks as Prof. of Chemistry. Lee H. Kalbus, Assoc. Dean of Academic Planning for Graduate Studies, returns to the ranks as Prof. of Chemistry. Richard T. Ackley, Assoc. Dean of Academic Administration (1974-83), returns to the ranks as Assoc. Prof. of Political Science. John M. Hatton, Act. Dean of Students, returns to his position of Assoc. Dean.

1 SEPT. 1983. As part of a major reorganization of the administration by Pres. Evans, Jerrold E. Pritchard is named Assoc. VP for Academic Programs, replacing Ralph H. Petrucci. Loralee MacPike is named Assoc. Dean for Graduate Programs, replacing Lee H. Kalbus. Catherine C. Gannon, Assoc. Dean of Academic Planning, is named Assoc. Dean for Undergraduate Programs. H. Stephen Prouty, Assoc. Dean of Admissions and Records, is named Assoc. Dean for Academic Programs. J. Cordell Robinson, Assoc. VP for Academic Affairs, is named Assoc. VP for Academic Personnel. James D. Thomas, Dean of Academic Administration, is named Assoc. VP for Academic Resources. Peter A. Wilson is named Dean of Students, replacing John M. Hatton. Florence Weiser, Asst. Dean of Academic Administration, is named Dir. of Sponsored Programs. Michael M. Rose, Relations with Schools Officer (1972-83), resigns. Sherri M. Deutchman Asst. Dir. of Housing (1981-83), is named Coordinator of the Student Union. Richard J. Bennecke, Student Affairs Administrator, is named first Dir. of the Alumni Affairs Off. The School of Administration is renamed the School of Business and Public Administration, and its 2 departments, Business Administration and Public Administration, are reconfigured into 4 new units: Public Administration, Accounting and Finance, Management, and Marketing and Management Science. Student fees increase from $189 to $232 per quarter. VP Scherba states that the change in designations is being undertaken to use titles found in similar positions at other CSU campuses, and to reflect more accurately the responsibilities of the individuals involved.

6 SEPT. 1983. The Student Services Building is reoccupied.

12 SEPT. 1983. At the annual convocation, Pres. Evans expresses appreciation of the sense of community at Cal State, its homogeneity in the midst of diversity, the quality and soundness of its academic programs, and the manner in which the campus has coped with a 3% budget cut. As soon as CSCSB reaches 5,081 students, the campus will immediately apply for university status. He announces a new budgeting/planning system to give more autonomy to individual units, the implementation of a Budget Planning and Priorities Committee and a major fund development program, and an increased emphasis on outreach. He stresses the need to improve the image of the College by revitalizing teacher training program, meeting the needs of the business community in nontraditional ways, and developing distinctive methods of better serving minorities. He states that the campus must develop new student markets, and move away from "an elite tradition" to become a "service institution." C. Donald Kajcienski is named Assoc. Dean of Admissions, Records, and Outreach, partially replacing H. Stephen Prouty.

15 SEPT. 1983. Alice Eleanor Wilson, Emer. Assoc. Libn. (1969-82), dies of cancer at age 69, being the first Emeritus faculty to die.

16 SEPT. 1983. Ansa Ojanlatva is named Act. Dir. of Sponsored Programs, replacing Florence Weiser. 2 large signs designating the "John M. Pfau Library" are installed at either end of the Library-Classroom Building.

19-20 SEPT. 1983. Allan W. Ostar, Pres. of the American Assoc. of State Colleges and Universities, visits the campus.

21 SEPT. 1983. Cal State graduate student Diana Lucille Wearne dies in Los Angeles at age 38.

23 SEPT. 1983. The campus receives a $23,130 grant from the Chancellor's Off. to fund the 2nd year of a special project for high school mathematics teachers. Campus enrollment hits a record high of 5,446 students (4,140 FTE), an increase of 7.6% over 1982, the highest in the CSU; this figure allows the campus to apply to the CSU System for University status.

28 Sept. 1983. Serrano Village, the campus residence hall, exceeds its 406-student capacity for the first time.

30 Sept. 1983. The campus receives a $52,892 grant from the National Endowment for the Humanities for an institute for high school teachers on "Rhetoric, Communication, and Freedom." Craig E. Henderson, Dir. of Housing, is named Student Affairs Administrator, with Doyle J. Stansel, Assoc. Dean of Students, assuming the added title of Act. Dir. of Housing.

1 Oct. 1983. Dr. James R. Savage, Act. Medical Dir. of Student Health Services, is named permanent Dir., replacing Dr. Ross L. Ballard.

3 Oct. 1983. George Martínez is named Dir. of the Upward Bound Program.

11 Oct. 1983. Lt. Gov. Leo T. McCarthy visits the campus. The Pfau Library enters the ten millionth bibliographical cataloging record in the OCLC database, under the direction of chief Library Cataloger, Michael Burgess.

13 Oct. 1983. Rep. George E. Brown speaks at a campus lunch for Private Industry Councils.

15 Oct. 1983. Cartoonist Mell Lazarus, actress Nedra Volz, and writer Alexandra Robbin speak at a seminar in UC.

16 Oct. 1983. The campus hosts "Love Your Heart" 5- and 10-kilometer runs, with 363 runners participating.

20 Oct. 1983. Artist Bob Zoell speaks about his work in VA-110.

21 Oct. 1983. The Art Dept. receives a $1,720 grant from the Calif. Arts Council to support an exhibition of materials from the Edward-Dean Museum of Decorative Arts.

23 Oct. 1983. The Fuchs Duo (pianist Louanne Fuchs and violinist Richard Fuchs) perform in RH.

24 Oct. 1983. The campus stops fingerprinting new employees, except for those working in "sensitive" areas.

26 Oct. 1983. Artist Gary Panter speaks about his work in VA-110.

1 Nov. 1983. C. Donald McKenzie is named 1st Budget Planning Analyst.

2 NOV. 1983. Phillip F. Straling, Bishop of the Catholic Diocese of S.B., speaks in SU.

4 NOV. 1983. Therapist Virginia Satir conducts a seminar in RH.

11 NOV. 1983. The campus hosts an Art Buffet Cabaret in LC, featuring Lawrence R. Smith.

12 NOV. 1983. Mezzo soprano Lisa Taylor and violinist Randy Fox perform in RH.

15-16 NOV. 1983. Cal State students vote 946-478 to double the instructionally related activity fee from $10-$20 per year to help fund an intercollegiate athletics program, and also recommend that the student newspaper change its name from *The Pawprint* to *The Cal State Chronicle* (the Publications Board approves the change on Nov. 30), and that the mascot change from St. Bernard to Coyote.

19 NOV. 1983. Lynn Fischer of the Jet Propulsion Laboratory speaks in PS-10 on the "Infrared Astronomy Satellite." The Trio dell'Arte chamber ensemble performs in RH.

22 NOV. 1983. Artist Mahamoud Omar speaks about his work in VA-110.

28 NOV.-12 DEC. 1983. The Art Gallery exhibits the work of the late Cal State student cartoonist, Roger Blakely Broadfoot, who died in Sept. in Alabama; a memorial scholarship is established in his name.

30 NOV. 1983. Mohamed Bakr speaks in VA-110 on "The Role of Papyrus in the Arts and History of Ancient Egypt."

2 DEC. 1983. The Pfau Library receives a $150 grant from the Jewish Chautauqua Soc. to purchase books on Judaism.

5 DEC. 1983. Pres. Evans appoints the first College Planning Advisory Council, including 15 representatives from the administration, faculty, staff, and students, to act as an advisory body for planning and budgetary activities.

16 DEC. 1983. Clifford LaRue McDonald Sr., Laboratory Support Technician (1977-83), dies in San Bernardino at age 47. Pres. Evans approves the recommendations of the Task Force on Intercollegiate Athletics, applies to the Chancellor's Off. for approval to inaugurate a program of NCAA Division III intercollegiate athletics by Fall 1984, and authorizes the hiring of an Athletic Director.

20 Dec. 1983. Pres. Evans testifies at a hearing on housing standards of the S.B. City Planning Commission that "a proliferation of unattractive, cheap, and inferior housing in the area" would seriously diminish the attractiveness of CSCSB.

30 Dec. 1983. Robert A. Blackey is named Outstanding Professor for 1983/84.

31 Dec. 1983. Catherine C. Gannon, Assoc. Dean for Undergraduate Programs, returns to the ranks as Prof. of English.

1984

1 Jan. 1984. Thomas J. Pierce is named Act. Assoc. Dean for Undergraduate Programs, replacing Catherine C. Gannon. A new Management Personnel Plan (MPP) takes effect in the CSU System under HEERA, the Higher Education Employer-Employee Relations Act, covering employees designated as "management," who will now be called Administrator I, II, III, or IV; all future raises for these classes will be based solely on merit; administrators hired after this date can no longer obtain attain tenure only as managers. Samuel Sid Kushner is named Dir. of Sponsored Programs.

2-4 Jan. 1984. Joan Dornemann of the Metropolitan Opera conducts a master class in RH.

3 Jan. 1984. Reginald L. Price, Chair of the Dept. of Physical Education and Recreation, is named first Athletic Dir.; he is charged with developing men's soccer and cross-country and women's volleyball and cross-country teams for Fall 1984, men's and women's basketball for Winter 1985, and men's and women tennis for Spring 1985; selecting coaches for these programs; and establishing an advisory board.

6 Jan. 1984. The Chancellor's Off. approves a new B.A. degree in Human Development.

9 Jan. 1984. William Vandament, CSU Act. Provost and Vice Chancellor of Academic Affairs, visits the campus.

10 Jan. 1984. Tenor Richard Barrett conducts an opera vocal technique class in RH.

12 Jan. 1984. The campus newspaper, *The Pawprint*, changes its name to *The Cal State Chronicle*, following a student poll recommending the move by a vote of 166-134. Sam García speaks in LC on "Capitalizing on Traditional Process in Corporate America."

16 JAN. 1984. The campus closes to observe Dr. Martin Luther King Jr. Day for the first time.

18 JAN. 1984. *The Cal State Chronicle* increases its physical size by an inch. Max Handy speaks in LC-241 on "From the Iron Curtain to the Berlin Wall."

21 JAN. 1984. The Off. of Continuing Education offers a Robotics Technology Workshop in SUMP.

23 JAN. 1984. German Consul Herbert Quelle speaks in PL-241.

1 FEB. 1984. Santa Ana winds exceeding 70 M.P.H. rip large sections of the roof from the Physical Plant, and blow out a window in the Pfau Library, while damaging several others.

4 FEB. 1984. The campus hosts its 2nd Annual Serving the Handicapped of Our Area in Recreation and Education Conference, "Special Education: Preparation for Life," with Patricia Madeiros Landurand giving the keynote address, "Multicultural Factors in Special Education."

5 FEB. 1984. The campus hosts a Teachers' Bach Festival in RH.

10 FEB. 1984. The Firebird Theatre Co. performs the play, *The Labors of Hercules*, in RH.

13 FEB. 1984. Robert Rewalt Roberts, Prof. of History and ex-Chair of the Social Sciences Div. and Chair of the Dept. of History (1963-84), dies in San Bernardino of leukemia at age 63.

17 FEB. 1984. Pres. Evans approves the coyote as the new official mascot, replacing the St. Bernard dog.

19 FEB. 1984. The gospel groups The San Bernardino Community Choir, The Poole Sisters, The Voices of Redemption, and The Christian Disciples perform in RH for Black History Week.

20 FEB. 1984. The campus hosts a panel of community leaders: *Black Voice* Editor Cheryl Brown, Deseret Homes Business Dir. David Horne, and Mabel Hariss.

21 FEB. 1984. Jackie Hempstead speaks in SUMP. Lauren Wasserman, City Manager of Rancho Cucamonga, speaks in SUMP on "Land Use Planning."

22 FEB. 1984. Lois J. Carson speaks in LC on "A Time to Come Together." Reginald Webb speaks in SUMP.

24 FEB. 1984. Ex-Rep. Yvonne Brathwaite Burke speaks in LC on "A Time to Come Together."

27 FEB. 1984. Poet Diane Wakoski reads from her work in RH.

29 FEB. 1984. Clarinetist Diane Lang Bryan performs in RH. Kathleen Edmunds, Secretary in Plant Operations, is injured when the electric cart she is driving overturns on her.

1 MAR. 1984. Karen Coleman and Zoe Ragan speak in SS-171 on "Child Molestation: What Can We Do?"

2 MAR. 1984. Clabe Hangan and Jon Rael perform "Music Americana" in RH.

2-3 MAR. 1984. Ceramic artist and sculptor Daniel Rhodes speaks and conducts a workshop in RH.

3 MAR. 1984. The campus hosts a festival for local grade and high school students in RH. The campus hosts its 8th Annual Reading Conference, "The Art of Comprehension," with Jerry Weiss giving the keynote address, "Reading in a *1984* World."

4 MAR. 1984. Jorun E. Johns meets Rudolf Kirchschlaeger, Pres. of Austria, in Vienna.

5 MAR. 1984. Women's study scholar Betty Brooks speaks in SUMP on "The Women's Movement: The Lesbian/Gay Movement, and Current Tide," as part of Women's History Week.

6 MAR. 1984. Noel Riley Fitch speaks in RH on "Transatlantic Sisterhood: Women Writers in Paris in the 1920s." Lynn Baxter speaks in LC on "Women's Lib Was Born in the Bible."

9 MAR. 1984. The campus hosts a Chicana workshop, "Building for the Future," with *El Chicano* Publisher Gloria Macías Harrison giving the keynote address. Althea Waites performs "Women in Music" in RH.

12 MAR. 1984. The Administrative Council authorizes the reactivation of the Campus Planning Committee.

14 MAR. 1984. Caesar J. Naples, CSU Vice Chancellor for Faculty and Staff Relations, visits the campus. Stan Trefren speaks in LC on "Investing for Tax Purposes."

15 MAR. 1984. Trumpeter David Washburn performs with the Cal State Wind Ensemble in RH.

16 MAR. 1984. The campus awards its first 22 research grants from the new Faculty Professional Development Program, providing $34,816 from the instructional budget to aid professional growth. B. H. "Pete" Fairchild wins First Prize in the Santa Cruz Writers' Union poetry competition with his poem, "The Woman at the Laundromat Crying 'Mercy'."

19 MAR. 1984. Michael W. Anderson, Exec. Dean for College Relations (1983-84), resigns to enter private industry.

29 MAR. 1984. San Val Engineering Inc. receives a $295,680 contract to reroof the Visual Arts Building.

4 APR. 1984. Welsh philosopher D. Z. Phillips speaks in LC on "The Devil's Disguises: Philosophy, Religion, and Cultural Divergence."

5 APR. 1984. Economist J. Fred Weston speaks in RH on "New Competition Among Financial Institutions."

6 APR. 1984. Kent M. Schofield and Thomas M. Meisenhelder receive a $3,000 stipend from the National Endowment for the Humanities. Roberta Stathis-Ochoa receives a $1,500 Winifred Hausam-Helen Fisk Award for Distinction in Higher Education at the Claremont Graduate School. The campus receives a $1,000 grant from the Chancellor's Off. to support math teaching.

7 APR. 1984. Mezzo soprano Claudine Carlson performs in RH.

9 APR. 1984. The campus alters its custodial work shift from a night to day schedule to save energy. Frances M. Berenson speaks in LC on "Can We Understand the Art of Other Cultures?"

11 APR. 1984. Clarinetist John Gates and pianist Gianna Pirelli perform in RH.

13 APR. 1984. The campus signs an agreement with Zagazig Univ. in Egypt to exchange faculty and students. The L.A. Moving Van and Puppet Co. performs *An Asian Fable: Tien Lee and the Fish of Gold and Other Stories* in RH. Susan Caroselli speaks in VA-110 on "The Last Extravagance: Italian Decorative Art of the Eighteenth Century," as part of the opening ceremony of an exhibit of decorative art from the Edward-Dean Museum in Yucaipa.

25 APR. 1984. Soprano Devy Barnett Buchen performs in RH, accompanied by pianist Robert Derick. Patrick L. Schul speaks in LC on "Winning the Salary Game and Getting the Job." Carol Wells speaks in SUMP on "The Role of Culture in the New Nicaragua."

27-28 APR. 1984. The campus conducts its 3rd Open House in conjunction with its 2nd Microtechnology for Everybody Festival, attracting 5,400 visitors. The festivities include an Army helicopter landing, camel rides, a demonstration of ROTC cadets rappelling off the top of the Library, a "Robot Olympics," etc.

30 APR. 1984. Janice Queener-Shaw speaks in VA-110 on "The Edward-Dean Collection: A Study in Curatorial Practice."

1 MAY 1984. Pulitzer Price-winning poet Louis Simpson reads from his work in RH. The campus hires its first athletics coaches: Gale L. Fitzgerald (women's basketball), James R. Ducey (men's basketball), Cherif Zein (soccer), and Michael Muscare (men's and women's tennis); additional coaches are hired on Jun. 9: Naomi Ruderman (women's volleyball) and Thomas Burleson (men's and women's cross-country).

3 MAY 1984. Pianist Gianna Pirelli performs in RH. Carol Nagy Jacklin speaks in RH on "Sex Differences."

4 MAY 1984. The campus receives a 2nd $4,000 grant from the Western Assoc. of Food Chains to support 4 $1,000 student scholarships in business administration. The Library begins implementing an automated circulation system, CL Systems LIBS 100 (CLSI). David H. Null receives a Governor's State Employee Safety Award. The Access Theater of Santa Barbara performs the musical sign-language revue, *Finger Talk*, in RH.

7 MAY 1984. Novelist Paul Gillette reads from his work in RH.

11 MAY 1984. The Free Flight Dance Co. performs in RH. Vivien Bull and Dean Buchen meet with students interested in the new Liberal Arts Program at the Coll. of the Desert.

13 MAY 1984. The Almont Ensemble performs in RH.

15 MAY 1984. Anne J. Davis speaks in RH on "The Future Responsibility of Nursing: An Ethical Perspective."

16 MAY 1984. Peter L. Ransom speaks in PL-500 on "Economic Security in the Twentieth Century: Some Thoughts on the Evidence."

17 MAY 1984. Peter L. Bouvier, Lect. in Management (1983-84), and Prof.

and Chair of the Dept. of Business Management at the Univ. of Redlands, who had accepted a permanent position at Cal State with the Fall 1984 term, dies at Redlands at age 41. Attorney William J. Winslade speaks in RH on his book, *The Insanity Plea*. Wendy Slatkin speaks in VA-110 on "Women Artists in History: From Antiquity to the Twentieth Century."

18 MAY 1984. The campus receives a $193,135 grant to fund a 2nd year of the Upward Bound Program.

19 MAY 1984. TV newscasters Liz Gonzáles and Maclovio Pérez participate in a Conference on Minorities' Access to the Media; other speakers include: Cheryl Brown and Hardy Brown, Editor and Publisher of *The Black Voice*; Alfredo Gonzáles, broadcaster with KVCR-TV and KCAL Radio; and Gloria Macías Harrison, Publisher of *El Chicano*. Carolyn Kubiak is named a CSU Administrative Fellow.

23 MAY 1984. The application by the campus to be renamed California State University, San Bernardino is unanimously approved by the CSU Board of Trustees, and is sent to the Calif. Postsecondary Education Commission for further action. CSU Chancellor Reynolds announces new system-wide admissions standards that require that teacher preparation programs admit only from the upper 50% of students, with other measures to raise the quality of the student teaching experience. Don Walsh speaks in BI-22 on "The Reagan Administration's Policy for a Maritime Economic Zone."

24 MAY 1984. The West Coast Brass Quintet performs in RH.

29 MAY 1984. Herbert Carter, CSU Vice Chancellor for Administration, visits the campus.

1 JUN. 1984. The acting group We Tell Stories performs "A Show for All Reasons" in RH.

5 JUN. 1984. The Chancellor's Off. approves the campus's 49th degree major, a B.A. in Communication, effective Fall 1984.

6 JUN. 1984. Cal State Business Administration student Cheryl Marie Stephens dies in Santa Monica in a car accident at age 21.

8 JUN. 1984. The campus honors 3 winners of the Outstanding Professor Award—Robert A. Blackey, Frances F. Berdan, and Frederick A. Newton—at a breakfast in the Commons. The Pfau Library announces that all faculty and students will need "zebra labels" affixed to their photo ID cards, beginning Jun. 20, as part of the implementation of a new automated circulation system, CLSI. The campus signs a memorandum of understanding with the U.S. Air Force to offer an M.A. degree in National Security Studies at George Air Force Base near Victorville.

11 JUN. 1984. The Committee on Policy Development of the Calif. Postsecondary Education Commission (CPEC) unanimously approves the request to grant university status to the College.

16 JUN. 1984. The 18th Commencement is held on the South Gymnasium Lawn, with Robert Middlekauff, Dir. of the Huntington Library, giving the keynote address; some 1,043 students are eligible to receive degrees. Attendees include CSU Trustee Robert K. Kully, and CAB members Robert Custer, Clarence R. Goodwin, Gloria Macías Harrison, Sister Ann Muckerman, Claude Noel, Richard Padilla, Wayne Scott, and Roberto Velásquez.

18 JUN. 1984. The Visual Arts Building is closed for reroofing.

20 JUN. 1984. The campus expands its summer school offerings to encompass 3 separate class sessions.

22 JUN. 1984. Theodore "Ted" Krug is elected to the Board of Directors of the S.B. Central Credit Union.

25 JUN. 1984. The campus adopts a policy allowing smoking only in the single-occupant offices, multiple-occupant offices where the employees unanimously agree to allow smoking, cafeterias, lounges, coffee rooms, and the Serrano Residence Hall common areas.

29 JUN. 1984. The campus receives a rare 10-year accreditation by the Western Assoc. of Schools and Colleges (WASC). Construction begins on a 20-by-16-ft. Bookstore addition.

30 JUN. 1984. Sandra Lyn Jensen, Campus Personnel Off., resigns.

1 JUL. 1984. Wendy A. Pederson is named Act. Campus Personnel Officer, replacing Sandra Lyn Jensen. The Offices of Budget Administration and Budget Planning are merged as the Off. of Budget Planning and Administration; C. Donald McKenzie, Budget Planning Analyst, is named Dir. of Budget Planning and Administration. John M. Hatton, Assoc. Dean of Counseling Services, is named Assoc. Dean of Counseling and Health Services, and the Student Health Center is placed under his control. C. Donald Kajcienski, Assoc. Dean of Admissions, Records, and Outreach, is named Assoc. Dean of Enrollment Services, and Financial Aid is moved from Student Services to his control. Doyle J. Stansel, Assoc. Dean of Student Services, is named Assoc. Dean of Student Life, and the Activities Off. is moved under his control.

2 JUL. 1984. Helga E. Scovel is named Dir. of the Student Union, replacing Sherri M. Deutchman, who reverts to Asst. Housing Dir.

9 JUL. 1984. Pres. Evans appoints an Ad Hoc Affirmative Action Steering Committee to help identify strategies to improve the racial mix of employees; members include Shirley Ealy, Grace Goodrich, Mildred M. Henry, Charles D. Hoffman, Sandra Lyn Jensen, George Martínez, Pola N. Patterson, Tom M. Rivera, J. Cordell Robinson, Pamela Stewart, and James H. Urata.

13 JUL. 1984. The Off. of Continuing Education is renamed the Off. of Extended Education, and the Dean's title is altered accordingly. The campus receives permission from the Federal Communications Commission to erect a transmitter for an instructional TV fixed station (ITFS).

19 JUL. 1984. *All for November*, play written by Cal State alumnus William Greeley, debuts at the Univ. of Redlands, with 8 CSCSB students, 2 staff members, and 2 faculty members participating.

20 JUL. 1984. KCBS-TV (Channel 2) brings its traveling Public Affairs Workshop to campus in PS-10.

23 JUL. 1984. The Calif. Postsecondary Education Commission approves the application of CSCSB to become a university, and the campus is officially renamed **California State University, San Bernardino** on this date. Buckley B. Barrett, Libn., carries the Olympic Torch through part of San Dimas on its way through Southern California to the L.A. Coliseum. At this turning point in its history, the campus has 5,450 students enrolled, 1,532 of them at the graduate level, with 400 residential students and 55 student organizations; offers 38 bachelor's degree and 9 master's degree programs, plus 32 certificates, 13 credentials, and 5 preprofessional certificates; employs 323 faculty; has 23 campus buildings on 430 acres of land; is accredited by the Western Assoc. of Schools and Colleges, the Calif. State Board of Education, the American Chemical Soc., the National League for Nursing, and the National Assoc. of Schools of Art and Design; and has a Library with 400,000 books (the largest ratio of books per student in the CSU System), 2,500 periodical subscriptions, 30 newspaper subscriptions, and 6,000 music recordings.

24 JUL. 1984. During a ceremony held at 9:00 A.M. at the main entrance to the campus, the large entryway sign ("California State College, San Bernardino") at State College Pkwy. and Northpark Blvd. is altered to remove the word "College" and insert the word "University." Gerald M. Scherba, VP for Academic Affairs, presides over the *fête*, together with Loralee MacPike, Chair of the Planning Committee, Pres. Evans, founding Pres.

Pfau, S.B. Mayor Holcomb and City Councilman Gordon Quiel (representing the city), Carol F. Goss (representing the faculty), Yolanda T. Moses (representing the alumni), Steve Winker (representing the student body), Luella Cohen and Gloria Macías Harrison (representing the Advisory Board), and Wilma Carter (representing the local community at large), among many others. Mary Williams, the University's longest-serving employee, strips the "College" name from the sign, and the special guests, beginning with Pres. Pfau and ending with Pres. Evans, insert the new letters to spell out "University." Quiel indicates that he will facilitate the changing of the name of State College Pkwy. to University Pkwy. Evans hails the elevation of the campus to university status as "an historic event which brings much joy to all of the institution's students, graduates, faculty, staff, and supporters. It is also a time of reassessment. Of necessity, we must maintain continuity with the past, but the new university's role is also to initiate, to change, to serve. By its very nature a university is universal, rather than regional, in scope and mission. Yet I am convinced that attaining university status will strengthen the institution's service to all people throughout the entire region. This is a time to recall John Masefield's observation that 'there are few earthly things more beautiful than a university' because it is 'a place where those who hate ignorance may strive to know, where those who perceive truth may strive to make others see'."

29 JUL. 1984. Cal State Political Science senior Lee Ann Gray is killed at age 30 near Perris in a skydiving accident when her parachute fails to open fully.

1 AUG. 1984 (?). The S.B. City Council changes the name of State College Pkwy. to University Pkwy.

3 AUG. 1984. Lee I. Porter is named a Fellow of the Academy of Continuing Education.

10 AUG. 1984. The campus receives a $5,706 grant from the U.S. Dept. of Education to hire a part-time veterans' affairs counselor. Michael Burgess is interviewed by Mike Hodel on the program, *Hour 25*, aired on radio station KPFK-FM in L.A.

22 AUG. 1984. The campus receives a $174,218 grant from the U.S. Dept. of Education to fund the 2nd year of a project to Train Bilingual/Cross-Cultural Teachers for Local Schools, and a $158,271 grant to fund a Bilingual Special Education Program.

24 AUG. 1984. The campus landscapes the area between the Pfau Library and the Physical Education complex—the last part of the academic core of the campus to be landscaped. Elliott Roofing Construction receives a

$16,989 contract to construct a training room in the Physical Education and Recreation Building.

31 AUG. 1984. Gerald M. Scherba, VP for Academic Affairs, returns to the ranks as Prof. of Biology. James D. Thomas, Assoc. VP for Academic Resources, returns to the ranks as Prof. of Political Science. Richard T. Ackley receives his 11th $500 grant from the National Strategy Information Center to purchase teaching materials.

1 SEPT. 1984. Ward M. McAfee, Dean of the School of Social and Behavioral Sciences, is named Act. VP for Academic Affairs, replacing Gerald M. Scherba. Judith M. Rymer is named Act. Exec. Dean for Univ. Relations, replacing Michael W. Anderson. Amer M. El-Ahraf, Chair of the Dept. of Health and Human Ecology, is named Assoc. VP for Academic Resources, replacing James D. Thomas. David J. Lutz is named Assoc. Dean for Graduate Studies, replacing Loralee MacPike. Diane F. Halpern is named Assoc. Dean for Undergraduate Studies, replacing Thomas J. Pierce, who is named Act. Dean of Social and Behavioral Sciences.

7 SEPT. 1984. The Chancellor's Off. approves renaming the campus weather station in honor of Marvin D. Frost, the late Cal State geographer (1939-83) who developed and managed it.

10 SEPT. 1984. The Visual Arts Building reopens for business.

11 SEPT. 1984. At the annual convocation, Pres. Evans states that the new academic year will be even better than the last. The nature of the Inland Empire affords the institution "unparalleled opportunities" to add student enrollment, to serve minorities, to prepare more teachers, and to respond to the special needs of today's students. He cites a "pivotal achievement" in the rare 10-year accreditation of the campus granted by WASC, plus the institution's elevation to university status. He commends the Office of Extended Education for its 45% growth, the revitalization of the School of Education, the automating and professionalization of admissions, the addition of new programs, concentrations, and certificates, the growth of off-campus offerings in the High Desert and the Coachella Valley, the introduction of intercollegiate athletics, the more sophisticated budgeting system, and the growth of grant applications, with $630,000 (16 grants) being received in 1983/84. He acknowledges an acute space problem, but notes that several buildings are in the works.

14 SEPT. 1984. The National Collegiate Athletic Assoc. (NCAA) accepts Cal State as a member of NCAA Division III, and authorizes the campus to compete in 8 intercollegiate sports.

20 SEPT. 1984. The campus changes from a 4-day class schedule to a 5-

day schedule, offering classes in 3-day (Monday, Wednesday, and Friday) and 2-day (Tuesday and Thursday) blocks to make better use of existing classroom space. The Pfau Library completes implementation of its first automated check-out system.

22 SEPT. 1984. The campus participates in its first NCAA-approved athletic contest, defeating the Univ. of Redlands in a soccer match by the score of 4-3, and also defeats Occidental College on the same day, 4-2. The men's and women's cross-country teams compete for the first time at Los Angeles Baptist College at LaVerne, Calif. Also appearing for the first time is the campus's cheerleading squad, comprised of 7 sophomores.

25 SEPT. 1984. The campus's women's volleyball team debuts in the Cal State Gymnasium against Pomona-Pitzer. *Newsweek* magazine editors and correspondents Maynard Parker, Thomas M. DeFrank, Susan Dentzer, Nicholas M. Horrock, and Gerald Lubenow speak before a World Affairs Council dinner in the Commons.

28 SEPT. 1984. Jean Peacock is named Dir. of SAIL and the Learning Center.

3 OCT. 1984. The Dept. of Marketing and Management Science opens a $100,000 IBM computer laboratory for its students.

5 OCT. 1984. Pres. Evans creates an Affirmative Action Advisory Committee to replace the Ad Hoc Committee, with 3 faculty, 3 staff, 3 administrators, and a student: Melvin G. Hawkins, Mildred M. Henry, Janice L. Loutzenhiser, Diana L. Mosqueda, Eula Barrios Brown, Carmen Murillo, Paul Frazier, H. Arthur Hoverland, and Doyle J. Stansel, plus ex-officio members J. Cordell Robinson and Dale T. West.

10 OCT. 1984. Alberto Arene speaks in SUMP on "Duarte's Showtime Is Over: An Analysis of the Current Situation in El Salvador."

15 OCT. 1984. The Library installs 2 electric doors at its north entrance.

25 OCT. 1984. Howard Dexter and Janet Coggins conduct a workshop, "Tuning and Temperament," in RH.

29 OCT. 1984. The campus begins Project Upbeat, a program to introduce gifted 6th-graders and the parents to the University.

2 NOV. 1984. Keith Johnson is named Dir. of Off-Campus State-Sponsored Programs. George Martínez, Dir. of the Upward Bound Program, is named Dir. of Community Affairs.

4 NOV. 1984. The campus hosts an open house, UniFest '84, for student families, with a performance by pop band The Unforgiven.

5 NOV. 1984. Dale T. West is named Campus Personnel Officer, replacing Wendy A. Pederson.

8 NOV. 1984. Folksinger Nick Pyzow performs in SU.

9 NOV. 1984. Frank T. Slaton, Manager of Data Processing Services (1975-84), is named Dir. of Computing. The Alden Ensemble performs in RH.

11 NOV. 1984. Melvin Chester speaks in SU on the Baha'i faith.

14 NOV. 1984. The American Culture and Language Program sponsors a seminar on "Cultural Differences and Culture Shock" under the direction of Sally Gardner.

16 NOV. 1984. The Inland Empire Student Services Consortium sponsors a conference "Student Outcomes" in LC.

17 NOV. 1984. The men's basketball team plays its first home game in the Gymnasium against California Institute of Technology; the women's team plays its first home game on Nov. 24, hosting Fresno Pacific College.

20 NOV. 1984. Ernest Partridge speaks in SU on "Nuclear Doctrine, Rationality, and the Moral Point of View."

26 NOV. 1984. Immigration attorney Maggie Popkin speaks in SUMP on "Changing Roles of Women in Central America." Mike Valles speaks in LC on "The Results of the Elections—Its Impact on the Hispanic Community."

28 NOV. 1984. Psychologist Henry B. Biller speaks in RH on "Parenting and Early Relationships."

30 NOV. 1984. Irving H. Buchen, Dean of the School of Humanities (1979-84), resigns to take a position at the Univ. of Wisconsin.

1 DEC. 1984. Stella T. Clark is named Act. Dean of the School of Humanities, replacing Irving H. Buchen.

4 DEC. 1984. CSU Trustee Robert D. Kully visits the campus.

7 DEC. 1984. The campus Bookstore begins selling computers.

12 DEC. 1984. The Women's Div. of the S.B. Chamber of Commerce names Jennifer McMullen, Administrative Aide to the Dean of Social and Behavioral Sciences, as its 1984 Woman of the Year.

14 DEC. 1984. The campus adopts Parkside Elementary School to use for teacher training. The campus begins construction on 4 energy-related projects totaling $174,625.

14-15 DEC. 1984. The campus hosts a High School Speech and Debate Tournament.

20-25 DEC. 1984. The campus closes for its first extended Christmas holiday break to save energy, using 3 holidays from earlier in the year to replace Dec. 20-21 and Dec. 24.

1985

4 JAN. 1985. Richard H. Rowland is named Outstanding Professor for 1984/85.

14 JAN. 1985. Humberto López and Carlos Ramos speak in SUMP on "The Hope for Peace in Nicaragua."

17 JAN. 1985. René Felix Dennemeyer, Emer. Prof. of Mathematics (1966-79), dies at Poway, Calif. at age 63. Robert Brosseau, Michael Tacchia, and Michele Brosseau-Tacchia perform in RH.

19 JAN. 1985. The campus hosts a free Family Reading Rally, with writer Jim Trelease giving the keynote address.

21 JAN. 1985. Violinist William Preucil gives a master class in RH.

24 JAN. 1985. The campus holds a reception to honor Abd el-Tawab Bahgat, VP of Zagazig Univ. (Egypt), and signs an agreement to exchange faculty and students with that school. Vernon Howe speaks in BI-129 on "Chaos and Stability in Populations."

25 JAN. 1985. The campus receives a $48,820 grant from the National Endowment for the Humanities to fund a conference on "Equality and the Constitution" for high school teachers; and a $5,000 grant from Ætna Life and Casualty Foundation to create a series of science-related workshops for high school students.

26 JAN. 1985. Alpha Kappa Alpha sponsors a 2nd annual Black Family Conference in SU, with keynote speaker ex-CSU Trustee Claudia Hampton, plus the Rev. Philip Nelson.

27 JAN. 1985. Violinist Carol Cheek, soprano Gwendolyn Lytle-Moors, cellist Catherine Graff MacLaughlin, and pianist Althea Mitchell Waites perform in RH.

1 FEB. 1985. The CSU implements an IRS ruling requiring that retirement contributions be deducted from an employee's salary before taxes are withheld. The Alumni Assoc. magazine, *Panorama*, increases in size from 8.5 x 11 inches to 11 x 17 inches.

6 FEB. 1985. The campus hosts an intramural College Bowl in SU.

7 FEB. 1985. The Campus Bookstore is renamed the Coyote Bookstore, after the students vote for the new designation.

8 FEB. 1985. Gerald M. Scherba, ex-VP for Academic Affairs, is named 3rd Dir. of the Desert Studies Consortium at Soda Springs (previously Zzyzx Mineral Springs), located in the Mojave Desert 13 miles southeast of Baker, Calif., replacing Lon McClanahan (1978-85). The Consortium comprises 7 CSU campuses with the U.S. Bureau of Land Management.

12 FEB. 1985. Susanne Jonas of the Institute for the Study of Militarism and Economic Crisis speaks in SU on "Rebellion and Repression in Guatemala."

14 FEB. 1985. Mathematician William Lucas speaks in BI-129 on "How to Divide a Cake or an Estate Fairly."

15 FEB. 1985. Lynda W. Warren receives a $47,100 grant from the Spencer Foundation to continue her research on gifted women. Clarinetist F. Gerard Errante performs in RH. A group of retired Cal State professors forms the CSU Assoc. of Emeriti Professors, the first such organization in the U.S.

16 FEB. 1985. Chandyn Productions performs the play, *Silhouette of Slavery*, in RH.

17 FEB. 1985. The gospel singers Niecie and Tim Watson's Group perform in RH.

18 FEB. 1985. Charles H. Weitz speaks in SUMP on "Famine and the Broader Issues of Agricultural Development."

20 FEB. 1985. Food sales are banned from the deck outside the first floor of the Pfau Library. Freeway signs on I-215 are changed to reflect "University Pkwy" as the new designation for the exit leading to Cal State. Cal State History major Douglas Alan Housel is killed in a car accident in Riverside at age 31.

21 FEB. 1985. Esteban L. Olmedo speaks in PS-122 on "New Frontiers in Professional Psychology: The Challenge of Cultural Diversity."

22 FEB. 1985. The campus receives a grant of $3,750 from Howard Grossman and TRW to create 2 scholarships for S.B. teachers. Cal State alumna Yolanda T. Moses speaks in SUMP on "Black American Political Factions: A Cultural Perspective."

1 MAR. 1985. Anderson J. Ward speaks in BI-101 on "New Trends in the Law and Funding Resources Affecting the Health and Biological Sciences." Pres. Evans appoints a 9-person Task Force on Minority Underrepresentation chaired by V.P. McAfee to suggest ways to increase minority faculty and students on campus.

2 MAR. 1985. The campus hosts its 9th annual Reading Conference, with Herbert Nickles giving the keynote address.

4 MAR. 1985. William Lutz speaks in LC and in SUMP on "Doublespeak." Dick Silk speaks in LC on "Cocaine: America's New High."

6 MAR. 1985. Robert Cohen speaks in the Theatre on "Acting Professionally."

7 MAR. 1985. Pianists Michael Redshaw and Lily Pan-Diehl perform in RH.

8 MAR. 1985. Pres. Evans approves the creation of an Outstanding Student Award to be given at Commencement.

9 MAR. 1985. The Cal State International Club sponsors a conference on Apartheid in South Africa, with speakers Clifford Cenge, Robert Bruce, and Ron Wilkins.

13 MAR. 1985. George Lipsitz speaks in RH on "Born to Run: Rock and Roll Music as Social History."

15 MAR. 1985. Sheldon E. Bockman, Donald Lindsey, and Barbara Sirotnik receive a $14,697 grant from the Friends of Copper Mountain College, Joshua Tree, to conduct a needs assessment study for that campus.

22 MAR. 1985. The campus installs a satellite receiver on the roof of the Pfau Library.

1 APR. 1985. The Off. of Academic Programs mails 10,000 flyers to residents of the Coachella Valley as part of a feasibility study to determine the higher education needs of Valley inhabitants, preparatory to establishing on off-campus educational facility there.

4 APR. 1985. Composer Sandy Feldstein speaks in RH. The Task Force on Minority Underrepresentation presents its *Final Report* to Pres. Evans, who accepts its findings and creates 4 faculty positions to be used solely for affirmative action hiring purposes, beginning with 1985/86, the program being renewed annually thereafter.

5 APR. 1985. Greg Price is named the 1st Golf Coach.

8-10 APR. 1985. The campus hosts a Conference on the Constitution in the Commons, sponsored by a $48,820 grant from the National Endowment for the Humanities. As part of the meeting, Pulitzer Prize-winning historian Leonard W. Levy speaks on Apr. 8 in LC on "Making the Constitution: 1776-1789"; and attorney Gerald Gunther speaks on Apr. 9 in RH on "The Role of the U.S. Supreme Court in Setting Forth Constitutional Norms."

13-14 APR. 1985. The campus hosts a Theatre Festival for Young Audiences, with more than 3,000 students attending, with performances by the Firebird Theatre, We Tell Stories, mime Judi Garratt, the Improvisational Theatre Project from the Mark Taper Forum, the South Coast Repertory Theatre, the Orange Co. Opera, the Twelfth Night Repertory Co., Little Broadway Productions, storyteller David Novak, the Patio Playhouse Youtheatre, the Webster Junior High Breakdancers, the John Glenn High School Touring Theatre, bagpipist Ron Murray, the Trinity Dance Ensemble, Clabe Hangan and Music Americana, the Univ. of Calif. Riverside Folk Dance Club, the Sweet Adelines of San Bernardino, the Sunshine Generations, the Butterfield Country Cloggers, clown Kelly Duro, juggler Joe Dunham, the Cloverleafs, and the Highlanders.

15 APR. 1985. CSU Trustee Lee Grissom visits the campus.

16 APR. 1985. Seismologist Clarence Allen speaks in RH on "San Bernardino's Earthquake Problem—Where Lies the Fault."

18 APR. 1985. Howard Wilkinson, Dir. of Corporate Affairs for Calif. Steel Industries, speaks in LC. Frank Rodríguez speaks in SU on "Recruiting Hispanics for the Corporate World."

19 APR. 1985. Therapist Richard A. Gardner speaks in RH on "Helping Families in Stress: Coping with Divorce." The campus receives a $5,000 gift from the Western Assoc. of Food Chains to sponsor scholarships for business students.

23 APR. 1985. Pat Michaels, owner of radio station KQLH, speaks in PL-241 on his experiences in communication. Holocaust survivor Elane Geller speaks in RH.

25 APR. 1985. Christopher Knight speaks in VA-110 on "The Role of the Critic and the Critical Response as It Relates to Contemporary Art."

26 APR. 1985. The Pfau Library receives a collection of 95 antiquarian books from noted L.A. dealer, Charles Salzman, including a leaf from a 1611 edition of the *King James Bible*, and a signed edition of Ray Bradbury's *Fahrenheit 451*. Cal State adopts Cajon High School as a partner in its teacher training efforts. The campus hosts a "Robot Olympics" as part of its annual Microtechnology for Everybody Festival.

27 APR. 1985. The campus hosts a Conference on Adoption in LC.

28 APR. 1985. Bands White Flag, Kushite Raiders, and The Sins perform in SUMP.

1 MAY 1985. The Special M.A. Degree in National Security Studies is honored with a federal award for excellence at the annual meeting of the Federal Executive Board/College Federation Council. The Almont Ensemble performs in RH.

3 MAY 1985. Arthur I. Saltzman receives a $17,317 grant from the S.B. Associated Governments to conduct a transit terminal study.

6 MAY 1985. Mexican guitarist Miguel Alcazar performs in RH.

7 MAY 1985. Pharmacologist Weldon B. Jolley speaks to the Accounting Assoc. in LC.

9 MAY 1985. Alumni pianist Michael Tacchia and cellist Michele Brosseau-Tacchia perform in RH.

10 MAY 1985. B. Jill Buroker receives $27,500 from the National Endowment for the Humanities to study in France in 1985/86.

12 MAY 1985. The Inland Empire Youth Symphony performs in RH.

16 MAY 1985. Nursing educator Carol A. Lindeman speaks in RH on "Conception for the Future." Nicaraguan musical group Grupo Pancasán performs on the SUP.

17 MAY 1985. Assemblyman Steve Clute visits the campus. Roberta Stathis-Ochoa is named a CSU Administrative Fellow for 1985/86.

19 May 1985. Mezzo soprano Faye Coates and bass baritone Wayne Shepperd perform in RH.

20 May 1985. The Administrative Council approves the addition of Greek fraternal organizations to the student social life program. The move is prompted by the informal establishment of a local chapter of Delta Sigma Phi (ΔΣΦ), which is soon followed by Sigma Chi Omicron (ΣΧΟ), Alpha Phi (ΑΦ), Phi Beta Sigma (ΦΒΣ), and Kappa Alpha Psi (ΚΑΨ).

23 May 1985. CSU Trustee Dale B. Ride visits the campus.

24 May 1985. The Activities Off. drafts guidelines to govern the recognition and activities of the first fraternities and sororities on campus. The campus receives a $200,000 grant from the U.S. Dept. of Education to fund the Upward Bound Program during 1985/86.

25 May 1985. Olympic medalist Alice Brown speaks in SU at the annual Upward Bound Banquet.

29 May 1985. Jim Beckman speaks in SU on "Careers in Business Economics." CSU Dir. of Analytical Studies William J. Mason visits the campus. CSUSB submits a proposal to the Chancellor's Office to establish a satellite campus at the Coll. of the Desert, with new funding of $500,000.

30 May 1985. Women's rights activist and attorney Gloria Allred speaks in RH on "Civil Rights, Gay Rights, and Social Change."

1 May 1985. John McNay is named the first Outstanding Student at CSUSB for 1984/85; presentation of the award takes place during Commencement on Jun. 15. Rep. George E. Brown and Meg Crahan speak at a panel on Central America in PS-10.

1 Jun. 1985. The Inland Master Chorale performs in UC.

3 Jun. 1985. Evlyn Wilcox takes office as S.B. Mayor, replacing W. R. "Bob" Holcomb.

5 Jun. 1985. The new Fitness Court is dedicated east of the Gymnasium between the swimming pool and the tennis court complex.

6 Jun. 1985. Pres. Evans sends a letter to CSU Chancellor Reynolds expressing his reservations over proposed reforms in Cal State admission standards, which he feels would limit minority student attendance.

7 Jun. 1985. Theodore R. McDowell receives a $17,468 grant from NSF for his project, "Instructional Instrumentation for Geography and Environmental Studies." Russell J. Barber receives a $5,846 grant from NSF for "Instructional Instrumentation for Archaeology in the Field and Laboratory." The campus holds its 1st Joe Thomas Invitational Golf Tournament at Shandin Hills Golf Course, in honor of Joseph K. Thomas, retired VP for Administration. The original dramas *Perspectives* by CSUSB student Valerie Smith and *A Day in the Life of America* by the Touring Theatre Group are performed in the Theatre.

9 JUN. 1985. Writer Ray Bradbury speaks in RH to inaugurate the Library Associates, a Pfau Library booster group.

11 JUN. 1985. Carolyn B. Rodríguez is elected the 1st Pres. of the Assoc. of Hispanic Faculty and Staff at CSUSB.

12 JUN. 1985. Carlos Márquez speaks in LC on "Career Enhancement."

14 JUN. 1985. Cal State Computer Science graduate student Kenneth Louis Miller dies in Redlands at age 36.

15 JUN. 1985. The 19th Commencement is held on the Library Lawn, with actress Carmen Zapata giving the keynote address.

18 JUN. 1985. The *San Bernardino Sun* states that "The university area is beginning to reflect a sardine-can style of planning, rather than anything approaching elegance or grace."

21 JUN. 1985. The campus receives a $37,000 grant from the Chancellor's Off. to help retrain 3 faculty members to teach courses in computer science.

27 JUN. 1985. The Pfau Library receives a gift of a run of *El Chicano* newspaper from Publisher Gloria Macías Harrison and her sister, Marta Macías McQueen (later Brown), at a reception held in PL.

28 JUN. 1985. Ballet Folklórico de San Bernardino performs in RH.

30 JUN. 1985. Wendy A. Pederson, Employee Relations Specialist, resigns.

SUM. 1985. Retirements: Nathan C. Kravetz, Prof. of Education (1976-85); Mary G. Patterson, Prof. of Nursing (1977-85).

12 JUL. 1985. Judith M. Rymer, Act. Exec. Dean for Univ. Relations, is named permanent Exec. Dean for Univ. Relations. The campus receives a $95,588 grant from the Chancellor's Off. to fund the Summer Transition and Enrichment Program (STEP).

14 JUL. 1985. The 84th Annual Dog Show of the Orange Empire Dog Club is held on the Library Lawn.

15 JUL. 1985. Frances L. Stromwall, Library Asst. (1968-85), retires.

18 JUL. 1985. Clabe Hangan and Music Americana perform on LCP.

18-20 JUL. 1985. A new play by William L. Slout, *The Burial of Alma*, debuts in RH, with Slout and his wife, actress Marte Boyle Slout, appearing in the starring roles.

21 JUL. 1985. Opera tenor William Olvis performs in RH.

22 JUL. 1985. Stephen Menzel Jr. is named Employee Relations Specialist, replacing Wendy A. Pederson.

26 JUL. 1985. The Student Assistant in Learning Program (SAIL) receives a $136,514 grant from the U.S. Dept. of Education to fund its operations for another year.

5 AUG. 1985. Cal State Education graduate student Leanna Ashley dies at Loma Linda at age 23.

8 AUG. 1985. Composer/singer Lalo Guerrero performs on LCP.

9 AUG. 1985. The Bilingual Education Training for Advancement (BETA) Center receives a $284,520 grant from the U.S. Dept. of Education to fund the program for another year. Joanna Roche is named Dir. of Alumni Affairs, replacing Richard J. Bennecke, who is named a financial aid advisor.

20-23 AUG. 1985. The campus hosts its "Teachers Are No. 1" Conference, with speakers Art Costa, Virginia Tooper, John Alston, and Tom Champoux.

23 AUG. 1985. The Civic Education Enhancement Project (CEEP) receives a $108,135 grant from the U.S. Dept. of Education to enhance the teaching of law-related education.

31 AUG. 1985. Ward M. McAfee, Act. VP for Academic Affairs, returns to the ranks as Prof. of History.

__ AUG. 1985. Pres. Evans appoints a Sexual Harassment Task Group under the chairmanship of Dale T. West to develop policies and to handle complaints; members include Pat Evertsen, Diane F. Halpern, Martha P. Kazlo, Gail Leininger, Stephen Menzel, J. Cordell Robinson, Judith M. Rymer, Linda L. Snyder, Lynda W. Warren, and Peter A. Wilson.

1 SEPT. 1985. Robert C. Detweiler is named VP for Academic Affairs, replacing Ward M. McAfee. Stella T. Clark, Act. Dean of the School of Humanities, is named Int. Dean. The Dept. of Physical Education and Recreation is renamed the Dept. of Physical Education. Parking fees increase from $5 to $7.50 per month.

3 SEPT. 1985. The new Academic Advising Center opens for business on the first floor of the Pfau Library.

6 SEPT. 1985. Individual dining and meeting areas in the Commons are renamed to make them more identifiable, with the President's Dining Room becoming the Oak Room, the New Dining Room the Eucalyptus Room, Room C-104 the Panorama Room, Room C-125 the Pine Room, and Room C-219 the Alder Room. Part of the external Plaza area of the lower level of the Commons is enclosed to form the new Sycamore Room.

9 SEPT. 1985. 5 new trailers housing faculty offices open between the Student Services Building and the Children's Center.

20 SEPT. 1985. All University outreach efforts are centralized under the Enrollment Services Dept. The campus receives a $23,000 grant from the Chancellor's Off. to add ethnic and women's studies to the curriculum. Marian Talley is named Dir. of the Learning Center, replacing Jean Peacock, who resumes being Dir. of the SAIL Program.

27 SEPT. 1985. The Affirmative Action Advisory Committee recommends that Pres. Evans create mentoring programs for the faculty, courses and workshops for employees, and a jobs data bank.

2 OCT. 1985. An earthquake measuring 4.9 on the Richter scale strikes Redlands, causing 5 times more movement than predicted on the 5th floor of the Pfau Library; this ultimately leads to replacement of the Library glass windows with unbreakable plastic, the strengthening of book shelves throughout the building, and the 1996-98 Seismic Retrofitting Project.

3 OCT. 1985. *The Black Voice* newspaper alleges that CSUSB has made insufficient efforts to recruit minority administrators, faculty, and students; Pres. Evans responds on Oct. 17. Cal State Administration student David Frank Montano dies at age 23 in S.B.

4 OCT. 1985. Alumnus Richard J. Bennecke, a graduate of CSUSB's first class of 1967, and first Student Activities Advisor, first Dir. of the Student Union, Dir. of Alumni Affairs, and Financial Aid Advisor (1967-85), resigns to join the staff of S.B. Mayor Wilcox. Retirements: Salvatore Bruno, Painter; William Harrigan, Custodian.

10 OCT. 1985. Actor George Plimpton speaks in SUMP on "An Amateur Among the Pros."

11 OCT. 1985. The BETA Center and Upward Bound relocate to new trailers behind the Student Services Building.

16 OCT. 1985. M. Jeanne Hogenson organizes the "Greek Council" to help establish fraternities and sororities on campus.

20 OCT. 1985. In a special supplement issued to commemorate the 20th anniversary of CSUSB, *San Bernardino Sun* writer Alan Mittelstaedt reviews Pres. Evans's 3-year tenure on campus, and notes some criticism of his management style, while also praising him for the changes that he has instituted in managing enrollment, instituting an athletics program, and increasing growth.

23 OCT. 1985. Printmaker Garner Tullis speaks about his work in VA-110.

24 OCT. 1985. The campus holds its annual convocation in the Gymnasium to mark the 20th anniversary of the opening of CSUSB, with CSU Chancellor Reynolds; CSU Trustees Chair Roy T. Brophy; CSU Trustees Wallace Albertson, Robert D. Kully, and Marianthi Lansdale; Pres. Evans; and Calif. Assemblyman Gerald Eaves among the 600 attendees. The Chancellor commends the university for its 20 years of service, and its ongoing efforts to become a "regional university. With an outward vision focusing on the future of your great institution, you—the academic community of faculty, staff, students, and alumni—have involved the great community in recasting the university as a servant of the cultural and educational needs of your regional service area." S.B. Mayor Wilcox proclaims Oct. 24 "Cal State Day."

28 OCT. 1985. Rep. George E. Brown speaks in ER on "New Technology, New Jobs, and New Educational Needs."

30 OCT. 1985. Dr. Jack Provonsha of the Center for Bioethics speaks in ER to a panel on "Bioethics and Human Experimentation." This is one of the first events sponsored by The Intellectual Life Committee, formerly the Lecturers and Artists Committee.

31 OCT. 1985. "A Little Light Reading," a horror story by Michael Burgess set in the Pfau Library, is published in the *San Bernardino Sun*, creating an urban legend that the building is haunted; a decade later, an English class signs a petition protesting the "fact" that the Library was built over an old Indian burial ground—it wasn't!

3 NOV. 1985. The S.B. Music Teachers Assoc. performs in RH.

5 Nov. 1985. Wilma M. Hanson, Library Asst. (1970-85), retires.

7 Nov. 1985. Robert Hastings speaks in RH on "UFOs—the Hidden History." Singer Mark Levy performs on the SUP.

12 Nov. 1985. In cooperation with several local Chambers of Commerce and corporate leaders, the campus launches a community Leadership and Development (LEAD) Program designed to stimulate civic involvement in the S.B. Valley, partly funded by a $5,000 grant from the *San Bernardino Sun*. Edna Bonacich speaks in ER to a panel on "South Africa: Country in Crisis."

13 Nov. 1985. The CSU Board of Trustees adopts new system-wide admission standards for Cal State students, and also seeks permission to offer an independent doctoral degree in Education. The motto on the CSU System seal is changed from "Vir, Veritas, Vox" to "Vox, Veritas, Vita." Criminologist Rita J. Simon speaks in ER on "The Defense of Insanity."

14 Nov. 1985. Margaret Szczepaniak speaks in ER on "The Comparable Worth of Women's Wages."

15 Nov. 1985. The campus receives grants of $2,000 and $5,000 from the S.B. Fine Arts Commission to exhibit Mexican and Indian folk costumes, and to stage a Theatre Festival for Young Audiences. Darleen K. Stoner and Renate M. Nummela receive a $4,200 grant from the State Dept. of Education.

18 Nov. 1985. Lee Gagnon speaks in SU on "Starting Your Own Business."

21 Nov. 1985. Conservative TV talk-show host Wally George speaks in SUMP. CSU Trustee Claudia Hampton visits the campus.

22 Nov. 1985. The Council of Academic Deans approves the creation of a Faculty Computer Users Committee to assess the computing needs of the campus faculty.

4 Dec. 1985. NBC executive Kenneth Raskoff peaks in CA-143 on "Careers in Television and Theater."

6 Dec. 1985. Andrew Schultz receives a $75,000 grant from the State Dept. of Consumer Affairs to evaluate the training program for emissions mechanics.

12 Dec. 1985. Li Kaiyun speaks in ER on "Principles of Enterprise Management in China."

13 DEC. 1985. Diane F. Halpern is named Outstanding Professor for 1984/85. The Council of Academic Deans approves plans for staffing off-campus programs.

15 DEC. 1985. Cal State student Joseph John Newman dies in S.B. at age 28.

16 DEC. 1985. The creation of the CSUSB Coachella Valley Center is approved by the Calif. Postsecondary Education Commission to open in Fall 1986, depending on the allocation of funds.

1986

10 JAN. 1986. The Data Gathering Center receives a $50,000 contract from the Redevelopment Agency of S.B. to develop a marketing strategy for the City's Enterprise Zone. The Dept. of Marketing and Management Science is renamed the Dept. of Marketing, Management Science, and Information Management. The campus forms a new Toastmasters Club.

13 JAN. 1986. Gov. Deukmejian's proposed 1986/87 state budget includes $350,000 to develop a satellite campus, the Coachella Valley Center (CVC), temporarily sited at the Coll. of the Desert, but later to have its own permanent location in the Palm Desert area.

15 JAN. 1986. The campus announces that it will debut its first intercollegiate baseball and softball teams in Spring 1987. Alumna Lois J. Carson speaks in PR on "The Life and Contributions of Dr. Martin Luther King."

16 JAN. 1986. Rudolph Schafer speaks in PR on "Environmental Education: For People or for the Birds?"

21 JAN. 1986. Jazz trumpeter Maynard Ferguson performs in RH. CSU Trustee Tom Stickel visits the campus.

23 JAN. 1986. Violinist John Golz and pianist Lily Pan-Diehl perform in RH.

24 JAN. 1986. The campus receives a $40,000 grant from the Chancellor's Off. to pave a 250-space dirt lot south of the tennis courts.

27 JAN. 1986. Bank of America VP Judy Maudsley speaks in SU on "Banking Relationships—What Your Bank Can Do for You." Mohamed Bakr speaks in ER on "The Solar Boat of King Cheops."

30 Jan. 1986. State Sen. Gary K. Hart speaks in PS-10 on "Educational Reform."

1 Feb. 1986. Tom M. Rivera is named Hispanic "Educator of the Year" by *Caminos* magazine in a ceremony held at the Bonaventure Hotel in L.A., with Lt. Gov. Leo McCarthy presenting the award.

7 Feb. 1986. The campus hosts a conference on special education, "Bridging for Success," with a keynote address by Lou Brown; the nearly 800 attendees set a new campus record for such events. 1985 CSU Outstanding Professor Reba Soffer speaks in SU on "English Universities from 1850-1930."

14 Feb. 1986. The campus receives a $990,381 grant (the largest to date) from the State Board of Education to establish a Summer Technology Training Institute for teachers.

14-15 Feb. 1986. The campus hosts its first Homecoming Weekend.

16 Feb. 1986. The gospel group Daz Patterson and the West Coast Singers performs in RH, and releases a record album, *Shout for Jesus—Recorded Live at Cal State*. William R. Coleman, Chair of the Library Associates, speaks in the PL on his collection of American presidential memorabilia.

17 Feb. 1986. Robert Pollin speaks in ER on "Changes in the Financial Section of the Economy Over the Past Decade."

20 Feb. 1986. The campus dedicates the PAL Center in San Bernardino, with S.B. Mayor Wilcox, Assemblyman Gerald Eaves, Rev. Elvin Ricks, and Pres. Evans attending.

21 Feb. 1986. The campus receives a $10,000 grant from the Economic Literacy Council of Calif. to improve economics instruction. CSU Trustee Thomas Bernard visits the campus.

24 Feb. 1986. The Early Music Academy performs in RH.

26 Feb. 1986. The campus hosts a Computer Fair in ER. William A. Cohen speaks in SUMP on "Making a Million in Mail Order."

27 Feb. 1986. The campus hosts a panel on "The Civil Rights Movement from a Black Perspective," with speakers SB City employee Anne Rhodes, Maurice Roberson, Alonza Thompson, and Rev. LeMar Foster.

28 Feb. 1986. The campus receives $202,571 in state lottery funds.

1 MAR. 1986. The campus hosts its 10th Annual Reading Conference, "Literacy in the Home," with keynote speaker Ralph Peterson.

4 MAR. 1986. S.B. Mayor Wilcox speaks in SUMP on "Women Supporting Women." Pres. Evans forms a Commission on the Status of Women, with 13 women elected to represent faculty, staff, management, students, and alumni. The minimum construction bid for the Faculty Office Building is 37% over budget; the contract will have to be rebid.

5 MAR. 1986. Shauna Clark speaks in SUMP on "Women in Local Government." David Richards Construction receives a $54,212 contract to construct a broadcast radio station booth in CA-187, using the call letters KSSB. Arthur Winer speaks in PS-10 on "How Toxic Is Our Air? Formation, Fate, and Impacts of Airborne Toxic Chemicals." Organist Carl Bertram Swanson performs in RH.

6 MAR. 1986. Wilmer D. Carter speaks in SUMP on "Is the Voucher Plan a Viable Tool for Our Children's Education?" Ex-Rep. Shirley Chisholm speaks in SUMP on "Black Perspectives from the Past for the Future," with S.B. Mayor Wilcox present.

7 MAR. 1986. Susan Reddy Butler speaks in SUMP on "A Look at the History of Women and Education."

8 MAR. 1986. The campus and the S.B. Commission on the Status of Women co-sponsor the conference, "Women: Buildings of Communities and Dreams," in the Commons.

10 MAR. 1986. Hollywood talent agent Claire Hiam speaks in CA-143 on "Casting for Commercials."

11 MAR. 1986. Diane F. Halpern is named 1 of 2 Outstanding Professors in the CSU System, receiving a cash award of $1,000.

19-20 MAR. 1986. The campus hosts the largest band and orchestra festival in Southern California, with over 2,000 participants from local schools. The campus hosts a conference on "Relieving African Famine," with Saaed Sumum giving the keynote address in LC, and TV reporter Miriam Hernández speaking later that day on "Logistics Lessons Learned from the Mexican Disaster Response."

28 MAR. 1986. The Intramurals Program is renamed the Recreational Sports Program, and is placed under the Student Services Div.

2 APR. 1986. Organist Malcolm Benson performs in RH.

10 APR. 1986. Ray Frauenholz of the Jet Propulsion Laboratory speaks in SUMP on "The Mysteries of Halley's Comet."

11 APR. 1986. Fred E. Jandt receives a $40,000 grant from the Calif. Dept. of Transportation to develop a motivational training program for mid-level managers. Cecil Holden Patterson is named the University's first Distinguishing Visiting Professor.

12-13 APR. 1986. The campus hosts the 12th annual Theatre Festival for Young Audiences, with 30 professional and semi-professional theatre companies, and 2,500 local school children attending.

15 APR. 1986. David P. DeMauro is named Dir. of Plant Operations, replacing James H. Urata, who goes on leave pending retirement.

17 APR. 1986. Roma Sill, Extended Education (1967-86), retires. The campus holds a reception in PR to honor Diane F. Halpern, one of CSU's Outstanding Professors of the Year. The campus receives approval to offer an M.A. degree in Health Care Administration, beginning Fall 1986.

18 APR. 1986. The Coachella Valley Community Coll. Dist. Board of Trustees approves an agreement to allow CSUSB to house temporary facilities for CVC on the Coll. of the Desert campus from July 1, 1986-June 30, 1991.

20 APR. 1986. TV newscaster Kelly Lange speaks in UC on "The TV Connection."

21 APR. 1986. Edward W. Harrison is named Police Services Manager with the rank of Lt.

22 APR. 1986. The campus holds a forum on Environmental Education, with participants Rhonda Reed, Don Hanson, and Lola Hanson.

24 APR. 1986. D. Z. Phillips speaks in LC-241 on "'Thou Shalt'—'What If I Don't?' Pirandello's *The Rules of the Game* and Beckett's *Waiting for Godot*."

25 APR. 1986. The campus hosts its 3rd annual Robot Olympics in the Gymnasium, with 2,000 students attending. The Faculty Senate Ad Hoc Committee on Preservation of Small Classes recommends the retention of small classes and the quarter system at CSUSB.

28 APR. 1986. Alumnus Jaga Nath Glassman speaks in ER on "Courses of Depression—Nature or Nurture? Modern Endocrinology in Psychiatric Disorders."

2 MAY 1986. TV weatherman Maclovio Pérez speaks on LCP on "Hispanics in the Media," as part of the Cinco de Mayo celebration, with Consul de México Emerenciano Rodríguez also speaking. Musical groups Mariachi Tequila and The Latin Society, and dancers Ballet Folklórico Mixcoacalli perform.

2-3 MAY 1986. The Southern Calif. Academy of Natural Sciences holds its annual meeting on campus.

8 MAY 1986. Comedians Marsha Warfield, Howie Gold, and Paul Provenza perform in a "Comedy Cabaret" in SUMP. Judge Carol Koppel speaks in SU on "Improving Civic Education: A View from the Bench."

9 MAY 1986. Susan and Thomas M. Meisenhelder receive Fulbright Fellowships to teach at the Univ. of Botswana during 1986/87.

10 MAY 1986. The campus hosts its 2nd Annual Conference for the Advancement of Mathematics Teaching, with V. Merriline Smith giving the keynote speech.

13-14 MAY 1986. Cal State students vote to increase their fees from $41-$70 annually to finance an addition to the Student Union, and from $20-$36 to provide more operating funds for the ASI.

14 & 21 MAY 1986. The Almont Ensemble and Anthony Lupica perform in RH.

15 MAY 1986. Stephen F. Morin speaks in SUMP on "Psychology and Public Policy," and also in RH on "Responding to the Psychological Crisis of AIDS." Nathaniel Davis, Fred Warner Neal, and Mohammed Al-Saadi speak in SUMP.

16 MAY 1986. The campus honors James H. Urata with a retirement dinner in the Commons.

18 MAY 1986. Magician Harry Blackstone Jr. speaks in RH on "The Awe-Inspiring Art of Illusion."

23 MAY 1986. Political activist Angela Davis speaks in RH on "At Home and Abroad: The Struggle for Peace," and conducts a Cross-Cultural Perspectives Workshop on May 24. Quentin J. Moses is named a CSU Administrative Fellow for 1986/87. Museum curator Charles Millard III speaks in VA-110 on "The Origins of Modern Sculpture." Ellen L. Kronowitz receives a Fulbright summer fellowship to study at the Japan Institute for Social and Economic Affairs. The campus implements a Computer Assisted Registration System (CARS) for students, based on the recommendation of the Task Force on Early Registration.

29 MAY 1986. Nielsen Construction Co. receives a $2,063,564 contract to construct the Faculty Office Building. Poet Sherod Santos reads from his work in RH.

31 MAY 1986. The gospel group Loveland Mass Choir of Fontana performs in RH.

1 JUN. 1986. James H. Urata, Dir. of Plant Operations and Dir. of Administrative Affairs (1963-86), retires.

4 JUN. 1986. Pres. Evans approves a Faculty Senate recommendation to discontinue the Ruml Plan, which since the beginning of the campus has awarded 5 credit units for 4 hours of class instruction. The conversion will take 2 years to implement.

6 JUN. 1986. Assemblyman Gerald Eaves visits the campus. The Learning Center receives a $10,000 grant from Anheuser-Busch to fund a developmental outreach program. Pres. Evans appoints a committee to draft a campus Educational Equity Plan.

12 JUN. 1986. Marjory Gordon speaks in RH on "Recent Developments in Nursing Diagnosis."

14 JUN. 1986. The 20th Commencement is held on the Library Lawn, with CSU Board of Trustees Chair Dale B. Ride giving the keynote address; some 1,170 students are eligible to receive degrees.

27 JUN. 1986. Assemblyman William R. "Bill" Leonard visits the campus. The Public Affairs Off. is split into two offices, with Edna L. Steinman, Dir. of Public Affairs, being named Dir. of Publications, Cynthia E. "Cindi" Pringle as Dir. of Media Relations and Public Information.

28 JUN. 1986. Cal State student John Raymond Heinz is shot and murdered by two of his roommates at age 20; his body is found on Aug. 2 in a shallow grave north of the campus.

30 JUN. 1986. H. Arthur "Hal" Hoverland, Dean of the School of Business and Public Administration (1972-86), returns to the ranks as Prof. of Accounting and Finance. Gladys Wilson, Switchboard Operator (1965-86), retires. Pres. Evans sends a letter to CSU Chancellor Reynolds discussing educational equity in the Inland Empire and at CSUSB (see Sept. 18).

1 JUL. 1986. William F. "Bill" Shum is named Dir. of Facility Planning and Policy Coordination, partially replacing James H. Urata.

3 JUL. 1986. John Edmond Fredricks, the campus's first Accounting Officer (1965-72), dies at Yountville, Calif. at age 67.

4 JUL. 1986. The campus begins offering a free annual Summer Concert Series, with the S.B. Community Concert Band giving the first performance on LCP. Catherine C. Gannon, soon-to-be-named Dir. of CVC, begins registering students at the Coll. of the Desert for the Fall 1986 term.

11 JUL. 1986. Groundbreaking is held for the $2,100,000, 30,800 sq. ft. Faculty Office Building, with Assemblyman William R. "Bill" Leonard and S.B. City Councilman Gordon Quiel participating.

15 JUL. 1986. Catherine C. Gannon is named first Dir. of CVC at the Coll. of the Desert.

16 JUL. 1986. Folk guitarist Sam Hinton performs on LCP.

24 JUL. 1986. Students working under the supervision of Prof. Russell Barber uncover the foundations of Fairview School, a one-room schoolhouse that existed near Badger Hill between 1887-91.

25 JUL. 1986. Reyes E. Ríos, Groundsworker, receives the Governor's Safety Award for his "outstanding efforts in employee safety."

30 JUL. 1986. Paraguayan harpist Alfredo Rolando Ortiz performs in RH.

31 JUL. 1986. Pamela D. Langford is named Dir. of Community Relations and Development.

1 AUG. 1986. David O. Porter is named Dean of the School of Business and Public Administration, replacing H. Arthur "Hal" Hoverland. M. Jeanne Hogenson, Dir. of Student Activities, is named Coordinator of International Student Programs. The Student Activities Off. is renamed the Off. of Student Life.

6 AUG. 1986. Flautist Jerrold Pritchard and guitarist Anthony Lupica perform on LCP.

8 AUG. 1986. The campus receives a $209,899 grant from the U.S. Dept. of Education to fund the Upward Bound Program, $118,812 from the U.S. Dept. of Education to fund the Law-Related Education Program, $130,643 from the U.S. Dept. of Education to fund the SAIL Program, $83,806 from the State Dept. of Education to fund 80% of the Children's Center budget for 1986/87, and $4,860 from the U.S. Agency for International Development to support a visiting scholar from Zagazig Univ. Darleen K. Stoner receives a $12,000 grant from the State Dept. of Education to fund an Environmental Education Materials Center.

13 AUG. 1986. Bluegrass group Phil Salazar Band performs on LCP.

17 AUG. 1986. Doris Marie Scott Allender, retired Secretary in Activities and Housing (1967-78), dies in Cherry Valley at age 69.

19-22 AUG. 1986. The campus hosts its 2nd Annual "Teachers Are #1" Conference, with Harry Wong, George McKenna III, Jo Stanchfield, and Roger Crawford giving the keynote addresses.

22 AUG. 1986. The Chancellor's Off. approves a B.S. degree in Foods and Nutrition, the 50th campus degree program, to be offered in 1986/87.

27 AUG. 1986. Folk guitarist Lalo Guerrero performs on LCP.

31 AUG. 1986. Stella T. Clark, Int. Dean of the School of Humanities, returns to the ranks as Prof. of Spanish. David J. Lutz, Assoc. Dean for Graduate Studies, returns to the ranks as Prof. of Psychology.

1 SEPT. 1986. Beverly L. Hendricks is named Dean of the School of Humanities, replacing Stella T. Clark. Julius D. Kaplan is named Assoc. Dean for Graduate Studies, replacing David J. Lutz. A temporary administration building for the new CVC opens on the Coll. of the Desert Campus in Palm Desert, and the campus begins offering regular classes there for the first time for 200 students; the campus begins beaming its first 3 Instructional Television Fixed Service (ITFS) courses to CVC, although problems with the service force further transmissions to be postponed until 1987/88. Diane F. Halpern, Assoc. Dean for Undergraduate Studies, is named Int. Dean for Undergraduate Studies. James J. Scanlon is named the first Dir. of Computing and Information Management Services.

4 SEPT. 1986. The Board of Directors of the CSUSB Foundation votes to divest itself of more than $500,000 in investments in companies doing business in South Africa, effective Oct. 1.

6 SEPT. 1986. Linda Long Riley, English Instructor in the Upward Bound Program (1983-86), dies at age 38.

15 SEPT. 1986. The annual convocation is held in RH.

18 SEPT. 1986. *The Black Voice News* prints the leaked text of a Jun. 30, 1986 private letter sent by Pres. Evans to Chancellor Reynolds (reprinted by *The Coyote Chronicle* on Oct. 15), in which he states that: "I am not sure just how many underrepresented students are ready, emotionally and intellectually, for a university experience. In short there are natural impediments over which we educators have limited control." These comments form the basis of later allegations by some African-Americans that Pres. Evans was a racist.

26 SEPT. 1986. The Chancellor's Off. approves an M.A. Degree in National Security Studies, the campus's 10th master's program, effective 1986/87; and also awards the campus a $67,152 budget supplement to help fund the Student Affirmative Action Program.

2 OCT. 1986. L.A. art dealer Garth Clark speaks in the Art Gallery.

6 OCT. 1986. Ex-White House aide G. Gordon Liddy and Hatem Hussaini, ex-head of the Palestine Liberation Organization Information Off. in Washington, DC, speak before a forum in UC on "Is One Man's Terrorist Another Man's Freedom Fighter?"

7 OCT. 1986. The Berkeley Shakespeare Festival performs the play, *The Tempest*, in RH.

10 OCT. 1986. The BETA Center receives 2 grants of $375,178 from Title VII funds to train bilingual teacher aides. The campus receives a 4th annual $5,000 grant from the Western Assoc. of Food Chains to fund 5 $1,000 scholarships for business students. R. James Charkins receives a $1,500 grant from the Economics Literacy Council of Calif. to support the Inland Empire Economics Project.

13 OCT. 1986. Leonard B. Farwell, Business Manager, is named VP for Administration and Finance, replacing James H. Urata.

16 OCT. 1986. The campus holds a forum to discuss alleged racially-biased incidents on campus.

23 OCT. 1986. Comedians Joe Alaskey, Paul Clay, and Andrea Carla Michaels perform in SUMP.

24 OCT. 1986. The Little Theatre of the Deaf performs in RH.

27 OCT. 1986. 5 new faculty office trailers are occupied north of the Student Services Building.

3 NOV. 1986. Don Walsh speaks in BI-22 on oceanography.

7 NOV. 1986. The new campus radio station, KSSB, begins broadcasting via Chambers Cable Co. at 106.3 megahertz on the FM band. On campus, the signal can be heard in SU, Serrano Village, and Audiovisual Services.

7-8 NOV. 1986. The Los Angeles Piano Quartet performs in RH.

13 NOV. 1986. U.S. Sen. William Proxmire speaks in RH on "The Coming Crisis: America's Troubled Economy".

24 NOV. 1986. Rep. C. Jerry Lewis speaks during a forum in PR.

29 NOV. 1986. Cal State Biology student Lynne Scott Schwab dies at age 21.

1 DEC. 1986. Velma Pollard speaks in SR on "Language and Identity: The Case of the Rastafarians of Jamaica."

2 DEC. 1986. Poet Robert Pinsky reads from his work in PR.

5 DEC. 1986. The Dept. of Special Programs in the School of Education is renamed the Dept. of Graduate Programs in Education. Josephine Mendoza receives a $40,000 grant from Prime Computer, Inc., to install ORACLE on the University's Prime Supermind computer.

12 DEC. 1986. Pat I. Stumpf, Head of the Payroll Off. (1971-86), retires.

19 DEC. 1986. Alice Coble, Head of Operations, Computer Center (1969-86), retires.

24 DEC. 1986. Robert F. "Bob" Lohnes, Asst. Dir. of Plant Operations (1967-86), retires.

25 DEC. 1986-4 JAN. 1987. To save energy, the campus for the first time closes for an entire week between Christmas and New Year's, bunching minor holidays together to create an extended break.

29 DEC. 1986. Cal State student Patrick Vernon Calvert dies at age 33.

1987

3 JAN. 1987. Peggy Janet Geane, retired Pharmacist in the Student Health Center (1979-86), dies in San Bernardino at age 50.

9 JAN. 1987. Margaret A. "Peggy" Atwell is named Outstanding Professor for 1986/87. Keith Johnson is named Assoc. Dean of Extended Education. Janice Ropp "Jan" Jackson is named Asst. Dean of Extended Education.

15 JAN. 1987. To celebrate Martin Luther King Jr.'s birthday, the campus hosts a gospel music group, Another Peace, with a keynote address by Frank Wilson, "I Need a Friend."

16 JAN. 1987. TV sports commentator Cheryl Miller conducts a basketball clinic in the Gymnasium.

20 JAN. 1987. Randy P. Harrell is named first Dir. of Student Life.

23 JAN. 1987. The Elementary Summer Technology Institute receives a $998,224 grant from the State Dept. of Education to continue its program for a 2nd year. Robert E. Cramer receives a $10,000 grant from Southern California Edison Co. to study Edison's program for customer service. A broken pipe floods part of the SU.

24 JAN. 1987. Campus radio station KSSB covers its first live sports event, the women's basketball game against UC San Diego in the Gymnasium. The campus hosts its Annual Black Family Conference, "Black Family United," in SU and Commons, with a keynote speech by Marian Talley.

27 JAN. 1987. Pianist Sergei Edelmann performs in RH.

30 JAN. 1987. Margaret Johnstone "Peggy" Lenz, Prof. of Education (1970-87), Pres. of the S.B. YWCA (1974-78), and member of the national YWCA Board of Directors (1979-87), dies in Tustin of a heart attack at age 57.

2 FEB. 1987. Maher el-Shinnawi speaks on "Soil and the Environment."

5-6 FEB. 1987. The campus hosts a conference, "Bridging for Success," with keynote speakers Lou Brown, Jeff Strully, and Wayne Sailor.

6 FEB. 1987. The campus requires students to obtain measles and rubella immunizations before registration.

12 FEB. 1987. Nobel Peace Prize winner Betty Williams speaks in RH on "World Peace Is Everyone's Business."

14 FEB. 1987. TV anchorman Larry Carroll speaks in RH on "Black Present, Black Future."

15 FEB. 1987. Soul groups X-pression and Divine Intervention perform in RH.

19 FEB. 1987. Comedians Howie Gold, Tim Jones, and Steven Greenstein perform in UC. William McClung speaks in VA-104 on "Imaging L.A." Sculptor Lilla Locurto and William Outcault speak in VA-110 on "Contemporary Bronze."

23 FEB. 1987. Artist Don Bachardy speaks about his work in VA-110.

Lynn Nadel speaks in SR on "New Discoveries About the Physiology of the Mind and Learning."

24 FEB. 1987. Rita J. Simon speaks in SR on "Comparative Patterns of Women in Crime."

25 FEB. 1987. A rare snowfall briefly covers the campus.

26 FEB. 1987. Atheist Gordon Stein and Catholic priest Rev. Michael Sweeney debate "Evolution vs. Creation: Does God Exist?" in SUMP.

27 FEB. 1987. Ex-Georgia State Sen. Julian Bond speaks in UC on "Echoes from the Past: Etching the Future."

28 FEB. 1987. The Preucil Family Players perform in RH.

3 MAR. 1987. Rep. Bella Abzug speaks in UC on "Political Power for American Women."

4 MAR. 1987. An article by Cassie MacDuff in the *San Bernardino Sun* examines the history of racism accusations against the campus and Pres. Evans by the Westside Action Group, a local organization of African-American businessmen, and others; a follow-up piece by MacDuff on Mar. 8 provides further details.

5 MAR. 1987. The campus plays its first NCAA Division III softball game at Calif. Lutheran College.

6 MAR. 1987. John F. "Jack" McDonnell is named Assoc. Dean of the School of Business and Public Administration; Adria F. Klein and Margaret A. Atwell are named Assoc. Deans of the School of Education and Joan Terry Hallett is named Assoc. Dean for the School of Natural Sciences—being the first Assoc. Deans created for the individual schools. Copies of the campus's first emergency plan are distributed. Frances F. Berdan receives a $3,500 summer stipend from the National Endowment for the Humanities. The Bella Lewitzky Dance Co. performs in RH.

7 MAR. 1987. The campus plays its first NCAA baseball game at Occidental College.

10 MAR. 1987. David Miller-Tiedeman and Anna Miller-Tiedeman speak in SR on "Life Career."

11 MAR. 1987. Ex-L.A. Dodgers baseball player Jay Johnstone speaks in UC.

12 MAR. 1987. Comedienne Kate Clinton and singers Ron Romanovsky and Paul Phillips perform in SUMP.

13 MAR. 1987. Pres. Evans meets with 50 faculty and staff to discuss ways to alleviate racial tensions on campus, and expresses "deep regret over [his] unfortunate choice of words" in his June 30, 1986 letter to CSU Chancellor Reynolds.

15 MAR. 1987. Conductor James Guthrie conducts the CSUSB Chamber Orchestra in RH.

20 MAR. 1987. John Cornelius Overton, Chief of Custodial Services (1970-87), dies at age 61. L.A. photographer William Giles is named Distinguished Visiting Prof. of Art for the Spring Quarter.

24-25 & 27 MAR. 1987. The campus hosts the Southern Calif. High School Band and Orchestra Festival, with some 2,000 participating.

28 MAR. 1987. Cal State Computer Science student Jamin Gomaidi is killed in a car accident in Arizona.

3 APR. 1987. Oakview Construction Inc. receives a $414,800 contract to build a 3,863-sq.-ft. annex to the Coyote Bookstore.

4-5 APR. 1987. The campus hosts a Young Audience Theatre Festival, with the Mark Taper Improvisational Theatre, Carmen Zapata's Children's Troupe from the Bilingual Foundation of the Arts, South Coast Repertory Theatre, and We Tell Stories Troupe.

8 APR. 1987. Writer Paul Zall speaks in RH on "We Too: Wives of the Founding Fathers: Voices of 1787."

10 APR. 1987. Van Deren Coke of the San Francisco Museum of Modern Art speaks in RH on "Time and Space in Twentieth Century Photography." Zorah Emami speaks in SUMP on "How to Economists Explain Women's Lower Earnings and Higher Unemployment?"

13 APR. 1987. Francisco J. Ayala speaks in SR on "Genetic Engineering." Hana Lostakova Ayala speaks on campus. Presidential advisor John P. Roche speaks in PR on "The Founding Fathers as a Reform Caucus in Action: A Retrospective View," and on 14 Apr. in PR on "A Postdoctoral Education with Lyndon Johnson: Two Years in the White House."

14 APR. 1987. Sheldon Messinger speaks in SU on "Regulating the Penal Enterprise."

15 Apr. 1987. Allen Strange speaks in RH on "The New Revolution in Music: Computers and Synthesizers." Maurice Naragon speaks in PL-27 on "The Latest in Desktop Publishing."

16 Apr. 1987. Writer John Molloy speaks in SU on "Live for Success." Jane Valentine speaks in PS-133 on "Population Health Responses to Potentially Toxic Levels of Selenium in Drinking Water." Elaine LaMonica speaks on "The Power of Helping Relationships in Nursing." Herman Belz speaks in SU on "Constitutionalism and the American Founding." Several local African-American community leaders call for the removal of Pres. Evans.

17 Apr. 1987. Bruce Cooperstein speaks in BI-129 on "Some Modern Problems in Algebra and Combinatorics."

20 Apr. 1987. Leonard W. Levy speaks in PR on "The Founder (Madison) and His Original Intent."

21 Apr. 1987. *Voyager* pilots Richard Rutan and Jeana Yeager speak in the Gymnasium about their around-the-world flight.

22 Apr. 1987. Assemblyman Gerald Eaves calls for the State Auditor General to investigate charges of racial discrimination at CSUSB.

23 Apr. 1987. Tatiana Galvan speaks in SR on "The Cultural Impact of Mass Media in the World Today." Charles Senn and José Tacal speak in PS-133 on "Health Science." Bertram Gross speaks in PR on "A Global Epidemic: Joblessness," and in SU on 24 Apr. on "The Rise and Fall of 'Full Employment'."

24 Apr. 1987. Groundbreaking is held for the Coyote Bookstore addition.

27 Apr. 1987. Fred A. López speaks in SR on "United States Intervention in Central America: A Chicano Perspective." Joyce O. Appleby speaks in PR on "Celebrating the Constitution." Frank Wykoff speaks in LC on the "Federal Budget."

28 Apr. 1987. Bea Hernández speaks in SR on "La Chicana: Woman of the Past, Heroine of Tomorrow."

30 Apr. 1987. Manuel Caldera and H. Frank Domínguez speak in SR on "Trends in the Hispanic Market." Ralph Cooper speaks in PS-133 on "Health Science." Harold Hodgkinson speaks in SR on "Educational Issues."

1 May 1987. Matich Corp. receives a $283,836 contract to build a 400-

space parking lot between the main entrance and the dorms. The Pfau Library receives a $28,325 grant from the U.S. Dept. of Education to reduce shelving earthquake hazards. Elliott R. Barkan receives a 2nd Fulbright Fellowship to study at the Univ. of Southampton in 1987/88. The Cinco de Mayo Festival features The Latin Society, Ballet Folklórico Mixcoacalli, and Teatro Aztlán presenting "The Decade of the '80s—A Broken Promise."

3 MAY 1987. *Los Angeles Times* TV critic Howard Rosenberg speaks in the Pfau Library on "How to Watch Eight Hours of TV a Day and Survive—Barely."

4 MAY 1987. Poet Carmen Tafolla speaks in RH. Alexander Austin speaks in RH on "Competition vs. Cooperation in Higher Education." Gary L. McDowell speaks in PR on "The Politics of Original Intent Jurisprudence."

5 MAY 1987. Writer Richard Cortez Day reads from his work in ER. Aaron Hass speaks in PR on his experiences as "A Child of Holocaust Survivors."

6 MAY 1987. San Antonio Mayor Henry Cisneros speaks in UC on "The Survival of American Cities in the 1980s."

8 MAY 1987. César Chávez, Pres. of the United Farmworkers of America, speaks in SUMP on "Wrath of Grapes: The Dangers Pesticides Pose to Farm Workers and Consumers." The UC Irvine Dance Touring Ensemble performs in RH. CSUSB becomes the first campus in the CSU System to require that all general education courses include materials on ethnic minorities and women.

11 MAY 1987. Historian Henry V. Jaffa speaks in PR on "The Intentions of the Framers of the Constitution."

14 MAY 1987. Playwrights Jerome Lawrence and Robert E. Lee perform *Under the Volcano* in the Theatre, and also speak in RH on "Which One Can't Spel?" [sic]. Cal State student Laura Ruth Major dies in Los Angeles at age 57.

15 MAY 1987. Oakview Construction Inc. receives a $136,700 contract to build a multipurpose room and kitchen in Serrano Village.

18 MAY 1987. Artist and photographer Joel-Peter Witkin speaks about his work in the Art Gallery.

19 MAY 1987. Kenneth Hama speaks in VA-110 on "Recent Excavations in Cyprus."

20 MAY 1987. Business analyst Fritz W. Scharpf speaks in PR on "The Political Economy of Macro-Economic Management: A Game-Theoretic Interpretation." Bernhardt Lawrence Mortensen, Emer. Assoc. Prof. of Sociology (1968-78), dies at age 71. Steven Red Buffalo speaks in SU Lounge on "Traditional Lakota Teachings."

21 MAY 1987. Comedians Jeff Mills, Monica Piper, and Larry Wilmore perform in UC. Robert Garfias speaks in PR on "Music: Thinking Globally, Acting Loyally."

26 MAY 1987. Donald Lagerberg speaks in VA-110 on "When Is an Illustration Not an Illustration, and Other Topics of Interest."

28 MAY 1987. Kathy Higgins speaks in SR on "Aesthetics and Music." The Upward Bound Program receives a $214,091 grant from the U.S. Dept. of Education to fund another year of operations.

29 MAY 1987. Guitarist Johnny Hickman performs in the Pub.

30 MAY 1987. The campus hosts its Law Day Conference, with S.B. Judge Kenneth Ziebarth giving the keynote speech.

1-5 JUN. 1987. The Nova Saxophone Quartet performs in RH (Jun. 1), and also conducts workshops later in the week.

2 JUN. 1987. Photographer Scott Peters speaks in VA-110 on "The Fine Art of Infra-Red Photography."

5 JUN. 1987. Part of the atrium in the Student Services Building is converted into 2 conference rooms; the 2 existing conference rooms are converted into offices.

6 JUN. 1987. The Iota Alpha (IA) Chapter of Sigma Chi (ΣX) fraternity is installed at a banquet at the Ontario Hilton Hotel.

17 JUN. 1987. Assemblyman Gerald Eaves releases a report from the State Auditor General, showing that CSUSB is matching or exceeding the efforts of other campuses in the CSU System in this area, with no need for a further review; however, W. H. "Bill" Jacocks, President of the Westside Action Group, rejects the report, saying that the University's work has been insufficient. In response, the campus issues a "Report from the President to the Campus Community" a week later, in which Pres. Evans states: "Since my arrival at CSUSB…, our university has made significant strides toward affirmative action and educational equity…we have attained important results in the areas of hiring women and minority faculty and staff, the recruitment of minority students, and the general implementation of affirmative action and educational equity policies and practices." Equipment Operator Rudolph "Rudy" Von Sydow is injured when a campus tram rolls over his legs.

19 JUN. 1987. The campus receives a $50,000 grant from the State to develop a pilot work-study program. *The San Bernardino Sun* publishes an editorial stating that charges of racism levied against the CSUSB are unproven and unfounded.

20 JUN. 1987. The 21st Commencement is held on the Library Lawn; William H. Pickens, Dir. of the Calif. Postsecondary Education Commission, gives the keynote address; also present are CSU Trustees Marianthi Lansdale and John Kashiwabara. William Haywood Merriett, who had completed a B.A. in Vocational Education, suffers a heart attack in the Gymnasium an hour before the graduation ceremony, and dies at age 54; his degree is awarded posthumously.

21 JUN. 1987. The campus hosts its annual Juneteenth celebration.

1 JUL. 1987. Dr. James R. Savage, Dir. of the Student Health Center (1978-87), retires. The Canto Bello Chorale singers perform on LCP.

8 JUL. 1987. Pianist Brian Shyer and singer Constance Cairo perform on LCP.

10 JUL. 1987. Arthur M. Butler, Dir. of Public Safety, is named Dir. of Administrative Services and Exec. Dir. of the CSUSB Foundation. Jim Hansen is named Asst. Dir. of Physical Plant. Edward W. Harrison, Police Lt. and Services Manager, is named Chief of Police Operations.

15 JUL. 1987. The Almont Ensemble performs on LCP.

22 JUL. 1987. The Diamano-Coura Dancers perform on the LC

24 JUL. 1987. The campus bans smoking in hallways and stairs.

29 JUL. 1987. Folksinger Ross Altman performs on LCP.

1 AUG. 1987. Herbert Nickles, Assoc. Dir. for Instructional Computing (1978-87), resigns.

4 AUG. 1987. The campus signs an agreement with the Westside Action Group to recruit more minority students, faculty, and staff.

5 Aug. 1987. The bluegrass group The Phil Salazar Band performs with fiddler Charl Ann Gastineau and the Cole Miners Clogging Club on LCP.

6 Aug. 1987. Actor Curtis Baldwin speaks on campus.

7 Aug. 1987. Elliott R. Barkan receives a $24,975 grant from the Institute for Academic Computer Enhancement to create social science instructional models in an in-class study on the computer.

12 Aug. 1987. The band Final Approach, an ensemble of the 15th Air Force at March AFB, performs on LCP.

17-19 Aug. 1987. The new Faculty Office Building is occupied by the Schools of Education and Social and Behavioral Sciences. New Public Safety Offices in the Physical Plant are occupied by Police Services and Parking Services.

18-21 Aug. 1987. The campus hosts its 3rd Annual "Teachers Are #1" Conference, with TV anchor Kelly Lange, Zachary Clements, Jim Kern, and Jim Trelease giving keynote speeches.

19 Aug. 1987. Irish folk band Reel to Reel performs on LCP.

21 Aug. 1987. The Financial Aid Accounting Off. is renamed the Student Aid Accounting Off.

26 Aug. 1987. Dixieland band The Fullertowne Strutters performs on LCP.

31 Aug. 1987. Thomas J. Pierce, Act. Dean of the School of Social and Behavioral Sciences, returns to the ranks as Prof. of Economics. Diane F. Halpern, Act. Dean of Undergraduate Studies, returns to the ranks as Prof. of Psychology.

1 Sept. 1987. Aubrey W. Bonnett is named Dean of the School of Social and Behavioral Sciences, replacing Thomas J. Pierce. Sidney A. Ribeau is named Dean of Undergraduate Studies, replacing Diane F. Halpern. The campus creates a Dept. of Information and Decision Sciences in the School of Business and Public Administration. Dr. John Preston Miller is named Dir. of the Student Health Center, replacing James R. Savage. The campus implements a new B.S. degree in Industrial Technology.

11 Sept. 1987. The campus hosts its Annual Children at Risk Conference, with Peter Alsop giving the keynote speech, and S.B. Co. Supervisors Robert Hammock and Larry Walker, and S.B. Judge Patrick J. Morris also appearing.

15 SEPT. 1987. At the annual convocation in the Gymnasium, Pres. Evans says that the administrators and faculty are working "vigorously" to develop new courses and revise existing ones to broaden CSUSB's academic base, including new B.A. programs in geology, physical science, leisure industry management, and legal studies, and new master's programs in social work, computer science, accounting, art, humanities, communication, mathematics, education, and educational administration, with an increased emphasis on the study of women and minorities. The campus is also trying, he says, to increase the number of women and minority faculty and staff. He notes that the University has increased enrollment 60% since 1982, has strengthened requirements for tenure and promotion, and has seen a 500% increase in grants received, with more than $2 million accruing in each of the previous 2 years. Evans stresses that his primary goal is producing a regional university known for its service: "A university's service, through primarily instructional in nature, takes many forms." He reemphasizes the 4 goals that he set on his arrival on campus: "Increase outreach activities in order to serve all qualified students in the area…; accelerate efforts to achieve more depth and breadth in the curriculum…; revitalize student life…; strengthen relationships with external audiences. Our university should be a major asset to regional economic development." He adds: "System executives in Long Beach describe our campus as one of the two best-managed universities in the CSU." "What is it that I envision for the future? My view is that there should be no single vision for the university; instead, there should be many dreams that complement one another."

18 SEPT. 1987. The campus occupies 4 modular classroom buildings north of the Pfau Library. A new 400-space parking lot south of the Commons opens for business. *The Bulletin* goes biweekly. Mexican Consul Emerenciano Rodríguez is honored at a dinner in SUMP, with Armando Navarro, Pres. of the Congress for United Communities, speaking. Rod Short speaks at the CSU Systemwide High School Counselor Conference on campus.

23 SEPT. 1987. The campus announces the formation of a new gospel singing group, the Reverence Singers.

1 OCT. 1987. The Oct./Nov. 1987 issue of *Panorama*, the University's alumni magazine, includes an article, "Cal State Faculty Are Not Closeted in Ivory Towers; They Too Are Out in the Real World—The Talents Which Make Them Excellent Teachers Also Make Them Valuable Members of the Community at Large."

2 OCT. 1987. The Chancellor's Off. approves a new M.S. degree in Health Services Administration, effective with Fall 1987. The campus restricts parking in the Science Lot to full-time employees working in the Pfau Library Building, the Physical Science Building, and the Biological Science

Building.

5 OCT. 1987. A ribbon-cutting ceremony marks the official re-opening of the newly redecorated Student Union Building.

10 OCT. 1987. The campus hosts a holistic symposium for today's woman, "Womansong," in SUMP.

16 OCT. 1987. The Center for Economics Education receives a $15,000 grant from the CSU to help train economics teachers.

20 OCT. 1987. Alan Dundes speaks in SUMP on "Folklore in the Modern World."

21 OCT. 1987. After losing its 3rd game of the season, the water polo team disbands for lack of players and forfeits the rest of its games. Peter Schlepelern speaks in SR on "Narratology and Film: How Stories Are Told in Cinema."

25 OCT. 1987. Pianist José Feghali conducts a master class in RH.

27 OCT. 1987. Accountant Donald A. Driftmier speaks in SUMP. Peter H. Salus speaks in RH on "Technology and the Arts as Mirrors of Society and Each Other."

31 OCT. 1987. The Serrano Village Multipurpose Room opens for business.

1 NOV. 1987. Juan C. González is named first Asst. to the President.

3 NOV. 1987. Australian Consul General Basil Teasey speaks in SR on "U.S. and Australian Relations."

4 NOV. 1987. 3 new modular classroom buildings are occupied by CVC at the Coll. of the Desert; CVC enrollment reaches 403 students, a 70% increase over 1986.

6 NOV. 1987. *The Bulletin* is renamed *Bulletin*. Daz Patterson and the West Coast Singers, with choirs from the Loveland Baptist Church, Community Missionary Baptist Church of Redlands, and Faith Apostolic Church, perform in RH.

7 NOV. 1987. Grover G. Hankins, General Counsel for the NAACP, speaks at the 25th Annual Freedom Funds Banquet on campus.

11 NOV. 1987. Psychologist and writer Dr. Joyce Brothers speaks in UC on "Discovering Your Hidden Powers." The CSU Board of Trustees approves the addition of 5 more temporary buildings north of the Pfau Library, to be occupied by Fall 1988.

12 Nov. 1987. Magician Lee Grabel performs in SUMP. Włodzimierz Dydzkowski speaks in PiR on "Contemporary Problems of European Waterways and Inland Navigation."

14 Nov. 1987. The men's soccer team wins the regional championship tournament at UC San Diego, and advances to the NCAA Division III Championship Tournament at the Univ. of North Carolina, Greensboro on Nov. 21-22.

16 Nov. 1987. Ex-Mormon activist Sonia Johnson speaks in RH on "Going Out of Our Minds: The Metaphysics of Liberation."

17 Nov. 1987. Nobel Prize winner George Wald speaks in UC on "Survival in a Lethal Society: How We Got Where We Are and What Lies Ahead."

18 Nov. 1987. Efraín Toro speaks in RH on "Electronic Percussion Through MIDI." William Minter speaks in RH on "King Solomon's Mines Revisited: Western Interests and the Burdened History of Southern Africa."

19 Nov. 1987. Peter Garvie speaks in RH on "The State of the Theatre."

21 Nov. 1987. The men's soccer team is defeated in a semifinals game in the NCAA Division III championship tournament.

24 Nov. 1987. The CSU publishes an asbestos abatement study of the Cal State System, showing 4 locations at CSUSB classified as "Category C—material is damaged with a potential for human exposure": the Gymnasium, Heating and Air Conditioning, the Animal House, and Room PS-10.

30 Nov. & 2 Dec. 1987. Tatiana Galvan speaks in LC-241 on "Hispanic Newspapers in California: Their Successes and Problems," and on 2 Dec. in PiR on "Communication Among Hispanics: Their Values and Culture."

2 Dec. 1987. Margaret Daly Hayes speaks in PS-10 on "Central America."

3 Dec. 1987. Singer Jello Biafra performs in UC.

4 Dec. 1987. Lynda W. Warren is named Outstanding Professor for 1987/88. George A. Weiny receives the College Swimming Coaches Assoc.'s 25-year Service Award.

4-5 DEC. 1987. The campus hosts a conference, "Caught in the Middle: Responding to Middle School Reform," with Joseph Bondi giving the keynote address.

10 DEC. 1987. A. Peter Burleigh speaks in SR on "The Persian Gulf."

11 DEC. 1987. Margaret Laird, Student Aid Accounting Off. (1965-87), retires.

18 DEC. 1987. The atrium in the Administration Building is remodeled into an outdoor eating and break area for employees.

1988

6 JAN. 1988. The campus begins beaming TV classes in Psychology and Communications to CVC.

8 JAN. 1988. The campus receives a $28,000 planning grant from the Calif. Student Aid Commission to promote higher education for low-income and minority students. The Coyote Bookstore addition opens for business. The campus limits parking in visitor spaces to 30 minutes. The campus creates a Behavioral Medicine and Integrative Health Studies Center.

14 JAN. 1988. Ex-UCLA basketball coach John Wooden speaks in the Gymnasium. Actor Felix Justice performs "Martin Luther King: Prophecy in America" in RH.

22 JAN. 1988. The University implements its 2nd joint Ph.D. program with Zagazig Univ. in Egypt.

25 JAN. 1988. Ex-White House counsel John Dean speaks in UC on "Blind Ambition."

28 JAN. 1988. Joan Mondale, wife of ex-VP Walter Mondale, speaks in SUMP on "The Arts and the Three R's: An Essential Partnership." Magician Harry Blackstone Jr. speaks in SUMP on "The Magic of the Humanities and the Humanity of Magic." Juanita Mantovani speaks on the Pfau Library steps on "The Humanities: Keys to Change."

3 FEB. 1988. Cheryl Charles speaks in RH on "Viewing Environmental Education: Rewind, Play, Fast Forward."

4 FEB. 1988. Patricia Miller speaks in SR on "Children as Amateur Psychologists."

4-5 FEB. 1988. The campus hosts a conference in SUMP on "AIDS and STDs," with William Yarber giving the keynote speech on "School-Based AIDS Education: Politics, Issues, and Responses."

5 FEB. 1988. The campus implements a new sexual harassment prevention policy, and appoints 13 faculty and staff members as sexual harassment advisors. The Learning Center receives an $11,000 grant from the Chancellor's Off. to help prepare students for the Entry-Level Mathematics (ELM) exam. The U.S.P.S. mail box is moved from the Bookstore to the circular drive at the Main Entrance.

6 FEB. 1988. Kathak Dancers of India perform in RH.

9 FEB. 1988. Gregory A. Daneke speaks in OR on "Managed or Unmanaged Growth in the Inland Empire." Cal State business major Marianne M. Whitehall dies at age 22.

10 FEB. 1988. Yolanda T. Moses speaks in SR on "The Black Woman as Scholar and Subject."

11 FEB. 1988. Jazz band Moses and Friends performs in SU Pub.

12 FEB. 1988. The campus hosts a Black Education Conference, "Strategies in Education: Black Is Back," in SUMP, with keynote speakers Wade W. Nobles and Shirley Thornton; other participants include Tommie Lakin, Carolyn Murray, Bill Ponder, Carolyn Lindsey, Yolanda T. Moses, and DeWanda Johnson.

13 FEB. 1988. Baritone Gene Brundage and soprano Arlene Brundage perform in RH.

15 FEB. 1988. Karen Brodkin Sacks speaks in SUMP on "Gender and Grassroots Leadership."

16 FEB. 1988. Timo Airaksinsen speaks in SU on "What Is Professional Ethics?"

18 FEB. 1988. The Student Union celebrates its 10th anniversary with day-long festivities. Bertram Miller performs in RH.

19 FEB. 1988. Günther Walch speaks in SR on "Life in the German Democratic Republic (Eastern Europe): A Personal View." Joe L. Martínez speaks in SUMP on "Do Hormones Affect Memory?"

23 FEB. 1988. CSU Trustee Chair Dale B. Ride visits the campus.

24 FEB. 1988. The campus hosts a reception in the Art Gallery to honor the 213-piece collection of Asian ceramic art donated by Pres. and Lois Evans. Ellis Rivkin speaks in SUMP at the 1st Morrow-McCombs Memorial Lecture on "A Hidden Revolution: Who Were the Pharisees?" Pianist Sergei Edelmann performs in RH.

25 FEB. 1988. U.S. Asst. Attorney General for Legal Policy Stephen J. Markman speaks in SR on "The Politics of Judicial Nominations."

2 MAR. 1988. Robert Fisher speaks in VA-110 on "Asian Ceramics." Michael Hamilton speaks in PS-10 on "Biopolitics for the Twenty-First Century: From Rainforests to Fast Foods."

3 MAR. 1988. Joyce Ladner speaks in RH on "Mixed Families: Adoption Across Racial Boundaries." Singer Deidre McCalla and comedian Tom Ammiano perform in SUMP.

5 MAR. 1988. The campus hosts its 12th Annual Reading Conference, "The Power of Literature: In the Midst of a Revolution," with Yetta Goodman giving the keynote speech.

8 MAR. 1988. Gerhard Zecha speaks in SR on "Value Neutrality and Responsibility in the Social Sciences." Barbara Reskin speaks in SR on "Sex Differentiation and the Devaluation of Women's Work: Implications for Occupational Progress and Pay Equity."

9 MAR. 1988. Actor Charles Shaughnessy speaks in SR on "From 'Soaps' to a World in Crisis: A Balance Between Illusion and Reality." Randy Silverston speaks in PL-211 on "An Overview of Current Studies and Research Perspectives in the Field of Child Abuse and Neglect."

10 MAR. 1988. The campus hosts Humanities Career Day, with Danny Bilson, Paul DeMeo, Joanne Fluke, Pete Peterson, Mary Frances Gómez, Jack Dexter, and Sherrie Connelly. The CSU System announces that implementation of tougher admissions standards for Cal State students, which many groups in the state had opposed as adversely affected minority students, will be phased in beginning with Fall 1988, with full implementation by Fall 1992.

16 MAR. 1988. Robert L. Brown speaks in VA-110 on "Social and Cultural Connections of Thai and Cambodian Ceramics." Yoshitomo Takahashi speaks in ER on "Suicide and Amnesia in the Mt. Fuji Forest."

17 MAR. 1988. New classrooms and offices for CVC on the east end of the Coll. of the Desert in Palm Desert are dedicated by CSU Trustee Marianthi Lansdale, Pres. Evans, and COD Pres. David A. George.

18 MAR. 1988. Wayne I. Boucher speaks at the Annual Economic Forecast Breakfast on "Alternative Scenarios for the Inland Empire in the Year 2000." *Wall Street Journal* reporters John Walcott and Alan Murray speak on "Politics, Business, and Foreign Relations in 1988: A Washington Perspective."

27 MAR. 1988. S. Lamont Waithe performs a "One-Man Show" in SR.

28 MAR. 1988. The campus announces a revitalized Ethnic Studies Program, with 8 courses debuting on Apr. 4.

29 MAR. 1988. New stop signs are installed at the corner of University Pkwy. and Northpark Blvd., to be replaced by traffic lights at the end of the year.

31 MAR. 1988. Arthur E. Nelson, Coll. Libn. and Library Dir. (1963-88), and the longest-serving Library Dir. in the Cal State System, returns to the ranks as Librarian.

1 APR. 1988. Max A. "Marty" Bloomberg, Assoc. Library Dir., is named Act. Library Dir., replacing Arthur E. Nelson.

6 APR. 1988. The campus experiences a one-hour power blackout.

7 APR. 1988. Writer Sally Gearhart speaks on "Why Reproduce in Captivity? What Are the Roots of Violence and How Do They Affect Women?"

11 APR. 1988. Leovigildo Anolin, Consul General of the Republic of the Philippines, speaks in SR on "U.S.-Philippine relations."

12 APR. 1988. Sarah Rushbrook speaks in ER on "Gender Images in Videogames: Portent to Computer Equity." Jack R. Peltason, Michael Riccards, and Lawrence Berman speak in SR as part of the discussion, "The American Presidency—A Roundtable."

13 APR. 1988. Lewis Baltz speaks in VA-110 about his art.

14 APR. 1988. Sjrdan Novac speaks in ER on "Biochemical Engineering."

15 APR. 1988. CSU Chancellor Reynolds visits the campus. Violinist Clayton Haslop and guitarist Jack Sanders perform in RH.

21 APR. 1988. Harpsichordist Beverly Briggs and oboist David Dutton perform in RH. Astronaut Pierre Thuot speaks in UC on "The Space Program—Today and in the Future."

22 APR. 1988. Traffic signals are installed at the corner of University Pkwy. and College Dr., not far from the campus, and the speed limit on University Pkwy. is lowered from 45 to 35 MPH.

25 APR. 1988. Clarence Thomas, Chair of the U.S. Equal Employment Opportunity Commission (and later a Justice of the U.S. Supreme Court), speaks in UC.

27 APR. 1988. Writer Martin E. Hellman speaks in RH on "Breakthrough: Soviet and Western Scholars Issue a Challenge in a Nuclear Age."

2 MAY 1988. Carmen Tafolla speaks in PR on being "A Chicana Poet," as part of the Cinco de Mayo celebration.

3 MAY 1988. TV news anchorman Frank Cruz speaks in UC on "Trends in the Hispanic Media."

4 MAY 1988. Healer Alice Saltzman speaks in SU on "Spiritual Healing in Brazil." Roberta Johnson speaks in PR on "Hispanic Women."

5 MAY 1988. Vons Pres. Bill Davila speaks in SUMP on "Building Your Formula for Success." Cal State student Brandii Schmitt is named Miss Rialto '88.

6 MAY 1988. The band Mariachi Vallarta and dancers Los Niños Ballarinos perform on LCP as part of Cinco de Mayo.

9 MAY 1988. Students hold an "End of the World" party in SU Pub to celebrate a "Great Quake" in Southern Calif. supposedly forecast by Nostradamus—alas, it doesn't happen!

10 MAY 1988. Harry Edwards speaks in RH on "Race and Sport," and again in PE-129 on "Educating Black Athletes."

12 MAY 1988. Donald Billingsley speaks in SR on "Black Youth in Crisis."

13 MAY 1988. Dancers Dennon and Sayhber Rawles perform in RH, and conduct a master class on May 21. The campus hosts a conference, "The Challenges of Growth in the Inland Empire: Shaping the Future Through Leadership," with speakers S.B. Mayor Wilcox, political columnist Dan Walters, ex-Fresno Mayor Daniel Whitehurst, and State Sen. Marion Bergeson.

14 MAY 1988. The campus hosts its 2nd Annual Environmental Expo, "Inland Empire at the Environmental Crossroads," with Rep. George E. Brown moderating a forum, "Living with Growth in the Inland Empire: What Are the Limiting Factors?", with speakers Riverside Co. Supervisor Norton Younglove, Joe Roth, Ray Becker, and Blase Bonpane.

16 MAY 1988. Gregory A. Daneke speaks in SR on "Managed or Unmanaged Growth in the Inland Empire." Joan Winser, Consul General of Canada, speaks in PR on "U.S.-Canada Relations."

18 MAY 1988. Richard Reeb speaks to the ASI Senate on "The Founding Fathers and the Media." The CSU Board of Trustees approves a new CSUSB master plan, the first revision in 20 years, projecting a future enrollment of 15,000 students and 16 new buildings.

19 MAY 1988. Theodore N. Ferdinand speaks in SR on "Juvenile Delinquency and Juvenile Justice."

20 MAY 1988. Cynthia Hamilton speaks in ER on "U.S. Contra Wars: The Case of Angola." The gospel group The Reverence Singers perform in RH.

21 MAY 1988. The campus hosts a conference, "South Africa," in PR, with Ruth Belonsky speaking on "A White South African's Experience of Apartheid," Mathabo Kunene on "The Impact of Apartheid on Women and Children," Helisi Price on "The Situation in Namibia," Vusi Shangasi on "The Situation in South Africa," and Duke More on "The Labor Movement in South Africa."

22 MAY 1988. *Los Angeles Times* cartoonist and Pulitzer Prize winner Paul Conrad speaks in PS-10 on "A Satirical Look at the World Through the Eyes of the Editorial Cartoonist." His talk is followed by a reception in the Pfau Library.

23 MAY 1988. Columnist Jack Anderson speaks in UC on "The News Behind the Headlines." Carol Thompson speaks in ER on "Frontline Response to Apartheid."

24 MAY 1988. Neva Makgetla speaks in SUMP on "U.S. Foreign Investments in South Africa." Leah Light speaks in ER on "Language and Memory in Old Age." Jim Kamusikiri speaks in PR on "Conflict Resolution in Southern Africa: The Example of Zimbabwe."

25 MAY 1988. Song Yufeng speaks in SR on "China's Education System." Roshen Kishun speaks in PR on "Education in South Africa." Patricia Anawalt speaks in VA-110 on "Textiles and Time Travel." Ron Wilkins speaks in PR on "Action Against Apartheid."

26 MAY 1988. Jazz trumpeter Freddie Hubbard performs in RH. Seph Makgetla speaks in ER on "Changes in the Liberation Movement in South Africa." Charles Marshall speaks in ER on "U.S. Angola Policy."

27 MAY 1988. Mazisi Kunene speaks in SR on "The Role of Literature in Political Change in South Africa."

31 MAY 1988. Nobel Peace Prize winner Glenn T. Seaborg speaks in UC on "Arms Control in the Johnson Years."

2 JUN. 1988. Educator Anita Taylor speaks in SR on "What Are We Doing Here? Education: the Real Agenda." Actor Tom Henschel directs the campus play, *A Flea in Her Ear*.

3 JUN. 1988. The Economics Dept. receives a $36,970 matching grant from NSF to create a computer lab for economics instruction.

4 JUN. 1988. The Academic Council creates the Major Events Logistics Committee to "bring about consistent, standardized coordination of all major University-funded events."

15 JUN. 1988. C. E. Tapie Rohm Jr. receives a Fulbright Fellowship to study in Tanzania in 1988/89, and Ellen L. Kronowitz receives a Fulbright grant to study the history of Indonesia and Singapore.

17 JUN. 1988. The campus receives authorization to offer a B.A. degree in Paralegal Administration at CVC, beginning in 1988/89.

18 JUN. 1988. The 22nd Commencement is held on the Library Lawn, with CSU Exec. Vice Chancellor Herbert L. Carter giving the keynote address.

19 JUN. 1988. The campus hosts its 5th Annual Juneteenth celebration in the Commons, with Marshall Thompson giving the keynote address.

22 JUN. 1988. The campus hosts a public reception in PR to discuss plans for a coordinated outreach program.

23 JUN. 1988. Daryl Ann Leonard is named Athletic Dir., effective Sept. 1, but abruptly resigns the position on Jul. 11 after encountering local smog and heat.

24 JUN. 1988. The campus Concert Choir, directed by Loren Filbeck, goes on a 2-week, 7-concert tour of Europe.

30 JUN. 1988. CSU Chancellor Reynolds declares a "fiscal crisis" in the

CSU System, and institutes a hiring freeze.

SUM. 1988. Retirements: Carol F. Goss, Prof. of Political Science (1971-88); C(harles) Frederick Kellers, Prof. of Physics (1968-88); Kenton L. Monroe, Prof. of Psychology and Assoc. Dean of Counseling and Dean of Students (1965-88); Mireille G. "Mimi" Rydell, Prof. of French (1968-88); Gordon E. Stanton, Prof. of Education (1968-88); Donald C. Woods, Prof. of Psychology and Counseling and Testing Officer (1968-88); Thomas E. Woods, Lect. in Education (1981-88).

6 JUL. 1988. The bluegrass group Shadow Mountain performs with the Butterfield County Cloggers on LCP.

13 JUL. 1988. The Celtic group Gael Force performs with harpist Dennis Doyle on LCP.

15 JUL. 1988. The campus receives a $22,503 grant from the Commission on the Bicentennial of the U.S. Constitution to fund a Jul. 25-29 seminar, and a 2nd grant of $27,635 to fund a conference on "Congress and the Separation of Powers."

20 JUL. 1988. The gospel group, Daz Patterson and the West Coast Singers, performs on LCP. Barbara A. Taylor, Bookkeeper in the Foundation (1977-88), dies.

25-29 JUL. 1988. The campus hosts a seminar for teachers, "Our Constitutional Heritage: Applications in the Classroom."

27 JUL. 1988. The Faculty Woodwind Quintet performs on LCP.

31 JUL. 1988. Joanna Roche, Dir. of Alumni Affairs (1986-88), resigns.

1 AUG. 1988. Mary Colacurcio is named Dir. of Alumni Affairs, replacing Joanna Roche. Pres. Evans announces that salary increases for campus employees will be eliminated or postponed for 1988/89 due to the budget crisis; $850,000 must be cut from the CSUSB operating budget.

3 AUG. 1988. The guitar duo Strings of Glass performs on LCP.

10 AUG. 1988. The folk group Marley's Ghost performs on LCP.

15 AUG. 1988. Linda R. Evans, Library Asst. (1963-88), retires on her 25th anniversary as the longest serving staff person on campus.

16-19 AUG. 1988. The campus hosts its "Teachers Are #1" Conference, with keynote speakers Terrence Deal, Susan Kovalik, Alvin Granowsky, and Rita Dunn.

17 AUG. 1988. The jazz group Latin Society performs on LCP.

19 AUG. 1988. The campus receives a $22,000 gift of computers from Apple Computers.

24 AUG. 1988. Folksinger Sam Hinton performs on LCP.

31 AUG. 1988. Max A. "Marty" Bloomberg, Act. Library Dir. and Assoc. Library Dir., returns to the ranks as Librarian. The San Diego Navy Brass Quintet performs on LCP.

1 SEPT. 1988. Johnnie Ann Ralph, Libn., is named Act. Library Dir., replacing Max A. "Marty" Bloomberg. The Pfau Library completes a project to reinforce its shelving against potential earthquake damage with a $55,726 grant from the U.S. Dept. of Education; the glass windows in the Library are all replaced with unbreakable plastic. The Library reoccupies the space at the north end of the 5th floor. Vicki Estelle is named first Dir. of the Calif. Student Opportunity and Access Program (Cal-SOAP). Parking fees increase from $7.50 to $12 per month for administrators and staff, and from $22.50 to $36 per quarter for students.

13 SEPT. 1988. At the annual convocation, Pres. Evans says that his "One major concern at this time is the state's revenue shortfall and its adverse impact on our campus." However, the campus is making steady progress toward its ultimate goal of "a balanced university noted for exemplary teaching, applied research, and broad service to the region." Increased enrollment makes possible the growth in faculty, staff, programs, and buildings, including the new Student Union addition. Over a 2-year period, CSUSB plans to add graduate programs in School Administration, Mathematics, Art, Accounting and Taxation, Computer Science, Social Science, and Communication. Cash contributions and donors reached new highs in 1987/88. "There are certain traditions of the campus," he adds, "which I hope will never change. I trust that [we] will forever remain service-oriented…that teaching will always be our primary emphasis…[that] the university sees the purpose of its existence as meeting basic educational needs." "We are committed only to necessary and orderly change. Change just for the sake of change has no place on our agenda." "We must work harder to communicate with each other. We must communicate more frequently and more effectively. We must elevate collegiality and not let it erode in any major way…. We need one another. We cannot afford dissention or lack of cooperation." The Pres. requested the assistance of all, especially the faculty, in helping to preserve "the superb liberal arts emphasis of our university…. Our region needs leaders with academic breadth as well as depth; it needs the liberating, civilizing effects which a liberal arts education provides."

14 SEPT. 1988. Assemblyman Tom Hayden speaks in PR on "Student Outcome Measurement and Performance-Based Funding for Improvement of California Higher Education."

21 SEPT. 1988. The campus receives a $225,000 grant from the U.S. Dept. of Education to train teachers of the handicapped at CVC.

26 SEPT. 1988. New York Gov. Mario Cuomo speaks in the Gymnasium about the forthcoming presidential election; also present are S.B. Mayor Wilcox, S.B. Co. Supervisor Larry Walker, S.B. City Councilmen Norine Miller, Jess Flores, and Jack Reilly, and Pres. of the S.B. Board of Education Hardy Brown.

30 SEPT. 1988. Margaret Lynam, Purchasing (1972-88), retires.

5 OCT. 1988. Superintendent of the Inglewood Unified School Dist. George J. McKenna III speaks in SU as part of the Conference, "Drug Abuse, Suicide, and Other Problems Facing Young People."

7 OCT. 1988. *The Bulletin* changes its name to *The Friday Bulletin*. Pres. Evans says that the new Athletic Dir., when hired, will report to the Exec. Dean for Univ. Relations instead of the President; the position had previously (until Fall 1987) reported to the Dean of Natural Sciences. The campus receives an award from Southern California Edison Co. for Outstanding Achievement in the Management of Electrical Energy.

10 OCT. 1988. 4 modular classrooms open for business north of the Pfau Library.

13 OCT. 1988. Ex-Calif. Gov. Edmund G. "Pat" Brown Sr. speaks in UC on "California: The Year 2000."

17 OCT. 1988. Spanish novelist Carmen Laforet speaks in RH on "The Role of Spanish Women in Post-Franco Spanish Society and Arts."

18 OCT. 1988. William "Buckey" Bush, brother of VP George H. W. Bush, speaks in RH about the Bush family.

19 OCT. 1988. Robert Blodget speaks in PR on "Using Laserdisc and Other Light-Based Technologies for Instructional Purposes."

20 OCT. 1988. Poet Sandra Sprayberry reads from her work in OR, as part of the 2nd Annual Humanities Day celebration, "The Humanities: The Art of Being Human."

24 Oct. 1988. Charmaine Della Neve speaks in PR on the "First Brain Compatible Learning School."

26 Oct. 1988. The campus signs an agreement with the Universidad Nacional Autónoma de México (UNAM) to assist faculty research and exchange. The campus establishes the Institute for Applied Research and Policy Analysis. Dense fog blankets the campus.

27 Oct. 1988. The campus receives a $75,000 grant from the U.S. Dept. of Education to recruit rehabilitation counseling students.

28 Oct. 1988. Comedian Max Martin and hypnotist James Downs perform in UC.

1 Nov. 1988. Campus radio station KSSB resumes broadcasting after a 4-month hiatus, being carried on 2 local TV cable networks. Judith M. Rymer, Exec. Dean for Univ. Relations, is named VP for Univ. Relations. Peter A. Wilson, Dean of Students, is named VP for Student Services.

8 Nov. 1988. CSUSB alumnus Paul A. Woodruff, a Republican, is elected to the 61st Dist., Calif. State Assembly.

9 Nov. 1988. The choral gospel group The Reverence Singers performs in RH.

10 Nov. 1988. Edward Feigenbaum conducts a TV symposium on "Artificial Intelligence" in PL-013. Reuben Hersh speaks in SR on "New Directions in the Philosophy of Mathematics." Judge Patrick J. Morris speaks in PR on "The Law and Young People," as part of the Social Sciences Law Day celebration.

17 Nov. 1988. CSU Trustee Lyman H. Heine visits the campus. M(argaret) Jeanne Hogenson, Coordinator of International Student Services (1978-88), dies in L.A. of cancer at age 43.

21 Nov. 1988. The campus hosts a TV conference, "Teaching and Learning in Transformation: The Silicon Evolution," in PL-087, with William H. Graves chairing a panel including Phillip Cartwright, Robert L. Davis, Loretta L. Jones, and James S. Noblitt.

30 Nov. 1988. The campus opens a handicapped access ramp at the south entrance to the Pfau Library and a wheelchair lift in the Theatre. Sister Rosa Marta speaks in PR on "Women in Central America." Filmmaker Alan Acker speaks in SUMP on "Reel Women: Pioneers of the Cinema."

1989

2 JAN. 1989. Johnnie Ann Ralph, Act. Library Dir., returns to the ranks as Librarian.

3 JAN. 1989. William Aguilar is named Univ. Libn., replacing Johnnie Ann Ralph.

4-6 JAN. 1989. The campus and the Off. of the Bicentennial of the U.S. Constitution sponsor an Institute on "Congress and the Separation of Powers."

6 JAN. 1989. The campus receives a $2,093 gift to establish the Barbara A. Taylor Memorial Scholarship Fund. The Off. of Media Relations and Public Information is renamed the Public Information Off. The Off. of Facility Planning and Policy Coordination is renamed the Off. of Physical Planning and Development. A 40-office modular faculty office building opens next to the new classrooms north of the Pfau Library.

11 JAN. 1989. Campus booster Emil Charles Hutchins, Chair of the School of Business and Public Administration's Board of Counselors, dies at Fontana of pneumonia at age 50.

13 JAN. 1989. The Inland Empire Division of the Future Leaders of American Program receives a $10,000 gift from Kraft Foods.

14 JAN. 1989. The campus hosts the Southern Regional United Black Students Union (UBSU) Conference.

17 JAN. 1989. Peter Meenan speaks in SR on "The Miracle of Corn: Cheating on the Agricultural Support Programs." Shifra Goldman speaks in VA-110 on "Contemporary Trends in Mexican Art."

18 JAN. 1989. Science educator Peter E. Yager speaks in SU on "New Goals for Science Education for the 21st Century" as part of a Science Education Conference.

19 JAN. 1989. CBS-TV newsman Kevin Phillips speaks at the Economic Forecast Breakfast in UC on "Business and the 1988 Elections"; also appearing are Joseph Wahed Sr. and David W. Ariss. Sonja K. Foss speaks in SR on "Gender and Communication."

20 JAN. 1989. Helene Wickham Koon is named Outstanding Professor for 1988/89. The campus forms a Gay, Lesbian, and Bisexual Faculty and Staff Assoc. The campus dedicates a new Center for Science Education.

24 JAN. 1989. Bruce E. Gronbeck speaks in SR on "Communications and the President."

26 JAN. 1989. L.A. Lakers Coach Pat Riley speaks in the Gym on "Mission: Motivation," as part of the first Winter Homecoming.

27 JAN. 1989. Comedians Lynn Lavner and Danny Williams perform in SUMP.

27-29 JAN. & 3-4, 10-11, & 17-18 FEB. 1989. *Ethel*, an original play based on the life of blues singer Ethel Waters by William L. Slout and Theatre Arts major Val Limar, debuts in RH, with Limar playing the lead role; it proves so popular that it returns for 4 more days.

30 JAN. 1989. The campus hosts a meeting between 27 Swedish and Norwegian government officials and 17 local officials in PR.

31 JAN. 1989. Gilbert Geis speaks in PR on "Good Samaritan Laws: Intent and Effect."

2 FEB. 1989. Hypnotist James Downs performs in SU. John Sanders speaks on "Sculpture" in VA-110.

3 FEB. 1989. The campus revives its Affirmative Action Advisory Committee after a 2-year absence, with representation being sought from various minority constituencies and groups on campus; Pres. Evans states: "I am quite hopeful that this new advisory body will serve the university well, and provide the campus community an additional opportunity for thorough consultation concerning affirmative action issues."

4 FEB. 1989. Donald W. Jordan, Trustee of the Foundation Board (1973-89), dies in San Bernardino at age 81. Jacque Wuertenberg gives the keynote speech at the 4th Annual Family Reading Rally on SUP.

5 FEB. 1989. Actress and singer Nichelle Nichols performs in RH.

7 FEB. 1989. Native American poet Georgiana Valoyce Sánchez reads from her work in OR.

9 FEB. 1989. Craig Blurton, Assoc. Prof. of Education, is named administrator of an $880,000 grant from the State Dept. of Education at the Office of the CSU Chancellor.

11 FEB. 1989. The campus hosts the conference, "A Common Venture: Aging in the Inland Counties," with speakers Edward L. Schneider and Victor Kassel.

15 FEB. 1989. Sarah Tamor speaks on "Sculpture" in VA-110.

17 FEB. 1989. The Chancellor's Off. approves a new M.A. degree in Teaching with a Major in Mathematics, to be offered in 1989/90. The campus receives a $162,803 grant from the U.S. Dept. of Education to continue funding of the SAIL Program.

23 FEB. 1989. Amy Shapiro speaks in PiR on "Women and Words."

24 FEB. 1989. Poet Nikki Giovanni reads from her work in UC.

25 FEB. 1989. Joy Nelson speaks in RH on "Creative Ideas for the Elementary Music Classroom."

27 FEB. 1989. The campus telephone number prefix changes from 887- to 880- with the installation of a new digital telecommunications system eliminating rotary dial phones. The campus adopts a new logo featuring a stylized outline of the San Bernardino Mountains, replacing the traditional round seal used for 20 years.

28 FEB. 1989. Sculptors Christopher Schumaker and Dustin Shuler speak about their work in VA-110.

1 MAR. 1989. The campus begins offering an escort service for students and staff from Monday through Saturday.

4 MAR. 1989. The campus hosts its 13th Annual Reading Conference, "Celebrating the Learner."

13 MAR. 1989. Jim Jenkins speaks on "Sculpture" in VA-110.

15 MAR. 1989. Softball pitcher Tanna Cash throws a perfect game as CSUSB defeats Cal Baptist College, 3-0.

16 MAR. 1989. Peter Lichtenstein speaks in SR on "Political Economy of Reform in the People's Republic of China."

18 MAR. 1989. Blues singer Dianne Davidson performs in SU Pub.

20 MAR. 1989. Tracy Cooper speaks in VA-110 on "Early Veronese: Style and Patronage."

21 MAR. 1989. Louise Burton receives a Fulbright Fellowship to study in Japan.

22 MAR. 1989. Egyptologist Zahi Hawass speaks in UC on "The History of the Pyramids."

29 MAR. 1989. The campus signs an agreement with Riverside Community Coll. to allow RCC students to transfer credits.

30 MAR.-1 APR. 1989. The campus hosts the 6th Annual Conference of the Calif. Glass Exchange in RH.

31 MAR. 1989. Reginald L. Price, Athletic Dir., returns to the ranks as Prof. of Physical Education.

1 APR. 1989. Johnnie Ann Ralph, Libn., is named Assoc. Univ. Libn., replacing Max A. "Marty" Bloomberg. David L. Suenram is named Athletic Dir., replacing Reginald L. Price.

5 APR. 1989. The campus radio station, KSSB, goes off the air due to lack of funding; it returns again in Fall 1989. A. Roy Eckardt and Alice Eckardt speak at the 2nd Annual Morrow-McCombs Memorial Lecture in RH on "Salient Christian-Jewish Issues of Today"; the event is sponsored by an endowment established in memory of Lilian Morrow and Ray McCombs to facilitate interfaith understanding between Christians and Jews.

7-9 APR. 1989. William Graham performs "The Sweetest Sounds," his one-man show about Richard Rodgers, in the Theatre.

7-10 & 13-16 APR. 1989. Duncan Macfarland and Clare Whistler of the Dance Art Co. perform and conduct master classes in RH.

8 APR. 1989. The campus hosts a conference, "Adelante Mujer Hispana," in SR to aid Hispanic women.

11 APR. 1989. Hans Spiegel speaks in PR on "Citizens in the Urban Development Process: Neighborhood Development from the Bottom Up."

14 APR. 1989. Cathy Schwichtenberg speaks in ER on "Post-Gender, Post-Modern." Archeologist Richard MacNeish speaks in SR on "The Origins of Agriculture."

17 APR. 1989. Jeffrey Burton Russell speaks in PR on "Glory in Time: The Cosmos' Yearning for God—an Historical Approach."

18 APR. 1989. Trumpeter Keith Johnson speaks and performs in RH.

19 APR. 1989. Walter Eder speaks in VA-110 on "Augustus and the Power of Tradition."

24 APR. 1989. Brian Patrick McGuire speaks in PL-271 on "Cistercian Monasticism," and also in PiR on "The Myths of the Valley of Fruitfulness and the City on the Hills: From Twelfth-Century Cistercians to Twentieth-Century Americans." Michael Allen Hoffman speaks in PR on "Hierakonpolis: Cradle of the Pharaohs."

26 APR. 1989. The campus hosts the Regional Educators Symposium, "Strengthening Connections: What Is? What Can Be?" with singer and humorist Peter Alsop as keynote speaker.

28 APR. 1989. Alumnus Assemblyman Paul A. Woodruff visits the campus. As part of Cinco de Mayo celebrations, a Cinco de Mayo Queen is crowned at a dance held in UC, with music by Los Genis. Margo McCaffery speaks in SUMP on "Pain Assessment and Intervention." Howard Frederick receives a Fulbright Fellowship to study at the Univ. of Salzburg in Austria during 1989/90.

29 APR. 1989. The campus hosts its 3rd Annual Environmental Expo, "Linking Citizens with Recycling, Waste, Management, and Resource Conservation," in the Gymnasium.

3 MAY 1989. Raymond Buriel speaks in SR on "La Cultura Latino-Americana—A Rich History of Traditions and Diversity." Peter Rhodes speaks in VA-110 on "Athenian Democracy." Bozenna Chylinska speaks in FO-177 on "Jews in Contemporary Poland.," and also in PL-271 on "Jews in Contemporary America."

4 MAY 1989. Historian Sherna Gluck speaks in SU on women's history. The quartet Son Cuatro and *canción nueva* composer Rosa Martha Zarate perform in UC.

5 MAY 1989. Mariachi California, Folklórico California, and Aztec dancers Xipe Totec perform on LCP. Richard Brilliant speaks in VA-110 on "Greek and Roman Classicism: The Creation and the Recollection of an Ideal," to inaugurate an exhibit (through Jun. 2) of 54 Greek vases from the collection of Hanita and Aaron Dechter.

5-6 MAY 1989. Dancers Jo Dierdorff, Paula Naggi, and Stephanie Gilliland perform in RH.

8 MAY 1989. Futurist Willis Harman speaks in UC on "What the Second Scientific Revolution Means for Business and Education."

9 MAY 1989. Ex-Calif. Gov. Edmund G. "Pat" Brown speaks in UC on "California: The Year 2000."

10 May 1989. W. R. "Bob" Holcomb takes office as S.B. Mayor for the 2nd time, replacing Evlyn Wilcox. C. Chan, Singapore's Ambassador to the United Nations, speaks in SUMP on "The Problems and Accomplishments of the United Nation."

11 May 1989. Poet Sherod Santos reads from his work in RH. Jay O'Brien speaks in CA-186 on "The Crisis in the Sudan."

12 May 1989. Artist William Wegman speaks in PS-10 about his whimsical portraits of his dog, Man Ray. Cal State student and U.S. Air Force Capt. David G. Campbell dies at age 28 when his F-4 fighter jet crashes during a training exercise south of Salinas in central California. The campus hosts a conference, "Time for Cooperation! Strategies for Directed Growth in the Inland Empire," in LC, featuring John E. Husing, John De-Grove, and Jane G. Pisano. The campus re-creates The Inland Empire Management Center with the help of an $80,000 contract from General Dynamics to train employees for a certification exam in production inventory management.

16 May 1989. A student is raped in a campus parking lot, the first such crime ever reported at CSUSB. The CSU Board of Trustees names Robert C. Detweiler, VP for Academic Affairs, as Pres. of CSU Dominguez Hills.

17 May 1989. Kenneth Hamma speaks in VA-110 on "The Dechter Collection of Greek Vases." Puerto Rican composer Hector Campos Parsi speaks in RH on "Latin American Influences on Band and Chamber Wind Ensembles."

17-20 May 1989. The campus hosts its 1st Music of the Americas Festival on Pfau Library Plaza, with performances on May 20 by jazz group UCLATINO, Mixcoacalli Folk Dance Ensemble, Los Peldanos Trio, INCA Folk Ensemble, and Poncho Sánchez and His Latin Jazz Ensemble.

19 May 1989. Ecuadorian soprano María Niles performs with the Palo Verde Trio in RH. Stephen Loza and Danilo Lozano speak and perform in RH on "Latin American Pop Music." Raymond Torres-Santos, Hector Campos Parsi, and Aurileo de la Vega speak and perform in RH on "Concern Music in Latin America."

20 May 1989. The rock group The Untouchables performs in the Gymnasium. The Newman Catholic Fellowship of CSUSB and the John XXIII Newman Ministry present the musical review, *Together Again*, featuring Jeanie Lamana and Kathy Fitzpatrick, in SR.

22 May 1989. Jerry Porras and Gus Cárdenas speak in SR on "Careers in Business and Business Education for Minorities," and also in RH on "Latinos in Contemporary Business Environments: Changing Trends."

24 MAY 1989. Latino Business Students Assoc. Pres. Claudia Hurtado and MEChA Pres. Eloisa Rivera speak in SR on "Issues of Minority Student Leaders in the 1990s." Colleen Fahey Fearn and Ethel Long-Scott speak in SR on "Welfare Reform: A Women's Issue."

30 MAY 1989. Ballet Folklórico Cultural performs on LCP. Panamanian poet Enrique Jaramillo-Levi reads from his work in PL-277.

31 MAY 1989. Christopher Donnan speaks in UC on "Discovery of a Moche Tomb in Sipán, Peru."

7 JUN. 1989. The pop group Cabazon Dinosaurs performs in SU; afterwards, 2 men cause $1,300 in vandalism.

11 JUN. 1989. Frank Aguirre, Lect. in Foreign Languages (1984-89), dies in Riverside at age 37.

15 JUN. 1989. The campus hosts a reception in SUMP to honor departing VP Robert C. Detweiler.

16 JUN. 1989. The campus installs 8 emergency phones inside 7 buildings, and 13 emergency phones at various outdoor locations.

17 JUN. 1989. The 23rd Commencement is held on the Library Lawn, with CSU Chancellor Reynolds giving the keynote address. Also present are Assemblymen Gerald Eaves and Paul A. Woodruff.

18 JUN. 1989. The pop group REAL performs at the 6th Annual Juneteenth celebration.

19 JUN. 1989. Zahir Ahmed is named Dir. of the International Student Services Program, replacing the late M. Jeanne Hogenson.

20 JUN. 1989. Gary A. Negin receives a Fulbright Fellowship to study in Jamaica during 1989/90.

26-30 JUN. 1989. The campus hosts the conference, "Teachers in Computer Integration in the Classroom," with speakers Lynne Anderson-Inman, Jenny Better-House, Ginger Britt, and Darlene Messinger.

30 JUN. 1989. Glenn Schroeder Dumke, ex-CSU Chancellor (1962-82), dies of a heart attack in L.A. at age 72.

SUM. 1989. Del LaVerne Watson, Prof. of Nursing (1981-89), retires.

5 Jul. 1989. Musical revue The Karousel Kids performs on LCP.

7 Jul. 1989. The Chancellor's Off. approves a new M.A. degree in School Administration, beginning with 1989/90. The campus moves the Athletics Program under the University Relations Division.

8 Jul. 1989. The Inland Alliance of Black School Educators and the Black Faculty and Staff Assoc. of CSUSB sponsor the conference, "Our Vision: Learning Achieving, Nurturing, Empowering." The campus signs an agreement with Citrus College guaranteeing admission to qualified CC transfer students attending CSUSB.

12 Jul. 1989. Bluegrass group Phil Salazar Band performs on LCP.

13 Jul. 1989. Rock group Camper Van Beethoven performs in SU.

16 Jul. 1989. The campus hosts the Orange Empire Dog Club All-Breed Dog Show and Obedience Trial.

19 Jul. 1989. The flute-guitar duo, Jan Borland and John Dowdall, perform on LCP.

26 Jul. 1989. The folk music group Shanachie performs on LCP.

31 Jul. 1989. Robert C. Detweiler, VP for Academic Affairs, resigns to become Pres. of CSU, Dominguez Hills.

1 Aug. 1989. Amer M. El-Ahraf, Assoc. VP for Academic Resources, is named Act. VP for Academic Affairs, replacing Robert C. Detweiler.

2 Aug. 1989. Dixieland band The Fullertowne Strutters performs on LCP.

9 Aug. 1989. The bluegrass group High Country performs on LCP.

12 Aug. 1989. The campus hosts the Bethune Youth Conference, featuring Rep. George E. Brown, Lois J. Carson, Debra Cooper, Wilmer D. Carter, and Beverly Powell.

16 Aug. 1989. Country western band The Bonners performs on LCP.

18-19 Aug. 1989. The campus hosts the 4th Annual Reading, Rhythms, and Rainbows Conference for elementary school teachers.

21 Aug. 1989. David Beyer is named first Sports Information Dir.

22-25 Aug. 1989. The campus hosts the conference, "1989 Teachers Are

No. 1," with anthropologist Jennifer James, *Oklahoma Observer* Editor Frosty Troy, author Dan Clark, and Carolyn Corbin giving the keynote speeches.

23 AUG. 1989. The jazz group Latin Society performs on LCP.

1 SEPT. 1989. The campus makes a major change in its curriculum, shifting from 5 unit credits granted for each course to the standard 4 units, thereby abandoning the Ruml Plan that had been in effect since 1965; this was the last remnant of the University's original curriculum plan to be discarded. The campus begins offering an M.S.W. degree in Social Work. Julius D. Kaplan, Assoc. Dean of Graduate Studies (1986-89), is named first Dean of Graduate Studies. The School of Education reorganizes, replacing the Depts. of Teacher Education and Graduate Programs with the Depts. of Elementary and Bilingual Education, Secondary and Vocational Education, and Advanced Studies. Edna L. Steinman, Dir. of Publications (1968-89), retires.

3 SEPT. 1989. The campus hosts the 3rd Annual Middle School Conference, "Bridging Tomorrow's Needs Through Today's Minds," at the Maruko Hotel, with Anthony Jackson, Dir. of the Carnegie Council on Adolescent Development, giving the keynote speech.

15 SEPT. 1989. The body of a murdered 15-year-old girl, Terri Ann Rodríguez, is found in a ditch near campus.

19 SEPT. 1989. At the annual convocation, Pres. Evans says that the Inland Empire's growing social and commercial needs are making it increasingly important that the campus "provide students with an education as broad as the issues that are sweeping the modern world." He notes that CSUSB implemented a new mandatory student advising policy in 1988/89: "Our current generation of students requires more nurturing, and I believe this new advising policy is the linchpin for one of the most essential services of a modern university." The campus also added 22,000 sq. ft. of temporary classrooms and office space during Summer 1989 to accommodate additional enrollment, and offered new degree programs in Commercial Music, Educational Administration, Teaching Mathematics, Social Work, and Environmental Education. In 1989/90 the campus will begin construction of University Hall and the Student Union Addition, plus 2 temporary parking lots.

23 SEPT. 1989. The campus and the Pomona Valley Writers' Assoc. sponsor a Writers' Conference, featuring Ray Bradbury, *Los Angeles Times* columnist Jack Smith, Monica Highland (aka Carolyn See, Lisa See, and John Espey), Carol Muske Dukes, Rodney J. Simard, Jason Rubinsteen, and Terry Dunnahoo.

25 Sept. 1989. The campus opens a 600-space temporary dirt parking lot southeast of the Serrano Village Residence Halls.

27 Sept. 1989. The campus hosts a "Conference on the Integration of Disabled Students."

28 Sept. 1989. The campus receives a $550,000 gift of computer equipment from AT&T.

3 Oct. 1989. Poet Thomas Lynch reads from his work in SR.

5 Oct. 1989. Will Roscoe speaks in UC on "The Zuni Man-Woman."

6 Oct. 1989. The campus hosts the 2nd Annual Conference on Preventing High Risk Behavior in Our Kids, with speakers Jack Cavanaugh and Lou Denti.

7 Oct. 1989. Violinist Peter Marsh performs in RH.

11 Oct. 1989. Writer Alex Haley speaks in the Gymnasium on "Find the Good…and Praise It."

12 Oct. 1989. Olga Kalbermatter speaks in ER on "The Process of Genetic Counseling." The campus signs an agreement with Coll. of the Desert to facilitate admittance of COD students into CSUSB.

13 Oct. 1989. The campus hosts the 6th Annual S.B. Chamber of Commerce Business Outlook Conference in UC, with speakers State Sen. William R. "Bill" Leonard, Matthew V. Scocozza, and Phillip E. Vincent.

16 Oct. 1989. Muneesh Joshi speaks in RH on "Women as the Savior: Discourse on Tantra."

17 Oct. 1989. Moustafa Gabal speaks in BI-129 on "Biological and Biochemical Effects of Aflatoxins on the Mammalian Host." The campus signs an agreement with Chaffey College to guarantee admittance of qualified CC students into CSUSB.

19 Oct. 1989. Gordon Ariel speaks in SUMP on "High Technology and Human Performance." Julie Sconza speaks in ER on "Gastrointestinal Tube Feeding." Herbert Aptheker speaks in SR on "The Life and Work of W. E. B. DuBois."

24 Oct. 1989. James F. Miles speaks in SR on "Strategic Planning: A View from the Top." Hana Ayala speaks in BI-129 on "Environmental Design for International Tourism: (Landscape Ecology and Design)."

25 OCT. 1989. Ex-Iranian Ambassador to the U.S. Mansour Farhung speaks in RH on "U.S.-Iranian Relations: The Making (and Unmaking) of a Quagmire." Andrew Leicester speaks in VA-110 on "Public Art and the Ways of Securing These Commissions." The campus signs an agreement with Mt. San Jacinto College to guarantee admittance of qualified MSJC students into CSUSB.

26 OCT. 1989. Stephen Ashwal speaks in ER on "Seizure Disorders, Medications, and the Role of the Special Education Teacher in Monitoring Seizures."

31 OCT. 1989. Vandals tag campus walks and buildings with graffiti.

1 NOV. 1989. The CSU Board of Trustees approves a $24.5 million, 121,239-square-foot addition to the Pfau Library.

3 NOV. 1989. 4 offices on the 5th floor of the Pfau Library are vandalized, with items worth $2,400 being stolen.

7 NOV. 1989. Sculptor Zeke Berman speaks about his work in VA-110. Dr. W. Benson Harer speaks in BI-129 on "The Health Care System in Ancient Egypt: Its Influences on Modern Medicine."

8 NOV. 1989. Poet Maurya Simon reads from her work in SR.

9 NOV. 1989. Poet Eloise Klein Healy speaks in OR on "Contemporary American Poets." Poet Jack Kendrick reads from his work in SR.

10 NOV. 1989. CSU Trustee Anthony M. Vitti visits the campus.

14 NOV. 1989. *Newsweek* editors and correspondents Thomas M. DeFrank, Doug Waller, Rich Thomas, and Margaret Warner discuss "Recent Events in the Warsaw Pact Nations" in UC. Children's writer Marilyn Cram Donohue speaks in SUMP on "How to Use Historical Fiction to Teach Literature and History in the Classroom."

15 NOV. 1989. The campus signs an agreement with Victor Valley Coll. to facilitate admittance of VVC students into CSUSB.

16 NOV. 1989. George Lipsitz speaks in RH on "A Life in the Struggle: Ivory Perry and the Culture of Opposition." Benoi Turyahikayo-Rugyema speaks in PiR on "Idi Amin's Uganda."

17 NOV. 1989. Artist Jerry Burchfield speaks about his work in VA-110. Assemblywoman Maxine Waters speaks at the annual Freedom Banquet of the S.B. Branch of the NAACP.

19 NOV. 1989. *Los Angeles Times* columnist Jack Smith speaks at the Library Lecture Series in RH on "My Times at the *Times*."

20 NOV. 1989. The campus installs a protective guardrail around the perimeter of the first floor of the Pfau Library after several employees are blown off the deck by Santa Ana winds.

26 NOV. 1989. Dorothy Robinson-Silas, retired Custodian, dies at age 62. The Palo Verde Trio performs in RH.

1 DEC. 1989. Patrick A. Areffi is named first Business Manager of ASI.

1-2 DEC. 1989. William Graham performs his one-man show, "Cole Porter: One of a Kind," in RH.

4 DEC. 1989. An arbitrator places a tenured CSUSB professor on 3 years' probation after he is found guilty of placing a racially tinged note on the windshield of an African-American student's vehicle; the professor denies knowing the student or writing the note.

5 DEC. 1989. Deborah Brouse speaks in SR on "Zero Population Growth."

8 DEC. 1989. Actor Ed Weston speaks in the Theatre.

1990

6 JAN. 1990. Assemblyman Paul A. Woodruff speaks to the Board of Directors of the Calif. Student Assoc. Alumni magazine *Panorama* reduces its size from 11 x 17 to 8.5 x 11 inches with its Winter issue.

10 JAN. 1990. The CSU Board of Trustees approves plans to construct the building that will become Jack H. Brown Hall. CSU Chancellor Reynolds notes that Gov. Deukmejian's proposed System budget for 1990/91 "is wholly inadequate to accommodate the number of students who are projected to enroll…[and] will require major cutbacks."

11 JAN. 1990. Elizabeth Clark speaks in SR on "Clinical Sociological Perspectives on Illness and Loss."

19 JAN. 1990. Robert E. Cramer is named Outstanding Professor for 1989/90. The campus hosts its 3rd Annual Economic Outlook Breakfast in UC, with Richard Rosenberg speaking on "Banking in the 1990s," and Michael Bazdarich on "The Economy in the Nineties: National and Local Perspectives."

26 JAN. 1990. As part of Homecoming, Olympic decathlon winner Rafer

Johnson speaks in the Gymnasium on "Being the Best You Can Be," and is honored with a dinner in PR. Artist Silvia Impert speaks about her work in VA-110.

26-28 Jan. & 2-4 Feb. 1990. A revised version of the musical play, *Ethel*, by Cal State student Val Limar with Prof. William L. Slout, begins its 2nd run in RH.

29 Jan. 1990. Jim Munro speaks in SR on "Entrepreneurship in Public Management."

3 Feb. 1990. Evelyn Forrester and Olga Loya speak to the Annual Family Reading Rally on the SUP.

5 Feb. 1990. Pres. Evans announces that CSUSB's intercollegiate athletic program will move from NCAA Division III to Division II, effective with school year 1991/92.

6 Feb. 1990. David Bunn speaks in VA-109 on "The History of Art to Produce Contemporary Works."

7 Feb. 1990. Traffic signals are installed at the corner of University Pkwy. and Northpark Blvd. Karen Kolehmainen receives a $9,487 grant to study quark-gluon plasma. Clifford O. Young Sr. receives a $16,990 grant from NSF to study "Redevelopment and the Redevelopment Process from Three Different Theoretical Perspectives in the Two Counties of the Inland Empire."

8 Feb. 1990. Robert Nideffer speaks in PE-129 on "Performance Enhancement and Concentration Techniques for High Level Athletes," and in TC-16 on "Sport Psychology Does Not Equal Sport Pharmacology."

8-9 Feb. 1990. The campus hosts a conference on AIDS, "Making Peace: Issues in Death and Dying," with speakers Dr. German Maisonet, Dr. Donald Francis, Rev. Carl Bean, and Gil Gerald.

12 Feb. 1990. Attallah Shabazz, daughter of the late Malcolm X, speaks in RH on "Positively You." Prexy Nesbitt, consultant to Mozambique, speaks in PS-10.

16 Feb. 1990. Richard Newman speaks in PS-10 on "Land, Water, Life Styles: The Impact of the *Valdez* on Prince William Sound."

20 Feb. 1990. The campus hosts the seminar, "Small Business Management Strategies for the 1990s," in SR, with speakers David Paulin and J. Casteel.

21 FEB. 1990. Sandra Lee Fredriksen, Cal State alumna and Lect. in English, dies at age 44. Mayme Clayton speaks in SUMP on "Black Films of the '20s, '30s, and '40s."

22 FEB. 1990. The campus hosts a teleconference on "Europe '92: The New American Challenge" in SR.

23 FEB. 1990. The campus and the Fontana Unified School Dist. receive a $264,000 grant from the State Dept. of Education and the State Commission on Teacher Credentialing to track the progress of 80 new teachers.

24 FEB. 1990. SECHABA performs in RH.

27 FEB. 1990. CSU Trustee Ted J. Saenger visits the campus.

28 FEB. 1990. Taylor Woodrow Construction California Ltd. receives a $15,997,000 contract to construct University Hall.

3 MAR. 1990. The campus hosts its 14th Annual Reading Conference, "Celebrating Literacy," in the Maruko Hotel, with Sims Bishop speaking on "Windows & Mirrors: Literature and Parallel Culture," and Charlotte Huck on "Celebrating Literature"; Charlotte Huck and Kristiana Gregory also sign their children's books.

8 MAR. 1990. Phillip Uri Treisman speaks in SR on "Academic Perestroika: Teaching, Learning, and the Faculty's Role in Turbulent Times."

9 MAR. 1990. Laura X, Dir. of the National Clearinghouse on Marital and Date Rape, speaks in PR on "Sexual Assault Issues."

10 MAR. 1990. The Honor Band performs in RH under the leadership of Don G. Wilcox.

13-14 MAR. 1990. Students defeat a referendum to increase fees to support the campus move from NCAA Division III to Division II.

14 MAR. 1990. Joseph Ghougassian, U.S. Ambassador to Qatar, speaks in PR on "The Gulf War and Its Impact on the United States." Poet Robert Mezey reads from his work in SR.

15 MAR. 1990. The Pfau Library sponsors a reception to honor the acquisition of its 500,000th volume, an 1891 map depicting the southwest portion of S.B. Co.; as part of the celebration, well-known writer Maya Angelou speaks in the Gymnasium as part of "An Evening with Maya Angelou."

18 MAR. 1990. Pianist Robert Palmer performs in RH.

21 MAR. 1990. A new 233-space parking lot opens near the Physical Education Building and Serrano Village. The campus receives a $30,000 grant from the Chancellor's Off. of the Calif. Community Colleges to increase minority students pursuing a teaching career.

21-23 MAR. 1990. The campus hosts The Renaissance Group at the Maruko Hotel, with CSU Chancellor Reynolds attending.

23 MAR. 1990. Pres. Evans creates a Task Force on Campus Safety.

26 MAR. 1990. Mildred M. Henry is named "1990 Woman of the Year" for the 66th Assembly Dist.

27 MAR. 1990. Eugene J. Fisher speaks in RH at the 3rd Annual Morrow-McCombs Memorial Lecture on "Christian and Jewish Relations: The Third Millennium." Tom M. Rivera receives a $5,000 grant from Target Discount Stores to support the Kiwanis Future Leaders Program. Nicole Bournias-Vardiabasis receives a $17,000 grant from the John Hopkins Center for Alternatives to Animal Testing to do research on the "Detection of Teratogens by Utilization of B-Galactosidase Reporter Gene Activity."

31 MAR. 1990. Catherine C. Gannon, Dean of CVC, goes on sabbatical leave.

1 APR. 1990. Susan E. Summers is named Act. Dean of CVC, replacing Catherine C. Gannon.

3 APR. 1990. Movie illustrator Drew Struzan speaks in RH.

4 APR. 1990. Poet Gary Soto reads from his work in SR.

8 APR. 1990. When his hang glider veers off course, Brad Bauer becomes entangled in 115,000-volt power lines near the campus.

9 APR. 1990. Carlos Lorrain de Ferari, ex-Chilean Ambassador to Switzerland, speaks in ER on "Chile: Human Rights and the End of the Pinochet Era."

11 APR. 1990. The pop group Polyhedra performs in WP in SU.

17 APR. 1990. Ecologist Anne H. Ehrlich speaks in the Gymnasium on "The Human Population Dilemma."

18 APR. 1990. Jack H. Brown, CEO and Pres. of Stater Brothers Markets, receives the first Arrowhead Distinguished Chief Executive Lecture

Award at a luncheon held in UC, and speaks on "Leadership for the '90s."

19 Apr. 1990. Norton Younglove speaks in UC on "Healthy Air vs. Healthy Economy: Can We Have Both?"

20 Apr. 1990. CSU Chancellor Reynolds announces her resignation effective 1 Oct. 1990, after questions are raised about recent administrative pay increases and the misuse of State funds.

21 Apr. 1990. The campus hosts its 4th Annual Inland Empire Environmental Expo, "Water: Earth's Precious Resource," with S.B. Mayor Holcomb moderating a forum on the city's water supply in PR, and G. Louis Fletcher giving the keynote address; other participants include Carlos Madrid, Neil Cline, Diana Barich, Herbert Wessell, Gerald J. Thibeault, and Cik Corneille. As part of the celebration, Frank Helling presents a drama, *Meet John Muir*, in PR.

24 Apr. 1990. Photographer Skeet McAuley speaks about his work in ER. The campus hosts a trainers' workshop for middle grade educators, "A World of Difference," in PR. Patricia Tefft Cousin receives an "Outstanding Dissertation Award" from the International Reading Assoc.

26 Apr. 1990. Writer, actor, and director Luis Valdez speaks in RH on "Theatre and Literature of Latin America," and also in UC on "The Emergence of the Hispanic Artist." Lazlo Garai speaks in SR on "Perestroika in Hungary: How the People View the Changes."

27 Apr. 1990. State Sen. Ruben S. Ayala speaks in PR on "The Effects of Organized Crime and Gangs on the County."

30 Apr. 1990. Folk musicians Agustín Lira and Grupo Musical Alma perform. The Palo Verde Trio performs in RH.

2 May 1990. Ramón Cortines speaks in SR on "Administration in the 1990s and Beyond."

4 May 1990. Aztec dancers Xipe Totec and Mexican folk group Son Cuatro perform on LCP.

5 May 1990. Jorun B. Johns receives the Austrian Medal of Honor for Arts and Letters from the Republic of Austria.

8 May 1990. The Women's Resource Center opens for business. The campus hosts a teleconference, "Introduction to Health and Safety for Educational Institutions," in PL-087, with James Unmack, Elaine Bild, Stanley H. Pine, and Jan Schienle participating.

10 MAY 1990. As part of Creative Writing Day, Writers Jay Gummerman and Michelle Latiolais speak to local students in RH.

12 MAY 1990. Judge F. Douglas McDaniel provides the keynote address at the 5th Annual Law Day celebration.

16 MAY 1990. W. Ann Reynolds, Chancellor of the CSU System, abruptly resigns at a Board of Trustees meeting (taking vacation time through 31 Jul.), and is replaced by Ellis E. McCune, Pres. of CSU, Hayward, as Act. Chancellor.

18 MAY 1990. The School of Education forms a campus chapter of Phi Delta Kappa (ΦΔK), an honorary international educational organization.

19 MAY 1990. Phil Crowley conducts a "Voice-Over Workshop" in the Theatre.

21 MAY 1990. Groundbreaking is held for University Hall, with CSU Trustee Ralph R. Pesqueira attending. Sterling Stuckey speaks in PiR on "African Influence on the Formation of Slave Culture."

22-25 MAY 1990. The Coyotes golf team finishes 4th in the NCAA Championships held in Jekyll Island, Georgia.

23 MAY 1990. The campus receives an Excellence in Energy Management Award from Southern California Edison Co. at the Maruko Hotel, together with a $4,975 rebate check. Salvador Torres speaks in VA-110 on "Chicano Park in the National Defense."

24 MAY 1990. The campus hosts a forum on "Malathion Spraying" in UC, with Jorge Mancillas, Joanne Wasbauer, and Gloria Anderson participating.

27 MAY 1990. The Coyotes baseball team competes for the first time in the NCAA Division III World Series at Battle Creek, Michigan, ultimately placing 4th.

30 MAY 1990. Jazz composer R. Murray Shafer speaks on "The Princess of the Stars," and performs in RH, as part of the 5-day Music of the Americas Festival.

31 MAY 1990. The campus installs a new chapter of Pi Lambda Theta (ΠΛΘ), a national honor society in education, in SR.

31 MAY-1 JUN. 1990. The campus co-sponsors the conference, "The Challenge of Growth in California and the Inland Empire: Shaping Solutions for the 1990s," at the Red Lion Inn in Ontario, Calif.

1 JUN. 1990. Denise Greenstein conducts a workshop in SR on "Appreciating Different Personality Types." The Jazz Ensemble performs in UC.

2 JUN. 1990. Maynard Ferguson and the Big Bop Nouveau Band perform on LCP. Patricia McNaughton speaks at a seminar on "How to Succeed in a Family Business."

8 JUN. 1990. The campus restricts vehicular traffic on most walkways.

16 JUN. 1990. The 24th Commencement is held on the Library Lawn, with Arnold Garson, Editor of the *San Bernardino County Sun*, giving the keynote address; among the graduates is 81-year-old Thomas Tortora; also attending are CSU Vice Chancellor Caesar Naples, Assemblyman Paul A. Woodruff, CSU Trustees Marian Bagdasarian and Scott Vick, and S.B. City Attorney and Alumni Assoc. Pres. James F. Penman.

20 JUN. 1990. Joe White, Gary Clark, and Chuck Felton conduct a seminar, "Profits from Real Estate in the '90s," in UC. The campus signs an agreement with Mt. San Antonio College to guarantee admittance of qualified MSJC students into CSUSB.

22 JUN. 1990. The campus hosts a dinner in UC honoring retiring VP Leonard B. Farwell. Deborah Kravitz is named the first Environmental Health and Safety Officer.

30 JUN. 1990. Leonard B. Farwell, VP for Administration and Finance (1962-90), retires, at 28 years being the longest-serving staff member at the time of his retirement, and the longest-serving member of the campus administration to date; he was the first employee hired by Pres. John M. Pfau in June 1962 to plan the development of the University. Stella T. Clark, Prof. of Spanish and Chair of the Foreign Languages Dept. and Assoc. Dean of Academic Administration and Int. Dean of the School of Humanities (1971-90), resigns. Senior Gena Philibert receives a $5,000 grant from the South Coast Air Quality Management Dist. to develop a "Clean Air Kit" to teach children how to protect their environment. Susan E. Summers, Act. Dean of CVC, returns to the ranks. Cal State sophomore Paul K. Carillo drowns in the Mendenhall River near Juneau, AK, at age 20.

1 JUL. 1990. David P. DeMauro, Dir. of the Physical Plant, is named Act. VP for Administration and Finance, replacing Leonard B. Farwell. The campus launches a new, 2-tiered employee recognition program that includes the annual presentation of an Outstanding Employee Award and 2

Performance Excellence Awards. Catherine C. Gannon returns to her position as Dean of CVC.

2 JUL. 1990. Helena Villacres Stanton, Assoc. Prof. of Education (1975-90), retires.

11 JUL. 1990. Pop group The GTE Connection performs on LCP.

17 JUL. 1990. Chris A. Topoleski, Custodian, suffers a heat stroke while bicycling near Perris Hill Park in S.B., and enters into a coma.

18 JUL. 1990. Irish harpist Dennis Doyle and the group Aisling perform on LCP.

20 JUL. 1990. Construction begins on a new electronic signboard at the Main Entrance, and on a new pedestrian walkway from Northpark Blvd. to the Perimeter Road.

25 JUL. 1990. Caribbean band Pandemonium performs on LCP.

31 JUL. 1990. Amer M. El-Ahraf, Act. VP for Academic Affairs, returns to his position of Assoc. VP for Academic Resources.

1 AUG. 1990. Dennis L. Hefner is named VP for Academic Affairs, replacing Amer M. El-Ahraf. Sidney A. Ribeau, Dean of Undergraduate Studies, resigns to take a post at Calif. Polytechnic State Univ., San Luis Obispo. The blues duo Tom Ball and Kenny Sultan perform on LCP.

2 AUG. 1990. Joel L. Nossoff, Asst. Dean of Undergraduate Studies, is named Act. Dean.

5 AUG. 1990. Frank Robert Beeman, Advanced Studies, dies at age 64.

8 AUG. 1990. The bluegrass group Sidesaddle performs on LCP with singer Julie Wingfield.

14 AUG. 1990. Ernest F. García, Prof. of Education and Dean of the School of Education (1968-90), retires.

15 AUG. 1990. John Dunworth, ex-Pres. of George Peabody College, is named Int. Dean of the School of Education, replacing Ernest F. García. The ensemble group Westwind Brass performs on LCP.

21-24 AUG. 1990. The campus hosts its 6th Annual "Teachers Are No. 1" Conference, with Hanoch McCarty, Carl Boyd, and Emmet Littleton giving the keynote addresses.

22 AUG. 1990. The Latin jazz group Flinting performs on LCP.

29 AUG. 1990. The group Latin Society performs on LCP.

31 AUG. 1990. Catherine C. Gannon, Dean of CVC, returns to the ranks as Prof. of English. Retirements: Helene W. Koon, Prof. of English (1970-90); Ralph H. Petrucci, Prof. of Chemistry, Chair of the Div. of Natural Sciences, Dean of Academic Planning (1964-90); Alexander D. Sokoloff, Prof. of Biology (1965-90); James D. Thomas, Prof. of Political Science, Assoc. Dean of Academic Administration, Dean of Academic Administration, Assoc. VP of Instruction Resources (1968-90).

1 SEPT. 1990. Peter A. Wilson, VP for Student Services, is named Int. Dean of CVC, replacing Catherine C. Gannon. Juan C. González, Asst. to the President, is named Int. VP for Student Services. Richard T. Ackley, Prof. of Political Science (1972-90), retires. The campus, facing a $3 million budget cut, slashes class sections, faculty, library books, computers, and lecturers. The campus initiates an Honors Program. The campus bans alcohol from its residence halls.

7 SEPT. 1990. The Social Work Dept., as part of a 10-school consortium, receives a $350,000 grant from the Ford Foundation to train graduate social workers for the needy. The campus opens a walkway from Northpark Blvd. to the Perimeter Rd.

13 SEPT. 1990. The campus hosts its 4th Annual Children's Network Conference, "Bridging the Gap: Schools and Services for At-Risk Youth," with keynote speaker Peter Alsop.

18 SEPT. 1990. At the annual convocation, Pres. Evans launches the celebration of the campus's 25th anniversary, with remarks by Prof. Ward M. McAfee, and the attendance of many of the individuals who were employed by the University from 1962-65.

21 SEPT. 1990. Amer M. El-Ahraf, Assoc. VP for Academic Resources and Act. VP of Academic Affairs (1973-90), resigns to become Exec. VP at CSU, Dominguez Hills.

27 SEPT. 1990. Writer Christopher Stone signs his book, *Re-Creating Your Self*, in the Coyote Bookstore. The campus hosts a reception for retiring Assoc. VP Amer M. El-Ahraf in UC.

3 OCT. 1990. Activist Ralph Nader, Wes Bannister, and Ken Reich speak in the Gymnasium at "A Forum on Car Insurance in California." *The Chronicle* campus newspaper increases its size to a bedsheet format.

5 Oct. 1990. The campus unveils an electronic signboard at the corner of Northpark Blvd. and University Pkwy. Cynthia Linton is named Int. Dir. of the Learning Center, replacing Sandra Clarkson. A Physics professor is removed from his class for disruptive behavior and taken to a mental health facility.

13 Oct. 1990. The Chinese Youth Goodwill Mission from Taipei performs in RH.

15 Oct. 1990. The campus welcomes 86 women from Yasuda Women's Univ. in Japan as part of a student exchange program.

19 Oct. 1990. Kruger McGrew Construction receives a $590,275 contract to construct a 235-space parking lot east of the Housing lot and a 567-space lot between the existing main lot and Northpark Blvd. east of University Pkwy. C. Donald Kajcienski, Assoc. VP for Enrollment Services, resigns.

23 Oct. 1990. Ron Daniels speaks in PR on "The Resurgence of Racism in America: The Causes and the Cure."

24 Oct. 1990. Carol Falk speaks in SUMP on "Case Management for Nurses and Nursing Administrators."

25 Oct. 1990. Actor and playwright Buddy Butler speaks in SU Lounge on "African-American Film Night." Biruté Ciplijauskaité speaks in SR on "Woman in Search of Her Language." Robert Meadow speaks in RH on "Where Have All the Voters Gone?"

26-27 Oct. 1990. The campus hosts its 5th Annual Black Family Conference in the Creative Arts Building, with State Sen. Diane E. Watson giving the keynote address.

27 Oct. 1990. The campus hosts a gala at the National Orange Show to celebrate the 25th anniversary of its opening, featuring the debut of new alma mater and fight songs, "Hail, Our Alma Mater," by Loren H. Filbeck, and "Cal State Fight Song," by Arthur A. Moorefield; participants include S.B. Mayor Holcomb, S.B. City Councilman Mike Maudsley, ex-Pres. Pfau, Suzanne Luck of Apple Computers, and Lois J. and Henry Carson. Actor and playwright Buddy Butler again speaks in the Commons on "Preserving the African-American Family." Oct. 27 is proclaimed "Cal State Day" by S.B. City.

28 Oct. 1990. Pianist Sergei Edelman performs in RH.

30 Oct. 1990. Jordanian legislator Fakhry Kawar speaks on campus.

31 Oct. 1990. The campus receives a $32,000 grant from the American Anti-Vivisection Society to find alternatives to the use of animal subjects in laboratory testing.

1 Nov. 1990. The CSUSB Emergency Loan Program is suspended due to lack of funds. The Head Start Program begins at the PAL (Provisional Learning Center) operated by Mildred D. Henry.

2 Nov. 1990. Carlos Márquez, Personnel Management Specialist (1984-90), retires.

4 Nov. 1990. Ward M. McAfee speaks on "CSUSB Celebrates 25 Years" in RH in conjunction with the publication of his book, *In Search of Community: A History of California State University, San Bernardino*.

6 Nov. 1990. Pres. Evans addresses the Faculty Senate, noting that the budget situation represents "by far the most difficult year our campus and system has seen," with cuts slated across the board for all campus divisions.

7 Nov. 1990. Comedians Lizette Mizelle, Greg Otto, and Doug Benson perform in WP. Tyrone Anthony Jazz Band performs on SUP.

8 Nov. 1990. Ex-Pres. Pfau speaks in SR on "Breaking Ground: The First Days of Cal State."

15 Nov. 1990. Artist Yolande McKay speaks in VA-109 on "Oxymoronics." Robert Robinson speaks in SR on "The Uptown Coalition: Philadelphia's Victory over R.J. Reynolds Tobacco Company."

16 Nov. 1990. Michael Parenti speaks in PR on "Media Bias and Coverage of the Persian Gulf Crisis."

19 Nov. 1990. The Digital Duo Band performs with singer Michael John in WP.

28 Nov. 1990. Mary Nichols speaks in SR on "Air Pollution: Is It the Limit to Growth?"

5 Dec. 1990. The campus installs the S.B. Desert Mountain Chapter of Phi Delta Kappa (ΦΔK), an international fraternity of educators.

7 Dec. 1990. Cheryl A. Smith, Dir. of Admissions, is named Assoc. VP for Enrollment Services, replacing C. Donald Kajcienski.

14 DEC. 1990. Wanda Pate, Administrative Secretary in Administration and Finance (1967-90), retires.

1991

1 JAN. 1991. The campus opens a 235-space parking lot east of the Serrano Village Residence Halls.

4 JAN. 1991. The campus receives a $10,000 grant from the Bank of America to train 30 volunteer "neighborhood advocates."

7 JAN. 1991. Pete Wilson takes office as Governor of California, replacing George Deukmejian.

10 JAN. 1991. Loralee MacPike is named Outstanding Professor for 1990/91. CSU Act. Chancellor McCune states, in response to the release of Gov. Wilson's projected 1991/92 state budget, that "This is a disastrous budget...[that] is going to make it very difficult for us to carry out our mission. I will consult with the campus presidents and all key constituencies to determine how we can still provide a quality education to our students."

11 JAN. 1991. Pres. Evans holds an emergency meeting with staff, faculty, students, and union representatives to share his initial plans in dealing with the budget crisis. "Next year's prospects are considerably more grim," he says. "We can expect uncertainty over the next few months. We will have to do things differently. I urge each of you to review all activities and programs."

14 JAN. 1991. Persi Diaconis speaks in BI-129 on "The Magic of Mixing Things Up," and also in UC on "Magic and Mathematics."

15 JAN. 1991. The rock group The Answer performs in WP. Cal State student Michail "Misha" Khokhlov, son of Prof. Nikolai E. Khokhlov, dies of kidney failure at age 25. 250 individuals march in a peace rally in front of the Pfau Library.

16 JAN. 1991. The CSU Board of Trustees approves construction of the Health and Physical Education Center and Visual Arts Center.

18 JAN. 1991. The campus hosts the 4th Annual Economic Outlook Breakfast in UC, with Jerry Grundhofer speaking on "Developments Affecting the Banking Industry," William R. "Bill" Leonard on "Transportation: Economic Key to the Inland Empire," Michael Bazdarich on "Economic Trends in the US," and John E. Husing on "The Economic Perspective from the Inland Empire's Point of View."

22 JAN. 1991. Legal scholar Erwin Chemerinsky speaks in SR on "The Rehnquist Court: The Future of Affirmative Action."

23 JAN. 1991. The Student Coalition for Peace in the Middle East holds a peace rally, causing a counter-protest by several students. Catholic priest Father Lawrence Martin Jenco, ex-hostage in Beirut, Lebanon, speaks in UC on "East Meets West."

24 JAN. 1991. Lillian Roybal Rose speaks in UC on "Connecting with Diversity."

25 JAN. 1991. The campus joins American Assoc. of Colleges for Teacher Education. Jazz musician Ronald Muldrow performs in WP.

28 JAN. 1991. Martin E. Marty speaks at the 4th Annual Morrow-McCombs Memorial Lecture in RH on "The Horror of Holocaust: Annihilating the Inharmonious."

30 JAN. 1991. Joel L. Nossoff, Act. Dean of Undergraduate Studies, returns to his position as Asst. Dean of Undergraduate Studies.

31 JAN. 1991. Lewis L. Jones is named Dean of Undergraduate Studies, replacing Joel L. Nossoff.

1 FEB. 1991. The Pfau Library displays books by Cal State alumni authors, including: Annette Annechild, Michelle Bancroft, Danny Bilson, Mary Wickizer Burgess, Prof. Juan Delgado, Paul DeMeo, James D. Elder Jr., Joanne Fluke, Robert Gordon, Susan Sterkel Haugh, Phillip Wayman Holdaway, Jonni Kincher, Jeffrey A. Kopang, Val Limar, Marsha Muscato, Linda Norman, Michael Reaves, and John L. Safford. Henry Louis Gates speaks in PR on "Multicultural Issues in Education." The Campus Media Commission fires the Editor of *The Chronicle*, the campus newspaper, over possible financial mismanagement. Ellen R. Gruenbaum receives a Fulbright Scholarship to study in Sweden during Fall 1991.

5 FEB. 1991. Attorney Derrick A. Bell Jr. speaks in UC on "Racism: A Prophecy for the Year 2000."

7 FEB. 1991. L.A. Rams Coach John Robinson is honored at a special Homecoming dinner in LC, and also speaks in the Gymnasium on "Tackling Tomorrow Today."

12 FEB. 1991. Thomas Rice speaks in SR on "Doing Something About the Cause of Homelessness."

14 FEB. 1991. *The Chronicle* reduces its physical size in half.

23 FEB. 1991. The Lambda Chi (ΛX) Chapter of Sigma Nu (ΣN) fraternity is inaugurated.

26 FEB. 1991. Cheryl Brown, co-Publisher of the *Black Voice News*, speaks in FO-177 on "Community Perspective in Minority Studies." Joe Epps speaks in SR on "Forensic Accounting."

27 FEB. 1991. Phillip E. Walker performs his one-man play, *Can I Speak for You Brother?*, in SUMP.

28 FEB. 1991. Army Major Thomas C. M. Zeugner, ex-Officer in Charge of Cal State's Military Science Dept. and ROTC Program for 4 years, is killed in action at age 36 in the Persian Gulf War while trying to deactivate a mine.

2 MAR. 1991. The campus hosts its 15th Annual Reading Conference, "The Politics of Change: Becoming a Whole Language Teacher," at the Maruko Hotel, with keynote speakers Kenneth Goodman, Barbara Flores, and Elena Castro.

6 MAR. 1991. Accountant Jim Farrell speaks in SR on "White Collar Crime."

6-8 MAR. 1991. The campus hosts the 1991/92 Calif. Academic Decathlon.

8 MAR. 1991. The reggae group Inner Secrets and punk rock group Power Trip perform on the SUP.

12 MAR. 1991. Kenneth I. Hanf speaks in SR on "Environmental Policy Making in Western Europe."

14 MAR. 1991. Pianist Max Lifchitz performs in RH.

19 MAR. 1991. Pres. Evans calls a meeting of campus administrators to discuss the growing state budget crisis, noting that the state deficit is projected to grow by as much as $10 million. "We'll have to look at all areas," he says. "Some services will be reduced and maybe some programs will be eliminated." The campus may also have to explore reductions in temporary and probationary personnel.

23 MAR. 1991. The campus hosts the 1st Annual Careers in Education Job Fair in the AR, with speakers Janet Young, Charles Jordan, Dan King, Henry Lee Kirk, and Joe Davis.

24 MAR. 1991. Chris Anthony Topoleski, Custodial Services (1980-91), dies at Lomita of the effects of a heat stroke at age 39, having been in a coma since the previous July.

31 MAR. 1991. Robert Dunworth, Int. Dean of the School of Education, resigns.

1 APR. 1991. Groundbreaking is held for the Foundation Building, with attorney Robert V. Fullerton and Lawrence L. Daniels attending. Margaret A. Atwell is named Act. Dean of the School of Education, replacing Robert Dunworth.

3-5 APR. 1991. The campus hosts a conference, "Managing Local Government Technology: The Year 2000," in Palm Springs.

6 APR. 1991. The campus hosts its first Celebrity Basketball Game in the Gymnasium, featuring Larry B. Scott, Stoney Jackson, Todd Bridges, Monica Calhoun, Kristoff St. John, Jon-Jon, Tina Yothers, Clyk Cozart, Willard Pugh, Larry O. Williams Jr., Nigel Miguel, and Kevin B. Benton.

8-12 APR. 1991. The campus hosts "Focus on the Persian Gulf" Week, featuring meetings, panels, forums, and lectures on the Persian Gulf War and its impact.

9 APR. 1991. Gene Berkman and Jane Henson speak in OR on "The Persian Gulf War: A Libertarian Perspective." Photographer Eileen Cowin speaks about her work in VA-109.

10 APR. 1991. Leila Brooks of the Union of Palestinian Women's Organizations speaks in PR on "The Palestinian Issue." Sherna Gluck speaks in PR on "'We Will Not Be Another Algeria': The Struggle for National Liberation and Women's Liberation in Occupied Palestine." Darrell Moellendorf speaks in OR on "'Just Wars' and the Gulf War."

11 APR. 1991. Philip Seff and Nancy Seff speak at the First Library Associates Lecture in RH on "Our Fascinating Earth." Gregory Bischak speaks in SR on "The War's Impact on the Domestic Economy." Attorney Howard Engelskirshen speaks in OR on "International Law and the Gulf War."

17 APR. 1991. ACLU attorney Steve Taneman speaks in SR on "Right to Privacy: Drug Testing and Abortion."

19 APR. 1991. The campus receives a $100,000 grant from the Calif. Arts Project to provide arts instruction to local teachers. Tony Ichsan is named Act. Environmental Health and Safety Officer. CSU Trustee Gloria S. Hom visits the campus.

20 APR. 1991. Actor Michael Goodrow and the group Amazing Music perform at the 5th Annual Environmental Expo, "Energy Choices and Challenges"; Todd "Hoss" McNutt performs special energy experiments in PR.

21 APR. 1991. Campus radio station KSSB begins broadcasting again at 106.3 megahertz on the FM dial.

24 APR. 1991. The Art Gallery begins exhibiting a set of 19th-century photos of Roman ruins by John Henry Parker. Ralph M. Lewis and Goldy Lewis are honored with the Arrowhead Distinguished Chief Executive Officer Award at a luncheon held in UC, with Ralph M. Lewis speaking on "The Outlook for Real Estate Development."

25 APR. 1991. The campus holds a reception in the Art Gallery Courtyard to celebrate its grant from the Calif. Arts Project. Sherry M. Howie receives a $48,000 grant from the U.S. Dept. of Education to create a pilot literacy program at S.B. High School.

26 APR. 1991. Pres. Evans announces that the campus Reserve Officer Training Corps (ROTC) Program will be retained; the Faculty Senate had recommended in a unanimous Jun. 1990 vote that the program be dropped for discriminating against homosexuals.

30 APR. 1991. The campus receives a $62,645 matching grant from NSF to buy an electron microscope.

1 MAY 1991. The campus opens a 567-space parking lot east of University Pkwy.

3 MAY 1991. The campus announces the formation of the Native American Students Assoc. Ballet Folklórico California, Mariachi Lucero, and the Aztec Dancers perform on LCP as part of Cinco de Mayo celebrations.

7 MAY 1991. Cellist Michele Brosseau-Tacchia and pianist Michael Tacchia perform at the annual Alumni Recital in RH.

8 MAY 1991. The campus unveils a new electronic marquee at the Main Entrance to the University.

9 MAY 1991. The campus hosts a Mexican fashion show, "Los Amigos Velada Literaria," in PiR.

10 MAY 1991. The campus announces a $7 million budget cut for 1991/92, including a $250,000 slash in the Library materials budget, permanently reducing its previous base of $1,014,000, plus the layoff of all 130 lecturers.

15 MAY 1991. Larry Echols, Toni Noel, and Bob Miller speak at a luncheon in PR on "Disabilities."

23 MAY 1991. James Steyer, Dir. of Children Now, speaks in SR on "California's Children: Crisis and Opportunity." Richard Saavedra speaks in RH on "Management of Group Dynamics."

24 MAY 1991. The Coyotes golf team finishes 5th in the NCAA Division III Championship Golf Tournament.

26 MAY 1991. The Coyotes baseball team loses 8-7 to Methodist Univ. of North Carolina in the NCAA Division III World Series tournament.

28 MAY-1 JUN. 1991. The campus hosts the 3rd Annual Music of the Americas Festival in RH.

29 MAY 1991. George Greco speaks at a luncheon in PR on "More Alike Than Different."

30 MAY 1991. Yolanda T. Moses speaks in FO-177 on "Issues of Race, Class, Gender, and Ethnic Studies for the 1990s."

31 MAY 1991. Guest composer Lloyd Pfautsch conducts the Univ. Choral Ensemble in a "Concert of American Choral Music" in RH.

1 JUN. 1991. Jazz trumpeter Bobby Shew performs with the Jazz Ensemble in RH.

2 JUN. 1991. Palancé Productions performs the musical drama *The High Life* in RH.

3 JUN. 1991. David P. DeMauro, Act. VP for Administration and Finance, is named permanent VP.

4 JUN. 1991. The campus hosts the Inland Council for Emergency Preparedness "Hands-On Emergency and Training Seminar."

6 JUN. 1991. Geoffrey Broadhead speaks in SR on "Meeting Special Education Needs Through Integrated Physical Education." Norman Meek receives the Warren J. Nystrom Award of the American Assoc. of Geographers.

11 JUN. 1991. Writer Diane Dunaway conducts a seminar in BK-103 on "Turning Myth and Magic into Novels That Sell."

13 JUN. 1991. Ralph Anttonen speaks in PR on "Why Students Should Stay in College: Benefits of Clubs and Other Student Organizations."

15-16 JUN. 1991. The 25th Commencement is held on the Library Lawn, with alumna Lois J. Carson giving the keynote address, "The Institution and the Individual: Enter to Learn, Depart to Serve," with the presence of CSU Chancellor McCune and Assemblyman Paul A. Woodruff. For the first time, a separate commencement ceremony is held at CVC (Jun. 16) at the McCallum Theatre for the Performing Arts in Palm Desert.

16 JUN. 1991. The campus hosts its 8th Annual Inland Empire Juneteenth Celebration.

24 JUN. 1991. The campus hosts the Coyote Basketball Camp, with ex-Olympic Gold Medalist Cheryl Miller participating.

SUM. 1991. Retirements: A. Vivien Bull, Prof. of French (1976-91); G. Keith Dolan, Prof. of Education (1967-91); Richard S. Saylor, Prof. of Music (1968-91); Gerald M. Scherba, Prof. of Biology, VP for Academic Affairs, VP in Charge, and Dir. of the Desert Studies Consortium (1962-91)—and at 29 years, the campus's longest-serving faculty member to date.

3 JUL. 1991. The campus appoints the first CVC Advisory Board: Paul Ames, Rolfe G. Arnhym, Palm Springs Mayor Sonny Bono, Steven W. Brummel, Ralph E. Hitchcock, Marc S. Homme, Sabby Jonathan, Ernest Moreno, J. M. "Manny" Sánchez, David E. Tschopp, and Elizabeth G. Williams.

5 JUL. 1991. C(arl) Michael O'Gara, Emeritus Prof. of Physical Education and Recreation and Chair of the Dept. of Physical Education (1964-77), dies in Humboldt Co. at age 79.

8 JUL. 1991. (Mer)lyn E. Young, Library Asst. (1967-91), retires.

10 JUL. 1991. The Celtic folk music group Shanachie performs on LCP. Mary Dye, President's Office (1966-91), retires.

14 JUL. 1991. James D. Crum, Dean of the School of Natural Sciences, returns to the ranks as Prof. of Chemistry.

15 JUL. 1991. Louis A. Fernández is named Dean of the School of Natural Sciences, replacing James D. Crum.

17 JUL. 1991. Gospel group Cal Poly Pomona Youth Gospel Choir performs on LCP.

24 Jul. 1991. Bluegrass fiddler Laurie Lewis and her Grant St. Band perform on LCP.

31 Jul. 1991. The rock group Popular Demand performs on LCP.

1 Aug. 1991. Barry A. Munitz is named Chancellor of the CSU System by the CSU Board of Trustees, replacing Ellis E. McCune (1990-91).

2 Aug. 1991. Hal Petersen, Building Maintenance (1981-91), retires.

7 Aug. 1991. Jazz band Tyrone Anthony Group performs on LCP.

10 Aug. 1991. Screenwriter David Trottier conducts a seminar in the Coyote Bookstore on "Writing and Selling Your Screenplay."

14 Aug. 1991. Jazz group The Latin Society performs on LCP.

15 Aug. 1991. The campus receives a $576,000 grant from the U.S. Dept. of Education to help boost the number of bilingual teachers in San Bernardino and Riverside Co. schools.

20-23 Aug. 1991. The campus hosts its 7th Annual "Teachers Are No. 1" Conference, with speakers Christy Marin, Mary Montle Bacon, and LeNise Jackson Gaertner.

22 Aug. 1991. The campus receives a $138,000 gift from the estate of Eva Mae Merchant to provide scholarships in nursing and teacher education.

23 Aug. 1991. The campus creates the Calif. Transition Center to aid autistic children and their families. Diane Rentfrow is named Dir. of the Student Assistance in Learning (SAIL) Program.

29 Aug. 1991. Margaret A. Atwell, Act. Dean of the School of Education, returns to her post as Assoc. Dean of Education.

30 Aug. 1991. Jean C. Ramage is named Dean of the School of Education, replacing Margaret A. Atwell. The University moves from NCAA Division III to Division II and joins the Calif. Collegiate Athletic Assoc.; the campus's first Division II games in men's soccer and women's volleyball are played on this date.

1 Sept. 1991. A budget shortfall of $2,596,000 forces the campus to drop its cross-country, tennis, and water polo teams, reduce 200 class sections and program offerings at off-campus sites, freeze equipment purchases, and cut personnel costs by 10%. The campus receives authorization to offer a new M.A. degree in Psychology with an industrial-organizational concentration, and a new emphasis in English-as-a-Second Language in the teaching of English composition. The Nursing Program changes from a 2-year upper division program to a 4-year baccalaureate program. The CSU System raises student fees by 20% ($240) to help cope with the budget crisis.

8 SEPT. 1991. The campus hosts the 3rd annual Youth Soccer and Coaches Clinic.

13 SEPT. 1991. Cal-Pac Construction Inc. receives a $15,489,000 contract to build Brown Hall.

14 SEPT. 1991. The campus hosts a Writers' Workshop, with speakers Judith Merkle Riley, Lawrence Block, Jacqueline Briskin, Carol Muske Dukes, Michael Hauge, Randee Phillips, Rick Pamplin, Reed Shelley, Chris Vogler, J. Randy Taraborrelli, Gordon Burgett, Anne Coyle, James Brown, Catherine Charlton, Rachel Ballon, Carol Bennett, and Anne Boe.

16 SEPT. & 6 OCT. 1991. 2 modular classrooms are installed at CVC at Coll. of the Desert.

17 SEPT. 1991. At the annual convocation in SUEC, Pres. Evans honors the first recipients of the Annual Staff Recognition Awards, and notes a number of campus achievements in 1990/91, including the 25th Silver Anniversary Gala, graduating 3,000 students, gaining $3.2 million in grants and $1.6 million in donations, achieving the accreditation of the Health Center, implementing Library automation, receipt of a super-computer, progress in numerous construction projects, and coping with the campus's worst budget crisis. Challenges for the future include: decline state financial support, reclaiming public confidence in higher education, strengthening teacher preparation, providing a multicultural role model that can assist the region in embracing and benefiting from ethnic diversity, and improving student retention rates.

19 SEPT. 1991. The campus hosts the 5th Annual Children's Network Conference, "Advocacy and Political Action for Children at Risk," with speakers Glenn A. Goldberg, Mary Ann Xavier, and Wendy Lazarus. The campus receives a $60,000 grant from the Exxon Education Foundation to help train Hispanic teachers.

20 SEPT. 1991. Thieves steal $3,000 worth of equipment from campus radio station KSSB, forcing it to go off the air for 10 days. The campus hosts a regional conference, "Meeting the Needs of the Homeless," with Lois J. Carson giving the keynote address.

25 SEPT. 1991. Cal State alumni and Hollywood screenwriters Paul De-

Meo and Danny Bilson visit the campus.

26 SEPT. 1991. A Cal State student is twice stabbed a mile off campus. CSU Trustee William D. Campbell visits the campus.

27 SEPT. 1991. Retirements: Arthur E. Nelson, Libn., Coll. Libn., and Library Dir. (1963-91); Dr. John Preston Miller, Physician and Dir. of the Univ. Health Center (1983/87-91); H. Stephen Prouty Jr., Assoc. Dean for Academic Services (1964-91); Laura J. Carbis, Secretary to the Univ. Libn. (1981-91); Loretta A. Campbell (1968-91), Budget Off.; Richard Ceballos (1966-91), Building Maintenance; Walter C. Erskine (1976-91, Housing Management; Richard Gilliam, Custodian Services (1979-91); Jorli R. Mast, Computer Center (1974-91); Lynn T. Moss, Career Development Center (1977-91); Robert Tinsley, Building Maintenance (1967-91); Jo Ann Von Wald, Records (1966-91); Reginald Williams, Heating, Air Conditioning, and Ventilation (1986-91).

28 SEPT. 1991. Dr. Jill E. Rocha, Physician (1987-91), is named Act. Dir. of the Student Health Center, replacing John Preston Miller.

2 OCT. 1991. *The Inland Empire Hispanic News* criticizes CSUSB's supposed inability to recruit and retain Latino faculty and administrators; VP Hefner publishes a response on Nov. 27, citing incorrect data used in the original article.

11 OCT. 1991. *The Friday Bulletin* increases its size from 8.5 x 11 inches to 11 x 17 inches.

15 OCT. 1991. The Boland and Dowdall Duo, featuring flautist Jan Boland and guitarist John Dowdall, perform in RH.

21 OCT. 1991. The Alder Room in UC reopens as a faculty and staff dining area.

23 OCT. 1991. Groundbreaking is held for the building that will become Jack H. Brown Hall, with the presence of CSU Trustee R. James Considine Jr., James Hlawek, and Donald I. Baker.

25 OCT. 1991. The campus reorganizes the Divisions of Academic Affairs and Student Services: Taft T. Newman Jr., Coordinator of EOP Counseling Services, is named Dir. of the EOP; Tom M. Rivera is named Assoc. Dean of Educational Programs; Walter S. Hawkins is named Dir. of Undergraduate Studies, Research, and Policy Analysis; Elinore H. Partridge is named Act. Assoc. Dean for Academic Services, replacing H. Stephen Prouty; Cynthia Linton is named Dir. of the Learning Center; Lydia Ortega is named Dir. of Admissions and Records; Elsa M. Ochoa-Fernández is named Dir. of International Student Services. The campus opens 3 modular buildings at CVC on the Coll. of the Desert campus, serving some 800 Cal State students.

31 OCT. 1991. Comedians John Henton and Colin Quinn perform in SUMP. Dr. Jill E. Rocha, Act. Dir. of the Student Health Center, is named permanent Dir.

8 NOV. 1991. Construction begins on traffic signals at I-215 and University Pkwy.

9 NOV. 1991. The Afro-Caribbean Dancers and Drummers perform in RH, under the direction of Matti Lascoe.

13 NOV. 1991. A Cal State student carrying 16 keys is arrested in the Pfau Library after tripping a silent alarm, and is charged with burglary and possession of stolen goods and illegal drugs after $20,000 in campus property is found in his car. CSU Trustee Claudia Hampton visits the campus.

15 NOV. 1991. The Foundation Building opens for business. The group Rampart Winds performs with the U.S. Air Force Academy in RH. The campus hosts an Academic Decathlon for local high schools in the Gymnasium. Cal State hosts the regional NCAA Division II soccer playoffs, but the Coyotes men's team loses 1-0 to Cal Poly San Luis Obispo, and is eliminated.

15-16 & 20-23 NOV. 1991. *A Warring Absence*, an original play by Cal State student Jody Duncan, premiers in RH.

19 NOV. 1991. At the 1st Faculty Author Recognition Reception, the campus honors faculty members Peter T. Robertshaw, Peter Holliday, Janet J. Woerner, Jennifer Randisi, Renate Carter, Bertram H. "Pete" Fairchild, and Ellen L. Kronowitz.

21 NOV. 1991. The campus receives a $90,000 grant from the Calif. State Dept. of Education, and is named the statewide site for master teaching training in reading recovery.

26 NOV. 1991. Pres. Evans tells senior administrators that campus employees will be challenged to "do things more effectively and efficiently" during the next 18 months. "We exist...to serve students. The heaviest priority must be classes. Some support services may have to be scaled back." Addressing the possibility of a mid-year budget cut, he says, "We can't deal with [that] without touching personnel. We will need to rethink programs and services for next year." He states that more vacant positions may remain unfilled.

10 DEC. 1991. University Hall opens for business, as faculty and staff begin occupying offices in the new building. State Superintendent of Public Instruction Bill Honig visits the campus.

12 DEC. 1991. The Chancellor approves a new M.S. degree in Educational Counseling, effective Winter 1992.

20 DEC. 1991 (?). Elva L. Kennedy, Children's Center (1988-91), dies of liver failure.

30-31 DEC. 1991 & 2-3 JAN. 1992. The campus hosts a baseball camp for children aged 8-15, with ex-California Angels player Ken Forsch, and Troy Kent, a relief pitcher with the S.B. Spirit.

1992

UNK. 1992. Grants: Billie Goode Blair receives $26,000 from the Danforth Foundation to help train school board candidates; Lynne Díaz-Rico receives $205,000 from the U.S. Off. of Bilingual Education and Minority Language Affairs to continue her Bilingual Educators' Career Advancement Program; Arturo Concepción, Kay Zemoudeh, and Owen Murphy receive a $100,000 matching grant from IBM to establish a laboratory for courses in computer architecture; Nicole Bournias-Vardiabasis receives a $16,000 renewal grant from Johns Hopkins Center for Alternatives to Animal Testing, and $23,000 from the Demeter Fund, both to analyze human birth defects; Chris Feiling and Dan Rinne receive $50,000 from NSF to investigate uniqueness results in trigonometric series; Tim Usher receives $13,000 from the Research Corp. to conduct research into ferroelectrics; Elizabeth Klonoff and Jan Fritz receive $150,000 from the Calif. Dept. of Health Services for "Action to Control Tobacco"; Marjorie McCabe and Dwight Sweeney receive $406,000 to train special education teachers.

8 JAN. 1992. The *San Bernardino Sun* publishes an article by Paul Oberjuerge criticizing the tenure of Athletic Dir. David L. Suenram.

8 JAN.-1 MAR. 1992. The Art Gallery, in conjunction with the S.B. Co. Museum, exhibits a collection of Egyptian artifacts from the collection of W. Benson Harer.

9 JAN. 1992. Robert A. Blackey is named VP of the American Historical Assoc.

12 JAN. 1992. A ribbon-cutting ceremony at the University Art Gallery marks the official unveiling of 300 Egyptian antiquities from the Harer Family Trust Collection.

14 JAN. 1992. Susan Jahoda speaks in SR on "Re-Representing the Body: Women Through Images."

16 JAN. 1992. Athletic Dir. David L. Suenram and women's basketball Coach Gary Schwartz meet with the press to discuss allegations of financial irregularities; Schwartz is suspended. Gloria A. Cowan is named Outstanding Professor for 1991/92. Doris Schattschneider speaks in UC on "M. C. Escher: Art and Mathematics."

17 JAN. 1992. Richard Farman, James Lents, and John E. Husing speak in UC to the 5th Annual Economic Forecast Breakfast, "Are Regulations and Taxes Driving Business from California?" The campus receives a $500,000 gift from Nicholas J. Coussoulis to help build the Health and Physical Education Complex and Arena.

19 JAN. 1992. The *San Bernardino Sun* publishes an article by Cindy Robertson and Paul Oberjuerge stating that ex-women's basketball Coach Gary Schwartz submitted questionable expense reports of more than $1,000 during 1990/91, and that these were approved by Athletic Dir. David L. Suenram; the campus denies the allegations. Oberjuerge also states that Schwartz harassed one of his players.

23 JAN. 1992. Hypnotist Bruce McDonald performs in WP. Bonnie Brunkhorst is named Pres. Elect of the Council of Scientific Society Presidents, to take office in 1993.

25 JAN. 1992. The campus hosts the United Black Student Union Southern Regional Conference.

29 JAN. 1992. The Ska group Orange Street Band performs in WP.

30 JAN. 1992. Christine Sleeter speaks in ER on "Infusing Multiculturalism in a Teacher Education Program," and also in UC on "A Framework for Conceptualizing a Multicultural Curriculum."

30-31 JAN. & 1-2 FEB. 1992. Cal State staff member Linda Stockham's play, *Heavy Shoes*, debuts in the Creative Arts Studio Lab.

31 JAN. 1992. The campus adopts a new affirmative action policy; Melvin G. Hawkins is named the first Affirmative Action Appeals Coordinator. The campus receives the first Annual Environmental Award from the S.B. Area Chamber of Commerce. Christine Sleeter discusses multicultural issues in education in PL-005 during an interactive session for faculty.

6 FEB. 1992. Ex-Rep. Shirley Chisholm speaks in the Gymnasium on "Unity Through Diversity."

7 FEB. 1992. A storm floods University Hall and the Coyote Bookstore. The campus hosts a conference, "Cutting Through the Red Tape: Local Government Summits on Coordinating Youth Police." Henry Smith conducts a master dance class in the Small Gymnasium.

8 FEB. 1992. The campus hosts the 1992 Family Reading Rally in SU, with keynote speaker Penny Hirschman.

9 FEB. 1992. Dancer Henry Smith performs "Warriors Don't Die" in RH.

12 FEB. 1992. Eleanor Guetzloe speaks in SR on "Depression and Suicide: Educators' Responsibility."

13 FEB. 1992. Nancy Thomas speaks in SR on "Private Egyptian Tombs: House of Eternity."

14 FEB. 1992. The reggae group Strongwill performs on LCP. M. L. Hansen Co. receives a $3,760,000 contract to expand the Student Union Building.

15 FEB. 1992. Pianist Stephen Prutsman teaches a master class in RH, and performs in RH on Feb. 16.

19 FEB. 1992. Dr. W. Benson Harer speaks in PS-10 on "Ancient Medicine and the Harer Family Trust Collection."

21 FEB. 1992. Antonio Loprieno speaks in UH-106 on "Government in Ancient Egypt."

24 FEB. 1992. Hans Gerhardt Jellen, Assoc. Prof. of Education (1989-92), dies of AIDS at age 49.

25 FEB. 1992. Robert C. Bailey speaks in UH-261 on "Coping with Uncertainty: Pygmies and Farmers in the Ituri Forest of Central Africa." Michael A. Signer and James A. Sanders speak in FB at the 5th Annual Morrow-McCombs Memorial Lecture, "Getting Our Story Straight: Jews and Christians Look at the Bible."

26 FEB. 1992. A ribbon-cutting ceremony marks the official opening of University Hall; Jan Roosevelt of the Southern California Edison Co. presents the University with a $50,000 rebate check to recognize the energy-saving devices in the new building. Gerry Scott III speaks in PS-10 on "Sculpture in the Ancient Egyptian Temple and Tomb." Kwame Ture (formerly Stokely Carmichael) speaks in SU.

27 FEB. 1992. The alternative group Lingo Band performs in WP.

28 Feb. 1992. Denise Benton, Dir. of the Upward Bound Program (1986-92), is named Dir. of Outreach Services.

29 Feb. 1992. Cal State student David Rojo López is murdered in S.B. at age 31.

4 Mar. 1992. The campus honors Ernesto Robles, Exec. Dir. of the National Hispanic Scholarship Fund, at a reception in UC. The hard rock group Nobody's Child performs in WP.

11 Mar. 1992. The hard rock group The Rebel Pebbles performs in WP. The campus holds a memorial service for Prof. Hans Jellen. Denese Shervington speaks in ER on "Reproduction Health Issues for Women—Liberty Versus Slavery."

12 Mar. 1992. Groundbreaking is held for the Student Union Building addition. The punk music group The Conditions performs in WP. The Chancellor's Off. approves a new M.A. degree in Education with an Instructional Technology Option, and a new B.S. degree in Vocational Education.

13 Mar. 1992. The campus closes the Student Health Center during July and August to save money. Paul Sweezy speaks in PR on "The Decline of the Soviet Union."

14 Mar. 1992. Kimball Newton "Kim" Hughes, Assoc. Prof. of Mathematics (1981-92), dies at age 38.

20 Mar. 1992. A storm floods the Coyote Bookstore.

26 Mar. 1992. Elliott R. Barkan receives his 3rd Fulbright Fellowship (a campus record) to study in Norway in 1992/93.

1 Apr. 1992. The campus conducts a "topping-off" ceremony for Business and Information Science Building.

10 Apr. 1992. The campus signs a memorandum with the Universidad Autónoma de Baja California to facilitate joint research and development opportunities.

15 Apr. 1992. Calvin Holder speaks in ER on "An Examination of West Indian Immigration to New York, 1900-1952."

17 Apr. 1992. The Persona Non Grata Band, Shake Mouse Band, and Banana Lizards Band perform in WP.

20 APR. 1992. Smoking is banned in all buildings on campus.

22 APR. 1992. State Sen. Gary K. Hart speaks on Proposition 153.

22-23 APR. 1992. CSU Trustee Bernard Goldstein visits the campus.

23 APR. 1992. The rock band The Penny Dreadfulls performs in WP.

24 APR. 1992. The campus launches a major fund-raising effort with its "Partnership 2000" campaign. The hard rock band Section 8 performs in WP. CVC celebrates 5 years of service with the unveiling of a new sign, with the participation of Indian Wells Mayor Richard Oliphant, Ralph E. Hitchcock, Rolfe G. Arnhym, Paul Ames, J. M. "Manny" Sánchez, Steven W. Brummel, Assemblywoman Tricia Hunter, and David E. Tschopp.

25 APR. 1992. Todd "Hoss" McNutt and folksinger Stephen Longfellow Fiske perform at the 6th Annual Environmental Expo, "Making a Difference for Earth's Sake," in the Gymnasium, with the presence of Rep. George E. Brown.

26 APR. 1992. The rock band Freaks Amour performs in RH.

27-28 APR. 1992. *A Warring Absence*, an original drama by Cal State grad student Jody Duncan, wins the $2,500 National Playwright Award at the American College Theater National Festival at the Kennedy Center in Washington, DC.

27 APR.-1 MAY 1992. The campus hosts "International Week," with cultural exhibits, a fashion show, foreign film showings, a food festival, and performances.

28 APR. 1992. Cal State student Amanda Sue Watson is named Miss Rancho Cucamonga.

30 APR. 1992. 200 students protest the Rodney King verdict in front of the Pub. The UCR Guitar Ensemble performs in RH. The NCAA announces that, following an investigation of supposed financial irregularities, it will levy no sanctions against the University.

7 MAY 1992. Cellist Michele Brosseau-Tacchia and pianist Michael Tacchia perform in RH.

8 MAY 1992. Martin A. Matich receives the Arrowhead Distinguished Chief Executive Officer Lecture Series Award at a banquet in UC, and speaks on "The Matich Corporation—Our History and Success." 3 members of the Sigma Chi fraternity begin painting a giant flag mural along the southbound side of the intersection of I-215 and State Highway 30.

12 MAY 1992. The trombone ensemble Dem Bones performs in RH.

13 MAY 1992. Comedienne Kathy Buckley performs in the Pub.

15 MAY 1992. The State Public Works Board approves construction of the Health and Physical Education Complex and Arena.

20 MAY 1992. The CSU Board of Trustees approves naming the Health and Physical Education Complex and Arena for James and Arianthi Coussoulis, parents of Nicholas J. Coussoulis, who donated $500,000 towards construction of the facility.

21 MAY 1992. Groundbreaking is held for the $22,698,000 Library Addition, to be built by Cal-Pac Construction Co., with the participation of ex-Pres. Pfau and Antreen Pfau, ex-Library Dir. Arthur E. Nelson, and ex-VP for Administration and Finance Leonard B. Farwell. The campus receives approval to offer an M.A. degree in Urban Planning, beginning in 1992/93.

28 MAY 1992. Alison Clark-Stewart speaks in SR on "Good News and Bad News About Day Care." The alternative music group Sista Marmalade performs in WP.

2 JUN. 1992. The Off. of Graduate Studies honors 10 faculty authors in the first of a series of annual receptions in LC. Abraham Monk chairs a panel, "Older Persons as a Community Resource: Can Older Volunteers Help High Risk Youth in the Inland Empire?" in RH, and later speaks in UC on "Problems and Potentials of an Aging Society: Bringing Generations Together."

3 JUN. 1992. Abraham Monk chairs a panel, "Future Directions for Gerontology at CSUSB," in SR.

5 JUN. 1992. Jean Saladino conducts an opera workshop in RH.

6 JUN. 1992. James Earl Cunningham, ex-S.B. Mayor (1947-50), State Sen., Superior Judge, and member of the first College Advisory Board, dies in Riverside at age 75.

13-14 JUN. 1992. The 26th Commencement is held on the Library Lawn, with CSU Chancellor Munitz giving the keynote address, "Next Step"; a 2nd ceremony is held at CVC on Jun. 14.

15 JUN. 1992. Sociologist Amitai Etzioni speaks on "Communitarian Philosophy: Strong Rights and Strong Responsibilities" at the Maruko Hotel to celebrate the accreditation of the University's Master of Social Work program. The campus begins a 4-day, 10-hour-per-day summer work schedule (through Sept. 11) to conserve energy costs. The campus receives the Christa McAuliffe Showcase for Excellence Award (one of 11 given nationwide) for its Hillside-University Demonstration School from the American Assoc. of State Colleges and Universities at the organization's "Teach American Conference," Washington, DC. The campus announces that the intercollegiate swimming program will be suspended for 1992/93.

21 JUN. 1992. Car-de-lite and D.J. Shon Boy, the City MCs, Prince Frosty and the Bed-Rock Posse, Spanky D, D.J. Fletch, Extended Version, My Brother's Keeper, the Mighty O.T., and Latisha and the Misfits Dance Team perform at the 9th Annual Juneteenth celebration on LCP; L.A. Rams running back David Lang, UNLV basketball player Melvin Love, Pastor Willie Hicks, Billy Johnson Jr., and Rev. Tom Gates speak at the event.

29 JUN. 1992. The Landers Quake knocks 50,000 volumes from the shelves of the upper floors of the Pfau Library, causing $80,000 worth of damage.

SUM. 1992. Retirements: Joe F. Bas, Prof. of Spanish (1968-92); Dominic M. Bulgarella, Prof. of Sociology (1969-92); James D. Crum, Prof. of Chemistry and Dean of the School of Natural Sciences (1966-92); Mary Dimon, Lect. in Education (1989-92); P(hilip) Leslie Herold, Assoc. Prof. of Sociology (1970-92); H. Arthur "Hal" Hoverland, Prof. of Accounting and Finance and Dean of the School of Business (1972-92); Nikolai E. Khokhlov, Prof. of Psychology (1968-92); Robert A. Lee, Assoc. Dean of Academic Affairs and Prof. of English (1968-92); Mary L. McGregor, Assoc. Prof. of Nursing (1975-92); Edward A. Nelson, Assoc. Prof. of Accounting and Finance (1987-92); Clifford T. Paynton, Prof. of Sociology (1968-92); William L. Slout, Prof. of Theatre Arts (1968-92); Bridget Tucker, Counselor (1987-92). Staff: Anne Crum, Secretary, Liberal Studies (1977-92); Nadine M. Horenburg, Property Clerk (1981-92); Pat Maietta, Instructional Support Technician (1969-92); Gerald Welch, Groundsworker (1971-92).

1 JUL. 1992. Juan C. González, Int. VP for Student Services, is named permanent VP. Stephen D. Christensen is named Dir. of Major Gifts.

8 JUL. 1992. The classic rock-and-roll band Popular Demand performs on LCP.

9 JUL. 1992. David N. Chalk conducts a seminar on "Legal Aspects of Supervision."

15 JUL. 1992. The bluegrass band Sidesaddle performs on LCP. The campus receives a $1 million gift from Jack H. Brown to help fund the new Business and Information Science Building, which is renamed Jack H. Brown Hall on 30 Jul. by the CSU Board of Trustees.

22 JUL. 1992. The rhythm-'n'-blues band Rick and the Recuperators performs on LCP.

23 JUL. 1992. Pres. Evans is named Chair of the Renaissance Group, a coalition of 17 universities that educate 8% of America's teachers, and are dedicated to promoting excellence in teacher education.

24 JUL. 1992. The campus lays off a full-time employee in the Public Relations Dept. in reaction to severe budget cuts.

29 JUL. 1992. The fiddle duo The Accousticats performs on LCP.

5-7 AUG. 1992. The British Broadcasting Co. (BBC) films a documentary on the Hillside-University Demonstration School.

6 AUG. 1992. Cal State professors A. I. Clifford Singh, Terry L. Rizzo, and Christopher C. Grenfell help arrest a burglar in the Physical Education Building. Judith M. Rymer is named 1992/93 Pres. of the National Orange Show Board of Directors.

12 AUG. 1992. The rock-'n'-roll group The LCR Band performs with jazz vocalist Angela Carole Brown on LCP.

15 AUG. 1992. Kathy L. O'Brien, Assoc. Prof. of Education (1984-92), dies of cancer at age 40; she bequeaths her children's book collection to the Pfau Library.

18-21 AUG. 1992. The campus hosts its 8th Annual "Teachers Are No. 1" Conference, with keynote speakers Dave Tansey, Denis Waitley, and S. Alan Cohen.

19 AUG. 1992. The jazz group The Latin Society performs on LCP.

26 AUG. 1992. Emerson George Webster, for whom the Rheubottom/Webster Lecture Series is later named, dies at age 89.

1 SEPT. 1992. The campus finishes landscaping the Mall in front of the Pfau Library. The campus alumni magazine, *Panorama*, published since 1980, is renamed *Cal State San Bernardino* with its Fall 1992/93 issue. Bonnie Brunkhorst and Herbert Brunkhorst become the first faculty couple to receive a joint appointment—in the schools of Education and Natural

Sciences. The Board of Trustees increases student fees in the CSU System by 40% to $1,308 per year.

15 SEPT. 1992. At the annual convocation in the Gymnasium, Pres. Evans notes that, on the eve of his 10th anniversary of assuming office, the campus is undergoing its worst financial meltdown ever, with a 9.2% drop in state support in 1992/93. "We'll need to spend a lot of time adjusting to the continuing fiscal crisis," he says. "We're going to have to work a little harder and a little smarter. I think we're going to have to keep the brakes on [spending] for another 12 months more." However, he also points to several achievements, including: the Theatre Dept. production of *A Warring Absence*, one of only 5 college plays to be staged at the Kennedy Center, Washington, DC; winning the Christa McAuliffe Showcase Award for Excellence in Education for the Hillside Demonstration School; securing $5 in external grant funds; and the start of several major construction projects. More help will be needed in education teachers, he adds, which is a "university-wide responsibility. We may need whole new models for schools and improved curriculums," particularly in the area of writing-across-the-curriculum strategies. He notes that computer capabilities must be advanced across the campus, that affirmative action efforts must be intensified, and that the Partnership 2000 development campaign must move forward. Maintaining quality around the university will be the challenge; the question that arises, he says, is "Quality for whom, at what cost, and at whose expense?"

16 SEPT. 1992. Cal State Marketing major Dino M. Tosolini is killed with his sister in a helicopter crash on Haleakala Mountain in Hawaii at age 24. The campus hosts the conference, "Adolescent Pregnancy and Parenting: Problems, Progress, and Promises," with keynote speaker Joycelyn Elders, Dir. of the Arkansas Dept. of Health.

17 SEPT. 1992. The campus hosts the 6th Annual Children's Network Conference, "Challenge and Change: Using the System to Preserve Families in the Year 2000," with keynote speaker Gene Bedley, writer and principal.

18 SEPT. 1992. The campus receives a $5,000 gift from Joseph Bailey to assist the Student Emergency Loan Fund.

23 SEPT. 1992. William Aguilar, Univ. Libn., is named VP of the newly created Information Resources and Technology (IRT) Div., which is split from Academic Affairs; the new unit incorporates the Computer Center, Audio-Visual Services, Telecommunications, and the Pfau Library. Aguilar also retains his previous title and responsibilities as Univ. Libn. until that position can be filled.

25 SEPT. 1992. The reggae band Strong Will performs at the Gymnasium Pool.

28 SEPT. 1992. A 20-acre brush fire on Wiggins Hill reaches within 700 yards of the campus.

1 OCT. 1992. The Personnel Off. is renamed the Human Resources Off.

7 OCT. 1992. Gayle Wilson, wife of Gov. Pete Wilson, visits the PAL Center on Highland Ave.

8 OCT. 1992. Film actor Claude Akins is honored by a dinner in the Commons, followed by a show and dance. Akins also appears at the 1992 Coyote Celebrity Golf Classic held on Oct. 9 at the Shandin Hills Golf Club, as part of an athletic scholarship benefit. Folk guitarist Tim Reis performs in WP.

14 OCT. 1992. Pianists Gustavo Tolosa and María Tolosa perform in RH. J. A. Jones Construction Co. makes a $19,900,000 bid to build the Physical Education Building and Sports Arena (later called the Health and Physical Education Complex and Coussoulis Arena), but later withdraws.

15 OCT. 1992 (?). Doyle J. Stansel, Asst. VP for Student Services (1966-92), retires.

17 OCT. 1992. Dancer Jeff Friedman performs in RH.

17 OCT.-17 DEC. 1992. The Art Gallery begins displaying a 90-piece African art collection donated by Jane Matthews.

21 OCT. 1992. Rep. George E. Brown visits the campus to see the University's new electron microscope. The rock group The Dead Milkmen perform on LCP.

27 OCT. 1992. The campus hosts a town-hall-style meeting on the welfare system in PR, with the participation of Norm Dollar, Bev Littlejohn, Al La Pinto, and Janette Arnquist.

28 OCT. 1992. The blues group Crazy Eight performs on LCP.

29 OCT. 1992. Comedienne Suzi Landolphi performs in the Commons Plaza. Hispanic writer Gary Keller (aka El Huitlacoche) meets with students in PR, and later reads from his work in SR.

30 OCT. 1992. The campus receives grants of $850,000 and $797,000 from NSF to hone teachers' science education skills.

31 OCT. 1992. Sue A. Ellis, Library Asst. (1966-92), retires.

2 NOV. 1992. The campus receives a $297,114 grant from the U.S. Office of Special Education to fund the Master's Program in Rehabilitation Counseling.

4 NOV. 1992. Catherine Stimpson speaks in SR on "Pains, Gains, and the Education of Women."

5 NOV. 1992. The reggae group King Arthur & the Royal Posse performs in WP.

11 NOV. 1992. Telewriter Fred Bronson speaks in PiR.

13 NOV. 1992. Karla Hallum, Dir. of the Credential and M.A. Off. in Education (1979-92), retires.

17 NOV. 1992. The campus cancels the scheduled appearance of white supremacist Tom Metzger at a forum on cultural diversity scheduled for Nov. 25, due to security concerns.

19 NOV. 1992. Billiards trick shot artist Jack White performs in WP.

22 NOV. 1992. Cal State sophomore Natasha Taylor is named Miss Jurupa for 1993.

23 NOV. 1992. Klaus R. Brasch receives a $92,000 grant from the National Institute of Health to research auto-antibodies.

1 DEC. 1992. Randy P. Harrell, Dir. of Student Life, is named Act. Asst. VP for Student Services, replacing Doyle J. Stansel. Norm Slosted is named Act. Dir. of Housing. Patricia Rodgers-Gordon is named Act. Dir. of the Career Development Center.

4 DEC. 1992. The Pfau Library creates the Pfau Addition Library Supporters (PALS) booster group, with initial members including Wilfrid Lemann, Marta Macías Brown, Ernest F. García, Penny Holcomb, and Thelma Press. The campus creates a Major Events Committee. Ashra Kwesi speaks in UC on "African Origin of Civilization and the Origin of Greek Philosophy."

6 DEC. 1992. Campus Police Officer Edward L. Brock is shot 3 times in the abdomen while assisting San Bernardino police in trailing a murder suspect near the campus; he is hospitalized for 6 days, but recovers and returns to duty.

10 DEC. 1992. The Provisional Accelerated Learning (PAL) Center receives a $7,000 grant from the S.B. Kiwanis Organization.

24 DEC. 1992. Willie Clark, Pres. of the S.B. branch of the NAACP, demands that Pres. Evans be reprimanded and terminated for allowing the forthcoming talk of white supremacist Tom Metzger.

1993

UNK. 1993. Kimberley R. Cousins receives a $32,200 grant from the Research Corp. to develop polymer-bond organo-aluminum reagents for organic synthesis. David M. L. Riefer receives a $250,000 grant from NSF for his project, "Multinomial Processing Tree Models of Cognition."

2 JAN. 1993. Virginia P. McKenzie, retired Secretary, Music and Theatre Arts (1971-83), dies at age 82.

4 JAN. 1993. Several students are injured while slipping on ice.

8 JAN. 1993. Ward M. McAfee is named Outstanding Professor for 1992/93. The Latin Society performs in UC.

11 JAN. 1993. White supremacist Tom Metzger is again barred from speaking at a campus forum set for Jan. 27. *S.B. Sun* columnist Paul Oberjuerge demands that Athletic Dir. David L. Suenram be fired.

14 JAN. 1993. Radio talk show hosts Kevin & Bean visit the campus.

15 JAN. 1993. The campus hosts its 6th Annual Economic Forecast Breakfast, "Will Gridlock and Recession Persist in 1993?", in UC, with Rep. George E. Brown, Assemblyman Jim Brulte, *Sacramento Bee* writer Dan Walters, and John E. Husing.

21 JAN. 1993. Melvin G. Hawkins, Prof. of Social Work and Affirmative Action Appeal Coordinator (1973-92), retires.

22 JAN. 1993. J. Milton Clark is named Affirmative Action Appeal Coordinator, replacing Melvin G. Hawkins.

27 JAN. 1993. The campus hosts a "Discrimination on Campus" forum in SR.

28 JAN. 1993. Arturo Ranfla González of the Universidad Autónoma de Baja California chairs a panel of 5 experts discussing "The North American Free Trade Agreement" in RH. The classic rock group The Waifs perform in WP.

29 JAN. 1993. Peter Detwiler speaks in SR on "Growth Management."

2 FEB. 1993. A campus parking services officer is kidnapped at gunpoint and driven to Devil Canyon, but escapes her attacker. ASI withdraws from the Calif. State Student Assoc. (CSSA).

5-7 & 10-14 FEB. 1993. The campus premieres *The Trial of Dr. Jekyll*, an original drama by William L. Slout; the text is later published by Borgo Press.

7 FEB. 1993. Michael Burgess receives the 1st Lifetime Collector's Award for his contributions to SF bibliography at a luncheon held at Pat's Restaurant in L.A., with the trophy being presented by antiquarian book dealer Barry R. Levin.

8 FEB. 1993. Pianist Donna Coleman performs and speaks in RH.

11 FEB. 1993. Groundbreaking is held for the Health and Physical Education Complex and the James and Arianthi Coussoulis Arena. Raymond Franklin speaks in SR on "Shadows of Race and Class: A Contemporary Analysis of Movements for Change." Rep. Maxine Waters speaks in RH. PBS televises the program, *All About Women*, featuring an interview with Sherry M. Howie. CSU Chancellor Munitz discusses the "State Budget Crisis" in UC.

19 FEB. 1993. *Reference Guide to Science Fiction, Fantasy, and Horror*, by Michael Burgess (Libraries Unlimited), is named an "Outstanding Academic Book, 1993" by *Choice Current Reviews for Academic Libraries*.

23 FEB. 1993. Katheryn Pfisterer Darr speaks in RH at the 6th Annual Morrow-McCombs Lecture on "Ruth Goes Gleaning."

25 FEB. 1993. Writer Terry McMillan speaks in RH on her book, *Waiting to Exhale*. Eunice Meyers speaks in SR on "Twentieth-Century Hispanic Women Authors."

1 MAR. 1993. Campus photographer Dan Moseley is beaten and robbed by 3 men in the Loading Dock of the Pfau Library.

4 MAR. 1993. Ex-National League umpire Dave Pallone and ex-Rep. John Le Boutillier debate gay rights in RH.

5 MAR. 1993. The campus issues contracts to build a Coyote Bookstore addition and a parking lot south of the Foundation Building.

8 MAR. 1993. Ex-State Sen. Stanford C. Shaw, who sponsored the legislation that created CSUSB, dies at Loma Linda at age 79.

11-12 MAR. 1993. Sonia Nieto speaks in UC on "Preparing Teachers to Work with Diverse Classrooms," and the next day conducts a workshop on "Teaching Diversity" in UH-261.

19 MAR. 1993. James M. Brown's short story, "Rat Boy," wins a *Chicago Tribune* Literary Award. Chuck Cervello and Richard Daniels are named to CVC Advisory Board.

31 MAR. 1993. The campus hosts an Energy Cost Reduction Conference for local school Districts.

1 APR. 1993. Lucas George Lawrence, ex-Dir. of Audio-Visual Services (1967-70), dies at age 68.

2 APR. 1993. Christine Ho speaks in FO-177 on "International Families: Child-Minding and Mothering Among Trinidadian Immigrants in Los Angeles."

6-10 APR. 1993. The campus's Model United Nations team wins a 2nd "Outstanding Delegation" Award in New York, representing Iran.

7 APR. 1993. Saxophonist Thom Bergeron performs in RH. The campus hosts a "Diversity, Justice, and Peace" rally between the Pub and University Hall, with speaker Wes Henderson.

13 APR. 1993. Andy Cleaves and Friends perform "An Evening of Jazz" in RH. The campus hosts a TV town meeting with U.S. Secretary of Education Richard W. Riley and U.S. Secretary of Labor Robert Reich.

15 APR. 1993. Reggae band Strong Will performs in WP.

22 APR. 1993. Los Guys perform on the University Hall Courtyard.

24 APR. 1993. Magician Steve "Trash" Richerson and group Naked Earth perform in the Gymnasium as part of the 7th Annual Environmental Expo, "Healthy Environment, Healthy Economy."

26 APR. 1993. The campus receives a $10,000 grant from GTE California to support Project UPBEAT.

29 APR. 1993. Alternative group Fighting Cause performs in WP.

30 APR. 1993. *Booklist/Reference Books Bulletin* names *Reference Guide to Science Fiction, Fantasy, and Horror*, by Michael Burgess, an Outstanding Reference Source for 1993. Faculty and students read Linda Stockham's play, *Divorce Sale*, out loud in UH-106.

1 MAY 1993. Arturo Madrid speaks at the 8th Annual Scholarship Awards Banquet of the CSUSB Assoc. of Hispanic Faculty and Staff in UC.

6 MAY 1993. Russ Edmonds of Walt Disney Feature Animation speaks in RH on "Integrating Biological Information into the Creation and Design of Disney Animated Characters." The Return of Disco Korruption Mobil Disc Jockey performs in WP.

8 MAY 1993. The Pueblo Eagle Dancers perform on the Library Lawn at the 2nd Annual Sweet Grass Gathering. Opera singer Mark Almy and pianist Michael Tacchia perform in RH.

9 MAY 1993. Pianist José Sandoval performs in RH.

11 MAY 1993. Adria F. Klein is elected VP/Pres. Elect of the Calif. Reading Assoc. The campus creates the Lawrence L. Daniel Award to honor a women's basketball player, the first recipient being Shandell Steen.

17 MAY 1993. Richard Salsgiver speaks in SR on "The American with Disabilities Act." Jim Collins speaks in SR on his life as an activist in the disabled movement.

19 MAY 1993. Elane Geller speaks in PS-10 on "Personal Lessons from the Holocaust." Mayfield Stew performs in Serrano Village.

20 MAY 1993. Reggae band Strong Will performs in WP. Alumna soprano Beverly Brule performs in RH. The campus establishes a quarterly health services student fee of $26, effective Fall 1993.

26 MAY 1993. The campus receives a $310,000 grant from the U.S. Dept. of Education and a $129,000 grant from the S.B. Co. Job and Employment Dept. to fund the Upward Bound Program.

27 MAY 1993. The reggae band Shaagnatty performs in the University Hall Courtyard. Taiwanese educators Menglin Chang, Yaw-Nan Chen, and Samuel F. Liu visit the campus to discuss possible educational exchanges.

28 MAY 1993. Alumnus baritone William Adams performs in RH. Magician Harry B. Blackstone Jr. and Gay Blackstone donate a collection of plays and scripts to the Theatre Dept. and the Pfau Library, in memory of their son, Harry B. Blackstone III.

1 JUN. 1993. Sue Greenfeld and Sherry M. Howie receive Fulbright Fellowships to teach in Taiwan during 1993/94.

3 JUN. 1993. The campus signs an agreement to establish an Air Force Reserve Officers' Training Corps program at Cal State.

7 JUN. 1993. Tom Minor takes office as S.B. Mayor, replacing W. R. "Bob" Holcomb. The School of Education dedicates its new Kathy O'Brien Literacy Center in University Hall, named in honor of the late Prof. of Advanced Studies.

11 JUN. 1993. *Reference Guide to Science Fiction, Fantasy, and Horror*, by Michael Burgess is named one of 30 "Outstanding Reference Sources: The 1993 Selection of Recent Titles" by the American Library Assoc.

12-13 JUN. 1993. The 27th Commencement is held on the Library Lawn, being split for the first time into 2 sessions, morning and evening, with CSU Trustee John E. Kashiwabara giving the morning keynote address, and Stater Bros. CEO Jack H. Brown the evening one. CVC Commencement takes place on Jun. 13 in the McCallum Theater in Palm Desert, with CSU Executive Vice Chancellor Molly Corbett Broad giving the keynote speech.

19 JUN. 1993. Michael Burgess receives the annual Pilgrim Award for lifetime contributions to SF scholarship from the Science Fiction Research Assoc. at its annual conference in Reno, Nevada.

20 JUN. 1993. The campus hosts its 10th Annual Juneteenth celebration in LC and on LCP.

24 JUN. 1993. Dolores Ballesteros is named to CVC Advisory Board.

SUM. 1993. P. Richard Switzer, Prof. of French and ex-Dean of the School of Humanities (1970-93), retires.

1 JUL. 1993. The campus receives a ¥100 million ($925,000) gift from Yasuda Institute of Education in Hiroshima, Japan, to help construct the Yasuda Extended Education Building. The campus receives a $217,000 grant from the U.S. Dept. of Education to continue funding for the SAIL Program.

4 JUL. 1993. David O. Porter, Dean of the School of Business and Public Administration, resigns to go to the Univ. of Fairbanks; Eldon C. Lewis is named Int. Dean of the School of Business and Public Administration, replacing David O. Porter.

6 JUL. 1993. The S.B. Fire Dept. responds to a report of smoke on the 2nd floor of the Biological Science Building, caused by an overheating exhaust fan.

7 JUL. 1993. The band Popular Demand performs on LCP.

14 JUL. 1993. The country group Marley's Ghost performs on LCP.

21 JUL. 1993. Jazz band Andy Cleaves and Friends perform on LCP.

23 JUL. 1993. Gary Eugene MacQuiddy, Support Technician (1977-93), dies at age 60.

24 JUL. 1993. Armando Ruben Rojas, retired Groundsman (1967-90), dies at age 58.

26 JUL. 1993. Jo-Ann Marie Minie, Accounting (1973-93), dies at age 49.

28 JUL. 1993. The Mariachi Internacional de America band performs on LCP.

30 JUL. 1993. The campus hosts the Inland Empire Future Leaders Program (IEFLP) banquet in UC.

4 AUG. 1993. The jazz group Pandemonium Steel Drum Band performs on LCP.

11 AUG. 1993. The bluegrass group Alan Munde and Country Gazette performs on LCP.

17-19 AUG. 1993. The campus hosts its 9th Annual "Teachers Are #1" Conference, with keynote speakers Bob Harris, Neal Shusterman, and Jon Pearson.

18 AUG. 1993. The pop group LCR Band performs on LCP.

25 AUG. 1993. The Latin Society performs on LCP. Bruce Golden wins the $700 1st Prize in the 4th Annual International Imitation Raymond Chandler Writing Contest.

31 AUG. 1993. Dr. Jill E. Rocha, Dir. of the Student Health Center, returns to the ranks as Physician.

1 SEPT. 1993. The Coyote Bookstore addition opens for business. A 100-space expansion of the Foundation Parking Lot opens for business. The track ring, soccer and baseball fields, and tennis courts open for business.

John M. Hatton, Dir. of Counseling and Test Center, is named Dir. of Counseling Services and the Student Health Center, replacing Dr. Jill E. Rocha, and the 2 areas are combined under his administration.

14 SEPT. 1993. At the annual convocation in SUEC, Pres. Evans focuses on "quality assurance" as a primary goal for the coming academic year. Because higher education has been criticized in the media, he says, for failing to improve the education levels of students graduating, now is the time to set firm quality assurance standards. He suggests examining the qualifications of instructors, testing requirements for students, the extent and quality of tutorial assistance, class size, the quality of time spent with students, and ways of measuring the quality of classrooms and facilities. We should focus special attention on students' writing skills: "I ask that we now implement a writing-across-the-curriculum requirement" that would have students bettering their communication skills. Tied to the need to quality is the need for diversity: "Diversity is the balance of quality and equity" in education, and diversity must become a primary mission of the university. The Pres. notes 12 constructions ongoing, and the acquisition of almost $8 million in grants. On the fiscal crisis, he states that "There's no opportunity at the moment to return to budget and operating levels of the past."

15 SEPT. 1993. The Children's Network holds its 7th Annual Conference, "A Concert of Colors: Meeting the Needs of Children in a Multi-Ethnic Society," on campus.

21 & 24 SEPT. 1993. Jack H. Brown Hall, the largest classroom-office building on campus, is dedicated at 2 ribbon-cutting ceremonies, with the attendance of Stater Brothers CEO and contributor Jack H. Brown.

26 SEPT. 1993. The Latin Society performs at the University Picnic on the Athletic Fields.

6 OCT. 1993. Screenwriter Randall Johnson speaks in ER.

11 OCT. 1993. Kevin Kennedy, Dir. of the Chesterfield Film Writers' Project, speaks in SR.

12 OCT. 1993. The campus receives a $962,000 grant from NSF to increase minorities in the natural sciences.

14 OCT. 1993. William Aguilar, VP of Information Resources and Technology, relinquishes his post as Univ. Libn.

15 OCT. 1993. Johnnie Ann Ralph, Assoc. Univ. Libn., is named Univ. Libn., replacing William Aguilar; the position of Assoc. Univ. Libn. is abolished. John Tate receives a $30,000 Cottrel Science Award for his project, "Transition Metal Complexes of Some New Attracting Macrocyclic Ligands."

18 OCT. 1993. The campus receives a $250,000 gift from S.B. attorney Robert V. Fullerton to help build the Univ. Art Museum. Palestinian educator Gabriel A. Baramki speaks in RH on the "Mideast Peace Accord."

20 OCT. 1993. Universal Studios Development Dir. Cary Granat speaks in SR.

29 OCT. 1993. The alternative rock group Small Tribe Band performs in SUEC.

30 OCT. 1993. Paula Kamen speaks to the CSU Women's Council in SUEC on "What Women in Their Twenties Really Think of Men, Sex, Orgasm, and Freedom."

2 NOV. 1993. Ed C. Krupp, Dir. of the Griffith Observatory, speaks in RH on "Under Stone Age Skies."

4 NOV. 1993. The reggae group Boomshaka Band performs on SU Pavilion.

6 NOV. 1993. The Univ. of Calif. at Santa Barbara Middle East Ensemble performs in RH.

9 NOV. 1993. The Associated Students Inc. Board of Directors votes to rejoin the Calif. State Student Assoc.

10 NOV. 1993. The pop group Monkey Siren performs on the SU Pavilion.

12 NOV. 1993. The campus receives a gift of 30 used IBM computers from GTE California to help track local energy use.

3 DEC. 1993. Randall Orton speaks in BI-102 on "Inventing the Public Trust Doctrine: California Water Law and the Mono Lake Controversy." The Student Services Building is renamed Sierra Hall (by Dec. 17).

7 DEC. 1993. The CSUSB Symphonic Band releases the first audio CD ever recorded by Cal State students, including Gustav Holst's "Second Suite in F, Op. 28b," and John Paulson's "Epinicion."

16 DEC. 1993. The campus receives a $486,458 grant from the South Coast Air Quality Management Dist. to help establish a distance learning network between the main campus, CVC, and sites in Joshua Tree and

Blythe.

30 DEC. 1993. Jackie A. Green, retired Library Asst. (1963-74), dies at age 75.

31 DEC. 1993. Retirements: Phyllis Adams, Prof. of Education (1989-93); Dalton D. Harrington, Prof. of Biology (1969-93). Staff retirements: Rita Cohn, Financial Aid (1975-93); Colleen Corbin, Humanities (1968-93); Elaine Haugen, Admissions (1974-93); Jim G. Martínez, Budget Officer (1970-93); Donald E. Sapronetti, Accounting Officer (1973-93). Dr. Jill E. Rocha, Physician and Dir. of the Student Health Center (1987-93), resigns.

1994

UNK. 1994. Ching-Hua Wang receives a $98,590 grant from the National Institutes of Health for research on "Early Intestinal B Cell Response to Helminthic Infection." The campus receives a $36,000 gift from Jim Rogers to establish scholarships for CVC.

1 JAN. 1994. Pat Quanstrom, Accounting Manager, is named Act. Dir. of Accounting, replacing Donald E. Sapronetti.

5 JAN. 1994. The campus receives a gift of 26 pieces of ancient Mediterranean ceramics from John W. Karnoff and Ellen Karnoff.

7 JAN. 1994. The campus hosts an Inland Empire Caucus, with Reps. C. Jerry Lewis, George E. Brown, Jim Kay, and Ken Calvert, State Sens. Ruben S. Ayala, Thomas Campbell, and William R. Leonard, Assemblyman Paul A. Woodruff, S.B. Co. Supervisor Gerald Eaves, Riverside Co. Supervisor Norton Younglove, Redlands Mayor Swen Larson, and Lake Elsinore Mayor Gary Washburn.

11 JAN. 1994. Claude Goldenberg speaks in UC on "Conversing and Teaching."

13 JAN. 1994. Alternative group Incognito Band performs in SUEC.

14 JAN. 1994. The alternative group Venus Wrecks performs in SUEC. Kathy Ervin, D. J. Watson, Rick Hoglund, Andy Cleaves, and Keith Fiddmont perform as part of "Jazzoetry" night in RH.

17 JAN. 1994. The Northridge Earthquake knocks thousands of volumes from the shelves on the upper floors of the Pfau Library. The new Parking and Information Building at the main entrance to campus opens for business.

18 Jan. 1994. Kenneth Edwin Aker collapses and dies on the landing outside of the Pfau Library at age 30. The campus implements the Student Information System (SIS+) registration software.

21 Jan. 1994. Edward M. White is named Outstanding Professor for 1993/94.

26 Jan. 1994. Writer Clarissa Estes reads from her work in the Women's Resource Center.

26-28 Jan. 1994. The campus hosts a Conference on Employment with Persons with Disabilities at the Hyatt Regency Suites in Palm Springs.

27 Jan. 1994. Richard Procida speaks on "Advertising That's Degrading to Women."

28 Jan. 1994. Sharon Yellowfly speaks in PS-107 on "Experiences of Native American Children Outside the Reservation." State Sen. Thomas Campbell and Howard L. Roth speak in SUEC at the 7th Annual Economic Forecast Breakfast, "Inland Empire '94: Prospects for Recovery." The campus hosts its 1st Annual Alumni Concert in RH, with performances by Dawn Giorgianni, Richard Wall, and James Myles.

29 Jan. 1994. Magicians John Engman, Robert Rodríguez, Tom Ferranti, Marc Bovee, and Ed Thomas perform in the Theatre.

1 Feb. 1994. *Los Angeles Times* writer Ralph Frammolino states that the Pfau Library tops a CSU list of 101 buildings vulnerable to earthquakes; other campus buildings needing repair include Physical Education and the Commons.

2-5 Feb. 1994. *The Dramatic Essentials*, an original play by Cal State student Christopher Thayer, debuts in the Drama Lab.

3 Feb. 1994. Campus radio station KSSB is fined $8,000 and forced to drop its call letters by the FCC, and officially becomes known as "Coyote Radio."

4 Feb. 1994. The campus begins seeking seismic retrofitting funds for the Pfau Library, Commons, and Physical Education buildings, which are listed among the top-20 priorities in the CSU. The Symphonic Band issues its first compact disk, *New Beginnings*, with pieces by modern and classical composers, orchestrated by Luis González. Assemblymen Paul A. Woodruff and Fred Aguiar, and State Sen. Ruben S. Ayala conduct an Education Roundtable.

11 FEB. 1994. A ribbon-cutting ceremony marks the official opening of the new Student Union addition.

12 FEB. 1994. The Alumni Assoc. dedicates a plaque in University Hall honoring the first 47 winners of its Distinguished Alumni Award.

15 FEB. 1994. Andrei G. Safirov speaks in SUEC on "The Present Political, Economic, and Social Situations in Russia."

17 FEB. 1994. Hazel Gold speaks in SR on "The Role of Women in the Nineteenth Century Spanish Novel."

22 FEB. 1994. Rabbi Elliot Dorff and James McClendon Jr. speak in RH at the 7th Annual Morrow-McCombs Memorial Lecture on "Faith and Law in Judaism and Christianity."

23 FEB. 1994. Jim Merod speaks in SR on "Critical Theory and Jazz as a Cultural Archive."

24 FEB. 1994. Rap artist Professor Griff and punk singers Exene Cervenka and Don Bajema perform in SUEC. The campus hosts a panel in SR, "Discerning the Emerging Features of NAFTA in the Local USA-Mexico Border Regions: Do You See What I See?" with participants from Universidad Autónoma de Baja California: Arturo González, Manuel Aguilera, Humberto Soto, Horacio López, Gonzalo Banuelos, and Daniel Beltrán. The campus hosts a Symposium of Fulbright Scholars in PR, with Profs. Elliott R. Barkan, Louise F. Fulton, Ellen R. Gruenbaum, John W. Heeren, Susan E. Meisenhelder, Thomas M. Meisenhelder, Gary A. Negin, J. C. Robinson, and C. E. Tapie Rohm Jr.

25 FEB. 1994. The Barstow High School Concert Band performs in RH.

28 FEB. 1994. Russell C. Coile Jr. speaks in SR on "The Future of Health Care."

5-6 MAR. 1994. The campus hosts its annual Family Reading Rally, featuring Linda Baguley, Katherine Thomerson, Elizabeth Jimínez, Angela Lloyd, Evelyn Forrester, Gloria Straight, Libby Williams, Shirley O'Morrow, and Virginia Castro.

6 MAR. 1994. Dominic Martin "Nick" Bulgarella, Emer. Assoc. Prof. of Sociology (1969-92), dies at age 64.

7-10 MAR. 1994. The campus hosts Sexual Harassment Prevention Week.

8 MAR. 1994. Singer Judy Gorman performs in SU. Robert McDowell,

Publisher of Story Line Press, speaks about his work in ER.

10 MAR. 1994. Writer and psychologist Nancy Gamble speaks in SU on "Date Rape and the Second Rape," and signs copies of her books at the Women's Resource Center. CSU Trustee Rosemary Thakar visits the campus. The campus hosts a multicultural show, "A World of Fashions," in SUEC.

11 MAR. 1994. The campus receives a $321,000 energy rebate from Southern California Edison Co. for its conservation efforts.

12 MAR. 1994. The Coyotes women's basketball team wins the NCAA Division II Western Regional Championship Tournament, and goes to the "Elite Eight" finals.

13 MAR. 1994. Peter James Wetterlind, Prof. of Computer Science and Chair of the Dept. of Computer Science (1987-94), dies in San Bernardino of cancer at age 51.

14 MAR. 1994. Ex-CIA agent Philip Agee speaks in SR on "Inside the Company: CIA Diary."

16 MAR. 1994. Comedians Margaret Cho, A. J. Jamal, and Shang perform in SUEC.

18 MAR. 1994. John Hallett speaks in PS-122 on "How Snow Crystals Get Their Shape."

21 MAR. 1994. CSU Trustee Joan Otomo-Corgel visits the campus.

21-23 MAR. 1994. The campus hosts the 27th Annual Meeting of the Cordilleran Section of the Geological Society of America at the S.B. Hilton.

24 MAR. 1994. Cal State student Mara Denise Simmons dies in her Serrano Village dorm room at age 21.

26 MAR. 1994. The Coyotes women's basketball team (29-4) loses the NCAA Division II championship game to North Dakota State, 89-56, in a televised broadcast at Fargo, North Dakota, effectively placing 2nd in the nation in Division II play. This is the furthest that any Cal State team has ever advanced in postseason competition. However, the team is later stripped of its title (see May 17).

28 MAR. 1994. Arthur Albert Moorefield, Prof. of Music and ex-Chair of the Dept. of Music (1973-94), dies of a heart attack in RH at age 65. The campus later creates an annual Arthur Moorefield Memorial Recital to honor his memory.

28 MAR.–2 APR. 1994. Cal State's Model United Nations team wins an "Outstanding Delegation" Award for the 2nd year in a row in New York City, with CSUSB representing Suriname.

29 MAR. 1994. The campus signs an agreement to offer a new degree in Restaurant Management at CVC, in cooperation with Calif. State Polytechnic Univ. Pomona and Coll. of the Desert.

1 APR. 1994. The Extended Education Off. moves from the 5th floor of the Pfau Library to Sierra Hall, and the Library reoccupies that space preparatory to a seismic retrofitting project, with the Technical Services and Collection Development Depts. relocating there from the basement. Dave Rolston is named to CVC Advisory Board.

6 APR. 1994. Raymond Buriel speaks in SR on "The Social Adjustment of Immigrant Teenagers and Adults."

7 APR. 1994. The Center for Correctional Education hosts a videoconference, "Newspapers in Correctional Education: The Newspaper as a Motivational Tool," in PR.

9 APR. 1994. Actor John Astin performs a reading of a play-in-progress, *Once Upon a Midnight: The Confessions of Edgar Allan Poe*, in the Theatre.

11 APR. 1994. The campus hosts a forum in JB-102 on "Racism in America," the 1st event from the Cultural Diversity Committee.

13 APR. 1994. Jewelle Taylor Gibbs speaks in RH on "Children of Color: Challenges for Clinical Practice and Social Policy."

14 APR. 1994. The alternative group Flatliner performs on SUC. The country western group Idyllwild performs in SUEC.

18-19 APR. 1994. Students vote (474-354) to approve a $54-per-year fee to bolster the athletics budget.

21 APR. 1994. Peter Holliday receives the Rome Prize in a ceremony at the White House, to study art in Rome during 1994/95.

23 APR. 1994. The local chapter of the Sigma Phi Epsilon ($\Sigma\Phi E$) fraternity receives its charter. Magician Steve "Trash" Richerson performs at the 8th Annual Inland Empire Environmental Expo, "Live Green for Life."

25 Apr. 1994. Kathy Pezdek speaks in SUEC on "The Illusion of False Memory."

29 Apr. 1994. The campus and Cal-Pac Construction are jointly awarded the 1993 Charles J. Pankow Award for construction quality and innovative design of the Pfau Library Addition.

30 Apr. 1994. Writer Victor Villaseñor speaks to the 9th Annual Scholarship Awards Banquet of the Assoc. of Latino Faculty, Staff, and Students in UC.

3 May 1994. The Faculty Senate Library Committee expresses its concern over the inadequate funding of Library personnel, resources, and the materials budget. The Faculty Senate unanimously passes a resolution (FSD 93-15) supporting the findings of the Library Committee, and urging the campus to rebuild the Library collection and restore its purchasing power to the levels of fiscal year 1989/90, the last fully funded budget year, when the Library materials budget was just over a million dollars. The combination of budget cuts and inflation, they say, will result in a "fiscal disaster" for the Library, unless addressed immediately. However, funding is never restored. Peter F. Drucker speaks in Brown Hall.

4 May 1994. The Women's Resource and Adult Re-Entry Center relocates to the SU. The Class of 1994 raises funds to purchase 4 clock faces to complete the SU Clock Tower. Louis Bosshart speaks in SUEC on "American Television Serials and Swiss Fairy Tales."

5 May 1994. Banda Sol Naciente, Mariachi los Gallos Reales, and Grupo Folklórico perform as part of the Cinco de Mayo celebration.

5-6 May 1994. The campus hosts a "Dance Kaleidoscope" in RH.

13 May 1994. The Chancellor's Off. approves a new M.S. degree in Computer Science, effective in 1994/95.

11 May 1994. Chilean writer Isabel Allende speaks and signs copies of her books in SUEC. Richard Salzgiver speaks at a Diversity Awareness Workshop in SR. George Iwanaga, ex-Asst. Prof of Spanish, dies of cancer in San Bernardino at age 56.

13 May 1994. Nicholas J. Coussoulis receives the Arrowhead Chief Executive Officer Award at a lunch held in SUEC.

14 May 1994. The campus hosts its 2nd Annual Sweet Grass Gathering on the Library Lawn, with Native American crafts and dance.

17 MAY 1994. David L. Suenram, Athletic Dir. (1989-95), announces his resignation effective Mar. 31, 1995, after stating that a member of its women's basketball team may have been ineligible to play for the entire season; the NCAA investigates.

18 MAY 1994. *The San Bernardino Sun* runs a front-page article criticizing David L. Suenram's years as Athletic Dir. Paul Watson speaks in Brown Hall on "Business Skills for Students."

19 MAY 1994. The ska music group The Skeletones perform in SUC.

20 MAY 1994. The Rim High School Concert Band performs in RH.

21 MAY 1994. The campus hosts its African American Family Conference in SUEC, featuring music, dance, food, and dress. The campus hosts its Career Connection Conference in SUEC.

22 MAY 1994. The Loveland Mass Choir, Voices of Praise from the Temple Missionary Baptist Church, and Voices of Inspiration from the Live Church of God in Christ perform in SUEC.

23 MAY 1994. Actor B. D. Wong speaks in the Creative Arts Building on "Change, Hope, and Equality for Asian Americans."

24 MAY 1994. Groundbreaking is held for the Visual Arts Center and the Fullerton Art Museum. The campus hosts the "Chuckle House Comedy Jam" in SUEC.

26 MAY 1994. Lewis L. Jones, Dean of Undergraduate Studies, resigns.

27 MAY 1994. Charles W. Martin is named Dean of Undergraduate Studies, replacing Lewis L. Jones. *Los Angeles Times* critic Charles Solomon speaks in BI-102 on "Early Animation."

2 JUN. 1994. The post-punk group The Meat Puppets performs in SUEC.

15 JUN. 1994. Retirements: Harriet P. Gibson and Nancy S. Mazza.

16 JUN. 1994. Groundbreaking is held for the building that will become the Yasuda Center for Extended Education.

18-19 JUN. 1994. The 28th Commencement is held on the Library Lawn and at CVC, with CSU Trustee Ralph R. Pesqueira giving the keynote address (morning), and R. Jim Considine, Vice Chair of the CSU Board of Trustees, the address for the afternoon; attendees include Assemblyman Paul A. Woodruff, S.B. City Councilmen Freddy Curlin, Jerry Devlin, and

David Oberhelman, S.B. Co. Supervisor Larry Walker. CVC's ceremony takes place on Jun. 19 at Coll. of the Desert, with June M Cooper, CSU Vice Chancellor for Human Resources and Operations, giving the address. Some 3,800 students are eligible to receive degrees.

19 JUN. 1994. The campus hosts its 11th Annual Juneteenth celebration, with Hedies Inc., Prince Frosty, Diamonds in the Rough, Car-de-lite, D.J. Spy & Cool Bay, Natural Love, Trina B, Teenie, C.J. Paige and Friends, James Musgrove, Norma Richardson, Christia Fields, Silver C., Jamin' with Swat Team, Gina, Bronica Nettles, Johnny Bell, Duane Ross, Jassy Morton, Solo B of Dab Productions, Boys' and Girls' Club Pacesetters, the Palmettes Side Steppers Drill Team, and King Soloman performing.

22 JUN. 1994. Retirements: Patricia V. D'Souza, Prof., Information and Decision Science; Joseph L. English; Alice Jean Glazier; Lee H. Kalbus, Prof., Chemistry (1965-94); Donald B. Lindsey, Prof., Criminal Justice.

23 JUN. 1994. Patricia Laflin and Ronald Meraz are named to CVC Advisory Board.

30 JUN. 1994. Beverly A. Ryan, Libn. (1985-94), resigns to take a position at UC Santa Barbara. Retirements: Sarojam Mankau, Prof. of Biology (1968-94); Donna M. Ziebarth, Assoc. Prof. of Nursing (1977-94).

1 JUL. 1994. Cheryl A. Smith, Assoc. VP for Enrollment Services, is named Act. VP for Student Services, replacing Juan C. González, who goes on vacation before leaving his position. Dale T. West, Coll. Personnel Officer, is named Dir. of Human Resources.

6 JUL. 1994. The '50s group Popular Demand performs on LCP.

13 JUL. 1994. Dennis L. Hefner, VP for Academic Affairs (1990-94), resigns. The Ancient Future duo, with magician Zhao Hui and guitarist Matthew Montfort, performs on LCP.

14 JUL. 1994. Louis A. Fernández, Dean of Natural Sciences, is named Act. VP for Academic Affairs, replacing Dennis L. Hefner. Joel L. Nossoff, Asst. Dean of Undergraduate Studies and ex-Act. Dean (1990-91), resigns.

15 JUL. 1994. Aubrey W. Bonnett, Prof. of Sociology and Dean of the School of Social and Behavioral Sciences (1987-94), retires to become VP for Academic Affairs at SUNY Old Westbury.

16 JUL. 1994. Ellen R. Gruenbaum, Asst. Dean of Social and Behavioral Sciences, is named Act. Dean of Social and Behavioral Sciences, replacing

Aubrey W. Bonnett.

20 JUL. 1994. The band Mariachi Huezar performs on LCP.

21 JUL. 1994. The John M. Pfau Library Addition is occupied.

27 JUL. 1994. The Celtic folk group Tempest performs on LCP.

28 JUL. 1994. Harry Franklin Rheubottom, for whom the Rheubottom/Webster Lecture Series is later named, dies at age 75.

30 JUL. 1994. William Takehara is named first Assoc. VP for Financial Operations. Retirements: Max A. "Marty" Bloomberg, Libn., Assoc. Library Dir., and Act. Library Dir. (1966-94); Rosalie E. Carpenter, Admissions and Records; Kathleen King; Elizabeth L. Kirkpatrick; B. Joyce Kluck; Kathleen Pettigrew; Patricia A. Quanstrom, Dir., Accounting.

3 AUG. 1994. The blues duo Eric and Suzy Thompson perform on LCP.

10 AUG. 1994. Edward W. Harrison, Dir. of Public Safety and Police Services Manager (1986-94), resigns to take a post at CSU, Northridge. The jazz group Andy Cleaves Band performs on LCP.

11 AUG. 1994. Stephen C. Nowicki, Police Lt. (1988-94), is named Act. Dir. of Public Safety, replacing Edward W. Harrison. Daryl Anderson is named Dir. of Accounting, replacing Pat Quanstrom. Daniel C. Ashley, Act. Dir. of Administrative Computing and Telecommunications (1992-94), is named permanent Dir.

13 AUG. 1994. Retirements: Paul J. Johnson, Prof. of Philosophy (1966-94); Lynda W. Warren; (staff) Marjorie Callaghan; Jackie J. Mansker, Custodian; Tena M. Nelson; Dennis R. Stover.

14 AUG. 1994. Juan C. González, VP for Student Services (1987-94), resigns to take a position at CPSU, San Luis Obispo.

17 AUG. 1994. The bluegrass folk group Flower and McLaren performs on LCP.

22 AUG. 1994. James E. Daniels is named Dir. of Academic Programs and Services at CVC.

24 AUG. 1994. The jazz group The Latin Society performs on LCP. Richard Mejia and Diego Romero speak in Brown Hall on "Local Opportunities Posed by the NAFTA Treaty Between the U.S. and Mexico."

31 AUG. 1994. The campus receives an $8,990 rebate from Southern California Edison Co. for the design of the Student Union Building.

1 SEPT. 1994. Klaus R. Brasch, Chair of the Biology Dept., is named Act. Dean of the School of Natural Sciences, replacing Louis A. Fernández. The campus begins offering an M.S. degree in Computer Science, an M.A. degree in Educational Technology, and an M.S. degree in Instructional Technology at CVC.

11 SEPT. 1994. Cheryl A. Smith, Act. VP for Student Services, returns to her position as Assoc. VP for Enrollment Services.

12 SEPT. 1994. Frank L. Rincón is named VP for Student Services, replacing Cheryl A. Smith.

14 SEPT. 1994. At the annual convocation, Pres. Evans and the five Vice Presidents highlight the gains the campus has made, including: the opening of a new Library Addition and the Women's and Multicultural Centers, reorganization of Information Resources and Technology, implementation of the SIS+ computer system, start of touch-tone registration and touch-tone access to review financial aid status, beginning of a recreational sports program, improved access for the disabled, the issuing of credit cards for small purchases by campus departments, the donation of $100,000 by faculty and staff to support the construction of the Robert V. Fullerton Art Museum, start of a general equity program by the Athletics Dept., the full accreditation of the campus by WASC, and the separate accreditation of the School of Business and Public Administration, and new school records for outside grants and contracts. The Pres. emphasizes the University's commitment to diversity: "Each of us has a responsibility to ensure that the campus climate is a positive one for all members of our student body, faculty, and staff."

16 SEPT. 1994. The campus hosts its 8th Annual Children's Network Conference, "Caring Hands: Creating a Safe Environment for Our Children," in the Commons, with Judge Patrick J. Morris giving the keynote address. The campus holds an academic retreat, "Building Community," led by Jeff Lustig, with 4 sessions revolving around the topics of creating community through participation, involvement, and commitment; redefining faculty roles and responsibilities; creating coherent, diverse curricula; and using technology and teaching strategies.

23 SEPT. 1994. Egyptologist Zahi Hawass speaks in RH on "Recent Discoveries in the Cheops Complex."

26 SEPT. 1994. A ribbon-cutting ceremony takes place on the Andrews-Hill Plaza (named for Anna Jane Hill Andrews and Herbert J. Andrews), marking the official opening of the John M. Pfau Library Addition, with ex-Pres. Pfau, Anna Jane Hill Andrews, Herbert J. Andrews, Pres. Evans, and S.B. Chamber of Commerce Exec. Judi Thompson participating.

28 SEPT. 1994. The campus hosts the "San Bernardino Economic Summit" in the Creative Arts Building, with participants S.B. City Mayor Minor, S.B. City Councilwoman Valerie Pope-Ludlam, José Gómez, Phil Robertson, and Ralph Korpman.

5 OCT. 1994. The ASI Board of Directors again votes to suspend its membership in the Calif. State Students Assoc. for 1994/95.

12 OCT. 1994. The campus launches a new support group, Business Partners, for the School of Business and Public Administration.

17-19 OCT. 1994. Japanese educators Susumu Harizuka, Ryzoh Shimizu, and Kazurori Kawahradal visit the campus.

19 OCT. 1994. Louis S. Adler speaks in UC at the Business Partners Leadership Seminar Luncheon on "Filling the Leadership Void: Why Companies Get into Trouble and How to Prevent It." The campus hosts its 2nd Annual Culturefest celebration, with a performance by the Scottish Highland Dancers, and a "Kultatami-O-Rama" in SUC of dance, dress, and food from around the world. Pres. Evans is named Chair of the St. Bernardine Medical Center Board of Directors.

23 OCT. 1994. After a school dance, 36 shots are fired at 1:40 A.M. in Parking Lot D, damaging several vehicles.

25 OCT. 1994. Rüdiger Löwe speaks in SUEC on "The United States of America in Germany: A Changing Relationship." The campus adds 4 new concentrations to the Ethnic Studies Program in American-Indian, Asian-American, African-American, and Latino studies. The campus receives energy rebates totaling $45,536 from Southern Calif. Edison Co. to fund conservation projects in Brown Hall, the Pfau Library, and SU Addition.

2 NOV. 1994. Robert L. Lindstrom speaks in JB-111 on "How to Create Multimedia Business Presentations Quickly."

4 NOV. 1994. The band Here Comes Everybody performs.

6 NOV. 1994. Harpsichordist Phyllis Benson performs in RH in the 1st Annual Arthur A. Moorefield Memorial Recital.

9 NOV. 1994. The CSU Board of Trustees votes to accept 40 acres of land donated by the City of Palm Desert at the corner of Frank Sinatra Dr. and

Cook St. to help establish a permanent site for CVC, with an adjoining 160-acre plot being set side for future growth.

22 NOV. 1994. The campus receives a matching $50,000 grant from Bank of America to help retain minority business students.

25 NOV. 1994. John Erven is named Dir. of the Multicultural Center.

1 DEC. 1994. Robert A. Senour, Dir. of Audiovisual Services, returns to the ranks as Prof. of Education.

2 DEC. 1994. Juan Negrín Fetter speaks at the Univ. Art Gallery on "The Stein Collection of Huichol Yarn Paintings." John Levin, Gerald Kominski, and Adrián Sánchez speak before the 8th Annual Economic Forecast Breakfast, "Health Care Reform: Payoffs and Price Tags," in SUEC. Susan M. Cooper is named Dir. of Academic Computing and Media, replacing Robert A. Senour. Michael V. Benton is named Chief of Custodial Services.

2-3 DEC. 1994. The campus hosts its first University Dance Concert in the Theatre.

6 DEC. 1994. Boris Gontarev speaks in PR on "The Current Political, Economic, and Spiritual Condition of Russia and How It Relates to America."

8 DEC. 1994. Barbara Caine speaks in the Women's Resource and Adult Re-Entry Center.

10-11 DEC. 1994. The campus hosts the Inland Area Native American Assoc. Inter-Tribal Traditional Pow-Wow in SUEC, with Orville Little Owl serving as master of ceremonies.

16 DEC. 1994. Mary F. Smith is named Outstanding Professor for 1994/95.

22 DEC. 1994. The IBM 4381 mainframe computer and IBM 9370 Library computer are moved into the Pfau Library Addition.

27 DEC. 1994. The Pfau Library is vandalized between Dec. 25-27, with 2 windows and a door being broken.

31 DEC. 1994. Jean C. Ramage, Dean of the School of Education, resigns.

1995

1 JAN. 1995. Phyllis F. Fernlund is named Act. Dean of the School of Education. Leo P. Connolly receives a $71,000 grant from NSF to continue his summer science program for high school students. The campus receives a $60,000 gift from Ted and Jo Dutton to help fund the Fullerton Art Museum; a display area is named the Dutton Gallery in their honor.

6 JAN. 1995. The campus hosts a "Meeting the Challenge" expo, with Sandra McBrayer giving the keynote address.

9 JAN. 1995. The campus begins offering e-mail advising to students.

11 JAN. 1995. Ira Jackson and Carla Jackson and the Expressions Youth Choir perform in SUEC. Cellist Franklin Cox performs in RH.

18 JAN. 1995. Actor Judd Winick speaks in SUEC about "AIDS in the Real World: Learning to Live with Diversity."

20 JAN. 1995. Nancy P. Simpson is named Act. Dir. of Athletics, substituting for retiring Dir. David L. Suenram, who goes on leave.

24 JAN. 1995. Australian writer Thomas Keneally speaks about his book, *Schindler's List*, in SUEC at the 2nd Library Associates Lecture.

25 JAN. 1995. The Orion Saxophone Quartet performs in RH.

30 JAN. 1995. HUD official Thelma Moore gives the keynote speech in SUEC at the conference, "The War on Homelessness II: Filling the Gaps in the Continuum of Care."

1 FEB. 1995. The SU presents its 1st Annual Black History Celebration. Traffic lights are installed at I-215 and University Pkwy.

3 FEB. 1995. Judith Rae Killgore, Secretary in the English Dept. (1987-95), dies in San Bernardino of breast cancer at age 42.

9 FEB. 1995. The Repertory Theater of America performs the romantic comedy, *It Had to Be You*, in SUEC.

15 FEB. 1995. Rosemary Ruether speaks in RH at the 8th Annual Morrow-McCombs Memorial Lecture on "Jewish-Christian Resources for Eco-Feminist Theology." Sondra Hale speaks in PiR on "After the War: Women Fighters in Eritrean People's Liberation Front."

16 FEB. 1995. Botswanan sociologist Patrick Molutsi speaks in JB-113 on "Southern Africa in the 1990s: Prospect for a Peaceful Transition."

17 FEB. 1995. The Library hosts a panel and reception in PL-4005 honoring alumni authors Sondra Anderson-Heimark, Paul DeMeo, J. Michael Reaves, and Linda Stockham.

18 FEB. 1995. Dancers Karl Schaffer, Erik Stern, and Scott Kim perform "Dances for the Mind's Eye" in RH.

22 FEB. 1995. Psychologist and writer Lenore Walker speaks in SU on "Current Perspectives on Spousal Abuse."

23 FEB. 1995. Akiko Tsuchiya speaks in SR on "Benito Pérez Galdós and the Nineteenth-Century Spanish Novel."

24 FEB. 1995. According to a study by Prof. Thomas J. Pierce and student Marcus Cole, CSUSB boosted regional output in the Inland Empire by $145 million in 1992/93, and raised regional earnings by $66 million.

27 FEB. 1995. Lenore Walker speaks in SUEC on "Current Perspectives on Spousal Abuse."

1 MAR. 1995. 2 thieves responsible for 19 car break-ins on campus are arrested on Northpark Blvd. after being trailed by students. The alternative rock groups Dag and Mother May I perform in SUEC.

3 MAR. 1995. An original play by Linda Stockham, *Fragments*, debuts in UH-106.

6 MAR. 1995. Women's Basketball Coach Luvina Beckley resigns effective May 31, but later rescinds her resignation, prompting accusations in the local media that she was fired for racial reasons. The campus receives a $49,775 grant from the Calif. Postsecondary Education Commission to fund a project, "The California Math Show: A Traveling Hands-On Math Museum."

9 MAR. 1995. The campus hosts a teleconference on "Students with Disabilities."

10 MAR. 1995. The Gamma Nu (ΓΝ) chapter of Epsilon Pi Tau (ΕΠΤ), an international organization dedicated to promoting excellence in technology and education, receives its charter.

13 MAR. 1995. Latino playwright Carlos Morton speaks in JB-102 about the film, *American Me*.

14 MAR. 1995. Comedienne Lydia Sargent performs "I Read About My Death in *Vogue Magazine*" in SUEC.

17 MAR. 1995. The body of murdered schoolteacher Sharon Turner Rich is found in a ditch a mile north of campus.

18 MAR. 1995. The John M. Pfau Library Addition is dedicated a 2nd time, with Peter Lyman, Univ. Libn. at UC Berkeley, giving the keynote address.

20 MAR. 1995. Peter T. Robertshaw receives an $88,863 grant from NSF to excavate sites in Uganda.

26 MAR. 1995. Margaret Sintetos Richards, retired Library Asst. (1966-83), dies at age 76.

27 MAR. 1995. George Azem Weiny, Prof. of Physical Education and ex-Chair of the Dept. of Physical Education (1967-95), dies in Colton of cancer at age 61.

28 MAR. 1995. Wallace Thomas Cleaves Sr., Emer. Prof. of Psychology (1971-95), dies at Claremont of multiple myeloma at age 52.

31 MAR. 1995. David L. Suenram, Athletic Dir. (1989-95), retires.

1 APR. 1995. Nancy P. Simpson, Act. Athletic Dir., is named permanent Athletic Dir., replacing David L. Suenram.

5 APR. 1995. Animator Glen Keane and anthropologist Elizabeth Rega speak in RH on "Disney's Animated Characters." Louis A. Fernández, Act. VP for Academic Affairs, is named permanent VP

8 APR. 1995. 10 local gospel groups perform in the annual Gospel Choir Fest in SUEC.

11 APR. 1995. Astronomer David Levy speaks on "Jupiter and Shoemaker-Levy 9: The Great Comet Collision" in SUEC.

12 APR. 1995. Valerie Miller speaks at the Univ. Art Gallery on "The Contemporary Art Scene: A Dealer's Perspective."

13 APR. 1995. Maryellen Weimer speaks in PL-013 on "Maximizing College Learning Experiences," and in UH-106 on "Students of the 1990s." The campus hosts its 3rd Annual Symposium on the North American Free Trade Agreement, "NAFTA's Second Year: Experiences, Challenges, and Opportunities for Medium and Small-Sized Business Ventures," in JB-

102, with Eduardo Durán, Rosa Zuniga-Green, and Arturo Ranfla González speaking.

17 APR. 1995. Eileen Stevens speaks in SUEC on "Hazing."

20 APR. 1995. Poet Nikki Giovanni reads from her work in SUEC.

21 APR. 1995. Edwin Carlow speaks in PS-202 on "Acoustics."

22 APR. 1995. Magician Paul Cash, folksinger Barbara Shields, and the groups Actual Size and Hot Mud perform at the 9th Annual Inland Empire Environmental Expo, "Healthy Habitat," in SUEC and LC.

24 APR. 1995. The campus signs a partnership agreement with Universidad Autónoma de Baja California (UNAM), formalizing an exchange program that had been ongoing for several years. The pact recognizes the working relationship between Cal State's School of Education and UNAM's Escuela de Ciencias Humanas. Rep. George E. Brown, Walter E. Massey, Becky Morgan, and Martha Krebs speak in SUEC at the conference, "Shaping Science Education to Meet the Industrial Needs of the 21st Century."

26 APR. 1995. CSUSB's Model UN team again wins an Outstanding Delegation Award at the national competition in New York, representing the country of Sudan.

1 MAY 1995. Stephen C. Nowicki, Act. Dir. for Public Safety, returns to the ranks as Police Lt. Charles Vincent Hartung, Emer. Assoc. Prof. of English (1969-77), dies in Ojai at age 81.

2 MAY 1995. Dennis W. Kraus is named Dir. for Public Safety, replacing Stephen C. Nowicki.

3 MAY 1995. The Ballet Folklórico de Guadalupe and the mariachi band Los a la Cranes perform on LCP.

5-6 MAY 1995. The campus hosts its 9th Annual Student Research Conference.

12 MAY 1995. Glenda Bayless receives the annual Arrowhead Distinguished Chief Executive Office Award at a banquet in SUEC.

17 MAY 1995. The campus sponsors its 1st Annual Scholarship Golf Classic at Shandin Hills Golf Club in San Bernardino.

18 MAY 1995. John Taylor speaks in UH-106 on "Diverse Populations and

Universities."

19 MAY 1995. Mark Nicholls is named to CVC Advisory Board. The ska music group The Skeletones perform on SUC.

20 MAY 1995. The campus hosts its 3rd Annual Sweet Grass Gathering on the Library Lawn, sponsored by ASI and the Native American Students Assoc.

22-23 MAY 1995. The campus unveils its new Marketing Resource and Learning Facility in JB-238.

23 MAY 1995. The Music Dept. and the Inland Empire Symphony jointly form a Symphonic Choir, to perform beginning Nov. 1995.

26 MAY 1995. Assemblyman Joe Baca meets with members of the Calif. Faculty Assoc. concerning its contract dispute with the CSU System. Richard Ball and his Colton High School Concert Band perform with the CSUSB Wind Ensemble in RH.

1 JUN. 1995. The rock band Sublime performs in SUEC.

5 JUN. 1995. The Full Fathom Five Woodwind Quintet performs in RH. Rev. Raymond Turner and his Community Task Force write to the CSU Board of Trustees calling for the removal of Pres. Evans for an alleged pattern of discrimination against minorities on campus; no action is taken.

7 JUN. 1995. Francisco Hidalgo is named Pres.-Elect of the Assoc. of American Teachers, with his term beginning in Feb. 1996.

17-18 JUN. 1995. The 29th Commencement is held on the Library Lawn and at CVC, with CSU Trustee Joan Otomo-Corgel giving the keynote address for the morning sessions, and Trustee William Hauck addressing the evening session. CVC's ceremony takes place on Jun. 18, with John S. Rogers giving the keynote address. Some 3,900 students are eligible to receive degrees.

18 JUN. 1995. The campus hosts its 15th Annual Juneteenth celebration, with performers C. J. Paige & Friends, Diamonds in the Rough, Counselor M.C., Prince Frosty, Natural Cause, Nachaka, Stephanie Watkins, Paschel and the Ghetto Scholars, Shang, the Dave and Richard ventriloquist team, KUCR-FM's "Teddy Bear" and Billy Johnson Jr., San Bernardino Boys' and Girls' Club Pacesetters Drill Team, and Rev. Dennis Brown.

26 JUN. 1995. The campus receives a $49,000 grant from NSF to purchase an X-ray diffraction system, and a $30,000 NSF grant to buy an Asynchronous Transfer Mode switch. The campus receives an $18,600 grant from The Research Corp. to fuel investigations into the syntheses of chemical compounds.

12 JUL. 1995. The group Popular Demand performs on LCP.

18 JUL. 1995. The campus receives an anonymous $1.2 million gift from a local business couple.

19 JUL. 1995. The CSU Board of Trustees names the new Extended Education Building the Yasuda Center for Extended Education. The swing era band The Swing Sisters perform on LCP.

26 JUL. 1995. The rhythm-'n'-blues group Faultline performs on LCP, but the sudden burst of a water line under the SR forces them to cut short their appearance.

31 JUL. 1995. Clifford O. Young Sr. is named an American Council on Education (ACE) Fellow for 1995/96.

2 AUG. 1995. Steel drum band Pandemonium performs on LCP.

9 AUG. 1995. Los Amigos Mariachi Band performs on LCP. Ex-Dean Ernest F. García is named Pres. of the National Orange Show for 1995/96.

11 AUG. 1995. Barbara Harrington, ex-employee in Academic Programs, dies in San Bernardino at age 62.

16 AUG. 1995. Andy Cleaves and Friends perform on LCP.

18 AUG. 1995. The campus signs an agreement with Birzeit Univ. in Palestine to exchange faculty and students.

22 AUG. 1995. A power outage darkens the campus for 2 hours.

23 AUG. 1995. The rock group LCR Band performs on LCP.

24 AUG. 1995. Pres. Evans creates a Strategic Planning Steering Council, which meets for the first time on this date.

27 AUG. 1995. The S.B. Area Chamber of Commerce extends a unanimous vote of confidence to Pres. Evans.

30 AUG. 1995. The Latin Society performs on LCP.

1 SEPT. 1995. The Calif. Transition Program is renamed the Univ. Center for Developmental Disabilities. Juan Delgado receives the Walter E. Dakin Fellowship in Poetry. The campus expands its CVC Advisory Committee, adding new members Palm Desert City Councilman Robert Spiegel, Palm Desert Asst. City Manager for Planning Ray Díaz, Pres. of First Bank David Tschopp, Palm Springs City Planner Claudia Salvatierra Gamlin, Martin Martínez, Coll. of the Desert Pres. David A. George, Dean Wilson, VP DeMauro, and CSU Dir. of Academic Affairs and Institutional Relations David Leveille.

13 SEPT. 1995. Rev. Raymond Turner and his Community Task Force launch a new campaign to uncover discrimination at CSUSB. At the annual convocation, Pres. Evans and the 5 Vice Presidents note that "Our budget restraints actually have become tighter and tighter over the last five [years]," with a projected shortfall in 1995/96 of $1.2 million, and no new buildings. However, seismic retrofits are in the works for the Pfau Library, Commons Building, and old Physical Education Building. On the positive side, both the Nursing Dept. and the School of Education were accredited, and new grants totaled $7.5 million. The campus also raised $5.2 million in gifts. Administration and Finance is working with Student Services to streamline the enrollment process. 1,100 parking spaces are being added near Brown Hall and the Extended Education facility. The campus mainframe was successfully relocated to the new Library Wedge, and telecommunication projects were completed for the new Health and Physical Education Complex and the Pfau Library. The new Coussoulis Arena will be overseen by the Student Services Division—"The facility has fantastic potential to bring residents of the region on campus," says VP Rincón. "I think it will become a recruitment boom for us." The campus will decentralize commencement ceremonies for the first time in 1995/96. In response to charges that the campus encourages a climate of fear and discrimination, the Pres. says: "Clearly, some groups express discomfort with certain features of campus life. Others indicate that they have experienced discrimination of one sort or another. There is no place for discrimination on a university campus."

15 SEPT. 1995. The campus hosts its 9th Annual Children's Conference, "We Are Family," in UC, with keynote speakers Paul Crissey and Peter Alsop.

22 SEPT. 1995. The campus hosts its 1st intercollegiate athletic event in the Arena, with the women's volleyball team beating UC Davis.

26 SEPT. 1995. A ribbon-cutting ceremony marks the opening of the Health and Physical Education Complex and the James and Arianthi Coussoulis Arena. Carol J. Dixon is named Dir. of the Coussoulis Arena and the Health and Physical Education Facilities.

27 SEPT. 1995. The campus receives a 4-year, $800,000 grant from the Ronald E. McNair Post Baccalaureate Achievement Program.

29 SEPT. 1995. The Strategic Planning Council begins meeting to revise the University's mission statement and establish areas for long-term planning. Mary Williams Ellis, Secretary (1964-95), retires, being the longest-serving staff member to date at 31 years.

30 SEPT. 1995. The campus hosts a conference in the Arena for the Inland Empire Unit of the Calif. Assoc. of Health, Physical Education, Recreation, and Dance.

7 OCT. 1995. The campus honors 50 regional NSF "Young Scholars."

7-8 OCT. 1995. The campus hosts its Annual Inter-Tribal Traditional Pow-Wow for local Native Americans.

9 OCT. 1995. (Perry) Richard Switzer, Emer. Prof. of French and Dean of the School of Humanities (1970-93), dies at age 70; he bequeaths his house and personal property to the University, and his French literature collection to the Pfau Library.

19 OCT. 1995. Gerald A. Fawcett speaks in UC at a Business Partners Breakfast Presentation on "The Rise and Fall of Kaiser Steel Corporation." Actor Charles Pace performs "W. E. B. DuBois" in the Theatre.

21-22 OCT. 1995. The campus hosts the Complex Societies Group, with Thomas Huffman giving the keynote speech on "Sacred Leadership at Great Zimbabwe" in SR.

23 OCT. 1995. A ribbon-cutting ceremony marks the opening of the Yasuda Center for Extended Education; attendees include: Chiaki Mukai, first Japanese woman in space; Rep. George E. Brown; Seiichiro Noboru, Consul General of the Japanese Consulate in L.A.; officials from the Yasuda Institute of Education, Hiroshima, Japan.

25 OCT. 1995. Lee Zeigler and Lucia Guerra speak in HP-124 on "Cuba: A Special Situation and the Third World."

26 OCT. 1995. Sandra Morgen speaks in SR on "Changes in the Women's Health Movement in the U.S."

3 NOV. 1995. The campus begins paving Coyote Dr. as a new 4-lane entrance to the University leading to Brown Hall and the Arena.

10 NOV. 1995. Writer Helena María Viramontes speaks in SR. 70 students and faculty are inducted into the new Gamma Lambda (ΓΛ) Chapter of the Phi Beta Delta (ΦBΔ) Honor Soc. for Scholars in a ceremony held in UC.

11-12 Nov. 1995. Pianist Stephen Prutsman conducts a master class and performs (Nov. 12) in RH.

14 Nov. 1995. The campus holds a memorial ceremony in RH for the late Dean P. Richard Switzer (1925-95).

20 Nov. 1995. Sharon Plowman speaks in HP-124 on "Children Aren't Little Adults."

27 Nov. 1995. An arson wildfire prompted by 75 M.P.H. Santa Ana winds sweeps through 280 acres of brush on the northern perimeter of the campus, forcing cancellation of classes and an evacuation of all students and staff. Massive traffic jams occur at the campus exits.

28 Nov. 1995. The campus celebrates the opening of the James and Arianthi Coussoulis Arena with a tribute to their son, Nicholas J. Coussoulis, who contributed $500,000 to its construction, with the Bud Light Daredevils performing acrobatics and gymnastics.

1 Dec. 1995. The campus hosts its Annual Economic Forecast Breakfast, "Pacific Rim: Opportunities for the Inland Empire," with John Goller and Adrián Sánchez speaking. The Loma Linda Roller Coasters plays the San Diego Express in a wheelchair basketball game in the Arena.

5 Dec. 1995. The campus receives a loan from UC Los Angeles of thousands of La Brea Tar Pit bones, including dire wolves, giant ground sloths, and saber tooth cats.

11 Dec. 1995. A one-act play by Linda Stockham, *Red Breams*, debuts in JB-111.

14 Dec. 1995. Collette Rocha is named Executive Dir. of University Development, replacing Stephen Christensen.

18 Dec. 1995. The Services to Students with Disabilities Off. relocates to the 1st floor of University Hall. The Student Services Dept. relocates from the 2nd to the 1st floor of University Hall.

19 Dec. 1995. John(ie) Dan Summers, retired Groundsman (1972-85), dies at age 64.

1996

1 JAN. 1996. Leslie M. Kong is elected VP and Pres.-Elect of the Calif. Academic and Research Libraries Assoc.

3 JAN. 1996. The computer laboratories in the wedge portion of the Pfau Library Building open for business.

18 JAN. 1996. Leo P. Connolly is honored when asteroid #6479 LeoConnolly (ex-1988 LC) is named for him.

20 JAN. 1996. Peter T. Robertshaw receives a $30,000 grant from the National Endowment for the Humanities for "The Evolution of Complex Societies in Tropical Africa: An Archaeological Approach to History."

23 JAN. 1996. The campus hosts a forum on "The California Civil Rights Initiative and Proposition 187" in PR.

25 JAN. 1996. Writer Michael Novick and Planned Parenthood representative Maggie Hawkins speak in SUEC.

26 JAN. 1996. S.B. City Councilwoman Betty Dean Anderson tours the campus.

30 JAN. 1996. The campus revives its women's tennis team for the first time since 1991.

1 FEB. 1996. Prof. Donna Gotch wins $60,000 on the TV program, *Wheel of Fortune*; the 3 programs on which she appears are broadcast on 4-6 Mar. 1996. Michael Dressler speaks in SA on "Toward the Great Attractor: Exploring Intergalactic Space."

2 FEB. 1996. S.B. City Councilwoman Rita Arias tours the campus.

5 FEB. 1996. Adria F. Klein is named Outstanding Professor for 1995/96.

10 FEB. 1996. The campus hosts the "Environmental Business Opportunities Conference" in LC.

13 FEB. 1996. Helene Wickham Koon, Emer. Prof. of English (1970-90), dies at Hollywood at age 70. The University announces plans to develop a separate satellite facility for CVC at the corner of Cook St. and Frank Sinatra Dr. in Palm Desert, with structures to be built from donated funds.

16 FEB. 1996. Ex-Gov. Edmund Gerald "Pat" Brown Sr., who signed legislature to create the campus, dies at Beverly Hills at age 90. Roberta Johnson speaks in SR on "Twentieth-Century Literary Currents in Spain."

17 FEB. 1996. Flautist Damien Bursill-Hall performs in RH.

20 FEB. 1996. Lewis M. Barth speaks at the 9th Annual Morrow-McCombs Memorial Lecture in YC on "Jewish Stories for Christians: Rabbinic Tales of Healing, Wonderworking, and Personal Growth."

22 FEB. 1996. Satoko Hamamoto of Yasuda Univ. speaks in SR on "Contemporary Japan."

23 FEB. 1996. The Faculty Senate hosts a forum on "Diversity and the RPT Process."

24 FEB. 1996. The campus hosts the S.B. Postal Employees Black Heritage Committee Evening of Celebration, with Hardy Brown giving the keynote speech, and performances by The Scrugg Sisters, Darryl Robinson, the "Soul Force," and Fashions and More.

28 FEB. 1996. Steel pan music group Caribbean Breeze, the Andy Cleaves Band, and the Philippe Vieux Quartet perform in SUEC.

29 FEB. 1996. David M. L. Riefer receives the Golden Apple Award for Best Teacher of 1995/96 at the San Bernardino Hilton.

5 MAR. 1996. Susan Curzon, VP for Information Resources and Technology and Dean of the Univ. Library at CSU, Northridge, speaks in PL-013 on the Northridge Earthquake. 50 Japanese exchange students dance in the Arena.

7 MAR. 1996. The campus receives a $10,000 gift from golf star Dave Stockton to create golf scholarships and buy equipment.

9 MAR. 1996. The campus hosts a forum in University Hall as part of International Women's Day.

12 MAR. 1996. Oğuz Çelikkol, Consul General of Turkey, speaks in PR about his country.

13 MAR. 1996. The campus receives a $2,700,000 gift of software from the Oracle Corp.

14 MAR. 1996. Stanley Sue speaks in ER on "Cross-Cultural Counseling Issues."

15 MAR. 1996. Rhodessa Jones of the Cultural Odessey Co. performs "Big Butt Girls, Hard-Headed Women" in RH.

23 MAR. 1996. The campus creates a Teaching Resource Center.

27 MAR. 1996. The campus hosts an AVID Conference.

28 MAR. 1996. The U.S. Army Field Band and Chorus performs in the Arena.

8 APR. 1996. Victor Johnson speaks in PR on "U.S.-Latin America Policy and Development."

9 APR. 1996. The Faculty Senate hosts a forum on "Staff Morale: The First Victim of Budget Cutbacks" in ER, with 75 attending.

10 APR. 1996. The L.A. Smart Girls perform in RH.

15 APR. 1996. Shelli Herman, Asst. Dir. of Student Services at Loyola Marymount Univ., speaks on the "Greek" lifestyle. Cal State students receive an Outstanding Delegation Award at the Model United Nations competition in New York, representing the United Arab Emirates.

20 APR. 1996. The campus hosts its 10th Annual Environmental Expo, "Resources for the 21st Century," in the Arena, with eco-magician Paul Cash performing.

1 MAY 1996. Robin Balthrope speaks at the Women's Resource and Adult Re-Entry Center on "Potential Allies: Women of the Anti-Lynching Crusaders and the Universal Negro Improvement Assoc. Against Lynching."

3 MAY 1996. William B. Wehrenberg is named Dean of the School of Natural Sciences, effective 1 Aug. 1996, but resigns at the end of May. Cynthia Gordon speaks in SR on "Patients as Decision Makers: Autonomy, Competence, and Informed Consent."

4 MAY 1996. Activist Angela Davis speaks in UH-106 on "Prisons and Women of Color." The campus hosts its 3rd Annual Gospel Fest in SUEC, with performances by St. Anthony's Gospel Choir, Jordan Gospel Group, Holy Persuasion Youth Choir, Ecclesia Christian Fellowship, Spiritual Awakening, the CSUSB Concert Choir, Da'Jhana Davenport, and Joe Reyes. Enrique Diemecke, Music Dir. of the Orquestra Sinfónica de México, performs in RH.

8 MAY 1996. Alfredo Mirande, Kevonne Small, and Leonard Ross speak in SUEC on "Drive-By Justice? Race and the Law." Pamela Harer speaks in PL-4005A on "Seventeenth-to-Nineteenth-Century Children's Literature."

9 MAY 1996. Michael Burawoy speaks in HP-124 on "The Color of Class: Africanization and Postcolonialism." Peter Y. Sussman signs copies of his book, *Committing Journalism*, in the Bookstore. Kenneth W. Goings speaks in SUEC on "Aunt Jemima and Uncle Moses: Black Collectibles as Barometers of Race."

10 MAY 1996. As part of its 30th anniversary celebration, the campus hosts a reception and book display in the Pfau Library to honor faculty authors and composers, and publishes *CSUSB Faculty Authors, Composers, and Playwrights: A Bibliography of Thirty Years of Published Monographs and Recordings, 1965-1995*, by Michael Burgess, a copy of which is presented to the attendees.

11 MAY 1996. In the 1st annual Harry Rheubottom/George Webster Local History Lecture (named for 2 deceased founding members of the Library Associates, and organized by Johnnie Ann Ralph), historians Larry E. Burgess and James Sandos speak on the 2nd floor of the John M. Library on "The Hunt for Willie Boy." The U.S. Olympic Women's Volleyball Team plays the Chinese Olympic Women's Volleyball Team in the Arena.

15 MAY 1996. Actor Edward James Olmos speaks in SUEC on "We're All in the Same Gang."

16 MAY 1996. Writer Peter Y. Sussman speaks in UH-106 on "Prisoner Access to Media." Henry Levin speaks in SUEC on "The Accelerated Schools Project." Anthony F. Grasha speaks at the 2nd Annual Arthur A. Moorefield Memorial Lecture in UH-106 on "More Than Method: Teaching with Style." Katie Feifer speaks on campus to various classes.

20 MAY 1996. Rep. George E. Brown speaks on campus.

21 MAY 1996. Halford H. Fairchild speaks in SR on "White Psychology, Black Psychology, and the Future of the World."

23 MAY 1996. Greek Consul-General Christos Panagopoulos speaks in PR on "The Current Situation in the European Union."

24 MAY 1996. The Bombrule Assoc. hosts a "Stop the Violence Day" in SUEC. Jeff Ferrell speaks in UH-106 on "The Graffiti Artist as Social Critic: Expressionism or Vandalism?" The golf team finishes in 11th place in the NCAA Division II championship.

29 MAY 1996. Neal T. Baker, founder of Baker's Drive-Thru Restaurants, receives the annual Arrowhead Distinguished Chief Executive Office Award at a banquet in SUEC. The campus announces that radio station KSSB will return to the air at 680 on the AM dial.

30 MAY 1996. Rap singer Sinbad performs in the Arena as part of the "End of the World Party."

31 MAY 1996. Matt Cartmill speaks in RH on "The Myths of Race."

1 JUN. 1996. Comedian Howie Mandel performs in the Arena.

4 JUN. 1996. The campus hosts the Pontiac Hot Wheels Fest '96 on the Library Lawn, with racing champion Randy Goodwin.

15-16 JUN. 1996. The 30th Commencement is held in the Arena (the first time there) and at CVC, with each school sponsoring its individual graduation ceremony; keynote speakers include: H. Arthur "Hal" Hoverland (Business and Public Administration); Harry Blackstone Jr. (Humanities); Sandra McBrayer (Education); Robert G. Stein (Natural Sciences); Sen. Barbara Boxer (Social and Behavioral Sciences); Riverside Co. Supervisor Roy Wilson (CVC).

16 JUN. 1996. The campus hosts its 13th Annual Juneteenth Celebration in LC.

23 JUN. 1996. Lee I. Porter is named Education Specialist of the Year by the Accrediting Commission of Career Schools and Colleges of Technology.

30 JUN. 1996. Ellen R. Gruenbaum, Act. Dean of the School of Social and Behavioral Sciences, returns to the ranks as Prof. of Anthropology. Loretta Adeline Campbell, retired employee in the Budget Off. (1968-91), dies at age 75.

SUM. 1996. Retirements: Stephen A. Bowles, Prof. of Psychology (1974-96); F. F. Liu, Prof. of Computer Sciences (1970-96); Edward M. White, Prof. of English (1965-96).

1 JUL. 1996. New parking fees and rules go into effect on campus, with visitors now having to buy temporary parking decals. John A. Conley is named Dean of the School of Social and Behavioral Sciences, replacing Ellen R. Gruenbaum. Quentin J. Moses is named Dir. of Parking Services.

8 JUL. 1996. The design of the University seal is updated to make the Pfau Library Building the central part of the emblem.

10 JUL. 1996. The band Popular Demand performs on LCP.

15 JUL. 1996. The School of Education reorganizes, creating 5 new departments to replace 3 existing ones: Educational Policy and Research; Educational Psychology and Counseling; Leadership, Curriculum, and Instruction; Learning, Literacy, and Culture; and Science, Mathematics, and Technology Education.

17 JUL. 1996. (Charles) Frederick "Fred" Kellers, Emer. Prof. of Physics and ex-Chair of the Dept. of Physics (1968-88), dies at age 65. The swing band The Notables performs on LCP.

24 JUL. 1996. Rhythm-'n'-blues band Faultline performs on LCP.

31 JUL. 1996. Mary Ellen Bobp, Libn. (1991-96), resigns. Eldon C. Lewis, Int. Dean of the School of Business and Public Administration, returns to the ranks as Prof. of Accounting and Finance. The band Pandemonium performs on LCP.

1 AUG. 1996. Steven M. Mintz is named Dean of the School of Business and Public Administration, replacing Eldon C. Lewis. The Campus Police Dept., Parking Services, and the Emergency Operation Center move from the Physical Plant to temporary office TO-209 north of the Pfau Library.

2 AUG. 1996. The campus receives a gift from CSU Chico Prof. James Kuiper of a 1-ton, 12-foot-high sculpture, "Cherokee," which is erected near the Visual Arts Center.

7 AUG. 1996. Andy Cleaves and His Band perform on LCP.

14 AUG. 1996. Bluegrass group Alive and Pickin' performs on LCP.

21 AUG. 1996. The '60s group The LCR Band performs on LCP.

26 AUG. 1996. The Technical Services and Collection Development Depts. of the Pfau Library complete their move to the 5th floor of that building, preparatory to the demolition of the Library basement as part of its seismic retrofitting project.

28 AUG. 1996. The Latin Society performs on LCP.

29 AUG. 1996. A parking officer is assaulted in the Creative Arts Building.

1 SEPT. 1996. The Dept. of Physical Education is renamed the Dept. of Kinesiology and Physical Education. Rowena S. Santiago, Secondary and Vocational Education, is named Coordinator of the Faculty Development

Program and Teaching Resource Center. The campus unveils a Nuclear Magnetic Resonance (NMR) spectrometer, partially funded by a $240,000 grant from NSF. The Pfau Library receives a gift of 2,000 English, Spanish, and Portuguese books from Carlos E. Cortés, Emer. Prof. of History at the Univ. of Calif., Riverside. The campus receives a $7,500 gift from golfer Dave Stockton to support a scholarship in the Coyote Athletics golf program. The alumni magazine, *Cal State San Bernardino*, increases its size from 8.5 x 11 inches to 10 x 12.5 inches, and changes its name to *Cal State SB*. Michael L. Ross is named Assoc. Dir. of Academic Computing and Media.

13 SEPT. 1996. The campus receives 5 grants from NSF totaling $204,315. The campus receives a $71,000 gift from Stater Bros. Markets and the Food Industry Council to establish a scholarship in honor of Stater Bros. VP Richard Moseley.

16 SEPT. 1996. The new Visual Arts Center opens for business.

17 SEPT. 1996. Pres. Anthony H. Evans announces his impending retirement in mid-1997. "Since the state of the university is good and improving each year, the timing seems right. We have attained many of our goals, and the university's growth and development have been so reassuring. I have taken such delight in my work here that it hardly seems possible that I have served...twice the national average for university presidents. The faculty and staff are strong, student enrollments are relatively stable, and budgetary challenges are more manageable. I am so pleased that CSUSB's facilities are now truly superb and that donor and alumni support is growing annually. I am grateful that the university's commitment to serving the region is firmly established."

18 SEPT. 1996. At the annual convocation, Pres. Evans states: "At this time, my 15th convocation, I want to request your special assistance in helping the university adjust to pending leadership changes. Change is not a stranger to us here, and because of the rapidity of change that characterizes our region and much of the world today, planning takes on more importance than ever before." The Pres. notes the important work of the Strategic Planning Council, chaired by VP Fernández, saying that its example of taking a more analytical and calculated approach to planning the future is crucial. Among notable achievements, the campus ranked first in the CSU in 1993-94 in the recruitment of minority faculty, and second in the hiring of women faculty. The Pfau Library is undergoing a noisy seismic retrofitting; the Library also plans to install a new on-line catalog system, Horizon. The campus plans to have all students apply for admission on-line, and to implement a direct student loan lending program. In the new academic year, the campus will focus on fundraising for CVC and the School of Humanities. Improving the university's outside relations and public image will also be a priority.

23 SEPT. 1996. The Off. of Student Housing is renamed the Off. of Residential Housing Services, and the Off. of Student Life is renamed the Off. of Student Leadership and Development. A Taco Bell franchise opens on the 2nd floor of the SU.

27 SEPT. 1996. A new traffic light at the corner of Coyote Dr. and Northpark Blvd. nears completion.

28 SEPT. 1996. Singer Vikki Carr performs with the band Mariachi Sol de México in the Arena.

1 OCT. 1996. The campus dedicates JB-102 as the Anheuser-Busch Auditorium to reflect a $150,000 gift from that company to the School of Business and Public Administration, with appearances by Jack H. Brown, Chair and CEO of Stater Bros., and the Anheuser-Busch Budweiser Clydesdale horses and carriage.

3 OCT. 1996. Philip Page receives the Eudora Welty Prize for his book, *Dangerous Freedom: Fusion and Fragmentation in Toni Morrison's Novels*.

4 OCT. 1996. Writer Jonathan Ned Katz speaks in UH-106 on "The Invention of Heterosexuality."

9 OCT. 1996. Diane F. Halpern receives a Career Achievement Award from the American Psychological Assoc. CSU Chancellor Munitz meets with the Faculty Senate concerning the selection of a new campus President.

10 OCT. 1996. A ribbon-cutting ceremony and banquet mark the official opening of the Visual Arts Center and Robert V. Fullerton Art Museum, with the attendance of CSU Chancellor Munitz and Anne Munitz. Among the collections housed in the Museum are 200 Egyptian artifacts on long-term loan from the Harer family; a full-sized replica of the tomb of Nefertari from the Getty Conservation Institute; 200 Asiatic ceramics donated by Pres. and Mrs. Evans; 95 pieces of African art from Jane Matthews; 55 yarn paintings rendered by the Huichol Indians from Joel A. Stein; and 26 Etruscan and Italian vases from the Karnoff Collection. The Museum unveils its first 2 exhibitions, "Selma Moskowitz: Recent Paintings" and "Minoru Ohira: Recent Sculptures." The ex-Visual Arts Building is renamed the Humanities Classroom Building.

14 OCT. 1996. Xiwen Zhang unveils her campus diversity webpage before the Administrative Council.

17 OCT. 1996. Painter Selma Moskowitz speaks about her work in SA.

20 OCT. 1996. Baritone Rodney Gilfry performs in RH at the 3rd Annual Arthur A. Moorefield Scholarship Recital.

25-26 OCT. 1996. Assemblyman Joe Baca sponsors an educational summit, "Excellence Through Technology."

26 OCT. 1996. A fire in the foothills of the San Bernardino Mountains briefly threatens the campus.

28 OCT. 1996. Jia-Rong "Jerome" Wen speaks in PR on "Computer-Assisted Instruction for Chinese." Dale Ulrich speaks in HP-124 on "Motor Development in Children."

28-29 OCT. 1996. CSU Trustees Martha C. Fallgatter [Walda], Bernard Goldstein, and Ali C. Razi meet with the UAB (Oct. 28) and engage in a forum in PR (Oct. 29).

1 NOV. 1996. John S. Rogers gives the campus $1.5 million from the Mary Stuart Rogers Foundation to establish 18 annual $3,300 endowed scholarships for CVC students.

6 NOV. 1996. Soprano Lauralyn Kolb performs "Women's Work" with pianist Rosemary Hyler in RH.

13 NOV. 1996. The campus celebrates Native American Day, with Earl Sisto giving the keynote address.

14 NOV. 1996. Writer Ellen Gootblatt speaks in SUEC on "Relationships." The 1st Annual Dave Stockton Coyote Classic Golf Tournament at Empire Lakes Golf Course in Rancho Cucamonga raises more than $35,000 for men's golf and athletic scholarships. Mystery writer Sharan Newman speaks in HP-124 on "Women in History: Researching and Writing Historical Novels."

18-19 NOV. 1996. CSU Trustee Frank Y. Wada visits the campus.

21 NOV. 1996. Architect Stephen William Harby speaks in SA on "Place Making for Campus and Community: The Architecture of Moore Ruble Yudell."

2 DEC. 1996. The Administrative Council changes the campus colors from blue and brown to Columbia blue and black.

3 DEC. 1996. The Seismic Retrofitting Project begins in the Library.

6 DEC. 1996. Howard L. Roth speaks in SUEC at the 10th Annual Economic Forecast Breakfast on "Inland Empire Economic Recovery: If It's Real, Prove It."

13 DEC. 1996. Construction begins on a $1.3 million parking project, with Phase I completing the paving of Coyote Dr. from Northpark Blvd. to Brown Hall and adding spaces to Lot F, and Phase II adding 800 spaces to Lot G near Physical Education and another 200 spaces to Lot A near the Physical Plant.

14 DEC. 1996. The campus hosts a wheelchair basketball game between the Inland Empire Roller Coasters and the San Diego Express in the Arena.

18 DEC. 1996. Linda Stockham's new one-act play, *Goddesses of the Western World*, is read in JB-111.

22 DEC. 1996. High Santa Ana winds damage 23 trees and a building roof.

1997

6 JAN. 1997. The campus closes after 75 M.P.H. Santa Ana winds knock down trees and students, and cause minor structural damage to several buildings. The campus begins offering a B.A. degree in Business Administration (Marketing) through Victor Valley Coll.

17 JAN. 1997. The campus chapter of Campus Crusade for Christ unveils its web page, one of the first created by a student group.

19 JAN. 1997. Writer Walter Moseley speaks and signs copies of his books at SUEC.

23 JAN. 1997. Writer Shifra Goldman speaks in SA on "The Influences of Mexican Muralist David Alfaro Siquieros."

24 JAN. 1997. The comedian Gallagher performs in the Arena.

27 JAN. 1997. The campus receives a $50,000 gift from ex-S.B. City Mayor Wilcox.

29 JAN. 1997. The Pfau Library unveils its on-line catalog, Horizon. The American Indian Movement (AIM) inaugurates a campus chapter in SUEC.

31 JAN. 1997. The campus receives a $75,000 grant from the Children's Fund to provide music education for 40 homeless youths.

1 FEB. 1997. Mark K. Day is named Assoc. Dir. of the Student Union.

5 FEB. 1997. Terry L. Rizzo is named Outstanding Professor for 1996/97. *San Bernardino Sun* Editor O. Ricardo Pimentel speaks on campus.

6 FEB. 1997. 200 faculty, staff, and students gather in SR to discuss a projected $3,500,000 campus budget deficit for 1997/98. Architectural historian Diane Favro speaks in SA on "Women's 'Writes' and Architecture: Women Authors on the Built Environment."

13 FEB. 1997. Steve Lilly speaks in JB-102 on "Changing the Culture of Teacher Preparation."

14 FEB. 1997. Zimbabwean political scientist Masipula Sithole speaks in UC on "Post-Mandela Southern Africa."

15 FEB. 1997. Kathy Pezdek speaks in PR on "Our Life Is Our Memory... but How Accurate Is That Memory?"

17 FEB. 1997. Cal State student Marie Grace Gottis dies in a fire in San Bernardino at age 28.

18 FEB. 1997. David L. Miller speaks in YC at the 10th Annual Morrow-McCombs Memorial Lecture on "Eggs & Apples: Paradox in Religious Dialogue/Dialogue in Religious Paradox."

19 FEB. 1997. Israeli Consul for Communication and Affairs Ido Aharoni speaks in UH-106 on "Israeli Media."

20 FEB. 1997. Painter Roland Reiss speaks about his work in SA. Fatma Ahmed Ibrahim speaks in JB-102 on "The Current Situation in Sudan and 'Islamic Terrorism'."

24 FEB. 1997. The Peking Acrobats perform in the Arena.

25 FEB. 1997. High Santa Ana winds injure a custodian at the Visual Arts Complex.

26 FEB. 1997. Children's literature critic Pamela Harer speaks at the 3rd Library Associates Lecture in PL-4005 on "Enjoying Children's Books the Second Time Around."

6 MAR. 1997. Mark Coughlin speaks in LC on his book, *Tokyo Daze*.

7 MAR. 1997. The campus proposes to set aside $750,000 as an ongoing contingency fund, as part of a plan to meet budget deficits.

8 MAR. 1997. Karin Higa, Curator for the Japanese American National Museum, speaks in SA on "One Curator's Odyssey: Japanese American Art from the Internment Camps."

14 MAR. 1997. A ribbon-cutting ceremony marks the unveiling of the permanent entrance sign at the new site of CVC in Palm Desert. The CVC master plan is submitted for approval to the Palm Desert City Council and Planning Commission.

19 MAR. 1997. The Strategic Planning Steering Council issues its report, "Project Cornerstone: Building for the 21st Century."

23 MAR. 1997. The Church of Jesus Christ of Latter-Day Saints holds its Regional Conference in the Arena.

28 MAR. 1997. Robert Rice Harrison, Emer. Prof. of Art (1965-72), dies at Yucaipa at age 88. Fook Fah Liu, Emer. Prof. of Computer Science (1970-96), dies of cancer at age 62. *The Friday Bulletin* adopts a new design.

31 MAR. 1997. Rodney Joe Simard, ex-Assoc. Prof. of English (1986-95?), is murdered at age 44.

4 APR. 1997. The Clock Tower over the Student Union Building is completed with the addition of 4 new clock faces.

5 APR. 1997. The campus hosts the Inland Empire Dance Invitational Step Show in the Arena.

9 APR. 1997. Retiring Pres. Evans is honored at a joint meeting of the Kiwanis and Rotary Clubs of S.B. in the National Orange Show Events Center. 120 faculty and staff rally against budget cuts.

10 APR. 1997. Artists Kim Koga and David Svenson speak in SA on "LIGHT-Headed: Working with Glass and Neon."

11 APR. 1997. University stationery is redesigned to provide more writing space on each sheet. The Friday *Bulletin* is now simultaneously published in color on the campus website.

12 APR. 1997. U.S. Asst. Secretary for Civil Rights Norma V. Cantu speaks at the 7th Annual Calif. Minority Graduate Education Forum.

13 APR. 1997. Ex-Cal State instructor Gerald Joseph McCall is arrested for murdering a prostitute.

14 APR. 1997. The Campus Budget Committee recommends a budget cut of $777,386, but spares any cuts to classes and teachers, and sets aside $500,000 as a reserve fund.

15 APR. 1997. Singer Linda Perry performs in SUC.

17 APR. 1997. A ribbon-cutting ceremony marks the unveiling of the new Clock Tower over the Student Union, with Marion Black of the S.B. Chamber of Commerce attending. Woodcarver Jim Lawrence speaks about his work in SA.

18 APR. 1997. The campus hosts a conference, "The Implications of Technology Development for Business Growth in the Inland Empire."

19 APR. 1997. Magician Paul Cash, musician Mark Lynn, and The Mountain Folksingers perform as part of the 11th Annual Environmental Expo in the Arena.

21 APR. 1997. Parking Lot E opens for business.

23 APR. 1997. James Schefter speaks in JB-280 on "All Corvettes Are Red."

24 APR. 1997. Critic Ed Earle speaks in SA on "New Frontier or Old Territory: Media Arts and the Internet."

1 MAY 1997. Ann Page speaks in SA on being the model of woodcarver and painter Jim Lawrence.

3 MAY 1997. Historian Edward Leo Lyman speaks at the 2nd Annual Rheubottom/Webster Historical Lecture in the Pfau Library on "San Bernardino: The Rise and Fall of a California Community."

5-9 MAY 1997. The campus hosts "Raza Culture Week" with performances by Mariachi Internacional de México, the Ballet Folklórico, and singer Rosa Marta Zarate; writer Simón Silva speaks about his work.

8 MAY 1997. TV weatherman Christopher Nance speaks in PL-013 on "Public Perceptions of Persons with Disabilities." Woodworker Connie Mississippi speaks in SA on "Turning to Space and Time: The Lathe-Turned Object as Art." Jesse Lerner speaks in UH-106 on "Frontierlandia."

9 MAY 1997. Activist Eldridge Cleaver speaks in RH.

10 MAY 1997. Writer Maya Angelou speaks at the Arena during a celebration of her work called "A Tribute to Mothers Everywhere," with 2,300 persons attending—but cuts her speech short due to illness.

14 MAY 1997. The CSU Board of Trustees names Albert K. Karnig the 3rd President of CSU, San Bernardino. The annual Faculty Book Launch is held in ER to honor faculty authors.

17 MAY 1997. Ernesto Robles, Pres. of the National Hispanic Scholarship Fund, speaks at the 12th Annual Latino Scholarship and Graduate Banquet and Dance in UC.

22 MAY 1997. Art collector Jane Matthews speaks at the 4th Library Associates Lecture in SA on "African Art: Old and New." Frederico Vigil speaks in SA on "Buon Fresco in New Mexico: Ancient Art/New Images."

23 MAY 1997. Cal State golfer Scott Householder wins the NCAA Division II Golf Individual Championship at Scottsdale, Arizona, the first (and only) time that any CSUSB athlete or team has won a national title.

31 MAY 1997. *Saturday Night Live* comedian Norm MacDonald performs in the Arena. The campus hosts its 2nd Annual Diversity Conference, "Successes and Challenges: Strategies to Overcome Historical Barriers," in SU and Commons, with Rep. George E. Brown welcoming participants, and Rev. Chuck Singleton giving the keynote address.

1 JUN. 1997. Coyote Dr., the 2nd major campus entrance, opens.

3 JUN. 1997. A campus honors retiring Pres. Evans at a reception in SUEC.

9 JUN. 1997. The campus receives a $3 million cash gift (the largest to date) from the Mary Stuart Rogers Foundation, to be paid in 3 annual increments of $1 million each, to help construct the first permanent building at CVC.

14 JUN. 1997. Cal State senior Sociology major Wardell Jermaine Epps dies at age 24.

14-15 JUN. 1997. The 31st Commencement is held in the Arena and at the McCallum Theatre in Palm Desert for CVC, with the following keynote speakers: Pres. Evans (CVC), alumnus Steve Mayering (Natural Sciences), alumnus USAF Col. Edward Sheeran (Social and Behavioral Sciences), alumnus Gerald A. Fawcett (Business and Public Administration), Emer. Prof. Edward M. White (Humanities), and Rabbi Marvin Heir (Education).

18 JUN. 1997. Retiring Pres. Evans is fêted with a dinner in the Arena. The Alumni Assoc. announces a $5,000 contribution to the newly established

Presidential Scholars Endowment, which has been erected in Evans's honor.

20 JUN. 1997. The campus cancels its summer entertainment series, due to budgetary constraints.

25 JUN. 1997. Rep. George E. Brown announces that the campus has received a 4-year, $960,000 grant from the U.S. Dept. of Education to help fund its Student Assistance in Learning (SAIL) program.

27 JUN. 1997. The campus hosts a "Conference on International Trade" at the Ontario International Airport.

SUM. 1997. Retirements: Ronald E. Barnes, Prof. of Theatre Arts and Chair of the Dept. (1965-97); Loralee MacPike, Prof. of English (1978-97); Amanda Sue Rudisill, Prof. of Theatre Arts (1969-97); David Shichor, Prof. of Criminal Justice (1976-97); Steven R. Wagner, Assoc. Prof. of Education (1974-97); Carl P. Wagoner, Prof. of Criminal Justice (1969-97).

1 JUL. 1997. Parking Lot F opens for business.

8 JUL. 1997. (Joseph) Patrick Watkins, Prof. of Theatre Arts and Chair of the Dept. (1994-97), dies at Paris, France of AIDS-related pneumonia at age 46.

11 JUL. 1997. *The Friday Bulletin* ceases to be distributed in printed form, becoming primarily an on-line publication, with a 5.5 x 8.5-inch printout being generated and distributed for those departments or individuals without web access (see also 11 Feb. 2000).

14 JUL. 1997. The campus agrees to purchase the bronze image of 3 coyotes by Xuanchang Guo to adorn the center strip of Coyote Dr., next to the new information booth being constructed there.

24 JUL. 1997. Retiring Pres. Evans is honored at a reception at the Arrowhead Credit Union sponsored by the Inland Empire Hispanic Chamber of Commerce; attendees include Assemblyman Joe Baca and Ray Quinto; IEHCC Pres. Marie Alonzo presents $1,000 to the campus to help create the Tony Evans Scholarship Fund.

31 JUL. 1997. Phyllis F. Fernlund, Act. Dean of the School of Education and Prof. of Education, resigns to become a Dean at Sonoma State Univ. Ellen Gruenbaum, ex-Act. Dean of the School of Social and Behavioral Sciences, resigns to become a Dean at CSU, Fresno.

1 AUG. 1997. Patricia K. Arlin is named Dean of the School of Education, replacing Phyllis F. Fernlund.

15 AUG. 1997. Anthony H. Evans, Prof. of History and 2nd Pres. of the University (1982-97), retires.

THE ADMINISTRATION OF
ALBERT K. KARNIG
16 AUGUST 1997 - DATE

ABOUT ALBERT K. KARNIG

ALBERT KOONDAKJIAN KARNIG was born Karnig Albert Koondakjian on 15 Apr. 1942 at New York, New York, the son of Avedis Koondakjian and Alice Manoukian, Armenian immigrants; he legally changed his name when he came of age. He married Marilyn Joan Vogelaar on 12 Jun. 1964 in Illinois, and they have 3 sons—Todd K., Eric V., and Brent D.—and several grandchildren. He earned his B.A. at Augustana College in 1968, his M.A. in Political Science at the Univ. of Illinois in 1969, and his Ph.D. there in 1972. He was a Woodrow Wilson Fellow, an NDEA Fellow, and a Kendric C. Babcock Fellow.

From 1972-77 he taught political science at Texas Technological Univ. He was hired to teach public administration at the Univ. of Arizona in 1977, eventually becoming Assoc. VP of Academic Affairs there. In 1988 he was named Provost at the Univ. of Wyoming. His writings include two books—*Black Representation and Urban Policy* (with Susan Welch; Univ. of Chicago Press, 1980), and *Urban Minority Administrators: Politics, Policy, and Style* (edited with Paula D. McClain, Greenwood Press, 1988)—and 60 refereed journal articles.

His philosophy of education was outlined in a speech he presented just a month after his arrival to a 19 Sept. 1997 convocation: "What we offer is an opportunity for a future to those who are less affluent, to those who are site-bound, to those who are changing careers, who wish to re-enter the work force, to those who are first-generation to attend college, who are late bloomers, and for those who don't make the foolish—and I want to underscore this—for those who don't make the foolish mistake of confusing selectivity and price on the one side with quality and value on the other."

1997 (continued)

16 Aug. 1997. Albert K. Karnig officially takes office as 3rd President of CSUSB, although he does not start work until Aug. 18.

25 Aug. 1997. Rep. George E. Brown appears at a reception in the Arena to inaugurate an America Reads Program at Cal State, funded through a $200,000 grant from that organization.

31 Aug. 1997. Klaus R. Brasch, Act. Dean of the School of Natural Sciences, returns to the ranks as Prof. of Biology.

1 Sept. 1997. J. Paul Vicknair is named Act. Dean of the School of Natural Sciences, replacing Klaus R. Brasch. The campus reinstates women's cross-country running as an intercollegiate sport.

2 Sept. 1997. Cheryl F. Fischer is named Pres. of the National Council of Professors of Educational Administration.

6 Sept. 1997. The campus hosts a "Karate for Kids" tournament, with 1,000 local children competing in a Tae Kwon Do dojo.

9 Sept. 1997. President Karnig addresses the Inland Action Group to set forth several goals for the campus, including the establishment of an engineering program and expansion of distance learning.

12 Sept. 1997. The campus hosts its 11th Annual Children's Network Conference, "Developing Resilience in Youth," with Bonnie Benard giving the keynote address, "It's Up to Us: Tapping the Innate Resilience of All Our Youth."

19 Sept. 1997. At the annual convocation in the SUEC, Pres. Karnig outlines his vision for the campus, stating that "Universities that operate best operate flat—not steeped in hierarchy." He stresses the need for each department to develop goals and a system of accountability for trying to meet them. "Our ultimate goal is to build an environment we can all flourish in." "One of the challenges we face as a university is that so many of our potential students out there are never going to go to college unless we find a way to intervene." He also announces that the Chancellor's Office is providing $600,000 in seed money to use for new programs or one-time expenses to improve the campus. He states that the campus can decide to do things better than other schools, do things differently than others, do different things than others, or wander into the future with no clear direction. "Politeness is better than rude," he notes. Conducting the business of the university amicably and with integrity, responsiveness, genuine concern, and a spirit that celebrates accomplishments are the characteristics that should mark the university's reputation. We must also adopt policies that promote community on campus, with clear goals that emphasize the development of staff, students, and faculty. The decentralization of decisions "to levels accountable for outcomes" will help in that development.

23 SEPT. 1997. A Faculty Senate retreat discusses the CSU's new strategic plan, Cornerstones.

1 OCT. 1997. The campus receives a $120,000 grant from S.B. County to study the effectiveness of its Home Run program.

9 OCT. 1997. The late Prof. J. Patrick Watkins is honored at a memorial service held in the Theatre.

14 OCT. 1997. Colombian writer René Rebétez speaks in SUEC on "Today's Latin American Cultures."

16 OCT. 1997. Artist Diana Shui-lu Wong speaks about her work in SA. Richard Young speaks in PL-013 on "The Acquisition of Interactional Competence in Different Subject Specializations." Vernon Bellecourt speaks in SUEC.

24 OCT. 1997. Ex-S.B. Mayor Wilcox receives the annual Arrowhead Distinguished Chief Executive Officer Award at a banquet held in SUEC.

28 OCT. 1997. Lex Luger and World Championship Wrestling perform in the Arena.

28 OCT.-2 NOV. 1997. The campus hosts a conference, "Education on the Edge of Possibility," in Idyllwild.

30 OCT. 1997. Alumni cellist Michele Brosseau-Tacchia and pianist Michael Tacchia perform in RH. Barbara Nolte, Student Accounts Off. (1976-97), retires.

1 NOV. 1997. Franklin P. Williams III begins a pilot program to calculate the risk of releasing inmates from state prisons. Rock singer Sammy Hagar performs in the Arena.

6 NOV. 1997. Taiwanese L.A. Consul Francias Lee speaks in SUEC on "Taiwan's Trade with Hong Kong and China After 1997."

9 NOV. 1997. Elsa O. Valdez is elected to the S.B. School Board. Russian pianist Kirill Gliadkovsky performs in the 4th Annual Arthur Moorefield Memorial Recital in RH.

12 NOV. 1997. Evelyn Nakano Glenn speaks in SUEC on "Race as a Social Construction: Implications for Asian American Politics and Identity." Mexican poet Juan Felipe Herrera reads from his work in RH.

13-15 NOV. 1997. The campus co-hosts with the Univ. of Redlands the annual Assoc. of College Unions International Conference.

15 NOV. 1997. Arlo Dean Harris, Emer. Prof. of Chemistry (1967-88), dies of cancer at age 63.

18 NOV. 1997. Paleontologist Robert Gonzáles speaks in PL-4005A on "The Oral Memoirs of Redlands Workers and Families."

19 NOV. 1997. Artist Richard Beckman speaks on his work in SA.

24 NOV. 1997. The campus hosts the 2nd Annual Grandmother's Council of Native American Women in SUEC.

25 NOV. 1997. Richard M. Eberst is named VP and Pres. Elect of the American School Health Assoc.

5 DEC. 1997. Howard L. Roth, Lee Redmond, James Mance, Noel Keen, and Deborah Acker speak in SUEC at the 11th Annual Economic Forecast Breakfast, "Taking Advantage of the Economic Recovery."

10 DEC. 1997. The campus Transportation Committee reverses itself to oppose $67,000 in funding for a bronze statue of 3 coyotes.

12 DEC. 1997. Larry E. McFatter wins the 1st annual Michael Hennagin Prize in Composition, being honored with a $5,000 prize and a performance of his work, "Hymn of the Earth."

1998

1 JAN. 1998. The campus debuts a 9-1-1 emergency dialing system with the assistance of a $200,000 state grant. Leslie M. Kong takes office as Pres. of the Calif. Academic and Research Libraries.

14 JAN. 1998. Deborah Hayes speaks in the Faculty Office Conference Room on "Multi-Ethnic Studies in Public Schools: K-12."

16 JAN. 1998. Geographer Stephen Cunha speaks on "Environment, People, and Politics in Central Asia," and on "The Environmental History of the Sierra Nevada." Mike Kelly speaks in PS-224 on "Increasing the Range of Cell Phones."

20 JAN. 1998. Thomas W. Churchill, Physical Plant (1973-98), dies of a heart attack near the Arena at age 58.

21 JAN. 1998. Cynthia J. Bird is named Outstanding Professor for 1997/98.

24 JAN. 1998. George A. Meneses, ex-Asst. Dir. of the EOP Program and Asst. Dean of Students (1970-71), dies at age 61.

29 JAN. 1998. Artist Laurel Rhoads speaks about her work in SA.

2 FEB. 1998. The Administrative Council recommends that the Humanities Classroom Building be renamed Chaparral Hall.

4 FEB. 1998. Pres. Karnig circulates a plan for decentralizing the campus budget at the Budget Committee meeting.

11 FEB. 1998. Renée M. Pigeon receives the Golden Apple Award for Best Teacher of 1997/98.

13 FEB. 1998. State Sen. Tom Hayden speaks in UH-232.

18 FEB. 1998. Robin Scott Peters performs "African Tragedian" in SUEC. TV host Hugh Hewitt and Rabbi Daniel Lapin speak in RH in the 11th Annual Morrow-McCombs Lecture on "What Christians and Jews Should Know About Each Other...but Are Afraid to Ask."

26 FEB. 1998. The Lana Walton Theatre Ensemble performs the play, *The Truth of the Matter*, dealing with the life of Sojourner Truth, in SUEC. Chad C. Wright speaks on "Current Issues in Modern Spanish Literature."

28 FEB. 1998. Barry A. Munitz, Chancellor of the CSU System, resigns. Cheryl A. Smith, Assoc. VP for Enrollment Services (1971-98), resigns to accept a position at Humboldt State Univ.

1 MAR. 1998. Charles B. Reed is named Chancellor of the CSU System by the CSU Board of Trustees, replacing Barry A. Munitz.

2 MAR. 1998. Judith A. Valles takes office as S.B. Mayor, replacing Tom Minor.

4 MAR. 1998. Writer and educator Carol Gilligan speaks in the Gymnasium on "The Impact of Educational Institutions on Female Development:

Finding a Voice."

6 MAR. 1998. Louis Fox, Int. Dir. of the Robert V. Fullerton Museum, resigns.

9 MAR. 1998. Eva Kirsch is named Dir. of the Robert V. Fullerton Museum, replacing Louis Fox.

17 MAR. 1998. Diane F. Halpern receives the 1998 Distinguished Teaching in Psychology Award from the American Psychological Foundation.

27 MAR. 1998. The campus hosts its 5th Annual Education Expo for Alternative Programs for Youths at Risk, with Ron Johnson giving the keynote address.

2 APR. 1998. Representatives of the Public Broadcasting Service speak at the 5th Library Associates Lecture in the Pfau Library on "Am I a Crook? Copyright Issues on the Internet."

5 APR. 1998. The campus wins its 2nd straight "Outstanding Delegation" Award at the Model United Nations Competition held in New York City, with CSUSB representing Malaysia.

7 APR. 1998. Writer Rudolfo Anaya speaks and signs his books in SUEC.

8 APR. 1998. S.B. Mayor Valles speaks in SUEC to a Business Partners Executing Briefing.

13 APR. 1998. Diane F. Halpern is elected Pres. of the Western Psychology Assoc.

15 APR. 1998. Writer Robin Ryan speaks as part of the Career Opportunities Fair on "24 Hours to Your Next Job, Raise, or Promotion" in UC, and on "Job Search: The Hidden Job Market"; Chris Ahearn speaks on "Résumés for Results," and Mary B. Nemnich on "Using the Internet and the World Wide Web in Your Job Search."

16 APR. 1998. Philip Q. Yang speaks in SU Multicultural Center on "Deconstructing the 'Model Minority' Myth."

21 APR. 1998. Sterling Stuckey speaks in SUEC on "Paul Robeson."

23 APR. 1998. The campus dedicates a "Stop the Violence" memorial bench for Anthony Martínez and Wardell Epps in front of University Hall, with Assemblyman Joe Baca and Shirley Goins present.

25 APR. 1998. S.B. Mayor Valles speaks in UC to the Assoc. of Latino Faculty, Staff, and Students. Magician Paul Cash, musician Mark Lynn, and group Toxic Jazz perform at the 12th Annual Environmental Expo in the Arena.

26 APR. 1998. Dr. W. Benson Harer speaks at the 6th Library Associates Lecture in the Fullerton Museum on "A Collector's Comments on Egyptian Antiquities at CSUSB."

29 APR. 1998. The campus holds a reception in PL-4005 for ex-Pres. Pfau and wife Antreen Pfau. Charles Solomon speaks on "The History of the Heroine: Women in Animation."

30 APR. 1998. Albert K. Karnig is installed as the campus's 3rd President in the Arena, with CSU Trustee Ralph R. Pesqueira presiding over the event, "Celebrating Our Past, Creating our Future," and CSU Chancellor Reed presenting the new executive with a bronze medallion designed by Cal State student David Ashby. Also attending are ex-CSUSB Presidents Pfau and Evans; CSU Trustees William D. Campbell, Laurence K. Gould Jr., James H. Gray, Ali C. Razi, and Michael J. Stennis; S.B. Trial Courts Presiding Judge John W. Kennedy; S.B. Superior Court Judge Patrick J. Morris, speaks at a campus-wide forum on developing university-community partnerships; and Alumni Assoc. Pres. Chris Ahearn. Prof. Larry E. McFatter composes the original musical accompaniment, *Fanfare*. Pres. Karnig presents the 1st President's Distinguished Achievement Awards to Yolanda T. Moses, ex-Assemblyman Paul A. Woodruff, and Ernesto Z. Robles. Jill Baldauf speaks in JB-283 on "The Socioeconomic Role of Advertising."

1 MAY 1998. Kim Miyoshi speaks in SUEC on "The Global Sweatshop."

3 MAY 1998. Actress Ann Jillian speaks at the Immaculate Mary '98 Conference in the Arena.

6 MAY 1998. Filmmaker Saul Landau speaks in UH-106 at the screening of his movie, *The Sixth Sun: Mayan Uprising in Chiapas*. Gary B. Nash speaks in SR on "History, Patriotism, and the Culture Wars of the 1990s."

7 MAY 1998. Olympic medalist Bonnie St. John Deane speaks in SUEC on "Pushing Through the Obstacles: The Art of Self-Motivation."

8 MAY 1998. The campus hosts the conference, "Child Care: Planning for Success," in SUEC.

12 MAY 1998. Writer William Glasser speaks in SUEC on "Choice Theory: A New Psychology of Personal Freedom."

14-17 MAY 1998. Sesame Street Live performs "Elmo's Coloring Book" in the Arena.

15 MAY 1998. The campus distributes recycling bins and trashcans.

29 MAY 1998. The Baseline Access, Training, and Support Initiative (BATS) receives most of the available one-time campus funds to provide computer support for the faculty.

29-30 MAY 1998. The campus hosts its 3rd Annual Diversity and Multicultural Conference, "Hearts and Minds: Excellence Through Diversity," in SUEC, with Thomas A. Parham (keynote speaker) and Samuel Betances participating.

30 MAY 1998. Robert González speaks at the 3rd Annual Harry Rheubottom/George Webster Historical Lecture in the Pfau Library on "Visions and Versions: Mexican Community in the East San Bernardino Valley."

31 MAY 1998. Janice L. "Jan" Lemmond, Support Services Officer (1978-98), retires.

1 JUN. 1998. Kathryn K. "Kathy" Shepard, Manager of Purchasing, is named Dir. of Procurement and Support Services, replacing Janice L. Lemmond.

3 JUN. 1998. *The Yeti*, the campus's first student-created feature film, premieres in JB-102, directed and co-written by biology student Ezequiel Martínez, and shot in the S.B. Mountains.

4 JUN. 1998. Pres. Karnig speaks to 100 community leaders in the Coachella Valley at the Marriott Desert Springs Resort on the progress of CSUSB's plans to build a permanent satellite campus at Palm Desert, with CSU Trustee Jim Gray attending.

11 JUN. 1998. Aurora Wolfgang receives a National Endowment of the Humanities Fellowship to study in France in 1998/99.

13-14 JUN. 1998. The 32nd Commencement is held in the Arena and at CVC, with keynote speakers William Kroonen (CVC), Pres. Karnig (Natural Sciences), Ruby L. Beale (Social and Behavioral Sciences), Jon Slater (Business and Public Administration), and Rep. George E. Brown (Education.

SUM. 1998. Retirements: Katharine M. Busch, Assoc. Prof. of Education (1984-98).

1 JUL. 1998. Patsy W. Oppenheim is named Asst. VP for Student Development, replacing Randy P. Harrell (who left Fall 1997).

5 JUL. 1998. 4 CSUSB students working under Stuart Sumida begin 6 weeks' work in Chicago to help restore the fossilized skeleton of "Sue," the largest *Tyrannosaurus rex* ever discovered.

10 JUL. 1998. Cal State graduate Francisco Ríos receives a $60,000 Ford Foundation Fellowship to work on a Ph.D. at UC Berkeley.

15 JUL. 1998. The campus resumes a shortened Summer Entertainment Series, with The Latin Society performing on LCP.

22 JUL. 1998. Rodents short out a 12,000-volt electric switch, causing a power outage that closes the campus for the day, and reschedules a concert by Andy Cleaves and the Summertime Big Band.

25 JUL. 1998. Nobel Prize-winning writer Toni Morrison reads from her work in SUEC. Also present is S.B. Mayor Valles.

27 JUL. 1998. During a power crisis, Southern California Edison Co. orders the campus to reduce electrical usage by 75%.

29 JUL. 1998. The country band Appaloosa performs on LCP.

1 AUG. 1998. C. Donald Kajcienski is named Assoc. VP for Enrollment Services and Dir. of Outreach Services.

4 AUG. 1998. The Pfau Library completes its seismic retrofitting project, and Technical Services, Collection Development, and Media Services move back into the redesigned basement.

5 AUG. 1998. Andy Cleaves and the Summertime Big Band perform on LCP.

14 AUG. 1998. Lee I. Porter, Dean of Extended Education (1981-98), retires.

15 AUG. 1998. Janice Ropp "Jan" Jackson, Assoc. Dean of Extended Education (1991-98), is named Dean of Extended Education, replacing Lee I. Porter.

19 AUG. 1998. Bryan Lee Pettit, Lect. of Information and Decision Sciences (1988-98), dies of a heart attack at Primm, NV, at age 52.

31 AUG. 1998. Charles W. Martin, Dean of Undergraduate Studies, returns to the ranks. Steven M. Mintz, Dean of the School of Business and Public Administration, returns to the ranks as Prof. of Accounting and Finance. Judith M. Rymer, VP for Univ. Relations, returns to the ranks as Prof. of Education.

1 SEPT. 1998. Eldon C. Lewis is again named Int. Dean of the School of Business and Public Administration, replacing Steven M. Mintz. Tom M. Rivera is named Int. Dean of Undergraduate Studies, replacing Charles W. Martin. Susan E. Summers is named Assoc. Dean of Extended Education, replacing Janice Ropp Jackson. The campus adds women's water polo as an intercollegiate sport, and drops men's volleyball. University Relations is renamed University Advancement.

11 SEPT. 1998. The campus hosts its 12th Annual Children's Network Conference, "Within Our Reach: Breaking the Cycle of the Disadvantaged," with Lisbeth B. Schorr giving the keynote address.

17 SEPT. 1998. At the annual convocation, Pres. Karnig announces that Louis A. Fernández, VP for Academic Affairs, is being named Provost. He states that becoming one of the nation's leading comprehensive universities and building community-based partnerships will be among the campus's highest goals. "It should be a living plan with improvements regularly made"—he then announces that 120 campus leaders will meet on Sept. 18 to produce concrete ideas that will give these goals wheels. Although the recent WASC review of the campus was positive, the agency recommended that the university place more emphasis on long-term planning and the decision-making that accompanies it, make student grievance procedures clearer, improve policy distribution, and create new ways to promote diversity. The Pres. notes that he has eliminated budget line items and position controls, and has allowed the rolling over of monies from one year to the next, giving the local departments much more flexibility. Still, he expects "links between the university plan and the budget." Faculty involvement to research and understand how students learn or to development community partnerships will be given high consideration in future hiring of tenure-track professors. With the crisis in student performance and a looming shortage of teachers, he says that CSUSB will focus more on teacher preparation. If legal, he would to form a "Staff Assembly" for employee feedback and participation. Some offices on campus will have their hours extended to better serve students. The quarter versus semester question deserves another look. Once the Pres. hires an Executive Asst., that individual might be involved in the administration of the Athletics Program and Governmental Relations area.

18 SEPT. 1998. The campus funds 5 University-community partnerships with $25,000 in seed money.

2 OCT. 1998. J. Milton Clark is named Int. Dean of Undergraduate Studies, replacing Charles W. Martin.

2 OCT. 1998. Klaus R. Brasch is named Exec. Dir. of Research Development and Technology Transfer.

9 OCT. 1998. Groundbreaking is held for the Corporation Yard, encompassing 50,000 square feet of renovated and expanded facilities, including a Duplicating Center, receiving, mail distribution center, Public Safety, and Maintenance Shops.

13 OCT. 1998. Billie P. Sessions receives the 1998 Outstanding Higher Education Art Educator Award from the Calif. Art Education Assoc.

15 OCT. 1998. Joseph Kovac Thomas, Emer. Prof. of Education and Exec. Dean and VP for Administration (1965-82), dies of pneumonia in Redlands at age 82.

20 OCT. 1998. A brush fire in Waterman Canyon burns 420 acres, and is not contained until Oct. 25.

21 OCT. 1998. Karen Savage speaks in PiR on "Remote Sensing Study of the San Andreas Fault in the San Bernardino Area and Associated Geologic Hazards."

22 OCT. 1998. Rev. Jesse Jackson speaks in LC on "Dignity Day."

23-24 OCT. 1998. Matthew Fox provides the keynote address at a celebration of the birth of composer Hildegard of Bingen. Anonymous 4 performs on campus.

29 OCT. 1998. Ceramics artist David Furman speaks about his work in SA.

30 OCT. 1998. Larry R. Sharp receives the Arrowhead Distinguished Chief Executive Officer Award at a banquet held in SUEC.

2 NOV. 1998. The campus renames the major academic divisions as "Colleges," and changes the School of Humanities to the Coll. of Arts and Letters, and the Extended Education Div. to the Coll. of Extended Learning, with the Deans' titles altering accordingly.

3 NOV. 1998. The campus hosts the national volleyball teams of Brazil and the U.S. (which wins 3-2) in the Arena.

5-6 NOV. 1998. While visiting the campus, CSU Chancellor Reed is picketed by faculty protesting "unfair employment contracts"; on Nov. 5 Reed is fêted at a dinner in YC honoring alumni, politicians, and donors, including Rep. George E. Brown.

8 Nov. 1998. The U.S. Army Field Band and Soldiers' Chorus performs in the Arena.

11 Nov. 1998. Adria F. Klein receives the 1998 Marcus Foster Memorial Reading Award.

17 Nov. 1998. B. H. Fairchild, whose *The Art of the Lathe* is one of 5 nominees for the National Book Award, participates in the "finalist's reading" in New York City.

24 Nov. 1998. A student is raped in the Creative Arts Building; a suspect is detained by students and arrested by campus police, but hangs himself in the county jail on Nov. 28. Ashante King and Edmund Sarpong speak in SUEC as part of African Culture Night.

3 Dec. 1998. The campus receives a $1,010,000 grant from NSF to create a Research Career Integration Program to help disadvantaged youth pursue computer careers.

4 Dec. 1998. The campus hosts its 12th Annual Economic Forecast Breakfast in SUEC, with Fred Latuperissa, State Sen. Jim Brulte, and John E. Husing speaking.

5 Dec. 1998. The campus hosts its Annual Gospel Christmas Concert, with St. Paul AME Church Revelations, Genesis Choirs, and Voices of Praise performing in SUEC.

9 Dec. 1998. The campus closes due to high Santa Ana winds, which cause $25,000 in damage and injure eight students.

11 Dec. 1998. J(oy) Cordell Robinson, Prof. of History and Assoc. VP for Academic Personnel (1971-98), is killed in an automobile accident on Baseline Rd. in Highland at age 58.

31 Dec. 1998. Eloise R. Hamilton, Library Asst. (1983-98), retires.

1999

4 Jan. 1999. Gray Davis takes office as Governor of California, replacing Pete Wilson.

12 Jan. 1999. Lance Duke, CEO of Landmark Building Products, receives the 1st Entrepreneur of the Year at the Entrepreneurial Success Conference in SUEC.

24 Jan. 1999. TV cameraman Luis Fuerte speaks at the 7th Library Associates Lecture in VA-101 on *"California's Gold* from Behind the Camera."

27 Jan. 1999. The CSU Board of Trustees approves a 10-year master plan for CSUSB, increasing the campus's enrollment base to 20,000 full-time equivalent students (27,000 bodies), and adding $245 million in 30 new building projects, including 10 academic buildings (an engineering building, a Univ. Distance Learning Center, an expanded theatre arts complex, 2 education buildings, and additions to the biology complex, Brown Hall, and the Pfau Library), an enlarged indoor arena, a running track with a 10,000-seat grandstand, a baseball diamond with 2,000 seats, an alumni center, the development of 15 acres for student housing and 5 acres for an experimental school, and 4,000 new parking spaces. In 2010 many of these goals have yet to be realized due to lack of funding.

29 Jan. 1999. CSUSB becomes the 32nd college named an Endorsed Internal Auditing Program by The Institute of Internal Auditors.

31 Jan. 1999. The Fullerton Museum reopens after a seismic retrofit with an exhibit of Egyptian antiquities from the collection of W. Benson Harer and Pamela Harer.

1 Feb. 1999. Cal State alumna Wilmer D. "Amina" Carter is named Coordinator of Governmental Relations in the President's Office.

2 Feb. 1999. Richard Santana speaks in the Cross Cultural Center on "A 'Gangbanger' Turned Educator."

3 Feb. 1999. Pres. Karnig speaks at an Executive Briefing Breakfast in SUEC about business and community partnerships.

6 Feb. 1999. The campus receives a $500,000 gift from the R. D. and Joan Dale Hubbard Foundation to help construct the first building at the permanent site for CVC, at the corner of Frank Sinatra Dr. and Cook St. in Palm Desert, Calif. Tim and Edra Blixseth host "Calypso Night" at their home in Rancho Mirage to raise funds supporting CVC development.

9 Feb. 1999. Susan M. Cooper, Dir. of Academic Computing and Media, is named Int. Dir. of Distributed Learning; Michael L. Ross, Assoc. Dir. of Academic Computing and Media, is named Int. Dir. of ACM.

11 Feb. 1999. Joan Harter speaks in SUEC on "Skeletons in the Closet: The Effects of Addiction on the Family."

12 FEB. 1999. The campus receives approval to offer a new concentration in Environmental Management for the B.A. degree in Business Administration, effective Fall 1999. Four students file a complaint with the U.S. Office of Civil Rights alleging discrimination.

16 FEB. 1999. John K. Papadopoulos, Assoc. Curator of Antiquities for the J. Paul Getty Museum, speaks in SUEC on "Virtual Reality and Classical Archaeology: The Forum of Trojan in Rome Revisited." Stuart Sumida is named Outstanding Professor for 1998/99.

17 FEB. 1999. Lana Walton and the Lana Walton Theatre Ensemble perform *The Truth of the Matter* in SUEC. Egyptian Consul Hagar Islambouly speaks in SR on "Facing Contemporary Challenges in the Middle East."

18 FEB. 1999. O. Ricardo Pimentel, Editor of the *San Bernardino County Sun*, and Orlando Ramírez, Food Editor of the *Riverside Press-Enterprise*, speak on "Artists as Editors" at the 8th Library Associates Lecture in SUEC. Psychologist Sidney J. Parnes speaks in LC on "Enhancing Innovative Thinking: Using Creative Problem Solving."

19 FEB. 1999. The campus holds a memorial honoring J. Cordell Robinson, late Assoc. VP for Academic Personnel, in SUEC. The Gymnasium fountain is refurbished and restored. Author Randall Robinson speaks in SUEC. Ex-instructor Gerald Joseph McCall is convicted of the 2nd-degree murder of a prostitute. Steven Pravdo speaks in PS-10 on "The Near-Earth Asteroid Tracking System."

23 FEB. 1999. Willard Daggett, Pres. of the International Center for Leadership in Education, speaks in the UC on "Skills Needed in a Technological, Information-Based Twenty-First Century, and What Young People Are Learning."

24 FEB. 1999. Violinist Todor Pelev and guitarist Terry Graves perform in RH. Rabbi David Saperstein speaks in YC at the 12th Annual Morrow-McCombs Memorial Lecture on "Walk the Talk: Applying Jewish Values to Contemporary Life." David M. L. Riefer receives his record 3rd Golden Apple Award for Best Teacher of 1998/99.

2 MAR. 1999. Benjamin Gómez Ramírez, Adjunct Prof. of Spanish, dies in Riverside of pneumonia at age 65.

3 MAR. 1999. The Harlem Globetrotters perform in the Arena.

4 MAR. 1999. Susan M. Cooper, Int. Dir. of Distributed Learning, is named the first permanent Director.

4-6 MAR. 1999. The Coyotes men's basketball team wins the NCAA Division II Western Regional Tournament.

5 MAR. 1999. Dr. W. Benson Harer speaks in the Fullerton Art Museum on his collection of Egyptian antiquities. B. H. "Pete" Fairchild receives the $50,000 Kingsley Tufts Poetry Award for his book, *The Art of the Lathe*, in addition to the William Carlos Williams Award from the Poetry Soc. of America.

12 MAR. 1999. María Contreras-Sweet, State Secretary of Business, Transportation, and Housing, provides the keynote speech at the 7th Annual Women's Conference, "Charting the Path Towards Millennium Empowerment," in UC, hosted by State Sen. Joe Baca. An accountant in the Student Aid Office is arresting for pandering, and then fired on Mar. 19; he pleads guilty to solicitation on Jul. 1.

18 MAR. 1999. The men's basketball team loses to Florida Southern 84-69 in the first round of the NCAA Division II Elite Eight Championship Tournament in Louisville, Kentucky, the furthest that the team has ever advanced in postseason play. Billy Goodson teaches a master dance class in HP-104.

20 MAR. 1999. Sugar Ray and Everlast perform in the Arena. Donna J. Boyd is named Asst. Dean of Marketing.

26 MAR. 1999. Stanley L. Swartz is named 1999 Distinguished Teacher Educator by the Assoc. of Teacher Educators.

28 MAR. 1999. Susan E. Meisenhelder is elected President of the Calif. Faculty Assoc.

31 MAR. 1994. James E. Daniels, Dir. of Academic Programs and Services at CVC, resigns to take a post at CSU Bakersfield.

14 APR. 1999. For the 3rd year in a row, the Cal State team, directed by Ralph Salmi, receives an "Outstanding Delegation" Award at the Model United Nations competition, while representing Egypt.

17 APR. 1999. The campus hosts a conference, "Reading to Unlock the Mysteries of History: Practical Classroom Strategies for Teaching Content—Area Reading," in UC. Sant Khalsa receives a $9,900 grant from the National Endowment for the Arts to photograph California's waterways.

20 APR. 1999. CSU Trustee Harold Goldwhite visits the campus.

22 APR. 1999. Diane F. Halpern wins a $20,000 Wang Family Excellence Award, the first CSUSB faculty member to do so. Writer Susan Straight reads from her work in PiR. The campus voids the student elections of Apr. 12-13 after discovering fraudulent voting, and schedules a new vote for Apr. 28-29. The murder conviction of ex-instructor Gerald Joseph McCall is voided, and he is granted a new trial.

24 APR. 1999. The campus hosts the 13th Annual Environmental Expo in the Arena, with musician and storyteller Mark Lynn and magician Paul Cash performing. Miguel A. Bretos speaks in UC at the annual Assoc. of Latino Faculty, Staff, and Students Scholarship Banquet and Dance.

30 APR. 1999. The campus hosts the conference, "Hearts and Minds: Connecting Through Diversity," in SUEC, with Bernita C. Berry giving the keynote address. The campus hosts a conference in UC, "Small Business Briefing with NASA," sponsored by Rep. George E. Brown, with a keynote address by NASA administrator Daniel Goldin.

1 MAY 1999. Sandra D. Kamusikiri speaks and performs at the 4th Annual Harry Rheubottom/George Webster Historical Lecture in the Pfau Library as "Biddy Mason: African-American Pioneer in Old San Bernardino."

5 MAY 1999. Writer Helena María Viramontes speaks at the SUEC.

7 MAY 1999. Cal State student Kwame Conkor wins a $25,000 scholarship with Merck Research Laboratories.

8 MAY 1999. Writer and psychologist Mary Pipher signs her books and speaks in the Coyote Den in the Gymnasium on "Media and Culture and Their Effects on Mental Health and the Family."

9 MAY 1999. REO Speedwagon performs in the Arena.

12 MAY 1999. Museum curator Kathleen B. Springer speaks at the 9th Library Associates Lecture in the Pfau Library on "Valley of the Mastodons."

13 MAY 1999. Ex-Chicago Bulls basketball player Bob Love speaks in SUEC on "The Winning Spirit." B. H. "Pete" Fairchild receives a Guggenheim Fellowship to study in Paris, France. The campus receives a $90,000 matching grant from the Ewing Kauffman Center for Entrepreneurial Leadership and Arrowhead Credit Union to sponsor internships in entrepreneurial leadership, leading to the creation of The Inland Empire Center for Entrepreneurship.

15 MAY 1999. The ska swing band Save Ferris performs on the SU Mall. Dance Hall Crushers and Freakdaddy perform in the Arena.

17 MAY 1999. Clifford O. Young Sr. is named the Asst. to the President.

18 MAY 1999. Sandra D. Kamusikiri again performs as "Biddy Mason" in PR.

22 MAY 1999. The campus hosts a retirement dinner in UC for Prof. Mildred M. Henry.

24 MAY 1999. The campus hosts a symposium on "Hate Crimes/Hate Speech: What Do We Do About It?" Rep. George E. Brown announces that the campus has received a $2.65 million, 5-year grant to fund its Upward Bound Program.

1 JUN. 1999. Jo Ann Hankin is named VP for Univ. Advancement, replacing Judith M. Rymer. Saudi Arabian Minister of Higher Education Khalid al-Ankary visits CSUSB, and the campus signs a memorandum of cooperation with Saudi Arabia to establish a faculty and student exchange program. The campus creates the Water Resources Institute with a $200,000 grant from the State, $550,000 from the U.S., $25,000 from the S.B. Municipal Water Dist., and $25,000 from the Inland Empire Utilities Agency; the facility is housed on the southeast corner of the 4th floor of the Pfau Library.

3 JUN. 1999. Psychologist Robert Karen speaks in SUEC on "Becoming Attached: Raising Children Who Feel That the World Is a Positive Place and That They Have Value." Artist Sally Elesby speaks about her work in the Fullerton Art Museum.

4 JUN. 1999. Richard Eichenbaum, General Manager of Ontario Mills Mall, is named Marketer of the Year at a banquet in UC by the campus chapter of the American Marketing Assoc.

10 JUN. 1999. Lucy Jones of the U.S. Geological Survey speaks in SUEC on "A Practical Approach to Predicting Earthquakes."

14 JUN. 1999. Cynthia Flores is named Assoc. Dean of CVC, replacing James E. Daniels.

15 JUN. 1999. Rep. George E. Brown announces that the campus has received an $830,000 grant from the U.S. Dept. of Education to fund Ronald E. McNair Postbaccalaureate Achievement grants.

18-20 JUN. 1999. The 33rd Commencement is held in the Arena and at

CVC, with Reps. C. Jerry Lewis and Maxine Waters, S.B. Mayor Valles, Martha Pinckney, Dick Heckman, and Stuart Sumida giving the keynote addresses.

22 JUN. 1999. The campus receives a $50,000 grant from GTE Foundation to facilitate a technology partnership with the Moreno Valley Unified School Dist.

25 JUN. 1999. Treadwell "Ted" Ruml receives a summer grant from the National Endowment for the Humanities to study at Yale Univ.

26 JUN. 1999. Mignon M. Schweitzer, a campus booster for whom Schweitzer Auditorium in the Visual Arts Center was named, dies a day before her 99th birthday.

30 JUN. 1999. Eldon C. Lewis, Int. Dean of the College of Business and Public Administration, returns to the ranks as Prof. of Accounting and Finance.

SUM. 1999. Retirements: Renate M. Nummela Caine, Prof. of Education (1978-99); Brij B. Khare, Prof. of Political Science (1968-99); Mildred M. Henry, Prof. of Education (1983-99); Arthur J. Townley, Prof. of Education (1990-99); William D. Warehall, Prof. of Art (1973-99).

1 JUL. 1999. Gordon L. Patzer is named Dean of the College of Business and Public Administration, replacing Eldon C. Lewis. Patricia M. Tefft Cousin, ex-Assoc. Prof. of Education (1987-96), dies of cancer at Nashville, Tennessee at age 48. The University Police Building in the new Corporate Yard is occupied by Facilities Management.

2 JUL. 1999. Frances L. "Fran" Stromwall, retired Library Asst. (1968-85), dies at age 76.

7 JUL. 1999. The Latin Society performs on LCP.

12 JUL. 1999. The Dept. of Athletics is moved for reporting purposes from the Dean of Natural Sciences to the VP for Univ. Advancement.

14 JUL. 1999. John York, formerly of The Byrds, performs '60s music on LCP.

15 JUL. 1999. Rep. George Edward Brown Jr., a strong booster of CSUSB, dies after heart surgery at Bethesda, Maryland, at age 79. The campus hosts a conference, "Home-Based Business Owners in the Inland Empire," in Jack Brown Hall.

21 JUL. 1999. Bluegrass group Squeakin' Wheels performs on LCP.

28 JUL. 1999. Jane Wachs Matthews, who donated a collection of African artifacts to the campus in 1992, dies at Williamsburg, Virginia. The surf rock group The Tornadoes performs on LCP.

4 AUG. 1999. John M. Tibbals, Libn. and Head of Public Services (1968-99), retires.

10 AUG. 1999. The campus receives a $5 million grant from the Federal Emergency Management Agency to test new technology in seismically retrofitting a building.

20 AUG. 1999. J. Paul Vicknair, Act. Dean of the School of Natural Sciences, is named Assoc. Provost of Academic Personnel, replacing the late J. Cordell Robinson. John H. Craig is named Int. Dean of Natural Sciences, replacing J. Paul Vicknair. The campus receives a $2 million Title V grant from the U.S. Dept. of Education to provide educational opportunities for Hispanic students, and the University is named a "Hispanic-Serving Institution."

31 AUG. 1999. Julius D. Kaplan, Dean of Graduate Studies, returns to the ranks as Prof. of Art.

1 SEPT. 1999. Sandra D. Kamusikiri is named Int. Assoc. VP for Assessment and Planning and Dean of Graduate Studies, replacing Julius D. Kaplan. William L. Slout wins the Antony Hippisley Coxe Award for the Year's Best Circus Book for *Olympians of the Sawdust Circle*. The campus begins offering a new B.A. in Criminal Justice degree at CVC.

10 SEPT. 1999. The campus hosts its 13th Annual Children's Conference, "The Future of Children in the 21st Century," with psychologist Peter Alsop giving the keynote address.

16 SEPT. 1999. At the annual convocation, Pres. Karnig says that the campus is well on its way to becoming a premier college for the Inland Empire, with a new master plan that includes 30 building projects totaling $245 million in costs through 2009, and a projected student enrollment of 25,000 students by 2004 (none of these goals are actually achieved, however, due to lack of state funding). "We should be ecstatic about the growth," states Karnig, "But the increases will stretch us as they normally do. I hope in your hearts you really understand that this is a university in contrast to others. I take enormous pride in who we are and who we're becoming."

18 SEPT. 1999. Taft Talmadge Newman Jr., alumnus, Counselor, and Dir.

of the EOP (1978-99), dies of cancer in Fontana at age 56. The Robert V. Fullerton Museum opens an exhibit of the ceramic works of Pablo Picasso (through Nov. 7).

19 SEPT. 1999. Nadine Chávez is named Int. Dir. of the EOP, replacing the late Taft T. Newman.

24-26 SEPT. 1999. The Cross Cultural Center hosts its 1st Native American Day and Calif. Indian Cultural Awareness Conference in SUEC, with 3,000 participants, including S.B. Mayor Valles, State Sen. Joe Baca, S.B. Superintendent of Schools Herb Fischer, and Riverside Co. Schools Superintendent David Long.

1 OCT. 1999. The campus hosts a lunch in UC for Charles D. and Shelby Obershaw, who donate $362,500 for campus scholarships. The campus receives a $165,000 gift from the Alumni Assoc. to support scholarships. The campus receives a $140,000 grant from Toyota USA Foundation to expand the Mathematics Institute.

7 OCT. 1999. *The Coyote Chronicle* increases its size by an inch.

10 OCT. 1999. Pianist Danae Linette Tetreau performs in RH.

13 OCT. 1999. Peter Schrag speaks in PR on "California at the Millennium," the first speaker in the WRI Lecture Series, sponsored by the Water Resources Institute.

14 OCT. 1999. The City Council of Palm Desert votes to transfer 40 acres of land for a permanent satellite campus site to CSUSB.

15 OCT. 1999. Writer and historian Howard Zinn speaks in RH on "Student Activism for Our Times." Dennis L. Ikenberry, Prof. of Computer Science (1965-99), retires.

16 OCT. 1999. The Hector Mine Earthquake knocks thousands of volumes off the shelves of the Pfau Library.

18 OCT. 1999. The campus receives a $644,705 grant from the CSU to help reduce the number of high school students requiring remedial education in mathematics and English. A 7.1 earthquake in Joshua Tree rattles the campus.

21 OCT. 1999. The campus announces a new M.S. degree in Nursing, partially funded by the U.S. Dept. of Health, Education, and Welfare, beginning with Winter 2000.

24 OCT. 1999. Vandals spray graffiti on campus buildings and the main entrance sign.

26 OCT. 1999. Athletes from World Championship Wrestling Live perform in the Arena. The campus signs an agreement with Theatrical Arts International to allow CSUSB Theatre Dept. productions to be presented at the California Theater on 4th St. in S.B.

28 OCT. 1999. Artist Fritz Dreisbach speaks about his work in SA. The campus hosts a forum, "Enterprise Vision…San Bernardino: The Private Sector Looks at the City," with S.B. Mayor Valles and economist Walter Williams.

2 NOV. 1999. Actor Henry Holden speaks in SUEC on "How the Media Represents People with Disabilities."

4 NOV. 1999. Frances F. Berdan receives a $122,000 grant from the National Endowment for the Humanities to design a CD-ROM to simulate field trips for anthropology majors.

5 NOV. 1999. CSU Chancellor Reed speaks at a lunch held at the Desert Falls Country Club, Palm Desert, on the creation of a satellite CSUSB campus at Palm Desert.

7 NOV. 1999. Pianists Frina Arschanska and Kenwyn Boldt perform in RH at the 6th Annual Arthur Moorefield Memorial Recital.

17 NOV. 1999. Writer Jervey Tervalon reads from his work in PiR.

19 NOV. 1999. William E. Leonard receives the Arrowhead Distinguished Chief Executive Officer Award at a banquet held in SUEC; attendees include his son, Assemblyman William R. Leonard, Assemblyman John Longville, Martin A. Matich, W. Benson Harer, Pamela Harer, S.B. Mayor Valles, ex-S.B. Mayor Holcomb, and ex-Dean of Education Ernest F. García.

22 NOV. 1999. Ex-Rep. Robert Edgar speaks in SUEC on "John F. Kennedy's Assassination."

1 DEC. 1999. Arthur M. Butler, Exec. Dir. of the Foundation (1987-99), is named Dir. of Risk Management. David Jones is named Int. Dir. of the Foundation, replacing Arthur M. Butler. Ghanaian Pastor Kodjoe Sumney speaks in SUEC.

3 DEC. 1999. The campus hosts its 13th Annual Economic Forecast Breakfast, "The Inland Empire's Real Y2K Problem: Upgrading the Labor Pool for the 21st Century Economy," in SUEC, with speakers Sen. Dianne Feinstein, Economic Development Corp. economist Jack Kyser, economist John E. Husing, and Dir. of Calif. Senate Relations and Labor Issues Bill A. Lloyd. High Santa Ana winds hit the campus with gusts of 90 M.P.H.

5 DEC. 1999. Melvin E. Artrup, ex-Supervising Custodian, dies in Olympia, Washington at age 80.

10 DEC. 1999. The campus receives a $1 million gift from Florence Rigdon, and a $4.5 million gift from the H. N. and Frances C. Berger Foundation, to help build the first permanent building at CVC, thereby completing the $9 million needed. This is the first campus structure to be constructed solely from donated funds (the Fullerton Museum, although built with donations, was an addition to the state-funded Visual Arts Center). The campus hosts a banquet at the Desert Springs Marriott Hotel to announce construction plans for the new satellite campus, with the attendance of Florence Rigdon, Palm Desert City Mayor Buford Crites, ex-Palm Desert City Mayor Robert Spiegel, campaign chair Richard R. Oliphant, Berger Foundation Pres. Ron Auen, and CSU Chancellor Reed.

12 DEC. 1999. The pop groups Suicidal Tendencies, Save Ferris, Ben Harper, and Lit and the Kottonmouth Kings perform in the Arena as part of radio station KCXX's X-Mas Fest 5.

13 DEC. 1999. Ex-golf coaches Bob Smith and Robert Flint win a $1.2 million judgment against CSUSB for age discrimination, but the amount is reduced to $120,000 by a judge on Feb. 4.

31 DEC. 1999. Retirements: Edward L. Brock, Campus Police Officer (1979-99); Dolores V. Tanno, Prof. of Communication Studies (1989-99).

2000

2 JAN. 2000. Elizabeth J. Barfield, Prof. of Nursing (1994-00), retires.

3 JAN. 2000. Pola Negri Patterson, Libn. and Head of Collection Development (1979-00), dies of bone cancer at age 64, 2 days after retiring. The campus is named a top Hispanic-serving institution by *Hispanic Outlook in Education*.

7 JAN. 2000. Helen P. Chinn, Asst. Libn. (1989-92, 1994-00), retires.

8 JAN. 2000. Marie E. Astor, acclaimed concert pianist and music instructor, dies at Loma Linda at age 68.

9-10 JAN. 2000. The Coll. of Education is among 50 colleges invited to participate in a National Conference on Teacher Quality held in Washington, DC.

13 JAN. 2000. Margaret Morgan speaks in the Fullerton Art Museum about her work.

22 JAN. 2000. Women's softball coach Roxanne Berch is suspended for four games for violating NCAA rules.

26 JAN. 2000. Jewish Defense League Dir. Irv Rubin speaks in SUEC.

28 JAN. 2000. Jo Ann Hankin wins the 1999 Terry McAdam Book Award of the Alliance for Nonprofit Managers for *Financial Management for Nonprofit Organizations*. Tenor Glenn Alpert and pianist Michael Tacchia perform in RH.

29 JAN. 2000. Comedian Alex Valdez performs in SUEC. The campus hosts its 2nd Annual Assistive Technology Expo.

31 JAN. 2000. The State institutes a requirement that faculty members who choose not to join the Calif. Faculty Assoc., the official bargaining agency for the Cal State faculty, must still pay a union fee amounting to 75-90% of membership dues. Dean John A. Conley and Prof. Ralph H. Salmi embark upon a week's journey to Saudi Arabia to meet with Ministry of Higher Education officials to discuss possible international exchanges between faculty and students. The Student Health Center receives a $6,000 grant to provide mammograms to low-income students.

1 FEB. 2000. Soltek Pacific receives a contract to construct the Social and Behavioral Sciences Building.

2 FEB. 2000. Violist Roslyn Young, cellist Michele Brosseau-Tacchia, and pianist Michael Tacchia perform in RH.

3 FEB. 2000. David Kamansky speaks in VA-101 on "Tibet: Holes in the Roof of the World."

5 FEB. 2000. The campus hosts the 17th Annual San Bernardino Co. Academic Decathlon, "Looking Forward: Creating the Future."

7 FEB. 2000. Writer Geoffrey Wolff reads from his work in PR. Senal Paz performs the drama, *Fresa y Chocolate*. Cal State student Jeffery Allen Berry dies in San Bernardino.

9 FEB. 2000. Pianist Kris Carlisle and soprano Dina Cancryn perform in RH. The campus signs an agreement with Dankook University, Seoul, Korea, to bring Korean students to CSUSB.

11 FEB. 2000. The CSU System purchases the Collaborative Management System (CMS) or PeopleSoft accounting system; the cost to CSUSB will exceed $10 million. The last physical issue of the (*Friday*) *Bulletin* is published.

14 FEB. 2000. Philip DeFeo speaks at a dedication luncheon for the Arrowhead Lab for Securities Analysis in Brown Hall, partially funded by a $27,600 grant from the Arrowhead Credit Union.

16 FEB. 2000. Helen M. García and Angela Louque speak in SUEC on "Emerging Profiles of High Achievement in Hispanic and Afro-American Women Scholars."

17 FEB. 2000. The campus celebrates Umoja Day as part of Black History Month. Forensic scientist Norman "Skip" Sperber speaks in SUEC. Earl "Ofari" Hutchison speaks in SUEC. Jim Hansen, Dir. of the Physical Plant (1990-00), resigns. David M. L. Riefer is named Outstanding Professor for 1999/00.

18 FEB. 2000. ASI buys a $44,900 bronze statue of 3 coyotes created by Chinese sculptor Guo Xuanchang, to be erected near the information booth at the Coyote Dr. entrance to the campus. Campus radio station KSSB returns to the air. Tony Simpson is named Int. Dir. of the Physical Plant, replacing Jim Hansen.

19 FEB. 2000. The Coyotes men basketball team clinches its first CCAA Conference championship by beating CSU Los Angeles.

21 FEB. 2000. N. Laura Kamptner receives the Golden Apple Award for best teacher of 1999/00. Amaryllis Hilao-Enríquez speaks in SUEC on "The Dictatorship of Filipino Dictator Ferdinand Marcos." The campus opens its Community Advancement Resource Enterprise (CARE) Center at 202 E. Airport Dr., Suite 155, San Bernardino.

23 FEB. 2000. Henry Hooks speaks at the 10th Library Associates Lecture in the Pfau Library on "Portrait of a Community." The campus receives a $2,000 gift from the Senior Citizens Foundation.

26 FEB. 2000. Assemblywoman Nell Soto debates Rob Guzman in the TV Studio.

28 FEB. 2000. Leonard Raines, Dave Barnett, and 12 other veterans read from their poetry in CA-102.

1 MAR. 2000. The Pacifica Chamber Artists perform in RH. Film director Gregory Nava speaks in SUEC on "The Influence of Latino Films in the Motion Picture Industry." Jorge Mariscal speaks in SUEC on "Aztlán and Vietnam: Chicano and Chicana Experiences of the War."

2 MAR. 2000. Chris Brochu speaks in RH on "Bringing a T-rex to Life."

4 MAR. 2000. The Harlem Globetrotters perform in the Arena. The campus hosts its Business Conference 2000, "Women as Leaders," with Rep. Joe Baca, Gerald García, and S.B. Mayor Valles speaking (keynote address).

7 MAR. 2000. Ex-Democratic Presidential candidate and Mass. Gov. Michael Dukakis speaks in PS-10 on "The 2000 Presidential Election: A Super Tuesday Perspective." Also present are S.B. City Councilpersons Betty Dean Anderson and José Suárez. Mary Louise Defender-Wilson speaks in SUEC on "Oral Traditions of Cultural Sovereignty."

8 MAR. 2000. Ruth Mayden, Pres. of the National Assoc. of Social Workers, speaks in UC on "Influencing Social Welfare Policy." WNBA star Sheryl Swoopes gives the keynote speech in SUEC at the Women's Research Conference.

13 MAR. 2000. Jerrold E. Pritchard receives a Fulbright grant to study in Germany in April. Rabbi Hillel Cohn, Rev. Peter Covas, Pastor William Loveless, and Rev. Sandra Tice speak in YC at the 13th Annual Morrow-McCombs Memorial Lecture on "The Ten Commandments for the 21st Century: Some Christian and Jewish Perspectives."

16 MAR. 2000. In his 2nd trial, ex-Instructor of Statistics Gerald Joseph McCall is convicted of manslaughter in the strangling death of a prostitute, and is sentenced on Apr. 14 to 11 years in prison. Guitarist Judy Gorman speaks and performs in the SU Fireside Lounge.

27 MAR. 2000. The campus renames the Creative Arts Building as the Performing Arts Building.

31 MAR. 2000. Arthur I. Saltzman, Prof. of Marketing (1984-2000), retires.

2 APR. 2000. Robert J. Greenfield, ex-Asst. Prof. of Sociology (1968-72), dies at St. Augustine Beach, Florida, at age 66.

7 APR. 2000. Sally J. Pederson, Lt. Gov. of Iowa, speaks in SR on "Autism, Inclusion, and Advocacy."

12 APR. 2000. Gay activist Keith Boykin speaks in SUEC. Astrophysicist

Virginia Trimble speaks in SUEC on "Man's Place in the Universe."

16-20 APR. 2000. The Cal State teams wins a 5th-straight "Outstanding Delegation" Award at the Model United Nations competition in New York, representing Uzbekistan.

17 APR. 2000. The Jin-Wen Institute of Technology, Taipei, Taiwan, signs an agreement with CSUSB to bring 150 Taiwanese students annually to the campus.

19 APR. 2000. Groundbreaking is held for the Social and Behavioral Sciences Building.

20 APR. 2000. Filmmaker Hector Galán speaks and shows his films, *New Harvest, Old Shame* and *Songs of the Homeland*, in SUEC.

22 APR. 2000. The campus hosts its 14th Annual Environmental Expo in the Arena, featuring magician Paul Cash, singer Mark Lynn, and the rock group Gayle & Co.

24 APR. 2000. Soprano Julie Makerov performs.

4 MAY 2000. Mariachi Lucero de Lupe Soría and Ballet Folklórico Alegria de México perform in SU Courtyard. The campus hosts a forum, "Changing the Face of Policing," in SUEC.

6 MAY 2000. S.B. Co. Museum curator Kathleen Springer speaks at the 5th Annual Harry Rheubottom/George Webster Lecture in the Pfau Library on "The Beasts Are Back: The Inland Empire's Lost World of Fossils of the Eastside Reservoir."

9 MAY 2000. The Joseph Andrew Rowe Collection of water documents is transferred from the Pfau Library to WRI.

10 MAY 2000. Writer Jane Elliott gives the keynote address in SUEC at the Annual Diversity Conference, "Hearts and Minds: Connecting Through Diversity in the New Millennium," in SUEC.

11 MAY 2000. The Inland Empire Center for Entrepreneurship and the Coll. of Business and Public Administration sponsor its 1st Entrepreneurship and the Academy Conference, "Building Bridges to the Future: Connecting the Academy to the Entrepreneurial Community in the New Millennium," with speakers Rep. Joe Baca, Al Lewis, Curt DeBerg, Sandy Sutton, Terri Ooms, and Bettye Burkhalter (keynote address).

12 MAY 2000. Ted Kennedy Jr. speaks in SUEC on "Facing the Challenge" for disabilities.

15 MAY 2000. C. Donald Kajcienski, Assoc. VP for Enrollment Services and Dir. of Outreach Services (1983-00), retires.

15-19 MAY 2000. The campus presents the Music of the Americas Festival, with Argentine pianist Manuel Rego and the UCLA Afro-Cuban Omo Ache Ensemble performing on May 15, guitarist Christopher Caliendo and flautist Sheridan Stokes and the West African Ensemble on May 16, soprano Teresa Radomski and pianist James Radomski and the UCLA Anglo-American Ensemble on May 17, pianist Ana Lía Lenchantín and the Camarata Tango on May 18, and the UCLA Mariachi Ensemble and Poncho Sánchez and His Latin Soul Ensemble on May 19.

17 MAY 2000. The remains of a *Tyrannosaurus rex* nicknamed "Sue" are unveiled at the Field Museum of Natural History in Chicago; Prof. Stuart Sumida and 8 Cal State students under his direction helped prepare the fossil for display.

18 MAY 2000. The Arrowhead Lab for Securities Analysis receives a $150,000 grant from the Leading Market Technology Corp., a $20,000 in-kind grant from Trader Training Corp. of Denmark, and a $5,000 grant from Citizen's Business Bank.

22 MAY 2000. J. Milton Clark, Int. Dean for Undergraduate Studies, is named permanent Dean.

23 MAY 2000. Cal State student Tanya Osborn dies of hepatitis B and liver cancer at Redlands at age 27. The campus unveils a website to allow students to register over the Internet. The WRI inaugurates its Lecture Series with Mark Reisner speaking on "The Age of Dams and Its Legacy."

25 MAY 2000. Pulitzer-Prize winning author Jared Diamond speaks in SUEC on "Why Have Europeans Settled So Much of the World Rather Than Other Groups?"

26 MAY 2000. New speed bumps installed in Parking Lots B and C cause a number of complaints over their height.

1 JUN. 2000. For the first time, the Theatre Dept. performs a play off-campus at the California Theatre in S.B.

3 JUN. 2000. Comedian and singer "Weird Al" Yankovic performs in the Arena.

5 JUN. 2000. Jeffrey W. Davis is named first Dir. of the Water Resources

Institute.

6 JUN. 2000. The campus erects a cast bronze statue of 3 coyotes by Chinese artist Guo Xuanchang (purchased by a $30,000 gift from the Associate Students Inc.) on the center strip of the Coyote Dr. Entrance to the campus; the 10-foot-high, 19-foot long artwork is dedicated on Jun. 9.

8 JUN. 2000. CSU Chancellor Reed announces that Cal State students will be redirected from the "crowded" campuses in the system to less impacted ones, including CSUSB.

17 JUN. 2000. Joseph A. Rowe, a local water engineer whose papers, photographs, books, journals, and maps form the core of the Water Resources Institute library, dies at age 82. Juan Delgado receives a $3,000 Whittenberger Fellowship in Poetry to teach 60 high school students at Albertson College in Idaho.

17-18 JUN. 2000. The 34th Commencement is held in the Arena and at CVC, with Assemblyman William R. Leonard, Rep. Joe Baca, Rep. Mary Bono, Marta Macías Brown, Margarita Benítez, and Sidney A. Ribeau giving the keynote addresses; 3,840 students are eligible to receive degrees.

22 JUN. 2000. Herbert Evans Brown, retired Dir. of the Physical Plant (1964-74), dies at age 85. The campus receives a 2nd $22,500 grant from the Ewing Kauffman Center for Entrepreneurial Leadership to sponsor internships in entrepreneurial leadership.

24 JUN. 2000. The campus hosts its Annual Juneteenth Jam, with performances by Hip Hop Xpo and Step Team Showcase; comedian and poet Richard O. Jones acts as emcee.

26 JUN. 2000. Lydia Ortega is named Act. Assoc. VP for Enrollment Services, replacing C. Donald Kajcienski.

30 JUN. 2000. Roger P. Lintault, Prof. of Art (1969-00), retires.

SUM. 2000. Retirements: Michael L. Boorom, Prof. of Marketing (1992-00); Morley David Glicken, Prof. of Social Work (1988-00); Joseph W. Gray, Assoc. Prof. of Education (1969-00); Richard W. Griffiths, Prof. of Education (1978-00); Jorun B. Johns, Prof. of Foreign Languages and Literature (1965-00); Marshall Jung, Prof. of Social Work (1994-00); Mary Beth Kelsey, Prof. of Sociology (1994-99); Adria F. Klein, Prof. of Education (1976-00); Barry A. Knight, Prof. of Accounting and Finance (1990-00); Janice M. Layton, Prof. of Nursing (1985-00); Steven M. Levy, Prof. of Management (1983-00); Denis R. Lichtman, Prof. of Mathematics (1969-00); Richard L. Moss, Prof. of Economics (1973-00); Cheryl A.

Stout, Student Services Professional (1986-00); Kenneth J. Thygerson, Prof. of Accounting and Finance (1990-00). Staff retirements: John A. Cervantes, Lead Groundsworker (1965-00); Gladys Chisom, Custodian (1980-00); Sandra Collins, Development (1992-00); Louis Díaz, Building Maintenance Worker (1986-00); Bennie R. García, Custodian (1980-00); Lillian E. Haskell, Academic Programs (1973-00); Richard Haskell, Operating Systems Analyst (1985-00); Maurice J. Huerter, Supervisor of Housing Maintenance (1983-00); Thelma Jackson, Custodian (1987-00); Edna Monroe, Custodian (1988-00); Rayanne Strait, Parking Officer (1987-00); Linda S. Vance, Administrative Support Coordinator, Philosophy (1986-00).

1 JUL. 2000. Michael L. Ross, Int. Dir. of Academic Computing and Media, is named permanent Dir.

3 JUL. 2000. The Facilities Management Dept. occupies the new Facilities Management Building in the new Corporation Yard, moving out of the University Police Building, which in turn is occupied by the Police Dept.

5 JUL. 2000. The Latin Society performs on LCP.

10-14 JUL. 2000. The campus hosts its Summer Music 2000 Camp for local students, including performances by the jazz band, the Side Street Strutters, and the Albert McNeil Jubilee Singers.

12 JUL. 2000. The blues quintet Mo' Betta Blues performs on LCP.

17-19 JUL. 2000. The campus hosts its 1st Annual International Conference on Geological Information Systems Education.

19 JUL. 2000. Anthony H. Evans is named President Emeritus by the CSU Board of Trustees. The San Francisco band The Waybacks performs on LCP.

26 JUL. 2000. The surf-rock band The Tornadoes performs on LCP.

31 JUL.-4 AUG. 2000. The campus hosts a conference, "Making the College Connection: Preparation, Motivation, and Innovation," for local high school mathematics and English teachers.

1 AUG. 2000. Robert A. Schwabe, Dir. of Institutional Research, retires.

2 AUG. 2000. Ross T. Moran is named Int. Dir. of Institutional Research, replacing Robert A. Schwabe.

7 AUG. 2000. The Administrative Council renames the Physical Plant as Facilities Services, and Physical Planning and Development as Capital Planning, Design, and Construction. A 3rd proposed name change, of Public Safety to the Univ. Police, is postponed. John M. Hatton, Dir. of Student Health Services and the Psychology Counseling Center, is also named Act. Assoc. VP for Student Affairs.

11 AUG. 2000. Rep. Joe Baca sponsors his 8th Annual Women's Conference, with speakers Tipper Gore, wife of VP Al Gore, María Eschaveste, Deputy Chief of Staff to Pres. Clinton, and Norma Cantu, Asst. Secretary for Civil Rights, U.S. Dept. of Education. The campus receives a $5 million grant from the U.S. government to establish The National Center for Excellence in Distance Learning in conjunction with the U.S. Navy.

11-13 AUG. 2000. The campus hosts the 2000 National Teen Leadership Program.

15 AUG. 2000. Beverly L. Hendricks, Prof. of Communication Studies and Dean of the Coll. of Arts and Letters (1986-00), retires.

16 AUG. 2000. Eri F. Yasuhara is named Dean of the Coll. of Arts and Letters, replacing Beverly L. Hendricks.

31 AUG. 2000. A Hollywood film crew visits the campus to shoot a scene from the movie *Slackers* in the Coyote Den. L. Lynn Judd, Prof. of Marketing (1987-00), retires.

1 SEPT. 2000. The alumni magazine, *Cal State SB*, changes its name to *Cal State San Bernardino Magazine*.

3 SEPT. 2000. Robert A. Senour, Prof. of Education and Dir. of Media Services (1970-2000), retires.

5 SEPT. 2000. Franklin P. Williams III, Prof. of Criminal Justice (1988-00), retires.

6 SEPT. 2000. Jeanette M. Bernthaler, ex-Libn. and Head of Public Services (1968-72), dies at age 77.

13 SEPT. 2000. Retirements: Joan H. Kritzberg, Prof. of Management (1987-00); John F. "Jack" McDonnell, Prof. of Information and Decision Sciences (1969-00). The campus receives a 5-year, $3,893,900 grant from the U.S. Dept. of Education to develop the federal Gaining Early Awareness and Readiness for Undergraduate Programs program.

14 SEPT. 2000. At the annual convocation, Pres. Karnig addresses the challenges facing the campus. He condemns a hate crime directed at a gay student living in the dormitories. "If we're going to blossom as an institution, we must have tolerance," he says. "Actions that diminish any one of us, diminish all of us." He notes that "If the region was a state, we'd rank 51st, dead last in the college-going rate. We'd rank 51st, dead last, in the high school graduation rates. There are few, if any, universities that are totally essential to their community. Few universities are as connected to the success of their community as we are." While the University is headed in the right direction, more work still needs to be done, Karnig says. "If we'd like to have as stimulating a campus as we'd like, there's general agreement that we need better participation by faculty and staff." The President also states that the University needs to raise additional money to cover such projects as the expansion of the Student Union Building and Cultural Center, and suggests that increasing student fees might be one way of doing so. Rep. Joe Baca announces that the campus has been awarded a $215,060 Community Oriented Policing Services grant.

18 SEPT. 2000. The campus dedicates new modular classrooms at Victor Valley College to expand its distance learning programs; the campus and Victor Valley College receive an $110,000 grant from the South Coast Air Quality Management Dist. to establish a video teleconferencing center at VVC.

18-22 SEPT. 2000. The campus co-hosts its 2nd Annual Calif. Indian Awareness Conference at the SUEC with the San Manuel Band of Serrano Mission Indians and S.B. Co. Schools, including a talk by Lt. Gov. Cruz Bustamante, a performance of the play *We Are Still Here* by Katherine Siva Saubel, and appearances by Rep. Joe Baca, S.B. Mayor Valles, S.B. Unified School Dist. Superintendent Arturo Delgado, and S.B. Co. School Superintendent Herbert Fischer.

22 SEPT. 2000. The campus hosts a banquet in UC to inaugurate the John M. Pfau Book Endowment for the Pfau Library, with the attendance of ex-Pres. Pfau, ex-Pres. Evans, and Pres. Karnig.

23 SEPT. 2000. The campus hosts a symposium, "Crisis in Minority Education: Gaining Access to College Dollars, Overcoming Test Score Obstacles," in the Cross Cultural Center, featuring Carolyn B. Murray, James Sandoval, and Michael Anderson.

27 SEPT. 2000. Friedrich Katz speaks in UC on "The Life and Times of Pancho Villa."

29 SEPT. 2000. Educator Temple Grandin speaks on campus. Rep. Joe Baca announces that the campus has received a $509,400 grant to help develop the Water Resources Institute.

2 Oct. 2000. The campus honors Cal State alumni Art Gallardo and Narciso Cardona with its first Outstanding Educator Awards.

4 Oct. 2000. Pianist Kris Carlisle performs in RH.

6 Oct. 2000. *The Coyote Chronicle* increases its physical size by 2 inches. Groundbreaking is held for the new apartment-style residence halls, Arrowhead Village.

8 Oct. 2000. Country western singer Jo Dee Messina performs in the Arena.

11 Oct. 2000. Writer Ron Arias reads from his work in PiR. Groundbreaking is held for the first permanent 3-story building to be constructed for CVC at the corner of Cook St. and Frank Sinatra Dr. in Palm Desert; the new structure is named the Mary Stuart Rogers Gateway Building to honor the initial donor for the project; the campus receives 2 grants of $250,000 each (one anonymous, one from Al Berry and Ed Meacham) to help support the project. Officials from 11 cities in S.B. Co. meet on campus to discuss creating a regional cable TV network.

12 Oct. 2000. 200 people gather on the Pfau Library steps to honor 2 gay men murdered in Laramie, Wyoming, 2 years earlier.

13 Oct. 2000. The Water Resources Institute sponsors its 1st Annual Conference, "The Future of Water in the Inland Empire," in SUEC; attendees include S.B. Mayor Valles, with Commissioner of the U.S. Bureau of Reclamation Eluid Martínez giving the keynote address.

18 Oct. 2000. Davida Fischman, Joan Terry Hallett, Dan Rinne, and Peter Williams receive a $175,000 grant from NSF to improve the retention and pass rate of students in lower division mathematics classes. The campus hosts the Bi-National Education Committee meeting in LC, with Mexican Consul Juan José Delgado, Superintendent of S.B. Co. Schools Herb Fischer, and S.B. City Unified School Dist. Superintendent Art Delgado attending.

19 Oct. 2000. Danny E. "Dan" Moseley, Campus Photographer, dies following heart surgery at age 52.

24 Oct. 2000. Manley A. Begay Jr. speaks in SR on "Native Nation Building: Sovereignty, Business, and Self-Government." The campus hosts a forum in SUEC on proposed S.B. City charter reform initiative, Measure M.

25 Oct. 2000. Darleen K. Stoner receives an award from the South Coast

Air Quality Management Dist. for 3 decades of dedication to environmental education.

26-28 OCT. 2000. The Center for Scholarship on Spirituality sponsors the "Rumi Conference," celebrating the life of the 13th-century poet and philosopher, with Coleman Barks giving the keynote address.

31 OCT. 2000. Retired Indian Air Force Vice Marshal Samir K. Sen speaks on security issues in the Indian subcontinent.

1 NOV. 2000. The Side Street Strutters jazz band performs in RH.

9 NOV. 2000. The campus hosts its 2nd Annual Inland Action Conference, featuring ex-Secretary of Housing and Urban Development Henry Cisneros and writer Ray Bradbury.

15 NOV. 2000. The campus hosts a symposium, "The Brave New Workplace: Strategies to Excel in a World of Change," at the Radisson Hotel, S.B., with insights (via satellite feed) from Nelson Mandela, Stephen Covey, Tom Peters, Martha Rogers, Martha Stewart, Andrew Grove, and Jerry Yang.

18 NOV. 2000. Larry Lester Kramer, Prof. of English (1968-00), dies in Fontana of multiple myeloma at age 61.

19 NOV. 2000. The women's volleyball team loses in the NCAA Division II Western Regional Tournament in L.A. The Pfau Library hosts the Grand Opening of the renovated Special Collections Dept. in PL-4005; John Weeks speaks about his book, *Inland Empire*.

30 NOV. 2000. A memorial service for Prof. Larry L. Kramer (1939-00) is held in PR. Oliver A. Ryder speaks in SR on "Genetic Research's Role in Helping to Save Endangered Species."

1 DEC. 2000. The campus receives a $50,000 gift from Jack H. Brown to establish the Rose Brown Expandable Scholarship Fund.

6 DEC. 2000. Traditional Mexican Jarocho group Conjunto Jarín performs with the Ballet Folklórico del Pacifico in RH.

8 DEC. 2000. The campus hosts a 35th anniversary celebration and luncheon, followed by a campus-wide reception, with CSU Chancellor Reed attending.

17-24 DEC. 2000. The campus closes offices an hour early to conserve energy.

21 DEC. 2000. The campus receives a $5 million gift from the City of Indian Wells to help fund construction of the Indian Wells Center for Educational Excellence at CVC. The campus receives a $1 million gift from Ron Auen to complete the funding for the Indian Wells Center at CVC.

2001

26 JAN.-15 AUG. 2001. The Robert V. Fullerton Museum exhibits 31 Greek antiquities from the J. Paul Getty Museum, funded by a $20,000 gift from the Arrowhead Credit Union, and $5,000 from the *Los Angeles Times*.

10 JAN. 2001. Guitarist Stuart Green performs in RH.

24 JAN. 2001. The CSU Board of Trustees approves naming the 2nd permanent building at CVC the Indian Wells Center for Educational Excellence.

5 FEB. 2001. Gerald Marron Scherba, Emer. Prof. of Biology, VP of Academic Affairs, VP in Charge, and Dir. of the Desert Studies Consortium (1962-91), dies in Santa Ana of congestive heart failure at age 73. Poet Kalamu Ya Salaam speaks in SUEC.

7 FEB. 2001. (Audrey) Vivien Bull, Emer. Prof. of French (1976-91), dies at Albuquerque, New Mexico, of a stroke at age 79. The Carl Schafer Quartet performs in RH.

12 FEB. 2001. Sandra D. Kamusikiri, Int. Assoc. VP for Assessment and Planning and Int. Dean of Graduate Studies, is named permanent Assoc. VP and Dean. Writer Iyanla Vanzant speaks in YC on her book, *Until Today*.

19 FEB. 2001. Ex-Air Force Col. Paul L. Green speaks at the 11th Library Associates Lecture in the Pfau Library on "Reminiscences of a Tuskegee Airman." Spanish writer Ona Siporín speaks in SR.

21 FEB. 2001. Michael Gazzaniga speaks in YC on "Automatic Brains/Interpretative Minds: Do We Have Free Will?"

23 FEB. 2001. The campus hosts the 13th Annual California State University-Production/Operations Management Conference at the Doubletree Inn, Ontario, with ESRI Pres. Jack Dangermond giving the keynote speech.

25 FEB. 2001. The Harlem Globetrotters perform in the Arena.

28 FEB. 2001. Frederick Jones and Curtis James speak about "The Buffalo Soldiers."

28 FEB.-1 MAR. 2001. Cal State students vote 1,285-483 to increase fees to expand the Student Union, build a Recreation Center, augment Cross Cultural programming, and add to athletics grants-in-aid.

2 MAR. 2001. Sanders A. McDougall is named Outstanding Professor for 2000/01. Zahid Z. Hasan receives the Golden Apple Award for teaching excellence for 2000/01.

3 MAR. 2001. The campus hosts its 2nd Annual Conference for Women, "Building Bridges for Success," in the Commons, with Gretchen M. Tibbits giving the keynote address.

4 MAR. 2001. Gloria Anzaldua speaks in SU.

5 MAR. 2001. Rabbi Elie Kaplan Spitz speaks in RH at the 14th Annual Morrow-McCombs Lecture on "Does the Soul Survive? A Jewish Journey to Belief in Afterlife, Past Lives, and Living with Purpose."

6 MAR. 2001. The campus announces that it will begin year-round operations in June 2001.

8 MAR. 2001. D. Linn Wiley receives the Arrowhead Distinguished Chief Executive Award at a banquet held in SUEC.

11 MAR. 2001. Violinist Andy Stein performs in RH.

29 MAR. 2001. The campus hosts its 8th Annual At-Risk Expo, "Our Youth, Our Community, Our Challenges: Seeing Beyond the Limitations," with comedian Alex Valdez giving the keynote address. The International Institute receives an $80,000 grant from the U.S. Dept. of Education to fund a minor in the Study of the Americas.

2 APR. 2001. Howard S. Wang is named Asst. VP for Student Affairs, replacing John M. Hatton. The CMS accounting system goes live on this date. Cuban poet César López Núñez is named Scholar in Residence for the Spring term.

4 APR. 2001. Guitarist Eric Cabalo performs in RH.

9 APR. 2001. James M. Monaghan is named Dir. of Distributed Learning. Elsa M. Ochoa-Fernández receives a $150,000 "180" Planning Grant from the State.

9-14 APR. 2001. For the 6th time in 7 years, the Cal State team receives an "Outstanding Delegation" award at the Model United Nations competition in New York City, representing Bangladesh.

12 APR. 2001. Elsa Ochoa-Fernández receives the Edward S. Blankenship Award from the honor society, Phi Beta Delta. Ross T. Moran, Int. Dir. of Institutional Research, is named permanent Dir.

18 APR. 2001. Kenneth E. Lane is named Director of the National Center for Excellence in Distance Education, a federally-funded center designed to offer distance learning to U.S. Naval personnel.

19 APR. 2001. Ben Lieberman and hypnotist Jason Nazar perform in SUEC.

21 APR. 2001. The campus hosts its 15th Annual Environmental Expo, "Pure Water: Our Lifeline to the Future," with TV weatherman Christopher Nance and magician Paul Cash appearing.

25 APR. 2001. The campus receives a $3 million gift from Walter and Leonore Annenberg and Annenberg Foundation to help build the Indian Wells Center for Educational Excellence at CVC. The campus creates the Center for the Study of Hate Crimes and Extremism.

4 MAY 2001. The campus holds a picnic on the Library Lawn to celebrate its 35th anniversary, with performances by Ballet Folklórico and the Westside Latin Band.

8 MAY 2001. Catherine Mulholland speaks in SUEC about her grandfather, "William Mulholland and the Rise of Los Angeles."

9 MAY 2001. The campus receives a $1 million gift from the H. N. and Frances C. Berger Foundation to help build the Indian Wells Center for Educational Excellence at CVC.

11 MAY 2001. The campus hosts its 4th Annual "Hearts and Minds: Diversity in Action Conference" in SUEC, with Angela E. Oh, Ballet Folklórico, and the "Living Voices" actors appearing.

12 MAY 2001. The rock group Save Ferris performs in the Arena. S.B. Co. Registrar Ingrid E. Gonzáles speaks in SUEC.

13 MAY 2001. James Edward Segesta, the first Libn. and Head of Technical Services, and the first faculty member at CSUSB not also an administrator (1963-66), dies at Bakersfield at age 66.

19 May 2001. Fireman Steven Shaw speaks at the 6th Annual Rheubottom/Webster Historical Lecture in the Pfau Library on "The History of the San Bernardino Fire Dept. Memorabilia Exhibit." The campus hosts the "Inland Empire Conference on Hate Crime: Characteristics and Community Responses" in JB-102, with Bonnie Jourhari, Ismael Ileto, and Morris Casuto speaking.

23 May 2001. Cal State student Coreen Ann Flores dies in San Bernardino after collapsing in class in University Hall at age 21.

24 May 2001. Judge Dana LaMon speaks at the 12th Annual Diversity Awareness Event in SUEC.

2 Jun. 2001. Cal State Education major Pearl Santos dies of a brain aneurysm in Valencia at age 28.

7 Jun. 2001. The campus receives a $1 million gift from the City of Rancho Mirage to help fund the Health Sciences Building at PDC.

8 Jun. 2001. Ja Rule and Brotherhood perform in the Arena.

16-17 Jun. 2001. The 35th Commencement is held in the Arena and at CVC, with Riverside Co. 4th Dist. Supervisor Roy Wilson, Refugio Rochín, W. Benson Harer (who also receives the campus's first honorary doctorate, a Dr. of Humane Letters degree), Jacquelyn L. Jackson, María Casillas, and Judge Patrick J. Morris giving the keynote addresses.

20 Jun. 2001. The campus hosts a "Conference on the Needs of Older Workers in the 21st Century" in SUEC. The campus receives a $50,000 gift from the West Valley Material Recovery Facility to establish 4-year scholarships.

27 Jun. 2001. The campus receives a $624,762 grant from the U.S. Dept. of Education to support enrollment of Hispanic students.

Sum. 2001. Retirements: Frank D. Benson, Prof. of Accounting and Finance (1986-01); Anand R. "Andy" Bhatia, Asst. Prof. of Information and Decision Sciences (1972-01); Jerry A. Freischlag, Prof. of Kinesiology (1987-01); Louise F. Fulton, Prof. of Education (1982-01); Diane F. Halpern, Prof. of Psychology (1981-01); Rauf A. Khan, Prof. of Accounting and Finance (1976-01); Eldon C. Lewis, Prof. of Accounting and Finance (1987-01); E. Clark Mayo, Prof. of English (1967-01); Walter C. Oliver, Prof. of Foreign Languages and Literature (1969-01); James G. Rogers, Prof. of Management (1974-01); Kent M. Schofield, Prof. of History (1966-01); David O. Stine, Prof. of Education (1988-01); Ruth C. Wilson (1971-01), Prof. of Biology; Don Woodford, Prof. of Art (1972-

01).

2 JUL. 2001. Peter T. Robertshaw receives a $23,650 grant from the National Geographical Society to study climate change in Uganda.

9 JUL. 2001. Lynda McNamara is named Assoc. VP for Univ. Advancement.

11 JUL. 2001. The pop group Popular Demand performs in LCP.

17 JUL. 2001. CSU Trustee Frederick W. Pierce IV visits CSUSB.

18 JUL. 2001. The Latin Society performs in LCP.

21 JUL. 2001. Shirley C. Booe, retired Library Asst. (1968-75), dies at age 79.

25 JUL. 2001. The Highway 111 Dance Band performs in LCP. Chris Naticchia receives a $24,000 grant from the National Endowment for the Arts for research on justice.

1 AUG. 2001. The r&b group Rhythm of Life performs in LCP.

6-16 AUG. 2001. The campus hosts a Conference on Police Work for Native American Teenagers.

20 AUG. 2001. Assemblyman Joe Baca hosts his annual Economic Summit on campus, with Calif. Public Utilities Commissioner Carl Wood, Pres. Karnig, and Tal Finney speaking.

29 AUG. 2001. Lydia Ortega, Act. Assoc. VP for Enrollment Management, returns to her previous position. Jennifer J. Zorn is elected Pres. of the Calif. Geographical Soc.

30 AUG. 2001. Robert McGowan is named Assoc. VP for Enrollment Management, replacing Lydia Ortega. Margaret Catherine King Gibbs, Emer. Prof. of Administration (1975-80), dies at Claremont at age 87.

31 AUG. 2001. John H. Craig, Int. Dean of the Coll. of Natural Sciences, returns to the ranks as Prof. of Chemistry and Biochemistry.

1 SEPT. 2001. B. Robert Carlson is named Dean of the Coll. of Natural Sciences, replacing John H. Craig. John S. Chaney is named Assoc. Dean for Administrative Affairs. Deletta R. "Del" Anderson is named Budget Officer. The campus begins offering courses in Arabic language studies, and an M.P.A. degree with an emphasis on Water Resources Management.

11 SEPT. 2001. The campus receives a $3 million Federal Education grant (with 4 other universities) to improve computer security.

13 SEPT. 2001. The new apartment-style dormitory building, Arrowhead Village Housing, opens for business. At the annual convocation, Pres. Karnig comments on the terrorist attack in New York 2 days earlier, stating: "I believe education offers the only possible long-term bridge over the chasm of beliefs and hatreds that now exist—beliefs so immutable and hatreds so white hot and intense that personal death—suicide—is a viable outcome.... I believe the best thing we can now do is to continue the essential work of education: of fighting ignorance; prejudice; class, race and ethnic hatred. It's fundamental to our enterprise that we teach our young to live successfully, with tolerance and forbearance for one another; to stand against hatred and violence; and to stand against those who preach hatred and violence." He notes rarely have "the planets lined up as well, with solid state economic expansion; strong student enrollments; general goodwill and collegiality on campus; excellent relationships with federal, state and local government officials; and virtually no town-gown conflict of any kind." He emphasizes that hate has no place on campus: "We will accept no bashing, no harassment, no intimidation—whether it's toward gays, lesbians, women, minorities, heterosexuals, members of religious groups or anyone else." He also outlines plans for development of a county-wide cable TV network for locally-oriented cultural and public affairs programming. He notes that the campus's enrollment continues to expand (announcing the first Winter graduate ceremony), that new buildings are planned, and that local demographics are changing, with a greater proportion of Latino students and a decline in older students. He emphasizes that the campus needs to develop additional resources for grants and fundraising.

25-28 SEPT. 2001. The campus hosts its 3rd Annual California Indian Cultural Awareness Conference with dances, songs, and storytelling.

27 SEPT. 2001. Margaret R. Summers, Library Asst. (1968-01), retires.

1 OCT. 2001. The campus receives an $885,982 grant from the U.S. Dept. of Education to fund the project, "Partnering to Prepare Tomorrow's Teachers to Use Technology." The campus receives a $213,843 grant from NSF to fund "Earth Science Pipeline: Recruiting Ethnic Groups in the Earth Sciences from Sixth Grade to Post-College," with additional funding (2 years) of $431,315. The campus forms the Coyote Arts Conservancy for junior high school students with the Theatre Dept. and S.B. City, with grants totaling almost $100,000 from the S.B. Fine Arts Commission, the federal government, private contributors, and the Presidential Fund for the Arts. Parking Lot H opens for business, adding 400 parking spaces near the dorms. The campus begins a $4.6 million telecommunications infrastructure upgrade project. Gonzalo Santos speaks in SR on "The Long March to Indigenous Rights in Mexico."

3 Oct. 2001. Singer Dina Cancryn and pianist Kris Carlisle perform in RH. A student is raped near the Children's Center.

8 Oct. 2001. After much campus discussion, Pres. Karnig decides to retain the quarter system at Cal State San Bernardino.

10 Oct. 2001. The campus signs an agreement with Instituto Mexicano Americano de Relaciones Culturales (IMARC) to facilitate bilingual education training.

11 Oct. 2001. The Coachella Valley Center (CVC) is renamed the Palm Desert Campus (PDC) of California State University, San Bernardino, and the titles of its Dean and Assoc. Dean change accordingly.

12 Oct. 2001. A ribbon-cutting ceremony marks the official opening of the new apartment-style dormitory building, adding 319 beds, the first new dorm to open since 1972. Wilmer D. "Amina" Carter, Coordinator of Governmental Relations, resigns.

12-14 Oct. 2001. The San Manuel Band of Mission Indians and Cross Cultural Center host the 1st People of the Pines Pow Wow in the Arena.

17 & 24 Oct. 2001. The campus hosts two forums in SUEC to deal with the aftermath of the 9/11 terrorist attacks in New York.

18-19 Oct. 2001. The WRI sponsors its 2nd Annual Water Resources Institute Conference, "Sharing the Waters," in SUEC, at which ex-State Sen. Ruben S. Ayala receives the 1st WRI Lifetime Achievement Award; WRI donates $10,500 to the campus to endow the Ruben S. Ayala Scholarship.

25 Oct. 2001. The campus hosts a Unity Forum Town Hall Conference in SUEC, with Gilberto Esquivel serving as master of ceremonies, and entertainment by Lalo Guerrero, Mariachi Estudiantes del Inland Empire, and Son Real.

29 Oct. 2001. The campus receives a $50,000 gift from Verizon and a $25,000 gift from the Southern California Edison Co. (in addition to $10,000 received from Edison in April) to help fund PDC.

31 Oct. 2001. Jo Ann Hankin, VP for Univ. Advancement, resigns; the position remains vacant until 2005, with the unit heads in this area reporting directly to Pres. Karnig.

2 NOV. 2001. A Cal State student is charged with murdering his pregnant girlfriend.

5 NOV. 2001. Robert A. Blackey is named to the National Academic Council of the College Board. Leslie M. Kong is named VP/Pres.-Elect of the Calif. Library Assoc.

7 NOV. 2001. The Music Dept. presents "Word for Word: Bringing Literature to Life" in RH.

8 NOV. 2001. Kellie Renée Rayburn, Lect. in English (1989-01), dies of cancer at age 39.

9 NOV. 2001. Cora Lee "Corky" Moffett, retired Secretary to the Dean of Students (1964-80), dies at age 78.

12 NOV. 2001. The campus receives a $100,000 gift from the San Manuel Indian Bingo and Casino to help establish a new TV station. David J. Bellis, K. Michael Clarke, and Guenther G. Kress receive a $453,000 grant from the U.S. Dept. of State and the Bureau of Educational and Cultural Affairs to fund a joint project with Calif. State Polytechnic Univ. Pomona, "Public Administration Curriculum and Capacity Development with the new Bulgarian University, Bulgaria." Larry K. Gaines receives a $22,592 grant from the Riverside Police Dept.

14 NOV. 2001. The Shakti Dance Company performs "Bharata Natyam" in RH, as part of International Education Week.

15 NOV. 2001. Teatro Milagro performs *Profecia* in SUEC. The Sarunay Filipino American Music Ensemble performs in UC. The Revolutionary Assoc. of Women of Afghanistan perform "I Am the Woman Who Has Awoken" in SUEC. Alain Boutet speaks in UC on "Environmental Education and Governance."

15-17 NOV. 2001. The campus hosts its 1st NCAA Division II tournament in the Arena, the Pacific Regional women's volleyball teams.

19 NOV. 2001. The campus receives a $300,000 grant from Riverside Co. to evaluate juvenile crime prevention programs.

20 NOV. 2001. Fantasy writer Katherine Kurtz speaks, signs her books, and is interviewed by Michael Burgess in PL-4005; published for this event is the original novelette, *Venture in Vain: A Tale of the Deryni* (Millefleurs, 2001). Ray Briggs and His Jazz Ensemble perform in RH.

26 NOV. 2001. The campus receives a $25,000 gift from Coeta Barker to establish the Donald R. Barker Endowment Scholarship Fund.

27 NOV. 2001. The WRI sponsors the conference, "California's Water Future," with Jim Costa giving the keynote speech.

28 NOV. 2001. Richard Dekmejian speaks in RH on "Terrorism and U.S. Foreign Policy."

30 NOV. 2001. The campus hosts its 15th Annual Economic Forecast Breakfast at the S.B. Radisson Hotel, with speakers Lon S. Hatamiya, Jay Moss, Christina Blenk, Jim Ritchie, and TV host Bob McCormick.

1 DEC. 2001. Rep. Maxine Waters speaks at the Pioneer Awards Dinner on campus. Delta Sigma Theta Sorority and the McNair Scholarship Program host the 2nd Annual African Culture Nite, with Pastor Kodjoe Sumney giving the keynote address. Country singer Dwight Yoakam performs in the Arena. Nadine Chávez, Int. Dir. of the Educational Opportunity Program, is named permanent Dir.

3 DEC. 2001. Campus booster Florence Rigdon dies at age 84.

5 DEC. 2001. The Boston Brass quintet performs in RH.

8 DEC. 2001. The first Winter Commencement is held in the Arena, with John M. Magness giving the keynote address; also present are CSU Trustee Debra S. Farar, *Inland Empire Business Journal* Pres. William Anthony, Nicholas J. Coussoulis, *Inland Empire Hispanic News* Publisher Graciano Gómez, Ray Quinto, S.B. Co. Schools Superintendent Herbert Fischer, S.B. Mayor Valles, and S.B. City Council members Esther Estrada and José "Joe" Suárez.

14 DEC. 2001. The campus receives a $213,800 grant from NSF to attract ethnic minorities in geology, to be followed by a 2nd-year, $430,000 grant to maintain the program.

20 DEC. 2001. The S.B. City Development and Environmental Review Committee reviews plans to build a 480-unit apartment dormitory complex across the street from the campus on Northpark Blvd.

24 DEC. 2001. Leila F. Shaw, campus booster and widow of State Sen. Stanford Shaw, dies at age 88.

31 DEC. 2001. Lynda K. Davaran, Library Asst. (1992-01), retires.

2002

1 JAN. 2002. Phillip Arthur Anderson, Lect. of Business and Public Administration, dies of a brain tumor at age 57.

2 JAN. 2002. Janet Honn-Alex is named Dir. of the Women's Resource Center and the Adult Re-Entry Center, replacing Karen Paton (1998-2001?) and Int. Dir. John Futch (2001-02).

4 JAN. 2002. Robert A. Blackey receives the Eugene Asher Distinguished Teaching Award of the American Historical Assoc.

7 JAN. 2002. The campus receives a $75,000 gift from Coeta Barker to help endow the Donald R. Barker Endowment Scholarship Fund.

9 JAN. 2002. Classical guitarist Alejandro Lazo performs in RH.

10 JAN. 2002. The campus receives a $12.8 million supplement grant from the Navy to offer courses to naval personnel around the globe.

17 JAN. 2002. Frank Wilkinson speaks in SUC on "Remembering Martin Luther King, Jr."

22 JAN. 2002. The Geological Science Dept. receives a $600,000 grant from NSF to recruit minority students. The campus receives a $12 million distance-learning grant from the federal government to help establish a new TV station. The men's basketball team becomes the first Cal State team to be rated #1 in a NCAA Division II poll. Laurie Flynn is named Dir. of Students with Disabilities, replacing Nicholas Erickson, who is named Dir. of Housing and Residential Life.

23 JAN. 2002. Peter T. Robertshaw is named Outstanding Professor for 2001/02.

24 JAN. 2002. Pres. Karnig announces that the campus will launch a community-oriented TV station for the Inland Empire in Sept.

26 JAN. 2002. The Arena marks an attendance record of 4,297 for the men's basketball game against Cal Poly Pomona, the team's 17th straight triumph in a so-far undefeated season.

29 JAN. 2002. Stephen Cunha speaks in SR on "The Geography of War: Life and Death on the Afghan Frontier."

31 JAN. 2002. Chilean economist Joan Garcés speaks in SUEC.

1 FEB. 2002. *The Coyote Chronicle* offers an on-line version of the newspaper. Chilean attorney Juan Garcés speaks in SUEC.

6 FEB. 2002. Awele Makeba performs "Rage Is Not a 1-Day Thing!" in RH.

8 FEB. 2002. Margaret S. Doane receives the Golden Apple Award for teaching excellence for 2001/02.

26 FEB. 2002. Writer DeWitt Henry reads from his work in SR.

27 FEB. 2002. Filmmaker John Milius speaks in UC on "The Difficulties in Producing Films Across Cultures." Harriet P. Gibson performs "Rosa Parks" in PL-4005. Frances Spivy-Weber speaks in UC on "The Future of Mono Lake."

5 MAR. 2002. Attorney Lee Rittenburg speaks in SUEC on "Traffic Violations." Jan Kollitz speaks in SUEC on "Intellectual Prosperity in the Twenty-First Century." Construction is completed on the Mary Stuart Rogers Gateway Building at PDC. Thomas Prendergast speaks in SUEC on "Public Health Issues."

6 MAR. 2002. Mariachi band Internacional de México performs in RH.

7 MAR. 2002. Tom M. Rivera receives the Sol Azteca International Hispanic Award.

7-9 MAR. 2002. The NCAA Division II Western Regional Basketball Tournament is held for the first time at CSUSB; the Coyotes win the contest, with an all-time best season record of 28-1; at Elite Eight Tournament on Mar. 20, they lose to Metro State.

11 MAR. 2002. A temporary Recreation Center opens northeast of the Library.

13 MAR. 2002. Robert Kain receives the Arrowhead Distinguished Executive Officer Award for 2002 at a banquet in SUEC. The campus receives approval to offer master's degrees in Child Development ('03), Public Health ('04), and Spanish ('05), and a B.S. in Information Systems ('04).

18 MAR. 2002. The campus receives a $100,000 gift from Verizon to help fund the ICTN TV station. The campus hosts "The Big Gala" black-tie event to celebrate the opening of the Mary Stuart Rogers Gateway Building at PDC, with CSU Chancellor Reed attending.

21 MAR. 2002. Pianist Michael Tacchia performs in RH.

23 MAR. 2002. The campus hosts its Annual Women to Women Conference in the Commons, with S.B. Mayor Valles giving the keynote speech.

3 APR. 2002. Living sculpture zin artist Sha Sha Higby performs in RH.

7 APR. 2002. Stephen C. Nowicki, Police Lt. and Int. Dir. of Public Safety, retires.

8 APR. 2002. Arthur M. Butler, Dir. of Risk Management, is also named Int. Dir. of Public Safety.

9 APR. 2002. Josh Valdez speaks in PiR on "Racial Disparities in Health."

12 APR. 2002. Theodore "Ted" Krug, Dir. of Financial Aid (1972-02), retires. The campus hosts its 3rd Annual Latin American Roundtable in UC.

13 APR. 2002. Henry F. "Hank" Kutak is named Int. Dir. of Financial Aid, replacing Theodore Krug. Aletha Fletcher, Libn. (1967-68), dies at Loma Linda, CA, at age 84. A team of MBA students takes top honors at the 38th Annual International Collegiate Business Strategy Competition.

14 APR. 2002. Cal State San Bernardino's Modern Arab League team wins its 13th "Outstanding Delegation" award, and its Model United Nations team its 7th "Outstanding Delegation" award in 8 years, representing India.

26 APR. 2002. Armando Navarro speaks in SUEC at the 26th Annual Statewide Student Research Conference, hosted by Cal State's Social Science Research and Instructional Council.

27 APR. 2002. The campus hosts its 16th Annual Environmental Expo, "Meeting the Challenge: Conserving Water & Energy," in the Arena, with TV weatherman Christopher Nance, magician Paul Cash, and music by Mark Lynn and Gayle and Company.

1 MAY 2002. Mexican writer Victor Villaseñor speaks in SUEC. A dedication ceremony marks the opening of the Recreation Center. For the first time ever, the campus sets this date as an application deadline for Fall term.

2 MAY 2002. Robert Lowell West, Emer. Prof. of Education and ex-Dean of the School of Education (1966-80), dies at age 84. Miguel Mora, "Dr. Equinox," speaks in SUEC on "The Aztec Calendar." B. H. "Pete" Fairchild receives the $20,000 Arthur Rense Poetry Prize.

3 MAY 2002. Olympic skater Derek Parra speaks in SUEC on "From San Bernardino to Salt Lake 2002."

7 MAY 2002. Ex-Israeli soldier Yossi Khen and historian Mahmood Ibrahim speak in PR on "Is Peace Possible in the Middle East?" Actress and screenwriter Evalina Fernández speaks in SUEC about her film, *Luminarias*, which is also screened.

8 MAY 2002. A 30-acre brush fire erupts about 4:50 P.M. in a canyon north of the University.

9 MAY 2002. The campus is ranked 25th among the top 100 universities nationwide in granting degrees to Latinos by *Hispanic Outlook in Higher Education*.

11 MAY 2002. Historian Kent M. Schofield speaks at the 7th Annual Harry Rheubottom/George Webster Historical Lecture in the Pfau Library on "The Flood of 1938: San Bernardino City and Community." Carolyn Jefferson-Jenkins, Pres. of the League of Women Voters USA, speaks about the 2000 elections. The campus hosts its "Hearts and Minds: Diversity in Action Conference" in SUEC, with attorney Angela E. Oh giving the keynote address, and with performances by Ballet Folklórico and Living Voices. The Coyotes baseball team defeats UC Davis twice to win the Calif. Collegiate Athletic Assoc. Tournament.

14 MAY 2002. Olympic runner John Carlos speaks in LC on "Why? John Carlos—The Fastest Man Alive." Carolyn Jefferson-Jenkins speaks in SUEC on "Reforming the Electoral Process."

15 MAY 2002. Faculty member Kent Hayward screens his film, *Homestead Artifact*, in SUEC. Victoria A. Seitz receives a Fulbright Fellowship to lecture at the Univ. of Iaşi in Romania in 2002/03.

16 MAY 2002. Tony Whittaker speaks in SUEC on "Successes of the Disabled."

19 MAY 2002. Spanish attorney Joan Garcés speaks on campus. The campus inaugurates its chapter of the Golden Key International Honour Society in UC.

21 MAY 2002. The campus signs a dual admissions agreement between PDC and Coll. of the Desert.

23 MAY 2002. Tim Usher receives a $300,000 grant from NASA to produce computer models of high displacement actuators. Sue Greenfeld receives a 2nd Fulbright Fellowship to lecture at Marmara Univ. in Ankara,

Turkey. Rev. Gregory Boyle speaks in PS-10 on "Keeping 'Homeboys' Off the Streets."

28 MAY 2002. Tibetan nuns Chuye Kunsang and Passang Llamo speak in SUEC about their experiences in Drapchi Prison.

4 JUN. 2002. Holocaust survivor Elane Norych Geller speaks in SUEC.

5 JUN. 2002. The Ray Briggs Jazz Quartet performs in RH.

6 JUN. 2002. Ward M. McAfee receives the Avery O. Craven Award for the most original book on the Civil War Era, for his editing of Don Fehrenbacher's *The Slaveholding Republic*.

13 JUN. 2002. Cal State student Kent Devol Ruffino dies in a car accident in Riverside at age 19.

15-16 JUN. 2002. The 36th Commencement is held in the Arena and at PDC; speakers include Tribal Chairman of the San Manuel Band of Mission Indians Derón Márquez, Calif. Lt. Gov. Cruz Bustamante, CSU Chancellor Reed, ex-CSU Trustee Ali C. Razi, entertainment exec Peggy Van Pelt, Asst. Superintendent for Curriculum and Instruction of the S.B. Co. Schools Francisca Sánchez, Crafton Hills Coll. Pres. Gloria Macías Harrison, and Coll. of the Desert Pres. Maria Sheehan.

17 JUN. 2002. The Mary Stuart Rogers Gateway Building, the initial structure at the permanent PDC site at the corner of Cook St. and Frank Sinatra Dr., is officially occupied by faculty and staff.

19 JUN. 2002. The first classes are held at the Mary Stuart Rogers Gateway Building at PDC.

20 JUN. 2002. The campus hosts a conference, "Addressing the Needs of Older Workers in the 21st Century," in SUEC.

27 JUN. 2002. Holocaust survivor Leon Leyson speaks in LC as part of a week-long conference, "Education for Democracy: The Role of the Educator in the 21st Century" (24-28 Jun.).

SUM. 2002. Retirements: Gene L. Andrusco (1977-02), Assoc. Prof. of Accounting and Finance; Elliott R. Barkan, Prof. of History (1968-02); Gloria A. Cowan, Prof. of Psychology (1973-02); John M. Hatton, Dir. of the Student Health and Counseling Center and Assoc. Prof. of Psychology (1967-02); Ward M. McAfee, Prof. of History (1965-02); T. Patrick Mullen, Prof. of Education (1975-02); David H. Null, Assoc. Prof. of Health Science and Human Ecology (1977-02); Stuart Michael Persell

(1967-02), Prof. of History; Judith M. Rymer, Prof. of Education and ex-VP for Advancement (1970-02); Dr. Alvin M. Wolf, Prof. of Education (1975-02).

1 Jul. 2002. Martha P. Kazlo is named Dir. of the Student Health and Psychological Counseling Center, replacing John M. Hatton.

3 Jul. 2002. The campus is named by *Black Issues in Higher Education* the 62nd top university in the United States awarding bachelor's degrees to minorities.

10 Jul. 2002. The Latin Society performs on LCP.

16 Jul. 2002. Margaret R. Summers, retired Library Asst. (1968-01), dies at age 65.

17 Jul. 2002. The pop group The Notables performs on LCP.

23 Jul. 2002. Dr. Ross Leonard Ballard, retired Dir. of the Health Center (1979-91), dies at Reno, Nevada at age 85.

24 Jul. 2002. The jazz group Nightfire performs on LCP.

29 Jul. 2002. Sidney A. "Sid" Robinson is named Dir. of Public Affairs, replacing Cynthia E. "Cindi" Pringle, who is named Exec. Dir. and Manager of the new campus TV station, KCSB-TV (ICTN).

31 Jul. 2002. Bennie R. García, retired Custodian (1980-00), dies at age 62. The surf-rock group The Tornadoes performs on LCP.

16 Aug. 2002. The campus hosts Rep. Joe Baca's 10th Annual Women's Conference in the Commons, with UC Riverside Chancellor France A. Córdova giving the keynote address.

19 Aug. 2002. Robert Albert Smith, Emer. Prof. of History (1965-82), dies at age 84.

19-22 Aug. 2002. The campus hosts a 4-day workshop on Egyptian antiquities for 30 6th-grade students.

22 Aug. 2002. Arsonists start a 40-acre fire north of the campus.

26 Aug. 2002. The Learning Channel sends an Australian TV crew to campus to film booster and physician Dr. W. Benson Harer for a segment called "The Ancient E.R.," to be aired on 27 Feb. 2003 on The Learning Channel.

31 AUG. 2002. Janice Ropp "Jan" Jackson, Dean of Extended Learning (1982-02), retires.

1 SEPT. 2002. The campus creates a Univ. Transportation Center. Susan E. Summers, Assoc. Dean of Extended Learning, is named Int. Dean of the Coll. of Extended Learning, replacing Janice Ropp Jackson, who is named Assoc. VP for Executive Affairs, partially replacing Clifford O. Young Sr., Asst. to the President, who is named Exec. Asst. to the President for Governmental Relations.

3 SEPT. 2002. The S.B. City Planning Commission amends its Development Code and General Plan to allow construction of student apartments, University Village, at an 11¼-acre site on Northpark Blvd. across the street from the campus.

4 SEPT. 2002. The campus receives a $10,813 gift from Lois Lauer to establish an endowed scholarship.

10 SEPT. 2002. The Social and Behavioral Sciences Building opens for business when faculty and staff occupy their offices.

12 SEPT. 2002. At the annual convocation, Pres. Karnig states that the campus will have to find new ways of saving money: "We can't rely as heavily, as historically we have, and as historically public universities have, on public appropriations." Statewide budget trends suggest a gradually slowing in the economy, and a diminution of state support. He also notes the continued expansion of the campus's enrollment base, and increases in fundraising and grants, and indicates that more work needs to be done in these areas. He states that the decentralization of campus budgets to the divisions and departments has resulted in greater efficiencies as well as more local autonomy in budgeting. The campus is also working to institute a Ph.D. in Experimental Psychology, and an Ed.D. in Education, and to bring several new buildings on line.

17 SEPT. 2002. PDC opens its own bookstore in the Mary Stuart Rogers Gateway Building. The new $32.8 million campus apartment complex, Arrowhead Village, opens for business.

19 SEPT. 2002. Caltrans widens the off ramp at I-215 and University Parkway from 1 lane to 2 to allow better access to the campus.

23 SEPT. 2002. The campus hosts the Calif. Indian Cultural Awareness Conference.

26-27 SEPT. 2002. The campus hosts Calif. Native American Day, with a performance by the Yurok Brush Dancers, a keynote speech by State Sen.

Jack O'Connell, and speeches by Derón Márquez, Rep. Joe Baca, and S.B. Co. School Superintendent Herb Fischer.

30 SEPT. 2002. Juan Delgado receives the Hispanic Caucus Award from the National Humanities Assoc. for Higher Education. CSU Student Trustee Erene S. Thomas visits the campus.

1 OCT. 2002. Greg Weissman is named the first employee of the Inland California Television Network (ICTN) or KCSB-TV. Campus booster and ex-U.S. Ambassador to Great Britain Walter Hubert Annenberg dies in Philadelphia, Pennsylvania, at age 94.

2 OCT. 2002. Lavay Smith and her Red Hot Skillet Lickers perform in RH.

4 OCT. 2002. Dimitrios "James" Coussoulis, for whom the Arena is named, dies in Redlands at age 93.

5 OCT. 2002. A man is shot 4 times during an attempted robbery and carjacking in Parking Lot D.

7 OCT. 2002. Rep. C. Jerry Lewis addresses a town hall meeting in SUEC; S.B. Mayor Valles also speaks.

8 OCT. 2002. The Women's Center hosts a "Women's Work" show in SUEC and SUC for singers, musicians, dancers, writers, photographers, and artists.

11 OCT. 2002. Singer Skott Freeman speaks about "Bisexuality" in the Cross Cultural Center. The campus hosts the annual San Manuel "People of the Pines Pow Wow" on the athletic fields.

18 OCT. 2002. The campus receives a $50,000 grant from the U.S. Dept. of Agriculture to establish a Southwest Border Initiative Center to develop programs to improve the economy and quality of life for Hispanics and Native Americans in rural towns in Southern Calif. The campus hosts the 3rd Annual Inland Empire Women in Focus Empowerment Conference in the Commons, with Rudy García-Tolson and Anita Starks speaking.

22 OCT. 2002. The campus co-hosts Family Violence Prevention Day with Option House Inc. in SUEC, with Rose Ann Parker giving the keynote address.

23 OCT. 2002. "Little Rock Nine" civil rights activist Terrence Roberts speaks at the Diversity Awards Reception in UC. Janet Peterson speaks about "Breast Cancer" in SU.

30 OCT. 2002. Jeffrey M. Thompson receives the Golden Apple Award for teaching excellence for 2002/03. Rep. C. Jerry Lewis speaks at a town hall meeting to 300 students and faculty.

1 NOV. 2002. Henry F. "Hank" Kutak, Dir. of Financial Aid, resigns.

2 NOV. 2002. Lois Madsen, Assoc. Dir. of Financial Aid, is named Act. Dir. Cynthia Linton is named Dir. of the Learning Center for the 2nd time.

4 NOV. 2002. Author and radio commentator Saul Landau speaks in PS-10 on "Eyewitness from Iraq." The S.B. City Council approves the construction of a student apartment complex, University Village, across the street from the campus on Northpark Blvd.

5-6 NOV. 2002. Pulitzer Prize-winning photographer José Gálvez speaks in PR (Nov. 5) and in PiR (Nov. 6) on "The Mexican-American Experience in Los Angeles."

6 NOV. 2002. The Boxtales Theater Co. performs *Mytos y Cuentos* and *Waters of the Earth* in RH.

7 NOV. 2002. Elaine Haglund speaks in PiR on her experience with international teaching. Cal State student Jerry Anderson dies of a heart attack on campus at age 21.

8 NOV. 2002. WRI sponsors its 3rd Annual Conference, "Drought: Yesterday, Today, and Tomorrow."

13 NOV. 2002. Poet Reza Barahani speaks about Iran in SR.

15 NOV. 2002. Denis Roger Lichtman, Emer. Assoc. Prof. of Mathematics (1969-00), dies at age 72. Anthropologist Ian Tattersall speaks in SUEC on "Becoming Human."

18 NOV. 2002. Leslie M. Kong takes office as Pres. of the Calif. Library Assoc.

20 NOV. 2002. Assemblyman John Longville speaks at a peace rally on campus.

21 NOV. 2002. Ex-soldier Anthony Chivas speaks in SUEC on "Windtalkers: Navajos and World War II."

23 NOV. 2002. The campus hosts an "Activism Conference" in SUEC, with Rosa Martha Zarate Macías, Chani Beeman, and Sonali Kolhatkar giving the keynote addresses.

24 NOV. 2002. The Stars of the Moscow State Circus perform in the Arena.

30 NOV. 2002. The campus hosts the Inland Empire "Best of the Best" R&B Hip Hop Showcase in SUEC.

1 DEC. 2002. Arthur M. Butler, Dir. of Risk Management and Int. Dir. of Public Safety (1971-02), retires.

2 DEC. 2002. Patrick T. McDonald is named Dir. of Public Safety and Chief of Police, replacing Arthur M. Butler.

4 DEC. 2002. Guitarist Stuart Green performs in RH.

7 DEC. 2002. The 2nd Winter Commencement is held in the Arena and at PDC, with ex-White House Chief of Staff Leon E. Panetta giving the keynote address.

12 DEC. 2002. The classic rock band Styx performs in the Arena.

13 DEC. 2002. The campus hosts the radio station KCXX-FM X-Mas Fest in the Arena, featuring the groups Adema, The Kottonmouth Kings, Bemus and Hollow, and 8STOP7.

13-14 DEC. 2002. The Inland Empire Symphonic Choir performs in RH.

18 DEC. 2002. Sant Khalsa receives the $10,000 Betty and Jim Kasson Center Award for her photography.

31 DEC. 2002. Lynda McNamara, Assoc. VP for Univ. Advancement, resigns.

2003

1 JAN. 2003. The Pfau Library closes its paper card shelf list.

8 JAN. 2003. The Inland Percussion Group performs in RH.

15 JAN. 2003. Pop band Same Way Again performs in SU Lounge.

16 JAN. 2003. Philosopher Alvin Plantinga speaks in RH on "Is Evolution Compatible with Design?" and also in University Hall. State Superintendent of Public Education Jack O'Connell speaks in SUEC to 300 local educators.

21 JAN. 2003. Groundbreaking is held for the Indian Wells Center for Excellence at PDC, with ex-Indian Wells Mayor Richard R. Oliphant, Indian Wells Mayor Rob Bernheimer, and Betty Barker participating. The S.B. City Council approves a new CSUSB access road, Campus Pkwy. (formerly Pepper Linden Dr.), from Kendall Dr. to Northpark Blvd. Amro Albanno speaks on "Life after CSUSB: A Graduate's Entrepreneurial Success Story" in PiR.

22 JAN. 2003. The campus hosts a forum, "Celebrating Our Right to Choose and Securing a Future with Choice," in SUEC, on the anniversary of the Roe v. Wade ruling of the U.S. Supreme Court, with Rep. Joe Baca, Elizabeth Sánchez, S.B. City Councilwoman Susan K. Lien Longville, Rialto City Councilman Kurt Wilson, and Sarah Palacios participating.

24 JAN. 2003. A Cal State student and his brother are arrested and charged with the murder and dismemberment of their mother.

25 JAN. 2003. Janice Ropp "Jan" Jackson, Assoc. VP for Executive Affairs (2002-03), resigns.

26 JAN. 2003. Howard S. Wang, Assoc. VP for Student Affairs, resigns.

27 JAN. 2003. Helga E. Kray, Dir. of the Student Union, is also named Act. Asst. VP of Student Affairs and Student Development.

28 JAN. 2003. Construction begins on the Indian Wells Center for Educational Excellence at PDC.

1 FEB. 2003. Pres. Karnig receives the 2003 Vision of Hope Award from the S.B. Catholic Diocese.

5 FEB. 2003. CSU Trustee Roberta Achtenberg visits the campus. The band Alma Melodiosa performs in SU. The Lula Washington Dance Theatre performs in RH.

6 FEB. 2003. Mike Tracey is named Int. Assoc. VP for Development.

6-7 FEB. 2003. The campus hosts a Web-Based Learning Conference at the Crowne Plaza Hotel, Redondo Beach.

8 FEB. 2003. Lois B. Krieger receives the 2nd Annual WRI Lifetime Achievement Award at a banquet in UC, which also raises $60,000 in scholarship funds. The campus receives a $25,000 gift from Stater Bros. Markets and Pepsi to support scholarships.

10 FEB. 2003. Poet Gary Young reads from his work in PiR.

11 Feb. 2003. Olympic medalist John Carlos speaks in SUEC.

16 Feb. 2003. Polyhedrist Joyce Frost speaks in UC on "Puzzles and Play for Art and Math."

19 Feb. 2003. Psychologist Mihály Csíkszentmihályi speaks in SUEC.

21 Feb. 2003. Fred E. Jandt is named Outstanding Professor for 2002/03.

23 Feb. 2003. The Harlem Globetrotters perform in the Arena.

24 Feb. 2003. James Sando is named Exec. Dir. of the Foundation at CSUSB.

25 Feb. 2003. Rev. Dennis Brown performs as "Martin Luther King, Jr." in SUEC.

26 Feb. 2003. B. H. "Pete" Fairchild receives both the National Book Critics Circle Award for Poetry for *Early Occult Memory Systems of the Lower Midwest*, and (in April) a Gold Medal from the California Book Awards. Journalist Bill Kahrl speaks in SUEC on "The Santa Ana Watershed."

27 Feb. 2003. The campus receives a $25,000 gift from the Palm Desert National Bank to fund a conference room at PDC.

28 Feb. 2003. Alumna Celeste Soderberry speaks in SUEC about serving in the Peace Corps as part of Peace Corps Day.

1 Mar. 2003. The men's basketball team wins its 21st consecutive victory, setting a new school record.

3 Mar. 2003. Pres. Karnig approves granting the title "Emeritus" to non-academic retired administrators who meet certain qualifications.

5 Mar. 2003. Cellist Ana María Maldonado performs with pianist Kris Carlisle in RH.

6 Mar. 2003. Alexandria LaFaye reads from her novels in PR. Donald A. Driftmeier receives the annual Arrowhead Distinguished Executive Officer Award at a banquet in SUEC.

8 Mar. 2003. The campus hosts the U.S.A. Cheerleading Competition in the Arena. The campus hosts the symposium, "Gather the Women: Envisioning the Future—Now!" in University Hall, with S.B. City Councilwoman Susan Lien-Longville giving the keynote speech.

19 Mar. 2003. The campus's California Council on Economic Education receives a $25,000 grant from the Bank of America to expand the existing program, "Choices and Changes." Lois Madsen, Act. Dir. of Financial Aid, is named permanent Dir.

29 Mar. 2003. Gil Navarro speaks at the 19th Annual Inland Empire Future Leaders Program Reunion in SUEC on "How to Be an Advocate for Your Child."

31 Mar. 2003. The campus closes for the first time to observe César Chávez Day.

2 Apr. 2003. Saxophonist Jeff Clayton performs in RH. Lydia Ortega, Dir. of Records, Registration, and Evaluation (1999-2003), is named Act. Dir. of Housing and Residential Services.

5 Apr. 2003. H(orace) Stephen "Steve" Prouty Jr., retired Assoc. Dean for Academic Services (1964-91), dies in Riverside of brain cancer at age 73.

7 Apr. 2003. The campus receives a $3 million gift from the San Manuel Band of Mission Indians to fund an expansion of the SU.

8 Apr. 2003. Rabbi Douglas Kohn, Rev. James Huffstutler, and Imam Yahya Abdul Rahman speak at the 16th Annual Morrow-McCombs Lecture, "What You Need to Know About Me and My Religion: Jewish, Christian, and Muslim Responses," at the First Presbyterian Church of S.B.

9 Apr. 2003. Robert A. Blackey becomes the 2nd Cal State recipient of the $20,000 Wang Family Excellence Award.

10 Apr. 2003. A ribbon-cutting ceremony marks the official opening of the Coll. of Social and Behavioral Sciences Building, with the attendance of former Dean Aubrey W. Bonnett; 25 demonstrators protest the event, alleging racism, sexism, and homophobia.

14-20 Apr. 2003. Cal State's Model United Nations Team wins its 8th consecutive "Outstanding Delegation Award" in the national competition held in New York City; the team represented Turkey.

17 Apr. 2003. Ex-Housing and Urban Development Secretary Henry Cisneros speaks in the Commons at the 1st Annual International Conference on Latin American Studies, "Redefining Latin American Identity in the 21st Century"; other speakers include Cuban poet Nancy Morejón and Raymond Williams.

18 Apr. 2003. Susan K. Lien Longville is named Assoc. Dir. of the WRI.

Guitarist Jesús Saiz Huedo performs in RH.

23 APR. 2003. Zeta Phi Beta Sorority, the SU Program Board, and ASI co-sponsor the 1st Annual CSUSB Talent Show in SUEC. Art critic Dave Hickey speaks in VA-101 on "The Role and Importance of Arts and Culture in a Democracy."

23-25 APR. 2003. The College of Extended Learning and the Division of Information Resources and Technology host the 1st Annual Secure IT Conference at the Pechanga Resort and Casino, Temecula.

24 APR. 2003. Historian Henry V. Jaffa speaks on "The Statesmanship of Abraham Lincoln."

26 APR. 2003. The campus hosts its 17th Annual Environment Expo in the Arena, featuring environmental magician Paul Cash; as part of the event, thousands of individuals form a giant image of the world and spell out the word "LOVE" on the Library Lawn.

2-4 MAY 2003. The campus hosts the State Debate Competition.

3 MAY 2003. Nicholas Cataldo speaks at the 8th Annual Harry Rheubottom/George Webster Historical Lecture in the Pfau Library on "Wyatt Earp: The Earp Clan in San Bernardino County."

5 MAY 2003. The Terremoto Latin Jazz Band performs in SU Courtyard, as part of the Cinco de Mayo celebration.

7 MAY 2003. The Magical Moonshine Theatre performs its puppetry magic in RH.

8 MAY 2003. Calif. State Secretary of Resources Mary Nichols speaks at the Water Resources Institute.

11 MAY 2003. The campus hosts its 11th Annual Women's Conference, "Local to Global: Everything You Need to Know About Women's Issues Today," in UC, with host Rep. Joe Baca, and Ramona Ripston giving the keynote address.

12 MAY 2003. Erlinda Alburo speaks in SR on "Women's Literature and Philippine Society."

13 MAY 2003. Poet Alix Olson performs with musician Pamela Means on the SU Courtyard.

14 MAY 2003. The CSU Board of Trustees renames the Student Union as the Santos Manuel Student Union.

15 MAY 2003. The campus receives a $100,000 gift from Verizon to better serve disabled students. Actress Geri Jewell speaks as part of the Access 2003 Expo in SUEC on disabilities. Larry K. Gaines receives a $35,751 grant from the S.B. Co. Probation Dept. to evaluate an intervention and management accountability program.

22 MAY 2003. Chris Chippindale speaks in UH-106 on "Art and Science in Aboriginal Australia."

30 MAY 2003. Comedian Mike Robles performs in SUEC.

2 JUN. 2003. The campus hosts a reception to honor the $3 million gift from the San Manuel Band of Mission Indians to help expand the SU (now renamed the Santos Manuel Student Union), with the attendance of Tribal Chairman Derón Márquez.

3 JUN. 2003. The campus receives a $206,124 grant from the Calif. Dept. of Transportation (Caltrans) to develop and implement an inventory method for 15,000 highway barriers.

5 JUN. 2003. The campus hosts the "60/91/215 Procurement Conference" in SUEC, co-sponsored by the Calif. Dept. of Transportation and the Inland Empire Center for Entrepreneurship.

13-15 JUN. 2003. The 37th Commencement is held in the Arena and at PDC, with Rep. Joe Baca, Assemblyman John J. Benoit, and Calif. Superintendent of Public Instruction Jack O'Connell giving the keynote addresses.

25 JUN. 2003. The Australian band The Waifs perform on LCP.

26 JUN. 2003. The campus hosts its 1st Transportation Marketplace Conference with the U.S. Dept. of Transportation at the Ontario Convention Center.

SUM. 2003. Retirements: Edward J. Bostley, Prof. of Music (1988-03); John S. Chaney, Prof. of Management (1972-03); Sherry M. Howie, Prof. of Education (1987-03); Julius D. Kaplan, Prof. of Art and Dean of Graduate Studies (1977-03); Steven M. Mintz, Prof. of Accounting and Finance and ex-Dean of the Coll. of Business and Public Administration (1996-03); Joseph R. Moran, Prof. of Art (1972-03); L. Theron Pace, Counselor and Coordinator of Special Programs and Services, Services to Students with Disabilities (1969-03); Elinore H. Partridge, Assoc. Prof. of English (1981-03); Peter R. Schroeder, Prof. of English (1967-03); Thomas C.

Timmreck, Prof. of Health Science and Human Ecology (1985-03); Michael E. Trubnick, Assoc. Prof. of Accounting and Finance (1982-03).

2 JUL. 2003. Beatles tribute band BackBeat performs on LCP.

9 JUL. 2003. The blues and reggae group Gregg Young and the Second Street Band performs on LCP.

16 JUL. 2003. Laura Young is named a Fellow in the U.S. Dept. of Agriculture's Hispanic-Serving Institutions Fellows Program. The Latin Society performs on LCP.

23 JUL. 2003. Marcia Luna Raines receives the Bautzer Faculty University Advancement Award.

30 JUL. 2003. Andre Arthur Maurel, retired Chief of Plant Operations (1965-78), dies at age 88.

13 AUG. 2003. Due to budget cuts, the campus halts all new student admissions for 2003/04.

28 AUG. 2003. The campus signs a dual admissions agreement with S.B. Valley Coll.

31 AUG. 2003. Peter A. Wilson, Dean of PDC, resigns to take a position with the Contra Costa Campus of CSU Hayward.

1 SEPT. 2003. Fred E. Jandt is named Int. Dean of PDC, replacing Peter A. Wilson. Fees for CSU students increase by 30%.

15 SEPT. 2003. Gordon L. Patzer, Prof. of Accounting and Finance and Dean of the Coll. of Business and Public Administration, retires to take a position at Roosevelt University.

16 SEPT. 2003. Norton E. Marks is named Int. Dean of the Coll. of Business and Public Administration, replacing Gordon L. Patzer.

18 SEPT. 2003. At the annual convocation, Pres. Karnig states, "Even given the budget problems, we're in good shape." Among the goals for 2003/04 is the creation of an ombudsman system, and renewing the five-year strategic plan. The campus, he says, set a new fund-raising record in 2002/03 with $11.6 million in gifts, plus $24 million in federal grants and contracts. "We need to keep on trucking: that's what we need to do."

23 SEPT. 2003. Groundbreaking is held for the Chemical Sciences Building.

25 SEPT. 2003. Arthur Edward Nelson, Emer. Libn., founding Coll. Libn., and Library Dir. (1963-91), dies of a series of strokes at age 76; a bibliophile and student of history, he was responsible for building a remarkable collection of books and other materials, and for designing the original Pfau Library Building.

26 SEPT. 2003. The campus hosts Native American Day.

27 SEPT. 2003. The campus hosts a "Today's Woman Inside/Out Conference" in UC, with S.B. Mayor Valles, author William R. Kellas, and Felice Willat giving the keynote addresses.

1 OCT. 2003. Masters of Harmony performs in RH.

6 OCT. 2003. *The Coyote Chronicle* increases its size to bedsheet format, and adds color to its pages for the first time.

9 OCT. 2003. Indian filmmaker Pankaj Rishi Kumar speaks in RH and screens several of his documentaries.

10-12 OCT. 2003. The campus hosts its 5th Annual Pow Wow of the San Manuel Band of Mission Indians on the old soccer field.

12 OCT. 2003. Pop bands 311 and Alien Ant Farm perform in the Arena.

17 OCT. 2003. The campus receives a $200,000 grant from the U.S. Dept. of Agriculture to help disadvantaged farmers.

17-18 OCT. 2003. The campus hosts its 4th Annual Women in Focus Forum in the Commons, with the participation of Letitia Wright, Amy Donovan, poet Dameon Wroe, and Anita Starks.

23 OCT. 2003. 28 alumni return to CSUSB as "Professors for a Day," including Assemblyman Russell Bogh, retired S.B. Co. Superior Court Judge Stanley Hough, filmmaker Paul J. DeMeo, and psychologist Frank Zizzo.

24 OCT. 2003. Rep. Joe Baca speaks at his Annual Economic Summit, "The Economics of Contracting with the Inland Empire," in UC, with UC Regents Velma Montoya and Monica Lozano, and Michael Bazdarich and Gary Zimmerman participating.

25 OCT. 2003. The Old Fire is set by arsonists in Waterman Canyon, and threatens the campus before burning towards Devore, into northern San Bernardino City, and into the S.B. Mountains. This is the largest and most dangerous firestorm to hit the campus since the Panorama Fire of Nov.

1980. The campus closes through Oct. 28, canceling all scheduled events. The temporary Recreation Center and a temporary office building (TC-28) are damaged, and one temporary classroom building (TC 13-18) north of the Library is destroyed; all are repaired or replaced within months. A number of faculty, staff, and students lose their homes, among them Bonnie L. Petry.

29 OCT. 2003. Prof. Susan E. Meisenhelder, ex-Pres. of the Calif. Faculty Assoc., is appointed to the CSU Board of Trustees by Gov. Davis, who is forced to withdraw her nomination on Nov. 5. The campus reopens after being closed since Oct. 25 for the Old Fire.

31 OCT. 2003. Herbert Brunkhorst is named a Fellow of the American Assoc. for the Advancement of Science.

4 NOV. 2003. Poet Lisa Steinman reads from her work in UH.

5 NOV. 2003. Guitarists Eric Cabalo and Stuart Green perform in RH.

5-6 NOV. 2003. The campus hosts a Symposium on the Middle East with Gazi University (Ankara, Turkey), in RH.

7-9 NOV. 2003. The campus hosts a Peace Symposium in SUEC with "Peace Troubadour" James Twyman and Pamela Pierce.

10 NOV. 2003. The Inland California Television Network (ICTN), KCSB-TV, broadcasts its first local news report, with co-anchors Greg Weissman and Tina Patel, weather forecaster Melissa Chávez, and sportscaster Terry McEachern.

13 NOV. 2003. Rodger Bybee speaks in SUEC on technology and literacy.

17 NOV. 2003. Gov. Davis is recalled by the voters, and actor Arnold Schwarzenegger takes his place.

18 NOV. 2003. The campus opens the Women's Business Center in downtown San Bernardino, partnering with the Inland Empire Center for Entrepreneurship, the Arrowhead Credit Union, and the U.S. Small Business Administration. Lanny B. Fields receives the Golden Apple Award for teaching excellence for 2003/04.

19 NOV. 2003. Screenwriter and producer Art Monterastelli speaks in PiR and also to an English class.

21 NOV. 2002. Rep. Joe Baca sponsors his Annual Education Summit, "Educational Excellence for All Students," in UC.

24-25 NOV. 2002. The campus hosts a Seminar on Criminal Justice and Anti-Terrorism in YC, with 25 Chinese officials attending.

25 NOV. 2002. The University Diversity Committee presents the play *Faces of America* in SUEC.

1 DEC. 2003. The Inland California Television Network (ICTN), or KCSB-TV, begins broadcasting its first news reports on local Channel 24 (KVCR-TV) in S.B.

4-6 DEC. 2003. The campus hosts the NCAA Division II National Women's Volleyball Tournament in the Arena, but the CSUSB team loses its semifinal match.

12 DEC. 2003. The campus honors ex-Pres. Pfau and wife Antreen Pfau at a reception at the Fullerton Art Museum as part of the Pioneer Alumni celebration.

13 DEC. 2003. The 3rd Winter Commencement is held in the Arena and at PDC, for the first time in 2 sessions (morning and afternoon), with Nicholas J. Coussoulis giving the keynote morning address.

14 DEC. 2003. The campus honors 200 firefighters and law enforcement personnel who helped save the University from the Old Fire on Oct. 25, with Rep. C. Jerry Lewis and Rep. Joe Baca attending.

19 DEC. 2003. The campus signs a dual-admission agreement with Palo Verde Coll.

21 DEC. 2003. The campus is named one of the "Publisher's Picks for 2003" by *Hispanic Outlook in Education Magazine*.

31 DEC. 2003. Rachel Adame Martínez, Library Asst. (1985-03), retires.

2004

4 JAN. 2004. The campus opens a modular classroom (TC 13-18) north of the Pfau Library to replace the one that burned in the Old Fire. The campus receives a $100,000 grant from Watson & Assocs. to fund the Watson Literacy Center, plus a $105,000 gift from Charles D. "Chuck" Obershaw to help endow the Obershaw Scholarship Fund.

7 JAN. 2004. The 562nd Air Force Band Dixieland Jazz Ensemble performs in RH.

9 JAN. 2004. Linda R. Evans, retired Library Asst. (1963-88), dies at age

79.

11 JAN. 2004. The campus renames the University Theatre as the Ronald E. Barnes Theatre in honor of the Emeritus Prof. who also served as the first Chair of the Theatre Arts Dept.

14 JAN. 2004. Actor Wilson Cruz speaks on campus.

17 JAN. 2004. The campus hosts a "Celebration of Languages and Cultures," with S.B. Mayor Valles giving the keynote address.

21 JAN. 2004. Psychologist Joan Rodman speaks in SUEC on "Writer's Block."

22 JAN. 2004. The campus co-sponsors (with King Saud University, Riyadh, Saudi Arabia) a conference in SUEC on "U.S.-Saudi Arabia Relations," with James Noyes, Khalil al-Khalil, and Thomas W. Lippman speaking. The Fly Dance Co. performs in RH.

28 JAN. 2004. Alumnus Sundip Doshi speaks in PiR on "Starting and Growing a Technology Company."

29 JAN. 2004. Scott L. Fedick speaks at PDC on "Ancient Mayan Relationships with Rain Forests: Implications for Modern Conservation."

31 JAN. 2004. The campus hosts its 2nd Annual Activism Conference in SUEC.

4 FEB. 2004. Clarinetists Jon Usher and Ana María Maldonado, and pianist Kris Carlisle perform in RH.

7 FEB. 2004. The campus hosts its 2nd Annual Gear Up Inland Empire Leadership Institute in SUEC, with Terrence "Little Rock Nine" Roberts speaking on "What It Means to Be a Leader."

9 FEB. 2004. Clifford O. Young Sr., Exec. Asst. to the President for Governmental Relations, is named Int. Supervisor of the 5th Dist. of the S.B. Co. Board of Supervisors to complete the term of Gerald Eaves.

10-15 FEB. 2004. The campus hosts the Region VIII Kennedy Center/American College Theatre Festival at the Calif. Theater of the Performing Arts, San Bernardino.

11 FEB. 2004. A student is arrested for shouting Nazi slogans at a Holocaust survivor speaking to a class in Chaparral Hall.

12 FEB. 2004. Romeo Ramírez and Bryan Payne speak on campus about the exploitation of American workers. The campus receives an $845,274 grant from the Calif. Postsecondary Education Commission to help train science teachers from the Coachella Valley.

13 FEB. 2004. Calif. Environmental Protection Agency Chief Terry Tamminen speaks in PiR on "State Water Issues."

18 FEB. 2004. Joyce Hanson speaks in SUEC on "Elaine Brown and the Black Panthers." In the first Mr. and Mrs. CSUSB Pageant, held in SUEC, Luis Martínez and Amanda Lindholm take top honors, with all their fees paid for Spring Quarter.

23 FEB. 2004. Richard F. Fehn is named Outstanding Professor for 2003/04. Richard M. Eberst receives the 8th Annual Ernest A. Lynton Award for Faculty Service and Academic Outreach from the New England Center for Higher Education, and also the Thomas Ehrlich Faculty Award for Serving Learning.

25 FEB. 2004. An all-CSUSB produced film, *Central Enforcement*, premieres in SUEC. Alan S. Kaufman speaks in SUEC on "IQ and Controversy: What Is the Role of Heredity and What Happens to Our Intelligence as We Age?"

26-28 FEB. 2004. The campus team wins a 14th consecutive "Outstanding Delegation" Award at the Model League of Arab States competition, Denver, Colorado, representing United Arab Emirates.

27 FEB. 2004. The men's basketball team wins a record-setting 22nd straight game, but loses its next.

1 MAR. 2004. During a special convocation, Pres. Karnig announces that CSUSB will cut enrollment by 1,000 students in Fall term in response to the state budget crisis, saving $13.3 million. "Anyone who has been around public education has been through this part of the roller-coaster ride in the past," he says. "Right now the budget is going through one of its valleys, but we expect it will rise again."

3 MAR. 2004. The eclectic vocal ensemble Zephyr-Voices Unbound performs in RH.

4 MAR. 2004. Xinyan Jiang speaks in PL-4005 on "Understanding Taoism." The campus signs an agreement with the Central City Lutheran Mission to provide services to the disadvantaged in S.B.

8 MAR. 2004. The campus receives a maximum 10-year accreditation from

Western Assoc. of Schools and Colleges.

11 MAR. 2004. Robert J. Sternberg speaks in SUEC on "A Model for Developing Leadership."

12-15 MAR. 2004. The campus hosts the NCAA Division II Western Regional Men's Basketball Tournament in the Arena.

13 MAR. 2004. The campus hosts its 2nd Annual Women's Conference, "Gather the Women: Weaving a World That Works," in SM SUEC. L.A. City Councilman and ex-Police Chief Bernard C. Parks gives the keynote speech at the Classic Upward Bound Program at the Radisson Hotel, S.B.

18-20 MAR. 2004. The campus and the U.S. Holocaust Memorial Museum host a forum, "Teaching About the Holocaust," in UC.

22 MAR. 2004. WRI hosts "Fire and Rain: A Forum on Flooding Hazards Following the California Wildfires" in SUEC.

29 MAR. 2004. Alemayehu G. "Al" Mariam is named Exec. Asst. to the Pres., replacing Clifford O. Young Sr.

1 APR. 2004. The campus hosts 11 scholars from Gazi University, Ankara, Turkey. Clifford O. Young Sr., Exec. Asst. to the Pres. for Government Relations (1999-04), resigns.

1-2 APR. 2004. The campus hosts a conference, "Understanding the Middle East: Perspectives on Politics, Culture, and History," in RH, with ex-U.S. Ambassador to Iraq Edward L. Peck and ex-U.S. Ambassador to Pakistan Tom Simmons giving the keynote addresses.

5 APR. 2004. Helga E. Kray, Act. Asst. VP for Student Affairs and Student Development and Dir. of the Santos Manuel Student Union, is named permanent Asst. VP; Mark K. Day, Assoc. Dir. of the Santos Manuel Student Union, is named Act. Dir.

6 APR. 2004. A non-student is arrested in Tokay Dorm for assault with a deadly weapon.

6-10 APR. 2004. The campus's Model United Nations Team wins an Outstanding Delegation Award for the 9th year in a row in New York City, representing the country of Yemen.

7 APR. 2004. The Boston Brass performs in RH.

9 APR. 2004. James R. Gooch, Duplicating Center Manager (Aug. 1965-

04), retires with 38+ years of service, being the campus's longest-serving staff person to date.

14 APR. 2004. Bruce Varner receives the Annual Arrowhead Distinguished Executive Officer Award in UC.

17 APR. 2004. John Brudin receives the 3rd Annual WRI Lifetime Achievement Award in UC.

18 APR. 2004. Terri Nelson receives the 2004 Outstanding Teacher Award from the Calif. Language Teachers Assoc.

22 APR. 2004. Writer Luis J. Rodríguez speaks about his life as a ex-gang member in PiR, as part of the 2nd Annual Latin American Roundtable.

23 APR. 2004. Astronomer Anneila Sargent speaks in SUEC on "Protoplanetary Disks—Clues to Our Origins?" The campus is ranked in the top 100 of the most successful entrepreneurship programs in the country by *Entrepreneur Magazine*. Producer Woodie King Jr. speaks in the Barnes Theatre.

24 APR. 2004. The campus hosts its 18th Annual Environment Expo, "Making a Wise Investment in Earth's Future," in the Arena, with magicians Paul Cash and Jon Sherman, and pop group Hobo-Jazz performing.

28 APR. 2004. The Upper Commons dining area is renamed the Charles and Shelby Obershaw Dining Room to honor the couple's generous donations to the University. The campus receives a 2nd $100,000 grant from the Bernard Osher Foundation to fund courses at PDC for retired persons in the Coachella Valley.

30 APR. 2004. Writers Susan and Stephen Perry speak in VA-101 on "Telling the Truth: Writing in the Flow: Using Your Own and Other's Stories."

1-2 MAY 2004. The Stars of the Moscow State Circus perform in the Arena.

5 MAY 2004. Deborah Prutsman performs in RH.

6 MAY 2004. Judith "Jack" Halberstam speaks on covert messages hidden within the mass media.

8 MAY 2004. Pauline Ormego Murillo and Clifford Tavser speak at the 9th Annual Harry Rheubottom/George Webster Historical Lecture in the Pfau Library on "San Manuel Band of Indians: History and Heritage."

12 May 2004. George Grose speaks at the 17th Annual Morrow-McCombs Memorial Lecture at Congregation Emanu El in San Bernardino on "The Abraham Connection: A Jew, Christian, and Muslim in Dialogue," with the participation of Rabbi Hillel Cohn and Mustafa Kuku.

13 May 2004. Comedian Fred Burns speaks in SUEC.

14 May 2004. 200 faculty and students rally to protest budget cuts.

15 May 2004. World Wrestling Entertainment performs in the Arena.

17 May 2004. Dorothy C. Chen-Maynard is named an Outstanding Dietetics Educator by the American Dietetics Assoc.

20 May 2004. The campus hosts its 11th Annual World Trade Conference, with Robert Bowen, John O'Doherty, and Fred Latuperissa.

21 May 2004. Comedians Freddy Soto and Jeff García perform in SUEC.

28 May 2004. As part of Memorial Day celebrations, vintage World War II aircraft fly over the campus.

5 Jun. 2004. Ronald Wilson Reagan, ex-Gov. of California and ex-Pres. of the United States, dies at age 93.

11-13 Jun. 2004. The 38th Commencement is held in the Arena and at PDC, with Larry R. Sharp, Florentino Garza, Richard F. Fehn, Patrick Ainsworth, and Michael Landes giving the keynote addresses.

14 Jun. 2004. The campus approves a new M.A. degree in Spanish, effective with Winter 2005.

15 Jun. 2004. Construction begins on the renovation and expansion of the Santos Manuel Student Union building.

Sum. 2004. Retirements: Cynthia J. Bird, Prof. of Accounting and Finance (1989-04); C. Charles Christie Jr., Prof. of Public Administration (1972-04); Esteban R. Díaz, Prof. of Education (1987-04); Richard M. Eberst, Prof. of Health Science and Human Ecology (1991-04); Stuart R. Ellins, Prof. of Psychology (1973-04); Lanny B. Fields, Prof. of History (1985-04); Loren H. Filbeck, Prof. of Music (1972-04); Bruce Golden, Prof. of English (1965-04), at 39 years the campus's longest-serving faculty and staff member to date; Linvol G. Henry, Prof. of Accounting and Finance (1985-04); Irvin Howard, Prof. of Education (1981-04); Kenneth M. Johns, Prof. of Education (1985-04); Ellen L. Kronowitz, Prof. of Education (1978-04); Kevin G. Lamude, Prof. of Communication Studies (1991-

04); Michael C. LeMay, Prof. of Political Science (1992-04); Carolyn A. Martin, Prof. of Kinesiology (1974-04); Thomas M. Meisenhelder, Prof. of Sociology (1975-04); Jerrold E. Pritchard, Prof. of Music and Assoc. Provost for Academic Programs (1983-04); John A. Scribner, Prof. of Accounting and Finance (1978-04); Hossein Shalchi, Prof. of Accounting and Finance (1989-04); Robert G. Stein, Prof. of Mathematics (1967-04); J. Brian Watts, Prof. of Public Administration (1989-04); L. Curtis Westbrook Jr., Prof. of Accounting and Finance (1989-04).

1 JUL. 2004. Jennifer J. "Jenny" Zorn is named Assoc. Provost for Academic Programs, replacing Jerrold E. Pritchard.

5 JUL. 2004. Cal State graduate Education student Barbara Ann Schnabel dies of cancer at Cherry Valley at age 41.

7 JUL. 2004. Friendz Band and the Phat Cat Swingers perform on LCP.

8 JUL. 2004. Cal State student Corey Jackson is named by Gov. Schwarzenegger to the CSU Board of Trustees.

14 JUL. 2004. The Latin Society performs on LCP.

18 JUL. 2004. Pres. Karnig is hospitalized for colitis, and undergoes surgery on Aug. 27.

21 JUL. 2004. Desperado performs on LCP.

24 JUL. 2004. David R. Bourquin, Libn. (1982-04), retires.

28 JUL. 2004. The surfing group Tornadoes performs on LCP.

31 JUL. 2004. Maria Titus, Secretary to the Univ. Libn. (1988-04), retires. Norton E. Marks, Int. Dean of the Coll. of Business and Public Administration, returns to the ranks as Prof. of Marketing.

1 AUG. 2004. Karen D. Dill Bowerman is named Dean of the Coll. of Business and Public Administration, replacing Norton E. Marks.

1-3 AUG. 2004. PDC hosts the annual Pacific and Asian Communication Assoc. conference, "Cultural Transformation and Convergence: East and West."

4-5 AUG. 2004. PDC hosts the annual Listening Assoc. Conference.

6-7 AUG. 2004. PDC hosts the annual World Communication Assoc. conference, "Culture, Self, and Communication: Teaching, Research, and

Practice."

17 AUG. 2004. The state cuts $6.6 million from CSUSB's budget.

24 AUG. 2004. The campus receives a $600,000 challenge grant from the W. M. Keck Foundation to help build an astronomical observatory on Badger Hill.

27 AUG. 2004. Campus employees Tony Simpson, Paul Frazier, Richard Hebert, Patrick Rogers, Joseph Hubbard, Phil Westbrook, Louis Cain, and James Boothe receive the Governor's State Employee Safety Award from Gov. Schwarzenegger for their firefighting actions during the Oct. 2003 Old Fire.

1 SEPT. 2004. The campus begins offering a B.S. degree in Nursing for registered nurses.

7 SEPT. 2004. The campus opens a Center for Alternative Media.

14 SEPT. 2004. The campus receives a $5,000 gift from the Agua Caliente Band of Cahuilla Indians to help fund the Palm Desert Health Sciences Building at PDC.

19 SEPT. 2004. The 480-unit University Village residence apartment complex, owned by a private company, opens on Northpark Blvd.

20 SEPT. 2004. Pres. Karnig returns to work following surgery, and addresses the annual convocation. He notes that the Facilities Services Volunteer Fire Response Team was honored with the 2003 State Employee Safety Award for its work in October 2003 Old Fire. He reminds attendees that education plays a crucial role in society: "Education is the single most powerful engine for change that exists today. Our role is vital." He also announces the creation of a $250,000 Presidential Investment Fund to assist funding projects, and notes numerous buildings either under construction or undergoing renovation, including the first two parking structures, renovations to the Biological and Physical Sciences Buildings, the Off. of Technology Transfer and Commercialization Building, the College of Education Building, a Student Recreation and Fitness Center, the second building at PDC, an apartment-style student housing, the Chemical Sciences Building, the Santos Manuel Student Union expansion; also planned is a new street—Campus Dr.—connecting Kendall Dr. and Northpark Blvd. He states that the campus raised $18 million in grants during 2003/04, a new record, but that the University faces continued economic challenges in the years to come, as state support continues to decline, with a loss of $6.7 million projected for 2004/05. He notes the rare 10-year accreditation of the University by WASC, and states that one of their recommendations—the creation of an Ombudsperson, is being implemented.

21-24 SEPT. 2004. The campus hosts the Calif. Indian Cultural Awareness Conference, featuring James Ramos, Dir. of the San Manuel Tribal Unity and Cultural Awareness Program; Rep. Joe Baca; Arturo Delgado, Superintendent of the S.B. City Unified School Dist.; Herbert R. Fischer, Superintendent of the S.B. Co. Schools; and S.B. Mayor Valles.

23 SEPT. 2004. The campus receives a 2nd $100,000 gift from Watson & Associates to help fund the Watson Literacy Center. Construction begins on the Santos Manuel Student Union renovation and expansion.

24 SEPT. 2004. The campus hosts its 3rd Annual California Native American Day celebration on LCP.

28 SEPT. 2004. The Office of Public Affairs unveils a new website with current and updated news about the campus.

1 OCT. 2004. With the help of donations, the campus purchases the 2,500-year-old coffin lid of Egyptian mummy Neter Heneb for the Fullerton Art Museum.

6 OCT. 2004. The campus receives a $296,354 grant from the U.S. Dept. of Agriculture to recruit bilingual students in environmental health, under the direction of Lal Mian. Incendio performs in RH.

8 OCT. 2004. Groundbreaking is held for the new Santos Manuel Student Union Building renovation and expansion.

8-10 OCT. 2004. The campus hosts its 3rd Annual Pow Wow of the San Manuel Band of Mission Indians.

9 OCT. 2004. Rep. Joe Baca speaks at his Annual Women's Conference in UC, with Phaedra Ellis-Lamkins giving the keynote address. PDC dedicates a 50-year time capsule inside a wall in IWT.

15 OCT. 2004. Nena M. Tórrez is named Educator of the Year by *Hispanic Lifestyle Magazine*.

18 OCT. 2004. Gov. Schwarzenegger signs 2 bills to facilitate the transfer of community college students into the CSU System.

20 OCT. 2004. Heavy rain and power outages force the campus to close for part of the day, with the Health Center and part of the Social and Behavioral Sciences Building being flooded.

21 OCT. 2004. The campus receives a $750,000 gift from the City of Indio to help fund the Health Sciences Building at PDC.

23 OCT. 2004. The campus hosts its 5th Annual Women in Focus Forum Conference in UC, with Letitia Wright acting as MC.

26 OCT. 2004. Rep. Gloria Negrete speaks in PR.

27 OCT. 2004. Groundbreaking is held for the Student Recreation and Fitness Center next to the Arena.

3 NOV. 2004. Economist Emma Porio speaks in SB-213 on The Philippines. Guitarists The Elgart/Yates Duo perform in RH. The campus receives a $100,000 gift from the Tatum Foundation and Citizens Volunteer Corps for scholarships.

11 NOV. 2004. Eugene H. Wong receives the Golden Apple Award for teaching excellence for 2004/05.

12 NOV. 2004. Rep. Joe Baca hosts his Annual Education Summit, "The Future of Higher Education: Golden Opportunities in California," in the Commons, with UC Riverside Chancellor France Córdova, Calif. Community College Chancellor Mark Drummond, S.B. Valley Coll. Pres. Denise Whittaker, Pres. Karnig, and moderator Marie Kane, Pres. of Chaffey Community Coll.

15 NOV. 2004. José Jara of José's Mexican Foods speaks in PiR. Balinese dancer Ni Wayan Ekarini performs in RH.

17 NOV. 2004. Walden Bello speaks in RH on "Empire and Resistance Today: An Asian Perspective."

18 NOV. 2004. Amanda Wilcox speaks in PiR on "Discipline in the Early Childhood Years."

20 NOV. 2004. The campus receives a $450,000 grant to develop the Center for the Commercialization of Advanced Technology. PDC unveils its Betty Barker Sculpture Garden.

22 NOV. 2004. Pres. Karnig denounces the Pres. of the Coll. Republicans Club for posting leaflets on campus that could be construed as anti-gay; members of the Club ask their Pres. to resign.

29-30 NOV. 2004. The Indian Wells Center for Educational Excellence and Indian Wells Theater at the Palm Desert Campus are dedicated in 2 ceremonies (private and public) on successive days, with the presence of CSU

Chancellor Reed.

30 NOV. 2004. The campus hosts a forum to discuss free speech, hate speech, and homosexuality. The campus receives a $20,000 gift from Renona Pennington to endow the Dora J. Prieto Scholarship.

1 DEC. 2004. The Redlands New Music Ensemble performs in RH. The annual Environment Expo receives the Governor's Environmental and Economic Leadership Award.

2 DEC. 2004. The women's volleyball team loses its quarter-finals match to Nebraska-Kearney in the NCAA Division II tournament.

9 DEC. 2004. 21 Chinese tourism officials visit the campus.

11 DEC. 2004. The 4th Winter Commencement is held in the Arena and at PDC.

22 DEC. 2004. The campus is again named a "Publisher's Pick" by *Hispanic Outlook in Higher Education*.

31 DEC. 2004. Retirements: Patricia (Rodgers-) Gordon, Dir. of the Career Development Center (1988-04); Martha P. Kazlo, Counselor and Dir. of Counseling and Health Services (1976-04).

2005

1 JAN. 2005. The campus begins offering an M.A. degree in Spanish.

3 JAN. 2005. Robert C. Aylmer is named Dir. of the Student Health and Psychological Counseling Center, replacing Martha P. Kazlo. Hamid Azhand, Assoc. Dir. of Capital Planning, Design, and Construction, is named Dir.

4 JAN. 2005. The campus buys the University Village apartments on the south side of Northpark Blvd. for $28,250,000 from American Campus Communities, Inc., thereby adding 6 buildings with 169,638 sq. ft. on 11.28 acres to CSUSB, after receiving approval from the CSU Board of Trustees on Nov. 17, 2004.

5 JAN. 2005. The Riverside Light Opera performs *Amahl and the Night Visitors* in RH.

13 JAN. 2005. Alexandria LaFaye receives the Scott O'Dell Award for Historical Fiction for her young adult novel, *Worth*.

17 JAN. 2005. The Mary Stuart Rogers Gateway Building at PDC wins the Redlands American Institute of Art Award for Architecture.

21 JAN. 2005. The Harlem Globetrotters perform in the Arena. Assemblywoman Carol Liu speaks about "The College Access Crisis."

24 JAN. 2005. Cal State places 2nd in the Western Regional Ethics Bowl competition at San Jose.

27 JAN. 2005. Dakota storyteller Mary Louise Defender-Wilson performs "Un De' Che Cha Pi: The Way We Are" in VA-101.

31 JAN. 2005. Mike Tracey, Int. Assoc. VP for Development, resigns. Mark K. Day, Act. Dir. of the Santos Manuel Student Union, resigns.

2 FEB. 2005. The Cancryn/Carlisle Duo perform in RH.

3 FEB. 2005. The campus signs a joint admissions agreement with Copper Mountain College in Joshua Tree.

11 FEB. 2005. Supreme Court Justice Anthony M. Kennedy, Rep. Mary Bono, and Assemblyman John J. Benoit speak at PDC at the dedication of the Annenberg Wing of the Indian Wells Center.

12 FEB. 2005. Dolores Huerta, co-founder of the United Farmworkers of America, gives the keynote address in UC at the 3rd Annual Women's Activism Conference. Ex-NFL player Mark Seay speaks at the Gear Up Inland Empire Leadership Institute in UC.

14 FEB. 2005. Fred E. Jandt, Int. Dean of PDC, is named permanent Dean.

15 FEB. 2005. Tim Wise speaks in LC on "Reflections on Race from a Privileged Son."

19-20 FEB. 2005. The campus hosts the Winter Guard International West Power Regional Color Guard Finals in the Arena.

22 FEB. 2005. The campus receives a $1 million gift from the Desert Healthcare District to fund the Palm Desert Health Sciences Building at PDC.

23 FEB. 2005. Sesh Velamoor speaks at PDC at its inaugural "Distinguished Scholar Series" lecture (co-sponsored with Coll. of the Desert) on "Looking Forward the Next 100 Years: What It Means for Our Society and Planet." Mary Soria and Bryan Devor are named Miss and Mr. CSUSB for 2005. The Inland California Television Network (ICTN) broadcasts for the last time at 10 P.M. The Coll. of Extended Learning begins offering an online registration system.

25 FEB. 2005. The Inland California Television Network (ICTN), which is operated by CSUSB, abruptly shuts down for lack of funding, after a key piece of equipment fails the day before.

25-26 FEB. 2005. The musical play *Ethel*, co-authored by Emer. Prof. William L. Slout and Cal State alumna Val Limar Jansen, begins a 2-day benefit encore in RH.

1 MAR. 2005. Rev. Dennis Brown speaks in LC. Margaret S. Doane is named Outstanding Professor for 2004/05. Diane F. Halpern speaks in VA-101 on "How Social Science Data Can Inform Public Policies About Work, Families, and Children." The San Manuel Band of Mission Indians reallocates $30,000 that had been pledge to support ICTN to the John M. Pfau Library to purchase materials on Native American sovereignty issues. Janet F. Gregoire, ex-Students with Disabilities, dies at age 62.

2 MAR. 2005. William Aguilar, VP of Information Resources and Technology, is named VP of Univ. Advancement, replacing Jo Ann Hankin (1999-01). Johnnie Ann Ralph, Univ. Libn., is named Dean of the John M. Pfau Library and Univ. Libn. Lorraine M. Frost, Dir. of Administrative Computing Services, is named Int. VP of Information Resources and Technology, replacing William Aguilar. The Pfau Library is moved from under the VP of Information Resources and Technology to the Provost and VP of Academic Affairs. The Water Resources Institute is moved from under the VP of Information Resources and Technology to the Dean of Natural Sciences. The contemporary vocal jazz group M-Pact performs in RH.

3 MAR. 2005. The campus unveils its Anthropology Museum on the 3rd floor of the Social and Behavioral Sciences Building.

8 MAR. 2005. Christopher Leighton speaks at the 18th Annual Morrow-McCombs Lecture on "Reaching Common Ground: The Challenge of Disarming Religious Hate" at the First Congregational United Church of Christ, S.B.

9 MAR. 2005. Spelman Coll. Glee Club performs in the Barnes Theatre.

14 MAR. 2005. Françoise B. Aylmer is named Act. Assoc. VP for Univ. Development, replacing Mike Tracey.

17 MAR. 2005. Yoga master Kauthub Desikichar speaks in the Arena.

18 Mar. & 6 May & 3 Jun. 2005. The campus hosts a conference, "Inland Region Goods Movement," at the Radisson Hotel, S.B.

19-20 Mar. 2005. Stars of the Moscow State Circus perform in the Arena.

25 Mar. 2005. The campus receives a 2nd $1 million gift from the City of Rancho Mirage to help build the Palm Desert Health Sciences Building at PDC.

28 Mar. 2005. John Dunworth, ex-Int. Dean of the School of Education (1990-91) and Pres. of Peabody College (1974-79), dies at Pensacola, Florida, at age 81.

2 Apr. 2005. The Cal State team wins the 2005 College Nutrition Bowl at the Riverside Convention Center.

5 Apr. 2005. Candace Hunter Wiest receives the annual Arrowhead Distinguished Executive Officer Award at a banquet at the Victoria Club, Riverside.

6 Apr. 2005. The Inland Percussion Group performs in RH.

7-10 Apr. 2005. The campus Model United Nations Team wins a "Distinguished Delegation" award at the national competition held in New York City, representing the country of Bahrain.

8-10 Apr. 2005. PDC hosts the California Desert Nature Festival.

13 Apr. 2005. Dr. Carmack Holmes speaks at PDC on "The Operating Room of the Future and the Twenty-First Century State-of-the-Art Hospital at UCLA."

14 Apr. 2005. The campus is named one of the top 75 entrepreneurship programs in the U.S. by *Entrepreneur Magazine*.

14-15 Apr. 2005. The campus hosts the Latin American Studies Conference, with featured speakers: artist Simón Silva; Carlos I. Giralt Cabrales, representative of the Consul General of México; Mexican poet Maricarmen Martínez Villalobos; and Chilean scholar Enrique Díaz.

15 Apr. 2005. Edward Lee Brock, retired Police Officer, dies at age 66.

19 Apr. 2005. Darui Long speaks in PiR on "What Is Confucianism?"

21 Apr. 2005. Gender outlaw performance artist Kate Bornstein speaks in RH "On Women, Men, and the Rest of Us."

23 APR. 2005. The campus hosts its 19th Annual Environmental Expo in the Arena, with actress Barbara Niven and magician Paul Cash.

25 APR. 2005. Madeline P. Terrazas, Library Asst. (1993-05), retires.

28 APR. 2005. Faculty poets Juan Delgado, Christi Rucker, B. H. "Pete" Fairchild, and Jackqueline Wilcoxen read from their works in UC, and Fairchild wins the $10,000 Rebekah Johnson Bobbitt National Prize for Poetry for 2004 for *Early Occult Memory Systems of the Lower Midwest*.

2 MAY 2005. The campus begins converting its phone system to a $3 million internet-based system, altering its dialing prefix from "880" to "537."

4 MAY 2005. Violinist Todor Pelev and cellist Ana María Maldonado perform in RH.

7 MAY 2005. Larry Sheffield speaks at the 10th Annual Harry Rheubottom/George Webster Historical Lecture in the Pfau Library on "Colton, California: The 'Hub' City."

16 MAY 2005. Sen. Barbara Boxer visits PDC.

17 MAY 2005. Mark Gonzáles and Asif Ullah speak in VA-101 about "The Power of Media in Creating Cultural Stereotypes." Maura Owens Townsend speaks in RH on "Culture and Gender Through Dance."

18 MAY 2005. Lawrence Baron speaks in PR on "Condemned Couples: Jewish Gentile Lovers in Holocaust Feature Films."

21 MAY 2005. The campus hosts *Break! The Urban Funk Spectacular* in the Arena.

24 MAY 2005. Romanian Chamber of Commerce official Cornelia Rotaru speaks in SR on "Romania: Exploring Great Opportunities for Small Business."

26 MAY 2005. The campus receives a $599,999 grant from the U.S. Dept. of Education's Rehabilitation Services Administration to provide scholarships to students enrolled in the master's or certificate programs in Rehabilitation Counseling.

1 JUN. 2005. Chizuko Judy Sugita de Queiroz speaks in PL-269 on "Camp Days, 1942-1945; her watercolors of the Japanese-American internment camps are simultaneously displayed on the 1st floor of the Pfau Library.

2 JUN. 2005. A mountain lion is spotted on campus.

4-5 JUN. 2005. The campus hosts its 25th Annual Juneteenth Coll. Expo and Festival.

5 JUN. 2005. Martha A. P. Cox, ex-Processor, dies in Highland at age 62.

6 JUN. 2005. The first Coll. of Education Literacy Center Golf Tournament is held at the Arrowhead Country Club.

14 JUN. 2005. The campus dedicates a 40-foot flagpole donated by Stater Bros. in the courtyard of Brown Hall.

15 JUN. 2005. The Fullerton Museum receives a $5,000 grant from the National Endowment for the Humanities to conserve artifacts.

17 JUN. 2005. Stephen Anthony Bowles, Emer. Prof. of Psychology (1974-96), dies of a heart attack in Crestline at age 71.

17-19 JUN. 2005. The 39th Commencement is held in the Arena and at PDC, with Jack H. Brown, Rep. Loretta Sánchez, and Paul F. Magana serving as keynote speakers, and Joriz de Guzmán receiving a B.S. in Mathematics and Computer Science at age 15, believed to be the youngest person ever to receive a degree at CSUSB.

SUM. 2005. Retirements: David J. Bellis, Prof. of Public Administration (1985-05); John H. Craig, Prof. of Chemistry and Biochemistry (1971-05); David L. Decker, Prof. of Sociology (1971-05); Bertram H. "Pete" Fairchild Jr., Prof. of English (1983-05); Sue Greenfeld, Prof. of Management (1987-05); Guenther G. Kress, Prof. of Public Administration (1987-05); Kenneth A. Mantei, Prof. of Chemistry and Biochemistry (1968-05); Norton E. Marks, Prof. of Marketing and Int. Dean of the Coll. of Public and Business Administration (1990-05); Frederick A. Newton, Prof. of Psychology (1975-05); James C. Pierson, Prof. of Anthropology (1971-05); Reginald L. Price, Prof. of Kinesiology and ex-Athletic Dir. (1971-05); Edward J. Schneiderhan, Counselor (1980-05).

1 JUL. 2005. The campus completes the transition of its telephone prefixes from "880-" to "537-". Parking fees increase from $12 to $22 per month and from $1.50 to $3.00 per day to help build the first 2 campus parking structures. Cal State student John Odis Demmer Jr. is killed by a hit-and-run driver in Rialto at age 19.

5 JUL. 2005. The Office of Technology Transfer and Commercialization Building (OTTC), built with the aid of a $600,000 federal grant, opens for business next to the Foundation Building.

6 JUL. 2005. The Latin Society performs on LCP. The CSU System reaches an agreement with the University of California to facilitate the awarding of educational doctorates in the CSU.

7 JUL. 2005. Jeffrey W. Davis, Dir. of the Water Resources Institute, resigns.

8 JUL. 2005. Susan K. Lien Longville, Assoc. Dir., is named Int. Dir. of the Water Resources Institute, replacing Jeffrey W. Davis.

11 JUL. 2005. Gloria Kapp is named Int. Dir. of Financial Aid. Gregory R. Lehr is named Exec. Dir. of the Santos Manuel Student Union, replacing Mark K. Day.

13 JUL. 2005. Gregg Young and the Second Street Band perform on LCP.

14 JUL. 2005. The campus receives a $4.5 million gift from the City of Palm Desert and a $1 million gift from the City of La Quinta to help build the Health Sciences Building at PDC.

20 JUL. 2005. The Basix performs on LCP. PDC receives a $27,705 grant from the Irene W. and Guy L. Anderson Children's Foundation to fund needy children.

25 JUL. 2005. The campus receives a $200,000 gift from the Portland Cement Co. to help build an astronomical observatory on Little Badger Hill.

27 JUL. 2005. The Bootie Shakers perform on LCP.

28 JUL. 2005. The campus opens its new Inland Empire Women's Business Resource Center of the Inland Empire Center for Entrepreneurship at 202 E. Airport Dr., Suite 155, in San Bernardino.

31 JUL. 2005. Susan E. Summers, Int. Dean of Extended Learning, returns to her position as Assoc. Dean of Extended Learning.

1 AUG. 2005. Jeetendra R. "Jeet" Joshee is named Dean of Extended Learning, replacing Susan E. Summers. The campus receives a $66,000 grant from the CSU to automate the Annual Fund Calling Center. Patricia A. "Patti" Smith is named Dir. of the Student Health and Psychological Center, replacing Robert C. Aylmer.

15 AUG. 2005. The campus receives a $2 million grant from the U.S. Army, and a $100,000 gift from Mrs. Lenore Annenberg for teaching scholarships.

19 AUG. 2005. Patrick Thomas McDonald, Dir. of Public Safety and Chief of Police (2002-05), dies in Redlands of cancer at age 61.

20 AUG. 2005. Brian D. Bodily, Police Lt., is named Int. Chief of Police, replacing Patrick T. McDonald.

1 SEPT. 2005. The Nursing Dept. joins with Riverside Community Hospital to launch the Elite Nursing Program, which in turn gives the campus $3,200,000 over a 4-year period to help graduate an additional 200 nursing students. The campus begins offering a Master of Public Health degree.

5 SEPT. 2005. Dorothy J. McCarthy, retired Library Asst. (1978-83), dies at age 83.

9 SEPT. 2005. Rep. Joe Baca hosts his Annual Women's Conference in YC, with Baca, Evelyn Erives, Kelly Hayes-Raitt, and Pamela Chute speaking. The campus receives a $250,000 gift from the City of Coachella to help build the Health Services Building at PDC.

12 SEPT. 2005. Jeffrey M. Thompson is named Assoc. Provost for Research.

14 SEPT. 2005. Michael Burgess, Libn., Head of Technical Services and Collection Development and Chief Cataloger (1970-05), retires.

19 SEPT. 2005. At the annual convocation, Pres. Karnig highlights the plans for the campus's 40th anniversary celebration throughout the year, launches a revision of the University's strategic plan, says that the campus will increase faculty and staff diversity, creates an ombudsman position, and seeks alternative sources of funding and better management of enrollment. On the down side, the campus has absorbed $27 million in cuts from the state over the last several years, with a slight uptick anticipated in 2005/06. It is essential, he says, that enrollment targets be met, and that recruitment of non-resident students be increased. Some means must be found of subsidizing new faculty housing. The campus plans several new degree programs, including a Master of Public Health, a B.S. in Computer Engineering, and an Ed.D. doctorate (the campus's first offering at that level) in Education. "What all of you do," Karnig states, "regardless of your role, is to give students life opportunities that they would not have otherwise."

22 SEPT.-10 DEC. 2005. As part of the campus's 40th anniversary celebration, the Fullerton Art Gallery displays "Coming Home: Art Alumni Exhibition," with 40 years of art by CSUSB alumni.

23 SEPT. 2005. Jackie Núñez and James Ramos speak in LC at the 7th Annual Calif. Native American Day. The Commons reopens after 2 months of remodeling.

26 SEPT. 2005. Ernest Siva is named Distinguished Guest Artist. The campus receives a FEMA grant to seismically retrofit the Biological Science and Physical Science Buildings.

28 SEPT. 2005. Due to high winds, the Pfau Library cancels a reception to celebrate the acquisition of its 750,000th volume, a 1929 map of the Atchison, Topeka, and Santa Fe Railway System from the estate of the late Library Dir. Arthur E. Nelson.

1 OCT. 2005. The campus receives permission to offer its first doctoral (Ed.D.) degree in Education, beginning with 2007/08.

5 OCT. 2005. Tenor saxophonist Robert Kyle and the Stew Undems Jazz Coalition perform in RH.

6 OCT. 2005. Elsa Ochoa-Fernández receives a Fulbright Fellowship to study in Germany. The campus signs agreements with Surindra Rajabhat Univ., Ubon Ratchathani Univ., Loei Rajabhat Univ., Rajabhat Rajanagarindra Univ., and Chulalongkorn Univ. in Thailand for cultural and educational exchanges.

7-9 OCT. 2005. The campus hosts its 9th Annual Pow Wow of the San Manuel Band of Mission Indians.

8 OCT. 2005. Arthur L. Littleworth receives the 4th Annual WRI Lifetime Achievement Award.

9 OCT. 2005. Historian Nick Cataldo speaks at the 12th Library Associates Lecture in the Pfau Library on "The Earps."

10 OCT. 2005. James Robert Savage, ex-Dir. of the Student Health Center (1983-87), dies in San Bernardino at age 91.

12 OCT. 2005. The campus receives a $2 million grant from the federal government to establish a Univ. Transportation Center, with Caltrans and other agencies donating a matching $2 million sum.

14 OCT. 2005. World Wrestling Entertainment (WWE) performs in the Arena.

22-23 OCT. 2005. Circus Vargas performs in the Arena.

24 OCT. 2005. The 5th floor of the Pfau Library is designated a "quiet zone." Ex-Muslim Army Chaplain Capt. James Yee speaks on campus.

25 Oct. 2005. Stanley L. Swartz is named Distinguished Professor in Human Sciences by Universidad Autónoma de Baja California.

31 Oct. 2005. The campus receives a $1,750,000 gift from the City of Rancho Mirage to build the Health Sciences Building at PDC.

1 Nov. 2005. CSU Trustee Craig Smith speaks in SR on "The Relevance of Classical Rhetoric to Contemporary Life."

2 Nov. 2005. Jazz saxophonist Robert Knot performs in RH.

3 Nov. 2005. Prof. Bret Anthony Johnston reads from his collection, *Corpus Christi*, which is also named a "Best Book of the Year" by the *Independent of London*. The campus receives a 6-year, $15.6 million grant from the U.S. Dept. of Education to fund the GEAR-UP program.

4 Nov. 2005. Ex-Presidents Pfau and Evans and their wives, Antreen Pfau and Lois Evans, are honored at a reception for campus retirees.

5 Nov. 2005. The campus holds a reception at the Fullerton Art Museum to present its 1st Alumni Awards of Distinction, with Antreen Pfau and Lois Evans receiving the first President's Awards and Nicholas J. and Tina Coussoulis the first Legacy Awards.

12 Nov. 2005. The campus hosts the Wisdom in Education Program.

15 Nov. 2005. John Bostick speaks in JB-114 on "Solving the World Hunger Problem: A Project in Honduras."

16 Nov. 2005. WRI celebrates its 5th anniversary with an open house.

17 Nov. 2005. Martin Fonkijom Fusi speaks in SR on "West African Theater and Culture in Action."

18 Nov. 2005. Rep. Joe Baca hosts his Annual Education Summit, "Health and Academics," with State Superintendent of Public Instruction Jack O'Connell and S.B. Co. Superintendent of Schools Herbert Fischer.

21 Nov. 2005. The campus is again named a "Publisher's Pick" by *Hispanic Outlook in Higher Education*.

22 Nov. 2005. The campus receives a mammoth fossil from an Irvine site for students to clean before its deposit in the Natural History Museum.

30 Nov. 2005. Alison Weir, Exec. Dir. of "If Americans Knew," speaks in UH-106 on the Israeli/Palestinian conflict. Campus Dr., the new road linking Kendall Ave. and Northpark Blvd., is completed; work begins on converting the remaining 2-lane portion of Northpark Blvd. on the southwest campus perimeter into a 4-lane road.

1 DEC. 2005. The campus's Inland Empire Center for Entrepreneurship receives a $70,000 grant from the Bank of America to establish the Coachella Valley Women's Business Center in Coachella.

2 DEC. 2005. The campus signs an agreement with the U.S. Dept. of Agriculture to provide a liaison office for 59 Hispanic Serving Institutions in Southern Calif., with Ramiro Porras Jr. serving as Dir.

7 DEC. 2005. Clarinetist Jon Usher performs in RH.

10 DEC. 2005. The 5th Winter Commencement is held in the Arena and at PDC, with ex-Pres. Evans giving the keynote speech.

21 DEC. 2005. The S.B. City Council votes 4-3 to provide $1 million in loans to assist entry-level professors at CSUSB to buy homes.

2006

6 JAN. 2006. The campus receives a $50,000 gift from Palm Desert National Bank to help build a Health Science Building at PDC. The campus begins offering a Latin American Studies Program.

9 JAN. 2006. Françoise B. Aylmer, Act. Assoc. VP for Univ. Advancement, is named permanent Assoc. VP. Sidney A. "Sid" Robinson is named Asst. VP for Public Affairs. The campus receives a $500,000 gift from the City of Desert Hot Springs to help build the Health Sciences Building at PDC. The campus discontinues the use of its "880" telephone prefix.

12 JAN. 2006. The campus receives a $12,000 grant from Best Buy Co. to help fund Rev. Martin Luther King Jr. Day events.

16 JAN. 2006. August W. "Augie" Hartung, Assoc. Dir. for Facilities Services (2001-06), dies of a heart attack at age 59.

18 JAN. 2006. A ribbon-cutting ceremony marks the official opening of the new Chemical Sciences Building, including the 3,000-sq.-ft. Natural History Museum.

20 JAN. 2006. As part of its 40th anniversary year celebration, the campus holds an Athletics Appreciation Day. Laurie Flynn, Dir. of Students with Disabilities, resigns.

21 Jan. 2006. The campus receives a $25,000 grant from Watson & Associates to plant 380 California native oak trees on Wiggins Hill and Northpark Blvd., the first being planted on this date by Paul Nota of Lost West Landscape Architecture and Construction.

23-24 Jan. 2006. The campus closes due to high Santa Ana winds.

25 Jan. 2006. The campus receives a $1.3 million grant from the U.S. Army to support a 5-year fellowship program, the Integrated Technology Transfer Network (ITTN), to promote a fusion of science and technology for the businesses of tomorrow.

30 Jan. 2006. Norm King is named 1st Dir. of the Univ. Transportation Center, with temporary offices in the Water Resources Institute in the Library-Classroom Building.

31 Jan. 2006. Int. Chief of Police Brian D. Bodily returns to the ranks as Police Lt.

1 Feb. 2006. Robert J. Miller is named Dir. of Public Safety and Chief of Police, replacing Brian D. Bodily.

2 Feb. 2006. Gerald R. Thrush receives the Golden Apple Award for teaching excellence for 2005/06.

3 Feb. 2006. The campus receives a $50,000 gift from Jack H. Brown, Chair and CEO of Stater Bros., to add to the Richard Moseley Scholarship Fund, established in 1997 by company employees.

7 Feb. 2006. Flautist Ernest Siva performs in RH. Ronald Edgar Barnes, Emer. Prof. of Theatre Arts (1965-97), dies of kidney failure in Riverside at age 75.

9 Feb. 2006. Ex-basketball star Vlade Divac visits campus to promote his Group Seven Project to bring foreign students to the U.S. to participate in basketball clinics. Paul K. Dixon is named Outstanding Professor for 2005/06.

10 Feb. 2006. The old Recreation Center closes to allow for the construction of the new College of Education Building; it reopens on Feb. 12 in the Coyote Den in the old Gymnasium.

11 Feb. 2006. The campus honors Nicholas and Christina Coussoulis during a banquet celebrating the 10th anniversary of the opening of the Arena. Also present are Jack H. and Debbie Brown of Stater Bros. Markets, Jerry and Ann Atkinson of Center Chevrolet, and Miguel Cepeda of Coca-Cola.

14 FEB. 2006. Art critic Peter Frank speaks to an art class.

16 FEB. 2006. Rose Girard speaks on starting a successful business. The campus hosts its 2nd Annual Asian/Asian-American Roundtable in PiR, with Tibetan monk Shi Chuan-Feng giving one keynote address, "Harmonious Worldview and Cosmology: A Concise Syntheses of Tai Chi, Feng Shui, and Tibetan Buddhism," and calligrapher Duan Changmin giving the other, "Chinese Calligraphy: A Lecture and Demonstration."

17 FEB. 2006. The campus hosts the 77th Annual Western States Communication Assoc. Convention at the Riviera Resort and Racquet Club, Palm Springs, with Palm Springs Mayor Ron Oden delivering the keynote address, "America: I Thought You Said!?"

23-24 FEB. 2006. Writer Ilán Stavans speaks at the Latin American Studies Conference on the Studies of the Americas in UC and UH.

24 FEB. 2006. Assemblywoman Gloria Negrete McLeod speaks at the Calif. Black Contributions Symposium.

1 MAR. 2006. The Capella group M-PACT performs in the Arena.

6 MAR. 2006. Beth Jaworski is named Int. Dir. of Services to Students with Disabilities. Judge Patrick J. Morris, son of ex-Cal State secretary Wilma Morris, takes office as S.B. Mayor, replacing Judith A. Valles.

6 & 10 MAR. 2006. Zhang Meiyun, VP of Shaanxi Univ. of Science and Technology in China, speaks, together with 17 other Chinese scholars and education administrators.

7 MAR. 2006. Sierra Club VP Bernard Zaleha speaks in PiR on "Death to Environmentalism." George H. Schnarre receives the annual Arrowhead Distinguished Executive Officer Award at a banquet in SUEC.

8 MAR. 2006. The campus receives a $10,000 grant from First American Title Corp. to provide labs in the new College of Education Building. The campus receives a 2nd $1 million gift from the Desert Healthcare District to fund the Health Sciences Building at PDC.

9 MAR. 2006. Chani Beeman is named 1st Univ. Ombudsperson.

15 MAR. 2006. Gerald A. Fawcett is named Executive-in-Residence for the Coll. of Business and Public Administration.

17 MAR. 2006. Michael Burgess, Librarian Emeritus, is named Editor of the new Borgo Press Imprint of Wildside Press.

23 Mar. 2006. The campus is named by *Hispanic Outlook in Education* as one of the top 20 universities nationwide awarding B.A. degrees to Hispanic women.

24 Mar. 2006. The campus hosts its Annual Women's Conference, "The NEW Women's Rights Issues: Celebrating the Advancements of Women," in UC, with Rep. Joe Baca.

28 Mar. 2006. The temporary Recreation Center opens for business. The interfaith musical group Yuval Ron Ensemble performs and speaks at the 19th Annual Morrow-McCombs Lecture on "Musical Bridges" at the First Congregational Church, S.B.

5 Apr. 2006. Alumni cellist Michele Brosseau-Tacchia and pianist Michael Tacchia perform in RH.

6 Apr. 2006. A ribbon-cutting ceremony marks the official opening of the expanded 83,000-sq.-ft. Santos Manuel Student Union. The campus hosts the statewide Economic Challenge in UC. Comedian Lew Lefton performs "Infinity Bottles of Beer on the Wall" in SA.

10 Apr. 2006. Alan Smith becomes the 3rd campus faculty member to win a $20,000 Wang Family Excellence Award.

18 Apr. 2006. Ellis Elmer McCune, Act. Chancellor of the CSU System (1990-91), dies in Palm Desert at age 84.

19 Apr. 2006. The campus receives the Institutional Award for Diversity from the Western Assoc. of Coll. and University Housing Officers. S.B. Mayor Morris speaks in YC.

21 Apr. 2006. Groundbreaking is held for the College of Education Building.

22 Apr. 2006. The campus hosts its 20th Annual Environmental Expo in the Arena, with magician Paul Cash.

25 Apr. 2006. Joel Alvin Stein, Prof. of Mathematics (1991-06), dies of heart failure in China at age 61.

26 Apr. 2006. The campus hosts its 17th Annual Access Disability Awareness/Assistitive Technology and Career Expo in the Arena, with Lawrence Silcock giving the keynote speech.

2 May 2006. As part of its 40th anniversary celebration, the campus holds a reception in the SU to honor faculty book authors, and to celebrate the publication of *CSUSB Faculty Authors, Composers, and Playwrights: A Bibliography of Forty Years of Published Monographs and Recordings, 1965-2005, 2nd Edition*, by Michael Burgess, a copy of which is presented to each of the attendees.

4 MAY 2006. The campus hosts a community forum on the future of the Santa Ana River, "Re-Envisioning Paradise," in VA-101.

6 MAY 2006. As part of its 40th anniversary celebration, the campus honors past Associated Student Inc. Presidents and former members of the SU Board with a black tie gala at SU; the event also includes silent and live auctions to raise endowment funds, and the unveiling of portraits of the 3 campus Presidents by artist Tom Pinch. Attendees include Nicholas J. Coussoulis, James and Judy Watson, 4 delegates from China, *San Bernardino Sun* Chief Executive Bob Balzer, Marie Alonzo of the Arrowhead Credit Union, Charles D. Obershaw, S.B. Mayor Morris, S.B. Catholic Diocese Bishop Gerald Barnes, ex-Pres. Pfau, ex-Pres. Evans, and CSU Chancellor Reed.

7 MAY 2006. A memorial service is held in the Barnes Theatre for Emer. Prof. Ronald E. Barnes. WrestleMania Revenge performs at the Arena.

8 MAY 2006. The campus partners with the S.B. Unified School Dist. to construct a new joint-use gymnasium at the César E. Chávez Middle School on Magnolia Ave. Pres. Karnig establishes a program of Executives in Residence/Artists in Residence for each of the colleges, beginning with the 2007/08 school year. The campus is ranked 21st in the nation among "Top Colleges for Hispanics" by *Hispanic Outlook in Education*.

13 MAY 2006. As part of its 40th anniversary celebration, the campus hosts a gala event, "A Legend of Pride and Promise," with ex-Presidents Pfau and Evans, Nicholas J. and Tina Coussoulis, ex-S.B. Mayor Valles, and Jack H. and Debbie Brown. *Cal State Cooks, 1965-2005: Selected Recipes from the Administration, Faculty, and Staff of California State University, San Bernardino, on the Fortieth Anniversary of the Founding of the Campus*, edited by Johnnie Ann Ralph and Michael Burgess, is published by the Pfau Library. Yolanda King, daughter of Rev. Martin Luther King Jr., speaks in the Arena.

16 MAY 2006. Actor B. D. Wong speaks in SUEC as part of the Conversations in Diversity series.

17 MAY 2006. The CSU Board of Trustees names the 3rd building at PDC the Palm Desert Health Sciences Center to recognize the $4.5 million gift from the city to help construct that building.

23 May 2006. Singer Harry Belafonte speaks in SUEC on "The State of the Union Address: Where Does American Stand in the Eyes of the World Today and in the Future."

25 May 2006. Harpist Celia Chan Valerio performs in RH.

1 Jun. 2006. Ex-Taliban hostage and reporter Yvonne Ridley speaks in SUEC on "In the Hands of the Taliban: A Captive's Account." The campus begins offering an on-line executive master's degree in Public Administration.

3 Jun. 2006. The Main Street Community Band performs in RH.

6 Jun. 2006. Agenor Mafra-Neto speaks on "From Research to Revenue" in PR.

10 Jun. 2006. Historian Ashra Kwesi speaks in SUEC as part of the campus's annual Juneteenth celebration; the band Hobo Jazz also performs on LCP.

15 Jun. 2006. Cal State alumnus Lou Monville III is named by Gov. Schwarzenegger to the CSU Board of Trustees.

16-18 Jun. 2006. The 40th Commencement is held in the Arena and on PDC.

19 Jun. 2006. Gregory R. Lehr, Exec. Dir. of the Santos Manuel SU, resigns. The campus begins offering a B.S. degree in Nursing.

27 Jun. 2006. The campus receives a $250,000 gift from Riverside Co. to help build the Palm Desert Health Sciences Building at PDC.

29 Jun. 2006. David J(ames) Bellis, Emer. Prof. of Public Administration (1985-05), dies of heart failure at Cedar Glen at age 62.

30 Jun. 2006. The campus receives a "Flex Your Power" Award from the State of California.

Sum. 2006. Retirements: Jacques Benzakein, Prof. of World Languages and Literatures (1985-06); Klaus R. Brasch, Prof. of Biology (1990-06); LuAnne Castle, Instructor, English; K. Michael Clarke, Prof. of Public Administration (1976-06); Frances S. Coles, Prof. of Criminal Justice (1978-06); Cheryl F. Fischer, Prof. of Education (1990-06); Mirta A. González, Prof. of World Languages and Literatures (1989-06); Joan Terry Hallett, Prof. of Mathematics (1981-06); Roger Harthrong, Lect., Nursing; Kenneth E. Lane, Prof. of Education (1989-06); Joseph E. Lovett, Prof. of

Health Science and Human Ecology (1989-06); Audrey L. Matthews, Prof. of Public Administration (1996-06); Susan E. Meisenhelder, Prof. of English (1982-06); Shari L. Oliver, Counselor (1993-06); Eugene Philip Page, Prof. of English (1989-06); Patricia D. Reed, Lect. in Management (1988-06); Daniel S. Whitaker, Prof. of World Languages and Literatures (1985-06). Staff: Gregory Baker, Facilities Services; Billie Bickmore, Administrative Support Coordinator; Brian Bodily, Public Safety; Noma Bradley, Facilities Services; Margaret Brasch, Research and Sponsored Programs; Diana Butler, Academic Personnel; Joan Caccavale, Public Affairs; Sara Corbett, Admin. Support Coordinator; Joan Dezember, Administrative Support Coordinator; Jim Eller, Coll. of Social and Behavioral Sciences; Anita Marlene Gaither, Student Accounts; Toni García, Career Development Center; Sandra Hall, Chemistry; Cindy Hopkins, Student Health Center; Pame Jones, Sociology; Tootie Killingsworth, PDC; Ronna Kivisto, Dir., Special Events; Susan Lloyd, Nursing; Irene Martínez, Coll. of Extended Learning; Debby McAllister, Coll. of Education; Lorney O'Connor, Theatre Arts; Sylvia Ramírez, Facilities Services; Linda M. Rogers, Supervisor, Records, Registration, and Evaluation (1984-2005); Diane Spencer, PDC; Robert Sperry, Testing Off.; Sandra Torres, Payroll; Arlan Wareham, Mathematics.

1 JUL. 2006. Roseanna Ruiz is named Financial Aid Dir. Maisie T. Conceicao, Library Asst. (1970-06), retires. Susan K. Lien Longville, Int. Dir. of the Water Resources Institute, is named permanent Dir.

4 JUL. 2006. John Edward Hafstrom, Emer. Prof. of Mathematics (1965-79), dies at Poulsbo, Washington at age 91.

5 JUL. 2006. The Latin Society performs on LCP.

12 JUL. 2006. The Rolling Stones tribute band Hot Rocks performs on LCP.

13 JUL. 2006. The campus receives a $7,500 gift from Citigroup Foundation to fund 15 scholarships.

17-21 JUL. 2006. The campus hosts the Group Seven Inland Empire Basketball Camp for foreign students.

18 JUL. 2006. The CSU Board of Trustees renames CSUSB's Transportation Center for William E. and Barbara Leonard, who contributed $2.1 million to support the activities of the center.

19 JUL. 2006. The swing group Phat Cat Swingers performs on LCP. The CSU Board of Trustees renames the Literacy Center in honor of Orange Co. developer Watson and Associates, who had contributed $1 million toward support of the center.

26 JUL. 2006. The jazz and blues group Friendz Band performs on LCP.

3 AUG. 2006. Marcia Luna Raines, Prof. of Nursing (1995-06), dies of cancer at Crestline at age 59. Lucy E. Hauer, Library Asst. (1967-78), dies at Sylvania, Ohio, at age 91.

7 AUG. 2006. The campus receives a $105,000 gift from Prem Reddy to endow scholarships at PDC. Risa E. Dickson is named Exec. Asst. to the President, replacing Alemayehu G. "Al" Mariam.

15 AUG. 2006. The campus receives a 4-year, $463,198 grant from NSF to help math and science students to become teachers.

24 AUG. 2006. TV producer, writer, and director Fern Field is named Artist-in-Residence for the 2006/07 school year at PDC.

29 AUG. 2006. The campus receives a 3rd-straight "Best in the West" designation from *The Princeton Review*, and is ranked 61st in the West in the annual "America's Best Colleges Guide" from *U.S. News & World Report*.

1 SEPT. 2006. The campus begins offering an M.A. Degree in Theatre Arts, and a B.S. degree in Computer Engineering.

12 SEPT. 2006. Alemayehu G. "Al" Mariam, ex-Exec. Asst. to the President (2004-06), returns the ranks as Prof. of Political Science.

14 SEPT. 2006. S.B. City Councilman Neil Derry speaks at the WorkAbility IV Program in SR.

17 SEPT. 2006. Leo P. Connolly receives the 1st Richard H. Emmons Award for Excellence in College Astronomy Teaching from the Astronomical Soc. of the Pacific.

18 SEPT. 2006. At the annual convocation, Pres. Karnig says that he wants the campus to maintain "an environment that sustains the collegiality I've experienced over the past several years, despite cuts to budgets and limited salary increases.... A college education fuels the economy and helps overcome past inequities." Campus priorities cited by the Pres. include: sustaining and promoting enrollment and student success, developing new academic programs, pushing the tenure-to-non-tenure faculty ratio to 3-to-1, assisting new faculty with subsidized housing, diversifying and enhancing the University's sources of funds, completing existing and beginning new planning efforts, and finishing existing capital projects. He notes $16.2 million in fundraising in 2005/06, almost twice the previous campus record, and an essential component of maintaining the educational quality of CSUSB, as well as a record $28 million in grants. However, meeting enrollment goals has become even more important, due to a new policy by the Chancellor's Office of pulling funding if enrollment targets are not met. Therefore the campus must focus on retaining the students it has, and increasing graduate and non-resident students. Karnig also announces the creation of the long-anticipated new road to loop through the north part of the campus.

18-22 SEPT. 2006. The campus hosts its Annual California Indian Cultural Awareness Conference in SU.

20 SEPT. 2006. The campus is ranked 4th nationally (out of 700) for graduate entrepreneurship programs by *The Princeton Review* and *Entrepreneur* magazine.

21 SEPT. 2006. Deborah Burns is named Int. Dir. of the Foundation.

21 SEPT.-9 DEC. 2006. The Fullerton Art Gallery exhibits "Golden Legacy: Ancient Jewelry from the Burton Y. Berry Collection."

22 SEPT. 2006. The campus hosts its Annual California Native American Day on LCP.

25 SEPT. 2006. The campus receives a 4-year, $500,000 grant from NSF to help attract students in mathematics and science. The Institute of Child Development and Family Relations receives a $3 million grant. The campus receives (with 7 other universities in S.B. Co.) a $3 million grant from the U.S. Off. of National Intelligence to expand their National Security Studies Programs; CSUSB (as host campus) receives $740,000.

1 OCT. 2006. Brian Levin is interviewed by Ed Bradley on a 60 *Minutes* TV segment.

4 OCT. 2006. Calif. Secretary of State Bruce McPherson and S.B. Co. Supervisor Josie Gonzáles speak in SUEC on "The Importance of Voting." The campus receives a $300,000 gift from James Watson for the creation of public art on and off campus.

10 OCT. 2006. Woodworker Sam Maloof speaks in SUT.

13 OCT. 2006. A freak rain and hail storm floods parts of the campus with 2.24 inches in an hour, causing $2 million in damage to the basements of 6 buildings.

13-15 OCT. 2006. The campus hosts its 7th Annual San Manuel Band of

Mission Indians Pow Wow on the athletic fields.

23 OCT. 2006. The campus receives approval to offer a B.S. degree in Computer Engineering, effective Winter 2007.

24 OCT. 2006. The Lumen Valo Finnish Choir performs in RH.

25 OCT. 2006. Economist John E. Husing speaks in YC on "The Labor Market in the Inland Empire." Cal State student Lauren Elizabeth Roberts is killed in an auto accident on Greenspot Road in Highland, CA, at age 22.

26 OCT. 2006. Michael Stoops, Exec. Dir. of the National Coalition for the Homeless, speaks in the Santos Manuel SU. The campus holds a memorial service for the late Prof. David J. Bellis in SUEC. The campus completes construction of a mobile launch platform by Lunar Rocket and Rover Co., Inc., a private rocket launch company in Los Alamitos.

27 OCT. 2006. John A. Kaufman III, ex-Assoc. Prof. of Communication, dies of cancer at Fontana at age 64.

30 OCT. 2006. Frances F. Berdan appears on the History Channel TV program, *Engineering an Empire: Aztecs*.

1 NOV. 2006. Sung-Heh "Sunny" Hyon receives the Golden Apple Award for teaching excellence for 2006/07. Pianist David Murray and soprano Michelle Murray perform in RH.

3 NOV. 2006. Henry F. Kutak, ex-Dir. of Financial Aid (2002), dies at age 70.

4 NOV. 2006. Rep. C. Jerry Lewis receives the 5th Annual WRI Lifetime Achievement Award at a banquet held in SUEC, with S.B. Mayor Morris serving as M.C. The campus hosts its 2nd Annual EdTech Conference in UH-039 and -043, with Mike Lawrence giving the keynote speech.

6 NOV. 2006. Groundbreaking is held for the Palm Desert Health Science Building at PDC, the 4th structure built there with donated funds, with the attendance of Palm Desert Mayor Jim Ferguson.

8 NOV. 2006. Dale A. Ulrich speaks in JB-144 and HP-125 on "Applications of the TGMD-2 for Assessing Children with and without Disabilities."

9 NOV. 2006. Gigi Hanna is named Assoc. Dir. of WRI.

13 NOV. 2006. The Travis Brass Quintet performs in RH.

14 NOV. 2006. Mark Zupan speaks in SUEC on "Murderball: Smashing Stereotypes." Eri F. Yasuhara is elected to the National Board of Colleges of Arts and Sciences.

17 NOV. 2006. Rep. Joe Baca holds his annual Economic Summit on math and science in UC, with Pamela Clute giving the keynote speech.

18 NOV. 2006. 16 Chinese government education officials visit the campus to sign an agreement for an exchange of science faculty and students between CSUSB and Yunnan University.

21 NOV. 2006. Jazz guitarist John Carey performs in RH.

27 NOV. 2006. Taiko drummers Ryohei and Kohei Inoue perform in RH.

28 NOV. 2006. Ramón Álvarez speaks in PiR about his business, "Álvarez Lincoln Mercury and Jaguar."

1 DEC. 2006. Dale T. West, Dir. of Human Resources, is named Asst. VP of Human Resources and Risk Management. The campus receives a $25,000 gift from James H. and Helen H. Urata to establish an endowed scholarship for the College of Arts and Letters. Stater Bros. CEO Jack H. Brown speaks on "Economic Development in the Inland Empire."

4 DEC. 2006. The campus receives a $500,000 Robert Noyce Scholarship grant to train math and science teachers for the S.B. Co. Unified School Dist.

6 DEC. 2006. The Tailgators Dixieland Band performs IN RH

9 DEC. 2006. The 6th Winter Commencement is held in the Arena and at PDC, with Rueben Martínez giving the keynote speech.

15 DEC. 2006. The campus is again named a "Publisher's Pick" by *Hispanic Outlook in Education*.

31 DEC. 2006. Retirements: Johnnie Ann Ralph, Libn., Act. Library Dir., Assoc. Univ. Libn., and Dean of the John M. Pfau Library and Univ. Libn. (1971-06; she returns as a retired annuitant for 6 more months); Paul J. Esposito, Counselor and Coordinator of Placement Services (1976-06); John M. Futch, Coordinator of the Cross Cultural Center (1997-06); Lois S. Hill, Library Asst. (1974-06); Antonio D. "Tony" Vilches, Library Stock Clerk (1976-06).

2007

1 JAN. 2007. The campus announces that it will now send official notices to students and staff only via email.

12 JAN. 2007. A storm blankets the campus with a rare half-inch of snow.

19 JAN. 2007. The campus receives a $75,750 grant from Kaiser Permanente to develop programs for disease prevention on campus, particularly diabetes.

22 JAN. 2007. Rev. Greg Boyle, S.J., speaks at PDC on "Jobs for a Future/Homeboy Industries."

29 JAN. 2007. The CSU Foundation announces the availability of $350,000 in funding for endowed scholarships for students attending any of the 23 CSU campuses for 2007/08. Cal State sophomore Steven Avila publishes his first novel, *Everything Changes: The Trevvlek War Trilogy, Volume 1*, from Xlibris Books. Lloyd E. Peake is named Outstanding Professor for 2006/07. The campus receives a $600,000 Work Force Development Grant to provide financial aid to nursing students.

31 JAN. 2007. Chani Beeman, Univ. Ombudsperson, resigns.

1 FEB. 2007. The Inland Empire Economic Partnership (IEEP) names Pres. Karnig as its Educator of the Year.

5 FEB. 2007. CSU Trustee Lou Monville III visits the campus. Rosemary Tilden Binney, alumna, Reading Specialist, EOP (-1986), dies at age 82.

8 FEB. 2007. The late singer Bob Marley is honored with a tribute at the Cross Cultural Center.

13 FEB. 2007. The Harlem Globetrotters perform in the Arena. Artist April Durham speaks in VA-101.

15 FEB. 2007. The Science Parking Lot is reduced in size by 32 spaces to accommodate the construction of the Education Building.

19 FEB. 2007. Construction begins on the Palm Desert Health Sciences Center at PDC. The campus receives a $700,000 Calif. Endowment from the State. Mark Hartley is named Dir. of Student Leadership and Development.

20 FEB. 2007. Artist Steven Carpenter speaks in VA-101.

21 FEB. 2007. Ramón Álvarez speaks in SU.

23 FEB. 2007. Donald I. Baker receives the annual Arrowhead Distinguished Executive Officer Award at a banquet in UC. Olympic gold medalist Julie Smith speaks in the Arena Lobby.

26 FEB. 2007. The campus receives a $1,240,000 gift from the Coachella Hospital to help establish a Nursing program at PDC.

27 FEB. 2007. Photographer Ciara Ennis speaks in VA-101.

28 FEB. 2007. Geologist Wesley R. Danskin speaks in PL-4005 on "Water Management Alternatives for the San Bernardino Area."

1 MAR. 2007. The last undeveloped portion of the center strip on Northpark Blvd. is landscaped. The campus hosts its 3rd Annual Asian Roundtable in PiR. Cal State students vote by a 70.6% margin to approve a fee increase to expand the Student Health Center. The campus holds a dinner in SU to launch a $100,000 textbook endowment fund in honor of John M. Futch, retired Dir. of Culture and Community Development. The campus hosts its 3rd Annual Asian Roundtable, with Linda Trinh Vö speaking.

2 MAR. 2007. Comedians Colin Mochrie and Brad Sherwood perform in the Arena.

3 MAR. 2007. The punk band A Fire Inside performs in the Arena.

6 MAR. 2007. Julia Chávez Rodríguez, daughter of the late labor leader César Chávez, speaks on labor issues in SUEC.

7 MAR. 2007. Guitarist Nicholas Lambson performs in RH. Photographer Douglas McCulloh speaks about his work in VA-101.

10 MAR. 2007. The campus hosts its 5th Annual Gather the Women Conference.

13 MAR. 2007. Activist Gloria Steinem speaks and signs books at SUEC during "An Evening with Gloria Steinem."

16 MAR. 2007. The campus receives a 3-year $240,000 grant from the Calif. Wellness Foundation to support nursing education at PDC.

18-22 MAR. 2007. The CSCSB Model United Nations team wins its 10th Outstanding Delegation and its 5th Outstanding Paper awards at the annual national competition in New York City, representing the country of Iraq.

19 Mar. 2007. The campus honors alumnus Michael Bracken as the inaugural 2007 Advocate of the Year.

22 Mar. 2007. Lt. Gov. John Garamendi visits the campus, where he hosts a forum in UC on his "Listening Tour."

24 Mar. 2007. In the NCAA Division II Elite Eight Tournament held at Springfield, MA, the Cal State men's basketball team is defeated 80-79 in the quarterfinals game. This is the furthest that any Coyotes men's squad has advanced in postseason play.

25 Mar. 2007. Selma S. "Jerry" Keller, ex-Libn. (1966-72), dies in Redlands at age 87.

25-30 Mar. 2007. PDC hosts its Biennial Virginia Waring International Piano Competition in IWT.

27 Mar. 2007. The Pfau Library introduces a new integrated library system, Millennium, which replaces Horizon.

28 Mar. 2007. Nicholas Arthur Erickson, ex-Dir. of Students with Disabilities and ex-Dir. of Housing and Residential Life, dies at Houghton, Michigan, at age 42.

3 Apr. 2007. A ribbon-cutting ceremony marks the official opening of the Student Recreation and Fitness Center.

4 Apr. 2007. The campus offers its first classes at the new CSUSB Downtown Center near 2nd and E Sts. in San Bernardino.

5 Apr. 2007. Coyote Radio Live debuts on local TV Channel 3.

6 Apr. 2007. Ron McCurdy and His Jazz Quartet perform in RH.

8 Apr. 2007. Cal State Theatre Arts major Megan Whitney Estrada-Miller dies in a car accident at age 21; she is commemorated in the "Pinecones & Pineapples" fundraiser on 8 July.

13 Apr. 2007. Rep. C. Jerry Lewis speaks at the unveiling of the new CSU Intelligence Community Center of Academic Excellence, together with Lonnie Henley, Deputy National Intelligence Officer of the East Asia Intelligence Council.

17 Apr. 2007. Chief of Police Robert J. Miller resigns to take a similar position with the City of Colton.

18 APR. 2007. Jimmie C. Brown, Police Lt., is named Int. Chief of Police, replacing Robert J. Miller. Blues artist John Carey performs in RH.

19 APR. 2007. Filmmaker Saul Landau speaks in UH-106 about his film, *We Don't Play Golf Here*.

21 APR. 2007. Eco-magician Paul Cash performs in the Arena as part of the 21st Annual Environmental Expo.

24 APR. 2007. Yehezkel Landau speaks at the 20th Annual Morrow-McCombs Memorial Lecture on "Religion, Conflict, and Peacemaking" at Congregation Emanu El, S.B.

26 APR. 2007. Dom Betro speaks in PR on "Social Entrepreneurship."

28 APR. 2007. Dan Abril speaks in VA-101 at Access Expo 2007.

30 APR. 2007. Walter S. Hawkins, Undergraduate Studies (1974-07), retires.

2 MAY 2007. Soprano Rebecca Tomlinson performs in RH.

5 MAY 2007. Susan E. Summers, Assoc. Dean for the Coll. of Extended Learning (1987-07), retires.

7 MAY 2007. Liz Murray speaks in SUEC on "Homeless to Harvard." The Biological Science Building is re-occupied following extensive remodeling and upgrading.

14 MAY 2007. Paul Iganski speaks in SR on "Hate Crime and Religious Intolerance: Lessons from London."

21 MAY 2007. The campus's Facilities Services Dept. receives an Award of Excellence in Facilities Management from APPA.

22 MAY 2007. Paul von Blum speaks in VA-302 on "Visual Politics: Critical Visions from African American and Latino Artists." John Boucard speaks in JB-287.

23 MAY 2007. Poets Ruth Nolan, Gayle Brandeis, Chrystine Julian, Alaska, and Cati Porter read from their work in SU Women's Center. The campus receives a 2-year, $122,000 grant from the U.S. Dept. of Education to support its Asian Studies Minor. The campus hosts a panel on "Immigration Policy and Its Effects on Our Community" in YC, with Carlos I. Giralt Cabrales (Consul General of Mexico), Father Pat Guillén (Libreria del Pueblo of San Bernardino), Mariana González (National Alliance for Human Rights), Barbara Flores, Elsa O. Valdez, and Michal Kohout.

2 JUN. 2007. Comedienne Lily Tomlin was scheduled to perform on this date in the Arena, but cancelled on May 22.

15 JUN. 2007. Colleen F. Artrup, ex- Custodian (1973-82), dies in Olympia, Washington at age 85.

15-17 JUN. 2007. The 41st Commencement is held in the Arena and at PDC, with Louise White giving the keynote speech at PDC.

17 JUN. 2007. Nancy P. Simpson, Athletic Dir. (1991-07), resigns.

18 JUN. 2007. Dwight P. Sweeney, Prof. of Education and Dir. of the Univ. Center for Developmental Disabilities, is named Int. Athletic Dir., replacing Nancy P. Simpson.

30 JUN. 2007. Johnnie Ann Ralph, Ex-Library Dean and Univ. Libn., relinquishes her office. Richard F. Fehn, Prof. of Biology (1983-07), dies of prostate cancer at age 55.

SUM. 2007. Retirements: Edna B. Domingo, Lect. in Nursing (2003-07); John W. Heeren, Prof. of Sociology (1971-07); Jeanne C. King, Prof. of Management (1990-07); Nancy L. Mary, Prof. of Social Work (1989-07); James L. Mulvihill, Prof. of Geography and Environmental Studies (1981-07); Maureen Newlin, Lect. in English (1998-07); Cynthia L. Paxton, Prof. of Health Science and Human Ecology (1979-07); S. E. Claire Purvis, Prof. of Accounting and Finance (1993-07); Richard H. Rowland, Prof. of Geography and Environmental Studies (1975-07); Elisabeth K. Ryland, Prof. of Management (1986-07); Ralph H. Salmi, Prof. of Political Science (1990-07); Christine M. Schalow, Prof. of Accounting and Finance (1991-07); David L. Schalow, Prof. of Accounting and Finance (1991-07); Beverly Shiflett, Lect. in Marketing; M. Alayne Sullivan, Assoc. Prof. of Education (2000-07); Michael Urmann, Lect. in Economics; Janet J. Woerner, Prof. of Education (1991-07). Staff: Marjorie Callaghan, Worker's Comp and Retirement Officer; James Fish, Analyst and Programmer for Administrative Computing; Deborah Grimsley, Grant Writer; Alinda King, Purchasing; Faliu Laulemaga, Grounds Maintenance; Cecilia McCarron, Student Health Center; Linda McCullough, Administrative Support Coordinator, Biology Dept.; Carolyn McDermid, Assoc. Dir., Accounting; Mary G. Moya, Univ. Advancement (1982-07); Margie Peltier, Student Health Center; Kenneth C. Reed, Instructional Support Technician, Art Dept. (1982-07); Fred Roybal, Supervising Electrician (1984-07); Carolyn Smits, Athletics; LeRoy A. Wilke, Chief Engineer and Energy Manager (1979-07).

1 JUL. 2007. César Caballero, Assoc. Univ. Libn. at CSU, Los Angeles, is named Dean of the John M. Pfau and Univ. Libn., replacing Johnnie Ann Ralph. Tera Bisbee is named Dir. of Ombuds Services and Equal Opportunity and Diversity Officer, replacing Chani Beeman. The campus begins installing solar panels on the Physical Education Building and Health and Physical Education Complex as part of a long-term partnership with Southern Calif. Edison Co. to reduce energy costs.

8 JUL. 2007. The campus receives $104,000 in gifts donated at the 5th Annual Pinecones & Pineapples event hosted by Neale and Patricia Perkins at their Lake Arrowhead home.

11 JUL. 2007. The surf rock group Tornadoes performs in LC.

18 JUL. 2007. The big band swing group Phat Cat Swinger performs in LC. S.B. City installs stop signs at the corner of Sierra Dr. and Northpark Blvd.

25 JUL. 2007. Blues group Rhythm of Life performs in LC.

31 JUL. 2007. John A. Conley, Prof. of Criminal Justice and Dean of the Coll. of Social and Behavioral Sciences (1996-07), retires.

1 AUG. 2007. Jamal R. Nassar is named Dean of the Coll. of Social and Behavioral Sciences, replacing John A. Conley. The group Latin Society performs in LC. David Wilson is named Custodial Supervisor, replacing Michael V. Benton.

14 AUG. 2007. The campus receives a $122,000 grant from the U.S. Dept. of Education to launch a new Asian Studies minor, effective Fall 2007.

16 AUG. 2007. WRI hosts its 1st San Bernardino Co. Water Conference in Ontario, with S.B. Co. Superintendent Brad Mitzelfelt giving the keynote address.

24 AUG. 2007. Cal State student Brandon Smith dies at the age of 19 in a motorcycle accident while racing in the Adelanto Grand Prix in the Nevada desert between Reno and Las Vegas.

27 AUG. 2007. Spencer A. Freund is named VP for Information Resources and Technology and Chief Information Officer, replacing Lorraine M. Frost, who is named Assoc. VP for Information Resources and Technology. WASC approves the Ed.D. degree for the campus. The campus receives a national silver medal for its *Come Here, Go Anywhere* student recruitment video from CASE, the Council for Advancement and Support of Education.

1 SEPT. 2007. The campus begins offering its 1st doctoral degree, an Ed.D. degree in Education.

5 SEPT. 2007. The campus receives a $1.5 million grant from The U.S. Dept. of Education to boost its "Quality Teachers for Quality Students" program. The campus receives a Diversity Award from Minority Access Inc.

17 SEPT. 2007. At the annual convocation, Pres. Karnig notes that he recently passed his tenth year as President, and was also reviewed during the previous year. The campus received $30 million in grants and contracts during 2006/07, more than 5 times the amount a decade earlier. "The CSU Trustees asked each campus to raise funds at least equal to 10% of the campus general fund budget; last year our goal was a bit over $9 million. We raised $10.4 million. Clearly, with successful grants and contracts and fundraising, we become less dependent and help define our own future. With funding for its Health Sciences Building, we closed the initial phase of the Palm Desert [Campus] campaign. Overall, we secured roughly $40 million in non-state resources to build the campus.... The Tools for Education campaign, which augments the College of Education's centers, labs, and institutes, has obtained nearly $3 million of its $4 million goal. We created the Presidential Academic Excellence Scholarship in 2002.... Ralph Salmi's Model UN Team's [won] its 10th Outstanding Delegate Award. The Coussoulis Arena will have its one millionth visitor this year. The students voted for higher fees to expand the Health Center, increase IRP, Athletics, and ASI funding, and provide sports' club insurance.... The [state budget] compact with the Governor was fully funded...[resulting in] a system increase of $300 or 7%; our campus budget will grow $13.9 million to nearly $160 million overall.... We'll enhance our marketing efforts [to promote the campus] and assess the University's image in the region.... We need to consider recruiting out of our area...we've accelerated our international recruitment, [and we need to increase retention, particularly of minority students].... Collegial approaches must be built on trust." Karnig also mentions the need to increase campus security, and that planning has begun for 2 Master of Fine Arts degrees in Studio Art and Creative Writing, and that CSUSB's first doctoral program, an Ed.D. degree, will begin within a few days. The campus is negotiating with developers to receive 4 acres of land to build about 70 homes for faculty, and a gift of 200 acres as a land preserve. The Education Building is under construction, and the Biology and Physical Science Buildings renovations are underway or completed, as is the Palm Desert Campus Health Sciences Building. Two parking structures are nearly finished, and the loop road will soon open. The Student Recreation and Fitness Center opened in April. Planning is underway for an expansion of the Nursing area. The Chancellor's Office has approved $10 million in bonds for disability access improvements. "A college education is the fuel for life's opportunities, raising incomes, increasing introspection, promoting civil involvement, and helping to overcome past inequities. Higher education is the engine for a healthy economy for all of us." For the 4th straight year, the campus receives a "Best in the West" designation from *Princeton Review*, and is again included in *U.S. News & World Report*'s 2008 edition of "America's Best Colleges." Nikolai Evgenievich Khokhlov, Emer. Prof. of Psychology (1968-92) and ex-Col. in the USSR KGB, dies in S.B. at age 85.

18 SEPT. 2007. The campus receives a $1 million gift from the Osher Lifelong Learning Institute to create an endowment to support the Institute at CSUSB. The campus unveils a new University logo featuring an outline in blue of the S.B. Mountains.

21 SEPT. 2007. The campus receives a 2007 Digital Education Achievement Award from the Center for Digital Education

22 SEPT. 2007. The campus honors 36 Latinos and Native Americans for their achievements at a recognition breakfast in SUEC, hosted by Assemblywoman Wilmer D. "Amina" Carter. The Fullerton Museum acquires several rare Egyptian artifacts from the Schwennesen Collection.

24 SEPT. 2007. The campus's Facilities Services Dept. receives the National Award of Excellence in Facilities Management from APPA (Association of Physical Plant Administrators).

24-28 SEPT. 2007. The campus hosts its Annual California Indian Cultural Awareness Conference in SUEC.

28 SEPT. 2007. The campus hosts its 5th Annual California Native American Day on LCP.

29 SEPT. 2007. The campus hosts the Annual Inland Empire African-American Educational Summit, "It Takes a Village."

4 OCT. 2007. The campus receives a 4th $1 million grant from the U.S. Dept. of Education to support its McNair Scholars Program.

6 OCT. 2007. The campus hosts its 1st DisAbility Sports Festival. The campus hosts The Inland Empire Dance Concert in RH.

9 OCT. 2007. KCBS newscaster Laura Díaz speaks in SUEC.

12-14 OCT. 2007. The campus hosts its 6th Annual Pow Wow of the San Manuel Band of Mission Indians.

18 Oct. 2007. The campus receives a $2.4 million Title V Hispanic-Serving Institution grant to help low-income Latino students. William C. Green receives the Golden Apple Award for Outstanding Teaching for 2007/08.

21-26 Oct. 2007. The campus closes its doors (save for a few hours on the morning of Oct. 22), because of high Santa Ana winds with gusts of 100 MPH, resulting in downed trees, flying debris, road closures, and smoke blowing from the Grass Valley and Slide fires in the San Bernardino Mountains. This is the longest period that Cal State has ever been shut down during an academic session. The winds damage the roof of Brown Hall, blow away panels on the Visual Arts Center, break windows in the Dance Studio, and damage carports in the Residence Halls. Several faculty lose their homes, including Lloyd E. Peake and Emer. Prof. Amanda Sue Rudisill.

23 Oct. 2007. University Police confront a suspect parked illegally on the north side of campus, and with the S.B. Police Dept., chase him into the foothills of the San Bernardino Mountains; when he rams a police car, he is shot and killed by the officers in self-defense.

29 Oct. 2007. Pres. Karnig announces that the campus will maintain its previously established academic schedule for the Fall Quarter, despite having lost a week's worth of classes.

29-30 Oct. 2007. Joseph P. Winnick speaks twice on "Helping Disabled Students and Adults Safely Participate in Physical Activities."

31 Oct. 2007. Yunsang Lee, Library Equipment Systems Specialist (2001-07), resigns. Dwight P. Sweeney, Int. Athletic Dir., returns to his position as Prof. of Education and Dir. of the Univ. Center for Developmental Disabilities.

1 Nov. 2007. Kevin L. Hatcher is named Athletic Dir., replacing Dwight P. Sweeney.

3 Nov. 2007. The campus hosts its Annual EdTech Conference in UH-106, with Stephanie Hamilton giving the keynote address.

4 Nov. 2007. World Wrestling Entertainment (WWE) performs "Raw Live!" in the Arena. Singer and comedienne Carol Channing performs "An Artful Journey" in RH.

5 Nov. 2007. Ash Dr., a short new connector road between Northpark Blvd. and Parking Lots A and B, opens for business.

9 NOV. 2007. The campus hosts its Global Warming/Climate Change Summit in SUEC, with William Patzert giving the keynote address. WRI hosts its Annual Conference, "Managing Drought in the Inland Empire," in UC, with Richard Minnich giving the keynote address, and gives the late Joseph A. Rowe its first-ever Water Hero Award.

14 NOV. 2007. The Martin A Matich family, the Matich Foundation, and the Matich Corp. receive the Lifetime Achievement Award at the 5th Annual Spirit of the Entrepreneur Awards at the Riverside Convention Center.

16 NOV. 2007. The campus holds a memorial service for the late Richard F. Fehn in SB-128. Nicaraguan poet Ricardo Barreto reads from his work in ER.

26 NOV. 2007. Audrey Mathews is named a Fellow of the National Academy of Public Administration. The campus adds 20 parking meters to Parking Lot G.

27 NOV. 2007. The campus receives a $4 million grant from the National Institute of Health to create a center promotion research and training on health inequities. The campus receives a $1 grant from the Coeta and Donald Barker Foundation to help train nurses of the Eisenhower Medical Center at the PDC Health Sciences Building under construction.

28 NOV. 2007. The group Mariachi Internacional de México de Francisco J. Jara performs in SUEC. Photographer Don Normark speaks about his work in the Art Gallery. *Los Angeles Times* reporter Sam Quinones speaks about Mexico in SMSU's The Bay.

29 NOV. 2007. Banker D. Linn Wiley is named Executive-in-Residence.

30 NOV. 2007. Rep. Joe Baca holds his Annual Education Summit, "No Child Left Behind: Time for a New Federal Response," in UC, with Carlos E. Cortés acting as moderator. Craig D. Henderson, Counselor and Judicial Affairs Officer (1976-07), retires.

1 DEC. 2007. Philip Ferrante speaks on "Hiking" in OA.

8 DEC. 2007. The 7th Winter Commencement is held in the Arena and on PDC.

10 DEC. 2007. The campus is again named one of the "Publisher's Picks of the Top 100 Four-Year Institutions in the U.S. in Graduating Hispanics" by *The Hispanic Outlook in Higher Education*.

15 DEC. 2007. Singer and actress Dana Adkins performs in the Indian Wells Theater at PDC.

21 DEC. 2007. Dorothy Hamill, Franc D'Ambrosio, and the Broadway on Ice troupe perform in the Arena.

31 DEC. 2007. Kristen Sanders, Library Asst. (1972-07), retires.

2008

5 JAN. 2008. Several buildings and rooms on campus are partially flooded by a major rainstorm, including JB-102, JB-124, the fourth and fifth floors of Brown Hall, and the BI basement.

7 JAN. 2008. The campus opens Parking Structure 2, adding 750 new parking spaces, plus the first segments of the new rear perimeter road, West Campus Circle and North Campus Circle. Tatiana V. Karmanova is named Assoc. Dean of Extended Learning, replacing Susan E. Summers.

10 JAN. 2008. Louis G. Pérez speaks in PiR and in IWT (Jan. 11) on "Should Japan Go Nuclear?"

11 JAN. 2008. The campus opens East Campus Circle and the rest of North Campus Circle, completing the new CSUSB interior perimeter road, which now terminates at a new entrance with traffic signals on the southeast edge of campus, at the corner of Northpark Blvd., Little Mountain Dr., and East Campus Circle.

14 JAN. 2008. The campus debuts a new website at www.csusb.edu.

15 JAN. 2008. Kim Ball, Dir. of the Coyote Bookstore, resigns. Assoc. Dean Cynthia Flores is appointed to the State Lottery Commission.

16 JAN. 2008. Writers Michael Craft and Thom Racina speak about their work in OA.

19 JAN. 2008. G. Louis Fletcher receives the 6th Annual WRI Lifetime Achievement Award in UC.

20 JAN. 2008. Samuel Maxwell Plaut, first Medical Dir. of the Student Health Center (1965-76), dies at Folsom at age 79.

23 JAN. 2008. The campus opens Parking Structure 1, adding 750 new parking spaces.

24 JAN. 2008. Lisa Marie Platske speaks in PL-4005 on "Designing Your

Destiny." The campus settles a class-action lawsuit brought against it by 9 disabled students and the Disability Rights Legal Center, in which it agrees to expend $11 million to provide better accessibility, training, and grievance procedures on campus, and to pay $505,000 in legal fees and $315,000 in compensation.

26 JAN. 2008. The campus hosts a 92nd birthday party for woodworker Sam Maloof in the Art Museum. Cal State student Kimberlee Benton is named Miss Black San Bernardino.

30 JAN. 2008. Toby Miller speaks in SUT on "Madeover Nation: The United States of Reinvention." The campus receives a $1.1 million gift of software from i2 to analyze terrorism intelligence.

31 JAN. 2008. Music executive Jomo speaks about her career in SUEC. Ex-MCI executive Walt Pavlo speaks in PL-4005 on "Wire Fraud and Money Laundering."

7 FEB. 2008. Jon Slater speaks in PL-4005 on "Teamwork: Independent Minds Working Together to Maximize Success."

8-10 FEB. 2008. The campus hosts the 16th Annual Western Regional Outdoor Leadership Conference in SUEC and SRFC, with Mike Libecki giving the keynote address.

13 FEB. 2008. Writer Bei Ling speaks on his work in PiR. Mathematician Yair Censor speaks in UH-250 on "Projection Methods."

14 FEB. 2008. *San Bernardino Sun* and *Inland Valley Daily Bulletin* Editor Steve Lambert speaks in PL-4005 on "Disruptive Innovation." Yuchin Chien is named Outstanding Professor for 2007/08.

15 FEB. 2008. (Sara) Jeanne Gordon Roberts, retired Secretary (-1984), dies at age 84. Philosopher Gary Watson speaks in SB-302-B on "Standing in Judgment."

18 FEB. 2008. The Harlem Globetrotters perform in the Arena.

19 FEB. 2008. Bernice Johnson Reagon speaks in SUEC on "The Song Culture of the Civil Rights Movement."

20 FEB. 2008. Beth Liebson Hawkins speaks in SB-516 on "Cultural Challenges: Forming a Family Identity." Linda Nichols speaks in PL-4005 on "Cardiac Care" as the 1st speaker in the revised John M. Pfau Library Lecture Series. Klaus Mueller speaks in UH-341 on "Real-Time 3D Computed Tomographic Reconstruction Using Commodity Graphics Hardware."

21 Feb. 2008. J. Corey Oliver speaks in JB-287 on "Traveler Guitar," as the 1st speaker in the Surado® Distinguished Entrepreneur Lecture Series of the CSUSB Inland Empire Center for Entrepreneurship. Writer and San Manuel Band of Mission Indians Elder Pauline Murillo speaks about her work in SU Cross Cultural Center. D. Linn Wiley speaks in PL-4005 on "Leadership in Tough Times." Haw-Jan "John" Wu is named Dir. of the William and Barbara Leonard University Transportation Center, replacing Norm King.

25 Feb. 2008. Julie A. Nelson speaks in PiR on "The Maritime Administration." Kevin Moffett receives a $25,000 fellowship from the National Endowment for the Arts.

26 Feb. 2008. Tanya Fisher speaks in PL-4005 on "Education in the African American Community." Daniel Beaty performs "Emergence—SEE!" in SUEC.

28 Feb. 2008. Gail Guge speaks in PL-4005 on "When Brands Leap, Business Bounds."

1 Mar. 2008. *The Coyote Chronicle* receives two awards from the California College Media Association at a gala awards ceremony in San Francisco: 1st-place award for "Best Special Section" and a 3rd-place for "Best News Page Design."

4 Mar. 2008. Miroslav Peric speaks in BI-009 on "Recent Progress in Electron Spin Exchange in Liquids." Takashi Hoshizaki speaks in SB-211 on "The Draft, War, and Conscience."

6 Mar. 2008. Noel L. Massie speaks in PL-4005 on "Strategies for Keeping an Organization Entrepreneurial." Alumna artist Katrin Wiese speaks about her work in the Art Gallery.

7 Mar. 2008. Michael Nelson speaks in SB-302-B on "Agent Causalism in a Casually Closed Physical World."

10 Mar. 2008. Writer DeWitt Henry speaks about his work in SR.

11 Mar. 2008. The Robert Kyle Latin/Brazilian Project performs in RH. María Elena Chávez speaks in PL-4005 on "César Chávez: His Life and Struggles."

12 Mar. 2008. Ellen Coleman speaks in PL-4005 on "Eat to Live." World War II aviator Iris Critchell speaks in SUEC.

13 MAR. 2008. Ursula Mentjes speaks in PL-4005 on "Selling with Intention." The campus holds a special assembly to discuss pending CSU budget cuts. Radio manager Jeff Parke speaks in SU.

17 MAR. 2008. Bagpiper Tim Riley performs in CCU.

21 MAR. 2008. Bonnie Brunkhorst receives the Robert H. Carleton Award from the National Science Teachers Assoc. Nick Nazarian, Asst. Dir. of Alumni Affairs (2001-08), resigns.

26 MAR. 2008. The campus receives a $200,000 gift from S.B. Co. Children's Fund to establish a scholarship to aid former foster youth.

27 MAR. 2008. The campus receives a $150,000 grant from the John F. Merrell Foundation to endow scholarships and fund faculty research in the Dept. of Accounting and Finance.

1 APR. 2008. Stuart Sumida becomes the 4th CSUSB faculty member to receive a $20,000 Wang Family Excellence Award. Elsa Ochoa-Fernández, Dir. of the International Institute (1991-08), retires.

5 APR. 2008. Tanya Atwater speaks at OA on "How the West Was Won."

7 APR. 2008. Jimmie C. Brown, Int. Chief of Police, is named permanent Chief. The campus receives a $340,000 grant from the Archaeological Survey Foundation to provide scholarships and research opportunities for anthropology students.

8 APR. 2008. Peter Kovach speaks in SR on "Learning Languages."

11 APR. 2008. Tomasz Owerkowicz speaks in CS-128 on "Respiratory Turbinates: Rosetta Bone in the Evolution of Endothermy in Mammals and Birds?" Jack H. Brown is named the 1st inductee into the CSUSB Food Industry Entrepreneurs Hall of Fame at a dinner in UC, with S.B. Mayor Morris conducting the ceremony.

13 APR. 2008. The men's hockey team loses in the semi-final game to Neumann College in the NCAA Division II Championships.

14 APR. 2008. Darleen K. Stoner receives the 2007 Environmental Achievement Award from the U.S. Environmental Protection Agency.

15 APR. 2008. The U.S. Army Jazz Septet performs in RH. David Coleman speaks in SUEC on "Making Relationships Matter."

16 APR. 2008. Robert Alan Lee, retired Assoc. Dean of Academic Affairs and Emer. Prof. of English (1968-92), dies in Santa Cruz of congestive heart failure at age 73.

17 APR. 2008. Jesse Billauer of Life Rolls speaks in SU on "Overcoming Adversity."

17-18 APR. 2008. The campus hosts its 6th Annual Latin American Studies Conference: Study of the Americas in the Commons, with Guatemalan novelist Gaspar Pedro González, Oaxacan filmmaker Yolanda Cruz, guitarist Eladio Scharrón, and Maya-Achí filmmaker Manuel Felipe Pérez.

22 APR. 2008. Chinese writer Anchee Min speaks in SUEC about her work.

22-27 APR. 2008. The campus team earns a 12th "Outstanding Delegation Award" at the Model United Nations competition in New York, representing The Philippines.

23 APR. 2008. The campus hosts "A Divided Community," a live performance by and about Japanese-Americans and their experiences during World War II, in SUT

24 APR. 2008. Artist Ava Brodsky de Gouttes speaks in VA-302 on "On Photography and Women in Paris."

26 APR. 2008. Country western singers Dana Adkins and Brian Scott perform "Two for the Road" in IWT.

29 APR. 2008. Local radio program Director Steve Hoffman and afternoon on-air personality "Daryl" speak in SUT on rock-'n'-roll radio.

29 APR. 2008. Amir Hussain speaks at the First Presbyterian Church of S.B. at the 21st Annual Morrow-McCombs Lecture Series on "Islam in North America: Separating Fact from Fiction."

1 MAY 2008. The campus creates an Admissions and Student Recruitment Advisory Board.

2 MAY 2008. The campus sponsors its 2nd Annual Leonard Transportation Center Forum, "For Whom the Road Should Toll? The Future of Toll Roads and Road Pricing in California," at the Hilton Ontario Airport in Ontario. Ex-Pres. Pfau, his wife Antreen, and daughters Elly and Madelaine, create the John M. Pfau Family Scholarship Endowment with a $12 million gift to the University, $10.8 million of which will be partially used to create the President's Academic Excellence Scholarship Program, and $1.2 million endowing the John M. Pfau Library.

3 MAY 2008. The campus Systems Analysis Team wins 1st place at the 12th Annual Information Technology Competition at Pomona.

6 MAY 2008. S.B. Mayor Morris hosts a VIP reception at the Fullerton Art Museum to honor its recent accreditation. Emeritus Prof. David Stine has a new school named after him in Montclair. The Mountain Fifes and Drums Corps performs in RH.

8 MAY 2008. Malaysian astronaut Muszaphar Shukor speaks about his experiences in PS-10. Edward Gómez speaks in PS-10 on "The Politics of Immigration." Steve Dunn speaks in SR on "The Journey from Lean to Green and Beyond." Tony Coulson receives the 2008 Award for Innovative Excellence in Teaching, Learning, and Technology.

9 MAY 2008. Dr. Dev A. GnanaDev is named 2008 Arrowhead Distinguished Executive Officer at the Ontario Convention Center.

11 MAY 2008. Elsa María Ochoa-Fernández, retired Dir. of International Student Services and the International Institute (1991-08) and wife of Provost Louis J. Fernández, dies in San Bernardino at age 67.

12 MAY 2008. Antronette "Toni" Yancey speaks in PR on "Culturally Targeted Physical Activity Promotion Approaches Between Settings and Regions: Everybody Needs a Little Push."

13 MAY 2008. Dorothy E. Inghram speaks in SUEC on "San Bernardino: Then and Now." Sherryl Vint speaks in SR on "Why Are There No Great Women Scientists? Gender and Genetics in Gwyneth Jones's Life."

14 MAY 2008. Larry E. Burgess speaks in PL-4005 at the revived 11th Rheubottom-Webster Local History Lecture series on "Challenges, Pitfalls, & Successes in Saving Local History."

16 MAY 2008. The campus holds a memorial service in UC for Elsa M. Ochoa-Fernández, late Dir. of International Student Services and the International Institute (1991-08). Greek Orthodox Archbishop of Sevastia Atallah Hanna and Palestinian Supreme Justice Sheikh Taiseer al-Tamimi speak in UC at the Gamma Lambda Chapter of Phi Beta Delta annual scholarship awards banquet.

17 MAY 2008. Glen Grayman speaks in IWT on "The Environmental Aspects of the Health of Eastern Riverside County."

20 MAY 2008. Peter Beyersdorf speaks in BI-104 on "Laser Interferometry for Gravitational Wave Detection."

21 May 2008. Students rally on the Library Lawn against budget cuts.

22 May 2008. Dick Rennick speaks in SU on "General Tips for Entrepreneurial Success."

23 May 2008. Tom Crisp speaks in SB-302-B on "Speaking Loosely About the Past." Sungkyoo Huh speaks in JB Dean's Conference Room on "The Effect of the Traits of Responsibility Center and the Traits of Job on Organizational Effectiveness."

27 May 2008. Sal Castro speaks in SUEC on "Brown and Proud: 40 Years of Chicano Activism." Columnist Gustavo Arrellano reads from his work in SUEC.

28 May 2008. Rep. C. Jerry Lewis attends a ceremony in SU to honor 9 minority students who have been named Fellows of the Integrated Technology Transfer Network.

29 May 2008. Adam Brisol speaks in SMSU's "The Bay" on "The Psychopharmacology of Creative Thinking." The campus is designated a National Center of Academic Excellence in Information Assurance Education by the National Security Agency and the Dept. of Homeland Security.

31 May 2008. Campus booster Neal T. Baker, founder and owner of Baker's Drive-Thru Restaurants, dies at Redlands at age 84. Retirements: Barbara Kerr, Facilities Services; Margaret DeGroff, SMSU (1990-08).

2 Jun. 2008. Robert A. Blackey is honored at the Faculty Awards Luncheon in UC as the first 40-year employee on campus. Tae-Hee Yoon speaks in PR on "Miracle and Paradox: The Revival of Korean, Inc."

3 Jun. 2008. Cellist Michele Brosseau-Tacchia and pianist Michael Tacchia perform in RH.

4 Jun. 2008. Cynthia Ann Amey, Administrative Asst. in the Career Development Center (1996-08), dies at age 44.

5 Jun. 2008. Campus booster William E. Leonard dies at San Bernardino at age 85.

7 Jun. 2008. Cal State graduate student Norene Tyus dies at age 57.

9 Jun. 2008. Kenton Lyle Monroe, Prof. of Psychology, Assoc. Dean of Counseling and Dean of Students (1965-88), dies in Loma Linda at age 74.

11 Jun. 2008. Janice L. "Jan" Lemmond, Support Services Officer (1978-

98), dies in Yucaipa of cancer at age 73. Cynthia Olivo, Assoc. Dir. of Admissions and Student Recruitment (1996-08), resigns.

13-15 JUN. 2008. The 42nd Commencement is held in the Arena and at PDC, with Jean Stephens giving the keynote address (Business & Public Administration ceremony).

SUM. 2008. Retirements: Carolyn B. Aldana, Prof. of Economics (1995-08); Otto H. Chang, Prof. of Accounting and Finance (1991-08); Charles D. Hoffman, Prof. of Psychology (1974-08); Janice L. Loutzenhiser, Prof. of Management (1976-08); Lee A. Lyons, Prof. of Theatre Arts (1990-08); James Mason, Asst. Prof. of Education (1992-08); Theodore R. McDowell, Prof. of Geography and Environmental Studies (1983-08); Dale K. Sechrest, Prof. of Criminal Justice (1990-08); Billie P. Sessions, Prof. of Art (1996-08); Darleen K. Stoner, Prof. of Education (1984-08). Staff: Jace Baker, Management; Peter Cleppe, Academic Computing and Media; Paula Cramer, Mathematics; Ellen Daroszewski, Nursing; Bruce Decker, Art; Ignacio Flores, Facilities Services; George Gibbs, EOP; Jeanette Janik, PDC; Helen Johnston, Coll. of Natural Sciences; Cita Jones, Athletics Dept.; Dennis Kroeger, Foreign Languages; Elizabeth Langenfeld, English; Diane Miller, Purchasing Dept.; Patricia Owens, Nursing Dept.; Eva Mae Pisciotta, Music; Judith Powell, Kinesiology; Sheryl Pytlak, Accounting; Ramona Rodríguez, Facilities Services; Daniel Tuckerman, Communication Studies; Russell Wheeler, Undergraduate Studies; William Whiting, Facilities Services; Paula Zaragossa, Management.

1 JUL. 2008. Parking fees increase from $24-$28 per month, and from $4-$5 per day. Follett Educational Services assumes management of the Coyote Bookstore from the Foundation.

2 JUL. 2008. The Latin Society performs on LCP. Jeffrey Thompson, Interim Assoc. Provost for Research (2005-08) and Prof. of Biology, is named permanent Assoc. Provost.

9 JUL. 2008. Laurie Lewis and Tom Rozum perform on LCP.

16 JUL. 2008. Blasphemous Rumours performs on LCP.

23 JUL. 2008. Mo' Better Blues performs on LCP.

30 JUL. 2008. The Beatles & The Monkees Tribute Band performs on LCP.

7 AUG. 2008. The campus receives a "Best in the West" designation from *The Princeton Review* for the 5th straight year.

8 AUG. 2008. Kathy Peigne (1998-08) retires.

14 AUG. 2008. The campus begins occupying the renovated Physical Sciences and Biological Sciences Buildings, and the Palm Desert Health Sciences Building at PDC.

17 AUG. 2008. Jeetendra R. Joshee, Dean of Extended Learning, resigns to take a position at CSU Long Beach.

18 AUG. 2008. Tatiana V. Karmanova, Assoc. Dean of Extended Learning, is named Act. Dean of Extended Learning, replacing Jeetendra R. Joshee.

21 AUG. 2008. Lynda Kristine Ludwig Davaran, retired Library Asst. (1992-01), dies of cancer at Twin Peaks at age 68. The campus signs a dual admissions agreement with Riverside Community Coll.

1 SEPT. 2008. The campus begins offering a B.A. degree in Arabic Language and Culture. Sodexo Inc. assumes operation of the Commons and the Coyote Café in SU.

3 SEPT. 2008. The campus is named one of "America's Best Colleges" by *U.S. News & World Report*.

8 SEPT. 2008. Cal State student Pamela Nobel stars in the film *Resurrection Mary*, using the screen name Pamela Jean.

16 SEPT. 2008. J. Paul Vicknair, Assoc. Provost for Academic Personnel, returns to the ranks as Prof. of Mathematics. Buckley B. Barrett, Libn. (1982-08), retires. The campus receives a gift from Inland Communities Corp. of 2 parcels of land, including 4 acres north of Badger Hill to be used for faculty housing, and 235 acres at the base of Badger Canyon to be known as the Akkad Natural Preserve, bringing the total campus area to 680 acres.

17 SEPT. 2008. Laurel A. Lilienthal is named Int. Asst. VP for Academic Personnel, replacing J. Paul Vicknair. Faculty members complain that Follett Educational Services, manager of the Coyote Bookstore, is pushing its own publications on the students.

22 SEPT. 2008. At the annual convocation, Pres. Karnig notes a deficit for 2008/09 of $2.1 million, which the campus will be able to cover from reserves and one-time funds; alas, 2009/10 is predicted to be another bad fiscal year. The university continues to improve energy and other efficiencies, cutting utility costs by reducing electrical consumption by 5 million kilowatt hours, and drilling a well that now supplies half of the irrigation water; additional solar panels will be added in the future. State funding must be supplemented with other outside revenues. The Inland Empire has been exceptionally impacted by the 2008 recession because it relied heavily on housing construction, and also because it has such low levels of educational attainment. Only 20% of adults have a college degree, with only one-third of graduating high school students here attending college. We need to improve these odds by producing quality K-12 teachers, since good teachers make a difference; by offering programs such as Gear Up and Upward Bound, which provide youth with academic skills and educational aspirations; and by promoting relevant research; by expanding outreach efforts that have promise, such as Tom Rivera's Inland Empire Future Leaders Program. We also need to increase the number of international students on campus, since for funding purposes they are separate from our state-budgeted enrollment targets, and represent extra revenue. During the coming year the campus will complete the shift of post-baccalaureate admissions to the Graduate School, thereby allowing the Admissions Office to focus on undergraduates. Given the costs of running the campus on a quarter system, the Faculty Senate again needs to assess the value of changing the academic schedule to semesters. The campus will explore the possibility of adding additional student housing. The Pres. notes that the campus membership in the Western Interstate Compact for Higher Education (WICHE) allows students from other Western states to attend classes by paying only 150% of in-state fees, less in many cases than it would cost to attend universities in their own areas. The campus needs to boost its efforts to provide programs and classes via distributed learning. The Presidential Academic Excellence Scholarship Program (PAES) has expanded from an initial 6 students to 46 this year. The Fullerton Art Museum was accredited by the American Association of Museums, one of only 4% institutions nationwide to be so honored. The campus was also accredited by the National Center of Academic Excellence in Information Assurance, one of just 4 schools in Calif. to receive this national distinction. The University raised $49 million in grants and gifts (4th in the CSU System), tripling that of the highest previous year, and intends to elicit funds to build a 60,000-sq.-ft. expansion of the Performing Arts Building and a Teaching Observatory, and also to double the size of the Student Health Center, add an addition to the Nursing complex, and spend $12 million to reduce campus barriers to access. Bookstore and commons functions were privatized to save money. The campus is developing a new strategic plan, building on previous efforts, to help increase the percentage of students actually graduating. The campus is implementing a new security system, featuring outdoor public loudspeakers, speaker phones in offices and classrooms, emergency messages sent via texting and voice messaging to cell phones, and security cameras in the parking lots and residence areas. Despite the bad budget news, he says, we have much to be thankful for.

22-26 SEPT. 2008. The campus hosts its Annual California Indian Culture

Awareness Conference in SU.

24 SEPT. 2008. Masaaki Yoshino, Pres. of Yasuda Women's University, Hiroshima, Japan, visits CSUSB to celebrate 20 years of cooperation between the two campuses.

25 SEPT. 2008. The Coll. of Education Building opens for business.

26 SEPT. 2008. The campus hosts its 10th Annual Native American Day celebration on LCP.

28 SEPT. 2008. Mary Gertrude Patterson, Emer. Prof. of Nursing (1977-85), dies in Desert Hot Springs at age 94.

30 SEPT. 2008. The campus signs a dual admissions agreement with Chaffey Coll.

1 OCT. 2008. Bob Wolf speaks in UC on "Business and Transportation in the Inland Empire."

2 OCT. 2008. Joshua Fredenburg hosts a forum, "Speak on It."

3 OCT. 2008. A ribbon-cutting ceremony marks the official opening of the Coll. of Education Building.

6 OCT. 2008. CSUSB's Coyote Radio is named an official iTunes station.

7 OCT. 2008. Pianist James Nalley performs in RH.

7-8 OCT. 2008. The Calif. Supreme Court holds a cession at PDC.

8 OCT. 2008. Victor Villanueva speaks in PR on "Writing and the Forgotten Canon of Memory."

10-12 OCT. 2008. The campus hosts its 10th Annual Pow Wow of the San Manuel Band of Mission Indians.

12 OCT. 2008. The Coll. of Business and Public Administration is named one of the "Best Business Schools" in *The Princeton Review*.

14 OCT. 2008. The campus closes for the day due to high Santa Ana winds and a nearby brush fire on Little Mountain. The WRI Archives are renamed the Joseph Andrew Rowe Water Resources Archives.

16 OCT. 2008. Ana M. Guevara speaks in SU on "Opportunities from the World Bank Green Technologies Fund." Christine Chávez, granddaughter of labor activist César Chávez, speaks on Propositions 4 and 8. The Pfau Library opens its Special Collections Dept. for public use, with an official dedication ceremony on Nov. 19.

16 & 18 OCT. 2008. A private dedication ceremony and public ribbon-cutting ceremony and health fair (Oct. 18) mark the official opening of the Palm Desert Health Sciences Building at PDC, including naming the building's plaza in honor of ex-Pres. Anthony H. Evans and his wife, Lois Evans, with the attendance of Palm Desert Mayor Jean Benson, Assemblyman John J. Benoit, and CNN reporter Thelma Gutiérrez.

23 OCT. 2008. Bo Laurent (aka Cheryl Chase) speaks in SUEC on "Sexual Ambiguity: The Patient-Centered Approach."

28 OCT. 2008. Greek writer Alexis Stamatis reads from his work in PiR.

5 NOV. 2008. Lisa Tucker speaks in the Art Museum on "New Directions in Contemporary Photography."

6 NOV. 2008. Director John Milius speaks in SUT on "Filmmaking in Hollywood." A ribbon-cutting ceremony marks the official re-opening of the upgraded Biological and Physical Sciences Buildings.

7 NOV. 2008. Chris Williams speaks in CS-122 on "Animation and Computer Gaming."

8 NOV. 2008. Environmentalist David T. Suzuki speaks on "A Vision for a Sustainable Future" at Palm Springs High School Auditorium in an event sponsored by PDC. Writer Michelle Moran speaks in SU at the whodunit murder dinner event, "Who Killed King Tut?"

10 NOV. 2008. Larry Geraty speaks in SUT on "Interfaith and Intercultural Communication."

12 NOV. 2008. Randal Pinkett speaks in UC on "How to Become a Successful Entrepreneur."

13 NOV. 2008. Margaret Serpico speaks in the Art Museum on "Half a Century of Excavating Egypt: William Flinders Petrie's Contributions to Egyptology." Tim Usher receives a Fulbright grant to teach at University College, Dublin (Ireland) in 2008/09.

15 NOV. 2008. Joseph Grindstaff, Dir. of the Calif. Bay Delta Authority, receives the 7th Annual WRI Lifetime Achievement Award at a banquet in SUEC; Hubert Webb receives the 2nd Water Hero Award.

17 NOV. 2008. Kimberley R. Cousins receives the Golden Apple Award for Teaching Excellence for 2008/09.

19 NOV. 2008. Meher McArthur speaks in SUEC on "Zen Buddhism and Its Arts." The Pfau Library dedicates its new Special Collections Room in PL-4005, with ex-Dean Johnnie Ann Ralph, VP William Aguilar, and *S.B. Sun* columnist John Weeks speaking.

21 NOV. 2008. Mohamad Nasser speaks in SUT on "Tolerance." Christ Brandt speaks in VA-101 on his film, *Independents*. The Rancho Belago Wind Ensemble performs with the CSUSB Symphonic Band in RH. The campus holds a memorial service for Mary Barnes, widow of the late Prof. Ronald E. Barnes.

22 NOV. 2008. The campus hosts a roundtable discussion on "The Promise of Women Leaders in Politics," with Ellen DuBois, Caroline Heldman, Lori Cox Han, Glenna Matthews, and moderator Karon Jolna.

22 NOV. 2008-15 FEB. 2009. The Fullerton Art Museum hosts an exhibit of 200 ancient Egyptian artifacts from the Petrie Museum, London.

24 NOV. 2008. For the first time in its history, the CSU System declares a systemwide "impaction," and announces a cut in its enrollment base of 10,000 students for 2009/10.

25 NOV. 2008. Timothy Havens speaks in SUT on "Selling Slavery Worldwide: On the Global Popularity of *Roots* and Industry Perceptions of Race." The Dept. of Social Work is renamed the School of Social Work, and Dept. Chair Teresa Morris is named Dir.

30 NOV. 2008. Karen Newman, Aide to VP, Student Affairs, retires.

1 DEC. 2008. Robert Wilson is named Assoc. VP for Financial Operations, replacing William Takehara (who retires at the end of the month). Guitarists Matthew Elgart and Peter Yates (Elgart-Yates Duo) perform in RH.

4 DEC. 2008. Barbara A. Quarton speaks about her book, *Christmas Stories Rediscovered*, in PL-4005A.

6 DEC. 2008. The women's volleyball team is defeated by Concordia-St. Paul in the NCAA Division II National Championship game.

9 DEC. 2008. Alumna opera soprano Julie Makerov performs in RH.

11 DEC. 2008. The campus, with the Ontario-Montclair School District, receives a $991,404 grant from the Calif. Postsecondary Education

Commission to aid elementary school math teaching.

12 DEC. 2008. Head women's volleyball coach Kim Cherniss is named 2008 American Volleyball Coaches Assoc. Division II National Coach of the Year.

13 DEC. 2008. The 8th Winter Commencement is held in the Arena and on PDC.

17 DEC. 2008. The Coll. of Education Building and Student Recreation and Fitness Center are both honored as "Outstanding Design" award winners by *American School & University Magazine*. The campus signs a dual admission agreement with Riverside Community Coll., Norco Campus.

18 DEC. 2008. The campus hosts a Summit on the Economic Crisis in the Education Building's Paul and Evelyn Magnuson Auditorium.

28 DEC. 2008. Harold Ales "Jim" Jambor, Emer. Lect. in Sociology (1975-80), dies in Olympia, WA, at age 95.

31 DEC. 2008. (Allen) Craig Monroe, ex-Prof. and Chair of Communications Studies (1993-03), dies of lung cancer at Glassboro, North Carolina, at age 66. Retirements: William Takehara, Assoc. VP for Financial Operations (1994-08); David P. DeMauro, VP for Administration and Finance (1986-08); John R. Camien, Library Asst. (1973-08); Georgia B. Durden, Library Asst. (1976-08); Nadine Chávez, Dir. of EOP; Simmie L. Jones, Facilities Services (1988-08).

2009

1 JAN. 2009. Helga E. Kray, Asst. VP for Student Affairs and Student Development, is named Assoc. VP.

6 JAN. 2009. The campus is named one of 119 best colleges in the U.S. by the Carnegie Foundation 2008 Community Engagement Classification. The Teaching Resource Center relocates to FO-182, and Community-University Partnerships to FO-228 through FO-233.

7 JAN. 2009. The campus announces a new M.F.A. degree in Creative Writing, effective Fall 2009.

8 JAN. 2009. Elizabeth Waraksa speaks in the Art Museum on "You Can Take It with You: Funerary Arts from the Petrie Museum."

9 JAN. 2009. The Chancellor's Office orders a hiring freeze at all 23 CSU campuses, halts all state-funded construction projects for 90 days, and freezes the pay of VP's and above.

16 JAN. 2009. Veronica R. Amerson is named Int. Dir. of EOP.

17 JAN. 2009. Stuart R. Hemphill, VP of Southern California Edison Co., speaks in OA on "Energy Alternatives for Southern California."

20 JAN. 2009. Lance Stacy and Amara Poolswasdi speak in VA-101 on "The Rainmaker Network."

23 JAN. 2009. Jim Normandin speaks in IWT on "Begin at the End: Ease and Clarity in Testamentary Planning."

27 JAN. 2009. Artist Alexandra Grant speaks about her work in VA-101.

29 JAN. 2009. Eddy Sumar speaks in UC on "A Treasure Hunt with Otis." Beatrice Gray speaks in PL-4005 on "The Dual Immersion Program: Fostering Empowerment in Bilingualism, Biliteracy, Multicultural and Academic Competence."

31 JAN. 2009. The men's basketball contest against Cal State Los Angeles is nationally televised by CBS from the Arena. The Inland Harp Ensemble performs in RH. An episode of *The Ambassadors*, a reality-based TV show, is filmed in the Art Museum.

5 FEB. 2009. Ronnie Kovach speaks about his books in UC.

6 FEB. 2009. The Leonard Transportation Center hosts its 1st Transportation Research Conference in SU.

9 FEB. 2009. Robert W. Gardner is named VP for Administration and Finance, replacing David P. DeMauro. CSUSB's Office of Technology Transfer and Commercialization announces 5 grants to 4 Southern California companies and a Pennsylvania firm, totaling more than $450,000, to help develop life-saving civilian and military medical applications.

10 FEB. 2009. Daniel Foster of the Community Foundation speaks in VA-101. Oscar H. Gandy Jr. speaks in SUT on "Rational Discrimination and Race: Engaging the Actuarial Assumption." Daniel McCarthy speaks in PL-4005 on "Who Created the Petroglyphs?"

11 FEB. 2009. For the 3rd straight year, the campus is named by the Corporation for National and Community Service to the President's Higher Education Community Service Honor Roll for exemplary service efforts and service to disadvantaged youth. In addition, the University is profiled in a 2009 publication, *Beyond the Books: A Guide to Service Learning Col-*

leges and Universities, as one of the nation's cutting-edge service learning programs in higher education. CSUSB is named by the Carnegie Foundation as one of 119 U.S. colleges and universities in its 2008 Community Engagement Classification. Robert George Fisk, ex-Dean of Students and Emer. Prof. of Education (1962-73), dies in Portland at age 93.

12 FEB. 2009. John M. Magness speaks in UC on his book, *Pilot Vision*. Edward Kulakowski speaks in SU on "Languages Mean Business." Kathlyn Mary Cooney speaks in the Art Gallery on "Sex and Death: The Religion of Resurrection in Ancient Egypt."

13 FEB. 2009. The campus holds a memorial service in PL-013 for the late Prof. A. Craig Monroe.

14 FEB. 2009. Michael Toman of RAND Corp. speaks in OA on "Energy Alternatives and Global Issues of Environment and Warming."

16 FEB. 2009. Janet Kottke is named Outstanding Professor for 2008/09.

18 FEB. 2009. Mark Landis speaks in PL-4005 at the 12th Rheubottom/Webster Local History Lecture on "The Tale of the Kite."

19 FEB. 2009. Dowell Myers speaks in SR on his book, *Immigrants and Boomers: Forging a New Social Contract for the Future of America*. Goro Toshima speaks in SUT on his film, *A Hard Straight*. Manfred B. Steger speaks in PS-10 on "No End of History: The Great Ideological Struggle of the 21st Century."

20 FEB. 2009. The campus signs a dual admissions agreement with Mt. San Jacinto Coll.

21 FEB. 2009. U.S. Air Force Band of the Golden West performs in RH.

23 FEB. 2009. Marta Van Loan speaks in PR on "Role of Genetics, Exercise, and Nutrition on Bone Health." James Kaufman receives the 2008 E. Paul Torrance Award from the National Assoc. of Gifted Children.

24 FEB. 2009. Curator Sam Mellon speaks in VA-101.

25 FEB. 2009. Gabor T. Herman speaks in CE-110 on "Finitely Convergent Sequential Algorithms and Their Applications to Intensity Modulated Radiation Therapy," and Yair Censor speaks on "Projection Methods: Perturbation Resilience and TV-Superiorization."

25-26 FEB. & 2 MAR. 2009. The campus hosts its 2nd Annual Asian Studies Symposium in PiR, SR, and CA-107.

26 FEB. 2009. Garner Holt speaks in UC about his animatronics company.

28 FEB. 2009. Linda Pella-Hartley retires.

3 MAR. 2009. Graphic designer Andrew Oakes speaks in VA-101. Journalist Macarión Schettino speaks in UC on "Mexico in the Twenty-First Century."

5 MAR. 2009. Attorney Danuta Tuszynska speaks in UC on "Employment Law."

9 MAR. 2009. Arthur J. Copley speaks in SB-127 on "Products and Learning—The Forgotten P of Creativity." A delegation from Dongguk University, Seoul, Korea, visits the campus.

12 MAR. 2009. Andy Taylor, Chairman of Enterprise Rent-a-Car, speaks in UC about his company. Will Keim speaks in SUT on "Welcome to the Time of Your Life."

13 MAR. 2009. The campus receives a Gold Medal in the 24th Annual Admissions Advertising Awards competition for the design of its new website. The campus receives an $800,000 gift from George and Pauline Murillo to help fund the observatory on Little Badger Hill, which will now be named the Murillo Family Observatory. Singer Andy Williams performs at IWT.

17 MAR. 2009. Artist Lewis deSoto speaks about his work in VA-101. Bagpiper Tim Riley performs in the SU.

19 MAR. 2009. Valmir Mundkur speaks in UC on "Doing Business with India." Nina Wallerstein speaks in SUEC on "Community Based Participatory Research." The campus signs a dual admissions agreement with Riverside Community Coll. Moreno Valley Campus.

20 MAR. 2009. The campus launches a weekly TV show, *myCSUSB*, on local access channel KCSB.

24 MAR. 2009. The campus signs an agreement with *Isla Radio*, an award-winning radio program, to help produce shows focused on ecology and green issues.

25 MAR. 2009. The campus and the Public Safety Academy establish Police Explorer Post 308 at CSUSB.

29 MAR.-3 APR. 2009. The campus hosts the annual Virginia Waring International Piano Competition.

31 MAR. 2009. Barbara Hallack, Secretary in the President's Office (2002-09), retires. Maura Oneill speaks at the 22nd Annual Morrow-McCombs Memorial Lecture on "Mending a Torn World: Women in Interreligious Dialogue" at the Church of Jesus Christ of Latter-Day Saints on Northpark Blvd., S.B.

1 APR. 2009. Paul Amaya is named Dir. of the International Center.

2 APR. 2009. The campus announces that it will begin offering an M.S. degree in Accounting, beginning Fall 2009.

5 APR. 2009. Kevin G. Lamude, Emer. Prof. of Communication Studies (1991-04), dies of bone cancer at Bakersfield at age 66.

7-12 APR. 2009. The Cal State team again earns an "Outstanding Delegation" Award at the Model United Nations Conference in New York, representing Egypt.

11 APR. 2009. Hank Plante speaks at OA on "Proposition 8."

14 APR. 2009. Dwight Douglas Gallo, Instructional Support Technician, Biology Dept. (1984-09), dies in S.B. at age 60.

15 APR. 2009. Rwandan Justice Hassan Bubacar Jallow speaks in IWT on "Bringing Accused Genocide Fugitives to Justice." AnaLouise Keating speaks in PiR on "Reaching Through the Wound: Transformational Identity Politics for the 21st Century."

16 APR. 2009. Ron McCurdy and his Jazz Quartet perform the music and words of poet Langston Hughes in SUEC.

17 APR. 2009. The Latino Community Leadership Committee accuses the campus of failing to recruit Latino faculty and students for its Ed.D. degree program. Four Latina professors file a grievance against the campus, alleging they have been denied opportunities for advancement by the Coll. of Education.

18 APR. 2009. Nick Cataldo speaks in PL-4005 at the 13th Rheubottom/Webster Local History Lecture Series on "The Legendary Earp Clan in San Bernardino County."

22 APR. 2009. Hussein Ibish speaks in SUT on "A New Course: Moving Forward Towards Israeli-Palestinian Peace."

23 APR. 2009. The campus hosts its Annual Latin American Studies Conference, "Study of the Americas," in SUT, with keynote speaker David Bacon.

25 APR. 2009. The campus hosts a Southern California Primate Research Forum in UH-106. The Cal State team wins 1st place at the 13th Annual Information Technology Competition in Pomona.

28 APR. 2009. Matt Glowacki speaks in SUEC on "Walking Is Overrated." Francisco E. Balderrama and Richard Santillán speak in PL-4005 on "The Mexican-American Baseball Project: From the Barrios to the Big Leagues to the University," to honor the housing of the Project at the John M. Pfau Library.

30 APR. 2009. Poet Jacqueline Osherow reads from her work at the inaugural Felix Guadalupe Valdez Creative Writing Series and Celebration in SU.

1 MAY 2009. John E. Husing is named 2009 Arrowhead Distinguished Executive Officer at a lunch held in UC. Kevin Padian speaks in PS-10 on "Dover, Darwin, and Intelligent Design: A View from the Trial."

6 MAY 2009. Philippine pianist Nita Abrogar-Quinto performs and composer María Christine Muyco speaks in RH.

7 MAY 2009. Fantasy writer Peter S. Beagle reads from his work in PL-4005. Edge Development Corp. receives a $6,886,000 contract to expand and renovate the Student Health Center.

8 MAY 2009. Pulitzer Prize-winning *New York Times* reporter Eric Lichtblau speaks in SUT on "Combating Terrorism: Not Quite Yesterday's News."

9 MAY 2009. Allen "Ali" Cayir receives an Ellis Island Medal of Honor award. The campus hosts its 3rd Annual Foster Care Summit in SU. The campus hosts the Inland Dance Concert in RH.

12 MAY 2009. Tomás Benítez speaks in PL-4005 on "Latino Baseball History Project: The Mexican-American Experience."

13 MAY 2009. CEO Ted Honcharik speaks in SR.

14 MAY 2009. The campus hosts its 4th Annual American Indian Women of Distinction Symposium in UC, with keynote speaker Juanita Majel-Dixon; tribal elders Renona Pennington of the Agua Caliente Band of Cahuilla Indians and Lorena Majel-Dixon of the Pauma Band of Luiseño Indians are honored by the Symposium.

16 MAY 2009. The Coll. of Social and Behavioral Sciences inducts the first 7 alumni into its new Hall of Fame.

19 MAY 2009. Holocaust survivors Eva Brown and Edith Eva Eger speak about their experiences in SU.

20 MAY 2009. Alan Gold speaks in PL-4005 during the unveiling of "The Charley Clayton Howe Collection." The Counseling Center relocates from the Student Health Center to TA-4 north of the construction zone.

21 MAY 2009. Cal State booster and woodworker Sam Maloof dies in Alta Loma at age 93.

22 MAY 2009. The Leonard Transportation Center hosts a regional dialogue, "Greener California: Impacts of Senate Bill 375 and Winning Strategies for Southern California," in the Doubletree Hotel, Ontario Airport. The men's golf team loses a finals round playoff to Sonoma State University in the NCAA Division II Championship.

27 MAY 2009. Director Catherine Hardwicke speaks in RH on "The Art of Filmmaking."

30 MAY 2009. Composer Chinary Ung performs in RH.

2 JUN. 2009. The campus hosts its 4th Annual Ethnic Studies Symposium, "Making Culture in the Inland Empire," in SUEC. The campus receives an $80,000 grant from STARTALK to fund the study of the Arabic language.

3 JUN. 2009. To honor the 25th anniversary of the establishment of intercollegiate athletics, the campus establishes a Coyote Athletics Hall of Fame, with 5 members being inducted at SUEC.

9 JUN. 2009. Sal Castro speaks in SU on "The Academic Status of Latino Students in California." Artist Marc Lathuillière speaks in VA-302 on his work. The campus unveils the image of a howling coyote head on the southeast corner of the running track at Northpark Blvd. and East Campus Circle.

12 JUN. 2009. Groundbreaking is held for the Murillo Family Observatory on Little Badger Hill. Four Latina Education professors hold a news conference to protest a "glass ceiling" at their college that they say keeps them from reaching their full potential.

17 JUN. 2009. Evans Kahuthu, Web Development Coordinator (2003-09), resigns. Campus booster and attorney Robert Victor Fullerton, who donated the funds to complete the Art Museum which bears his name, dies at age 91.

19-21 JUN. 2009. The 43rd Commencement is held in the Arena and at PDC.

30 JUN. 2009. Louis A. Fernández, Provost and VP for Academic Affairs and Dean of the School of Natural Sciences (1991-09), retires, but returns as a retired annuitant for another month.

SUM. 2009. Retirements: Linda Burgess, Lect. in English; Mary Cannon, Lect. in Nursing (1998-09); Susan M. Finsen, Prof. of Philosophy (1986-09); Carol P. Haviland, Prof. of English and Writing Center (1987-09); Frederick J. Hebein, Prof. of Marketing (1989-09); José S. Hernández, Prof. of Language, Literacy, and Culture (1991-09); Randi L. Miller, Prof. of Sociology (1987-09). Staff: Maureen Hixson, Extended Learning (1972-09).

1 JUL. 2009. Suavé performs on LCP.

2 JUL. 2009. The Foundation for CSUSB receives a first-year Federal Women's Education Equity Grant of $164,911 from the U.S. Dept. of Education to improve the math skills of female students at Bloomington Middle School, Bloomington.

6 JUL. 2009. The Duplicating Center is renamed Printing Services.

8 JUL. 2009. Jumping Jack Flash performs on LCP.

9 JUL. 2009. The campus receives a $1,546,866 grant from the National Institute of Health to help prepare minority students to pursue doctoral degrees in biology, chemistry, kinesiology, physics, and psychology.

13 JUL. 2009. The CSU System announces that it will not accept new students for Spring term 2010.

14 JUL. 2009. Louis A. Fernández, Act. Provost and VP for Academic Affairs, relinquishes his office, but continues on the payroll through July 31.

15 JUL. 2009. Andrew R. Bodman is named Provost and VP for Academic Affairs, replacing Louis A. Fernández.

16 JUL. 2009. The Members Lonely Band performs on LCP.

21 JUL. 2009. The CSU Board of Trustees adopts drastic cost-cutting measures in the CSU System to meet a $584 million deficit, including: a 2-day-per-month furlough of most employees, with a 9.3% pay decrease; a 32% student fee increase (to $4,857 annually); and a $183 million reduction imposed directly upon the 23 campuses ($7 million at CSUSB). The campuses are ordered to reduce enrollments for the next 2 school years.

22 JUL. 2009. The Best of Everything Band performs on LCP

23 JUL. 2009. The campus receives a $100,000 grant from the U.S. Dept. of Defense's Information Assurance Scholarship Program to train students to fight electronic terrorist assaults.

28 JUL. 2009. The campus unveils a new Strategic Plan to address its financial, building, and other needs into the future.

29 JUL. 2009. The Latin Society performs on Upper Commons Patio, as part of a "Latino Baseball Reunion." Pres. Karnig presides over a Budget Council meeting attended by 400 faculty and staff members, in which he outlines $26 million (25%) in cuts that the University will have to make during the next 2 academic years, reducing its baseline from $105 to $79 million, and slashing the number of students by 2,300. Cost-cutting measures include a salary freeze for executives, a hiring freeze on non-essential positions (leaving vacation positions open), the cancellation of all non-critical equipment and supply purchases, and employee travel restrictions. Most employees will be furloughed 2 days per month in 2009/10.

31 JUL.-2 AUG. 2009. The CSUSB Spirit Team (cheerleaders and dance) is name Grand Champion at the 2009 USA Collegiate and Pro Dance Camp.

3 AUG. 2009. The campus earns a 6th consecutive "Best in the West" designation from the *Princeton Review*'s "2010 Best Colleges."

12 AUG. 2009. Pres. Karnig appoints a University Advisory Committee on Efficiency and Effectiveness, chaired by ex-Provost Fernández, "To develop recommendations regarding CSUSB future organization, policy, processes, revenue and/or expenditure patterns, which would help make the institution more efficient, effective, and/or provide budget savings without compromising achievement of the University's instructional research and service missions."

14 AUG. 2009. The campus takes the first of a series of "State Budget Closure" [i.e., furlough] days, to cut employee costs by 9.3% for fiscal year 2009/10.

24 AUG. 2009. PDC receives a $190,000 grant from the U.S. Dept. of Education to buy lab equipment for nurses' training.

25 AUG. 2009. The campus receives an $857,328 grant from the American Recovery and Reinvestment Act to fund the CSUSB Minority Drug Abuse Research Program.

25 AUG. 2009. The Student Recreation and Fitness Center installs 20 Precor Elliptical fitness machines that generate energy from exercise as users walk, jog, or run on the machines.

30 AUG. 2009. Clifford O. Young is named a Fellow of the W. K. Kellogg Foundation Minority Serving Institutions/National Assoc. for Equal Opportunity in Higher Education Leadership Program.

1 SEPT. 2009. The campus begins offering an M.S. degree in Accounting, and an M.F.A. degree in Creating Writing. The CSU Chancellor's Office distributes a new system-wide travel policy. Mark K. Day is named Exec. Dir. of the Santos Manuel Student Union, having previously served as Assoc. Dir. from 1997-04.

2 SEPT. 2009. The campus dedicates a new flagpole at Coyote Premier Field, donated by Local 891 of the Professional Firefighters Union in S.B.

3 SEPT. 2009. Daniel Robinson, Music Dept. Technician, retires.

12 SEPT. 2009. The campus hosts a Constitution Day conference, "Taking Liberties: A Celebration of America's Constitutional Freedoms," in the Arena.

18 SEPT. 2009. The PDC hosts a forum on hunger and its impact on healthcare in the Coachella Valley, "Coachella Valley's Healthy Menu for Change."

21 SEPT. 2009. At the annual convocation, Pres. Karnig focuses on the unprecedented budget cuts that have affected the CSU System, saying: "This will be the most challenging year the institution has encountered in the more than 12 years I've served at CSUSB and in more than 40 years since this campus's inception.... According to the Public Policy Institute of Calif., at our current college graduation rate, by 2025 California will be one million college graduates short of what the economy will need. This is a colossal mistake.... In the chaos of this last legislative session, the CSU was slashed $564 million, and CSUSB experienced a shortfall of $26 million. Our state appropriation is the lowest amount in the last five years. And despite inflation over the period, state support per FTES is lower than [at] any time in the past decade.... By 2010/11, there will be a systemwide 9.5% reduction in target FTES...from roughly 14,900 to 13,050 FTES.... A bit over $10 million [was] taken as furloughs or layoffs...approximately two-thirds in Academic Affairs. The Trustees approved a 32% package of fee increases for students....

"It's time to get past rigid ideology and, just as we do in each of our disciplines, more objectively examine the data and the steps we must take to be successful in assuring quality education and protecting our employees' future. We must look at a system of higher fees joined at the hip with protection of those with less ability to pay.... It's not possible to know next year's budget, but a reasonable guess is that we'll have to find somewhere in the area of $10-$14 million to cut.... So the slashed higher education budgets will have both personal and statewide implications for decades to come.... The state's financial crisis is likely to remain, and state revenues are already trailing budget projections by over 3%.... Let's talk about strategies we can employ to treat that [$10-$14 million] level of cut next year. First, we'll continue to exercise control over expenditures. We'll have 400 few class sections this year. We'll continue a freeze on non–essential hires, class sizes will grow, and reassigned time will diminish. Each Vice President [will] examine [his] operations to identify opportunities for merger, streamlining, and/or elimination of infrastructure.... We've established a goal of 10% infrastructure savings over the next 2 years. I've also appointed an effectiveness-efficiency committee.... It will closely examine a few items that have long-term benefit in terms of effectiveness and cost savings.... We also need to be more focused on revenue-generating activity. We simply need to reduce our dependence on unreliable state funding. To that end, I've asked relevant units to seek a 10% increase in revenue generated for the university.... We'll seek a similar 10% increase in Congressional special project funding.... We'll reconstruct our Foundation operation by dramatically increasing its membership, and by creating a number of committees that will have a clear focus on philanthropy to benefit CSUSB. We'll also concentrate on recruiting and retaining non-resident students.... We will seek to furnish coursework for 13,050 FTES during [next] academic year, and operate the Summer Session under our Coll. of Extended Learning.... Last year I appointed a Strategic Planning Committee. The plan [it prepared] establishes the principal University goals for the next 3-5 years within the context of formidable budget and other challenges. With the University plan now in place, a first priority is for each of the vice presidential areas to either formulate their own new division plans or reconfigure existing plans in order to identify how their units will meet relevant goals of the University plan.... A second priority consists of an ongoing focus on being green and cost efficient. The strategies include installation of additional solar units both on ground and on roof tops, a fuel cell which will provide clean energy, metering of all buildings to determine where problems exist, consolidation of servers to reduce energy consumption and hardware costs, converting selective areas of turf to ground cover needing only low water maintenance, expanding use of software to better maintain computer electrical costs, and formulating as many paperless processes as possible.... A third goal is completing...the Murillo Family Observatory [and]...the Water Conservation Garden....

"This year we'll introduce the Master of Fine Arts in Creative Writing. Tony Coulson [secured a] $2 million, 4-year NSF Data Security Program Development Grant. Cynthia Crawford [received] a $857,000 grant to increase campus research on drug abuse. Our $29 in extramural funding ranks No. 5 among the 23 CSU campuses.... We can't depend on anyone to help us. If we're going to succeed, we'll need to help ourselves. There's good reason to believe we can help ourselves, as we have in the face of adversity before. We've confronted financial challenges without sacrificing students and our personnel. It's that kind of attitude we need to build on.

21-25 SEPT. 2009. The campus hosts its 11th Annual California Indian Cultural Awareness Conference.

25 SEPT. 2009. The campus hosts its annual California Native American Day celebration in LC, co-sponsored by the San Manuel Band of Serrano Mission Indians and the Agua Caliente Band of Cahuilla Indians.

1-2 OCT. 2009. The campus hosts its Annual Counselor Conference at the Ontario Convention Center, Ontario.

3 OCT. 2009. The campus hosts its DisAbility Sports Festival in the Arena.

7 OCT. 2009. Ex-English Prof. Alexandria LaFaye reads from her work in PL-4005. Daniel Griswold speaks in SMSU on "Mad About Trade: Should Main Street America Embrace Globalization?" The campus receives the first of 3 annual installments of a $36,000 grant from the Catholic Charities San Bernardino/Riverside to help train graduate and undergraduate Social Work students.

8 OCT. 2009. CSUSB's Coyote Radio is recognized by the website mtvU.com as one of the top 25 college radio stations in the U.S.

9 OCT. 2009. The campus holds a memorial service for campus booster Robert V. Fullerton (1918-2009) in VA-101.

9-10 OCT. 2009. The campus hosts its 11th Annual Pow Wow of the San Manuel Band of Mission Indians.

17 OCT. 2009. The campus hosts a Financial Education Fair in the Commons. The campus hosts a Young Women's Health Conference, with TV writer Luisa Leschin speaking.

19 OCT. 2009. Ex-Prof. Stella T. Clark and Alfonso González speak in

PL-4005 on "Fernando del Paso's *Noticias del Imperio* (*News from the Empire*)."

20 OCT. 2009. S.B. Co. Deputy Coroner David Van Norman speaks in PL-4005 on "Myth vs. Reality—Forensic Investigation." Tom Vanderbilt speaks in SMSU on "Traffic: Why We Drive the Way We Do (and What It Says About Us)." S.B. Mayor Morris speaks in UC about his accomplishments as Mayor.

22 OCT. 2009. The campus takes a State Budget Closure [furlough] Day on what would normally have been an instructional day, the first of 6 such days scheduled during 2009/10.

25 OCT. 2009. Hiking expert Philip Ferrante speaks in OA.

28 OCT. 2009. Writer/producer Skye Dent speaks in PiR on "I'm Not Just a Black Sci Fi Chick!!!"

29 OCT. 2009. The campus receives a $2.5 million bequest from the estate of Evelyn Magnuson to help fund scholarships and building. The campus hosts a symposium in the Fullerton Museum on "Graphic Design in Europe," with Robert Flynn Johnson, Victoria Martino, Peter Frank, and Museum Dir. Eva Kirsch.

30 OCT. 2009. Well-known actor Hal Linden stars in the play *Tuesdays with Morrie* at IWT. David Krentz speaks in JB-102 on "How to Draw *Tyrannosaurus rex*," and in CE-105 on "Dinosaurs: From Scientific Discovery to the Big Screen: How the Process Works."

1 NOV. 2009. Karen K. Fosdick, Lect. of Health Science and Human Ecology, dies at age 69.

3 NOV. 2009. CSUSB's Coyote Radio is voted one of the top 5 collegiate radio stations in the U.S.

4 NOV. 2009. The campus's Energy Efficiency and Infrastructure Upgrade Project is awarded the 2009 Energy Project of the Year Award: National from the Assoc. of Energy Engineers.

5 NOV. 2009. Kristin Tillquist speaks in CH-135 and VA-101 on "Be Nice: Get Ahead." Andrea Reyes speaks in PiR on "Outraged Citizens: Mexican Women Journalists Make Their Voices Heard," as part of International Education Week. Katherine Thomerson speaks in PL-4005 on "They Painted Their Own Stories: Illustrators of Picture Books."

6 NOV. 2009. Ross T. Moran, Dir. of Institutional Research (2000-09), retires. Simmie L. Jones, Facilities Services (1988-08), dies at age 61. The CSUSB William and Barbara Leonard Transportation Center hosts its 2nd Annual Transportation Research Conference, "Going to San Bernardino: A Symposium on Intermodal Transit Stations," and "Transit-Oriented Design," in the Obershaw Dining Room, featuring S.B. Mayor Morris; the Conference is renamed the Jack R. Widmeyer Transportation Research Conference at a luncheon ceremony. The campus announces that it will begin offering a new Certificate Program in E-Learning, effective Spring 2010.

9 Nov. 2009. Rabbi Hillel Cohn speaks in PL-4005 on "San Bernardino's Bicentennial! May 20, 1810-May 20, 2010."

11 Nov. 2009. Susan Nona García, Athletics Equipment Room Technician, dies at age 70.

12 Nov. 2009. Groundbreaking is held for the 2,566-sq.-ft. Nursing Laboratory.

14 Nov. 2009. Richard McInnis speaks in PL-4005 as part of the Rheubottom/Webster Lecture Series on "Rialto Citrus: From the Label to the Grove." Gerard J. "Gerry" Thibeault receives the 8th Annual WRI Lifetime Achievement Award, and ex-S. B. Mayor W. R. "Bob" Holcomb is named 2009 Water Hero, at a banquet held in UC.

17 Nov. 2009. Kimiko Ford speaks in PL-4005 on "Community Hospital of San Bernardino: 1910-2010."

19 Nov. 2009. Blues musician B. B. King and Gregory Adamson perform in the Arena. Lane Ryo Hirabayashi speaks in SMSUEC on "The Mass Incarceration of Japanese Americans." Eric J. Newman receives the Golden Apple Award for Teaching Excellence for 2009/10. Ernest Siva speaks in SB-514 on "The Global Need to Preserve Native and Endangered Languages and Cultures: Focus on the Serrano Language of the San Manuel Band of Mission Indians."

20 Nov. 2009. Ex-CSUSB Prof. Elizabeth Klonoff speaks in JB-111 on "Can I Have a Pack of Marlboros? Research Ideas Come from Strange Places."

21 Nov. 2009. Dhekra Toumi speaks in UH-058 on "Tunisia Today: Faithful to My Heritage, Open to the World."

1 Dec. 2009. Pres. Karnig announces that, due to system-wide mandates imposed by the state budget crisis, the campus will limit enrollment in 2009/10 to 13,026 FTES, a reduction of 1,101 full-time equivalent students, or more than 2,000 headcount students. Carol Gil speaks in SMSUT on "Balinese Temple Attire," and in the Fullerton Museum on "Bringing the Museum to Public School Classrooms: Educational Outreach Boxes from the Petterson Collection."

2 DEC. 2009. Namy Yi Gilmore, Facilities Services (1980-09), retires.

4 DEC. 2009. Alan Stacy speaks in JB-111 on "An Associative Memory Framework for Health Behavior and Prevention." The Coyotes women's volleyball team loses to Concordia-St. Paul in the NCAA Div. II national semifinal game.

8 DEC. 2009. Harpist Vanessa R. Sheldon speaks and performs "Celtic Harps Playing Holiday Music" in OA. The College of Education receives a 7-year accreditation from the National Council for Accreditation of Teacher Education.

11 DEC. 2009. Richard Samuel Saylor, Emer. Prof. of Music (1968-91), dies in Arcadia at age 83.

12 DEC. 2009. The 9th Winter Commencement is held in the Arena and at PDC. TV soap opera actors Jed Allen and Frank Furino speak in IWT.

15 DEC. 2009. The campus stops accepting undergraduate applications for the Fall 2010 term. The campus receives a $25,000 grant from the UPS Foundation to support the Inland Empire Center for Entrepreneurship.

18 DEC. 2009. Margaret "Margo" Chávez, Budget Officer, IRT (1972-09), retires. The campus receives a $1.1 million grant from the Calif. Institute for Regenerative Medicine to provide 6-month internships for 10 students to become researchers in the stem cell industry.

31 DEC. 2009. Retirements: William Aguilar, VP for University Advancement, VP for IRT, University Librarian, and Librarian (1989-09); S. Sid Kushner, Dir. of Research and Sponsored Programs (1984-09); Michael Murphy, Asst. Athletic Dir. & Sports Information Dir. (1999-09).

2010

1 JAN. 2010. Françoise Aylmer, Assoc. VP for University Advancement, is named Int. VP, replacing William Aguilar.

5 JAN. 2010. The campus and the City of San Bernardino agree to move the Coyotes baseball games for the coming season to Fiscalini Field.

7 JAN. 2010. Carolyn M. Stevens, Counselor, retires.

9 JAN. 2010. The John M. Pfau Library reduces its hours of operations in response to the budget crisis.

10 JAN. 2010. Filmmaker Saul Landau speaks and shows his film, *Syria: Between Iraq and a Hard Place*, in IWT.

17 JAN. 2010. The Inland Empire Center for Entrepreneurship receives the Entrepreneurship Education Award for "Outstanding Entrepreneurship Program" from the U.S. Assoc. for Small Business and Entrepreneurship.

19 JAN. 2010. The campus receives a $10,000 Challenge America grant from the National Endowment for the Arts to support a spring series of events, "Timeless Enchantment: Retelling Richard Wagner's *Ring of the Niebelung* in Music, Visual Arts, Movies, Literature, and Popular Culture" in the Art Museum. Construction begins on the Murillo Family Observatory on Little Badger Hill.

20 JAN. 2010. Lynne K. Miyake speaks in PL-4005 on "*Shōjo* Girls/Ladies/Gag and More: Japanese *Manga* Comics Looks at the 11th Century *Tale of Genji*."

25 JAN. 2010. William C(raig) Green, Assoc. Prof. of Political Science (1995-10), dies at age 53 of a pulmonary embolism while on leave at Stuttgart, Germany, serving as a Reserve Naval Commander.

27 JAN. 2010. Prof. James M. Brown speaks in PL-4005 on "Writing a Memoir: The Fine Line Between Fact and Fiction."

1 FEB. 2010. David Noblett is named Asst. Athletic Dir. for Sports Information, replacing Michael Murphy.

2 FEB. 2010. *The EverGreen Show*, an environmental program hosted and produced by Prof. Darleen K. Stoner, debuts on Coyote Radio.

5 FEB. 2010. The campus hosts a panel on "Healthcare Reform and the Impact on Your Business" in SMSUEC, with speakers Stephen Inrig, Dev A. GnanaDev and Chuck Carlsen.

10 FEB. 2010. Writer Kate Gale speaks about her work in PL-4005,

11 FEB. 2010. The campus, with four other CSU campuses, receives part of a $2.88 million grant from the U.S. Strategic Language Initiative to education students in Arabic, Persian, Russian, and other languages considered crucial to natural security, commerce, and cultural understanding.

13 FEB. 2010. TV host Peter Marshall speaks in IWT.

18 FEB. 2010. Linguist John Baugh speaks in SMSUEC on "Linguistic Profiling and Discrimination." John Hockaday speaks in PL-4005 on "Trails and Tails of the Cajon Pass from Indian Footpath to Modern Highway."

20 FEB. 2010. The San Diego Presidio Brass Quintet performs with the CSUSB Symphonic Band in RH.

22 FEB. 2010. Ellen Shimakawa is named Int. Dir., Research and Sponsored Programs, replacing Sid Kushner.

24 FEB. 2010. For the first time in its history, the campus declares a campus-wide enrollment impaction for Fall 2010, in preparation for cutting 1,900 FTES students (13%) from its enrollment base for 2010/11.

25 FEB. 2010. Activist Angela Davis speaks in SMSUEC on "Activism and Diversity in Higher Education: How Change Happens."

26 FEB. 2010. JoAnn Oliver, Lib. Asst. (1989-10), retires. The campus holds a memorial service in SMSUEC for Prof. William C. Green.

27 FEB. 2010. Heather Hendershot speaks in PL-4005 on "From *Captain Video* to iCarly: The Shifting Paradigms of Children's Television and the Scholars Who Study It."

28 FEB. 2010. Robert McGowan, Assoc. VP for Enrollment Services (2001-10), retires.

1 MAR. 2010. Olivia Rosas, Dir. of Admissions and Student Recruitment, is named Acting Assoc. VP for Enrollment Services, replacing Robert McGowan.

3-4 MAR. 2010. The campus hosts its 3rd Annual Asian Studies Symposium in PiR, with Takeshi Miike speaking on "Surrealism and Cinema: Some Thoughts on Contemporary Expressions in Japanese Film," Soko Osumi and Kazutaka Osumi demonstrating the Japanese tea ceremony, Chado, and a screening of the film, *Big Bang Love, Juvenile A*.

4 MAR. 2010. The campus receives the President's 2009 Higher Education Community Service Honor Roll with Distinction, for its commitment to volunteering, service-learning, and civic engagement.

5 MAR. 2010. Arturo Zavala speaks in PR on "Involvement of AMPA Glutamate Receptors in an Animal Model of Cocaine Craving."

6-7 MAR. 2010. The campus hosts its 23rd Annual Rainbows to Understanding Children Conference in SMSUEC, with Lisa "The Ooey Gooey Lady" Murphy and Jim "Mr. Stinky Feet" Cosgrove speaking and performing.

8 MAR. 2010. Veronica R. Amerson, Int. Dir. of EOP, is named permanent Dir.

9 MAR. 2010. Children's writer Diane Adams speaks in PL-4005 on "The ABC's of Writing for Children."

10 MAR. 2010. C. E. Tapie Rohm is named Outstanding Professor for 2009/10. N. Laura Kamptner and Faith McClure receive a $100,000 grant from First 5 of S.B. County to develop a program to help educate incarcerated mothers of young children.

11 MAR. 2010. The campus receives 2 Awards of Merit in the 25th Annual Admissions Advertising Awards national competition.

16 MAR. 2010. Herbert Brunkhorst receives the Distinguished Service Award of the National Science Teachers Assoc.

17 MAR. 2010. Rabbi Hillel Cohn speaks in SMSUEC at the annual Morrow-McCombs Memorial Lecture on "Can't We All Just Get Along?—Reflections on 200 Years of Religious Life in San Bernardino."

18 MAR. 2010. Steven Shaw speaks in PL-4005 on "The History of the San Bernardino Fire Department." Eyes Set to Kill performs in SMSUEC.

25 MAR. 2010. Linda M. Rogers, retired Supervisor of the Records Unit (1984-05), dies of cancer at age 60.

26 MAR. 2010. Rep. Joe Baca holds his Annual Education Summit, "Race to the Top," in the Obershaw Dining Room, with speakers Greg Johnson, National Education Assoc.; Jane Robb, Calif. Teachers' Assoc.; State Sen. Gloria Romero; Jim Solano, State Legislative Analyst's Office; Barbara Flores; and Beth Higbee, S.B. Co. Superintendent of Schools Office.

27 MAR. 2010. Patti Gribow interviews 4 former members of The Golddiggers musical group—Maria Lauren, Linda Eichberg, Joyce Garro, Linda Snook-Bott, and Marie Halton in IWT. John Francis "Jack" McDonnell, Emer. Prof. of Information and Decision Sciences (1969-00), dies of a heart attack at Upland at age 77.

29 MAR. 2010. The campus hosts its 1st Latino Education and Advocacy Day (LEAD) in SMSUEC, with speakers Juan Sepúlveda, Dir., White House Initiative on Educational Excellence for Hispanic Americans;

Dolores Huerta, co-founder of the United Farm Workers; and activist Sylvia Mendez. The campus receives a $192,000 grant from the State Office of Statewide Health Planning and Development.

1 APR. 2010. Happy Almogela is named Acting Judicial Affairs Officer.

3 APR. 2010. The campus team receives its 14th Outstanding Delegation Award in 17 years at the National Model U.N. Conference in New York.

5 APR. 2010. The Student Health Center Annex opens for business, and the old section of the Center closes for renovation.

7 APR. 2010. The campus announces that Summer Session in 2010 will be conducted by the Coll. of Extended Learning.

8 APR. 2010. The Calif. Public Utilities Commission approves the installation by Southern California Edison Co. of a megawatt FuelCell Energy system on campus.

10 APR. 2010. Nicholas Cataldo speaks in PL-4005 on "From Wagon Road to Mother Road: The Story of Route 66 in the San Bernardino Valley"—and the Library sponsors a car show in front of the Pfau Library Building.

11 APR. 2010. For the 18th straight year, the campus team receives an Outstanding Delegation Award from the West Coast Model Arab League Conference.

12 APR. 2010. Pauline Murillo speaks in PL-4005 on "San Manuel Serrano People: Commemorating the Bicentennial."

13 APR. 2010. Construction begins in the Nursing Skills Lab Addition.

14 APR. 2010. David Shirinyan, UCLA Center for Autism Research and Treatment, speaks in UH-261 on "Neuroimaging the Autistic Brain with an Eye Towards Improving Treatments." The campus hosts the 10th Annual Calif. Economics Challenge for high school students.

16-25 APR. 2010. Olympic diving gold medalist Greg Louganis stars in the play, *The Little Dog Laughed*, at IWT.

17 APR. 2010. Symphonie Jeunesse Youth Orchestra performs in RH in a tribute to the late Prof. Richard S. Saylor. Cal State students capture 1st place in the Web Development Category of the 14th Annual Information Technology Competition at Pomona.

20 APR. 2010. Marisa Ugarte, Exec. Dir., Bilateral Safety Corridor Coalition, speaks in SMSUT on "Human Trafficking: The Reality of Modern Day Slavery." *American Idol* finalist Scott MacIntyre speaks in SMSUEC on "Living Your Dream." Diane Podolske, Dir., CSUSB's Community-University Partnerships and Service Learning Programs, is selected to participate in the U.S. Dept. of Agriculture's Eligio (Kika) de la Garza Fellowship Program.

22 APR. 2010. BreAnda Northcutt, Deputy Secretary for Communications, Calif. Environmental Protection Agency, speaks in SB-361 on her agency. Terje Manger and Arve Asbjornsen of the University of Bergen, Norway, speak in CE-310 on "Prisoners' Educational Needs." The campus is named one of 10 institutions in the U.S. to participate in the 2010 International Academic Partnership Program, designed to increase partnerships between higher education institutions in the U.S. and those in India.

23 APR. 2010. Groundsmen Jesse O. Garza and Robert C. García retire.

24 APR. 2010. Rosa Margarita González, Lect. in Education, Program Dir., Title V Grant (1998-03), dies at Victorville at age 62. The campus hosts Clay Day, with 100 local high school students participating in the Ceramics Studio.

28 APR. 2010. Bill Sapp speaks in PL-4005 on "The Great Southern California Gold Rush of 1860: Historical Archaeology and the CSUSB Field School." Writer Thomas E. Kennedy speaks about his work in PL-4005. Chris Evans, Dir., Hatos Center for Neuropharmacology in the Semel Institute, and Dir., UCLA Brain Research Institute, speaks in UH-261 on "Opioids: Battleships or Destroyers." SunEdison begins installing 2 new solar panel projects on the grounds north of the University Police Building and on the roof of the College of Education Building.

29 APR. 2010. The campus announces that it will cut its intercollegiate women's tennis program beginning in Fall 2010, and slash $45,000 from its athletic scholarships.

30 APR. 2010. Steve Abbott of Avizio speaks in JB391 on "New Technology to Detect the Presence of Potentially Dangerous Substances Through an Attachment to a Cellular Phone." Quentin J. Moses, Dir. of Parking Services (1996-10), retires.

1 MAY 2010. Ron Profeta is named Act. Dir. of Parking Services, replacing Quentin J. Moses.
3-5 MAY 2010. The campus hosts the 2010 NCAA Division II Men's Golf West/Central Super Regional Tournament, at the Classic Club, Palm Desert.

6 MAY 2010. The campus hosts its Annual Latin American Studies Conference on Study of the Americas in SMSUT, with Armin Schwegler giving the keynote speech, "Black Magic: Ritual Spanish and African Tongues in Cuba." Joseph W. Gray, Emer. Assoc. Prof. of Education (1969-00), dies in Redlands at age 73.

7 MAY 2010. Noel L. Massie, VP of United Parcel Service, receives the Arrowhead Distinguished Executive Officer Award at a lunch held in the Obershaw Dining Room. Frances Leslie speaks in JB-113 on "Adolescent Vulnerability to Nicotine."

11 MAY 2010. Capt. Raymond Gregory, Riverside Co. Sheriff's Dept., speaks in PL-4005 on "The Changing Face of Law Enforcement: Embracing Diversity in the Ranks."

13 MAY 2010. David Hayes-Bautista speaks in PL-4005 on "La Nueva California—Latinos in the Golden State."

14 MAY 2010. Leonard Transportation Center sponsors its 4th Annual Leonard Transportation Center Forum at the Doubletree Hotel, Ontario, with speakers Greg Deveraux, Chief Accounting Officer, S.B. County; Gregg Albright, Calif. Dep. Sec. for Business; and Ty Schuiling, Dir. of Policy and Planning, S.B. Associated Governments. Charles "Stan" Stanley, Dir., Sponsored Programs Administration, Foundation (1992-10), retires.

17 MAY 2010. Diane Trujillo is named Dir., Sponsored Programs Administration, Foundation, replacing Charles "Stan" Stanley.

19 MAY 2010. Carmela Reichel speaks in UH-261 on "Cognitive and Motivational Consequences Following Chronic Methamphetamine Self-Administration: Impact of Modafinil."

21 MAY 2010. The campus hosts the "Community Visioning Conference 2010" in SMSU. Senate candidate Chuck DeVore speaks in SMSUEC.

22 MAY 2010. The campus entry for the San Bernardino Bicentennial Parade—"Educating for the Future"—wins an award for best float.

22-23 MAY 2010. The PDC campus hosts its 1st Environmental Science Education Expo for local high school students.

23 MAY 2010. David Cropley speaks in PS-223 on "Functional Creativity: One Man's Shopping Bag Is Another Man's Shank."

24 MAY 2010. Mohamed Tavakoli-Targhi speaks in the Obershaw Dining

Room of UC on "From Islamic Revivalism to Cultural Engineering in Iran." Nick Navaroli speaks in JB-356 on "Machine Learning Techniques Applied to Freeway Traffic Patterns."

26 MAY 2010. Historian Russell L. Keller speaks in PL-4005 on "The History of Lake Arrowhead." John Walsh speaks in UH-261 on "Balancing Careers in Education and Research: Networking and Collaboration in Neuroscience."

27 MAY 2010. John Levin speaks at the Spring Scholarship Banquet of the Gamma Lambda Chapter of Phi Beta Delta in the Obershaw Dining Room of UC on "Globalization and the Flow of Cultures to Our Colleges and Universities."

1 JUN. 2010. Peter Bradley speaks in PL-4005 on "The Naming of San Bernardino Valley." Lori Krueger, Photographer, retires. Michael Burgess, Libn. (1970-2010), and the author of this book, leaves the campus.

2 JUN. 2010. The campus receives a gift of 8 metal sculptures from artist Simi Dabah, to be installed at outdoor locations around the campus.

3 JUN. 2010. Mary-Alice Welshon speaks in PL-4005 on "Hispanic History in Greater San Bernardino: 1810-Present." The Nursing Program at PDC receives a $192,000 Song-Brown Registered Nurse Capitation Grant from the Calif. Health Data Planning Fund.

4 JUN. 2010. The Leonard Transportation Center sponsors its 2010 Transportation and Logistics Seminar at the Doubletree Hotel, Ontario, Calif.,, with speakers Paul Bingham, Managing Dir., Global Commerce and Transportation; Hasan Ikhrata, Exec. Dir., Southern Calif. Assoc. of Governments; John E. Husing; and Patty Senecal, International Warehouse Logistics Assoc. Groundbreaking takes places for the San Bernardino Valley Water Conservation Garden near the swimming pool, with the presence of C. Patrick Milligan, Pres., SB Valley Municipal Water Dist.

9 JUN. 2010. The campus receives a gift from CareFusion Corp. of 3 critical care ventilators for the Nursing Program at PDC.

12 JUN. 2010. Singer Deborah Prutsman performs in RH.

17, 19-20 JUN. 2010. The 44th Commencement is held in the Arena and at PDC, with Juan Sepúlveda, Dir. of the White House Initiative on Educational Excellence for Hispanic Americans, providing the keynote speech at the Social and Behavioral Sciences and College of Education ceremonies. The campus awards its first engineering degrees.

18 Jun. 2010. CSU Board of Trustees raises student fees for 2010/11 by 5% to $4,230 annually. Facilities Services begins installing 2 wind turbines generating 5 KW each of electricity near the Observatory and the East Parking Structure (#2). The Art Gallery celebrates its 40th anniversary of operation with an exhibition of Student Art.

30 Jun. 2010. Patricia K. Arlin, Dean of the Coll. of Education (1997-10), returns to the ranks as Prof. of Education. Stephen Villaseñor is named Dir. of Upward Bound. Retirements: Michael V. Benton, ex-Chief of custodial Services (1978-10); Peggy L. Kindschy, Off. of Records, Registration, and Evaluations. *The Coyote Chronicles: A Chronological History of California State University, San Bernardino, 1960-2010*, by Michael Burgess, is completed.

Sum. 2010. Retirements: Gregory R. Bassiry, Prof. of Management; Frances F. Berdan, Prof. of Anthropology; Sarah M. Boeh, Assoc. Prof. of Kinesiology; Mary Jean Comadena, Lect. of Education; Steve A. Comadena, Lect. in Education; Leo P. Connolly, Prof. of Physics; Margaret H. Cooney, Prof. of Education; Christopher C. Grenfell, Prof. of Kinesiology; James E. Hill, Lect. in Education; Jotindar S. "Vic" Johar, Prof. of Marketing; Robin Larsen, Prof. of Communications Studies; Larry E. McFatter, Prof. of Music; George McGinnis, Prof. of Art; Mary E. Molle, Prof. of Nursing; Clark Molstad, Prof. of Management; Ruth A. Norton, Prof. of Education; Lloyd E. Peake, Prof. of Management; Dennis M. Pederson, Prof. of Chemistry; Gregory L. Price, Prof. of Kinesiology; Nancy E. Rose, Prof. of Economics; Gary Sherwin, Assoc. Prof. of Education; A. I. Clifford Singh, Prof. of Kinesiology; Mary Jo Skillings, Prof. of Education; Joanna S. Worthley, Prof. of Psychology. Staff: Rebecca M. Botting, PDC; Dieter B. Braune, Building Maintenance; Bonnie Butterfield, Library Asst., PDC; Sharon D. Cady, Academic Research; Diana Catalano, Business & Public Administration; Pegeen J. Davidson, Payroll; Laura Duarte, Education; Anna Guthrie, English; Janetha A. Hamre, Teacher Education Off.; Moises Hernández, Information Technology Specialist; Joseph Hubbard, Heating & Air Conditioning; Maria L. Lootens, Capital Planning, Design & Construction; Dennis Mori, Education; Dorothea D. Niessen, Business & Public Administration; John C. Paige, University Police; Anthony Pritchett, Parking Services; Homer O. Prudholm, Building Maintenance; Davida G. Villalobos, Natural Sciences.

16 Jul. 2010. Françoise Aylmer, Int. VP and Assoc. VP for Advancement, resigns, and is replaced by Cynthia E. "Cindi" Pringle as Assoc. VP, Development.

MAJOR CAMPUS ADMINISTRATORS

THE PRESIDENT'S OFFICE

PRESIDENTS OF THE UNIVERSITY

1962-1982	John M. Pfau
1982	Gerald M. Scherba (Vice President in Charge)
1982-1997	Anthony H. Evans
1997-	Albert K. Karnig

EXECUTIVE ASSISTANTS TO THE PRESIDENT

1987-1990	Juan C. González (Asst. to the President)
1990-1999	*vacant*
1999-2001	Wilmer D. "Amina" Carter (Coordinator of Governmental Relations)
1999-2004	Clifford O. Young Sr. (Asst. to the President 1999; Exec. Asst. to the President for Governmental Relations 2002)
2004-2006	Alemayehu G. "Al" Mariam (Exec. Asst. to the President for Federal Relations)
2006-	Risa E. Dickson (Exec. Asst. to the President)

ASSOCIATE VICE PRESIDENT FOR EXECUTIVE AFFAIRS
(Position abolished 2003)

2002-2003	Janice Ropp "Jan" Jackson

ACADEMIC AFFAIRS

PROVOSTS AND VICE PRESIDENTS OF ACADEMIC AFFAIRS

1962-1966	George L. McMichael (Dean of Instruction 1962; Dean

	of Faculty 1963?)
1966-1984	Gerald M. Scherba (Act. Dean of Academic Affairs 1966; Perm. 1967?; VP of Academic Affairs 1968)
1984-1985	Ward M. McAfee (Act.)
1985-1989	Robert C. Detweiler
1989-1990	Amer M. El-Ahraf (Act.)
1990-1994	Dennis L. Hefner
1994-2009	Louis A. Fernández (Act. 1994; Perm. 1995; Provost and VP 1998; Act. 2009)
2009-	Andrew R. Bodman

ASSOCIATE PROVOSTS FOR ACADEMIC PROGRAMS

1969-1971	Robert D. Picker (Dean of Instruction; Dean of Academic Planning 1970?)
1971-1972	Lee H. Kalbus (Act. Dean of Academic Planning)
1972-1983	Ralph H. Petrucci (Dean of Academic Planning)
1983-2004	Jerrold E. Pritchard (Assoc. VP for Academic Programs; Assoc. Provost 1998)
2004-	Jennifer J. "Jenny" Zorn

ASSOCIATE DEANS FOR ACADEMIC SERVICES
(Position abolished 1992?)

1983-1991	H. Stephen Prouty (Assoc. Dean for Academic Programs 1983; Assoc. Dean for Academic Services 1987?)
1991-1992?	Elinor H. Partridge (Act.)

ASSOCIATE VICE PRESIDENTS FOR ASSESSMENT AND PLANNING & DEANS OF GRADUATE STUDIES

1975-1983	Lee H. Kalbus (Assoc. Dean of Academic Planning for Graduate Studies)
1983-1985	Loralee MacPike (Assoc. Dean for Graduate Programs)
1985-1986	David J. Lutz (Assoc. Dean for Graduate Studies)
1986-1999	Julius D. Kaplan (Dean of Graduate Studies 1989)
1999-	Sandra D. Kamusikiri (Int. Assoc. VP for Assessment and Planning & Dean of Graduate Studies; Perm. 2001)

Associate Provosts for Research

2005-   Jeffrey M. Thompson

Directors of Research and Sponsored Programs

1974-1983   Florence Weiser (Asst. Dean of Academic Administration 1974; Dir. of Sponsored Programs 1983)
1983-1984   Ansa T. T. Ojanlatva (Act.)
1984-2009   S. Sid Kushner (Dir. of Research and Sponsored Programs 1994?)
2010-   Ellen Shimakawa (Int.)

Associate Provosts for Academic Personnel

1973-1979   Robert A. Lee (Assoc. Dean for Academic Affairs)
1979-1998   J. Cordell Robinson (Assoc. Dean 1980; Assoc. VP for Academic Personnel 1983)
1998-2008   J. Paul Vicknair (Act. Assoc. Provost for Academic Personnel; Perm. 1999)
2008-   Laurel A. Lilienthal (Int. Asst. VP for Academic Personnel)

Directors of Academic Resources

1966-1967   Peter T. Marcy (Assoc. Dean for Academic Administration)
1968-1984   James D. Thomas (Assoc. Dean 1968; Dean 1969; Assoc. VP for Academic Resources 1983)
1984-1990   Amer M. El-Ahraf
1990-1992?   Phillip A. Taylor (Int.)
1992?-1999? *vacant*
1999?-   Olga J. Morales (Dir. of Academic Resources)

Associate Deans for Academic Skills
(Position abolished 1990?)

1990?   Sandra Clarkson

Associate Deans of Academic Administration
(Position abolished 1983)

1974-1983   Richard T. Ackley

DEANS OF THE COLLEGE OF ARTS AND LETTERS

1965-1966   Robert H. Ross (Chairman of the Humanities Div.)
1966-1969   Jesse Hiraoka (Act. 1966; Perm. 1967)
1969-1970   Ronald E. Barnes (Act.)
1970-1979   P. Richard Switzer (Dean of the School of Humanities 1972)
1979-1980   Irving H. Buchen
1980   Helene W. Koon (Act.)
1980-1984   Irving H. Buchen
1984-1986   Stella T. Clark (Act. 1984; Int. 1985)
1986-2000   Beverly L. Hendricks (Dean of the Coll. of Arts and Letters 1998)
2000-   Eri F. Yasuhara

DEANS OF THE COLLEGE OF BUSINESS AND PUBLIC ADMINISTRATION

1968-1970   Richard W. Graves (Chairman of the Dept. of Business Administration)
1970-1971   Edward J. Carlson (Coordinator and Act. Chair of the Dept. of Administration)
1971-1972   Edward J. Carlson (Chairman)
1972-1986   H. Arthur "Hal" Hoverland (Chairman of the Dept. of Administration 1972; Dean of the School of Administration 1974; Dean of the School of Business and Public Administration 1983)
1986-1993   David O. Porter
1993-1996   Eldon C. Lewis (Int.)
1996-1998   Steven M. Mintz
1998-1999   Eldon C. Lewis (Int. Dean 1998; Int. Dean of the Coll. of Business and Public Administration 1998)
1999-2003   Gordon L. Patzer
2003-2004   Norton E. Marks (Int.)
2004-   Karen D. Dill Bowerman

DEANS OF THE COLLEGE OF NATURAL SCIENCES

1962-1966   Gerald M. Scherba (Chairman of the Natural Sciences Div.)
1966-1971   Ralph H. Petrucci (Act. 1966; Perm. 1967)
1971   John E. Hafstrom (Act.)
1971-1972   Ralph H. Petrucci

1972-1991	James D. Crum (Chairman 1972; Dean of the School of Natural Sciences 1972)
1991-1994	Louis A. Fernández
1994-1997	Klaus R. Brasch (Act.)
[1996	*William B. Wehrenberg (appointed, never served)]*
1997-1999	J. Paul Vicknair (Act.; Act. Dean of the Coll. of Natural Sciences 1998)
1999-2001	John H. Craig (Int.)
2001-	B. Robert Carlson

DIRECTORS OF THE WATER RESOURCES INSTITUTE

2000-2005	Jeffrey W. Davis
2005-	Susan K. Lien Longville (Int. 2005; Perm. 2006)

ASSOCIATE DIRECTORS OF THE WATER RESOURCES INSTITUTE

2003-2006	Susan K. Lien Longville
2006-	Gigi S. Hanna

DEANS OF THE COLLEGE OF EDUCATION

1966-1974	Robert L. West (Chairman of the Education Dept.; Dean of the School of Education 1972)
1974-1975	Ronald G. Petrie
1975-1976	Florence A. Mote (Act.)
1976-1979	Nathan C. Kravetz
1979-1990	Ernest F. García
1990-1991	John Dunworth (Int.)
1991	Margaret A. Atwell (Act.)
1991-1994	Jean C. Ramage
1995-1997	Phyllis F. Fernlund (Act.)
1997-2010	Patricia K. Arlin (Dean of the Coll. of Education 1998)

DEANS OF THE COLLEGE OF SOCIAL AND BEHAVIORAL SCIENCES

1963-1971	Robert R. Roberts (Chair of the Social Sciences Div.)
1971-1974	Ward M. McAfee (Dean of the School of Social Sciences 1972)
1974-1975	Freeman J. Wright
1975-1984	Ward M. McAfee (Act. 1975; Perm. 1976; Dean of the

School of Social and Behavioral Sciences 1977)
1984-1987   Thomas J. Pierce (Act.)
1987-1994   Aubrey W. Bonnett
1994-1996   Ellen R. Gruenbaum (Act.)
1996-2007   John A. Conley (Dean of the Coll. of Social and Behavioral Sciences 1998)
2007-   Jamal R. Nassar

DEANS OF EXTENDED LEARNING

1966-1967   Peter T. Marcy (Dir. of Summer Session)
1967-1969   Robert L. West (Dir. of Summer Session; Dir. of Extension 1968?)
1969-1974   Fred Roach (Dean of Continuing Education)
1974-1981   Stephen A. Bowles
1981   Sherrie R. Bartell (Act.)
1981-1998   Lee I. Porter (Dean of Extended Education 1984)
1998-2002   Janice Ropp "Jan" Jackson (Dean of Extended Education 1998; Dean of Extended Learning 1998)
2002-2005   Susan E. Summers (Int.)
2005-2008   Jeetendra R. Joshee
2008-   Tatiana V. Karmanova (Act.)

ASSOCIATE DEANS OF EXTENDED LEARNING

1987-1991   Keith Johnson (Assoc. Dean of Extended Education)
1991-1998   Janice Ropp "Jan" Jackson
1998-2002   Susan E. Summers (Assoc. Dean of Extended Learning)
2002-2006   Jacques Benzakein (date correct)
2005-2007   Susan E. Summers (date correct; title overlapped)
2008-   Tatiana V. Karmanova

ASSISTANT DEAN OF EXTENDED EDUCATION
(Position abolished 1991)

1987-1991   Janice Ropp "Jan" Jackson

ASSISTANT DEANS OF MARKETING

1999-   Donna Boyd

DEANS OF UNDERGRADUATE STUDIES

1971-1972	Carl P. Wagoner (Assoc. Dean for Academic Planning)
1972-1973	Kent M. Schofield
1973	Carl P. Wagoner (Act.)
1973-1976	Kent M. Schofield (Assoc. Dean of Academic Planning)
1976-1984	Catherine C. Gannon (Assoc. Dean for Undergraduate Programs 1983)
1984	Thomas J. Pierce (Act.)
1984-1987	Diane F. Halpern (Assoc. Dean for Undergraduate Studies; Int. Dean 1986)
1987-1990	Sidney A. Ribeau (Dean of Undergraduate Studies)
1990-1991	Joel L. Nossoff (Act.)
1991-1994	Lewis L. Jones (Dean)
1994-1998	Charles W. Martin
1998	Tom M. Rivera (Int.)
1998-	J. Milton Clark (Int. 1998; Perm. 2000)

ASSISTANT DEANS OF UNDERGRADUATE STUDIES
(Position abolished 1994)

1990?-1994	Joel L. Nossoff

DEANS OF THE CSUSB PALM DESERT CAMPUS

1986-1990	Catherine C. Gannon (Dir. of the Coachella Valley Center; Dean 1989?)
1990	Susan E. Summers (Act.)
1990	Catherine C. Gannon
1990-2003	Peter A. Wilson (Int. 1990; Perm. 1992; Dean of the Palm Desert Campus 2001)
2003-	Fred E. Jandt (Int. 2003; Perm. 2005)

ASSOCIATE DEANS OF THE CSUSB PALM DESERT CAMPUS

1994-1999	James E. Daniels (Dir. of Academic Programs and Services at CVC)
1999-	Cynthia Flores (Assoc. Dean of CVC 1999; Assoc. Dean of the Palm Desert Campus 2001)

DEANS OF THE JOHN M. PFAU LIBRARY AND UNIVERSITY LIBRARIANS

1963-1988   Arthur E. Nelson (Coll. Libn.; Library Dir. 1972)
1988   Max A. "Marty" Bloomberg (Act.)
1988   Johnnie Ann Ralph (Act.)
1989-1993   William Aguilar (University Libn.)
1993-2007   Johnnie Ann Ralph (Dean of the John M. Pfau Library & University Libn. 2005; Act. 2007)
2007-   César Caballero

ASSOCIATE LIBRARY DIRECTORS
(Position abolished 1993)

1979-1988   Max A. "Marty" Bloomberg (Asst. Library Dir. 1979, Assoc. Library Dir. 1982)
1988-1989   *vacant*
1989-1993   Johnnie Ann Ralph

DIRECTORS OF DISTRIBUTED LEARNING

2001-   James M. Monaghan

DIRECTORS OF INSTITUTIONAL RESEARCH

1967-1969   James T. Freeman (Dir. of Institutional Studies; Dir. of Institutional Research 1968?)
1969-2000   Robert A. Schwabe
2000-2009   Ross T. Moran (Int. 2000; Perm. 2001)

DIRECTORS OF THE TEACHING RESOURCE CENTER

1996-   Rowena S. Santiago

EXECUTIVE DIRECTORS OF RESEARCH DEVELOPMENT AND TECHNOLOGY TRANSFER
(Position abolished 2006)

1998-2006   Klaus R. Brasch

ADMINISTRATION AND FINANCE

VICE PRESIDENTS FOR ADMINISTRATION AND FINANCE

1962-1965   Kenneth Phillips (Executive Dean)
1965-1982   Joseph K. Thomas (VP for Administration 1971)
1982-1986   James H. Urata (Act. Executive Dean 1982; Dir. of Administrative Affairs 1983)
1986-1990   Leonard B. Farwell (VP for Administration and Finance)
1990-2008   David P. DeMauro (Act. 1990; Perm. 1991)
2009-   Robert W. Gardner

ASSOCIATE VICE PRESIDENTS FOR FINANCIAL OPERATIONS

1994-2008   William Takehara
2009-   Robert Wilson

BUSINESS MANAGER
(Position abolished 1986)

1962-1986   Leonard B. Farwell

DIRECTORS OF ACCOUNTING

1966?-1971   John E. Fredricks (Coll. Accounting Officer)
1971-1973   Bernard Higuera
1973-1993   Donald E. Sapronetti (Accounting Officer)
1994   Pat Quanstrom (Act. Dir. of Accounting)
1994-1998   Daryl Anderson (Dir. of Accounting)
1998?-2007   Sheryl Pytlak
2007-   Deletta R. "Del" Anderson

DIRECTOR OF THE BUDGET

1983-1994?   C. Don McKenzie (Budget Planning Analyst 1983; Dir. of Budget Planning and Administration 1984; Dir. of Budget and Telecommunications 1989?; Dir. of the Budget 1993?)

Budget Officers

-1970 Arthur Gage
1970-1993 Jim G. Martínez
1993?-2000? Andrea W. Beechko (Budget Analyst 1993?; Budget Officer 1997?)
2000?-2001 Carolyn McDermid
2001-2004 Deletta R. "Del" Anderson
2004-2008 Robert Wilson
2008- *vacant*

Directors of Procurement and Support Services

1966-1978 R. Joy Robertson (Purchasing Officer; Business Services Officer 1972?)
1978-1998 Janice L. "Jan" Lemmond (Support Services Officer)
1998- Kathryn K. "Kathy" (Shepard) Hansen (Dir. of Procurement and Support Services)

Assistant Vice Presidents for Human Resources

1965-1969 Joseph Jerz (Coll. Personnel Officer)
1969-1981 Oscar C. Jackson, Jr.
1981-1984 Sandra Lyn Jensen
1984 Wendy A. Pederson (Act.)
1984- Dale T. West (Dir. of Human Resources 1994; Asst. VP for Human Resources 2006, with added title of Risk Management)

Executive Directors of the Foundation

1987-1999 Arthur M. Butler
1999-2003? David Jones (Int.)
2003-2006? James F. Sando
2006- Deborah Burns (Int.)

Senior Directors of Facilities Services

1964-1974 Herbert E. Brown (Dir. of Physical Plant)
1974-1978 Andre A. Maurel (Chief of Plant Operations)
1979-1986 James H. Urata (Dir. of Plant Operations)
1986-1990 David P. DeMauro
1990-2000 James "Jim" Hansen (Act. 1990; Perm. 1994?)

2000-   Tony Simpson (Int. Dir. of Facilities Services 2000;
               Sen. Dir. of Facilities Services 2007?)

BUILDING COORDINATOR
(Position abolished 1979)

1963-1979   James H. Urata

DIRECTOR OF RISK MANAGEMENT
(Merged with Asst. Vice President of Human Resources 2006)

1987-2002   Arthur M. Butler (Dir. of Administrative Services
               1987; Dir. of Risk Management 1999?)
2002?-2006   Dale T. West (Int.)

CHIEFS OF POLICE

1967-1968   C. Carl Johnson (Chief of Campus Security)
1968-1975   Walter S. Kadyk (Dir. of College Police)
1975-1981   Michael A. Gómez
1981-1987   Arthur M. Butler (Act. Dir. of Public Safety 1981;
               Perm. 1982)
1987-1994   Edward W. Harrison (Chief of Police Operations and
               Dir. of Public Safety)
1994-1995   Stephen C. Nowicki (Act.)
1995-2000   Dennis W. Kraus
2000-2002   Stephen C. Nowicki (Int.)
2002   Arthur M. Butler (Int.)
2002-2005   Patrick T. McDonald (Chief of Police)
2005-2006   Brian D. Bodily (Act.)
2006-2007   Robert J. Miller
2007-   Jimmie C. Brown (Int. 2007; Perm. 2008)

STUDENT SERVICES

VICE PRESIDENTS FOR STUDENT SERVICES

1962-1966   Robert G. Fisk (Dean of Students)
1966-1983   Kenton L. Monroe
1983   John M. Hatton (Act.)
1983-1990   Peter A. Wilson (VP for Student Services 1988)
1990-1994   Juan C. González (Int. 1990; Perm. 1992)

1994   Cheryl A. Smith (Act.)
1994-   Frank L. Rincón

ASSOCIATE VICE PRESIDENTS FOR STUDENT AFFAIRS AND STUDENT DEVELOPMENT

1966-1992   Doyle J. Stansel (Dir. of Placement and Financial Aid 1966; Assoc. Dean 1969; Assoc. Dean of Student Services 1979?; Assoc. Dean of Student Life 1984; Assoc. Dean of Student Development and Dir. of Housing 1986?; Asst. VP for Student Services and Dir. of Housing 1989?)
1992-1997   Randy P. Harrell (Act. 1992; Perm. 1995?)
1997-1998   John M. Hatton (Act.)
1998-2000   Patsy W. Oppenheim (Asst. VP for Student Development)
2000-2001   John M. Hatton (Act. Assoc. VP for Student Affairs)
2001-2003   Howard S. Wang (Assoc. VP for Student Affairs)
2003-   Helga E. Kray (Act. Asst. VP for Student Affairs and Student Development 2003; Perm. 2004; Assoc. VP 2009)

ASSISTANT DEANS OF STUDENTS
(Position abolished 1975)

1968-1970   Robert F. Gentry
1971   George A. Meneses
1971-1972   *vacant*
1972-1975   D. Gaye Perry

ASSOCIATE DEANS OF EDUCATIONAL PROGRAMS

1972-1981   Tom M. Rivera (Assoc. Dean of the Educational Opportunity Program; Assoc. Dean of Special Services 1976; Assoc. Dean of Educational Support Services 1980)
1981-1983   Walter S. Hawkins (Act.)
1983-   Tom M. Rivera (Assoc. Dean of Educational Programs 1991)

DIRECTORS OF COUNSELING AND TESTING CENTER
(Merged with the Student Health Center 1993)

1965-1966   Kenton L. Monroe
1967-1993   John M. Hatton (Assoc. Dean of Counseling and Testing 1967; Assoc. Dean of Counseling Services 1979?; Assoc. Dean of Counseling and Health Services 1984; Dir. of Counseling and Testing Center 1984)

DIRECTORS OF THE STUDENT HEALTH CENTER
(Merged with the Counseling and Testing Center 1993)

1965-1976   Samuel M. Plaut (Dir. of the Student Health Center)
1976-1983   Ross L. Ballard
1983-1987   James R. Savage (Act. 1983; Perm. 1983)
1987-1991   John Preston Miller
1991-1993   Jill E. Rocha (Act. 1991; Perm. 1991)

DIRECTORS OF STUDENT HEALTH SERVICES AND THE PSYCHOLOGICAL COUNSELING CENTER

1993-2002   John M. Hatton
2002-2004   Martha P. Kazlo
2004-2005   Robert C. Aylmer
2005-   Patricia A. "Patti" Smith

ASSOCIATE VICE PRESIDENTS FOR ENROLLMENT SERVICES

1964-1983   H. Stephen Prouty (Dir. of Admissions and Records 1964; Assoc. Dean of Admissions and Records 1969)
1983-1990   C. Donald Kajcienski (Assoc. Dean for Admissions, Records, and Outreach 1983; Assoc. Dean for Enrollment Services 1984; Assoc. VP for Enrollment Services 1989?)
1990-1998   Cheryl A. Smith
1998   Lydia Ortega (Int.)
1998-2000   C. Donald Kajcienski
2000-2001   Lydia Ortega (Int.)
2001-2010   Robert McGowan
2010-   Olivia Rosas (Act.)

ASSOCIATE DEANS FOR ACTIVITIES AND HOUSING

1966-1968　G. William Hume
1968-1978　Russell J. DeRemer
1978-1983　M. Jeanne Hogenson (Act. Dir. & Dir., Student Activities)
1983-1996　Randy P. Harrell

EXECUTIVE DIRECTORS OF THE SANTOS MANUEL STUDENT UNION

1984-2004　Helga E. (Scovel Lingren) Kray (Dir. of the Student Union; Exec. Dir. of the Santos Manuel Student Union 2003)
2004-2005　Mark K. Day (Int.)
2005　Helga E. Kray (Int.)
2005-2006　Gregory R. Lehr
2006-2009　Helga E. Kray (Int.)
2009-　Mark K. Day

UNIVERSITY ADVANCEMENT

VICE PRESIDENTS FOR UNIVERSITY ADVANCEMENT

1984-1998　Judith M. Rymer (Act. Exec. Dean for University Relations 1984; Perm. 1985; VP for University Relations 1988)
1998-1999　*vacant*
1999-2001　Jo Ann Hankin (VP for University Advancement)
2001-2005　*vacant* (dept. heads reported directly to the President)
2005-2009　William Aguilar
2010　Françoise B. Aylmer (Int.)
2010-　*vacant* (dept. heads reported directly to the President)

ASSOCIATE VICE PRESIDENTS FOR UNIVERSITY DEVELOPMENT

2001-2002　Lynda McNamara
2002-2005　*vacant*
2005-2010　Françoise B. Aylmer (Act. 2005; Perm. 2006)
2010-　Cynthia E. "Cindi" Pringle

Assistant Vice Presidents for Public Affairs

1967-1968	James H. McKone (Publications Manager)
1968-1989	Edna L. Steinman (Dir. of College Publications 1968; Dir. of Public Affairs _; Dir. of Publications 1986)
1986-2002	Cynthia E. "Cindi" Pringle (Dir. of Media Relations and Public Information 1986; Dir. of Public Affairs _)
2002-	Sidney A. "Sid" Robinson (Asst. Vice President 2006)

Athletic Directors

1984-1989	Reginald L. Price
[1988	*Daryl Ann Leonard (appointed, never served)]*
1989-1995	David L. Suenram
1995-2007	Nancy P. Simpson (Act. 1995; Perm. 1995)
2007	Dwight P. Sweeney (Int.)
2007-	Kevin L. Hatcher

INFORMATION RESOURCES & TECHNOLOGY

Vice Presidents for Information Resources and Technology & Chief Information Officers

1993-2005	William Aguilar
2005-2007	Lorraine M. Frost (Int.)
2007-	Spencer A. Freund (with added title of CIO)

Associate Vice Presidents for Information Resources and Technology

2007-	Lorraine M. Frost

Directors of Academic Computing and Media

1967-1970	Lucas G. Lawrence (Dir. of Audio-Visual Services)
1970-1994	Robert A. Senour (Dir. of Audiovisual Services)
1994-1999	Susan M. Cooper (Dir. of Academic Computing and Media)
1999-	Michael L. Ross (Int. Dir. 1999; Dir. 2000)

DIRECTORS OF COMPUTING AND TELECOMMUNICATIONS
(Position abolished 1996?)

1975-1986 Frank T. Slaton (Manager of Data Processing Services; Dir. of Computing Services 1984)
1986-1992 James J. Scanlon (Dir. of Computing and Information Management)
1992-1996? Daniel C. Ashley (Act. Dir. 1992; Dir. of Administrative Computing and Telecommunications 1994)

FACULTY OFFICES AND AWARDS

CHAIRS OF THE FACULTY SENATE

1966-1967 Fernando Peñalosa
1967-1969 Ronald E. Barnes (2 terms)
1969-1970 Jesse Hiraoka
1970-1971 Mary A. Cisar
1971-1972 C. Frederick Kellers
1972-1973 John M. Hatton
1973-1975 Paul J. Johnson (2 terms)
1975-1976 Carol F. Goss
1976-1978 Eugene Garver (2 terms)
1978-1979 John F. "Jack" McDonnell
1979-1980 Edward J. Erler
1980-1982 Judith M. Rymer (2 terms)
1982-1984 Joe F. Bas (1st time; 2 terms)
1984-1986 Carol F. Goss (2 terms)
1986-1987 Carl P. Wagoner
1987-1990 John H. Craig (3 terms)
1990-1992 Joe F. Bas (2nd time; 2 terms)
1992-1995 Walter C. Oliver (3 terms)
1995-1997 Teresa Morris (2 terms)
1997-2000 Jeanne C. King (3 terms)
2000-2003 Treadwell "Ted" Ruml II (3 terms)
2003-2004 C. E. Tapie Rohm
2004-2007 Lloyd E. Peake (3 terms)
2007-2010 Dorothy C. Chen-Maynard (3 terms)

OUTSTANDING PROFESSORS OF THE YEAR
(*=Also named a CSU System Outstanding Professor)

1980-1981	Robert M. O'Brien (Sociology)
1981-1982	Frederick A. Newton (Psychology)
1982-1983	Frances F. Berdan (Anthropology)*
1983-1984	Robert A. Blackey (History)
1984-1985	Richard H. Rowland (Geography)
1985-1986	Diane F. Halpern (Psychology)*
1986-1987	Margaret A. "Peggy" Atwell (Education)
1987-1988	Lynda W. Warren (Psychology)
1988-1989	Helene W. Koon (English)
1989-1990	Robert E. Cramer (Psychology)
1990-1991	Loralee MacPike (English)
1991-1992	Gloria A. Cowan (Psychology)
1992-1993	Ward M. McAfee (History)
1993-1994	Edward M. White (English)
1994-1995	Mary F. Smith (Marketing)
1995-1996	Adria F. Klein (Advanced Studies)
1996-1997	Terry L. Rizzo (Kinesiology and Physical Education)
1997-1998	Cynthia J. Bird (Accounting and Finance)
1998-1999	Stuart S. Sumida (Biology)
1999-2000	David M. L. Riefer (Psychology)
2000-2001	Sanders A. "Sandy" McDougall (Psychology)
2001-2002	Peter T. Robertshaw (Anthropology)
2002-2003	Fred E. Jandt (Communication Studies)
2003-2004	Richard F. Fehn (Biology)
2004-2005	Margaret S. Doane (English)
2005-2006	Paul K. Dixon (Physics)
2006-2007	Lloyd E. Peake (Management)
2007-2008	Yuchin Chien (Psychology)
2008-2009	Janet L. Kottke (Psychology)
2009-2010	C. E. Tapie Rohm (Decision and Information Sciences)

GOLDEN APPLE AWARDS
FOR EXCELLENCE IN TEACHING

1994-1995	David M. L. Riefer (Psychology)
1995-1996	David M. L. Riefer (Psychology; 2nd time)
1996-1997	Terry L. Rizzo (Kinesiology)
1997-1998	Renée M. Pigeon (English)
1998-1999	David M. L. Riefer (Psychology; 3rd time)
1999-2000	N. Laura Kamptner (Psychology)

2000-2001   Zahid Z. Hasan (Mathematics)
2001-2002   Margaret S. Doane (English)
2002-2003   Jeffrey M. Thompson (Biology)
2003-2004   Lanny B. Fields (History)
2004-2005   Eugene H. Wong (Psychology)
2005-2006   Gerald R. Thrush (Biology)
2006-2007   Sung-Heh "Sunny" Hyon (English)
2007-2008   William T. Green (Political Science)
2008-2009   Kimberley R. Cousins (Chemistry & Biochemistry)
2009-2010   Eric J. Newman (Marketing)

STUDENT OFFICES AND AWARDS

PRESIDENTS OF THE ASSOCIATED STUDENTS INC. (ASI)

1965-1967   Richard J. Bennecke (2 terms; Chair of the Student Organization Committee, Oct. 1965; Pres. of the Associated Student Body [ASB], Inc., from Jan. 1966)
1967-1968   James F. Penman
1968-1969   Jerry Rohde
1969-1970   Barry B. Thompson
1970-1971   Harold J. "Skip" Rush
1971-1972   Breck Nichols
1972   Van C. Andrews (4 months)
1972-1973   Bruce Prescott (from 27 Sept. 1972)
1973-1974   Eddie Baca
1974   Juan Torres (4 months)
1974-1975   Judith A. "Judi" Jones (from 1 Oct. 1974)
1975-1976   Raul R. Ceja
1976-1978   Kevin Gallagher (2 terms)
1978-1979   Sydney(e) Moser-James (Pres. of the Associated Students, Inc. [ASI], from 9 Nov. 1978)
1979-1980   Kathryn "Kathy" Fortner
1980-1981   Timothy C. Hamre
1981-1982   Pauline Barbour
1982-1983   Elyse Traynum
1983-1984   Rod Hendry
1984   Chris Phelps (4 months)
1984-1985   Sheryl Hammer (from 26 Sept. 1984)
1985-1986   Joani George
1986-1987   Penni K. Overstreet
1987-1988   Stephen B. Hekman

1988-1989	F. Larry Hetter
1989-1990	Aaron Watson
1990-1991	Patrick Cooney
1991-1992	Michele Miller
1992-1993	Sheri L. Major
1993-1994	Larisa R. Tompkins
1994-1995	Lou Monville III
1995-1996	Christy Hearne
1996-1997	Shannon Stratton
1997-1998	Ose Amafidon
1998-1999	T. J. Wood
1999-2000	Mary Ellen Ábilez
2000-2002	Luis Portillo (2 terms)
2002-2003	Erik Fallis
2003-2005	Ezekiel Bonillas (2 terms)
2005-2006	Rubén Díaz
2006-2008	Anthony Conley (2 terms)
2008-2009	Jeremy Vásquez
2009-2010	James Fukazawa

ALUMNI ASSOCIATION PRESIDENTS
(Alumni Assoc. officers replaced with Advisory Board in 2006)

1968-1970	Richard J. Bennecke
1970-1972	John Skeete
1972-1974	René Jacober
1974-1976	Cheryl Ciabattini
1976-1977	Stanley W. Hodge
1977-1978	Marlin Brown
1978-1982	Lawrence L. Daniels (2 terms)
1982-1984	Kathryn "Kathy" Fortner
1984-1987	John Kirwan (1½ terms; resigned)
1987-1990	James F. Penman (1½ terms; from 21 Oct. 1987)
1990-1994	James N. Kennedy (2 terms)
1994-1996	Terry E. May
1996-1998	Chris Ahearn
1998-2000	Deborah Daniel
2000-2002	Harold J. Vollkommer
2002-2004	Gerald A. Fawcett
2004-2006	Lou Monville III

OUTSTANDING STUDENTS OF THE YEAR

1984-1985   John McNay
1985-1986   Lee G. Kinney
1986-1987   Sharon Younkin (graduate), Paul Mata (undergraduate)
1987-1988   Alison Jaffe-Karp (graduate), Cherlynn A. Rush (undergraduate)
1988-1989   Marguerite Dragna (graduate), Rebecca Hodde (undergraduate)
1989-1990   Ilona Marie Eubank (graduate), Paul Soo Dee Naik (undergraduate)
1990-1991   Joseph V. Fengler (graduate), Debra Kay Ledford (undergraduate)
1991-1992   Julie LaMay Abner (graduate), Tae-Wook Chun (undergraduate)
1992-1993   Jill Kuhn (graduate), Suzanne Reid (undergraduate)
1993-1994   Eileen Payne (graduate), Kerry Branch (undergraduate)
1994-1995   Carlos Bolanos (graduate), Kristine Nicholls (undergraduate)
1995-1996   Graduate: Paul Cook (B&PA), Anne Johnson-Curtis (E), Kimberly Manning (H), Ratnasri Adharpurapu (NS), Rudolph Sánchez (S&BS); Undergraduate: Judith Wood (B&PA), Eric Porter (H), Nerissa Concepción (NS), Janet Long (S&BS).
1996-1997   Graduate: Kristi Manclow (B&PA), Merrill "Doc" Heim (E), Heidi Lockhart (H), Paula Estrada (NS), Laura Davis (S&BS); Undergraduate: Cindy Ashley-Navaroli (B&PA), Lucinda Smith (H), Masashi Kitazawa (NS), Gale Koch (S&BS).
1997-1998   Graduate: Nancy Jo McIntosh (CVC), Leslie Bryan (H), Sharon Newman-Gómez (NS), Kathie Lynne Pelletier (NS), Roby Hartono (B&PA); Undergraduate: Christine Van Cleave Newkirk (CVC), Susan Peloza (H), Fernando Villarruel (NS), Donovan Rinker-Morris (S&BS), Deborah Knight-Moreno (B&PA).
1998-1999   Graduate: Natsuki Yamamoto (A&L), Bonnie O'Connor (B&PA), Tina Marie Walker (CVC), James Walliser (NS), Robert Collins (S&BS); Undergraduate: Shane Churchill (A&L), Robert Brooks (B&PA), Alen Velagic (CVC), Scott Phillips (NS), Celesta Atkins (S&BS).
1999-2000   Graduate: Kristine L. Potter (A&L), Yuan Patricia

	Song (B&PA), Tinya Holt (S&BS), Rick Allen (NS), Marguerite Dover (CVC); Undergraduate: Misty Burruel (A&L), Tammy L. DuPree (B& PA), Victoria Santimaw (S&BS), Kwame Donkor (NS), Scott Hord (CVC).
2000-2001	Graduate: Annette Bell (CVC), Joe Notarangelo (A&L), Scott Parker (NS), KaMala Thomas (S&BS), Andrew M. Brammer (B&PA); Undergraduate: Gary Graves (CVC), Myron Ávila (A&L), Tracie Rivera & Kristin García (NS), Hal Shorey (S&BS), Kathryn Kent (B&PA).
2001-2002	Graduate: Bobbi Goldstein (PDC), Dino Bozonelos (S&SB), Erin Thomson (B&PA), Jessica Flynn (NS), Richard Colby (A&L); Undergraduate: Pamela Gabbay (PDC), Jill Messing (S&BS), Ronda Shutt (B&PA), Natalia Wideman (NS), Liliana Guevara & Brian Stanley (A&L).
2002-2003	Graduate: Kathryn Hansler (A&L), Khozette Bracken (PDC), Kitima Kanlayaphichet (B&PA), Gavan Albright (NS), Leanne Graff (S&BS); Undergraduate: Mary Bohen (A&L), Victor Sciortino (NS), Linda Wright Theriault (PDC), Jacqueline Wantz-Sutton (S&BS).
2003-2004	Graduate: Susan Berilla (A&L), Fiona Choi (S&BS), Richard Gagnon (NS), Matías Farre (B&PA), and Jory Kirchhevel (PDC); Undergraduate: Callie Kettman & Elisabeth Joy Villareal (A&L), Suzzane McLay (NS), Jesse Zinn (S&BS), Kaori Takeda (B&PA), and Emmanual C. Manríquez (PDC).
2004-2005	Graduate: John García (A&L), Lucy Soo Yon Jun (NS), Farah Meadows (PDC), Leijie Yao (B&PA), Amanda De Vries Liabeuf (S&BS; Undergraduate: Alba Cruz-Hacker & Sheryl Teal (A&L), Joriz de Guzmán & Ali Rejali (NS), Travis Lee Mahan (PDC), Faradean C. Frawley (B&PA), Erik Fallis (S&BS).
2005-2006	Graduate: Lee Dionne (A&L), Jason C. Mackay (B&PA), Thomas Benson (NS), Nancy Stuart (PDC), Maren Oslund (S&BS); Undergraduate: Laura Loper & Chani Lewis (A&L), Sotheary Tep (B&PA), Daniel Havey (NS), Cynthia Spence (PDC), Heather Marshall-Pyle (S&BS).
2006-2007	Graduate: Angela Asbell (A&L), Samuel "Alex" Na-

jera (B&PA), Tom Lee (NS), La Tanya Strange (PDC), Julie Humphrey (S&BS); Undergraduate: Rosie Bautista and Kenneth Hanour (A&L), Leah McLain (B&PA), Lyudmila Shved (NS), Max Panchuk (PDC), Christopher Pérez (S&BS).
2007-2008 Graduate: Cynthia Spence (PDC), Mary Melissa Flesher (S&BS), Chris Duran (NS), Lee Scott Catlett (B&PA), Sarah Antinora (A&L); Undergraduate: Gerry Morrow (PDC), Vanessa Segura (S&BS), Lyudmila Shved (NS), Christine Gibson (B&PA), April Van Bibber & Tina Hansen (A&L).
2008-2009 Graduate: Shane Churchill (A&L), Majda Elhams (B&PA), Ken Noriega (NS), Cynthia Bradley (PDC), Valerie Laws (S&BS); Undergraduate: Adriana Vargas & Bryce Holgate (A&L), Clifford Adikuono (B&PA), Nicholas Navaroli (NS), Jesseca Valcazar (PDC), Keeonna Harris (S&BS).
2009-2010 Graduate: Kimberly Aguilar (A&L), Susan Powell (B&PA), Erin Strong (NS), Lynda Kerney (PDC), Heather Fikas (S&BS); Undergraduate: Aaron Brock & Nadine Hanhan (A&L), Rachel Wolfinbarger (B&PA), Matthew Strader (NS), Antonio Salcedo (PDC), Mark Ocegueda (S&BS).

OTHER AWARDS

ALUMNI AWARDS OF DISTINCTION
(To 2004 called Distinguished Alumni Awards)

1975 Richard J. Bennecke (special one-time award)
1980 Robert E. Botts, Lois J. Carson, Deborah Daniel Tharaldson, James F. Penman, Glenn G. Rymer (listed as "first" awards in contemporaneous accounts)
1981 Concetta C. Arnone, Alan A. Breslow, Wilmer D. Carter, Loretta R. Martínez Gómez
1982 Rosemary T. Binney, Cheryl Minter Brown
1983 Very Rev. Chrysostomos (A. E. J. González-Alexopoulos), Virginia Comstock, Lawrence L. Daniels (Alumnus of the Year), Charlotte (Elder) Gusay, Yolanda T. Moses
1984 Thomas R. Ahrens, Frances "Fancy" Lodge Davis, Rudolpho Robles, Wallace A. Sánchez, Col. Edward J. Sheeran

Year	Recipients
1985	Daniel Carrasco, Richard F. Fehn, Dr. Richard D. McAllister, Vernon R. Stauble, Robin Valles
1986	Jennifer Vaughn Blakely, Nicholas J. Coussoulis, Dr. Elka K. Kelly, Gerald M. Newcombe, Anna María Rodríguez, V. Merriline Smith
1987	Dr. Marlin L. Brown, Dr. D. Steven Meyering, Linda J. Lingo, Enrique N. Martínez, Kathleen Williams Rager
1988	David Álvarez, Shauna Clark, Mary Frances Gómez, Marcia Lentz, Elyse Traynum
1989	none
1990	Cheryl A. (Hill) Flowers
1991	Luis Salazar Gómez
1992	Paul A. Woodruff
1993	Wesley A. Krause
1994	John Winn Kennedy Sr.
1995	Danny Bilson, Paul DeMeo
1996	Kat Grossman, Samuel C. Scott
1997	James N. Kennedy, Michele Tacchia, Michael Tacchia, Robert J. Hodges, Ruby L. Beale, Teresa Germany
1998	Deborah L. Crowley, Erma J. Nichols, Jody D. Duncan, Lee D. Roberts, Stephen T. Lilburn
1999	J. Michael Reaves, Dianne L. Wilkman, John P. Wood, Stanley W. Hodge
2000	Lois Clark, Toni L. Robinette, Talmadge Wilson, William A. Jenson, Dr. Dennis J. Wourms
2001	Aurora Tenorio-Kerr, Jacquelyn L. Jackson, Patrick A. Ainsworth, Laxman "Lex" Reddy, Patricia Márquez Sandoval, Linda J. Blessing
2002	David F. Maynard, Steven K. Messerli, Jean Pfeiffer Leonard, D. Brian Reider, M. Jean Snell, Brenda A. Soulliere
2003	Amro Albanna, Ellen Gaynor Weisser, Edward B. "Ned" Cooney, Dr. Patrick García, John J. Benoit, Harold J. Vollkommer
2004	Adam N. Torres, Ann Vessey, Travis Huxman, Kent Paxton, Deborah Greer Currier
2005	Gerald A. Fawcett, Jeffrey S. Shockey, Jean M. Stephens

No awards presented after 2005.

HONORARY DEGREE RECIPIENTS

June 2001   W. Benson Harer, Jr., Doctor of Humane Letters (Arts & Letters ceremony)
June 2002   Ali C. Razi, Doctor of Humane Letters (Business & Public Administration ceremony)
June 2003   Dorothy E. Inghram, Doctor of Humane Letters (Education ceremony)
June 2004   Florentino Garza, Doctor of Humane Letters (Arts & Letters ceremony)
June 2005   Jack H. Brown, Doctor of Humane Letters (Business & Public Administration ceremony); Bing Sum Wong, Doctor of Humane Letters (Education ceremony)
June 2006   Richard R. Oliphant, Doctor of Humane Letters (Palm Desert Campus ceremony); Charles Obershaw and Shelby Obershaw, Doctors of Humane Letters (Education ceremony)
June 2007   William E. Leonard, Doctor of Humane Letters (Business & Public Administration ceremony); Sam Maloof, Doctor of Fine Arts (Arts & Letters ceremony)
June 2008   Neale Perkins, Doctor of Humane Letters (Social & Behavioral Sciences ceremony); Larry R. Sharp, Doctor of Humane Letters (Business & Public Administration ceremony)
June 2009   Nicholas J. Coussoulis, Doctor of Humane Letters (Social & Behavioral Sciences ceremony); Ernest Siva, Doctor of Fine Arts (Arts & Letters ceremony)
June 2010   Betty M. Barker, Doctor of Humane Letters (PDC ceremony); James R. Watson, Doctor of Humane Letters (Education ceremony)

PRESIDENT'S AWARDS

2005   Antreen Pfau, Lois Evans
No awards presented after 2005.

LEGACY AWARDS

2005   Nicholas J. Coussoulis, Christina Coussoulis, and the Coussoulis Family
No awards presented after 2005.

ARROWHEAD DISTINGUISHED EXECUTIVE OFFICER AWARDS

1990   Jack H. Brown, Chair/CEO, Stater Bros. Markets
1991   Ralph M. Lewis and Goldie Lewis, Founders, Lewis Operating Corp.
1992   Martin A. Matich, Chair of the Board, Matich Corp.
1993   no award
1994   Nicholas J. Coussoulis, Pres., Coussoulis Development Co.
1995   Glenda Bayless, Owner, Bayless Accountancy Corp.
1996   Neal T. Baker, Pres./CEO, Baker's Drive-Thru Restaurants
1997   E. Evlyn Wilcox, ex-S.B. Mayor and Pres., Manpower Staffing Services
1998   Larry R. Sharp, Pres./CEO, Arrowhead Credit Union
1999   William E. Leonard, Owner, San Gorgonio Land Co.
2000   no award
2001   D. Linn Wiley, Pres./CEO, Citizen's Business Bank
2002   Robert Kain, Chair of the Board, HMN Architects
2003   Donald A. Driftmier, Partner, Vaurinek, Trine, Day & Co., LLP
2004   Bruce Doyle Varner, Partner, Varner & Brandt LLP
2005   Candace Hunter Wiest, ex-Pres./CEO, Inland Empire National Bank
2006   George H. Schnarre, Pres./CEO, George H. Schnarre Real Estate
2007   Donald I. Baker, Senior Consultant and ex-Pres./CEO, Stater Bros. Markets
2008   Dr. Dev A. GnanaDev, Pres.-Elect of the Calif. Medical Assoc.
2009   John E. Husing, economist
2010   Noel L. Massie, VP, United Parcel Service

PRESIDENT'S ADVANCEMENT COUNCIL

(College Advisory Board Members to July 1984,
University Advisory Board Members to 2004)
(With Years of Appointment)

1965   Judge James E. Cunningham Sr., Wilma Goodcell, James A. Guthrie (d. 1966), Leroy Hansberger, Leslie I. Harris, Hayes Hertford, Dr. Henry W. Holder, Earl "Tiny" Wilson

1966	James K. Guthrie, Hayes Hertford (2nd time), Dr. Ernst H. Krause, Martin A. Matich
1967	Judge James E. Cunningham (2nd time), Leslie I. Harris (2nd time), Earl "Tiny" Wilson (2nd time)
1968	Shibli S. Damus, Arthur J. Forbes, Florentino Garza, Nancy (Mrs. C. Lowell) Smith
1969	none
1970	Florentino Garza (2nd time), Martin A. Matich (2nd time)
1971	Shibli S. Damus (2nd time), Leslie I. Harris (3rd time), Barbara R. (Mrs. William E.) Leonard, Verne F. Potter Jr., Nancy E. (Mrs. C. Lowell) Smith (2nd time), Earl "Tiny" Wilson (3rd time)
1972	William H. Baughn, Wilma Goodcell (2nd time), Leroy Hansberger (2nd time), Barbara R. Leonard (2nd time)
1973	none
1974	Harold C. Harris Jr., Martin A. Matich (3rd time), Verne F. Potter Jr. (2nd time)
1975	none
1976	Robert J. Bierschbach, Robert J. Mitton, Eliseo G. Ruiz, Dr. Wayne Scott
1977	Luella M. (Mrs. Theodore M.) Cohen
1978	Charles R. Ford, Edith (Mrs. Le Mon) Smith
1979	Regina (Mrs. Florentino) Garza, William Honeysett, George M. Hubbard
1980	none
1981	none
1982	Dannie M. Hayes
1983	Virginia Brown, Mary Curtin, Robert Custer, Clarence R. Goodwin, Gloria Macías Harrison, Medley Jeansonne, Sister Ann Muckerman, Richard Padilla, Roberto Velásquez
1984	Dr. Claude E. Noel
1985	Lois J. Carson, Homer G. Peterson
1986	Robert C. Lee
1987	Nicholas J. Coussoulis, Dr. Luis Salazar Gómez, Dr. Norman C. Guith, Lee G. Kinney, Larry McMillan, Raúl Mercado, Richard R. Oliphant, Margaret Ollerton, Rev. Charles E. Singleton, Elyse Traynum, Bruce Varner
1988	Barbara R. "Bobbie" Leonard, Gordon Quiel, Mignon M. Schweitzer
1989	none
1990	Mary Drury, Dr. Don Iman, Darlene Johnson, Gordon Quiel, James Robinson, W. P. Wylie

1991	Karen Craig, Don Ecker, Joe Frazier, Milton Johnson, James R. Mulkey, Vivian Nash Dukes, Gerald Newcombe, Kenneth Patterson, Valerie Romero, Lawrence Winking
1992	Richard F. Crail, Dr. Taewoong Kim, Dr. Robert Percy
1993	Marion Black, Edward Dunagan, Edward Hill Jr.
1994	Bruce Bartells, Robert E. Botts, Gloria Cutler, Ted Dutton, Ronald Evans, Lynn Hirtz, Ray Quinto, Larry R. Sharp, Paul A. Woodruff
1995	Gregory Adams, Darrol Groven, Robert J. Mitton, Richard Padilla, James Previti, D. Brian Reider, Adrian Sánchez, Dr. Wayne Scott, James White
1996	Kathleen Mitchum-McIntosh
1997	David DeValk, Debbie Guthrie Huffman, Brooks Johnson, Dr. Dilip Kelekar, Barbara McGee, Neale Perkins
1998	Dr. W. Benson Harer Jr., Lois Lauer, Martin A. Matich
1999	William Anthony, Marta Brown, Deborah Daniel, Herbert Fischer, Graciano Gómez, Al Sabsevitz, Jon Slater
2000	Dr. Michael Miller
2001	Jim Ferguson, Garner Holt, James N. Kennedy, Mary Tenorio, Harold J. Vollkommer, D. Linn Wiley
2002	Gerald A. Fawcett, Mark Schnitzer
2003	Lou Monville III
2004	Dennis Craig, Edward C. Teyber
2005	William Anthony, Donald Baker, Glenda Bayless, Theodore Dutton, Gerald A. Fawcett, Jim Ferguson, Robert V. Fullerton, Michael Gallo, Florentino Garza, Herbert Fischer, George Gorian, Scott Laurie, Wilfried Lemann, Dobbin Lo, Martin A. Matich, Lou Monville III, April Morris, Charles Obershaw, Neale Perkins, Ray Quinto, D. Brian Reider, Judith Rymer, Phil Savage III, George H. Schnarre, Larry R. Sharp, James R. Watson, Ellen Weisser, D. Linn Wiley
2006	Ann Atkinson, John Brudin, Arthur Butler, Gloria Cutler, John Egan, G. Louis Fletcher, Graciano Gómez, Allen B. Gresham, James E. Henwood, Barbara McGee, Michael R. Miller, Richard R. Oliphant
2007	Mark Edwards, Bruce Varner
2008	Steve I. Chiang, Greg Christian, Stephen Saleson

FACULTY PASSINGS

FACULTY WHO HAVE DIED IN SERVICE
(with Years Hired and Ages at Death)

Mary A. Cisar (1965)—d. 6 Dec. 1971 (age 39)
Jack A. Sullivan (?)—d. 25 Nov. 1973 (age 43)
Walter O. Zoecklein (1969)—d. 27 Jun. 1975 (age 57)
Florence A. Mote (1967)—d. 17 Apr. 1977 (age 64)
Neville J. Spencer (1968)—d. 22 Nov. 1977 (age 37)
James J. Finley (1973)—d. 22 Mar. 1980 (age 61)
William D. Gean (1976)—d. 27 Oct. 1980 (age 44)
F. Eugene Mueller (1973)—d. 25 Dec. 1981 (age 77)
Alfred S. Egge (1966)—d. 17 Oct. 1982 (age 49)
Marvin D. Frost (1976)—d. 17 Apr. 1983 (age 43)
Robert R. Roberts (1963)—d. 13 Feb. 1984 (age 63)
Peter L. Bouvier (1983)—d. 17 May 1984 (age 41)
Margaret J. Lenz (1970)—d. 30 Jan. 1987 (age 57)
Frank Aguirre (1984)—d. 11 Jun. 1989 (age 37)
Sandra L. Fredriksen (?)—d. 21 Feb. 1991 (age 44)
Hans G. Jellen (1989)—d. 24 Feb. 1992 (age 49)
Kimball N. Hughes (1981)—d. 14 Mar. 1992 (age 38)
Kathy L. O'Brien (1984)—d. 15 Aug. 1992 (age 40)
Peter J. Wetterlind (1987)—d. 13 Mar. 1994 (age 51)
Arthur A. Moorefield (1973)—d. 28 Mar. 1994 (age 65)
George A. Weiny (1967)—d. 27 Mar. 1995 (age 61)
Wallace T. Cleaves (1971)—d. 28 Mar. 1995 (age 52)
J. Patrick Watkins (1994)—d. 8 Jul. 1997 (age 46)
Bryan L. Pettit (1988)—d. 19 Aug. 1998 (age 52)
J. Cordell Robinson (1971)—d. 11 Dec. 1998 (age 58)
Benjamin G. Ramírez (?)—d. 2 Mar. 1999 (age 65)
Taft T. Newman Jr. (1978)—d. 18 Sept. 1999 (age 56)
Pola N. Patterson (1979)—d. 3 Jan. 2000 (age 64)
Larry L. Kramer (1968)—d. 18 Nov. 2000 (age 61)
Pierrette M. Serna (?)—d. 21 Apr. 2001 (age 61)
Kellie R. Rayburn (1989)—d. 8 Nov. 2001 (age 39)
Phillip A. Anderson (?)—d. 1 Jan. 2002 (age 57)
Joel A. Stein (1991)—d. 25 Apr. 2006 (age 61)
Marcia L. Raines (1995)—d. 3 Aug. 2006 (age 59)
Richard F. Fehn (1983)—d. 30 Jun. 2007 (age 55)
William C. Green (1995)—d. 25 Jan. 2010 (age 53)

EMERITI FACULTY WHO HAVE DIED POST-RETIREMENT
(with Years Served and Ages at Death)

Alice E. Wilson (1969-82)—d. 15 Sept. 1983 (age 69)
René F. Dennemeyer (1966-79)—d. 17 Jan. 1985 (age 63)
C. Michael O'Gara (1964-77)—d. 5 Jul. 1991 (age 79)
Dominic M. Bulgarella (1969-92)—d. 6 Mar. 1994 (age 64)
Charles V. Hartung (1969-77)—d. 2 May 1995 (age 81)
P. Richard Switzer (1970-93)—d. 9 Oct. 1995 (age 70)
Helene W. Koon (1970-90)—d. 13 Feb. 1996 (age 70)
C. Fred Kellers (1968-88)—d. 17 Jul. 1996 (age 65)
Robert R. Harrison (1965-72)—d. 28 Mar. 1997 (age 88)
F. F. Liu (1970-95)—d. 28 Mar. 1997 (age 62)
Arlo D. Harris (1967-88)—d. 15 Nov. 1997 (age 63)
Joseph K. Thomas (1965-82)—d. 15 Oct. 1998 (age 82)
Gerald M. Scherba (1962-91)—d. 5 Feb. 2001 (age 73)
A. Vivien Bull (1976-91)—d. 7 Feb. 2001 (age 79)
Margaret K. Gibbs (1975-80)—d. 30 Aug. 2001 (age 87)
Robert L. West (1966-80)—d. 2 May 2002 (age 84)
Robert A. Smith (1965-82)—d. 19 Aug. 2002 (age 84)
Denis R. Lichtman (1969-2000)—d. 15 Nov. 2002 (age 72)
Arthur E. Nelson (1963-91)—d. 25 Sept. 2003 (age 76)
Stephen A. Bowles (1974-96)—d. 17 Jun. 2005 (age 71)
Ronald E. Barnes (1965-97)—d. 7 Feb. 2006 (age 75)
David J. Bellis (1985-2005)—d. 29 Jun. 2006 (age 62)
John E. Hafstrom (1965-79)—d. 4 Jul. 2006 (age 91)
Nikolai A. Khokhlov (1968-92)—d. 17 Sept. 2007 (age 85)
Robert A. Lee (1968-92)—d. 16 Apr. 2008 (age 73)
Mary G. Patterson (1977-85)—d. 28 Sept. 2008 (age 94)
Harold A. Jambor (1975-80)—d. 28 Dec. 2008 (age 95)
Robert G. Fisk (1962-73)—d. 11 Feb. 2009 (age 93)
Richard S. Saylor (1968-91)—d. 11 Dec. 2009 (age 83)
John F. "Jack" McDonnell (1969-2000)—d. 27 Mar. 2010 (age 77)
Rosa M. González (1989-2003)—d. 24 Apr. 2010 (age 62)
Joseph W. Gray (1969-2000)—d. 6 May 2010 (age 73)

CAMPUS ENROLLMENT BY YEAR (Fall Term)

1965/66	293	
1966/67	605	+ 106%
1967/68	983	+ 62%
1968/69	1,308	+ 33%

1969/70	1,723	+ 32%
1970/71	2,269	+ 32%
1971/72	2,556	+ 13%
1972/73	2,657	+ 4%
1973/74	3,043	+ 15%
1974/75	3,489	+ 15%
1975/76	4,017	+ 15%
1976/77	4,065	+ 1%
1977/78	4,443	+ 9%
1978/79	4,383	- 1%
1979/80	4,231	- 3%
1980/81	4,659	+ 10%
1981/82	4,961	+ 6%
1982/83	5,060	+ 2%
1983/84	5,450	+ 8%
1984/85	5,847	+ 7%
1985/86	6,513	+ 11%
1986/87	7,423	+ 14%
1987/88	8,366	+ 13%
1988/89	9,673	+ 16%
1989/90	10,873	+ 12%
1990/91	11,927	+ 10%
1991/92	12,561	+ 5%
1992/93	12,485	- 1%
1993/94	12,121	- 3%
1994/95	11,864	- 2%
1995/96	11,957	+ 1%
1996/97	12,153	+ 2%
1997/98	13,280	+ 9%
1998/99	13,600	+ 2%
1999/00	14,280	+ 5%
2000/01	14,909	+ 4%
2001/02	15,985	+ 7%
2002/03	16,341	+ 2%
2003/04	16,927	+ 4%
2004/05	16,194	- 5%
2005/06	16,431	+ 1%
2006/07	16,479	+ 0.3%
2007/08	17,066	+ 3.5%
2008/09	17,646	+ 3.4%
2009/10	17,852	+ 1.2%

OTHER OFFICIALS

MAYORS OF THE CITY OF SAN BERNARDINO
(Thanks to Paul Garrity of the S.B. Public Library)

1905-1907	Hiram M. Barton
1907-1909	John J. Hanford
1909-1911	S. B. W. McNabb (1st term)
1911-1913	Joseph S. Bright
1913-1915	Joseph W. Catick (1st term)
1915-1917	George S. Wixom
1917-1919	Joseph W. Catick (2nd term)
1919-1921	John A. Henderson
1921-1925	S. B. W. McNabb (2nd term)
1925-1927	Grant Holcomb
1927-1929	Ira N. Gilbert (1st term)
1929-1931	John C. Ralphs Jr.
1931-1933	Ira N. Gilbert (2nd term)
1933-1935	Ormonde W. Seccombe
1935-1939	Clarence T. Johnson (1st term)
1939-1941	Henry C. McAllister
1941-1947	William C. Seccombe
1947-1950	James E. Cunningham
1950-1951	Clarence T. Johnson (2nd term)
1951-1955	George C. Blair
1955-1957	Raymond H. Gregory (1st term)
1957-1959	Elmer D. Kremer
1959-1961	Raymond H. Gregory (2nd term)
1961-1965	Donald G. Mauldin
1965-1971	Al C. Ballard
1971-1985	W. R. "Bob" Holcomb (1st term)
1985-1989	(E.) Evlyn Wilcox
1989-1993	W. R. "Bob" Holcomb (2nd term)
1993-1998	Tom Minor
1998-2006	Judith A. Valles
2006-	Patrick J. Morris

CHANCELLORS OF THE CALIFORNIA STATE UNIVERSITY

1961-1962	Buell G. Gallagher
1962-1982	Glenn S. Dumke
1982-1990	W. Ann Reynolds

1990-1991	Ellis E. McCune (Act.)
1991-1998	Barry A. Munitz
1998-	Charles B. Reed

GOVERNORS OF THE STATE OF CALIFORNIA (from 1960)

1959-1967	Edmund G. "Pat" Brown Sr.
1967-1975	Ronald W. Reagan
1975-1983	Edmund G. "Jerry" Brown Jr.
1983-1991	(C.) George Deukmejian
1991-1999	Pete (i.e., Peter B.) Wilson
1999-2003	Gray (i.e., Joseph Graham) Davis
2003-	Arnold A. Schwarzenegger

LIEUTENANT GOVERNORS OF THE STATE OF CALIFORNIA

1959-1967	Glenn M. Anderson
1967-1969	Robert H. Finch
1969-1974	Edwin Reinecke
1974-1975	John L. Harmer
1975-1979	Mervyn M. Dymally
1979-1983	Michael Curb
1983-1995	Leo T. McCarthy
1995-1999	Gray (i.e., Joseph Graham) Davis
1999-2007	Cruz M. Bustamante
2007-2009	John R. Garamendi
2009-2010	*vacant*
2010-	Abel Maldonado

AFTERWORD:
OF THE MAKING OF BOOKS

Of the making of books there is no end, a wise man once said, but of course we all come to our ends sooner or later—and usually sooner than we would wish. Hence, my time at the University is rapidly expiring, and I suspect that the remaining sandy orts in my own little globe of hours are running a tad shy as well. No matter.

I've spent three and one-half years putting this book together—neither my longest nor my most difficult work, but a great deal of effort nonetheless. For helping me to achieve it, I owe a big tip of the hat to Johnnie Ralph and César Caballero, to Lou Fernández and Al Karnig, to my dear Mary; and to all those other folks who came before, beginning forty-five years ago with my friend and mentor, the late Dr. Fran Polek, who was the first to give me permission to unleash my demons upon an innocent world. Thank you so very much, each and every one.

I had the idea for this work many years before I started it. I wanted to compile a chronological record of what had happened here—of the great and small things and the great and small people that together made this institution something worth remembering and worth championing. I've spent my entire adult life here, trying most assiduously to fashion something better—of myself, of the students and staff and faculty that I encountered, and of this singular place of learning. I have no idea at this point whether I've had any impact at all that's worth remembering, *but at least I will have remembered the campus itself.*

This is not the kind of history that's intended to be read and savored and contemplated. I'd thought about taking that more conventional approach, as I'd done with *Tempest in a Teapot: The Falkland Islands War*; but after my experience with that tome, I decided that I didn't want to spend my remaining years fighting others over my opinions. That I do have such opinions, a few of you are most certainly aware; but they're hidden from this text, and I chose and choose deliberately to leave them unvoiced, now and in the future. Let someone wiser than I make such *pronunciamentos*.

At least my successors will know *what* happened here, if not necessarily *why*. Those "whys" are surprisingly well hidden beneath mounds of academic verbiage in the dry, abbreviated renditions of the surviving *Administrative Council Minutes* and such, and require a context that I don't have and didn't particularly want to research. There were heroes and there were villains and there were plenty of folks who just slogged along, doing the best they could; but almost all of them are already fading into the gray concrete walls, and perhaps that's for the best. We're here to serve our students, after all, and not ourselves.

I've written—and continue to write—many other works of fact and fable, and each of them has a voice of its own. As I give birth to this particular godchild of my imagination, I wish it—and all of you—"*bon chance*." We live in interesting times, as the old Chinese curse intimates; but someone else will need to face the challenges yet to come, and to make a record of them in one fashion or another.

My record, my account, is now done.

—Michael Burgess
San Bernardino, California
13 November 2006-4 July 2010
Afterword written 16 April 2010

ABOUT THE AUTHOR

MICHAEL BURGESS received his A.B. from Gonzaga University in 1969, and his M.S. from the University of Southern California in 1970. He joined the faculty at California State College, San Bernardino, on Sept. 1, 1970, and worked in the John M. Pfau Library in Reference, Periodicals, Technical Services, and Collection Development. He retired from state service in Sept. 2005, and continued working part-time in the Faculty Early Retirement Program until June 1, 2010.

As a writer and editor, often under the pseudonym Robert Reginald, he has written more than 115 fiction and nonfiction books and 13,000 short pieces, and has edited some 1,500 volumes for a half-dozen publishers. With his wife, Mary, and assorted critters, he lives and works in San Bernardino, California.

INDEX

ABBREVIATIONS

Act.=Acting
ASB=Associated Student Body
ASI=Associated Students Inc.
Assoc.=Associate or Association
Asst.=Assistant
CA=California
CAB=Campus Advisory Board
Co.=Company or County
CSCSB=California State College, San Bernardino
CSU=California State University System
CSUC= California State University and Colleges System
CSUSB=California State University, San Bernardino
CVC=Coachella Valley Campus
Dept.=Department
Dir.=Director
EOP=Educational Opportunity Program
Gov.=Governor
Int.=Interim
IRT=Information Research and Technology
Lect.=Lecturer
Libn.=Librarian
Lt.=Lieutenant
PAC=President's Advisory Counsel
PDC=Palm Desert Campus
Pres.=President
Prof.=Professor
SB=San Bernardino
Sec.=Secretary
UAB=University Advisory Board
Univ.=University
US=United States
VP=Vice President.

"1", rock group, 64
8STOP7, musical group, 388
9-1-1 emergency phone system, 340
60 Minutes (TV show), 144, 159
"60/91/215 Procurement Conference," 393
311, musical group, 395
562nd Air Force Band Dixieland Jazz Ensemble, musical group, 397
2000 National Teen Leadership Program, 366
Abbott, Steve, Avizio, 470
ABC Radio, 72
ABC TV, 136
Abdul Rahman, Yahya, Imam, 391
Abernathy, Tom, basketball player, 133
Abileah, Benjamin, Israeli Consul-General, L.A., 70
Ábilez, Mary Ellen, Pres., ASI, 492
Abner, Julie LaMay, Outstanding Student, 493
"Abortion: Ethical Considerations," symposium, 65
Abril, Dan, speaker, 431
Abrogar-Quinto, Nita, pianist, 456
Abzug, Bella, US Rep., 226
Academic Administration, Office of, 145
Academic Advising Center, 212
Academic Affairs, Division of, 278, 288, 409
Academic Council, 242, 327
Academic Decathlon, 279
Academic departments, formation of, 65
Academic Senate of the CSC, 56
Academy of Continuing Education, 172, 200
Access Disability Awareness/Assistitive Technology and Career Expo, 393, 420, 431
Access Theater of Santa Barbara, theatre group, 196
Accounting, Dept. of, 76
Accounting and Finance, Dept. of, 189
Accousticats, musical group, 286
Accrediting Commission of Career Schools and Colleges of Technology, 324
Achtenberg, Roberta, CSU Trustee, 389
Acis and Galatea (Handel), 180

Acker, Alan, speaker, 246
Acker, Deborah, speaker, 340
Acker, Jack E., Admissions Officer, 101
Ackley, G. David, campus booster, 60
Ackley, Richard T., Prof., Assoc. Dean, Academic Administration, 99, 107, 173, 188, 201, 266, 476
ACLU, 272
Acosta, Oscar, Chicano activist, 75
Activities Office, 198-99, 209
"Activism Conference," 387, 398
Actos de la Vida (play), 75
Actual Size, musical group, 314
Acuña, Arlene, flamenco dancer, 51
Adams, Diane, children's writer, 468
Adams, Frank P., CSUC Trustee, 110
Adams, Greg, trumpeter, 141
Adams, Gregory, UAB Member, 500
Adams, Marjorie M., SB landowner, 28, 33
Adams, Phyllis, Prof., 299
Adams, William, singer, 294
Adamson, Gregory, performer, 464
"Addressing the Needs of Older Workers in the 21st Century," conference, 383
"Adelante Mujer Hispana," conference, 250
Adelanto Grand Prix, motorcycle race, 433
Adema, musical group, 388
Adharpurapu, Ratnasri, Outstanding Student, 493
Ad-Hoc Committee to Review the Academic Goals and Programs of the College—see: Task Force on Academic Goals and Programs
Adikuono, Clifford, Outstanding Student, 495
Adkins, Dana, singer and actress, 438, 442
Adler, Leta M., Prof., 69
Adler, Louis S., speaker, 309
Administration Building, 13, 17, 34, 36, 45, 49, 95, 150, 160-61, 188, 236
Administration, School of, 117, 188
Administrative Council, 79, 88, 209, 328, 341
Administrative Council Minutes, 6
Administrative Services, 13

Admissions, 76
Admissions Advertising Awards, 454, 468
Admissions and Records Office, 105, 447
Admissions and Student Recruitment Advisory Board, 442
Admissions standards, 238
"Adolescence in Crisis," conference, 68
"Adolescent Pregnancy and Parenting: Problems, Progress, and Promises," conference, 288
Adult College Opportunity Program, 156
"Advancement Through Education," conference, 73
"Advocacy and Political Action for Children at Risk," conference, 277
Advocate of the Year Award, 430
Aerospace Corp., 35, 37
Ætna Life and Casualty Foundation, 204
Affirmative Action Advisory Committee, 202, 212, 248
Affirmative action and racism, 59, 65, 80, 87-88, 99, 114, 132, 149, 153, 165, 184, 199, 202, 207, 209, 212, 220, 222-23, 226-31, 248, 278, 281, 291, 303, 308, 312, 315, 317, 350, 391, 406-07, 455, 457
Affirmative Action Program, 80, 132, 153, 165, 223
Affirmative Action Steering Committee, 199
"African American Family Conference," 305
African Culture Night, 348, 378
Afro-Caribbean Dancers and Drummers, 279
Agee, Philip, CIA agent, 302
"Agent Orange," workshop, 149, 152, 159
Agnew, William C. "Bill," Bookstore Book Buyer, 147
Agoura High School Wind Ensemble, 151
Agran, Larry, Dir., History of Cancer Control Project, UCLA, 120
Agriculture U.S.A. (TV show), 158
Agua Caliente Band of Cahuilla Indians, 404, 456, 462

Aguiar, Fred, Assemblyman, 300
Aguilar, Andrew, filmmaker, 83-84
Aguilar, Kimberly, Outstanding Student, 495
Aguilar, William, Libn., University Libn., VP, Information Resources and Technology, VP, University Advancement, 9, 247, 288, 297, 409, 450, 465, 481, 487-88
Aguilera, Manuel, speaker, 301
Aguirre, Frank, Lect., 253, 501
Aharoni, Ido, Israeli Consul, 330
Ahearn, Chris, Pres., Alumni Assoc., 342-43, 492
Ahl, Ingrid, art collector, 70
Ahmed, Zahir, Dir., International Student Services Program, 253
Ahrens, Thomas R., Alumni Award, 495
Aidman, Charles, writer, 63
"AIDS and STDs," conference, 237
Ainsworth, Patrick A., Alumni Award, 402, 496
Air Force Magazine, 92
Airaksinsen, Timo, speaker, 237
Aisling, musical group, 265
Akar, violinist, 164
Aker, Kenneth Edwin, student, 300
Akins, Claude, actor, 289
Akkad Natural Preserve, 446
Alan Munde and Country Gazette, musical group, 296
Al-Ankary, Khalid, Saudi Arabian Minister of Higher Education, 353
Alarcón Cruz, Evelina, Dir., Instituto del Pueblo, 119
Alaska, poet, 431
Alaskey, Joe, comedian, 223
Alback, Stan, basketball coach, 133, 141
Albanno, Amro, Alumni Award, 389, 496
Albert C. Martin & Assocs., CSCSB architects, 27, 29-30, 33, 52
Albert McNeil Jubilee Singers, musical group, 365
Albertson College, 364
Albertson, Wallace, CSUC Trustee, 160, 185, 213
Albright, Gavan, Outstanding Student, 494

Albright, Gregg, Calif. Secretary for Business, 471
Alburo, Erlinda, speaker, 392
Alcazar, Miguel, guitarist, 208
Alcohol on campus, 266
Aldano, Carolyn B., Prof., 445
Alder Room, Commons, 11, 212, 278
Aldrich, Kenneth, speaker, 158
Aldrin, Edwin E. "Buzz," astronaut, 125
Aleshire, Frank, City Manager, Palm Springs, 60
Alexander, Ann, singer, 100
Alexander, Ashley, trombonist, 157
Alfred F. and Chella D. Moore Scholarship Fund, 58, 78, 161
Alien Ant Farm, musical group, 395
Alive and Pickin', musical group, 325
al-Khalil, Khalil, speaker, 398
All About Women (TV show), 292
All for November (Greeley), 199
Allen, Clarence, seismologist, 207
Allen, Jack, speaker, 72
Allen, Jed, actor, 465
Allen, Joyce, student, 65
Allen, Rick, Outstanding Student, 494
Allende, Isabel, writer, 304
Allender, Doris Marie Scott, Secretary, 222
Alliance for Nonprofit Managers, 359
Allis Chalmers, musical group, 72, 78
Allred, Gloria, activist, 147, 209
Allward, Tony, speaker, 118
Almay, Mark, singer, 294
Almogela, Happy, Act. Judicial Affairs Officer, 469
Almont Ensemble, musical group, 196, 208, 219, 231
Alonzo, Marie, Pres., Inland Empire Hispanic Chamber of Commerce, Arrowhead Credit Union, 334, 421
Alpert, Glenn, singer, 359
Alpha Kappa Alpha, honor society, 204
Alpha Kappa Delta, sociology honor society, 85
Alpha Kappa Psi, Business Honor Society, 85, 123
Alpha-Omega Players of the Repertory Theater of America, 92
Alpha Phi, 209
Al-Saadi, Mohammed, speaker, 219

Alsop, Peter, singer/speaker, 232, 251, 266, 317, 355
Alston, John, speaker, 211
al-Tamimi, Taiseer, Palestine Supreme Justice, 443
Altman, Ross, folksinger, 231
Alumni Assoc., 6, 45, 47, 51, 55, 58, 147, 182, 205, 301, 333-34, 356
Alumni Awards of Distinction, 416
Alumni Chorus, 186
Alumni Concert, 300
Alumni Recital, 273
Álvarez, David, Alumni Award, 496
Álvarez, Ramón, auto dealer, 427, 429
Álvarez, Rudolfo, Dir., UCLA Chicano Studies Center, 112
Amafidon, Ose, Pres., ASI, 492
Amahl and the Night Visitors (musical play), 407
Amaya, Paul, Dir., International Center, 455
Amazing Music, musical group, 273
The Ambassadors (TV show), 452
Amberg, Paul Michael, student, 66
Ambroson, David, violinist, 101
America Reads Program, 338
American Academy of Arts and Sciences, 171
American Anti-Vivisection Society, 268
American Asphalt Paving Co., contractors, 50, 55, 86
American Association for the Advancement of Science, 396
American Association of Colleges for Teacher Education, 270
American Association of Geographers, 274
American Association of Museums, 447
American Association of State Colleges and Universities, 138, 189, 286
American Association of University Professors, 73
American Association of University Women, 109
American Campus Communities, Inc., 407
American Chemical Society, 199
American College Theater National Festival, 284
American Council on Education, 181
American Culture and Language Pro-

gram, 161, 203
American Dietetics Assoc., 402
American Drum Feather Club, dancers, 72
American Historical Assoc., 280, 379
American Idol (TV show), 470
American Indian Movement (AIM), 329
American Indian Tribal Dancers, 72
"American Indian Women of Distinction Symposium," 456
American Library Assoc., 295
American Marketing Assoc., 353
American Me (film), 312
American Philosophical Assoc., 33
American Psychological Assoc., 327
American Psychological Foundation, 342
American Recovery and Reinvestment Act, 460
American School and University (magazine), 55, 451
American School Health Assoc., 340
American Veterans Movement, 103
American Volleyball Coaches Assoc., 451
Amerson, Veronica R., Dir., EOP, 452, 468
Ames, Paul, CVC Advisory Board member, 275, 284
Amey, Cynthia Ann, Career Development Center, 444
Los Amigos Mariachi Band, musical group, 316
"Los Amigos Velada Literaria," fashion show, 273
Ammiano, Tom, comedian, 238
Among the Valiant (Marín), 126
Amy, Frank Mardis, student, 46
Anawalt, Patricia, speaker, 241
Anaya, Rudolfo, writer, 342
Ancient Future Duo, musical group, 306
Anderson, Betty Dean, SB City Councilwoman, 320
Anderson, Bruce, percussionist, 101
Anderson, Daryl, Dir., Accounting, 307, 482
Anderson, Deletta R. "Del," Budget Officer, Dir., Accounting, 374, 482-83

Anderson, George Jr., student, 47
Anderson, Glenn M., Lt. Gov., CA, 40, 505
Anderson, Gloria, speaker, 263
Anderson, Guy L., campus booster, 413
Anderson-Heimark, Sondra, alumna author, 312
Anderson-Inman, Lynne, speaker, 253
Anderson, Irene W., campus booster, 413
Anderson, Jack, columnist, 241
Anderson, Jerry, student, 387
Anderson, John, poet, 102
Anderson, Michael, speaker, 367
Anderson, Michael W., Exec. Dean, College Relations, 188, 195, 201
Anderson, Newton E., SB landowner, 28
Anderson, Phillip K., Lect., 379, 501
Anderson, William, Mechanic, 136
Andrews, Anna Jane Hill, campus booster, 308-09
Andrews, Herbert J., campus booster, 308-09
Andrews-Hill Plaza, John M. Pfau Library Building, 308-09
Andrews, Michael, pianist, 56
Andrews, Van C., Pres., ASB, 87, 491
Andromedan! (campus film), 160
Andrusco, Gene L., Prof., 383
Andy Cleaves and Friends Band, musical group, 293, 296, 307, 316, 321, 325, 345
Anemometer, 115
Angelou, Maya, writer, 260, 332-33
Angel's Construction Co., builders, 167
Anheuser-Busch, 220, 327
Anheuser-Busch Auditorium, 327
Anheuser-Busch Budweiser Clydesdale horses and carriage, 327
Animal Greenhouse, 13
Animal House, 13, 235
Annechild, Annette, alumna writer, 270
Annenberg, Lenore, campus booster, 372, 413
Annenberg, Walter, US Ambassador to Great Britain, campus booster, 372, 386
Annenberg Wing, Indian Wells Center for Educational Excellence, PDC, 408
Anniversary celebrations—

Tenth Anniversary, 110
Fifteenth Anniversary, 150
Twentieth Anniversary, 213
Twenty-Fifth Anniversary, 266-68
Thirtieth Anniversary, 323
Thirty-Fifth Anniversary, 369, 371-73
Fortieth Anniversary, 420-21
Annual Fund Calling Center, 413
Anolin, Leovigildo, Consul General, Philippines, 239
Anonymous 4, musical group, 347
Another Peace, musical group, 224
Answer, musical group, 269
Antelope Valley Concert Band, 65
Anthony H. and Lois Evans Plaza PDC, 449
Anthony, Tyrone, musician, 268
Anthony, William, UAB & PAC Member, Pres., *Inland Empire Business Journal*, 378, 500
Anthropology Museum, Social and Behavioral Sciences Building, 409
Antinora, Sarah, Outstanding Student, 495
Antony Hippisley Coxe Award for the Year's Best Circus Book, 355
Anttonen, Ralph, speaker, 275
Anzaldua, Gloria, speaker, 371
"Apartheid in South Africa," conference, 206
Appaloosa, musical group, 345
Apple Computers, 244, 267
Appleby, Joyce O., speaker, 228
Aptheker, Herbert, speaker, 256
Arabatzis, Demetrios "Jim," Manager, Bookstore, 145-46
Arbolado, Camp, 59, 67
Archaeological Survey Foundation, 441
Archuletta, (Anna) Marchand, student, 51, 56
Areffi, Pat, Business Manager, ASI, 258
Arene, Alberto, speaker, 202
Arias, Rita, SB City Councilwoman, 320
Arias, Ronald, writer, 119, 368
Ariel, Gordon, speaker, 256
Ariss, David W., speaker, 247
Arkansas Dept. of Health, 288
Arlin, Patricia K., Prof., Dean, Education, 335, 473, 478

Armacost, Michael H., US State Dept., 109
Armour, Richard, humorist, 144
Army Corps of Engineers, 37
Arnone, Concetta C., Alumni Award, 495
Arnott, Catherine, speaker, 69
Arnhym, Rolfe G., CVC Advisory Board member, 275, 284
Arnquist, Janette, speaker, 289
Arrellano, Gustavo, columnist, 444
Arrowhead Building Corp., 26
Arrowhead Country Club, 82, 121
Arrowhead Credit Union, 352, 360, 370, 396, 421, 498
Arrowhead Distinguished Chief Executive Lecture, 262, 273, 284, 304, 314, 323-24, 339, 347, 357, 371, 380, 390, 401, 410, 419, 429, 443, 456, 471
Arrowhead Elementary School, 163
Arrowhead Hall, 17, 87
Arrowhead Lab for Securities Analysis, 360, 363
Arrowhead School District, 32
Arrowhead United Fund, 25
Arrowhead Village Housing, 13, 18, 368, 375-76, 385
Arschanska, Frina, pianist, 357
Art Buffet Cabaret, 191
Art Facility, Cafeteria Building, 67, 70
Art Gallery, 49, 62, 90, 142, 147, 238, 273, 280, 289
"The Art of Comprehension," conference, 194
Art Week (magazine), 144
Arts and Letters, College of, 347
The Art of the Lathe (Fairchild), 348, 351
Arthur A. Moorefield Memorial Recital, 302-03, 309, 328, 340
Arthur Rense Poetry Prize, 381
Artrup, Colleen F., Custodian, 144, 173, 432
Artrup, Melvin E., Supervising Custodian, 158, 358
ASB—SEE: Associated Student Body
Asbell, Angela, Outstanding Student, 494
Asbestos abatement on campus, 235
Asbjornsen, Arve, speaker, 470
ASCAP, 128

Asco, artist group, 160
Ash Dr., 14, 436
Ashby, David, student, 343
Ashley, Daniel C., Dir., Administrative Computing and Telecommunications, 307, 489
Ashley, Leanna, student, 211
Ashley-Navaroli, Cindy, Outstanding Student, 493
Ashwal, Stephen, speaker, 257
ASI—SEE: Associated Students, Inc.
Asian/Asian-American Roundtable, 419, 429
Asian Conference of Southern California, 94
An Asian Fable (play), 195
"Asian Studies Conference," 111
"Asian Studies Symposium," 453-54, 467
Asoka, dancer, 111
Assistive Technology Expo, 359
Associated Student Body (ASB), 11, 37-39, 58, 60, 139
Associated Students, Inc. (ASI), 11, 139, 219, 258, 292, 298, 309, 315, 360, 391, 421
Association of American Teachers, 315, 351
"Association of College Unions International Conference," 340
Association of Energy Engineers, 463
Association of Hispanic/Latino Faculty and Staff at CSUSB, 210, 294, 304, 342, 352
Astin, John, actor, 303
Astor, Marie E., pianist, Instructor, 48, 358
Astronomical Observatory—SEE: Murillo Family Observatory
Astronomical Society of the Pacific, 424
AT&T, 256
At-Risk Expo, 371
Athletics Appreciation Day, 417
Athletics, Dept. of, 308, 354
Athletics Dr., 14
Athletics fee, 303
Athletics Program, 254, 346
Atkins, Celesta, Outstanding Student, 493
Atkins, William J., speaker, 79

Atkinson, Ann, PAC Member, 418, 500
Atkinson, Jerry, campus booster, 418
Atterbury, Jean, Manager, Cafeteria, 47, 64
Atwater, Tanya, speaker, 441
Atwell, Margaret A. "Peggy," Prof., Assoc. Dean & Act. Dean, School of Education, 224, 226, 272, 276, 478, 490
Audio-Visual Dept./Services, 76, 288
Auen, Ron, Pres., H. N. and Frances C. Berger Foundation, 358, 370
Augustana College, 337
Auto Fleet Services, 13
Auxier, Gwen, Dr., physician, 64-65
Avery O. Craven Award, 383
"AVID Conference," 322
Ávila, Myron, Outstanding Student, 494
Ávila, Steven, student writer, 428
Avizio, 470
Ayala, Francisco J., speaker, 227
Ayala, Hana Lostakova, speaker, 227, 256
Ayala, Ruben S., State Sen., 104-05, 121, 123, 130, 156, 262, 299-300, 376
Aylmer, Françoise B., Assoc. VP and Int. VP, University Development, 409, 417, 465, 473, 487
Aylmer, Robert C., Dir., Student Health and Psychological Counseling Center, 407, 413, 486
Azhand, Hamid, Assoc. Dir., Dir., Capital Planning, Design, and Construction, 407
Aztec Dancers, 273
B, Trina, performer, 306
Baca, Eddie, Pres., ASB, 491
Baca, Gene, singer, 137
Baca, Joe, Assemblyman, State Sen., US Rep., 315, 328, 334, 342, 351, 356, 361-62, 364, 366-67, 374, 384, 386, 389, 392-93, 395-97, 405-06, 414, 416, 420, 427, 437, 468
Bachardy, Don, artist, 226
Bacher, Ulf, Austrian Press Attaché, 181
BackBeat, musical group, 394
Bacon, David, speaker, 456
Bacon, Mary Montle, speaker, 276
Badger Canyon, 35, 446

Badger Hall, 14, 17, 87, 154
Badger Hill (Mount McPherson) and Little Badger Hill, 28-30, 221, 404, 413, 446, 454, 466
Baer, Donald, speaker, 69
Baez, Joan, singer, 91
Bagdasarian, Marian, CSU Trustee, 264
Baguley, Linda, speaker, 301
Bahgat, Abd el-Tawab, VP, Zagazig University, 204
Bail, Homer M., attorney, 99
Bailey, Joseph, campus booster, 288
Bailey, Kenneth, speaker, 64
Bailey, Robert C., speaker, 282
Bajema, Don, singer, 301
Baker, Donald I., PAC Member, Arrowhead Award, Pres. & CEO, Stater Bros. Markets, 278, 429, 498, 500
Baker, Gregory, Facilities Services, 423
Baker, Jace, Management, 445
Baker, Neal T., Arrowhead Award, Pres. & CEO, Baker's Drive-Thru Restaurants, 323-24, 444, 498
Baker, Sarah, Libn., 9
Baker's Drive-Thru Restaurants, 323-24, 444, 498
Bakr, Mohamed, speaker, 191, 215
The Bald Soprano (Ionesco), 39
Bald, Suresht, speaker, 94
Baldauf, Jill, speaker, 343
Balderrama, Francisco E., speaker, 456
Baldwin, Curtis, actor, 232
Ball, Kim, Dir., Coyote Bookstore, 438
Ball, Richard, orchestra director, 315
Ball, Tom, singer, 265
Ballard, Al C., Mayor, SB, 35, 38-39, 47, 75, 504
Ballard, Ross L., Dir., Student Health Center, 117, 158, 184, 187, 190, 384, 486
Ballesteros, Dolores, CVC Advisory Board member, 295
Ballet Folklórico, dancers, 137, 332, 372, 382
Ballet Folklórico Alegria de México, dancers, 362
Ballet Folklórico California, dancers, 273
Ballet Folklórico Cultural, dancers, 253
Ballet Folklórico de Blythe, dancers, 94
Ballet Folklórico de Guadalupe, dancers, 314
Ballet Folklórico de San Bernardino, dancers, 143, 210
Ballet Folklórico del Pacifico, dancers, 369
Ballet Folklórico ITZ, dancers, 119
Ballet Folklórico Mixcoacalli, dancers, 219, 229
Ballet Folklórico Teotihuacán, dancers, 127
Ballon, Rachel, writer, 277
Balthrope, Robin, speaker, 322
Baltz, Lewis, artist, 239
Balzer, Bob, Chief Executive, *San Bernardino Sun*, 421
Banana Lizards Band, musical group, 283
Bancroft, Michelle, alumna author, 270
Band and Orchestra Festival, 126, 135, 142, 149
Band Directors Clinic, 165
Banda Sol Naciente, musical group, 304
Bank of America, 121, 215, 269, 310, 391, 417
Banks, William, psychologist, 141
Bannatyne, Alex, speaker, 131
Bannatyne, Maryl, speaker, 147
Banning Unified School District, 109
Bannister, Wes, speaker, 266
Banquet for the Executive Women International, 152-53
Banuelos, Gonzalo, speaker, 301
Barahani, Reza, poet, 387
Baramki, Gabriel A., educator, 298
Barbara A. Taylor Memorial Scholarship, 247
Barber, Louis, speaker, 181
Barber, Russell J., Prof., 210, 221
Barbour, Pauline, Pres., ASI, 185, 491
Barfield, Elizabeth J., Prof., 358
Bargman, Lorne, speaker, 69, 105
Barkan, Elliott R., Prof., 67, 72, 74, 187, 229, 232, 283, 301, 383
Barkan, Esther, wife of Elliott R., 67
Barker, Betty M., Hon. Ph.D., sculptress, 389, 406, 497
Barker, Coeta, campus booster, 377-79, 437
Barker, Donald R., campus booster, 377-79, 437
Barkin, Kenneth D., historian, 156

Barks, Coleman, speaker, 369
Barnes, Gerald, Bishop, SB Catholic Diocese, 421
Barnes, Mary, wife of Ronald E., 450
Barnes, Ronald E., Prof., Act. Chair, Humanities Div., 41, 55, 59, 67, 71, 334, 398, 418, 421, 450, 477, 489, 502
Barnett, Dave, poet, 360
Barnett, Thomas, guitarist, 100
Baron, Lawrence, speaker, 411
The Barons, musical group, 165
Barreto, Ricardo, poet, 437
Barrett, Buckley B., Libn., 199, 446
Barrett, Richard, tenor, 192
Barron, Kayce, actress, 100
Barstow College Band, 120
Barstow Freeway (I-15E), 30, 35, 38, 164
Barstow High School Concert Band, musical group, 301
Bartell, Sherrie R., Act. Dean, Continuing Education, 145, 160, 162, 479
Bartells, Bruce, UAB Member, 500
Barth, Lewis M., speaker, 321
Barthol, Richard P., speaker, 117
Barton Flats, 59, 67
Barton, Hiram M., Mayor, SB, 504
Bas, Joe F., Prof., 71, 286, 489
Baseline Access, Training, and Support Initiative (BATS), 344
Basham, A. L., speaker, 123
Basix, musical group, 413
Bassiry, Gregory R., Prof., 473
Bauer, Brad, hang glider, 261
Baugh, John, linguist, 467
Baughn, William H., CAB Member, 499
Bautista, Rosie, Outstanding Student, 495
Bautzer Faculty University Advancement Award, 394
Baxter, Lynn, speaker, 194
Bayless Accountancy Corp., 498
Bayless, Glenda, PAC Member, Arrowhead Award, accountant, 314, 498, 500
Bazdarich, Michael, economist, 258, 269, 395
BBC (British Broadcasting Co.), 95, 99, 287

B-C Construction, builders, 51
The Beach Boys (Golden), 118
Beagle, Peter S., writer, 456
Beal, Brenda U., speaker, 159
Beal, Robert, speaker, 105
Beale, Ruby L., Alumni Award, 344, 496
Bean, Carl, Rev., 259
Beane, Jeff, speaker, 100
Beatles & The Monkees Tribute Band, musical group, 445
Beaty, Daniel, performer, 440
Becker, Ray, speaker, 241
Beckett, Samuel, playwright, 92
Beckley, Luvina, Coach, 312
Beckman, Jim, speaker, 209
Beckman, Richard, artist, 340
Bedley, Gene, writer, 288
Beechko, Andrea W., Budget Analyst, Budget Officer, 482
Beeman, Chani, University Ombudsperson, 387, 419, 428, 433
Beeman, Frank R., Advanced Studies, 265
Beer Garden Patio, Student Union, 160
Beer on campus, 111
Begay, Manley A. Jr., speaker, 368
Behar, Joseph V., speaker, 74
Behavioral Medicine and Integrative Health Studies Center, 236
Behrens, Jack, pianist, 116
Behrens, Sonja, pianist, 116
Belafonte, Harry, singer, 422
Belden, Burr, historian and booster, 57
Bell, Annette, Outstanding Student, 494
Bell, Chuck, speaker, 150
Bell, Derrick A. Jr., attorney, 270
Bell, Johnny, performer, 306
Bell, Joseph, Grounds Worker, 144
Bell, Marvin, poet, 81, 126
Bella Lewitzky Dance Company, dancers, 226
Bellecourt, Vernon, speaker, 339
Bellis, David J., Prof., 377, 412, 422, 426, 502
Bello, Walden, speaker, 406
Belonsky, Ruth, speaker, 241
Belser, Richard, Grounds Worker, 188
Beltrán, Abe, Mayor, Colton, 119
Beltrán, Daniel, speaker, 301
Beltrán, George, artist, 106

Belz, Herman, speaker, 228
Bemus and Hollow, musical group, 388
Benard, Bonnie, speaker, 338
Benavides, Emilio, speaker, 111
Bender, Eugene I., speaker, 146
Bengelsdorf, Irving S., columnist, 51, 62, 83, 151
Benítez, Margarita, speaker, 364
Benítez, Tomás, speaker, 456
Benjamin, Karl, artist, 155
Bennecke, Richard J., Pres., ASB, Pres., Alumni Assoc., Activities Advisor, Coordinator, Student Union, Dir., Alumni Affairs Assoc., Alumni Award, 37-38, 47, 49, 52, 124, 133-34, 185, 188, 211-12, 491-92, 495
Bennett, Carol, writer, 277
Bennis, Phyllis, US Committee in Solidarity with the People of El Salvador, 158
Benoit, John J., Alumni Award, Assemblyman, 393, 408, 449, 496
Benson, Doug, comedian, 268
Benson, Frank D., Prof., 373
Benson, Gustavo, Rev., speaker, 136, 142
Benson, Jean, Mayor, Palm Desert, 449
Benson, Malcolm, organist, 217
Benson, Phyllis, harpsichordist, 133, 173, 309
Benson, Thomas, Outstanding Student, 494
Benton, Denise, Dir., Upward Bound Program, Dir., Outreach Services, 180, 283
Benton, Kevin B., 272
Benton, Kimberlee, student, 439
Benton, Michael V., Chief, Custodial Services, 310, 433, 473
Benzakein, Jacques, Prof., 422
Berch, Roxanne, Coach, 359
Berdan, Frances F., Prof., 180, 182, 197, 226, 357, 426, 473, 490
Berenson, Frances M., philosopher, 154, 195
Berger Circle Dr., PDC, 14
Berger, Frances C., campus booster, 358
Berger, H. N., campus booster, 358
Berger, Stephen E., psychologist, 131
Bergeron, Thom, saxophonist, 293

Bergeson, Marian, Assemblywoman, State Sen., 167, 240
Bergstrand, Sandra, Secretary, ASB, 38
Berilla, Susan, Outstanding Student, 494
Berk, Susan, speaker, 120
Berkeley Shakespeare Group, theatre group, 223
Berkman, Gene, speaker, 272
Berman, Lawrence, speaker, 239
Berman, Zeke, sculptor, 257
Bermingham, Ann, speaker, 178
Bernard, Carl F., US Army Col., 111
Bernard Osher Foundation, 401
Bernard, Thomas, CSU Trustee, 216
Bernheimer, Rob, Mayor, Indian Wells, 389
Berns, Walter, speaker, 177
Bernthaler, Jeanette M., Libn., 89, 366
Bero, Francesca, speaker, 184
Berry, Al, campus booster, 368
Berry, Bernita C., speaker, 352
Berry, Jeffery Allen, student, 359
Berry, Ray, speaker, 64
Bersch, Blanche C., CSU Trustee, 168, 185
Best Buy Company, 417
Best of Everything Band, musical group, 459
BETA Center 211, 213, 223
Betances, Samuel, speaker, 344
Bethelaires, musical group, 98
Bethune Youth Conference, 254
Betro, Dom, speaker, 431
Better-House, Jenny, speaker, 253
Betty and Jim Kasson Center Award, 388
Betty Barker Sculpture Garden, PDC, 406
Beydler, Gary, artist, 118
Beyer, David, Dir., Sports Information, 254
Beyersdorf, Peter, speaker, 443
Beyond the Books: A Guide to Service Learning Colleges and Universities (book), 453
Bhajan, Yogi, Kundalini yoga master, 91
Bhatia, Anand R. "Andy," Prof., 373
Biafra, Jello, singer, 235
Bialosky, Marshall, Musical Dir., CSU

Dominguez Hills, 94
Biblical Gospel Singers, 125
Bickham, musical group, 101
Bickmore, Billie, Administrative Support Coordinator, 423
Bicycle stands, 73
Biddle, W. Craig, State Sen., 97, 105
Biden, Joseph R., US Sen., US Vice President, 105
Bieber, David, Pres., La Sierra Coll., 40
Bielfeldt und Greis, musical group, 100, 107
Bierschbach, Robert J., CAB Member, 499
Big Bang Love, Juvenile A (film), 467
Big Bop Nouveau Band, musical group, 264
Biggs, Bernice, speaker, 127
Bigley, George Patrick, student, 139
Bilateral Safety Corridor Coalition, 470
Bild, Elaine, speaker, 262
"Bilingual/Bicultural Education," symposium, 124
Bilingual Bicultural Teacher Corps Training Program, 122, 129
Bilingual Education Training for Advancement Center—see: BETA
Bilingual Educators' Career Advancement Program, 280
Bilingual Foundation of the Arts, 227
Bilingual Special Education Program, 200
Bilingual Teacher Corps Program, 122, 142, 146, 153
Billauer, Jesse, Life Rolls, 442
Biller, Henry B., psychologist, 203
Billingsley, Donald, speaker, 240
Bilson, Bruce, speaker, 128
Bilson, Danny, Alumni Award, TV writer, 134, 238, 270, 278, 496
Bi-National Education Committee, 368
Bingham, Paul, Managing Dir., Global Commerce and Transportation, 472
Binney, Rosemary Tilden, Alumni Award, Reading Specialist, EOP, 428, 495
Biological Science(s) Building, 13, 17, 34, 39, 41, 47-49, 51, 55, 60, 99, 171, 188, 234, 296, 404, 415, 431, 434, 438, 446, 449
Bird, Cynthia J., Prof., 341, 402, 490

Birns, Beverly, psychologist, 149
Birzeit University, Palestine, 316
Bisbee, Tera, Dir., Ombuds Services, Equal Opportunity and Diversity Officer, 433
Bischak, Gregory, speaker, 272
Bishop, Sims, speaker, 260
Bits and Bytes (play), 184
Black and Brown Bibliography (Library booklets by Meade), 62, 64-65
"Black Career Day," 100
Black Cultural Festival, 91
Black Education Conference, 237
Black Faculty and Staff Assoc. of CSUSB, 254
Black Family Conference, 204, 225, 267
"Black Family United," conference, 225
Black History Celebration, 311
Black History Month, 360
Black History Week, 108, 125, 148, 156, 165, 180, 193
Black Issues in Higher Education (magazine), 384
Black, Marion, UAB Member, SB Chamber of Commerce, 332, 500
Black Renaissance Week, 108
Black Representation and Urban Policy (Karnig & Welch), 337
Black Student Union, 78, 88, 157
The Black Voice News (newspaper), 193, 197, 212, 222-23, 271
Black, White, and Mrs. Green (play), 72
"Black Women in America" program, 125
Blackey, Robert A., Prof., Relations-with-Schools Officer, 80, 86, 192, 197, 280, 377, 379, 391, 444, 490
"Blacks in the Arts" festival, 141
Blackstone, Gay, wife of Harry Jr., 294
Blackstone, Harry B. Jr., magician, 219, 236, 294, 324
Blackstone, Harry B. III, son of Harry Jr., 294
Blair, Albert, Equipment Technician, 128
Blair, Billie Goode, Prof., 280
Blair, Don, speaker, 123
Blair, George C., Mayor, SB, 504
Blake, Robert D., Pres., Scientific Methods Inc., 116

Blakely, Jennifer Vaughn, Alumni Award, 496
Blanchard, William G. "Doc," organist, 77
Blander, Milton, chemist, 61
Blasphemous Rumors, musical group, 445
Blenk, Christina, speaker, 378
Blessing, Linda J., Alumni Award, 496
Bliss, A. Harry, speaker, 112
Blitz, Mark, speaker, 177
Blixseth, Edra, campus booster, 349
Blixseth, Tim, campus booster, 349
Block, Janie, National Organization of Women, 92
Block, Lawrence, writer, 277
Blockbusters (TV show), 155, 166
Blodget, Robert, speaker, 245
Bloomberg, Max A. "Marty", Libn., Asst. & Assoc. Library Dir., Act. Library Dir., 141, 166, 239, 244, 307, 481
Bloomington Middle School, Bloomington, 458
Blount, Gilbert L., musician, 147
Blumer, Herbert, sociologist, 93
Blurton, Craig, Prof., 248
Bluth, Louis, Pres., Eckankar, 82
Board of Counselors, Dept. of Business Administration, 60
Bob Field Construction Co., builders, 160
Bobo, Roger, musician, 158
Bobp, Mary Ellen, Libn., 325
Bockman, Sheldon E., Prof., 206
Bodie Mountain Express, musical group, 134
Bodily, Brian D., Police Lt., Int. Chief of Police, 414, 418, 423, 484
Bodman, Andrew R., Provost and VP, Academic Affairs, 458, 475
Boe, Anne, writer, 277
Boeh, Sarah M., Prof., 473
Boese, Raymond, organist, 173
Bogatin, Matt, speaker, 105
Bogen, James, philosopher, 137
Bogh, Russell, alumnus Assemblyman, 395
Bohen, Mary, Outstanding Student, 494
Boland and Dowdall Duo, musical group, 278

Boland, Jan, flautist, 278
Bolanos, Carlos, Outstanding Student, 493
Bolasky, Glenn, Riverside County Deputy Sheriff, 151
Boldt, Kenwyn, pianist, 357
Bombarry, Dan, speaker, 72
Bombrule Assoc., 323
Bonacich, Edna, speaker, 214
Bond, James G., Pres., CSU Sacramento, 95
Bond, Julian, Georgia State Sen., 226
Bondi, Joseph, speaker, 236
Bones, musical group, 91
Bonillas, Ezekiel, Pres., ASI, 492
Bonneau, Ron, magician, 135
Bonners, musical group, 254
Bonnett, Aubrey W., Prof., Dean, School of Social and Behavioral Sciences, 232, 306-07, 391, 479
Bono, Mary, US Rep., 364, 408
Bono, Sonny, singer, Mayor, Palm Springs, CVC Advisory Board member, 275
Bonoff, Karla, folksinger, 118
Bonpane, Blase, speaker, 241
Bonton, George, elementary student, 73
Booe, Shirley C., Lib. Asst., 113, 374
Book Collectors' Club, 50
Booklist (magazine), 293
Boomshaka Band, musical group, 298
Boorom, Michael L., Prof., 364
Boothe, James, Facilities Maintenance Worker, 404
Bootie Shakers, musical group, 413
Borgo Press, 114, 419
Boring, Shirley, speaker, 105
Borland, Jan, flautist, 254
Bormann, Emma, Austrian scholar, 51
Bornstein, Kate, artist, 410
Bosshart, Louis, speaker, 304
Bostain, James C., linguist, 92
Bostick, John, speaker, 416
Bostley, Edward J., Prof., 393
Boston Brass, musical group, 378, 400
Botting, Rebecca M., PDC, 473
Botts, Robert E., Alumni Award, UAB Member, 79, 150, 495, 500
Boucard, John, speaker, 431
Boucher, Wayne I., speaker, 239
Bournias-Vardiabasis, Nicole, Prof.,

261, 280
Bourquin, David R., Libn., 403
Boutet, Alain, speaker, 377
Bouvier, Peter L., Prof., 196-97, 501
Bovee, Marc, magician, 300
Bowen, Robert, speaker, 402
Bowerman, Karen D. Dill, Prof., Dean, College of Business and Public Administration, 403, 477
Bowers, Ron, Cafeteria Manager, 90
Bowles, Stephen A., Prof., Dean, Continuing Education, 104, 160, 324, 412, 479, 502
Bowling for Dollars (TV show), 105
Box and Cox (play), 92
Boxer, Barbara, US Sen., 324, 411
Boxtales Theater Company, theatre group, 387
Boyd, Carl, speaker, 265
Boyd, Donna J., Asst. Dean, Marketing, 351, 479
Boykin, Keith, activist, 362
Boyle, Gregory, S.J., Rev., 383, 428
Boys' and Girls' Club Pacesetters Drill Team, dancers, 306, 315
Bozonelos, Dino, Outstanding Student, 494
Bozzi, Pat, speaker, 100
Bracken, Khozette, Outstanding Student, 494
Bracken, Michael, alumnus, 430
Bradbury, Ray, writer, 63, 208, 210, 255, 369
Bradley, Cynthia, Outstanding Student, 495
Bradley, Ed., TV interviewer, 425
Bradley, Noma, Facilities Services, 423
Bradley, Peter, historian, 472
Bradshaw, Ralph, Pres., Riverside City Coll., 40
Braga, Thomas, ex.-Prof., 98
Brame, Geraldine Ruth, student, 45
Brammer, Andrew M., Outstanding Student, 494
Branch, Kerry, Outstanding Student, 493
Brandeis, Gayle, poet, 431
Brandt, Christ, speaker, 450
Branscomb, Albert, speaker, 159
Brasch, Klaus R., Prof., Act. Dean, School of Natural Sciences, Executive Dir., Research Development and Technology Transfer, 290, 308, 338, 347, 422, 478, 481
Brasch, Margaret, Research and Sponsored Programs, 423
Braune, Dieter B., Building Maintenance, 473
"The Brave New Workplace: Strategies to Excel in a World of Change," symposium, 369
Break! The Urban Funk Spectacular, 411
Breslow, Alan A., Alumni Award, 495
Bretos, Miguel A., speaker, 352
Brickley, James H., Mich. Supreme Court Justice, 185
Bridges, Todd, 272
"Bridging for Success," conference, 216, 225
"Bridging the Gap: Schools and Services for At-Risk Youth," conference, 266
"Bridging Tomorrow's Needs Through Today's Minds," conference, 255
Briggs, Beverly, harpsichordist, 239
Briggs, John, Assemblyman, 123
Briggs, Ray, musician, 377, 383
Brighouse, Gilbert, psychologist, 93
Bright, Joseph S., Mayor, SB, 504
Brightman, Lehman, speaker, 72
Briley, Dianne, 155
Brilliant, Richard, speaker, 251
Brinegar, Paul, actor, 61, 77, 94
Brinkley, David, TV newscaster, 157
Briscoe, Charles A., 64
Briscoe, Peter M., Libn., 138
Briskin, Jacqueline, writer, 277
Brisol, Adam, speaker, 444
Britt, Ginger, speaker, 253
Britto, Anthony "Tony," Supervisor, Campus Stores, 152
Broad, Molly Corbett, CSU Executive Vice Chancellor, 295
Broadfoot, Roger Blakely, student, 191
Broadhead, Geoffrey, speaker, 274
Broadway on Ice, performers, 438
Brochu, Chris, speaker, 361
Brock, Aaron, Outstanding Student, 495
Brock, Edward L., Police Officer, 290, 358, 410

Brodsky de Gouttes, Ava, artist, 442
Bronson, Fred, telewriter, 290
Bronx Museum of the Arts, 119
Brooks, Betty, women's studies scholar, 194
Brooks, Leila, Union of Palestine Women's Organizations, 272
Brooks, Robert, Outstanding Student, 493
Brophy, Roy T., CSU Trustee, 213
Brosseau, Robert, musician, 204
Brosseau-Tacchia, Michele, Alumni Award, cellist, 131, 204, 208, 273, 284, 339, 359, 420, 444, 496
Brotherhood, musical group, 373
Brothers, Joyce, psychologist, 235
Brouse, Dorothy, speaker, 258
Brown, Alice, Olympic medalist, 209
Brown, Angela Carole, singer, 287
Brown, Cheryl Minter, Alumni Award, Editor, *Black Voice*, 193, 197, 271, 495
Brown, David G., presidential candidate, 169
Brown, Debbie, wife of Jack H., campus booster, 418, 421
Brown, Dennis, Rev., 315, 390, 409
Brown, Doreen Ann, student, 67
Brown, Edmund G. Sr. "Pat", Gov., CA, 15, 20, 27, 33-34, 43, 245, 251, 320-21, 505
Brown, Edmund G. Jr. "Jerry", Gov., CA, 107, 135, 140, 155-56, 178, 505
Brown, Eula Barrios, Admissions Counselor, 202
Brown, Eva, Holocaust survivor, 457
Brown, George E. Jr., US Rep., 62, 83, 105, 139, 154, 163, 174, 182, 187, 190, 209, 213, 241, 254, 284, 289, 291, 299, 314, 318, 323, 333-34, 338, 344, 348, 352-54
Brown, Gillian, photographer, 177
Brown, Hardy, Publisher, *Black Voice*, Pres., SB Board of Education, 197, 245, 321
Brown, Harrison, geochemist, 51
Brown, Herbert E., Dir., Physical Plant, 34, 37, 104, 364, 483
Brown, Jack H., Hon. Ph.D., Arrowhead Award, CEO/Pres., Stater Brothers Markets, 261-62, 278, 295, 297, 327, 369, 412, 418, 421, 427, 441, 497-98
Brown, James M., Prof. & writer, 277, 293, 466
Brown, Jimmie C., Int. Chief & Chief of Police, 431, 441, 484
Brown, Lou, speaker, 216, 225
Brown, Marlin L., Alumni Award, Pres., Alumni Assoc., 492, 496
Brown, Marta—SEE: Macías Brown, Marta
Brown, Michael R., Libn., 94
Brown, Robert L., speaker, 238
Brown, Rose, campus booster, 369
Brown Society, musical group, 136
Brown, Virginia, CAB Member, 499
Brown, Willie, State Assemblyman, 87
Browne, Michael Dennis, poet, 72
Bruce, Robert, speaker, 206
Brudin, John, PAC Member, 401, 500
Brulte, Jim, Assemblyman, State Sen., 291, 348
Brummel, Steven W., CVC Advisory Board member, 275, 284
Brundage, Arlene, soprano, 237
Brundage, Gene, baritone, 237
Brunkhorst, Bonnie, Prof., 281, 288, 441
Brunkhorst, Herbert, Prof., 288, 396, 468
Bruno, Salvatore, Painter, 212
Bruton, Al, speaker, 139
Bryan, Diane Lang, clarinetist, 116, 194
Bryan, Leslie, Outstanding Student, 493
Buchen, Devy Barnett, soprano, wife of Irving H., 156, 196
Buchen, Irving H., Prof., Dean, School of Humanities, 145, 153, 155, 196, 203, 477
Buchla, Donald, synthesizer builder, 85
Buckley, Kathy, comedienne, 285
Bud Light Daredevils, performers, 319
Budapest, Z., wiccan, 120
Buddy Buddy (film), 157
Budget Administration, Office of, 198
Budget crisis and cuts, 269, 271, 273-74, 276-77, 279, 288, 297, 330-32, 385, 394, 399, 402, 404, 414, 424-25, 434, 441, 444, 446-47, 451-52, 459-61, 464, 466
Budget Planning and Administration,

Office of, 198
Budget Planning and Priorities Committee, 189
Budget Planning, Office of, 198
Buena Vista Cable, 181
Building abbreviation codes, 71, 127
"Building Bridges for Success," conference, 371
"Building Bridges to the Future," conference, 362
"Building for the Future," workshop, 194
Bulgarella, Dominic M., Prof., 63, 286, 301, 502
Bulgarella, Rosaria, Dir., Human Learning Center, 63
Bull, A. Vivien, Prof., 142, 196, 275, 370, 502
(The) Bulletin (campus newsletter), 6, 9, 38, 55, 149, 156, 233-34, 245, 278, 359—SEE ALSO: *Friday Bulletin*
Bunn, David, speaker, 259
Burawoy, Michael, speaker, 323
Burchfield, Jerry, artist, 257
Burdon, Eric, singer, 60
Burgess, Gordon, Southern California Edison Co., 80
Burgess, Larry E., Dir., Redlands Public Library, 323, 443
Burgess, Linda, Lect., 458
Burgess, Mary A. Wickizer, Purchasing Agent & alumna author, 114, 138, 144, 162, 270, 506, 508
Burgess, Michael, Libn., 75, 89-90, 96-97, 114, 158, 172, 190, 200, 213, 292-95, 323, 377, 414, 419, 421, 472-73
Burgett, Carol, writer, 277
The Burial of Alma (Slout), 211
Buriel, Raymond, speaker, 251, 303
Burke, Yvonne Brathwaite, US Rep., 194
Burkhalter, Bettye, speaker, 362
Burleigh, A. Peter, speaker, 236
Burleson, Thomas, Coach, 196
Burns, Deborah, Int. Dir., Foundation, 425, 483
Burns, Fred, comedian, 402
Buroker, B. Jill, Prof., 182, 208
Burruel, Misty, Outstanding Student, 494
Bursill-Hall, Damien, flautist, 321

Burton, Louise, Prof., 249
Bus Stop, 46, 132
Busch, Katharine M., Prof., 344
Buse, Courtney S., speaker, 102
Bush, George H. W., VP and Pres., US, 245
Bush, William "Buckey," brother of Pres. George H. W. Bush, 245
Business and Public Administration, College of, 362, 419, 448
Business and Public Administration, School of, 189, 308-09
Business Administration, Dept. of, 189
Business Management Club, 63
Business Partners, support group, 309
Buss, Claude, speaker, 94
Bustamante, Andrés, guitarist, 136
Bustamante, Cruz, Lt. Gov., CA, 367, 383, 505
Butler, Arthur M., Environmental Health and Safety Officer, Act. Dir. & Dir., Public Safety, Int. Chief, Police Operations, Dir., Administrative Services, Exec. Dir., CSUSB Foundation, Dir., Risk Management, PAC Member, 146, 162, 166, 231, 357, 381, 388, 483-84, 500
Butler, Buddy, actor/playwright, 267
Butler, Daws, TV writer, 54
Butler, Diana, Academic Personnel, 423
Butler, John J., campus booster, 60
Butler, Susan Reddy, speaker, 217
Butterfield, Bonnie, Library Asst., PDC, 473
Butterfield Country Cloggers, dance group, 207
Bybee, Rodger, speaker, 396
Byington, Diane, violinist, 113
Byrd, Charles E., Watchman, 52
Byrds, musical group, 354
Caballero, César, Libn., Dean and University Libn., John M. Pfau Library, 433, 481, 506
Cabalo, Eric, guitarist, 371, 396
Cabazon Dinosaurs, musical group, 253
Cabrera, Armando, artist, 106
Caccavale, Joan, Public Affairs, 423
Cadiz Valley, 129
Cady, Sharon D., Academic Research, 473
Cafeteria Building, 17, 67, 70, 87

Cain, Louis, Lead Plumber, 404
Caine, Barbara, speaker, 310
Caine, Renate M. Nummela, Prof., 214, 354
Cairo, Constance, singer, 231
Cajon Blvd., 35
Cajon High School, 208
Cajon High School Wind Ensemble, 168
Cal-Pac Construction Inc., builders, 277, 285, 304
Cal State All-Stars (amateur basketball team), 108, 152
Cal State Associates, 151, 164
Cal State San Bernardino (alumni magazine), 6, 287, 326, 366
Cal State SB (alumni magazine), 6, 326, 366
Cal State Chronicle (student newspaper), 6, 191-93, 266-67, 270, 356
Cal State Concert Choir, 100, 140, 159, 242, 322
Cal State Cooks, 1965-2005: Selected Recipes from the Administration, Faculty, and Staff of California State University, San Bernardino, on the Fortieth Anniversary of the Founding of the Campus (Ralph & Burgess), 421
"Cal State Day," 213, 267
Cal State International Club, 206
Cal State Jazz Ensemble, 115, 157
Cal State Student Presidents Assoc. Conference, 138
Cal State Wind Ensemble, 136-37, 140, 180, 315
Caldera, Manuel, speaker, 228
Caldera, musical group, 118
Caldiron, Carla, poet, 127
Caldwell, George, speaker, 64
Caldwell, Liston, student, 95
Calhoun, Monica, 272
Caliendo, Christopher, guitarist, 363
California Academic and Research Libraries Assoc., 320
California Academic Decathlon, 271
California Angels, baseball team, 280
California Art Education Assoc., 347
California Arts Council, 162, 190
California Arts Project, 272-73
California Association of Health, Physical Education, Recreation, and Dance, 318
California Baptist College, 89, 249
California Bay Delta Authority, 449
California Book Awards, 390
"The California Civil Rights Initiative and Proposition 187," forum, 320
California College Media Assoc., 440
California Collegiate Athletic Assoc., 276
California Collegiate Athletic Assoc. Tournament, 382
California Community Colleges, 261, 406
California Continuing Education Assoc. Conference, 79
California Coordinating Council for Higher Education, 75
California Council for the Humanities in Public Policy, 126
California Council on Economic Education, 391
California Department of Education, 61, 117
California Department of Transportation (Caltrans), 393, 415
California Desert Natural Festival, 410
California Economics Challenge, 469
California Faculty Assoc.—SEE: CFA
California Folklore Society, 110
California Geological Society, 374
California Glass Exchange, 250
California Health Data Planning Fund, 472
California High Education Employer-Employee Relations Act (HEERA), 144
"California Indian Cultural Awareness Conference," 356, 367, 375, 385, 405, 425, 435, 448, 462
California Indoor Clean Air Act, 128
California Institute for Regenerative Medicine, 465
California Institute of Technology, 203
California Language Teachers Assoc., 401
California Library Assoc., 377, 387
California Lutheran College, 226
"The California Math Show: A Traveling Hands-On Math Museum," project, 312

California Mathematical Project, 187
California Medical Assoc., 498
California Minority Graduate Education Forum, 331
California Native American Day, 385, 405, 414, 425, 435, 462
California Organization of Women, 135
California Polytechnic State University, San Luis Obispo, 265, 279, 307
California Postsecondary Education Commission, 15, 197-99, 215, 231, 312, 399, 450-51
California Probation, Parole, and Correctional Assoc., 106
California Public Relations Board, 181
California Public Utilities Commission, 469
California Reading Assoc., 294
California Retired Teachers Assoc., 70, 91, 101, 111
California School Counselors Assoc., 162
California State Colleges Board of Trustees, 21, 25-35, 37-38, 46-47, 66, 68
California State Colleges System, 20, 79
California State Employees Assoc. (CSEA), 43-44, 48-49, 76, 104
California State Polytechnic University, Pomona, 303, 377, 379
California State Polytechnic University, Pomona Youth Gospel Choir, 275
California State Student Assoc., 172, 177, 292, 298
California State University and Colleges Board of Trustees, 82, 95, 106, 110-11, 115, 133, 135, 138, 140, 163
California State University and Colleges Chancellor's Office, 121, 460
California State University and Colleges High School Counselor Conference, 162
California State University and Colleges System, 11, 79, 164
California State University Assoc. of Emeriti Professors, 205
California State University, Bakersfield, 42, 351
California State University Board of Trustees, 169, 178, 188, 197, 214, 241, 257, 269, 276, 285, 287-88, 309-10, 316, 333, 349, 370, 392, 396, 403, 407, 421, 423, 458-59, 473
California State University, Chico, 24
California State University Committee on Academic Planning and Program Review, 173
California State University Committee on the Future, 164
California State University, Dominguez Hills, 20, 28, 31, 94, 252, 254, 266
California State University Foundation, 428
California State University, Fresno, 334
California State University, Fullerton Wind Ensemble, 131
California State University, Hayward, 394
California State University, Long Beach, 446
California State University, Los Angeles, 111, 360, 452
California State University, Northridge, 147, 307, 321
California State University, Northridge Dance Troupe, 91
"California State University-Productions/Operations Management Conference," 370
California State University, Sacramento, 95
California State University, San Bernardino name change, 197-200
California State University System, 11, 164, 412-13, 450
California State University System-Wide Advisory Committee on the Student Services Fee, 172
California State University System-Wide High School Counselor Conference, 233
California State University Women's Council, 298
California Steel Industries, 207
California Student Assoc., 258, 309
California Student Opportunity and Access Program (Cal-SOAP), 244
California Supreme Court, 448
California Teachers' Assoc., 468
California Theater of the Performing Arts, San Bernardino, 357, 363, 398

California Transition Center, 276, 316
California Wellness Foundation, 429
Californians Quartet, musical group, 180
"California's Water Future," conference, 378
Callaghan, Marjorie, Workmen's Comp and Retirement Officer, 307, 432
Calvert, Ken, US Rep., 299
Calvert, Patrick Vernon, student, 224
Camarata Tango, musical group, 363
"Cambodia Today, Vietnam Yesterday," conference, 167
Cameron, Colin, speaker, 128
Campbell, David G., Capt., student, 252
Campbell, Frank D. Jr., student, Lib. Asst., 92, 124, 126
Campbell, Lloyd, Prof., 121
Campbell, Loretta A., Budget Office, 278, 324
Campbell, Stuart, speaker, 128
Campbell, Thomas, State Sen., 299-300
Campbell, William D., CSU Trustee, 278, 343
Camper Van Beethoven, musical group, 254
Camien, John R., Lib. Asst., 451
Campos Parsi, Hector, composer, 252
Campos, Tony, SB City Councilman, 85
Campus Archives, 6, 9
Campus Budget Committee, 331-32, 341
Campus Circle, 425
Campus Crusade for Christ, 329
Campus Dr., 14, 389, 404, 416-17
Campus Mall, 129-30, 139, 287
Campus Media Commission, 270
Campus Map, 133
Campus medallion, 343
Campus Planning Committee, 194
Campus Police Dept., 325, 365
Campus Stores Receiving Dept., 102
Can I Speak for You Brother? (Walker), 271
Cancryn, Dina, singer, 359, 376, 408
Canfield, J. Douglas, speaker, 89
Cannon, Mary, Lect., 458
Cannon, Terrence, activist, 54
Cantlay, Claire, Secretary, 33, 106, 118, 122

Canto Bello Chorale, singers, 231
Cantu, Norma V., US Asst. Secretary for Civil Rights, 331, 366
Capital Planning, Design, and Construction, Dept. of, 366
Carawan, Guy, folksinger, 57
Carbis, Laura J., Secretary, 278
Car-de-lite and D.J. Shon Boy, musical group, 286, 306
Cárdenas, Gus, speaker, 252-53
Cardona, Narciso, alumnus, 368
"Career Connection Conference," 305
Career Day, 123
Career Marketplace, 143
Career Opportunity Fair, 342
Careers in Job Education Fair, 271
CareFusion Corp., 472
Carey, John, guitarist, 427, 431
Caribbean Breeze, musical group, 321
Carillo, Paul K., student, 264
"Caring Hands: Creating a Safe Environment for Our Children," conference, 308
Carl Schafer Quartet, musical group, 370
Carlisle, Kris, pianist, 359, 368, 376, 390, 398, 408
Carlos, John, Olympic runner, 382, 390
Carlow, Edwin, speaker, 314
Carlquist, Sherwin, naturalist, 64
Carlsen, Chuck, speaker, 466
Carlson, B. Robert, Prof., Dean, College of Natural Sciences, 374, 478
Carlson, Bill, folksinger, 81, 93
Carlson, Claudine, soprano, 195
Carlson, Edward J., Prof., Chair, Dept. of Administration, 67, 77, 85, 477
Carmen Zapata's Children's Troupe, theatre group, 227
Carmona, María, play director, 137
Carnegie Council on Adolescent Development, 255
Carnegie Foundation Community Engagement Classification, 451, 453
Carno, Zita, pianist, 158
Carns, Mickey, Police Sergeant, 63
Caroselli, Susan, speaker, 195
Carpenter, Rosalie E., Evaluator, Admissions and Records, 307
Carpenter, Steven, artist, 428
Carpooling, 67

Carr, Vikki, singer, 327
Carrasco, Daniel, Alumni Award, 496
Carrasco, David, student, 95
Carrasco, Pete Sr., student, 95
Carroll, Larry, TV anchorman, 225
Carson, Henry, campus booster, 267
Carson, Lois J., Alumni Award, UAB Member, 125, 150, 194, 215, 254, 267, 275, 277, 495, 499
Carter, Gaylord, organist, 51
Carter, George F., geographer, 115
Carter, Grant, speaker, 121
Carter, Herbert, CSU Vice Chancellor, Administration, 197
Carter, Renate, Prof., 279
Carter, Wilmer D. "Amina," Alumni Award, Coordinator of Governmental Relations, Assemblywoman, 217, 254, 349, 376, 435, 474, 495
Cartmill, Matt, speaker, 324
Cartwright, Phillip, speaker, 246
Carver, Venita L., speaker, 149, 152
Casabo Dance, 44
Casabo (yearbook), 6, 46
Casanova, Aldo, speaker, 142
Casas, Tony, speaker, 110
Casem, Edward, clarinetist, 103
Cash, Paul, magician, 314, 322, 332, 343, 352, 362, 372, 381, 392, 401, 411, 420, 431
Cash, Tanna, student, 249
Casillas, María, speaker, 373
Castaneda, Lorna, soprano, 72
Casteel, J., speaker, 259
Castellanos, Leonard, artist, 106
Castle, LuAnne, Instructor, 423
Castro, Elena, speaker, 271
Castro, Sal, speaker, 444, 457
Castro, Virginia, speaker, 301
Casuto, Morris, speaker, 373
Catalano, Diana, Business & Public Administration, 473
Cataldo, Nicholas, historian, 392, 415, 455, 469
Catholic Charities San Bernardino/Riverside, 462
Catick, Joseph W., Mayor, SB, 504
Catlett, Lee Scott, Outstanding Student, 495
Caughey, John, historian, 118
"Caught in the Middle: Responding to Middle School Reform," conference, 236
Cauley, Harry, actor, 96, 98, 143, 164
Causey, Jack, architect, 151
Cavanaugh, Jack, speaker, 256
Cayir, Allen "Ali," 456
CBS, TV network, 452
Ceballos, Richard, Building Maintenance, 278
Ceja, Raul R., Pres., ASB, 491
"Celebrating Literacy," conference, 260
"Celebrating Our Right to Choose and Securing a Future with Choice," forum, 389
"Celebrating the Learner," conference, 249
"Celebration of Languages and Culture," 398
Celebrity Basketball Game, 272
Çelikkol, Oğuz, Turkish General Consul, 321
Cenge, Clifford, speaker, 206
Censor, Yair, mathematician, 439, 453
Center Chevrolet, 418
Center for Alternative Media, 404
Center for Bioethics, 213
Center for Correctional Education, 303
Center for Digital Education, 435
Center for Economics Education, 234
Center for General Education, 181
Center for New Directions, 123
Center for Professional Development, 107
Center for Scholarship on Spirituality, 369
Center for Science Education, 247
Center for the Commercialization of Advanced Technology, 406
Center for the Study of Hate Crimes and Extremism, 372
Center on Economic Education, 140
Centerwall, Siegfried, speaker, 98
Central City Advisory Board, 112
Central City Lutheran Mission, 399
Central Enforcement (campus film), 399
Central Labor Council, 37
Cepeda, Miguel, Coca-Cola, 418
Cervantes, John A., Lead Groundsworker, 52, 365
Cervantes, Robert A., speaker, 124

Cervello, Chuck, campus booster, 293
Cervenka, Exene, singer, 301
César E. Chávez Day, 391
César E. Chávez Middle School, 421
CFA (Congress of Faculty Associations/Calif. Faculty Assoc.), 167, 181, 188, 315, 351, 359, 396
Chaffey College, 256, 406, 448
Chakterian, John, mathematician, 62
Chalk, David N., speaker, 286-87
"Challenge and Change: Using the System to Preserve Families in the Year 2000," conference, 288
"The Challenge of Growth in California and the Inland Empire: Shaping Solutions for the 1990s," conference, 264
"The Challenges of Growth in the Inland Empire: Shaping the Future Through Leadership," conference, 240
Chamber Choir of Fort Hayes State University, 186
Chamber Orchestra of CSCSB, 84, 128, 166, 227
Chamber Players of CSU Northridge, 107
Chamber Singers, 149, 151, 163
Chambers Cable Co., SB, 223
Champoux, Tom, speaker, 211
Chan, C., Singapore Ambassador to United Nations, 252
Chandler, Harold, speaker, 98
Chandrasekhar, S., Indian Minister of Health, 111
Chandyn Productions, theatre group, 205
Chaney, John S., Prof., Assoc. Dean, Administrative Affairs, 374, 393
Chang, Menglin, educator, 294
Chang, Otto H., Prof., 445
The Changing College (Report of the Task Force to Review Educational Goals and Programs), 88
"Changing Dimensions in Reading," conference, 159
"Changing the Face of Policing," forum, 362
"The Changing World of Women," conference, 69
Channing, Carol, performer, 436
Chaparral Hall, 13-14, 17, 341

Charkins, R. James, Prof., 140, 148, 223
Charles and Shelby Obershaw Dining Room, Commons Building, 401, 464
Charles, Cheryl, speaker, 236
Charles J. Pankow Award, 304
Charley Clayton Howe Collection, 457
"Charting the Path Towards Millennium Empowerment," conference, 351
Charlton, Catherine, writer, 277
Chávez, César E., Pres., United Farmworkers of America, 229, 391, 429, 440, 449
Chávez, Christine, daughter of César E., 449
Chávez, Margaret "Margo," Budget Officer, IRT, 465
Chávez, María Elena, daughter of César E., 440
Chávez, Nadine, Dir., EOP, 356, 378, 451
Chávez, Melissa, weather forecaster, KCSB-TV, 396
Cheek, Carol, violinist, 181, 205
Cheek, Donald, educator, 134
Cheerleading Squad, 202
Chekhov, Anton, writer, 131
Chemerinsky, Erwin, legal scholar, 270
Chemical Sciences Building, 13, 18, 394, 404, 417
Chemistry Dept., 33
Chen-Maynard, Dorothy C., Prof., 402, 489
Chen, Yaw-Nan, educator, 294
Cherniss, Kim, Coach, 451
"Cherokee" (Kuiper), 325
Chesney, John, Dir., Upward Bound Program, 130
Chesterfield Film Writers' Project, 297
Chevy, folksingers, 93
Chiang, Steve I., PAC Member, 500
Chiapelli, Fredi, speaker, 100
Chicago Book Clinic, 79
Chicago Bulls, basketball team, 352
Chicago, Teacher's College, 24
Chicago Tribune Literary Award, 293
"The Chicano in a White Society," symposium, 64
El Chicano (newspaper), 69, 124, 127, 194, 197, 210
"The Chicano: Now and the Future,"

forum, 142
Chico State College, 24, 147, 171
Chien, Yuchin, Prof., 439, 490
"Child Abuse," seminar, 116
Child Care Center—see: Children's Center
"Child Care: Planning for Success," conference, 343
Child Development Center, 117
"Child in the Middle Years," conference, 114
"Children at Risk Conference," 232
Children Now, 274
Children's Center, 13, 17, 94, 118, 120, 124, 138, 147, 149, 151, 156, 158, 161, 212, 221
Children's Conference, 317, 355
Children's Festival, 135
Children's Fund, 329
Children's Network Conference, 266, 277, 288, 297, 308, 338, 346
Children's Opera Factory, musical group, 183
Childress, Leon, fashion designer, 141
Childs, Barney, musician, 145
Chimbole, Larry, Assemblyman, 123
Chinese Olympic Women's Volleyball Team, 323
Chinese Youth Goodwill Mission, musical group, 267
Chinmoy, Sri, Esraj player, 138
Chinn, Helen P., Libn., 358
Chino Basin Metropolitan Water District, 141
Chinn, Tom, speaker, 74
Chippindale, Chris, speaker, 393
Chisholm, Shirley, US Rep., 217, 281
Chisom, Gladys, Custodian, 365
Chivas, Anthony, soldier, 387
Cho, Margaret, comedienne, 302
Choi, Fiona, Outstanding Student, 494
Choice Magazine, 158, 292
Choinière, Raymond, speaker, 79
Choral Ensemble, 274
Choral Festival, 142, 150
Choral Society, 69
Chouinard, Joseph J., Libn., 97
Christa McAuliffe Showcase Award for Excellence in Education, 286, 288
Christensen, Stephen D., Dir., Major Gifts, Executive Dir., University Development, 286, 319
Christian Disciples, musical group, 193
Christian, Greg, PAC Member, 500
Christianson, Lawrence, choral director, 107
Christie, C. Charles Jr., Prof., 402
Christmas holiday break closure, 204, 224
Christmas Stories Rediscovered (Quarton), 450
The Chronicle (student newspaper)—SEE: *Cal State Chronicle*
Chrysostomos, Very Rev., Alumni Award, 495
Chuckle House Comedy Jam, 305
Chulalongkorn University, Thailand, 415
Chun, Tae-Wook, Outstanding Student, 493
Chung, Connie, TV newscaster, 151
Church of Jesus Christ of Latter-Day Saints, 455
Church of Jesus Christ of Latter-Day Saints Regional Conference, 331
Churchill, Shane, Outstanding Student, 493, 495
Churchill, Thomas W., Physical Plant, 341
Chute, Pamela, speaker, 414
Chylinska, Bozenna, speaker, 251
Ciabattini, Cheryl, Pres., Alumni Assoc., 492
Cid, Armando, artist, 106
Cinco de Mayo celebration, 51, 94, 111, 119, 136, 142, 151, 167, 219, 229, 240, 251, 304, 392
Ciplijauskaité, Birutė, speaker, 267
Circle K Club of CSCSB, 69-70, 73
Circle K International, 70
Circus Vargas, 415
Cisar, Mary Ann, Prof., 79, 489, 501
Cisneros, Henry, Mayor, San Antonio, Texas, US Secretary, Housing and Urban Development, 229, 369, 391
Citigroup Foundation, 423
Citizen's Business Bank, 363, 498
Citrus College, 254
City MCs, musical group, 286
Civic Education Enhancement Project (CEEP), 211
"Civil Disobedience," forum, 100

"The Civil Rights Movement from a Black Perspective," panel, 216
C.J. Paige and Friends, musical group, 306, 315
Clark, Dan, writer, 255
Clark, Elizabeth, speaker, 258
Clark, Garth, art dealer, 223
Clark, Gary, speaker, 264
Clark, J. Milton, Affirmative Action Appeal Coordinator, Int. Dean & Dean, Undergraduate Studies, 291, 347, 363, 480
Clark, Lois, Alumni Award, 496
Clark, Shauna, Alumni Award, 217, 496
Clark, Stella T., Prof., Assoc. Dean, Academic Administration, Act. Dean, School of Humanities, 88, 203, 212, 222, 264, 463, 477
Clark-Stewart, Alison, speaker, 285
Clark, T. J., artist, 142
Clark, Todd, speaker, 79
Clark, William D., chemist, 61
Clark, Willie, Pres., SB Branch of NAACP, 291
Clark, Woodrow W., anthropologist, 143
Clarke, K. Michael, Prof., 377, 422
Clarkson, Sandra, Dir., Learning Center, Assoc. Dean, Academic Skills, 267, 476
Claussen, Karen, poet, 137
Clay, Paul, comedian, 223
Clayton, Frank, student, 89
Clayton, Jeff, saxophonist, 391
Clayton, Mayme, speaker, 260
Cleaver, Eldridge, activist, 332
Cleaves, Andy, musician, 293, 296, 299
Cleaves, Wallace T., Prof., 107, 313, 501
Clements, Zachary, speaker, 232
Cleppe, Peter, Academic Computing and Media, 445
Cless, Elizabeth, speaker, 69
Cline, Neil, speaker, 262
Clinkscale, Martha Novak, pianist, 101, 180
Clinton, Kate, comedienne, 227
Clock Tower, Student Union Building, 304, 331-32
Close, Jayne, flautist, 167
Cloverleafs, musical group, 207
CLSI automated circulation system, 196, 198
Clute, Pamela, speaker, 427
Clute, Steve, Assemblyman, 208
CNN (Cable News Network), 449
Coachella, Calif., 414
Coachella Hospital, 429
Coachella Valley Center Advisory Board, 275, 317
Coachella Valley Center/Campus (CVC), 11, 180, 206-07, 215, 218, 221-22, 234, 236, 238-39, 245, 275, 277, 279, 284, 295, 298, 303, 309-10, 320, 326, 328, 330, 344, 349, 356-58, 368, 370, 376
Coachella Valley Community College District Board, 218
Coachella Valley Women's Business Center, 417
"Coachella Valley's Healthy Menu for Change," forum, 460
Coast State Builders, builders, 44
Coates, Faye, soprano, 209
Cobb, John B., theologian, 86
Coble, Alice, Head, Operations, Computer Center, 155, 224
Coca-Cola, 418
Coeta and Donald Barker Foundation, 437
Coggins, Janet, speaker, 202
Cohen, Ellie, speaker, 185
Cohen, Luella M., CAB Member, 200, 499
Cohen, Robert, speaker, 206
Cohen, S. Alan, speaker, 287
Cohen, William A., speaker, 216
Cohn, Hillel, Rabbi, 65, 160, 361, 402, 464, 468
Cohn, Rita, Financial Aid, 299
Coile, Russell C. Jr., speaker, 301
Coke, Van Deren, San Francisco Museum of Modern Art, 227
Colacurcio, Mary, Dir., Alumni Affairs, 243
Colby, Richard, Outstanding Student, 494
A Cold Day in Hell (play), 180
Cole, Marcus, student, 312
Cole Miners Clogging Club, dancers, 232

Coleman, David, speaker, 441
Coleman, Donna, pianist, 292
Coleman, Ellen, speaker, 440
Coleman, Julia, speaker, 79
Coleman, Karen, speaker, 194
Coleman, William R., Chair, Library Associates, 216
Coles, Frances S., Prof., 422
Collaborative Management System (CMS), 360, 371
College Advisory Board, 11, 37, 285
College and University Business (magazine), 55
College Board, 377
College Bookstore (Building), 17, 126, 130, 132, 198, 203, 205
College Bowl, 205
College Courses (Pfau & Robinson), 83
College Courses II (Pfau & DeRemer), 121
College Dale Baptist Church, 126
College Dr., 240
College Information Center, 54, 60
College Nutrition Bowl, 410
College of Education Building, 13, 18, 404, 418-20, 434, 448, 451, 470
College of Education Literacy Center Golf Tournament, 412
College of the Desert, 96, 196, 209, 215, 218, 221-22, 234, 239, 256, 277, 279, 303, 306, 382, 408
College of the Desert Band, 120
College Planning Advisory Council, 191
College Police, 56, 58, 142
College Republicans Club, 406
College Skills Learning Center, 90
College Swimming Coaches Assoc., 235-36
College Union Committee, 44
Collegiate Choral Festival, 149
Collegiate Chorus, 160, 168
Collegium Musicum of UCR, 142, 148, 155
Collins, Brian R., student, 86
Collins, Jim, activist, 294
Collins, Richard, pianist, 133
Collings, Robert, Outstanding Student, 493
Collins, Sandra, Development, 365
Cologne, Gordon, State Sen., 40, 43

Colors, campus, 38, 40, 328
Colton Chamber of Commerce, 68
Colton High School Concert Band, musical group, 315
Colton High School Wind Ensemble, musical group, 136, 151
Colton Joint Unified School District, 160
Colton Youth Soccer Club, 178
Comadena, Mary Jean, Lect., 473
Comadena, Steve A., Lect., 473
Come Here, Go Anywhere (campus recruitment video), 433
"Come to the Cabaret," show, 92
Commencement, 15-16, 45, 52, 58, 65, 76, 85, 95, 103, 112, 121, 129, 137, 152, 160, 168, 186, 198, 206, 210, 220, 231, 242, 253, 264, 275, 285, 295, 305, 315, 324, 333, 344, 353-54, 364, 373, 383, 393, 402, 412, 422, 432, 445, 458, 472-73
Commencement, Winter, 375, 378, 388, 397, 407, 417, 427, 437, 451, 465
Commission on the Bicentennial of the U.S. Constitution, 243, 247
Commission on the Status of Women, 217
Committee on Computer Affairs (Faculty Senate), 79
Committee on Ethnic Studies Program, 56
Committee to Develop an Affirmative-Action Plan, 99
Committing Journalism (Sussman), 323
"A Common Venture: Aging in the Inland Counties," conference, 248
Commons Building, 13, 17, 66, 70-73, 75, 87, 90, 115, 145, 172-73, 300, 317, 401, 414-15, 446
Communique (student newspaper), 6, 37, 42
Community Advancement Resource Enterprise (CARE) Center, 360
Community College Chorus of Victor Valley College, 152, 163
Community Counseling Center, 154
Community Foundation, 452
Community Missionary Baptist Church, Redlands, 234
Community Task Force, 315, 317
Community University, 57

Community University Partnerships, 451
"Community Visioning Conference 2010," 471
"Competencies in the '80s," conference, 150
Complex Societies Group, 318
Comprehensive exam requirement for graduation, 56
Computer Assisted Registration System (CARS), 219
"Computer Carpooling," conference, 74
Computer Center, 116, 145, 161, 288
Computer Fair, 216
Comstock, Virginia, Alumni Award, 495
Conceicao, Maisie T., Lib. Asst., 423
Concepción, Arturo, Prof., 280
Concepción, Nerissa, Outstanding Student, 493
Concert Choir, 117, 163, 177
Concierto de Aranjuez (Rodrigo), 74
Concordia-St. Paul, 450, 465
Conditions, musical group, 283
"Conference for the Advancement of Mathematics Teaching," 219
"Conference for Women," 371
"Conference of the California Glass Exchange," 250
"Conference on Adoption," 208
"Conference on Electoral Reform," 105
"Conference on Employment with Persons with Disabilities," 300
"Conference on International Trade," 334
"Conference on Police Work for Native American Teenagers," 374
"Conference on Preventing High Risk Behavior in Our Kids," 256
"Conference on Strengthening Family Life," 97
"Conference on the Constitution," 207
"Conference on the Integration of Disabled Students," 256
"Conference on the Junior High-Middle School," 105
"Conference on the Needs of Older Workers," 373
"Conference on the Use of Computer, Media, and Library Resources in the Classroom," 166

Congregation Emanu El, San Bernardino, 402
"Congress and the Separation of Powers," conference, 243, 247
Congress for United Communities, 232
Congress of Faculty Associations—see: CFA
Conjunto Jarín, musical group, 369
Conkor, Kwame, student, 352
Conley, Anthony, Pres., ASI, 492
Conley, John A., Prof., Dean, School of Social and Behavioral Sciences, 324, 359, 433, 479
Connelly, Sherrie, speaker, 238
Connolly, Leo P., Prof., 311, 320, 424, 473
Connors, William J., SB landowner, 28
Conrad, Paul, cartoonist, 241
Considine, R. James, CSU Trustee, 278, 305
Constitution Day, 460
Contino, Fiora, conductor, 180
Continuing Education, Office of, 199
Contreras-Sweet, María, State Secretary of Business, 351
Control Data Corp., computer vendor, 154
Conversations in Diversity Series, 421
Cook, Carl L. Jr., physician, 118
Cook, Paul, Outstanding Student, 493
Cook St., Palm Desert, 14, 309-10, 320, 349, 368, 383
Cooley Ranch site, 26-27
Coombs, William E., State Sen., 61, 83, 105
Cooney, Edward B. "Ned," Alumni Award, 496
Cooney, Kathlyn Mary, speaker, 453
Cooney, Margaret H., Prof., 473
Cooney, Patrick, Pres., ASI, 492
Cooper, Debra, speaker, 254
Cooper, June M., CSU Vice Chancellor for Human Resources and Operations, 306
Cooper, Melvin Dwight, helicopter pilot, 160
Cooper, Ralph, speaker, 228
Cooper, Susan M., Prof., Dir., Academic Computing and Media, Int. Dir. & Dir., Distributed Learning, 310, 349, 351, 488

Cooper, Tracy, speaker, 249
Cooperstein, Bruce, speaker, 228
COPE Foundation, 61
Copley, Arthur J., speaker, 454
Copper Mountain College, 206, 408
Corbett, Sara, Administrative Support Coordinator, 423
Corbin, Carolyn, speaker, 255
Corbin, Colleen, Humanities, 299
Córdova, France A., Chancellor, UC Riverside, 384, 406
Cordova, Fred, Plumber, Pres., Badger Hill No. 184 Chapter, CSEA, 43-44, 48-49, 105, 144, 152
Core Student Affirmative Action Program, 153
Corneille, Cik, speaker, 262
Cornerstones strategic plan, 339
Corona, Burt, speaker, 64
Corona-Norco School Board, 147
Corporation for National and Community Service, 452
Corporation Yard, 17, 51-52, 56, 347, 363
Corpus Christi (Johnston), 416
Cortés, Carlos E., Prof., UC Riverside, 326, 437
Cortines, Ramón, speaker, 262
Cory, Alicia, folksinger, 83
Cosgrove, Jim "Mr. Stinky Feet," speaker, 468
Cosi fan tutte (Mozart), 137
Costa, Art, speaker, 211
Costa, Jim, speaker, 378
Cottrel Science Award, 298
Coughlin, Mark, writer, 330
Coulson, Tony, Prof., 443, 462
Council for Advancement and Support of Education (CASE), 433
Council of Academic Deans, 214-15
Council of Scientific Society Presidents, 281
Counseling and Test Center, 297, 457
Counselor M.C., musical group, 315
Cousin, Patricia M. Tefft, Prof., 262, 354
Cousins, Kimberley R., Prof., 291, 450, 491
Coussoulis Arena—see: James and Arianthi Coussoulis Arena
Coussoulis, Christina "Tina," Legacy Award, 416, 418, 421, 497
Coussoulis Development Co., 498
Coussoulis, Dimitrios "James," campus booster, 386
Coussoulis Family, Legacy Award, 497
Coussoulis, Nicholas J., Hon. Ph.D., Legacy Award, Arrowhead Award, Alumni Award, UAB Member, son of Dimitrios, 281, 304, 319, 378, 397, 416, 418, 421, 496-99
Cousteau, Jean-Michel, oceanographer, 115
Covas, Peter, Rev., 361
Covey, Stephen, speaker, 369
Cowan, Gloria A., Prof., 138, 281, 383, 490
Cowin, Eileen, photographer, 272
Cox and Box (Gilbert & Sullivan), 159
Cox, Franklin, cellist, 311
Cox, Jack, puppeteer, 184
Cox, James L., City Manager, Victorville, 119
Cox, Martha A. P., Processor, Financial Aid, 412
Coyle, Anne, writer, 277
Coyote Arts Conservancy, 375
Coyote Athletics Hall of Fame, 457
Coyote Basketball Camp, 275
Coyote Bookstore, 13, 17, 205, 227-28, 236, 282-83, 292, 296, 445-46
Coyote Café, Commons, 446
Coyote Celebrity Golf Classic, 289
Coyote Chronicle (campus newspaper), 368, 380, 395, 440
The Coyote Chronicles: A Chronological History of California State University, San Bernardino, 1960-2010 (Burgess), 473
Coyote Den, Gymnasium, 418
Coyote Dr., 14, 318, 327, 329, 333-34, 360, 364
Coyote head emblem on running track, 457
Coyote mascot, 191, 193
Coyote Premier Field, 460
Coyote Radio (Live) (formerly KSSB), 300, 430, 448, 462-63, 466
Coyote Research Laboratory, 122
Coyotes athletic teams:
  baseball, 263, 274, 294, 382, 466
  basketball, 302, 305, 312, 351, 360,

379-80, 390, 399, 430, 452
cross-country, 338
golf, 263, 274, 323, 326, 457
hockey, 441
soccer, 279
tennis, 320, 470
volleyball, 317, 346, 369, 397, 407, 450-51, 465
water polo, 346
Cozart, Clyk, 272
Craft, Michael, writer, 438
Crafton, Alan, speaker, 185
Crafton Hills College, 98, 383
Crahan, Meg, speaker, 209
Craig, Dennis, UAB Member, 500
Craig, John H., Prof., Int. Dean, Natural Sciences, 78, 355, 374, 412, 478, 489
Craig, Karen, UAB Member, 500
Crail, Richard F., UAB Member, 500
Cramer, James, SB District Attorney, 119
Cramer, Paula, Mathematics, 445
Cramer, Robert E., Prof., 225, 258, 490
Cranston, Alan, US Sen., 112
Crawford, Cynthia, Prof., 462
Crawford, Roger, speaker, 222
Crazy Eight, musical group, 289
The Creation (Haydn), 159
Creative Arts Building, 13, 17-18, 110, 112-13, 115, 125, 128-30, 132, 135, 139, 161, 188, 325, 348, 361
"Creative Writing Conference," 101, 111, 136, 143
Creative Writing Day, 263
Credibility Gap, satirical group, 91
"Crime Prevention Week," 186
"Crisis in Minority Education," conference, 367
"Crisis in Public School Finance," conference, 64
"Crisis Intervention," conference, 106
Crisp, Tom, speaker, 444
Crissey, Paul, speaker, 317
Crist, Rose, student, 57, 73
Critchell, Iris, World War II aviator, 440
Crites, Buford, Mayor, Palm Desert, 358
Cromise, Robert, literary critic, 107
Cropley, David, speaker, 471-72
Cross Cultural Center, Santos Manuel Student Union, 11, 356, 376, 428
Crowley, Deborah L., Alumni Award, 496
Crowley, Phil, speaker, 263
Crum, Anne, Secretary, 286
Crum, James D., Prof., Chair, Natural Sciences Div., Dean, School of Natural Sciences, 71, 86, 275, 286, 478
Cruz, Frank, TV news anchorman, 240
Cruz-Hacker, Alba, Outstanding Student, 494
Cruz, Wilson, actor, 398
Cruz, Yolanda, filmmaker, 442
CSCS Bulletin, 38
Csíkszentmihályi, Mihály, psychologist, 390
CSUSB Downtown Center, 430
CSUSB Faculty Authors, Composers, and Playwrights: A Bibliography of Thirty Years of Published Monographs and Recordings, 1965-1995 (Burgess), 323
CSUSB Faculty Authors, Composers, and Playwrights: A Bibliography of Forty Years of Published Monographs and Recordings, 1965-2005 (Burgess), 421
CSUSB Food Industry Entrepreneurs Hall of Fame, 441
CSUSB Foundation, 107, 222, 458
CSUSB Magazine, 6
CSUSB Minority Drug Abuse Research Program, 460
CSUSB Spirit Team, 459
CSUSB Symphonic Band, 298, 300, 450, 467
CSUSB Talent Show, 391
Cuellar, Ruday, artist, 106
Culberson, Larry, student, 73
Cultural Center, 367
Cultural Diversity Committee, 303
Cultural Odyssey Company, musical group, 322
"Cultural Transformation and Convergence: East and West," conference, 403
"Culture, Self, and Communication: Teaching, Research, and Practice," conference, 403-04
Culturefest celebration, 309
cummings, e. e., writer, 48

Cummins, Thomas Jay, student, 186
Cumulative Paperback Index, 1939-1959 (Burgess), 96
Cunha, Stephen, geographer, 340-41, 379
Cunningham, James E., Mayor, SB, State Sen., Superior Court Judge, CAB Member, 40, 285, 498-99, 504
Cuomo, Mario, Gov., New York, 245
Curb, Michael, Lt. Gov., CA, 505
Curlin, Freddy, SB City Councilman, 305
Curriculum and curriculum reform, 16, 32, 35-36, 220, 255
Currier, Deborah Greer, Alumni Award, 496
Curry, Donna, musician, 73
Curry, Paul, SB County Sheriff's Sergeant, 146
Curtin, Mary, CAB Member, 499
Curtis, Lanse Palmer, student, 104
Curzon, Susan, VP, Information Resources and Technology, CSU Northridge, 321
Custer, Robert, CAB Member, 198, 499
Cutler, Gloria, UAB & PAC Member, 500
"Cutting Through the Red Tape: Local Government Summits on Coordinating Youth Police," conference, 282
CVC—see: Coachella Valley Campus
D. J. Fletch, musical group, 286
D. J. Stine Co., builders, 131
Dabah, Simi, sculptor, 472
Dag, musical group, 312
Daggett, Willard, Pres., International Center for Leadership in Education, 350
Dainko, Edward, physician, 82
Damaske, Frederick H., Prof., 74
D'Ambrosio, Franc, ice skater, 438
Damus, Shibli S., CAB Member, 499
Danby Lake, 129
Dance Art Co., 250
Dance Hall Crushers, musical group, 353
Dance Kaleidoscope, 304
Danchuk, George, sixth grade teacher, 73
Daneke, Gregory A., speaker, 237, 241
Danforth Foundation, 280

Dangermond, Jack, Pres., ESRI, 370
Dangerous Freedom: Fusion and Fragmentation in Toni Morrison's Novels (Page), 327
Daniel, Deborah (Tharaldson), Pres., Alumni Assoc., Alumni Award, UAB Member, 150, 492, 495, 500
Daniels, James E., Dir., Academic Programs and Services, CVC, 307, 351, 353, 480
Daniels, Lawrence L., Pres., Alumni Assoc., Alumni Award, 272, 492, 495
Daniels, Richard, campus booster, 293
Daniels, Ron, speaker, 267
Dankook University, Seoul, Korea, 359-60
Danskin, Wesley R., geologist, 429
Danz, Walter N., Plant Operations, 169
Dark Root of a Scream (play), 68
Daroszewski, Ellen, Nursing, 445
Darr, Katheryn Pfisterer, speaker, 292
Dartmouth Plan, 31
Daryl, radio personality, 442
Data Gathering Center, 215
Data Processing Center, 74, 76
Data Security Program Development Grant, 462
Davaran, Lynda K., Lib. Asst., 378, 446
Dave and Richard Ventriloquist Team, ventriloquist, 315
Dave Stockton Coyote Classic Golf Tournament, 328
Davenport, Da'Jhana, singer, 322
Davey and the Corvettes, musical group, 101
David Brinkley's Magazine (TV show), 157
David Richards Construction, builders, 217
Davidson, Dianne, singer, 249
Davidson, Pegeen, Payroll, 473
Davila, Bill, Pres., Vons, 240
Davis, Angela, activist, 219, 322, 467
Davis, Anne B., actress, 61
Davis, Anne J., speaker, 196
Davis, Frances Lodge "Fancy," Alumni Award, 495
Davis, Gray, Lt. Gov. & Gov., CA, 348, 396, 505
Davis, James V., Owner, Schaffner Players, 61

Davis, Jeffrey W., Dir., Water Resources Institute, 364, 413, 478
Davis, Joe, speaker, 271
Davis, Laura, Outstanding Student, 493
Davis, Nathaniel, speaker, 219
Davis, Robert L., speaker, 246
A Day in the Life of America (play), 210
Day, Mark K., Assoc. Dir., Int. Dir., & Dir., Santos Manuel Student Union, 330, 400, 408, 413, 460, 487
Day, Richard Cortez, writer, 229
Daz Patterson and the West Coast Singers, musical group, 216, 234, 243
De Anza College Chorale, music group, 64
de Bellis, Frank, book collector, 99
de Bellis, Serena, book collector, 99
de Coteau, Denis, musical director, 74
de Ferrari, Carlos Lorrain, Chilean Ambassador to Switzerland, 261
de Guzmán, Joriz, Outstanding Student, 412, 494
de la Torre, Rey, guitarist, 74
de la Vega, Aurileo, musician, 252
De Lozier, Nancy, student, 49
Deacon, Walter K., campus booster, 60
Dead Milkmen, musical group, 289
Deal, Terrence, speaker, 244
Dean, John, White House counsel, 236
Deane, Bonnie St. John, Olympic medalist, 343
Deathbird Stories (Ellison), 127
DeAvila, Edward A., speaker, 124
DeBerg, Curt, speaker, 362
DeBerry, Clyde E., Lect., 87
DeBranch, Charlene Kaye, student, 45
Deception, Mr., magician, 119, 121
Dechter, Aaron, art collector, 251
Dechter, Hanita, art collector, 251
Decisive Battles of the U.S.A. (Fuller), 57
Decker, Bruce, Art, 445
Decker, David L., Prof., 412
Defender-Wilson, Mary Louise, storyteller, 361, 408
DeFeo, Philip, speaker, 360
DeFrank, Thomas M., *Newsweek* correspondent, 202, 257
Degler, Carl, historian, 108
DeGroff, Margaret, Santos Manuel Student Union, 444

DeGrove, John, speaker, 252
DeJong, Angelikia, student, 177
Del Rosa Grange Number 711, 43
Delamar, Jim, U.S. Secret Service, 172
Delgado, Arturo, SB Unified School District Superintendent, 367-68, 405
Delgado, Juan, Prof. & alumnus author, 270, 317, 364, 386, 411
Delgado, Juan José, Mexican Consul, 368
Della Neve, Charmaine, speaker, 246
Dellaguardia, M., French Commercial Attaché, 181
Delmore Schwartz Memorial Poetry Award, 182
Delta Sigma Phi, 209
Delta Sigma Theta, sorority, 378
Dem Bones, musical group, 285
DeMauro, David P., Dir., Plant Operations, Act. VP & VP, Administration and Finance, 218, 264, 274, 317, 451-52, 482-83
Demento, Dr., radio broadcaster, 111
DeMeo, Paul, Alumni Award, TV writer, 134, 238, 270, 277-78, 312, 395, 496
Demeter Fund, 280
Demmer, John Odis Jr., student, 412
Dennemeyer, René F., Prof., 48, 144, 204, 502
Dent, Skye, writer and producer, 463
Denti, Lou, speaker, 256
Dentzer, Susan, *Newsweek* correspondent, 202
Department chairs, 71
DeRemer, Kyla, wife of Russell J., 121
DeRemer, Russell J., Assoc. Dean, Activities & Housing, 39, 52, 79, 138, 487
Derick, Robert, pianist, 196
Derry, Neil, SB City Councilman, 424
Desert Healthcare District, 408, 419
Desert Hot Springs, Calif., 417
Desert Studies Center/Consortium, Soda Springs, 116, 171, 205
Desikichar, Kauthub, yoga master, 409
Deslonde, James, speaker, 83
deSoto, Lewis, artist, 454
Desperado, musical group, 403
Detweiler, Robert C., VP, Academic Affairs, Pres., CSU Dominguez Hills,

212, 252-54, 475
Detwiler, Peter, speaker, 292
Deukmejian, George, Gov., CA, 178, 187, 215, 269, 505
Deutchman, Sherri M., Asst. Dir., Housing, Coordinator, Student Union, 189, 199
Deval, Jacques, playwright, 129
DeValk, David, UAB Member, 500
"Developing Resilience in Youth," conference, 338
Deveraux, Greg, Chief Accounting Officer, S.B. County, 471
Devil Canyon, 67, 292
Devils Canyon Channel Bridge, 37
Devils Canyon Road, 38, 139
Devine, Jim, economist, 184
Devlin, Jerry, SB City Councilman, 305
Devor, Bryan, student, 408
DeVore, Chuck, US Senate candidate, 471
Dewar, Jackie, SB Rape Crisis and Assault Services Program, 146
Dexter, Howard, alumnus, 185, 202
Dexter, Jack, speaker, 238
Dezember, Joan, Administrative Support Coordinator, 423
"Diabetics," conference, 123
Diaconis, Persi, speaker, 269
Diamano-Coura Dancers, 231
Diamond, Jared, writer, 363
Diamonds in the Rough, musical group, 306, 315
The Diary of Adam and Eve (Twain), 92
Díaz, Enrique, Chilean scholar, 410
Díaz, Esteban R., Prof., 402
Díaz, Hiram, 126
Díaz, Laura, TV newscaster, 435
Díaz, Louis, Building Maintenance Worker, 365
Díaz, Ray, Asst. City Manager, Palm Desert, 317
Díaz-Rico, Lynne, Prof., 280
Díaz, Rubén, Pres., ASI, 492
Dibble, Don, speaker, 71
Dickey, James, writer, 41
Dickson, Risa E., Prof., Executive Asst. to the President, 424, 474
Diemecke, Enrique, Music Dir., Orquesta Sinfónica de México, 322
Dierdorff, Jo, dancer, 251
Dietzen, W. N. Jr., US Navy Rear Admiral, 119
Diez, Richard, speaker, 167
Digital Duo Band, musical group, 268
Digital Education Achievement Award, 435
Dilworth, Nelson S., State Sen., 20-21
Dimon, Mary, Lect., 286
Dinitz, Simon, criminologist, 136
Dionne, Lee, Outstanding Student, 494
Disabled access on campus, 439
Disability Rights Legal Center, 439
DisAbility Sports Festival, 435, 462
Disabled Performers in Television and Films, 181
"Discrimination on Campus," forum, 291
Distance learning, 338
Distance Learning Center, 349
Distinguished Alumni Award, 301
Distinguished Scholar Series, PDC, 408
District Five Commissioners Cup in Soccer, 178
Divac, Vlade, basketball player, 428
"Diversity and the RPT Process," forum, 321
"Diversity (and Multicultural) Conference," 333, 343, 362
Diversity Award, 434
Divine Intervention, music group, 225
Divorce Sale (Stockham), 294
Dixieland Band, 157
Dixon, Carol J., Dir., James and Arianthi Coussoulis Arena & Health and Physical Education Complex, 317
Dixon, Fred, Campus Guard, 120
Dixon, Paul K., Prof., 418, 490
D.J. Books (SB), 118
D.J. Spy & Cool Bay, musical group, 306
Doane, Margaret S., Prof., 380, 409, 490-91
Dobbs, Ben, speaker, 185
Dobzhansky, Theodosius, geneticist, 82
Dockstader, Dennis, pianist, 61, 94
Doctoral degree on campus, 413-15, 433-34
Dogs restrained by leash, 79
Dolan, G. Keith, Prof., 275
Dollar, Norm, speaker, 289

Dolmetsch, Carl, singer, 47
Dolmetsch-Schoenfeld Ensemble (music group), 47
Domhoff, G. William, sociologist, 139, 157
Domingo, Edna B., Lect., 432
Domínguez, H. Frank, speaker, 101, 228
Dominik, Carl, harpsichordist, 166
Donald R. Barker Endowment Scholarship Fund, 377-79
Donald Roberts & Co., singers, 125
Dongguk University, Seoul, Korea, 454
Donker, Kwame, Outstanding Student, 494
Donnan, Christopher, speaker, 253
Donohue, Marilyn Cram, writer, 257
Donovan, Amy, speaker, 395
Donovan, Duncan, speaker, 143
Dora J. Prieto Scholarship, 407
Dorff, Elliot, Rabbi, 301
Dorman/Munselle Associates, CSC architects, 52
Dornemann, Joan, opera singer, 178
Dorra, Henri, art historian, 151
Dortch, Pamela I., Dir., Children's Center, 166
Las Dos Caras del Patroncito (Guerrero), 143
Doshi, Sundip, alumnus, 398
Douglas, Charlotte, actress, 100
Douglas, Jack D., sociologist, 81
Douglas, Paul, speaker, 97
Dover, Marguerite, Outstanding Student, 494
Dowdall, John, guitarist, 254, 278
Downs, James, hypnotist, 246, 248
Downtown Democratic Club (SB), 35
Downtown Exchange Club of SB, 42
Doyle, Dennis, harpist, 243, 265
Doyle, Gerald, speaker, 139
Dr. Martin Luther King Jr. Day, 193, 417
Dr. Snootful's Medicine Show, 118
Dragna, Marguerite, Outstanding Student, 493
Drago, Ross, sculptor, 57
Drama Dept., 129
Drama Workshop, 103, 128
The Dramatic Essentials (Thayer), 300
Drapchi Prison, Tibet, 383

Drayton, Joyce, Secretary, 26, 43
Dreisbach, Fritz, artist, 357
Dressler, Michael, speaker, 320
Drickey, Darrell J., physicist, 80
Driftmier, Donald A., Arrowhead Award, accountant, 125, 234, 390, 498
"Drought: Yesterday, Today, and Tomorrow," conference, 387
Drucker, Peter F., management expert, 100, 304
"Drug Abuse, Suicide, and Other Problems Facing Young People," conference, 245
Drummond, Mark, Chancellor, California Community College System, 406
Drury, Mary, UAB Member, 499
D'Souza, Patricia V., Prof., 306
Duan, Changmin, calligrapher, 419
Duarte, Laura, Education, 473
DuBois, Ellen, speaker, 450
Ducey, James R., Coach, 196
Duffy, Carolyn, 155
Dukakis, Michael, Gov., Mass., Pres. candidate, 361
Duke, Lance, CEO, Landmark Building Products, 348-49
Dukes, Carol Muske, writer, 255, 277
Dukes, Vivian Nash, UAB Member, 500
Dulaney, Charles W., Maintenance Mechanic, 144, 186-87
Dumke, Glenn S., Chancellor, CSC, 21, 25, 30, 37, 40, 50, 56, 59, 67-68, 86, 88, 115, 125, 127, 154, 161-62, 164, 168-69, 172, 253, 504
Dunagan, Edward, UAB Member, 500
Dunaway, Diane, writer, 274
Duncan, Jody D., Alumni Award, writer, 279, 284, 288, 496
Dundes, Alan, speaker, 234
Dunham, Joe, juggler, 207
Dunlap, Carol, Manager, Bookstore, 153
Dunn, Rita, speaker, 244
Dunn, Steve, speaker, 443
Dunnahoo, Terry, speaker, 255
Dunworth, John, Int. Dean, School of Education, 265, 272, 410, 478
Duplicating Center, 347, 458
DuPree, Tammy L., Outstanding Stu-

dent, 494
Duran, Chris, Outstanding Student, 495
Durán, Eduardo, speaker, 314
Duran, Mike, Dir., Minority Information Center, 99
Durden, Georgia B., Lib. Asst., 451
Durio, Greg, folksinger, 81, 93
Duro, Kelly, clown, 207
Dutton, David, oboist, 239
Dutton Gallery, Art Museum, 311
Dutton, Jo, campus booster, 311
Dutton, Theodore, UAB & PAC Member, 311, 500
Dydzkowski, Włodzimierz, speaker, 235
Dye, Mary A., Secretary, President's Office, 52
Dymally, Mervyn M., Lt. Gov., CA, 97, 505
"The Dynamism of an Atom" (Hetrick sculpture), 46
Eagle Forum, 1351
Ealy, Shirley, Secretary, 199
Earhart Foundation, 117
Earle, Ed, critic, 332
Earley, James, economist, 145
"Early Childhood Development," conference, 106
Early Music Academy, musical group, 216
Early Occult Memory Systems of the Lower Midwest (Fairchild), 390, 411
Earth Day, 64, 74, 150
Earth, Wind, and Fire, musical group, 84
Eason Construction Inc., builders, 145
East Asia Intelligence Council, 430
East Campus Circle, 14, 438, 457
East of the Mountains of the Moon (film), 48
East Texas Baptist College, 176
Eastern Michigan University, 173, 176
Eastman, Janice, harpsichordist, 89
Eastman, Shirley, speaker, 173, 186
Eastvold, Ike, speaker, 150
Eaves, Gerald, Assemblyman, SB County Supervisor, 213, 216, 220, 228, 230, 253, 299, 398
Eberst, Richard M., Prof., 340, 399, 402
Eby, Karlin, flautist, 144
Ecclesia Christian Fellowship, musical group, 322
Echols, Larry, speaker, 274
Eckankar, 82
Ecker, Don, UAB Member, 500
Eckhardt, A. Roy, speaker, 250
Eckhardt, Alice, speaker, 250
Eckstrom, Gordon, 155
Ecology Pond, 82
"Economic Challenge," 420
Economic Development Corp., 358
Economic Forecast/Outlook Breakfast, 239, 247, 258, 269, 281, 291, 300, 310, 319, 340, 348, 357-58, 378
Economic Literacy Council of California, 216, 223
Economic Summit, 374, 395-96, 427
Economics Dept., 242
"The Economics of Contracting with the Inland Empire," conference, 395
Edelman, Sergei, pianist, 225, 238, 267
Eder, Walter, speaker, 250
Edgar, Robert, US Rep., 357
Edge Development Corp., builders, 456
Edmonds, Russ, Walt Disney animator, 294
Edmonson, Leonard, speaker, 99
Edmunds, Kathleen, Secretary, 194
"EdTech Conference," 426, 436
Education, College of, 358, 465
Education, Dept. of, 76, 87
Education Expo for Alternative Programs for Youths at Risk, 342
"Education for Democracy: The Role of the Educator in the 21st Century," conference, 383
Education Lane, 14
"Education on the Edge of Possibility," conference, 339
Education, School of, 87, 224, 232, 255, 314, 317, 325
Education Summit, 406, 416, 437, 468
Educational Equity Plan Committee, 220
Educational Opportunity Program (EOP), 11, 44, 76
Educational Policy and Research, Dept. of, 325
Educational Psychology and Counseling, Dept. of, 325
Educational Support Services, Dept. of, 153

Edward-Dean Museum of Decorative Arts, 190, 195
Edward S. Blankenship Award, 372
Edwards, Harry, sociologist, 240
Edwards, Marie B., psychologist, 75
Edwards, Mark, PAC Member, 500
"Effective Thinking in the Social Studies," conference, 79
Egan, John, PAC Member, 500
Eger, Edith Eva, Holocaust survivor, 457
Egge, Alfred S., Prof., 49, 71, 81, 173, 501
Egge, Björn, Norwegian Army Maj., 127
Ehrlich, Anne H., ecologist, 261
Eichberg, Linda, singer, 468
Eichenbaum, Richard, General Manager, Ontario Mills Mall, 353
Eisenhower, Dwight D., Pres., US, 56
Eisenhower Medical Center, Palm Desert Health Sciences Building, PDC, 437
Eisner, Elliot W., speaker, 120
Ekaitis, Frances A., Lib. Asst., 106, 188
Ekarini, Ni Wayan, dancer, 406
El-Ahraf, Amer M., Assoc. VP, Academic Resources, Act. VP, Academic Affairs, 201, 254, 265-66, 475-76-76
Elder, James D. Jr., alumnus author, 270
Elders, Joycelyn, Dir., Arkansas Dept. of Health, 288
Electronic Music Studio, 85
Elementary and Bilingual Education, Dept. of, 255
Elementary Summer Technology Institute, 225
Elesby, Sally, artist, 353
Elgart, Matthew, guitarist, 450
Elgart/Yates Duo, musical group, 406, 450
Elhams, Majda, Outstanding Student, 495
Eligio (Kika) de la Garza Fellowship Program, 470
Elite Nursing Program, 414
Elizondo, Sergio D., Prof., 75
Ellena Brothers, SB vintners, 29
Eller, Jim, Social and Behavioral Sciences, 423
Ellins, Stuart R., Prof., 114, 122, 158, 402
Elliott, Jane, writer, 362
Elliott, Jo Eleanor, Dir., Div. of Nursing, U.S. Public Health Service, 168
Elliott Roofing Construction, builders, 201
Ellis, Albert, psychotherapist, 185
Ellis Island Medal of Honor, 456
Ellis-Lamkins, Phaedra, speaker, 405
Ellis, Mary Williams—SEE: Williams, Mary
Ellis, Sue, Lib. Asst., 144, 155, 290
Ellison, Harlan, writer, 127
Elsen, Albert, art historian, 56-57
el-Shinnawi, Maher, speaker, 225
Elson, Dave, pianist, 69
Email advising, 311
Email notification of staff and students, 428
Emami, Zorah, speaker, 227
Emergency Loan Program, 268
Emergency Operation Center, 325
Emergency phones, 81, 141, 253
Emergency Plan, 134
Emeritus faculty parking, 169
Empey, LaMar T., sociologist, 151
Empire Lakes Golf Course, Rancho Cucamonga, 328
Employee furloughs, 459, 463
"End of the World Party," 240
The Endgame (Beckett), 92
Endorsed Internal Auditing Program, 349
Energy conservation, 95, 155, 161, 178, 204, 224, 281, 286, 302, 309, 345, 369, 433, 460, 463, 469-70, 473
"Energy Cost Reduction Conference," 293
Energy Efficiency and Infrastructure Upgrade Project, 463
Energy Project of the Year Award: National, 463
Engelskirshen, Howard, attorney, 272
Engineering an Empire: Aztecs (TV show), 426
Engman, John, magician, 300
Ennis, Ciara, photographer, 429
Enrollment, 502-03
Enrollment cuts, 450, 458-59, 465, 467
Enrollment impaction, 467

Enrollment Services Dept., 212
Entrepreneur Magazine, 401, 410, 425
"Entrepreneurial Success Conference," 349
"Entrepreneurship and the Academic Conference," 362
Entrepreneurship Education Award, 466
Enterprise Rent-a-Car, 454
Environmental Achievement Award, 441
"Environmental Business Opportunities Conference," 320
"Environmental Education," forum, 218
Environmental Education Materials Center, 221-22
Environmental Expo, 241, 251, 262, 273, 284, 293, 303, 314, 322, 332, 343, 352, 362, 372, 381, 392, 401, 407, 411, 420, 431
Environmental Health and Safety, 13
Environmental Science Expo, PDC, 471-72
Epps, Joe, speaker, 271
Epps, Wardell Jermaine, student, 333, 342
Epsilon Pi Tau, technology and education honors group, 312
Epstein, Edwin M., speaker, 177
Erickson, Nicholas A., Dir., Students with Disabilities, Dir., Housing and Residential Life, 379, 430
Eriksson, E. John, attorney, 99
Erives, Evelyn, speaker, 414
Erler, Edward J., Prof, 117, 168, 489
Ernest A. Lynton Award for Faculty Service and Academic Outreach, 399
Errante, F. Gerard, clarinetist, 205
Erreca, John, Dir., CA State Finance Dept., 31
Erskine, Walter C., Housing Management, 278
Erven, John, Dir., Multicultural Center, 310
Ervin, Kathy, musician, 299
Eschaveste, María, Deputy Chief of Staff to Pres. Clinton, 366
Escort service for students, 249
Escuela de la Raza Unida, dance group, 94, 101, 136, 167
Esposito, Paul J. Jr., Counselor, Coor-dinator, Placement Services, 121, 427
Esquivel, Gilberto, speaker, 376
ESRI, 370
Estelle, Vicki, Dir., California Student Opportunity and Access Program, 244
Estes, Clarissa, writer, 300
Estrada, Esther, SB City Councilwoman, 378
Estrada-Miller, Megan Whitney, student, 430
Estrada, Paula, Outstanding Student, 493
Ethel (Limar & Slout), 248, 259, 409
Ethics Bowl, 408
Ethnic Studies Program, 58, 67, 239
"Ethnic Studies Symposium," 457
Ettinger, Torma, Vice Counsel for Information, Israeli Consul General's Office, 94
Etzioni, Amitai, sociologist, 285-86
Eu, March Fong, Calif. Secretary of State, 158
Eubank, Ilona Marie, Outstanding Student, 493
Eucalyptus Room, Commons, 11, 212
Eudora Welty Prize, 327
Eugene Asher Distinguished Teaching Award, 379
Eulau, Heinz, political scientist, 146
"Europe '92: The New American Challenge," teleconference, 260
European Community Information Service, 111
Evans, Anthony H. "Tony," President, 9, 16, 173, 343, 367, 416, 421, 474
administration, 175-335
affirmative action, 209, 212, 220, 222-23, 226-28, 230-31, 278, 291, 312, 315, 317
Asian art donations, 238, 327
budget crisis, 269, 271, 273-74, 276-77, 279, 288
inauguration, 185
personal background, 176
Plaza dedication at PDC, 449
President Emeritus, 365
retirement, 326, 331, 333-35
Evans, Chris, neuropharmacologist, 470
Evans, Gary, psychologist, 124, 134
Evans, Jody, Chair, Staff Council, 52
Evans, Linda R., Lib. Asst., 106, 243,

397-98
Evans, Lois Fay Kirkham, President's Award, wife of Anthony H., 176, 178, 238, 327, 416, 449, 497
Evans, Ronald, UAB Member, 500
Evans, Thelma Fay Crews, 176
Evans, Thomas F., 47
Evans, William Raymond, 176
Evening Service Center, 97
The EverGreen Show (Coyote Radio), 466
Everlast, musical group, 351
Evers, Medgar, civil rights activist, 60
Evers-Williams, Myrlie Beasley, civil rights activist, 60
Evertsen, Pat, Secretary, 211
Everything Changes: The Trevvlek War Trilogy (Ávila), 428
Ewing Kauffman Center for Entrepreneurial Leadership, 352, 364
Executive Assistant to the President position, 346
Executive Briefing Breakfast, 349
Executive in Residence/Artist in Residence Program, 421
Expressions Youth Choir, musical group, 311
Extended Education, Office/Division of, 199, 303
Extended Learning, College of, 347, 392, 409, 469
Extended Version, musical group, 286
Extension Program, 61, 67-68, 82
External Degree Program, 96
Extreme Flash, musical group, 71
Exxon Education Foundation, 277
Eyring, Henry, chemist, 101
F. M. Thomas Air Conditioning, builders, 157
Faces of America (play), 397
Facilities Management Building, 13, 18, 365
Facilities Management, Dept. of, 365
Facilities Services, Dept. of, 366, 404, 431
Facilities Services Storage, 13
Facility Planning and Policy Coordination, Office of, 247
Faculty Author Recognition Reception/Faculty Book Launch, 279, 333
Faculty collective bargaining, 144, 188

Faculty Computer Users Committee, 214
Faculty Dining Room, Commons, 145
Faculty Early Retirement Program (FERP), 169
Faculty housing, 434
Faculty Office Building, 13, 17, 217, 220-21, 232
Faculty Professional Development Program, 195
Faculty Senate, 79, 84-85, 130, 158, 304, 321-22, 327, 339, 447
Faculty Wind Quintet of the University of Redlands, 151
Faculty Wives Club, 40-41, 50, 62, 66, 83, 104, 107, 116, 133, 148, 151
Faculty Woodwind Quintet, 243
Fagan, Brian M., anthropologist, 133
Fahrenheit 451 (Bradbury), 208
Fairchild, Bertram H. "Pete," Prof. and poet, 195, 279, 348, 351-52, 381, 390, 411-12
Fairchild, Halford H., speaker, 323
Fairview Dr., 14
Fairview School, 221
Fairview School District, 32
Faith Apostolic Church, 234
Falk, Carol, speaker, 267
Fallgatter, Martha C. (Walda), CSU Trustee, 328
Fallis, Erik, Pres., ASI, Outstanding Student, 492, 494
Falzalore, Richard, speaker, 142
Family Reading Rally, 204, 248, 282, 301
Fanfare (McFatter), 343
Farar, Debra S., CSU Trustee, 378
Farhinger, James, baritone, 69
Farhung, Mansour, Iranian Ambassador to U.S., 257
Farley, Harriet S., SB landowner, 28, 33
Farley, Venner, speaker, 182
Farman, Richard, speaker, 281
Farre, Matías, Outstanding Student, 494
Farrell, Jim, accountant, 271
Farwell, Leonard B., Business Manager, VP, Administration and Finance, 26, 28, 36, 105-06, 173, 223, 264, 285, 482
Fashions and More, 321

Faultline, musical group, 316, 325
Favro, Diane, architectural historian, 330
Fawcett, Gerald A., UAB & PAC Member, Alumni Award, Pres., Alumni Assoc., Executive-in-Residence, 318, 333, 419, 492, 496, 500
Fay, Joe, artist, 143
Fay, Paul B. Jr., U.S. Secretary of Navy, 44
Fearn, Colleen Fahey, speaker, 253
Federal Communications Commission (FCC), 199
Federal Emergency Management Agency, 355
Federal Executive Board/College Federation Council, 208
Fedick, Scott L., speaker, 398
Feeley, Diane, labor activist, 69
Feghali, José, pianist, 234
Fehn, Richard F., Prof., Alumni Award, 399, 402, 432, 437, 490, 496, 501
Feifer, Katie, speaker, 323
Feigenbaum, Edward, speaker, 246
Fehrenbacher, Don, 383
Feiling, Chris, Prof., 280
Feinstein, Dianne, US Sen., 358
Feldheym, Norman, Rabbi, 82, 92
Feldstein, Sandy, composer, 207
Felix Guadalupe Valdez Creative Writing Series and Celebration, 456
Felton, Chuck, speaker, 264
Felton, Jean S., speaker, 168
Fengler, Joseph V., Outstanding Student, 493
Fennell, Bill, Bill, Dir. of Operations, Manager, Commons, 158, 161
Fennell, Frederick, conductor, 156
Fenton, Helen, speaker, 69
Ferdinand, Theodore N., speaker, 241
Ferguson, James L., speaker, 64
Ferguson, Jim, UAB & PAC Member, Mayor, Palm Desert, 426, 500
Ferguson, Maynard, trumpeter, 215, 264
Fernández, Evalina, actress, 382
Fernández, Louis A., Prof., Dean, School of Natural Sciences, VP & Provost, Academic Affairs, 8-9, 275, 306, 308, 313, 326, 346, 458-59, 475, 478, 506
Fernlund, Phyllis F., Prof., Act. Dean, School of Education, 311, 334-35, 478
Ferrante, Philip, hiking expert, 437, 463
Ferranti, Tom, magician, 300
Ferrell, Jeff, speaker, 323
Fess, Robert C., campus booster, 60
Festival of the Arts and Humanities, 117
Fiddmont, Keith, musician, 299
Field Cablevision, 178
Field, Fern, TV writer and director, Artist-in-Residence, 424
Field Museum of Natural History, 363
Fields, Christia, performer, 306
Fields, Lanny B., Prof., 396, 402, 491
Fierro, Charles, pianist, 72
"La Fiesta de Educación y Carreras en Aztlán," conference, 101
"Fiesta de la Revolución" festival, 111
Fifteenth Air Force Band, 51, 232
Fighting Cause, musical group, 293
Fikas, Heather, Outstanding Student, 495
Filbeck, Loren H., Prof., 126, 242, 267, 402
Final Approach, musical group, 232
Financial Aid Office, 76, 168, 172, 198, 232
Financial Education Fair, 462
Financial Management for Nonprofit Organizations (Hankin), 359
Finch, Robert H., Lt. Gov., CA, 505
Fine Arts Building, 13, 17, 87, 90, 129, 145, 151, 153
Finger Talk (play), 196
Fingerprinting of employees, 190
Finley, James J., Prof., 117, 149, 501
Finn, James, Head, Dept. Instructional Technology, University of Southern California, 55
Finney, Tal, speaker, 374
Finsen, Susan M., Prof., 458
Fire and Ice, musical group, 116
"Fire and Rain: A Forum on Flooding Hazards Following the California Wildfires," 400
Fire Inside, musical group, 429
"Fireball '75" festival, 111
Firebird Theatre Company, 174, 193,

207
Firestone, Renée, speaker, 183
First 5 of San Bernardino County, 468
First American Title Corp., 419
First Bank, 317
First Baptist Loveland Church of Fontana Choir, 156
First Congregational United Church of Christ, San Bernardino, 409
First Presbyterian Church of San Bernardino, 391, 442
Fiscalini Field, San Bernardino, 466
Fischer, Cheryl F., Prof., 338, 422
Fischer, Herbert R., SB Co. Superintendent of Schools, UAB & PAC Member, 356, 367-68, 378, 386, 405, 416, 500
Fischer, Lynn, Jet Propulsion Laboratory, 191
Fischman, Davida, Prof., 368
Fish, James, Administrative Computing, 432
Fisher, Duke, psychiatrist, 47
Fisher, Eugene J., speaker, 261
Fisher, John, Custodian, 103
Fisher, Robert, speaker, 238
Fisher, Rowland, speaker, 149
Fisher, Tanya, speaker, 440
The Fisherman and His Wife (Grimm Bros.), 174
Fisk, Robert G., Prof., Dean, Students, 25-26, 28, 36-37, 42, 95, 453, 484, 502
Fiske, Stephen Longfellow, performer, 284
Fitch, Noel Riley, speaker, 194
Fitness Court, 209
Fitzgerald, Gale L., Coach, 196
Fitzgerald-Richards, Dell, poet, 120
Fitzpatrick, Kathy, singer, 252
Five Centuries Ensemble, musical group, 165
Flagpole, Coyote Premier Field, 460
Flagpole, Jack H. Brown Hall, 412
Flatliner, musical group, 303
A Flea in Her Ear (play), 242
Flesher, Mary Melissa, Outstanding Student, 495
Fletcher, Aletha, Libn., 381
Fletcher, G. Louis, PAC Member, 262, 438, 500

"Flex Your Power" Award, 422
Flint, David, speaker, 71
Flint, Robert, Coach, 358
Flinting, musical group, 266
Floan, Tina, speaker, 100
Flores, Barbara, speaker, 271, 432
Flores, Coreen Ann, student, 373
Flores, Cynthia, Assoc. Dean, CVC, 9, 353, 438, 480
Flores, Ignacio, Facilities Services, 445
Flores, Jess, SB City Councilman, 245
Florida Southern University, 351
Flournoy, Houston I., State Controller, 105
Flower and McLaren, musical group, 307
Flowers, Cheryl A. Hill, Alumni Award, 496
Fluke, Joanne, alumna writer, 238, 270
Fly Dance Company, 398
Flynn, Jessica, Outstanding Student, 494
Flynn, Laurie, Dir., Students with Disabilities, 379, 417
"Focus on the Persian Gulf War" Week, 272
Fog on campus, 246
Fogg, Betty, Secretary, 177
Folger Library, 93
Folk Fest Hootenanny, 69
Folklórico California, musical group, 251
Folklórico el Instituto de Bellas Artes, musical group, 119
Folklórico Lindo, dance group, 151
Follett Educational Services, 445-46
Fonda, Jane, actress, 93, 97
Fontana Paving Inc., contractors, 59
Fontana Unified School District, 260
Food Industry Council, 326
For the Use of the Hall (Hailey), 115
"For Whom the Road Should Toll? The Future of Toll Roads and Road Pricing in California," forum, 442
Forbes, Arthur J., CAB Member, 499
Ford, Charles R., CAB Member, 499
Ford, Don, basketball player, 141
Ford Foundation, 266, 345
Ford, Kimiko, speaker, 464
Ford, Larry, trumpeter, 181
Foreign Language Field Day, 119

Foreign language requirement for graduation, 80
Forest Home Conference Center, 53
Forrester, Evelyn, speaker, 259, 301
Forsberg and Gregory, builders, 39
Forsch, Ken, baseball player, 280
Fort Hayes State University, 186
Fort Ord, 66
Fortner, Kathryn "Kathy," Pres., ASI, Pres., Alumni Assoc., 185, 491-92
Forty Years of English at CSUSB (Schroeder), 6, 9
Fosdick, Karen K., Lect., 463
Foskey, Dawnell, Dir., Woodbridge School, 124
Foss, Sonja K., speaker, 247
"Foster Care Summit," 456
Foster, David, Community Foundation, 452
Foster, LeMar, Rev., speaker, 216
Foundation Board, 248
Foundation Building, 13, 17, 272, 279, 292, 412
Foundation Parking Lot, 296
Fouts, Rogers S., primate researcher, 167
Fox, Douglas C., geophysicist, 78
Fox, Fred, Los Angeles Philharmonic Orchestra, 139
Fox, Louis, Int. Dir., Robert V. Fullerton Museum, 342
Fox, Matthew, speaker, 347
Fox, Randy, violinist, 191
Foy, Jim, KNBC, 130
Fragments (Stockham), 312
Frammolino, Ralph, *Los Angeles Times* writer, 300
Francis, Donald, physician, 259
Frank E. Scully Piano Trio, 113
Frank, Peter, art critic, 419, 463
Frank Sinatra Dr., Palm Desert, 14, 309-10, 320, 349, 368, 383
Franklin, Raymond, speaker, 292
Fraternities and sororities, 209
Frauenholz, Ray, Jet Propulsion Laboratory, 218
Frawley, Faradean C., Outstanding Student, 494
Frazier, Joe, UAB Member, 500
Frazier, Paul, Supervisor, Grounds Maintenance, 202, 404

Freakdaddy, musical group, 353
Freaks Amour, musical group, 284
Fredenburg, Joshua, speaker, 448
Frederick, Howard, Prof., 251
Fredricks, John E., Accounting Officer, Asst. Business Manager, 48, 76, 221, 482
Fredriksen, Sandra Lee, alumna & Lect., 260, 501
Free Flight Dance Company, dancing group, 196
Free Speech Area, 49, 68
Freedom Funds Banquet, 234, 257
Freeman, James T., Dir., Institutional Studies, Dir., Institutional Research, 46, 59, 481
Freeman, Skott, singer, 386
Freidel, Frank, historian, 110
Freischlag, Jerry A., Prof., 373
French, Kazuko Shibasaki, student, 115
French Students' Day, 98
Fresa y Chocolate (play), 359
Fresno Pacific College, 203
Freund, Spencer A., VP, Information Resources and Technology & Chief Information Off., 433, 488
Friday Bulletin (campus newsletter), 38, 55, 245, 331, 334—SEE ALSO: *Bulletin*
Friedman, Harvey, student, 76
Friedman, Jeff, dancer, 289
Friedman, Melvin J., critic, 74
Friedman, Norman, sociologist, 141
Friedrich, Gerhard, CSC Dean, Academic Planning, 79
Friends of Nancy E. Smith Committee, 138
Friendz Band, musical group, 403, 424
Fritz, Jan, Prof., 280
Frost, Joyce, polyhedrist, 390
Frost, Lorraine M., Dir., Administrative Computer Services, Int. VP and Assoc. VP, Information Resources and Technology, 409, 488
Frost, Marvin D., Prof., 183-84, 201, 501
Frye, David, impressionist, 85
Fuchs, Louanne, pianist, 190
Fuchs, Richard, violinist, 190
Fuerte, Luis, TV cameraman, 349
Fukazawa, James, Pres., ASI, 492

Full Fathom Five Woodwind Quintet, musical group, 315
Fuller, J. F. C., historian, 57
Fullerton, Robert V., PAC Member, SB attorney, 25, 272, 298, 458, 462, 500
Fullertowne Strutters, musical group, 232, 254
Fulton, Louise F., Prof., 301, 373
Furino, Frank, actor, 465
Furman, David, artist, 347
Fusi, Martin Fonkijom, speaker, 416
Futch, John M., Int. Dir., Women's Resource Center and Adult Re-Entry Program, Coordinator, Cross Cultural Center, 379, 427, 429
Futterman, Susan, Manager, Children's Programs, ABC TV, 136
Future Leaders of America, 247
"The Future of Children in the 21st Century," conference, 355
"The Future of Higher Education: Golden Opportunities in California," conference, 406
"The Future of Water in the Inland Empire," conference, 368
Gabal, Moustafa, speaker, 256
Gabbay, Pamela, Outstanding Student, 494
Gabler, Sharon, speaker, 135
Gael Force, musical group, 243
Gaertner, LeNise Jackson, speaker, 276
Gage, Arthur, Budget Officer, 63, 483
Gage Canal Co., 37
Gagnon, Lee, speaker, 214
Gagnon, Richard, Outstanding Student, 494
Gaines, Larry K., Prof., 377, 393
Gaining Early Awareness and Readiness for Undergraduate Programs Program, 366
Gaither, Anita Marlene, Student Accounts, 423
Galán, Hector, filmmaker, 362
Gale, Kate, writer, 466
Gallagher, Buell G., Chancellor, CSC, 21, 25, 138, 504
Gallagher, comedian, 329
Gallagher, Kevin, Pres., ASB, 127, 135, 491
Gallardo, Art, alumnus, 368
Galles, Arie, artist, 157
Gallo, Dwight D., Instructional Support Technician, 455
Gallo, Michael, PAC Member, 500
Galvan, Tatiana, speaker, 228, 235
Gálvez, José, photographer, 387
Gamble, Nancy, writer, 302
Gamlin, Claudia Salvatierra, City Planner, Palm Springs, 317
Gamma Lambda Chapter of Phi Beta Delta, 319, 443, 472
Gamma Nu Chapter of Epsilon Pi Tau, 312
Gandhi, Indira, Prime Minister, India, 156
Gandy, Oscar H. Jr., speaker, 452
Gannon, Catherine C., Prof.., Assoc. Dean, Academic Planning, Assoc. Dean, Undergraduate Programs, Dir., Coachella Valley Center, 122, 188, 192, 221, 261, 265-66, 480
A Gap in Generations (play), 117
Garai, Lazlo, speaker, 262
Garamendi, John, Lt. Gov., CA, 430, 505
Garcés, Joan, economist, 379, 382
García, Bennie R., Custodian, 365, 384
García, Ernest F., Prof., Dean, School of Education, 108, 110, 114, 122, 124, 136, 145, 265, 290, 316, 357, 478
García, Gerald, speaker, 361
García, Helen M., speaker, 360
García, Jeff, speaker, 402
García, John, Outstanding Student, 494
García, Kristin, Outstanding Student, 494
García, Patrick, Alumni Award, 496
García, Richard A., CSUC Trustee, 110
García, Robert C., Grounds Maintenance, 470
García, Sam, speaker, 192-93
García, Susan N., Athletics Equipment Room Technician, 464
García-Tolson, Rudy, speaker, 386
García, Toni, Career Development Center, 423
Gardner, Richard A., therapist, 207
Gardner, Robert W., VP, Administration and Finance, 452, 482
Gardner, Sally, speaker, 203
Garfias, Robert, speaker, 230

Garratt, Judi, mime artist, 182, 207
Garrity, Paul, Libn., SB Public Library, 9
Garro, Joyce, singer, 468
Garry, Ann, philosopher, 133
Garson, Arnold, *SB Sun* Editor, 264
Garver, Eugene, Prof., 156, 489
Garvie, Peter, speaker, 235
Garza, Florentino, CAB & PAC Member, Hon. Ph.D., 402, 497, 499-500
Garza, Jesse O., Groundsman, 470
Garza, Regina, CAB Member, wife of Florentino, 499
Gastineau, Charl Ann, fiddler, 232
Gates, Henry Louis, speaker, 270
Gates, John, clarinetist, 195
Gates, Tom, Rev., 286
Gates, Yoko Ito, Koto player, 166
"Gather the Women," conference, 429
"Gather the Women: Envisioning the Future—Now!", symposium, 390
"Gather the Women: Weaving a World That Works," conference, 400
Gatheral, Mary Ann, speaker, 127
Gathings, John, speaker, 79
Gauguin, Vincent, artist, 150
Gay, Lesbian, and Bisexual Faculty and Staff Assoc., 247
Gayle & Co., musical group, 362, 381
Gazi University, Ankara, Turkey, 396, 400, 400
Gazzaniga, Michael, speaker, 370
Gean, William D., Prof., 133, 142, 154, 501
Geane, Peggy J., Pharmacist, Student Health Center, 224
GEAR-UP Program, 416, 447
"Gear Up Inland Empire Leadership Institute," 398, 408
Gearhart, Sally, writer, 239
Geis, Gilbert, criminologist, 98, 143, 248
Gelbaum, Bernard R., mathematician, 56
Geller, Elane Norych, Holocaust survivor, 208, 294, 383
Gendrop, Paul, adventurer, 62
General Dynamics, 252
General Education Program, 81, 84-85, 154, 181
Genesis Choirs, musical group, 348

Los Genis, musical group, 251
Gentry, Robert F., Asst. Dean of Students, 67, 73, 485
Geological Science, Dept. of., 379
Geological Society of America, 302
Geology Lab, 13
George Air Force Base, 198
George, David A., Pres., College of the Desert, 239, 317
George H. Schnarre Real Estate, 498
George, Joani, Pres., ASI, 491
George Peabody College, 265
George, Wally, TV talk-show host, 214
Gerald, Gil, speaker, 259
Gerald T. Sullivan Co., builders, 53
Geraty, Larry, speaker, 449
Geraway, William R., Mafia informer, 106
Germany, Teresa, Alumni Award, 496
Gharavi, Seyed Hamid, student, 187
Ghougassian, Joseph, U.S. Ambassador to Qatar, 260
Gibbs, George, EOP, 137, 445
Gibbs, Jewelle Taylor, speaker, 303
Gibbs, Margaret C. K., Prof., 143, 152, 374, 502
Gilbert, William S., librettist, 159
Gibson, Christine, Outstanding Student, 495
Gibson, Harriet P., Counselor, EOP, 305, 380
Gibson, Luther E., State Sen., 31
Gibson, Marie, soprano, 43
Gil, Carol, speaker, 465
Gilbert, Ira N., Mayor, SB, 504
Giles, William, Distinguished Visiting Prof. of Art, 227
Gilfry, Rodney, singer, 328
Gillen, John, sculptor, 160
Gillette, Paul, writer, 196
Gilliam, Richard, Custodian, 278
Gillig, Susan, Information Officer, British Consulate General in L.A., 106
Gilligan, Carol, writer, 341-42
Gilliland, Stephanie, dancer, 251
Gillis, John, psychologist, 148
Gilmore, Namy Yi, Facilities Services, 465
Giorgianni, Dawn, alumna, 300
Gilpin, Chester, speaker, 64
Gina, performer, 306

Giovanni, Nikki, poet, 249, 314
Giralt Cabrales, Carlos I., Mexican Consul General, 410, 431
Girard, Rose, speaker, 419
Giulio Cesare (Handel), 180
A Glass of Water (Scribe), 132
Glasser, William, writer, 343
Glassman, Jaga Nath, alumnus, 218
Glazier, Alice Jean, staff, 306
Glenn, Evelyn Nakano, speaker, 340
Glenn, Jack, art dealer, 96
Gliadkovsky, Kirill, pianist, 340
Glicken, Morley D., Prof., 364
Glines, Don, speaker, 105
Global Commerce and Transportation, 472
"Global Warming/Climate Change Summit," 437
Glowacki, Matt, speaker, 456
Gluck, Sherna, historian, 251, 272
Glyndebourne Opera, 131
GnanaDev, Dev A., Arrowhead Award, Pres., Calif. Medical Assoc., 443, 466, 498
Gneck, Tony, karate expert, 102
Goddesses of the Western World (Stockham), 329
Godinez, Robert, speaker, 157
Goedeck, Kathleen L., Custodian, 137
Goff, William, speaker, 183
Goggin, Terry, Assemblyman, 123
"Going to San Bernardino: A Symposium on Intermodal Transit Stations," conference, 464
Goings, Kenneth W., speaker, 323
Goins, Shirley, speaker, 342
Gold, Alan, speaker, 457
Gold, Hazel, speaker, 301
Gold, Howie, comedian, 219, 225
Gold, Phillip, physician, 118
Goldberg, Glenn A., speaker, 277
Golddiggers, musical group, 468
Golden, Bruce, Prof., 73, 93, 118, 136, 296, 402
Golden Key International Honor Society, 382
Goldenberg, Claude, speaker, 299
Goldin, Daniel, NASA administrator, 352
Goldman, Joseph S., speaker, 149, 152
Goldman, Shifra, writer, 247, 329
Goldstein, Bernard, CSU Trustee, 284, 328
Goldstein, Bobbi, Outstanding Student, 494
Goldwhite, Harold, CSU Trustee, 352
Goller, John, speaker, 319
Golz, John, violinist, 215
Gomaidi, Jamin, student, 227
Gomen, J. R., speaker, 74
Gómez, Edward, speaker, 443
Gómez, Graciano, UAB & PAC Member, Publisher, *Inland Empire Hispanic News*, 378, 500
Gómez, José, speaker, 309
Gómez, Laura, Outreach Counselor, 132
Gómez, Loretta Martínez, Alumni Award, 495
Gómez, Luis Salazar, Alumni Award, UAB Member, 496, 499
Gómez, Mary Frances, Alumni Award, 238, 496
Gómez, Michael A., Dir., College Police and Public Safety, 113, 162, 484
Gontarev, Boris, speaker, 310
Gonzaga University, 508
Gonzáles, Alfredo, TV broadcaster, 197
Gonzáles, Edward, elementary student, 73
Gonzáles, Josie, SB County Supervisor, 425
Gonzáles, Ingrid E., SB County Registrar, 372
Gonzáles, Liz, TV newscaster, 197
Gonzáles, Mark, speaker, 411
Gonzáles, Roberto, paleontologist, 340
Gonzáles, Rosemarie, 44
González-Alexopoulos, A. E. J.—SEE: Chrysostomos
González, Alfonso, speaker, 463
González, Arturo, speaker, 301
González, Gaspar Pedro, writer, 442
González, Juan C., Asst. to the President, Int. VP & VP, Student Services, 234, 266, 286, 306-07, 474, 484
González, Luis, orchestrator, 300
González, Mariana, National Alliance for Human Rights, 431-32
González, Mirta, Prof., 422
González, Robert, historian, 344
González, Rosa M., Lect., 470, 502

Gooch, James R., Manager, Duplicating Center, 55, 400-01
Good News Singers, 80
Goodcell, Wilma, CAB Member, 37, 498-99
Goodman, Kenneth, speaker, 271
Goodman, Yetta, speaker, 238
Goodrich, Grace, Lecturer, 199
Goodrow, Michael, actor, 273
Goodson, Billy, dancer, 351
Goodwin, Clarence R., CAB Member, 198, 499
Goodwin, Randy, racer, 324
Gootblatt, Ellen, writer, 328
Gordon, Cynthia, speaker, 322
Gordon, Gerald I., speaker, 137
Gordon, Marjory, speaker, 220
Gordon, Robert, alumnus author, 270
Gore, Al, US VP, 366
Gore, Tipper, wife of Al, 366
Gorian, George, PAC Member, 500
Gorkowski, Anton, Custodian, 152
Gorman, Judy, guitarist, 301, 361
Gortov, Melvin, speaker, 94
Gospel Christmas Concert, 348
Gospel Concert, 181
Gospel Choir Fest, 313, 322
Gospel Five, music group, 60
Goss, Carol F., Prof., 137, 200, 243, 489
Gossett, Maxie N., student, 70
Gotch, Donna, Prof., 320
Gottis, Marie Grace, student, 330
Gould, Brian, pianist, 99
Gould, Laurence K., CSU Trustee, 343
Gower, Charles, oboist, 56
Governmental Relations Advisor to the President, 346
Governor's Employee Safety Award, 404
Governor's Environmental and Economic Leadership Award, 407
Grabel, Lee, magician, 235
Graber, Ethel, speaker, 105
Graduate Programs, Dept. of, 224, 255
Graduate Studies, Office of, 285
Graff, Catherine, cellist, 94
Graff, Leanne, Outstanding Student, 494
Graham, William, musician, 250, 258
Gramlich, Bernice Marie, student, 73

Granat, Cary, Dir. of Development, Universal Studios, 298
Granat, Endre, violinist, 72
Grandin, Temple, educator, 367
Grandmother's Council of Native American Women, 340
Granowsky, Alvin, speaker, 182, 244
Grant, Alexandra, artist, 452
Grant St. Band, musical group, 276
"Graphic Design in Europe," symposium, 463
Grasha, Anthony F., speaker, 323
Grass Fire (2007), 436
Graves, Gary, Outstanding Student, 494
Graves, Richard W., Prof., Chair, Business Administration Dept., 53, 67, 477
Graves, Terry, guitarist, 350
Graves, William H., speaker, 246
Gray, Beatrice, speaker, 452
Gray, James H., CSU Trustee, 343-44
Gray, Joseph W., Prof., 364, 471, 502
Gray, Lee Ann, student, 200
Grayman, Glen, speaker, 443
Greco, George, speaker, 274
Greek Council, 213
Greek Theatre, 130
Greeley, William, student, 199
The Green, 68
Green, Jackie A., Lib. Asst., 102, 299
Green, Mary Elizabeth, speaker, 89
Green, Paul L., US Air Force Col., 370
Green, Stuart, guitarist, 370, 388, 396
Green, William C., Prof., 436, 466-67, 491, 501
Greenburg, William, newspaper columnist, 111
"Greener California: Impacts of Senate Bill 375 and Winning Strategies for Southern California," conference, 457
Greenfeld, Sue, Prof., 295, 382
Greenfield, Robert J., Prof., 361
Greenstein, Denise, speaker, 264
Greenstein, Steven, comedian, 225
Greenspot Road, Highland, 426
Greenwood Press, 337
Gregg Young and the Second Street Band, musical group, 394, 413
Gregoire, Janet F., Students with Disabilities, 409
Gregory, Betty J., Equipment Atten-

dant, 152
Gregory, Kristiana, writer, 260
Gregory, Norris, speaker, 108
Gregory, Raymond, Riverside Co. Sheriff's Dept., 471
Gregory, Raymond H., Mayor, SB, 20-21, 504
Grenfell, Christopher C., Prof., 286, 473
Gresham, Allen B., PAC Member, 60, 500
Gribow, Patti, interviewer, 468
Grice, Frances, speaker, 69
Grier, Barnett, speaker, 148
Griff, Professor, musician, 301
Griffin, Jonathan, poet, 114
Griffith Observatory, 298
Griffiths, Eldon W., British MP and Ed., *Newsweek*, 49
Griffiths, Richard W., Prof., 185, 364
Grimm, Brothers, writers, 174
Grimsley, Deborah, Grant Writer, 432
Grindstaff, Joseph, Dir., California Bay Delta Authority, 449
Grissom, Lee, CSU Trustee, 207
Griswold, Daniel, speaker, 462
Gronbeck, Bruce E., speaker, 248
Grose, George, speaker, 402
Gross, Bertram, speaker, 228
Grossman, Howard, booster, 206
Grossman, Kat, Alumni Award, 496
Group Seven Inland Empire Basketball Camp, 423
Group Seven Project, 418
Group W Cable, 181
Grove, Andrew, speaker, 369
Groven, Darrol, UAB Member, 500
Groves, James R., speaker, 89
Grubb, Everett, General Manager, Western Municipal Water Dist., 29
Gruenbaum, Ellen R., Prof., Act. Dean, Social and Behavioral Sciences, 270, 301, 306, 324, 334, 479
Gruening, Ernest, US Sen., 85
Grundhofer, Jerry, speaker, 269
Grupo Folklórico, musical group, 304
Grupo Musical Alma, musical group, 262
Grupo Pancasán, musical group, 208
GTE California, 293, 298
GTE Connection, musical group, 265
GTE Foundation, 354
Gubrud, Irene, singer, 116
Guerra, Lucia, speaker, 318
Guerrero, Lalo, composer/guitarist, 143, 211, 222, 376
Guetzloe, Eleanor, speaker, 282
Guevara, Ana M., speaker, 448-49
Guevara, Liliana, Outstanding Student, 494
Guge, Gail, speaker, 440
Guggenheim Fellowship, 186, 352
Guhin, Alan, SB City Councilman, 38-39
Guillén, Manuel, speaker, 64
Guillén, Pat, Father, Libreria del Pueblo, 431
Guith, Norman C., UAB Member, 499
Gumbleton, Don, social worker, 148
Gummerman, Jay, writer, 263
Gunther, Gerald, attorney, 207
Guo, Xuanchang, sculptor, 334, 360, 364
Gusay, Charlotte Elder, Alumni Award, 495
Gutek, Barbara A., speaker, 163
Guthrie, Anna, English, 473
Guthrie, James, conductor, 227
Guthrie, James A., CAB Member, Editor, *SB Sun*, 37, 42, 498
Guthrie, James K., CAB Member, Publisher, *SB Sun*, 45, 134, 168, 499
Gutiérrez, Frank, 126
Gutiérrez, Thelma, CNN TV reporter, 449
Guttmacher, Alan F., Pres., Planned Parenthood, 57
Los Guys, musical group, 293
Guzman, Rob, speaker, 360
Gymnasium, 39-40, 44, 53, 209, 235, 350
H. N. and Frances C. Berger Foundation, 358, 372
Hacettepe University, Turkey, 72
Hadlock, O. P., student, 160
Hafstrom, John E., Prof., Act. Chair, Natural Sciences Div., 71, 144, 423, 502
Hagar, Sammy, singer, 339
Hahn, Barbara Evelyn, student, 118
"Hail, Our Alma Mater" (Filbeck), 267
Hailey, Oliver, playwright, 115

Halberstam, Judith "Jack," speaker, 401
Hale, Sondra, speaker, 311
Hales, Diane, badminton champion, 106
Hales, Stan, badminton champion, 106
Haley, Alex, writer, 256
Hall, John, chess master, 91
Hall, Sandra, Administrative Support Coordinator, 423
Hallack, Barbara, Secretary in the President's Office, 455
Hallett, Joan Terry, Prof., Assoc. Dean, School of Natural Sciences, 226, 368, 422
Hallett, John, speaker, 302
Hallum, Karla, Dir., Credential & M.A. Office in Education, 290
Halmos, Paul, mathematician, 136
Halpern, Diane F., Prof., Assoc. Dean & Int. Dean, Undergraduate Studies, 201, 211, 215, 217-18, 222, 232, 327, 342, 352, 373, 409, 480, 490
Halstead, Bruce, Dir., World Life Research Institute, 74
Halton, Marie, singer, 469
Ham, MaryLou, soprano, 50
Hama, Kenneth, speaker, 229-30
Hamada, potter, 74
Hamamoto, Satoko, Yasuda University, 321
Hamill, Dorothy, ice skater, 438
Hamilton, Cynthia, speaker, 241
Hamilton, Eloise R., Library Asst., 348
Hamilton, Michael, speaker, 238
Hamilton, Stephanie, speaker, 436
Hamma, Kenneth, speaker, 252
Hammer, Sheryl, Pres., ASI, 491
Hammock, Robert, SB County Supervisor, 151, 232
Hammond, Peter R., US Naval Weapons Center, 50
Hampshire Ave., SB, 147
Hampton, Claudia H., CSUC Trustee, 110, 185, 204, 214, 279
Hamre, Janetha A., Teacher Education Off., 473
Hamre, Timothy C., Pres., ASI, 185, 491
Han, Lori Cox, speaker, 450
Hancer, Kevin, writer, 172
Handel, George, composer, 177, 180
Handicapped access on campus, 246

Handy, Max, speaker, 193
Haney, William L., painter, 49
Hanf, Kenneth I., speaker, 271
Hanford, John J., Mayor, SB, 504
Hangan, Clabe, singer and guitarist, 47, 55, 110, 194, 207, 211
Hanhan, Nadine, Outstanding Student, 495
Hankin, Jo Ann, VP, University Advancement, 353, 359, 376, 409, 487
Hankins, Grover C., General Counsel, NCAAP, 234
Hanna, Atallah, Greek Orthodox Archbishop of Sevastia, 443
Hanna, Gigi, Assoc. Dir., Water Resources Institute, 426, 478
Hanour, Kenneth, Outstanding Student, 495
Hansberger, Leroy, CAB Member, Pres., Tri-City Concrete Co., 37, 498-99
Hansel and Gretel (Humperdinck), 183
Hansen, James "Jim," Asst. Dir., Physical Plant, Act. Dir. & Dir., Plant Operations, 231, 360, 483
Hansen, Kathryn K. Shepard "Kathy," Dir., Procurement and Support Services, 344, 483
Hansen Plumbing and Heating Co., contractors, 43
Hansen, Tina, Outstanding Student, 495
Hansler, Kathryn, Outstanding Student, 494
Hanson, Don, speaker, 218
Hanson, Joyce, speaker, 398
Hanson, Lola, speaker, 218
Hanson, Wilma M., Lib. Asst., 214
Harby, Stephen William, architect, 328
A Hard Straight (film), 453
Harding, Peggy, speaker, 105
Hardwicke, Catherine, film director, 457
Hare, Nathan, educator, 84
Harer, Pamela, literary critic, 322-23, 327, 329, 349, 357
Harer, W. Benson, physician, Hon. Ph.D., UAB Member, 15, 257, 280, 282, 327, 343, 349, 351, 357, 373, 384, 497, 500
Hariss, Mabel, speaker, 193
Harizuka, Susumu, educator, 309

Harkins and Larson, musical group, 142
Harlem Globetrotters, comedy basketball team, 350, 361, 370, 390, 408, 428, 439
Harman, Willis, futurist, 251
Harmer, John L., State Sen., Lt. Gov., CA, 62, 505
Harmon, Harry, CSC Facilities Planner, 31, 39
Harnish, Jay Dewey, architect, 125
Harper, Ben, musician, 358
Harrell, Randy P., Dir., Student Life, Act. Asst. VP & Asst. VP, Student Services, 225, 290, 345, 485, 487
Harrigan, William, Custodian, 212
Harrington, Barbara, Academic Programs, 316
Harrington, Dalton D., Prof., Dir., Desert Studies Center, 116, 123, 299
Harris, Arlo D., Prof., 50, 54, 151, 340, 502
Harris, Bob, speaker, 296
Harris Co., 37
Harris, David, activist, 85
Harris, Harold C. Jr., CAB Member, 60, 499
Harris, John Reece, student, 143
Harris, Leslie I., CAB Member, Pres., Harris Co., 37, 79, 93, 498-99
Harrison Canyon, SB, 147
Harrison, Edward W., Police Services Manager, Dir., Public Safety, Chief, Police Operations, 218, 231, 307, 484
Harrison, Robert R., Prof., 71, 85, 331, 502
Harry Rheubottom/George Webster Local History Lecture Series—SEE: Rheubottom/Webster Local History Lecture Series
Hart, Gary K., State Sen., 216, 284
Harter, Joan, speaker, 349-50
Harthrong, Roger, Lecturer, 423
Hartley, Joellen, psychologist, 134
Hartley, Mark, Dir., Student Leadership and Development, 428
Hartman Construction Co., builders, 60
Hartono, Roby, Outstanding Student, 493
Hartung, August W. "Augie," Assoc. Dir., Facilities Services, 417
Hartung, Charles V., Prof., 129, 314, 502
Harvey, Dana, Judge, Fontana Municipal Court, 147
Harvey, Peggy, speaker, 135
Harwood, William, fencer, 60
Hasan, Zahid Z., Prof., 371, 491
Haselkorn, Avigdor, speaker, 135
Haskell, Lillian E., Academic Programs, 365
Haskell, Richard, Operating Systems Analyst, 365
Hass, Aaron, Holocaust expert, 229
Hass, Robert, poet, 157
Hastings, Robert, speaker, 214
Hatamiya, Lon S., speaker, 378
Hatcher, Kevin L., Dir., Athletics, 436, 488
"Hate Crimes/Hate Speech: What Do We Do About It?" conference, 353
Hate crimes on campus, 367
Hatos Center for Neuropharmacology, 470
Hatt, David, harpsichordist, 110, 118
Hatton, John M., Assoc. Dean, Counseling & Testing (Center), Act. Dean, Student Services, Assoc. Dean, Counseling (and Health) Services, Act. Assoc. VP, Student Affairs, Dir., Student Health Services & Psychological Counseling Center, 45, 109, 155, 166, 179, 188, 198, 297, 366, 371, 383-84, 484-86, 489
Hauber, Joyce, Manager, Cafeteria, 45, 47
Hauck, William, CSU Trustee, 315
Hauer, Lucy E., Lib. Asst., 140, 424
Hauge, Michael, writer, 277
Haugen, Connie Lee, student, 129-30
Haugen, Elaine, Admissions, 299
Haugh, Susan Sterkel, alumna author, 270
Hauser, Tom, writer, 174
Havasupai Indian Reservation, 77
Havens, Timothy, speaker, 450
Havey, Daniel, Outstanding Student, 494
Haviland, Carol P., Prof., 458
Haviland, Susan, psychologist, 133
Hawass, Zahi, Egyptologist, 249-50, 308
Hawkins, Beth Liebson, speaker, 439

Hawkins, Maggie, Planned Parenthood, 320
Hawkins, Melvin G., Affirmative Action Appeals Coordinator, 148, 202, 281, 291
Hawkins, Robbin, speaker, 148
Hawkins, Walter S., Dir., Upward Bound Program, Act. Assoc. Dean, Education Support Services, Dir., Undergraduate Studies, Research, and Policy Analysis, 104, 113, 161, 180, 278, 431, 485
Hay, Edward M., Supervising Custodian, 109
Hayden, Tom, Assemblyman, State Sen., 245, 341
Haydn, Joseph, composer, 159
Hayes-Bautista, David, speaker, 471
Hayes, Dannie M., CAB Member, 499
Hayes, Deborah, speaker, 340
Hayes, Margaret Daly, speaker, 235
Hayes-Raitt, Kelly, speaker, 414
Haynes and Ramey, musical group, 135
Hayward, Kent, Prof., 382
Head Start Program, 268
Health and Physical Education Complex, 13, 18, 269, 285, 289, 292, 317, 433
Health services student fee, 294
"Healthcare Reform and the Impact on Your Business," panel, 466
Healy, Eloise Klein, poet, 257
Hearn, Vicki, writer, 168
Hearne, Christy, Pres., ASI, 492
"Hearts and Minds: Connecting Through Diversity," conference, 352
"Hearts and Minds: Connecting Through Diversity in the New Millennium," conference, 362
"Hearts and Minds: Diversity in Action," conference, 372, 382
"Hearts and Minds: Excellence Through Diversity," conference, 344
Heating and Air Conditioning Plant, 13, 35, 43, 48, 58, 75, 115, 155, 157, 159, 235
Heavy Shoes (Stockham), 281
Hebein, Frederick J., Prof., 458
Hebert, Richard, Maintenance Mechanic, 404
Heckman, Dick, speaker, 354

Hector Mine Earthquake, 356
Hedies Inc., musical group, 306
HEERA—see: California Higher Education Employee-Employee Relations Act
Heeran, John W., Prof., 301
Hefner, Dennis L., VC, Academic Affairs, 265, 278, 306, 475
Heilbron, Louis H., Chair, CSC Board of Trustees, 58
Heim, Merrill "Doc," Outstanding Student, 493
Heine, Lyman H., CSU Trustee, 246
Heinz, John Raymond, student, 220
Heir, Marvin, Rabbi, 333
Hekman, Stephen B., Pres., ASI, 491
Heldman, Caroline, speaker, 450
Helinski, Donald, speaker, 135
Helling, Frank, speaker, 262
Hellman, Martin E., writer, 240
Heltzel, Henrietta, book collector, 124
Hemisphere Constructors, builders, 58, 67, 75
Hemphill, VP, Southern California Edison Co., 452
Hempstead, Jackie, speaker, 193
Hendershot, Heather, speaker, 467
Henderson, Craig E., Counselor, Housing Coordinator, Dir., Housing, 124, 190, 437
Henderson, John A., Mayor, SB, 504
Henderson, Wes, speaker, 293
The Hendersons, folksingers, 93
Hendricks, Beverly L., Prof., Dean, School of Humanities, 222, 366, 477
Hendry, Rod, Pres., ASI, 491
Henley, Lonnie, Deputy National Intelligence Officer, East Asia Intelligence Council, 430
Henley, Robert D., SB City Councilman, 38
Henry, DeWitt, writer, 380, 440
Henry, Linvol G., Prof., 402
Henry, Mildred M., Prof., 199, 202, 261, 268, 353-54
Henschel, Tom, actor, 242
Henson, Jane, speaker, 272
Henton, John, comedian, 279
Henwood, James E., PAC Member, 500
Here Comes Everybody, musical group, 309

Herman, Gabor T., speaker, 453
Herman, Shelli, Asst. Dir., Student Services, Loyola Marymount University, 322
Herms, George, speaker, 142
Hern, Chick, sportscaster, 105
Hernández, Bea, speaker, 228
Hernández, Miriam, TV reporter, 217
Hernández, Moises, Information Technology Specialist, 473
Hernández, Pete, 126
Hernández, Ralph, SB City Councilman, 145
Herold, P. Leslie, Prof., 286
Herrbach, Joseph, Custodian, 139
Herrera, Juan Felipe, writer, 340
Hersh, Reuben, speaker, 246
Hertford, Hayes, CAB Member, Pres., Gage Canal Co., 37, 498-99
Herzberg, Frederick L., behavioral scientist, 101
Heseman, Leon S., campus booster, 56, 63
Hesse, Everett W., speaker, 135
Hetrick, Richard Manchester, sculptor, 46
Hetter, F. Larry, Pres., ASI, 492
Hewitt, Alan, actor, 106
Hewitt, Hugh, TV host, 341
Hiam, Claire, talent agent, 217
Hickey, Dave, art critic, 392
Hickman, Johnny, guitarist, 230
Hicks, Willie, Pastor, 286
Hidalgo, Francisco, Prof., 315
Higa, Karin, Curator, Japanese American National Museum, 330
Higbee, Beth, S.B. County Superintendent of Schools Office, 468
Higby, Sha Sha, artist, 381
Higgins, Kathy, speaker, 230
High Country, musical group, 254
High Desert Symphony, 159
The High Life (musical), 274
High pressure sodium lamps, 161
High School Choral Festival, 109
"High School Counselors' Conference," 183
High School Speech and Debate Tournament, 204
High School Theatre Workshop, 85, 94, 160

Highland, Monica, writer, 255
Highlanders, musical group, 207
Highway 111 Dance Band, musical group, 374
Higuera, Bernard, Accounting Officer, 76, 91-92, 482
Hilao-Enríquez, Amaryllis, speaker, 360
Hill, Arthur, speaker, 72
Hill, Charles Eugene, student, 88
Hill, Edward Jr., UAB Member, 500
Hill, James E., Lect., 473
Hill, Jerry, speaker, 72
Hill, Lawrence S., speaker, 102
Hill, Lois S., Lib. Asst., 427
Hillside-University Demonstration School, 286-88
Hinckley, Stewart, Assemblyman, 40
Hine, Robert, historian, 133
Hino, Dorothea, Secretary, 187
Hinton, Sam, guitarist, 44, 221, 244
Hip Hop Xpo, musical group, 364
Hirabayashi, Lane Ryo, speaker, 464
Hiraoka, Jesse, Prof., Chair, Humanities Div., 42-43, 59, 86, 477, 489
Hiring freeze, 243, 451-52
Hirschman, Penny, speaker, 282
Hirtz, Lynn, UAB Member, 500
Hispanic Caucus Award, 386
Hispanic Lifestyle Magazine, 405
Hispanic Outlook in Education (magazine), 358, 382, 397, 407, 416, 420-21, 427, 437
"Hispanic-Serving Institution" designation, 355, 358, 417
L'Histoire du Soldat (Stravinsky), 107
History Channel (TV network), 426
History of Cancer Control Project, UCLA, 120
"History of the Blues," conference, 142
Hitchcock, Ralph E., CVC Advisory Board member, 275, 284
Hixson, Maureen, Extended Learning, 458
Hlawek, James, campus booster, 278
HMN Architects, 498
Ho, Christine, speaker, 293
Hobbs, John D., SB City Councilman, 108, 180
Hobo-Jazz, musical group, 401
Hock, George J., Custodian, 125, 134-

35
Hockaday, John, speaker, 467
Hodde, Rebecca, Outstanding Student, 493
Hodek, Antonin, pantomimist, 77
Hodel, Mike, radio show host, 200
Hodgdon, Warner W., SB builder, 26
Hodge, Stanley W., Alumni Award, Pres., Alumni Assoc., 492, 496
Hodges, Robert J., Alumni Award, 496
Hodgkinson, Harold, speaker, 228
Hodnett, Louis C., Prof., 87
Hoffman, Charles D., Prof., 199, 445
Hoffman, Michael Allen, speaker, 251
Hoffman, Steve, radio program director, 442
Hogenson, M. Jeanne, Act. Dir. & Dir., Student Activities, Coordinator, International Student Program, 137, 213, 221, 246, 253, 487
Hogland, Rick, musician, 299
Holcomb, Grant, Mayor, SB, 504
Holcomb, Penny, wife of W. R., 290
Holcomb, W. R. "Bob", Mayor, SB, 28, 71, 75, 79-80, 96, 104, 110, 120, 124, 200, 209, 252, 262, 267, 295, 357, 464, 504
Holdaway, Phillip Wayman, alumnus author, 270
Holden, Henry, actor, 357
Holder, Calvin, speaker, 283
Holder, Henry W., CAB Member, physician, Patton State Hospital, 37, 498
Holgate, Bryce, Outstanding Student, 495
Holguín, Ámparo, speaker, 136
Holiday Inn (SB), 45, 69
Holliday, Peter, Prof., 279, 303
Holloway, William H., psychiatrist, 163
Holmes, Carmack, physician, 410
Holmes, Dallas, speaker, 74
Holt, Garner, UAB Member, 454, 500
Holt, Helen A., Lib. Asst., 143-44
Holt, Tinya, Outstanding Student, 494
Holy Persuasion Youth Choir, musical group, 322
Hom, Gloria S., CSU Trustee, 272
"Home-Based Business Owners in the Inland Empire," conference, 354
Home of Neighborly Service, 54
Home Run Program, 339

Homecoming, 58, 216, 248
Homestead Artifact (film), 382
Homme, Marc S., CVC Advisory Board member, 275
Honcharik, Ted, business executive, 456
Honeysett, William, CAB Member, Publisher, *San Bernardino Sun*, 130, 499
Honig, Bill, State Superintendent of Public Instruction, 280
Honn-Alex, Janet, Dir., Women's Resource Center and Adult Re-Entry Program, 379
Honor Band, musical group, 260
Honors Program, 266
Hooks, Henry, speaker, 360
Hoover, David, mathematician, 165
Hopkins, Cindy, Student Health Center, 423
Hord, Scott, Outstanding Student, 494
Horenburg, Nadine M., Property Clerk, 286
Horizon (online library catalog), 326, 329, 430
Horne, David, Business Dir., Deseret Homes, 193
Horrock, Nicholas M., *Newsweek* correspondent, 202
Horseshoe pits, 155
Hoshizaki, Takashi, speaker, 440
Hospers, John, Libertarian Party Presidential candidate, 105
Hot Mud, musical group, 314
Hot Rocks, musical group, 423
The Houdini Deception (DeMeo & Bilson), 134
Hough, Stanley, alumnus SB County Superior Court Judge, 395
Hour 25 (radio show), 200
Hour Glass and Mirror Inc., builders, 172
Housel, Douglas Alan, student, 205-06
Householder, Scott, student, 333
Houseman, John, actor, 162
Housing Office, 162-63
Hoverland, H. Arthur "Hal," Prof., Chair, Administration, Dean, School of Administration, Dean, School of Business and Public Administration, 86, 104, 121, 202, 220-21, 286, 324,

477
"How to Survive College," conference, 105
Howard C. Edmiston Co., builders, 126
Howard, Irvin, Prof., 402
Howard, Laurie, Manager, Cafeteria, 45
Howe, Vernon, speaker, 240
Howell, F. Clark, paleoanthropologist, 126
Howie, Sherry M., Prof., 273, 292, 295, 393
Hubacher, John, speaker, 119
Hubbard, Freddie, trumpeter, 242
Hubbard, George M., CAB Member, 499
Hubbard, Gladys M., Placement Advisor, 59, 93
Hubbard, Joan Dale, campus booster, 349
Hubbard, Joseph, Building Service Engineer, 404, 473
Hubbard, R. D., campus booster, 349
Hubbell, Ned S., speaker, 114
Hubert, Renée, speaker, 152
Huck, Charlotte, writer, 260
Hudson, Lionel, SB City Councilman, 80
Hudson, Robert P., medical historian, 140
Huerta, Dolores, co-founder, United Farm Workers of America, 408, 469
Huerta, Ray, labor activist, 83
Huerter, Maurice J., Supervisor, Housing Maintenance, 365
Huffman, Debbie Guthrie, UAB Member, 500
Huffman, Thomas, speaker, 318
Huffstutler, James, Rev., 391
Hughes, Kimball N. "Kim," Prof., 283, 501
Hughes, Langston, poet, 455
Hughes, Michael, photographer, 177
Huh, Sungkyoo, speaker, 444
Hui, Zhao, magician, 306
Human Learning Center, 63
Human Resources Office, 289
Humanities Career Day, 238
Humanities Classroom Building, 17-18, 341
Humanities Day, 245
Humanities, Division of, 71, 76, 87

Humanities, School of, 87, 326, 347
Hume, G. William, Assoc. Dean, Activities & Housing, 42, 52, 487
Humperdinck, Engelbert, composer, 183
Humphrey, Bobby, musician, 99
Humphrey, Julie, Outstanding Student, 495
Humphries, John, Activities Advisor, 49, 52
Hunt, Robert, speaker, 111
Hunter, Tricia, Assemblywoman, 284
Huntington Library, 198
Hurtado, Claudia, Pres., Latino Business Students Assoc., 253
Husing, John E., Arrowhead Award, economist, 139, 252, 269, 281, 291, 348, 358, 426, 456, 472, 498
Huskey, Ken, speaker, 102
Hussain, Amir, speaker, 442
Hussain, Zakir, musician, 70, 94
Hussaini, Hatem, Palestine Liberation Organization, 223
Hutcherson, Bobby, musician, 99
Hutchings, Raymond, British diplomat, 146
Hutchins, Emil C., campus booster, 247
Hutchinson, Bud, Secretary, Coll. Council, American Federation of Teachers, 46
Hutchison, Earl "Ofari," speaker, 360
Hutchison, John A., philosopher, 110
Hutto, Elgar, RCA Co., 114
Huxman, Travis, Alumni Award, 496
HVAC Building, 13
Hyman, Cecelia, speaker, 100
Hyon, Sung-Heh "Sunny," Prof., 426, 491
i2, 439
Ibish, Hussein, speaker, 455
IBM, 75-76, 280
Ibrahim, Fatma Ahmed, speaker, 330
Ibrahim, Mahmood, historian, 382
ICE, musical group, 153
Ichsan, Tony, Environmental Health and Safety Officer, 272
Idyllwild, musical group, 303
Iganski, Paul, speaker, 431
Ikenberry, Dennis L., Prof., 356
Ikhrata, Hasan, Exec. Dir., Southern California Assoc. of Governments,

472

Ikiru (film), 39
Ileto, Ismael, speaker, 373
Illegitimate Theatre, theatre group, 64
Imagination Players, theatre group, 182
Iman, Don, UAB Member, 499
Immigrants and Boomers (Myers), 453
"Immigration Policy and Its Effects on Our Community," panel, 431
Impert, Silvia, artist, 259
"The Implications of Technology Development for Business Growth in the Inland Empire," conference, 332
In Search of Community: A History of California State University, San Bernardino (McAfee), 6, 9, 268
INCA Folk Ensemble, musical group, 252
Incendio, musical group, 405
Incognito Band, musical group, 299
Independent of London (newspaper), 416
Independents (film), 450
Indian Day, 72
Indian Wells, Calif., 370
Indian Wells Center for Educational Excellence, PDC, 13, 18, 370, 372, 388-89, 404, 406
Indian Wells Theater at Palm Desert Campus, 13, 18, 406
Indio, Calif., 406
Industry-Education Council of San Bernardino and Riverside Counties, 97, 123
Infant Care Center, 126
Information and Decision Sciences, Dept. of, 232
Information Assurance Scholarship Program, 459
Information Center Kiosk #1, University Parkway Main Entrance, 13, 90, 116, 133
Information Center Kiosk #2, Coyote Dr., 13, 334
Information Resources and Technology (IRT), Division of, 288, 308, 392, 409
Information Technology Competition, 443, 456, 470
Ingalls, Walter, Assemblyman, 112, 123
Ingles, Lloyd G., naturalist, 48

Inglewood Unified School Dist., 221, 245
Inghram, Dorothy E., Hon. Ph.D., 443, 497
Inland Action Conference, 369
Inland Action Group, 338
Inland Alliance of Black School Educators, 254
Inland Area Native American Association Inter-Tribal Traditional Pow-Wow, 310, 318
Inland Area Personnel Management Assoc., 111
Inland Area Urban League, 165
Inland Brass Quintet, 154, 165, 177
Inland California Television Network—SEE: KCSB-TV
Inland Communities Corp., 446
Inland Council for Emergency Preparedness, 274
Inland Dance Concert, 456
Inland Empire (Weeks), 369
Inland Empire Academic Library Cooperation (IEALC), 105
Inland Empire African-American Educational Summit, 435
Inland Empire "Best of the Best" R&B Hip Hop Showcase, 388
Inland Empire Business Journal (magazine), 378
Inland Empire Caucus, 299
Inland Empire Center for Entrepreneurship, 352, 362, 393, 396, 413, 417, 440, 465-66
Inland Empire Chapter, Southern California Assoc. for the Education of Young Children, 88
Inland Empire College Library Cooperative, 89
"Inland Empire Conference on Hate Crime: Characteristics and Community Responses," conference, 373
Inland Empire Council for the Social Studies, 79
Inland Empire Dance Concert, dancers, 435
Inland Empire Dance Invitational Step Show, 331
Inland Empire Division, Future Leaders of America, 247
Inland Empire Economic Partnership,

428
Inland Empire Economics Project, 223
Inland Empire Future Leaders Program, 296, 391, 447
Inland Empire Hispanic Chamber of Commerce, 334
Inland Empire Hispanic News (newspaper), 278, 378
"The Inland Empire in 1980 and the Coming Decade," forum, 148
Inland Empire Management Center, 85, 90, 96, 98, 115, 118, 252
Inland Empire Library Tech Teachers, 80
Inland Empire National Bank, 498
Inland Empire Roller Coasters, wheelchair basketball team, 329
Inland Empire Student Services Consortium, 203
Inland Empire Symphonic Choir, 388
Inland Empire Symphony, 315
Inland Empire Utilities Agency, 353
"Inland Empire Women in Focus Empowerment Conference," 386
Inland Empire Women's Business Resource Center, 413
Inland Empire Youth Symphony, 208
Inland Harp Ensemble, musical group, 452
Inland Manpower Assoc., 123
Inland Master Chorale, musical group, 209
Inland Percussion Group, musical group, 388, 410
"Inland Regional Goods Movement," conference, 410
Inland Science Fair, 50, 82, 92, 100
Inland Valley Daily Bulletin (newspaper), 439
Inland Youth Forum (radio program), 76-77
Inner Secrets, musical group, 271
Innovative Excellence in Teaching, Learning, and Technology Award, 443
Inoue, Kohei, drummer, 427
Inoue, Ryohei, drummer, 427
Inouye, Daniel, US Sen., 183
Inrig, Stephen, speaker, 466
The Insanity Plea (Winslade), 197
In-Service Institute in Sociology, 66
Institute for Academic Computer Enhancement, 232
Institute for Applied Research and Policy Analysis, 246
Institute for Contemporary Studies, 172
Institute for the Study of Militarism and Economic Crisis, 205
Institute of Child Development and Family Relations, 425
Institute of Internal Auditors, 349
Institute on Bilingual Communication Skills, 71
Institutional Award for Diversity, 420
Institutional Research, 145
Instituto del Pueblo, 119
Instituto Mexicano Americano de Relaciones Culturales (IMARC), 376
Instructional Television Fixed Service (ITFS), 222
Instructionally Related Activity Fee, 133, 191
Integrated Business System (IBS), management software, 184
Integrated Technology Transfer Network (ITTN), 418, 444
Intellectual Life Committee, 213
Intelligence Community Center of Academic Excellence, 430
Interactors of San Bernardino, theatre group, 72
Intercollegiate athletics, 69, 180, 184, 186, 191-92, 201-03, 215, 259, 276, 286, 317, 338, 346, 379, 457, 470
Internacional de México, musical group, 380
International Academic Partnership Program, 470
International Center for Leadership in Education, 350
International Collegiate Business Strategy Competition, 381
"International Conference on Geological Information Systems Education," 365
"International Conference on Latin American Studies," 391
International Education Week, 377, 463
International Festival, 70
International Hobbes Tercentenary Congress, 141
International Imitation Raymond Chan-

dler Writing Contest, 296
International Institute, 371
International Warehouse Logistics Assoc., 472
International Week, 284
International Women's Day, 321
Inter-Organization Council, 116
Interstate Highway 15E, 38, 164, 167
Interstate Highway 215, 164, 279, 285, 311, 385
Intramurals Program, 217
"Introduction to Health and Safety for Educational Institutions," teleconference, 262
Ionesco, Eugène, playwright, 39
Iota Alpha Chapter of Sigma Xi, 230
Iota Omicron Chapter of Alpha Kappa Psi, 85
Irene W. and Guy L. Anderson Children's Foundation, 413
IRT—SEE: Information Resources and Technology, Division of
Irving, Janne, pianist, 162, 166
Irwin, Harvey, speaker, 64
Iskin, Ruth, artist, 93
Isla Radio (radio show), 454
Islambouly, Hagar, Egyptian Consul, 350
Islamic Club, 165
"Issues '72," program, 89
It Had to Be You (play), 311
Italian Opera Theatre Festival, 178
Iyer, Raghuvan, speaker, 75
Iwanaga, George, Prof., 304
J. A. Jones Construction Co., builders, 289
J. D. Stine Co., builders, 135, 138
J. F. Diffenbaugh Inc., contractors, 34
J. Paul Getty Conservation Institute, 327
J. Paul Getty Museum, 350, 370
J. Putnam Henck Co., builders, 39, 42-43, 48
Ja Rule, musical group, 373
Jack H. Brown Hall, 13, 17, 277-78, 283, 287, 297, 309, 318, 329, 349, 412, 436, 438
"Jack R. Widmeyer Transportation Research Conference," 464
Jack Stines, builders, 152
Jacklin, Carol Nagy, speaker, 196

Jackson, Anthony, Dir., Carnegie Council on Adolescent Development, 255
Jackson, Betty, singer, 91, 102
Jackson, Carla, performer, 311
Jackson, Corey, student & CSU Trustee, 403
Jackson, Horace, speaker, 105
Jackson, Ira, performer, 311
Jackson, Jacquelyn L., Alumni Award, 373, 496
Jackson, Janice Ropp "Jan," Asst. Dean, Assoc. Dean, & Dean, Extended Education, Dean, Extended Learning, Assoc. VP, Executive Affairs, 224, 345-46, 385, 389, 474, 479
Jackson, Jesse, Rev., 347
Jackson, Oscar C. Jr., Coll. Personnel Officer, 61, 159, 483
Jackson, Stoney, 272
Jackson, Thelma, Custodian, 365
Jacob, Barbara, Deputy Dir., European Community Information Service, 111
Jacober, René, attorney, Pres., Alumni Assoc., 123, 135, 492
Jacobs, William, philosopher, 125
Jacobson, Betty, speaker, 73
Jacocks, W. H. "Bill," Pres., Westside Action Group, 230
Jacques, Truman, broadcaster, 150
Jacquett, Rosalyn, student, 73
Jaffa, Henry V., historian, 229, 392
Jaffe-Karp, Alison, Outstanding Student, 493
Jahoda, Susan, speaker, 281
Jallow, Hassan Bubacar, Rwandan Justice, 455
Jamal, A. J., comedian, 302
Jambor, Harold A. "Jim," Lect., 152, 451, 502
James and Arianthi Coussoulis Arena, 11, 13, 18, 281, 285, 289, 292, 317-19
James, Charity, educator, 81
James, Curtis, speaker, 371
James I. Barnes Construction Co., builders, 52
James, Jennifer, anthropologist, 255
James, Scott, Duplicating, 162
Jamin' with Swat Team, musical group, 306
Jandt, Fred E., Prof., Int. Dean & Dean, PDC, 218, 390, 394, 408, 480, 490

THE COYOTE CHRONICLES: CSUSB, BY MICHAEL BURGESS * 559

Jane's Fighting Ships, 114
Janick, Jeanette, PDC, 445
Japanese American Citizens League, 133
Japanese American National Museum, 331
Jara, José, Pres., José's Mexican Foods, 406
Jaramillo-Levi, Enrique, poet, 253
Jarvis-Gann Initiative (Proposition 13), 137
Jasper, Barbara, speaker, 134
Jaworksi, Beth, Int. Dir., Services to Students with Disabilities, 419
Jayalakshmi, Salem S., singer, 177
Jayaraman, Lalgudi G., violinist, 78
Jazz Ensemble, 264, 274
Jazz Festival, 134
Jazzoetry Night, 299
Jean, Pamela, student & actress, 446
Jeansonne, Medley, CAB Member, 499
Jefferson-Jenkins, Carolyn, Pres., League of Women Voters USA, 382
Jellen, Hans G., Prof., 282-83, 501
Jenco, Lawrence, Father, ex-hostage priest, 270
Jenkins, Ed, M.C., 181
Jenkins, Jim, speaker, 249
Jensen, Sandra Lyn "Sandi," Coll. Personnel Officer, 159, 198-99, 483
Jenson, William A., Alumni Award, 496
Jerz, Joseph, Coll. Personnel Officer, 59, 61, 483
Jet Propulsion Laboratory, 116, 191, 218
Jewell, Geri, actress, 393
Jewish Chautauqua Society, 191
Jewish Defense League, 359
Jiang, Xinyan, speaker, 399
Jillian, Ann, actress, 343
Jimínez, Elizabeth, speaker, 301
Jin-Wen Institute of Technology, Taipei, Taiwan, 362
Joe Thomas Invitational Gold Tournament, 210
Johansen, Judith, harpsichordist, 79
Johansen, Lawrence "Larry," trumpeter, 79, 154
Johar, Jotindar S. "Vic," Prof., 473
John D. MacDonald and the Colorful World of Travis McGee (Campbell), 92, 126
John F. Merrell Foundation, 441
John Glenn High School Touring Theatre, theatre group, 207
John M. Futch Textbook Endowment Fund, 429
John M. Pfau Book Endowment, 367
John M. Pfau Family Scholarship Endowment, 442
John M. Pfau Library, 183, 191, 197, 202, 208, 210, 212, 229, 260, 270, 286-87, 290, 294, 304, 318, 325-26, 329, 362, 367, 369, 388, 409, 415, 430, 442, 449-50, 466
John M. Pfau Library Building, 12, 14, 17, 168, 172, 187-89, 193, 200, 206, 212-13, 233-34, 246-47, 257-58, 279, 287-88, 292, 299-300, 303, 309-10, 317, 324, 326, 328, 345, 349, 353, 356, 395, 418, 469
John M. Pfau Library Building Addition, 17, 257, 285, 290, 304, 307-10, 313, 320
John M. Pfau Library Lecture Series, 439
John, Mavis A., student, 109
John, Michael, singer, 268
John XXIII Newman Ministry, 252
Johns Hopkins Center for Alternatives to Animal Testing, 261, 280
Johns, Jorun B., Prof., 51, 194, 262, 364
Johns, Kenneth M., Prof., 402
Johnson, Billy Jr., speaker, 286, 315
Johnson, Brooks, UAB Member, 500
Johnson, C. Carl Jr., Chief, Campus Security, 48, 54, 484
Johnson, Clarence T., Mayor, SB, 504
Johnson-Curtis, Anne, Outstanding Student, 493
Johnson, Darlene, UAB Member, 499
Johnson, DeWanda, speaker, 237
Johnson, Dorothy, Prof., 155, 186
Johnson, Harvey M., Prof., 87
Johnson, Jim, Walnut Properties Inc., 130
Johnson, Keith, Dir., Off-Campus State-Sponsored Programs, Assoc. Dean, Extended Education, 202, 224, 250, 479

Johnson, L. Keating, tubist, 162
Johnson, Lawrence E. "Larry," Dir., Financial Aid, Dir., Experimental Admissions Program; Dir. of EOP, 53, 58, 87
Johnson, Lyndon B., Pres., US, 37
Johnson, Marshall, speaker, 125
Johnson, Milton, UAB Member, 500
Johnson, Nancy Sue, statistician, 125
Johnson, Oliver, speaker, 127
Johnson, Paul, 9
Johnson, Paul J., Prof., 141, 307, 489
Johnson, Rafer, Olympic athlete, 258-59
Johnson, Randall, screenwriter, 297
Johnson, Robert Flynn, speaker, 463
Johnson, Roberta, speaker, 240, 321
Johnson, Ron, speaker, 342
Johnson, Rudolph A. Jr., Dir., Supportive Services, EOP, 95, 110
Johnson, Sherry, speaker, 123
Johnson, Sonia, Mormon activist, 235
Johnson, Victor, speaker, 322
Johnston, Becky, puppeteer, 184
Johnston, Bret Anthony, Prof. and writer, 416
Johnston, Helen, Natural Sciences, 445
Johnstone, Jay, baseball player, 226
Joint Committee on the Master Plan for Education (Calif. State Legislature), 84
Jolley, Weldon B., pharmacologist, 208
Jolna, Karon, speaker, 450
Jomo, music executive, 439
Jon-Jon, 272
Jonas, Susanne, Institute for the Study of Militarism and Economic Crisis, 205
Jonathan, Sabby, CVC Advisory Board member, 275
Jones, Cita, Athletics, 445
Jones, David, Int. Dir., Foundation, 357, 483
Jones, Frederick, speaker, 371
Jones, Geraldine "Jerry," Secretary, 106
Jones, James W., Publisher, *Rialto Record*, 29, 33
Jones, Judith A. "Judi," Pres., ASB, 185, 491
Jones, Lewis L., Dean, Undergraduate Studies, 270, 305, 480
Jones, Loretta L., speaker, 246
Jones, Lucy, US Geological Survey, 353
Jones, Pame, Administrative Support Coordinator, 423
Jones, Reginald, psychologist, 78
Jones, Rhodessa, Cultural Odyssey Co., 322
Jones, Richard O., performer, 364
Jones, Simmie L., Facilities Services, 451, 464
Jones, Tim, comedian, 225
Joosten, S. Paul A., campus boosters, 52
Jordan, Charles, speaker, 271
Jordan, Donald W., Pres., Foundation Board, 248
Jordan Gospel Choir, musical group, 322
Joseph Andrew Rowe Collection, 362
Joseph Andrew Rowe Water Resources Archives, 448
José's Mexican Foods, 406
Joshee, Jeetendra R. "Jeet," Dean, Extended Learning, 413, 446, 479
Joshi, Muneesh, speaker, 256
Joshua Hall, 14, 17, 87
Jourhari, Bonnie, speaker, 373
Journey into Blackness (play), 134
Judd, L. Lynn, Prof., 366
Julian, Chrystine, poet, 431
Jumping Jack Flash, musical group, 458
Jun, Lucy Soo Yon, Outstanding Student, 494
Juneteenth Celebration, 231, 242, 275, 286, 295, 306, 315, 324, 364, 412
Jung, Marshall, Prof., 364
Jupe, Rachel, harpsichordist, 75-76
Jurina, Rob, speaker, 143
Justice, Donald, poet, 75
Justice, Felix, actor, 236
'Justments (play), 180
K. L. Neff Construction Co., builders, 130, 149
Kabak, Robert, artist, 109
Kadyk, Walter S., Dir., College Police, 54, 78, 113, 484
Kagan, Spencer, speaker, 103
Kahrl, Bill, journalist, 390
Kahuthu, Web Development Coordinator, 457-58

Kain, Robert, Arrowhead Award, architect, 380, 498
Kaiser Permanente, 428
Kaiser Steel, 109
Kajcienski, C. Donald, Assoc. Dean, Admissions, Records, and Outreach, Assoc. Dean & Assoc. VP, Enrollment Services, Dir., Outreach Services, 189, 198, 267-68, 345, 363-64, 486
Kalbermatter, Olga, speaker, 256
Kalbus, Lee H., Prof., Act. Dean and Assoc. Dean, Academic Planning, 77, 86, 107, 155, 188, 306, 475
Kamansky, David, speaker, 359
Kamen, Paula, speaker, 298
Kamptner, N. Laura, Prof., 360, 468, 490
Kamusikiri, Jim, speaker, 241
Kamusikiri, Sandra D., Prof., Assoc. VP, Assessment and Planning, Dean, Graduate Studies, 9, 352-53, 355, 370, 475
Kane, Marie, Pres., Chaffey College, 406
Kanlayaphichet, Kitima, Outstanding Student, 494
Kaplan, Julius D., Prof., Assoc. Dean & Dean, Graduate Studies, 222, 255, 355, 393, 475
Kaplowitz, Karen, attorney, 93
Kapp, Gloria, Int. Dir., Financial Aid, 413
Kappa Alpha Psi, 209
"Karate for Kids" tournament, 338
Karen, Robert, psychologist, 353
Karmanova, Tatiana V., Assoc. Dean & Act. Dean, Extended Learning, 438, 446, 479
Karmen, Harvey, psychologist, 93
Karnig, Albert K., President, 7, 9, 16, 333. 474, 506
  administration, 336-465
  affirmative action, 350, 391, 406-07, 455, 457
  budget cuts, 385, 394, 399, 402, 404, 414, 424-25, 434, 441, 444, 446-47, 451-52, 459-61, 464, 466
  disabled access on campus, 439
  hospitalization and illness, 403-04
  inauguration, 343
  personal background, 337
  television station KCSB-TV, 368, 375, 379-80, 384, 408-09
Karnig, Brent D., son of Albert K., 337
Karnig, Eric V., son of Albert K., 337
Karnig, Marilyn Joan Vogelaar, wife of Albert K., 337
Karnig, Todd K., son of Albert K., 337
Karnoff, Ellen, art collector, 299, 327
Karnoff, John W., art collector, 299, 327
Karousel Kids, musical group, 254
Kasen, Jill, Prof., 138
Kashiwabara, John, CSU Trustee, 231, 295
Kassel, Victor, speaker, 248
Kathak Dancers, 237
Kathy O'Brien Literacy Center, 295
Katz, Friedrich, speaker, 367
Katz, Jonathan Ned, writer, 327
Kaufman, Alan S., speaker, 399
Kaufman, James, Prof., 453
Kaufman, John A. III, Prof., 426
Kaufmann, William J. III, physicist, 116, 142
Kawahradal, Kazurori, educator, 309
Kawar, Fakhry, Jordanian legislator, 268
Kay, Jim, US Rep., 299
Kazlo, Martha P., Counselor, Dir., Student Health and Psychological Counseling Center, 211, 384, 407, 486
KBON (radio station), 76-77
KCAL (radio station), 197
KCBS-TV (TV station), 199, 435
KCSB-TV (TV station), 384, 386, 396-97, 409, 454
KCXX-FM (radio station), 358, 388
Keane, Glen, animator, 313
Keating, AnaLouise, speaker, 455
Keaton, Buster, actor, 77
Kedding, Leon, speaker, 123
Keen, Noel, speaker, 340
Keene, Fred, Prof., 142
Kegley, Charles, speaker, 119
Kehoe, James W. Jr., US Navy Capt., 126
Keim, Will, speaker, 454
Kelch, Jim, speaker, 89
Kelekar, Dilip, UAB Member, 500
Kellas, William R., writer, 395

Keller, Ed, SB Bar Assoc., 130
Keller, Gary, writer, 289
Keller, Russell L., historian, 472
Keller, Selma S. "Jerry," Libn., 84, 430
Kellers, C. Frederick "Fred," Prof., 71, 243, 325, 489, 502
Kelln, Elmer, physician, 123
Kellogg Chamber Singers, 117
Kelly, Elka K., Alumni Award, 496
Kelly, James, Instructional Support Technician, 188
Kelly, Mike, speaker, 341
Kelly, Willie Ruth, Housing Maintenance, 186
Kelsey, Mary Beth, Prof., 364
Kemp, Anthony, speaker, 71
Kendrick C. Babcock Fellowship, 337
Keneally, Thomas, writer, 311
Kendall Dr. (SB), 30, 46, 54, 63, 75, 77, 90, 97, 139, 167-68, 184, 187, 389, 404, 417
Kendall Elementary School, 118, 120
Kendrick, Jack, poet, 257
Kennan Institute for Advanced Russian Studies, 126
Kennedy Center/American College Theatre Festival, 398
Kennedy Center for the Performing Arts, Washington, DC, 284, 288
Kennedy, Anthony M., US Supreme Court Justice, 408
Kennedy, Elva L., Children's Center, 280
Kennedy, James N., Alumni Award, Pres., Alumni Assoc., UAB Member, 492, 496, 500
Kennedy, John Winn, Alumni Award, SB Trial Court Presiding Judge, 78, 343, 496
Kennedy, Kevin, Dir., Chesterfield Film Writers' Project, 297
Kennedy, Ted Jr., speaker, 363
Kennedy, Thomas E., writer, 470
Kent, Carolee, student & dancer, 130, 165
Kent, Kathryn, Outstanding Student, 494
Kent State University, 64-65
Kent, Troy, baseball player, 280
Kern, Jim, speaker, 232
Kerney, Lynda, Outstanding Student, 495
Kerr, Barbara, Facilities Services, 444
Kessel, Barbara, speaker, 69
Kettman, Callie, Outstanding Student, 494
Kevin & Bean, radio talk show hosts, 291
KGB, 99
Khalsa, Sant, Prof., 351, 388
Khan, Ashish, musician, 70
Khan, Pranesh, musician, 70
Khan, Rauf A., Prof., 373
Khare, Brij B., Prof., 71, 156, 354
Khen, Yossi, Israeli soldier, 382
Khokhlov, Michail "Misha," student, son of Nikolai E., 269
Khokhlov, Nikolai E., Prof., 66-67, 72, 95, 98, 100, 122, 144, 157, 269, 286, 435, 502
Killgore, Judith R., Secretary, 311
Killingsworth, Tootie, Dir., Credential and Graduate Programs, PDC, 423
Kim, Scott, dancer, 312
Kim, Taewoong, UAB Member, 500
Kime, Sandy, Cafeteria Manager, 64
Kincher, Jonni, alumna author, 270
Kindschy, Peggy, Off. of Records, Registration, and Evaluations, 473
Kinesiology and Physical Education, Dept. of, 325
King, Alinda, Purchasing, 432
King Arthur and the Royal Posse, musical group, 290
King, Ashante, speaker, 348
King, B. B., musician, 464
King, Charles, philosopher, 124
King, Dan, speaker, 271
King, David, artist, 117
King, Edward L., chemist, 65
King James Bible, 208
King, Jeanne C., Prof., 432, 489
King, Kathleen, Dispatcher, Public Safety, 307
King, Martin Luther Jr., Rev. Dr., 50, 193, 224
King, Norm, Dir., University Transportation Center, 418, 440
King, Rodney, 284
King Saud University, Riyadh, Saudi Arabia, 398
King Soloman, musical group, 306

King, Wayne, speaker, 163
King, Woodie Jr., producer, 401
King, Yolanda, daughter of Martin Luther, 421
Kingsley Tufts Poetry Award, 351
Kinney, Lee G., Outstanding Student, UAB Member, 493, 499
KIOT, radio station, 182
Kirchhevel, Jory, Outstanding Student, 494
Kirk, Henry Lee, speaker, 271
Kirkpatrick, Elizabeth L., Piano Accompanist, 307
Kirkwood, Gray, musical director, 67
Kirsch, Eva, Dir., Robert V. Fullerton Museum, 342, 463
Kirchschlaeger, Rudolf, Pres., Austria, 194
Kirwan, John, VP, ASB, Pres., Alumni Assoc., 38, 492
Kitazawa, Masashi, Outstanding Student, 493
Kivisto, Ronna, Dir., Special Events, 423
Kiwanis Club (SB), 108, 331
Kiwanis Future Leaders Program, 261
Klein, Adria F., Prof., Assoc. Dean, School of Education, 226, 294, 320, 348, 364, 490
Klein, Malcolm W., speaker, 128
Klein, Sidney, speaker, 94
Klonoff, Elizabeth, Prof., 280, 464
Kluck, Bernice Joyce, Administrative Analyst, 307
KNBC (TV station), 130, 158
Knight, Barry A., Prof., 364
Knight, Christopher, speaker, 208
Knight, Goodwin J., CA Gov., 20
Knight-Moreno, Deborah, Outstanding Student, 493
Knight, Morris, speaker, 102
Kniss, Ray, speaker, 64
Knot, Robert, saxophonist, 416
Knott, Bill, poet, 63
Knowles, Linda, soprano, 89
KNXT-TV (TV station), 150
Koch, Gale, Outstanding Student, 493
Kochenderfer, Lee, speaker, 148
Koeller, Shirley, Prof., 132
Koga, Kim, artist, 331
Kohn, Douglas, Rabbi, 391

Kohout, Michal, speaker, 432
Kolb, Lauralyn, singer, 328
Kolehmainen, Karen, Prof., 259
Kolhatkar, Sonali, speaker, 387
Kollitz, Jan, speaker, 380
Kominski, Gerald, speaker, 310
Kong, Leslie M., Libn., 320, 340, 377, 387
Koon, Helene W., Prof., Act. Dean, School of Humanities, 152-53, 155, 247, 266, 320, 477, 490, 502
Koondakjian, Alice Manoukian, 337
Koondakjian, Avedis, 337
Kopang, Jeffrey A., alumnus author, 270
Koppel, Carol, Judge, 219
Korpman, Ralph, speaker, 309
Kottke, Janet L., Prof., 453, 490
Kottonmouth Kings, musical group, 388
Kovach, Peter, speaker, 441
Kovach, Ronnie, writer, 452
Kovalik, Susan, speaker, 244
Kozel, Chuck, speaker, 123
KPFK (radio station), 200
KQLH (radio station), 208
Kraft Foods, 247
Kramer, Larry L., Prof., 369, 501
Kraus, Dennis W., Dir., Public Safety, 314, 484
Krause, Ernst H., CAB Member, 499
Krause, Wesley A., Alumni Award, 496
Krausher, Phillip, mathematician, 135
Kravetz, Nathan, Prof., Dean, School of Education, 122, 145, 210, 478
Kravitz, Deborah, Environmental Health and Safety Officer, 264
Kray, Helga E. (Scovel Lingren), Dir., Student Union, Int. Dir. & Exec. Dir., Santos Manuel Student Union, Act. Asst. VP, Asst. VP, & Assoc. VP, Student Affairs and Student Development, 199, 389, 400, 451, 485, 487
Krebs, Martha, speaker, 314
Kremer, Elmer D., Mayor, SB, 20, 504
Krentz, David, speaker, 463
Kress, Guenther G., Prof., 377, 412
Kreter, Leo, Second VP, CSCSB CSEA Chapter, 43, 48
Krieger, Lois B., speaker, 389
Kritzberg, Joan H., Prof., 366

Kroeger, Dennis, Foreign Languages, 445
Kronos Quartet, musical group, 183
Kronowitz, Ellen L., Prof., 219, 242, 279, 402
Kroonen, William, speaker, 344
Krueger, Lori, Photographer, 472
Krug, Theodore "Ted," Financial Aid Advisor, Dir., Financial Aid, 82, 198, 381
Kruger McGrew Construction, builders, 267
Krupp, Ed C., Dir., Griffith Observatory, 298
Krushenick, Nicholas, painter, 106, 108
KSCI (TV station), 150
KSSB (campus radio station), 217, 223, 225, 246, 250, 273, 277, 300, 324, 360—SEE ALSO: Coyote Radio
Kubiak, Carolyn Rae, Prof., 197
Kuchel, Thomas H., US Sen., 76
KUCR-FM, radio station, 315
Kuhn, Jill, Outstanding Student, 493
Kuiper, James, sculptor, 325
Kuku, Mustafa, speaker, 402
Kulakowski, Edward, speaker, 453
Kully, Robert K., CSU Trustee, 185, 198, 203, 213
"Kultatami-O-Rama," 309
Kuman, Pankaj Rishi, filmmaker, 395
Kunene, Mathabo, speaker, 241
Kunene, Mazisi, speaker, 242
Kunsang, Chuye, Tibetan nun, 383
Kuppuswamy, Gowri, singer, 158
Kurtz, Katherine, writer, 377
Kurzweil Computer Products, 169
Kushite Raiders, musical group, 208
Kushner, Samuel Sid, Dir., Sponsored Programs, 192, 465, 467, 476
Kutak, Henry F. "Hank," Dir., Financial Aid, 381, 387, 426
Kutania People, 114
KVCR (TV station), 107, 150, 197
Kwesi, Ashra, speaker, 290, 422
Kyle, Robert, saxophonist, 415, 440
Kyser, Jack, Economic Development Corp., 358
La Brea Tar Pits, 319
L.A. Moving Van and Puppet Company, theatre group, 195
L.A. Smart Girls, musical group, 322
La Pinto, Al, speaker, 289
La Quinta, Calif., 413
The Labors of Hercules (play), 193
Lacey, Walter, musician, 99
Lachaise, Gaston, artist, 154
Ladner, Joyce, speaker, 238
"Lady Beware," seminar, 173
LaFaye, Alexandria, Prof. and writer, 390, 407, 462
Laffin, Patricia, member, CVC Advisory Board, 306
Laforet, Carmen, novelist, 245
Lagerberg, Donald, speaker, 230
Laird, Margaret, Student Aid, 236
Lakin, Tommie, speaker, 237
Lamana, Jeanie, singer, 252
Lambda Chi Chapter of Sigma Nu, 271
Lambert, Steve, Editor, *San Bernardino Sun*, 439
Lambson, Nicholas, guitarist, 429
LaMon, Dana, Judge, 373
LaMonica, Elaine, speaker, 228
Lampel, Anita, psychologist, 93, 116-17
Lamplighters (music group), 41
Lamude, Kevin G., Prof., 402-03, 455
Lana Walton Theatre Ensemble, theatre group, 341, 350
Lancaster, Winifred H., CSUC Trustee, 110
Landau, Saul, filmmaker, 343, 387, 431, 466
Landau, Yehezkel, speaker, 431
Landers Quake, 286
Landes, Michael, speaker, 402
Landis, Mark, historian, 453
Landmark Building Products, 349
Landolphi, Suzi, comedienne, 289
Landurand, Patricia Madeiros, speaker, 193
Lane, Kenneth E., Prof., 372, 422
Lang, David, football player, 286
Lange, Kelly, TV newscaster, 218, 232
Langenfeld, Elizabeth, English, 445
Langford, Pamela D., Dir., Community Relations and Development, 221
Langhammerer, Stephen A., booster, 118
Langley, Clifford, builders, 42
"Language Day," festival, 94
Language Lab, 71, 76

Lansdale, Marianthi, CSU Trustee, 213, 231, 239
Lantz, Teresa, Act. Dir., Children's Center, 140, 145
Lapin, Daniel, Rabbi, 341
LaPre, Larry, speaker, 150
Lara, Gilbert B., Dir., Upward Bound Program, 96, 109
Larsen, Robin, Prof., 473
Larson, Swen, Mayor, Redlands, 299
Lascoe, Matti, dancer, 279
Lathuillière, Marc, artist, 457
Latin American Roundtable, 381, 401
"Latin American Studies Conference: Study of the Americas," 410, 419, 442, 456, 471
Latin Society, musical group, 219, 229, 244, 255, 266, 276, 287, 291, 296-97, 307, 316, 325, 345, 354, 365, 374, 384, 394, 403, 412, 423, 433, 445, 459
Latino Baseball Reunion, 459
Latino Business Students Assoc., 253
Latino Community Leadership Committee, 455
Latino Education and Advocacy Day, 469
Latino Scholarship and Graduate Banquet and Dance, 333
Latiolais, Michelle, writer, 263
Latisha and the Misfits Dance Team, 286
Latuperissa, Fred, speaker, 348, 402
Lauer, Lois, UAB Member, real estate agent, 385, 500
Laulemaga, Faliu, Grounds Maintenance, 432
Lauren, Maria, singer, 469
Laurent, Bo, speaker, 449
Laurie, Greg, singer, 91
Laurie, Scott, PAC Member, 500
Lavin, Angela, 172
Lavner, Lynn, comedian, 248
Law Day Celebration, 263
"Law Day Conference," 230
Law-Related Education Program, 221
Lawrence, David, speaker, 94
Lawrence, Jerome, playwright, 229
Lawrence, Jim, woodcarver, 332
Lawrence L. Daniel Award, 294
Lawrence, Lucas G., Dir., Audio-Visual Services, 43, 66-67, 293, 488
Lawrence, Mike, speaker, 426
Lawrence, Stephen B., Prof., 59
Laws, Valerie, Outstanding Student, 495
Lawson, John, 155
Lawton, Chukia, activist, 89
Layton, Janice M., Prof., 364
Lazarus, Mell, cartoonist, 190
Lazarus, Wendy, speaker, 277
Lazo, Alejandro, guitarist, 379
LCR Band, musical group, 287, 296, 316, 325
Le Boutillier, John, US Rep., 292
Leach, Britt, actor, 100
Leadership and Development Program (LEAD), 214
Leadership, Curriculum, and Instruction, Dept. of, 325
Leading Market Technology Corp., 363
League of Women Voters USA, 382
Learning Center, 220, 237
Learning Channel, 384
Learning Laboratory, 78
Learning, Literacy, and Culture, Dept. of, 325
Leathers, Larry, Custodian, 128
Lecturers and Artists Committee, 213
Ledford, Debra Kay, Outstanding Student, 493
Lee, Beatrice, Clerical Asst., 188
Lee, Eleanor, actress, 92
Lee, Francias, Taiwanese Consul, 339
Lee, Robert A., Prof., Assoc. Dean, Academic Affairs, 54, 73, 90, 145, 286, 441-42, 476, 502
Lee, Robert C., UAB Member, 499
Lee, Robert E., playwright, 229
Lee, Tom, Outstanding Student, 495
Lee, Yunsang, Library Equipment Systems Specialist, 436
Lefton, Lew, comedian, 420
Legacy Awards, 416
Legislative Forum, 123, 130
Lehr, Gregory R., Exec. Dir., Santos Manuel Student Union, 413, 422, 487
Lehmann, Wilfrid, campus booster, 290
Leicester, Andrew, speaker, 257
Leighton, Christopher, speaker, 409
Leininger, Gail, staff, 211
Leithner, Paul, Treasurer, ASB, 38

Lemann, Wilfried, PAC Member, 500
LeMay, Michael C., Prof., 403
Lemmon, Jack, actor, 157
Lemmond, Janice L. "Jan," Support Services Officer, 138, 344, 445, 483
Lenchantín, Ana Lía, pianist, 363
Lents, James, speaker, 281
Lentz, Marcia, Alumni Award, 496
Lenz, Margaret J. "Peggy," Prof., 101, 121, 225, 501
Lenz, Milo, Painter, 185
LeoConnolly (asteroid), 320
Leonard, Barbara R. "Bobbie," wife of William E., CAB & UAB Member, 112, 423, 499
Leonard, Daryl Ann, appointed Athletic Dir., 242, 488
Leonard, Jean Pfeiffer, Alumni Award, 496
Leonard, William E., Hon. Ph.D., Arrowhead Award, Owner, San Gorgonio Land Co., 357, 423, 444, 497-98
Leonard, William R. "Bill," Assemblyman & State Sen., 146, 154, 156, 220-21, 256, 269, 299, 357, 364
Lerner, Jesse, speaker, 332
LeRoy Crandall Assocs., soil testers, 31
Leschin, Luisa, writer, 463
Leslie, Francis, speaker, 471
Leslie I. Harris String Quartet, 93-94, 103
Let's Make a Deal (TV show), 61
Leveille, David, CSU Dir., Academic Affairs and Institutional Relations, 317
Leviege, Vernon O. "Ollie," Prof., 59, 71, 87-88
Levin, Barry R., book dealer, 292
Levin, Brian, Prof., 425
Levin, Harry, speaker, 323
Levin, John, speaker, 310, 472
Levy, David, astronomer, 313
Levy, Heather, 155
Levy, Leonard W., historian, 207, 228
Levy, Mark, singer, 214
Levy, Steven M., Prof., 364-65
Lewein, Laura, speaker, 173
Lewis, Al, speaker, 362
Lewis, Birdene, Exec. Secretary, CSCSB CSEA Chapter, 48
Lewis, C. Jerry, Assemblyman and US Rep., 61, 88, 104-05, 117, 121-23, 130, 132, 154, 223, 299, 354, 386-87, 397, 426, 430, 444
Lewis, Chani, Outstanding Student, 494
Lewis, Eldon C., Prof., Int. Dean, School & Coll. of Business and Public Administration, 294, 325, 346, 354, 373, 477
Lewis, Goldy, Arrowhead Award, 273, 498
Lewis, Laurie, fiddler, 276, 445
Lewis Operating Corp., 498
Lewis, Ralph M., Arrowhead Award, 273, 498
Lewis, Victoria Ann, actress, 181
Leyson, Leon, Holocaust survivor, 383
Li, Kaiyun, speaker, 215
Liabeuf, Amanda De Vries, Outstanding Student, 494
Libecki, Mike, speaker, 439
Liberty Cable, 178
Library Associates, 210, 216
Library Associates Lecture, 272, 311, 330, 333, 342-43, 350, 352, 360, 370, 415
Library, College, 76, 99, 119, 122, 124, 127, 129, 151, 168
Library Building (old), 17, 76, 103
Library-Classroom Building (new), 13, 17, 34, 45, 50, 52-53, 55, 58-59, 68, 71-74, 76, 129, 132
Library Staff Assoc., 55
Libreria del Pueblo, San Bernardino, 431
Lichtblau, Eric, *New York Times* reporter, 456
Lichtenstein, Peter, speaker, 249
Lichtman, Denis R., Prof., 71, 365, 387, 502
Liddy, G. Gordon, presidential aide, 223
Lieberman, Ben, performer, 372
Life Rolls, 442
Lifetime Collector's Award, 292
Light, Leah, psychologist, 127, 133, 241
Lightbone, Leonard, speaker, 98
Lilburn, Stephen T., Alumni Award, 496
Lilienthal, Laurel A., Int. Asst. VP, Academic Personnel, 9, 446, 476

Lilly, Steve, speaker, 330
Limar Jansen, Val, alumna author, 248, 259, 270, 409
Lincoln, Abbey, actress, 141
Lindeman, Carol A., nurse educator, 208
Linden, Hal, actor, 463
Lindholm, Amanda, student, 399
Lindman, Erick L., 64
Lindorff, Joyce, harpsichordist, 162
Lindsey, Carolyn, speaker, 237
Lindsey, Donald B. Prof., 206, 306
Lindstrom, Robert L., speaker, 309
Ling, Bei, writer, 439
Lingo Band, musical group, 282
Lingo, Linda J., Alumni Award, 496
Lingren, Paul, speaker, 94
Lintault, Roger P., Prof., 62, 142, 364
Linton, Cynthia, Dir., Learning Center, 267, 278, 387
Lippman, Thomas W., speaker, 398
Lipsey, Mark, speaker, 137
Lipsitz, George, speaker, 206, 257
Lira, Agustín, musician, 262
Liss, Martha, Prof., 161
"Listening Association Conference," 403
Lit and the Kottonmouth Kings, musical group, 358
"Literacy in the '80s: Reading, Writing, and Technology," conference, 182
"Literacy in the Home," conference, 217
Little Broadway Productions, theatre group, 207
The Little Dog Laughed (play), 469
"A Little Light Reading" (Burgess), 213
Little Mountain, 448
Little Mountain Dr., 14, 438
Little Owl, Orville, speaker, 310
Little, Paul, speaker, 103
Little Theatre, Fine Arts Building, 129
Little Theatre of the Deaf, theatre group, 223
Littlejohn, Bev, speaker, 289
Littleton, Emmet, speaker, 265
Littleton, Harvey, sculptor, 109
Littleworth, Arthur L., speaker, 415
Litwack, Leon F., speaker, 123
Liu, Carol, speaker, 408

Liu, F. F., Prof., 101, 324, 331, 502
Liu, Samuel F., educator, 294
"Living for the City," conference, 114
"Living Voices," theatre group, 372, 382
Llamo, Passang, Tibetan nun, 383
Lloyd, Angela, speaker, 301
Lloyd, Bill A., Dir., Calif. Senate Relations and Labor Issues, 358
Lloyd, Susan, MSN Coordinator, Nursing, 423
Lo, Dobbin, PAC Member, 500
Lobb, Delbert, speaker, 64
Local Agency Formation Commission, 33
"Local to Global: Everything You Need to Know About Women's Issues Today," conference, 392
Lockhart, Heidi, Outstanding Student, 493
Loei Rajabhat University, Thailand, 415
Loer, Steven P., speaker, 125
Logo, campus, 249, 435
Logsdon, Robert, Central City Advisory Board, 112
Lohlmuller, Dale, First VP, CSCSB CSEA Chapter, 48, 50
Lohnes, Robert F. "Bob," Asst. Dir., Physical Plant, 116, 187, 224
Loma Linda Roller Coasters, wheelchair basketball team, 319
Loma Linda University, 76, 89
Loma Linda University Medical Center, 160
Long, Darui, speaker, 410
Long, David, Riverside County Schools Superintendent, 356
Long, Janet, Outstanding Student, 493
Long-Scott, Ethel, speaker, 253
Longville, John, Assemblyman, 357, 387
Longville, Susan K. Lien, Prof., Assoc. Dir. & Dir., Water Resources Institute, SB City Councilwoman, 389-91, 413, 423, 478
Lootens, Frank, Equipment Technician, 144
Lootens, Maria L., Capital Planning, Design & Construction, 9, 473
Loper, Laura, Outstanding Student, 494

López, Alvado, artist, 106
López, David Rojo, student, 283
López, Fred A., speaker, 228
López, Horacio, speaker, 301
López, Humberto, speaker, 204
López, José, activist, 93
López Núñez, César, poet, 371
López Saenz, Lionila, activist, 89
Loprieno, Antonio, speaker, 282
Lorber, Aletha, Secretary, Alumni Assoc., 45, 47
Loreman, Shirley, accountant, 131
Los a la Cranes, musical group, 314
Los Angeles Baptist College, 202
Los Angeles County Agricultural Commissioner, 114
Los Angeles County Superior Court, 29, 33
Los Angeles Dodgers baseball team, 226
Los Angeles Lakers, basketball team, 133, 141, 248
Los Angeles Piano Quartet, music group, 224
Los Angeles Philharmonic Orchestra, 139
Los Angeles Police Revolver and Athletic Club, 108
Los Angeles Rams, football team, 270, 286
Los Angeles Suicide Center, 68-69
Los Angeles Times (newspaper), 51, 62, 119, 140, 229, 241, 255, 258, 300, 305, 370, 437
Lost West Landscape Architecture and Construction, 418
Lotakov, Yuri, pianist, 153
Louganis, Greg, Olympic diving gold medalist, 469
Louque, Angela, speaker, 360
Loutzenhiser, Janice L., Prof., 202, 445
Love, Bob, basketball player, 352
Love, Melvin, basketball player, 286
Love (Skillings), 98
Love Train Ltd., musical group, 108
Loveland Baptist Church, 234
Loveland Mass Choir of Fontana, 220, 305
Loveless, William, Pastor, 361
Lovett, Joseph E., Prof., 422
Löwe, Rüdiger, speaker, 309
Lower Commons, Commons, 12, 89
Lower Commons Plaza/Patio, Commons, 12
Loveridge, Ronald, speaker, 74
Loya, Olga, speaker, 259
Loya, Raúl, speaker, 64
Loyola Marymount University, 322
Loza, Stephen, musician, 252
Lozano, Danilo, musician, 252
Lozano, Monica, UC Regent, 395
Lubenow, Gerald, *Newsweek* correspondent, 202
Lubin, Georges, French scholar, 151
Lucarto, Lilla, sculptor, 225
Lucas, George, educator, 79
Lucas, William, mathematician, 205
Los Luceros, musical group, 127
Luck, Suzanne, Apple Computers, 267
Luckman, Charles, CSC Trustee, 40
Luetcke, Linda, student, 46
Luger, Lex, wrestler, 339
Luján, Gilberto, artist, 106
Lula Washington Dance Company, 389
Lumen Valo Finnish Choir, musical group, 426
Lumian, Dave, speaker, 166
Luminarias (film), 382
Lunar Rocket and Rover Co., Inc., 426
Lunchtime (play), 76
Lung Association of San Bernardino, Inyo, and Mono Counties, 143
Lupica, Anthony, guitarist, 219, 221
Lustig, Jeff, retreat manager, 308
Lutz, David J., Assoc. Dean, Graduate Studies, 201, 222, 475
Lutz, William, speaker, 206
Luxton, Larry, speaker, 123
Lybarger, Mary Helen, Secretary, 26, 48
Lyman, Edward Leo, historian, 332
Lyman, Peter, University Libn., University of California, Berkeley, 313
Lynam, Margaret, Purchasing, 245
Lynch, Thomas, poet, 256
Lynn, Mark, musician & storyteller, 332, 343, 352, 362, 381
Lyons, Lee A., Prof., 445
Lytle-Moors, Gwendolyn, soprano, 149, 205
M. L. Hansen Co., builders, 282
M-Pact, musical group, 409, 419

Macbeth (Shakespeare), 93
MacDonald, Bruce W., speaker, 151
MacDonald, Norm, comedian, 333
MacDuff, Cassie, *SB Sun* writer, 226
Mace, bronze campus, 183, 185
Macfarlane, Duncan, dancer, 250
Machalski, Bronisław "Miko," mime artist, 181
Machiavelli, Niccolò, writer, 100
Macías Harrison, Gloria, Publisher, *El Chicano*, CAB Member, Pres., Crafton Hills College, 124, 127, 194, 197-98, 200, 210, 383, 499
Macías McQueen/Brown, Marta, UAB Member, 210, 290, 364, 500
Mackay, Jason C., Outstanding Student, 494
MacIntyre, Scott, singer, 470
MacLaughlin, Catherine Graff, cellist, 205
MacNeish, archeologist, 250
MacPike, Loralee, Prof., Assoc. Dean, Graduate Programs, 186, 188, 199-201, 269, 334, 475, 490
MacQuiddy, Gary E., Support Technician, 296
Mademoiselle (magazine), 51
Madrid, Arturo, speaker, 294
Madrid, Carlos, speaker, 262
Madsen, Lois, Assoc. Dir., Act. Dir. & Dir., Financial Aid, 387, 391
Mafra-Neto, Agenor, speaker, 422
Magana, Paul F., speaker, 412
Magical Moonshine Theatre, theatre group, 392
Magness, John M., speaker, 378, 453
Magnus, Bernd, philosopher, 132
Magnuson, Evelyn, campus booster, 463
Magnuson, George E., speaker, 79
Mahan, Travis Lee, Outstanding Student, 494
Maietta, Pat, Instructional Support Technician, 286
Mail box, 237
Main Entrance, 90, 111-12, 114, 116, 132, 138, 183, 265, 273
Main Street Community Band, musical group, 422
Maintenance Shops, 347
Maisonet, German, physician, 259
Majel-Dixon, Juanita, speaker, 456
Majel-Dixon, Lorena, Elder, Pauma Band of Luiseño Indians, 456
Major Events (Logistics) Committee, 242, 290
Major, Laura Ruth, student, 229
Major, Sheri L., Pres., ASI, 492
Makeba, Awele, performer, 380
Makerov, Julie, alumna singer, 362, 450
Makgetla, Neva, speaker, 241
Makgetla, Seth, speaker, 242
"Making Culture in the Inland Empire," symposium, 457
"Making Peace: Issues in Death and Dying," conference, 259
"Making the Connection: Preparation, Motivation, and Innovation," conference, 365
"Malathion Spraying," forum, 263
Maldonado, Abel, Lt. Gov., CA, 505
Maldonado, Ana María, cellist, 390, 398, 411
Maleson, Al, speaker, 74
Malone, James, speaker, 110
Maloof, Sam, Hon. Ph.D., woodworker, 425, 439, 457, 497
Mamakos, Peter, actor, 100
"Management by Goals and Results," conference, 96
Management, Dept. of, 189
Management Personnel Plan, 192
"Managing and Motivating Members of the Organization," seminar, 101
"Managing Drought in the Inland Empire," conference, 437
"Managing Local Government Technology: The Year 2000," conference, 272
Mance, James, speaker, 340
Mancilla, Jorge, speaker, 263
Manclow, Kristi, Outstanding Student, 493
Mandatory retirement age, 140
Mandel, Howie, comedian, 324
Mandela, Nelson, Pres., South Africa, 369
Mandragola (Machiavelli), 100
Manger, Terje, speaker, 470
Mankau, Sarojam K., Prof., 56, 306
Mann, Nancy, Rockwell International Science Center, 128

Manning, Kimberly, Outstanding Student, 493
Mannion, Elizabeth, soprano, 179
Manpower Staffing Services, 498
Manríquez, Emmanual C., Outstanding Student, 494
Mansker, Jackie J., Custodian, 307
Mantei, Kenneth A., Prof., 87, 107, 412
Mantovani, Juanita, speaker, 236
Marable, Elaine, speaker, 139
Maranatha Singers, 91
March Air Force Base Band, 40, 232
Marcus Foster Memorial Reading Award, 348
Marcy, Arie L., Pres. Faculty Wives Club, wife of Peter T., 41
Marcy, Peter T., Prof., Assoc. Dean, Academic Administration, Dir., Summer Session, 39, 41, 44, 53, 476, 479
Mariachi California, musical group, 251
Mariachi Cocula, musical group, 143, 151
Mariachi de Valley de Indio, musical group, 119
Mariachi Estudiantes del Inland Empire, musical group, 376
Mariachi Huezar, musical group, 307
Mariachi Internacional de America, musical group, 296
Mariachi Internacional de México, musical group, 332
Mariachi Internacional de México de Francisco J. Jara, musical group, 437
Mariachi los Gallos Reales, musical group, 304
Mariachi Lucero, musical group, 273
Mariachi Lucero de Lupe Soría, musical group, 362
Mariachi Sol de México, musical group, 327
Mariachi Tequila, musical group, 219
Mariachi Vallarta, musical group, 240
Mariam, Alemayehu G. "Al," Prof., Exec. Asst. to the President, 400, 424, 474
Marin, Christy, speaker, 276
Marin, Peter, speaker, 79
Marín, Ramona, wife of Raúl, 126
Marín, Raúl, writer, 126
Mariscal, Jorge, speaker, 361
Mark Cox Electric, contractors, 43
Mark Taper Forum, 207
Marketing and Management Science, Dept. of, 189, 202, 215
Marketing, Management Science, and Information Management, Dept. of, 215
Marketing Resource and Learning Facility, 315
Markman, Stephen J., US Asst. Attorney General, 238
Marks, Norton E., Prof., Int. Dean, College of Business and Public Administration, 394, 403, 412, 477
Marley, Bob, singer, 428
Marley's Ghost, musical group, 243, 296
Marmara University, Ankara, Turkey, 382-83
Márquez, Carlos, Personnel Management Specialist, 210, 268
Márquez, Derón, Tribal Chairman, San Manuel Band of Mission Indians, 383, 386, 393
Marsh, Peter, violinist, 256
Marsh, William L., Plant Operations, 187
Marshall, Charles, speaker, 242
Marshall, Peter, TV host, 467
Marshall-Pyle, Heather, Outstanding Student, 494
Marta, Rosa, Sister, speaker, 246
Martin, Carolyn A., Prof., 403
Martin, Charles W., Dean, Undergraduate Studies, 305, 345-47, 480
Martin, Dorothy, speaker, 73
Martin, D'Urville, actor, 163
Martin, Gina, speaker, 100
Martin, Joseph M., mathematician, 91
Martin Luther King Day, 224
Martin, Max, comedian, 246
Martín Meléndez, Guadalupe, student, 180
Martínez, Anthony, crime victim, 342
Martínez, Eliud, *El Chicano*, Commissioner, U.S. Bureau of Reclamation, 127, 368
Martínez, Enrique N., Alumni Award, play director, 137, 496
Martínez, Ezequiel, student, 344
Martínez, George, Dir., Upward Bound Program, Dir., Community Affairs,

190, 199, 202
Martínez, Irene, Extended Learning, 423
Martínez, Jim G., Budget Officer, 63, 299, 483
Martínez, Joe L., psychologist, 127, 237
Martínez, Luis, student, 399
Martínez, Martin, member, CVC Advisory Board, 317
Martínez, Rachel Adame, Lib. Asst., 397
Martínez, Rueben, speaker, 427
Martínez, Sergio, speaker, 106
Martínez Villalobos, Maricarmen, poet, 410
Martino, Victoria, speaker, 463
Marty, Martin E., speaker, 270
Marvin D. Frost Weather Station, 201
Mary Cisar Memorial Fund, 79
Mary, Nancy L., Prof., 432
Mary Stuart Rogers Foundation, 328, 333, 368
Mary Stuart Rogers Gateway Building, PDC, 14, 18, 333, 368, 380, 383, 385, 408
Masefield, John, poet, 200
Mason, James, Prof., 445
Mason, William J., CSU Dir., Analytical Studies, 209
Massey, Walter E., speaker, 314
Massie, Noel L., Arrowhead Award, VP, United Parcel Service, 440, 471, 498
Mast, Jorli R., Computer Center, 278
Master Plan for CSCSB/CSUSB, 95, 241, 349
Master Plan for Higher Education in California, 22, 84
Master's degree, first, 82, 95
Masters of Harmony, musical group, 395
Mata, Paul, Outstanding Student, 493
Mathias, Theophane A., Rev., Jesuit priest, 78
Math-Science Day, 83
Mathematics Institute, 356
Mathews, Audrey, Prof., 437
Matich Corp., builders, 228-29, 437, 498
Matich Foundation, 437
Matich, Martin A., CAB & UAB & PAC Member, Arrowhead Award, Pres., Matich Corp., 284, 357, 437, 498-500
Matranga, James, actor, 100
Matranga, Leo V., actor, 92, 100, 132
Matthau, Walter, actor, 157
Matthews, Audrey L., Prof., 422-23
Matthews, Glenna, speaker, 450
Matthews, Jane Wachs, art collector, 289, 327, 333, 355
Maudsley, Judy, VP, Bank of America, 215
Maudsley, Mike, SB City Councilman, 267
Mauel, Ed, newspaper columnist, 111
Mauldin, Donald G., Mayor, SB, 21, 26, 28, 34-35, 172, 504
Maurel, Andre A., Chief, Plant Operations, 104, 140, 394, 483
May, Terry E., Pres., Alumni Assoc., 492
Mayden, Ruth, Pres., National Assoc. of Social Workers, 361
Mayering, Steve, alumnus, 333
Mayfield, James L., SB Co. Supervisor, 134, 137
Mayhew, Wilbur W., zoologist, 64
Maynard, David F., Alumni Award, 496
Mayo, E. Clark, Prof., 373
Mazur, Michael, painter, 52
Mazza, Nancy S., Secretary, 305
Mbogua, Leonard S., Prof., 59
McAfee, Lois, wife, Ward M., 126
McAfee, Ward M., Prof., Chair, Social Sciences Div., Dean, School of Social Sciences, Act. VP, Academic Affairs, 6, 9, 77, 104, 113, 122, 125, 184, 201, 206, 211-12, 266, 268, 291, 383, 475, 478-79, 490
McAllister, Debby, Systems Analyst, 423
McAllister, Harry C., Mayor, SB, 504
McAllister, Richard D., Alumni Award, 496
McArthur, Greg, meditation expert, 92
McArthur, Meher, speaker, 450
McAuley, Skeet, photographer, 262
McBrayer, Sandra, speaker, 311, 324
McCabe, Marjorie, Prof., 280
McCaffery, Margo, speaker, 251
McCall, Gerald J., Lect., 331, 350, 352,

361
McCalla, Deidre, singer, 238
McCallum Theatre for the Performing Arts, Palm Desert, 275, 295
McCarron, Cecilia, Student Health Center, 432
McCarthy, Daniel, speaker, 452
McCarthy, Dorothy J., Lib. Asst., 187, 414
McCarthy, Leo J., CA Lt. Gov., 190, 216
McCarty, Hanoch, speaker, 265
McClain, Paula D., writer, 337
McClanahan, Lon, Dir., Desert Studies Consortium, 205
McClendon, James Jr., speaker, 301
McClung, William, speaker, 225
McClure, Faith, Prof., 468
McClure, Rosemary, *San Bernardino Sun*, 123
McCombs, Ray, 250
McCormick, Bob, TV host, 378
McCullough, Linda, Administrative Support Coordinator, 432
McCulloh, Douglas, photographer, 429
McCune, Ellis E., CSC Dean, Academic Planning, Pres., CSU Hayward, Act. Chancellor, CSU, 39, 263, 269, 275-76, 420, 505
McCurdy, Ron, jazz performer, 430, 455
McDaniel, F. Douglas, Judge, 263
McDaniels, Edison P., writer, 64
McDermid, Carolyn, Budget Officer, Assoc. Dir., Accounting, 432, 483
McDonald, Bruce, hypnotist, 281
McDonald, Clifford L., Laboratory Support Technician, 191
McDonald, Patrick T., Dir. of Public Safety and Chief of Police, 388, 413-14, 484
McDonnell, John F. "Jack," Prof., Asst. to Dean, Academic Administration, Dir., Inland Empire Management Center, Assoc. Dean, Business and Public Administration, 80, 99, 117, 226, 366, 468-69, 489, 502
McDougall, Sanders A. "Sandy," Prof., 371, 490
McDowell, Gary L., speaker, 177, 229
McDowell, Robert, Publisher, Story Line Press, 301-02
McDowell, Theodore R., Prof., 209, 445
McEachern, Terry, sportscaster, KCSB-TV, 396
McEachern, Vivian, Nurse, 36
McFatter, Larry E., Prof., 340, 343, Prof., 473
McFerrin, Robert, baritone, 135
McGaugh, James, psychobiologist, 108
McGee, Barbara, UAB & PAC Member, 500
McGill, Ormond, hypnotist, 91
McGinnis, George, Prof., 473
McGovern, George, US Sen., 85
McGowan, Robert, Assoc. VP, Enrollment Management,/Enrollment Services, 374, 467, 486
McGraff, Tom, CSC Asst. Vice-Chancellor, 55
McGregor, Mary L., Prof., 286
McGrievy, Susan, speaker, 143
McGuckian, Trish, Libn., 9
McGuire, Brian Patrick, speaker, 251
McGuire, John, Standard Oil Co. of Calif., 80
MCI, 439
McInnis, Richard, historian, 464
McIntosh, Nancy Jo, Outstanding Student, 493
McKay, Yolande, artist, 268
McKenna, George J. III, Superintendent, Inglewood Unified School Dist., 221, 245
McKenna, Robert, speaker, 128
McKenney, Jack, skin diver, 135
McKenzie, Bob Jr., speaker, 108
McKenzie, C. Donald, Budget Planning Analyst, Dir., Budget Planning and Administration, Dir., Budget and Telecommunications, Dir. of the Budget, 191, 198, 482
McKenzie, Virginia P., Secretary, 187, 291
McKone, James H., Publications Manager, Dir., College Relations, 46, 53, 59, 488
McLain, Leah, Outstanding Student, 495
McLay, Suzzane, Outstanding Student, 494

McLellan, Elizabeth, speaker, 109
McLeod, Gloria Negrete, Assemblywoman, 419
McMichael, George L., Dean, Instruction, Dean, Faculty, 25-26, 28, 36, 42, 48, 51, 82, 474-75
McMichael, James, poet, 115
McMillan, Larry, UAB Member, 499
McMillan, Terry, writer, 292
McMullen, Jennifer, Administrative Aide, 204
McMullen, Tim, comedian, 117, 120
McNabb, S. B. W., Mayor, SB, 504
McNair scholars—SEE: Ronald E. McNair Post Baccalaureate Achievement Program
McNamara, Lynda, Assoc. VP, University Advancement, 374, 388, 487
McNassor, Don, speaker, 96
McNaughton, Patricia, speaker, 264
McNay, John, Outstanding Student, 209, 493
McNeil, Keith, folksinger, 65
McNeil, Rusty, folksinger, 65
McNutt, Todd "Hoss," energy experimenter, 273, 284
McPharlin, Eldon G., SB landowner, 28-29
McPherson, Bruce, CA Sec. of State, 425
McPherson, Charles R., Engineer, 139
McQueen, Marta Macías, Editor, *El Chicano*, 69
McVittie, William, Assemblyman, 112, 123, 130
Meacham, Ed, campus booster, 368
Meade, Mary Jo, Libn., 62, 64, 66
Meadow, Robert, speaker, 267
Meadows, Farah, Outstanding Student, 494
Meat Puppets, musical group, 305
MEChA (Movimiento Estudiantil Chicano de Aztlán), 70, 73, 94, 111-12, 119, 253
Media Luncheon, 102
Media Relations and Public Information Office, 220, 243
Mednick, Sarnoff A., speaker, 168
Medved, John, speaker, 118
Meek, Norman, Prof., 274
Meenan, Peter, speaker, 247

Meet John Muir (play), 262
"Meeting the Challenge" expo, 311
"Meeting the Fears of the In-Between Years," conference, 96
"Meeting the Needs of the Homeless," conference, 277
Meisenhelder, Susan E., Prof., Pres., CFA, 219, 301, 351, 396, 423
Meisenhelder, Thomas M., Prof., 195, 219, 301, 403
Mejia, Richard, speaker, 307
Mellon, Sam, curator, 453
Melmed, Paul, education researcher, 53
Members Lonely Band, musical group, 458
Mendez, Sylvia, activist, 469
Mendoza, Josephine, Prof., 224
Mendoza, Ricardo, *El Chicano*, 127
Meneses, George A., Asst. Dean, Students, 67, 73, 77-78, 88, 341, 485
Mentemeier, Ailien, speaker, 123
Mentjes, Ursula, speaker, 441
Menzel, Stephen Jr., Employee Relations Specialist, 211
Meraz, Ronald, member, CVC Advisory Board, 306
Mercado, Raúl, UAB Member, 499
Merchant, Eva Mae, campus booster, 276
Merck Research Laboratories, 352
Mercury vapor lamps, 161
Merod, Jim, speaker, 301
Merrell, John F., campus booster, 441
Merriett, William Haywood, student, 231
Merritt, Virginia R., student, 183
Messerli, Steven K., Alumni Award, 496
Messiah (Handel), 177
Messina, Jo Dee, singer, 368
Messing, Jill, Outstanding Student, 494
Messinger, Darlene, speaker, 253
Messinger, Sheldon, speaker, 227
Metcalf, Allan, speaker, 143
Metcalf, Robert L., entomologist, 51
Metfessel, Newton, speaker, 105
Methodist University of North Carolina, 274
Metro State University, 380
Metropolitan Opera, 135
Metternich, Henry C., speaker, 164

Metzger, Tom, white supremacist, 290-91
Meyering, D. Steven, Alumni Award, 496
Meyers, Eunice, speaker, 292
Mezey, Robert, poet, 260
Mian, Lal, Prof., 405
Michael Hennagin Prize in Composition, 340
Michaels, Andrea Carla, comedienne, 223
Michaels, Pat, owner, KQLH radio, 208
Michigan State University, 63
"Microtechnology for Everyone Festival," 184, 196, 208
Middle Earth, music group, 60
Middle School Conference, 255
Middlekauff, Robert, Dir, Huntington Library, 198
Mighty O.T., musical group, 286
"Migrant Education," conference, 183
Miguel, Nigel, 272
Miike, Takeshi, speaker, 467
Miklac Players, theatre group, 141
Miles, James F., speaker, 256
Milius, John, filmmaker, 380, 449
Mill Creek County Folk Group, 85
Millard, Charles III, speaker, 219
Millennium (online library catalog), 430
Miller, Bertram, musician, 237
Miller, Bob, speaker, 274
Miller, Cheryl, TV sportscaster & Olympic medalist, 225, 275
Miller, David L., speaker, 330
Miller, Diane, Purchasing, 445
Miller, John Preston, Dir., Student Health Center, 232, 278, 486
Miller, Julius Sumner, physicist, 110, 117
Miller, Kenneth Louis, student, 210
Miller, Larry, poet, 127
Miller, Linda D., Libn., 152
Miller, Michael, UAB & PAC Member, 500
Miller, Michele, Pres., ASI, 492
Miller, Norine, SB City Councilwoman, 245
Miller, Patricia, speaker, 236-37
Miller, Randi L., Prof., 458
Miller, Rita, speaker, 135
Miller, Robert J., Dir., Public Safety and Chief of Police, 418, 430-31, 484
Miller-Tiedeman, Anna, speaker, 226
Miller-Tiedeman, David, speaker, 226
Miller, Toby, speaker, 439
Miller, Valerie, speaker, 313
Milligan, C. Patrick, Pres., SB Valley Municipal Water Dist., 472
Mills, Jeff, comedian, 230
Mills, Shari, student, 172
Min, Anchee, writer, 442
Minces, Juliette, writer, 90
Minie, Jo-Ann M., Accounting, 296
Minnich, Richard, speaker, 437
Minor, Tom, Mayor, SB, 295, 309, 341, 504
Minority Access Inc., 434
Minority Information Center, 99
Minter, William, speaker, 235
Mintz, Steven M., Prof., Dean, School of Business and Public Administration, 325, 346, 393
Mirande, Alfredo, speaker, 322
Mission Inn, Riverside, 41
Mississippi, Connie, woodworker, 332
Mitchell, Candice, flautist, 128
Mitchum-McIntosh, Kathleen, UAB Member, 500
Mittelstaedt, Alan, *SB Sun* writer, 213
Mitton, Robert J., CAB & UAB Member, 499-500
Mitzelfelt, Brad, SB County Supervisor, 433
Mixcoacalli Folk Dance Ensemble, 252
Mixed Motion Dance Co., 130
Miyake, Lynne K., speaker, 466
Miyoshi, Kim, speaker, 343
Mizelle, Lizette, comedienne, 268
Mo' Better Blues, musical group, 365, 445
Mobile Launch Platform, 426
Mochrie, Colin, comedian, 429
"Model Congress," 167
Model United Nations Team/Program, 101, 293, 303, 314, 322, 342, 351, 362, 372, 381, 391, 400, 410, 429, 434, 442, 455, 469
Modern Arab League Team, 381, 399, 469
Moellendorf, Darrell, speaker, 272
Moeller, Hans-Bernard, speaker, 166

Moffett, Cora Lee "Corky," Secretary, 106, 150, 377
Moffett, Kevin, Prof., 440
Mojave Hall, 14, 17, 87
Molière, playwright, 98
Molina, Carmen, student, 49
Molinaro, Al, actor, 92
Molle, Mary E., Prof., 473
Mollet, Mark, Junior Class Pres., ASB, 38
Molloy, John, writer, 228
Molstad, Clark, Prof., 473
Molutsi, Patrick, sociologist, 312
Monaghan, James M., Dir., Distributed Learning, 371, 481
Mondale, Joan, wife of VP Walter Mondale, 236
Mondolini, Jules-Pierre, Asst. Cultural Attaché, French Consulate in L.A., 166
Monk, Abraham, speaker, 285
Monkey Siren, musical group, 298
Monroe, A. Craig, Prof., 451, 453
Monroe, Edna, Custodian, 365
Monroe, Kenton L., Prof., Dir., Counseling, Dean, Students, 36, 42, 179, 243, 444, 484, 486
Montáñez, Larry, Mail Room Supervisor, 141
Montano, David Frank, student, 212
Monte Corona Conference Center, 80
Montenegro, Raquel, Assoc. Dir., Project MAESTRO, 72
Monterastelli, Art, screenwriter, 396
Monterey Pop, musical group, 72
Montez, Rosa, speaker, 120
Montfort, Matthew, guitarist, 306
Montoya, José, artist, 106
Montoya, Velma, UC Regent, 395
Monville, Lou III, UAB & PAC Member, Pres., ASI, Pres., Alumni Assoc., CSU Trustee, 422, 428, 492, 500
Monzon, Raoul, Groundsworker, 147
Moore, Alfred Finley, astronomer and booster, 58, 78, 161
Moore, Chella Dean, campus booster, 43, 58, 78, 161
Moore, Douglas R., Pres., University of Redlands, 184
Moore, Sherri, pianist, 128
Moore, Thelma, US Dept. of Housing and Urban Development official, 311
Moore, Thomas, speaker, 117
Moorefield, Arthur A., Prof., 135, 267, 302, 501
Moorehead, Lora, speaker, 83
Mora, Miguel, speaker, 381
Morales, Olga J., Dir., Academic Resources, 476
Moran, Joseph R., Prof., 106, 114, 121-22, 393
Moran, Michelle, writer, 449
Moran, Ross T., Int. Dir. & Dir., Institutional Research, 9, 365, 372, 464, 481
More, Duke, speaker, 241
More, V., speaker, 94
Morejón, Nancy, poet, 391
Moreno, Edward V., speaker, 64
Moreno, Ernest, CVC Advisory Board member, 275
Moreno Valley Unified School District, 354
Morey, John, Dir. of Admissions, 97
Morgan, Becky, speaker, 314
Morgan, Margaret, artist, 359
Morgen, Sandra, speaker, 318
Mori, Dennis, Education, 473
Morin, Stephen F., speaker, 219
Morongo Hall, 14, 17, 87
Morris, April, PAC Member, 500
Morris, Patrick J., SB Superior Court Judge, Mayor, SB, 232, 246, 308, 343, 373, 419-21, 426, 441, 443, 463, 504
Morris, Teresa, Prof., Chair and Dir., Social Work, 450, 489
Morris, Wilma, Secretary, President's Office, 121, 419
Morrison, Donald H., education planner, 32
Morrison, Toni, writer, 345
Morrow Field airport, 26
Morrow, Gerry, Outstanding Student, 495
Morrow, Lilian, 250
Morrow-McCombs Memorial Lecture, 238, 250, 261, 270, 282, 292, 301, 311, 321, 330, 341, 350, 361, 371, 391, 402, 409, 420, 431, 442, 455, 468
Morrow, Meredith, Administrative

Aide, 178
Morrow site, 26
Morse, David, speaker, 157
Mortensen, Bernhardt L., Prof., 138, 230
Morton, Carlos, playwright, 312
Morton, Jassy, performer, 306
Mosby, Robert, speaker, 148
Moseley, Dan, Photographer, 292, 368
Moseley, Richard, VP, Stater Bros., 326, 418
Moseley, Walter, writer, 329
Moser-James, Sydney(e), Pres., ASB & ASI, 491
Moses and Friends, musical group, 237
Moses, Jesse D., Dir., Supportive Services, EOP; Placement Officer, 91, 95, 113, 121
Moses, Quentin J., Dir., Parking Services, 219, 324, 470
Moses, Yolanda T., Alumni Award, Dean, School of Arts, CSPU Pomona, 167, 200, 206, 237, 274, 343, 495
Moskowitz, Selma, painter, 328
Mosqueda, Diana L., Secretary, 202
Moss, Jay, speaker, 378
Moss, Lynn T., Career Development Center, 278
Moss, Richard L., Prof., 365
Mote, Florence A., Prof., Asst. Dean, Academic Administration, Act. Dean, School of Education, 98, 113, 122, 126-27, 159, 478, 501
Mother Bear's, Commons, 89
Mother May I, musical group, 312
Motor Enthusiasts Club, 43
Moulder Brothers, contractors, 85, 90
Mounce, Wallace, architect, 39
Mount McPherson—see: Badger Hill
Mountain Fifes and Drums Corps, musical group, 443
Mountain Folksingers, musical group, 332
Mountain lion on campus, 411
Movimiento Estudiantil Chicano de Aztlán—see: MEChA
Moya, Mary G., Secretary, 432
Mozart, Wolfgang, composer, 137
Mr. and Mrs. CSUSB Pageant, 399
Mrozinski, Jan, speaker, 120
Mt. San Antonio College, 264
Mt. San Jacinto College, 257, 453
mtvU.com, 462
Muchnic, Susanne, art critic, 142
Muckerman, Ann, Sister, CAB Member, 198, 499
Mudd, Brian, speaker, 158
Mueller, F. Eugene, Lect., 163, 501
Mueller, Klaus, speaker, 439-40
Mukai, Chiaki, astronaut, 318
Muldrow, Ronald, musician, 270
Mulholland, Catherine, speaker, 372
Mulkey, James R., UAB Member, 500
Mulla, Mir S., entomologist, 39
Mullen, T. Patrick, Prof., 383
Multicultural Center, 308
"Multiethnic Education," seminar, 83
Mulvihill, James L., Prof., 432
Munde, Alan, performer, 296
Mundkur, Valmir, speaker, 454
Munitz, Anne, wife of Barry A., 327
Munitz, Barry A., Chancellor, CSU, 276, 285, 292, 327, 341, 505
Munn, Harriet, SB landowner, 28
Munro, Jim, speaker, 259
Murillo, Carmen, Clerical Assistant, 202
Murillo Family Observatory, 404, 413, 447, 454, 457, 462, 466, 473
Murillo, George, campus booster, 454
Murillo, Pauline Ormego, historian, 401, 440, 454, 469
Murphy, Lisa "The Ooey Gooey Lady," speaker, 468
Murphy, Michael, Asst. Athletic Director, Sports Information Dir., 465-66, 473
Murphy, Owen, Prof., 280
Murphy, Richard, oceanographer, 115
Murphy, Robert, speaker, 73
Murray, Alan, *Wall Street Journal* reporter, 239
Murray, Alma, speaker, 69
Murray, Carolyn B., speaker, 237, 367
Murray, David, pianist, 426
Murray, Liz, speaker, 431
Murray, Michelle, singer, 426
Murray, Ron, bagpipist, 207
Muscare, Michael, Coach, 196
Muscato, Marsha, alumna author, 270
Museum Dr., 14
Musgrove, James, performer, 306

Music Americana, musical group, 207, 211
Music Dept., 56, 315
Music from Oberlin Trio, musical group, 164
Music of the Americas Festival, 252, 274, 362
Musical Offering, musical group, 174
Musick's Recreation, musical group, 155
Mutual-use library agreement, 86
Muyco, María Christine, composer, 456
My Brother's Keeper, musical group, 286
myCSUSB (TV show), 454
Myers, Dowell, speaker, 453
Myers, Hector, psychologist, 119
Myers, Lynne, CSU Trustee, 185
Myles, James, alumnus, 300
Mytos y Cuentos (play), 387
NAACP (National Association for the Advancement of Colored People), 234, 257, 291
Nachaka, performer, 315
Nadel, Lynn, speaker, 226
Nader, Ralph, activist, 266
"NAFTA's Second Year: Experiences, Challenges, and Opportunities for Medium and Small-Sized Business Ventures," symposium, 313-14
Naggi, Paula, dancer, 251
Nagy, Ferenc, Prime Minister, Hungary, 54
Naik, Paul Soo Dee, Outstanding Student, 493
Najera, Samuel "Alex," Outstanding Student, 494-95
Naked Earth, musical group, 293
Nalley, James, pianist, 448
Nance, Christopher, TV weatherman, 332, 372, 381
Naples, Caesar J., CSU Vice Chancellor, Faculty and Staff Relations, 194, 264
Naragon, Maurice, speaker, 228
NASA, 352
Nash, Gary B., speaker, 343
Nash, J. Richard, playwright, 77
Nash, Richard, Rev., speaker, 102
Nassar, Jamal R., Prof., Dean, College of Social and Behavioral Sciences, 433, 479
Nasser, Mohamad, speaker, 450
Nathan-Elaine, folksingers, 93
Naticchia, Chris, Prof., 374
National Academy of Public Administration, 437
National Alliance for Human Rights, 431-32
National Assoc. of Gifted Children, 453
National Assoc. of Schools of Art and Design, 199
National Assoc. of Social Workers, 361
National Board of Colleges of Arts and Sciences, 427
National Book Award, 348
National Book Critics Circle Award for Poetry, 390
National Boys AAU Cross Country Championships, 97
National Center for Excellence in Distance Learning, 366, 372
National Center for the Exploration of Human Potential, 97-98
National Center of Academic Excellence in Information Assurance Education, 444, 447
National Clearinghouse on Marital and Date Rape, 260
National Coalition for the Homeless, 426
National Collegiate Athletic Assoc.—see: NCAA
"National Conference on Teacher Quality," 359
National Council for Accreditation of Teacher Education, 465
National Endowment for the Arts, 374, 440, 466
National Endowment for the Humanities, 320
National Geographical Society, 374
National Hispanic Scholarship Fund, 283, 333
National Humanities Assoc. for Higher Education, 386
National Institute of Health, 437, 458
National League for Nursing, 147, 199
National Orange Show, 40, 56, 267, 287, 316, 331
National Organization of Women, 92
National Science Foundation, 171, 289

National Science Teachers Assoc., 441, 468
National Society for the Preservation of Tent, Folk, and Repertoire Theatre, 61
National Shakespeare Company, 166
Native American Day, 328, 356, 395, 448
Native American Students Alliance, 72
Native American Students Assoc., 273, 315
Native Sons of the Golden West, 139
Natural Beauty Program, 80
Natural Cause, musical group, 315
Natural History Museum, 416-17
Natural Love, musical group, 306
Natural Sciences, College of, 354, 409
Natural Sciences, Division of, 26, 71, 87
Natural Sciences, School of, 87, 140
Nava, Gregory, film director, 361
Nararoli, Nicholas, Outstanding Student, 472, 495
Navarro, Armando, Pres., Congress for United Communities, 136, 142, 232, 381
Navarro, Gil, speaker, 391
Navarro, Ramón, Escuela de la Raza Unida, 94
Nazar, Jason, hypnotist, 372
Nazarian, Nick, Asst. Dir., Alumni Affairs, 441
NBC, 214
NCAA Division II Men's Gold West/Central Super Regional Tournament, 471
NCAA Division II National Women's Volleyball Tournament, 397
NCAA Division II Western Regional Basketball Tournament, 380, 400
NCAA (National Collegiate Athletic Assoc.), 16, 186, 191, 201-02, 226, 259-60, 263, 274, 276, 279, 284, 302, 305, 323, 333, 351, 359, 369, 377, 379-80, 397, 400, 407, 430, 441, 450, 457, 465, 471
Neal, Fred Warner, speaker, 219
Negin, Gary A., Prof., 253, 301
Negrín Fetter, Juan, speaker, 310
Nelson, Arthur E., Libn., College Libn., Library Dir., 28, 31, 36, 50, 86, 239, 278, 285, 395, 415, 481, 502

Nelson, Edward, sociologist, 120
Nelson, Elizabeth, sociologist, 120
Nelson, Jeanie, student, 95
Nelson, Joy, speaker, 249
Nelson, Julie A., speaker, 440
Nelson, Michael, speaker, 440
Nelson, Philip, Rev., speaker, 204
Nelson, Tena M., Lect., 307
Nelson, Terri, Prof., 401
Nemnich, Mary B., speaker, 342
Nesbitt, Prexy, speaker, 259
Nethery, James, physician, 123
Nettles, Bronica, performer, 306
Neumann College, 441
New Beginnings (CSUSB Symphonic Band), 300
New Decade, musical group, 72
New Dining Room, Commons, 212
"New Directions in Special Education," conference, 181
New England Center for Higher Education, 399
New Harvest, Old Shame (film), 362
New Minds, musical group, 64
New Miss Alice Stone Ladies Society Orchestra, 120
"The NEW Women's Rights Issues: Celebrating the Advancements of Women," conference, 420
New York Times (newspaper), 456
Newcastle Publishing Co., Inc., 75
Newcombe, Gerald M., Alumni Award, UAB Member, 496, 500
Newkirk, Christine Van Cleave, Outstanding Student, 493
Newlin, Maureen, Lect., 432
Newman Catholic Fellowship of CSUSB, 252
Newman, Eric J., Prof., 464, 491
Newman-Gómez, Sharon, Outstanding Student, 493
Newman, Janne Irvine—see: Irvine, Janne
Newman, Jerzy, statistician, 81
Newman, Joseph John, student, 215
Newman, Karen, Aide, VP, Student Affairs, 9, 450
Newman, Marvin R., Plant Operations, 186
Newman, Mary, Graphic Artist, 188
Newman, Richard, speaker, 259

The Coyote Chronicles: CSUSB, by Michael Burgess

Newman, Sharan, writer, 328
Newman, Taft T. Jr., Prof., Coordinator, EOP Counseling Services, Dir., EOP, 278, 355-56, 501
Newmannis, Joan, student, 85
Newsweek (magazine), 202, 257
Newton, Frederick A., Prof., 165, 197, 412, 490
Next Time for Real (Cauley), 164
Nicholls, Kristine, Outstanding Student, 493
Nicholls, Mark, member, CVC Advisory Board, 315
Nichols, Breck, Pres., ASB, 491
Nichols, Erma J., Alumni Award, 496
Nichols, Linda, speaker, 439
Nichols, Mary, State Secretary of Resources, 268, 392
Nichols, Nichelle, actress, 248
Nichols, Penny, singer, 91
Nicholson, Freshman Class Pres., ASB, 38
Nick Pokrajac Inc., builders, 110, 112, 115, 121
Nickles, Herbert, Assoc. Dir., Instructional Computing, 206, 231
Nideffer, Robert, speaker, 259
Niecie, musical group, 205
Niehoff, Tom, speaker, 149
Nielsen Construction Co., builders, 220
Niessen, Dorothea D., Business & Public Administration, 473
Nieto-Gómez, Ana, speaker, 142
Nieto, Sonia, speaker, 293
Nightfire, musical group, 384
Nightspore, musical group, 166
Niles, María, soprano, 252
Los Niños Ballarinos, dancers, 240
Nisbet, Eugene G., State Sen., 40
Nisbet, Robert A., sociologist, 65
Niven, Barbara, actress, 411
Nix, Dottie Ogle, pianist, 47
Nixon, Norm, basketball player, 141
Nixon, Richard M., Pres., US, 58
"No Child Left Behind: Time for a New Federal Response," conference, 437
No Exit (Sartre), 41
Noah and the Ark '76 (musical play), 118
Nobel, Pamela—SEE: Jean, Pamela
Nobles, Wade W., speaker, 237

Noblett, David, Asst. Athletic Dir. for Sports Information, 466
Noblitt, James S., speaker, 246
Nobody's Child, musical group, 283
Noboru, Seiichiro, Japanese Consul General, 318
Nobuyuki, Karl, Exec. Dir., Japanese American Citizens League, 133
Noches de Aztlán (musical), 159
Noel, Claude E., CAB Member, 198, 499
Noel, Toni, speaker, 274
Nolan, Ruth, poet, 431
Nolte, Barbara, Dir., College Relations Office, Student Accounts Office, 149, 339
Noriega, Ken, Outstanding Student, 495
Norman, Linda, alumna author, 270
Normandin, Jim, speaker, 452
Normark, Don, photographer, 437
North Campus Circle, 14, 438
North Dakota State University, 302
Northcutt, BreAnda, speaker, 470
"Northern Ireland: Where the Heart Turns," symposium, 107
Northpark Blvd. [North Park Circle Dr.] (SB), 14, 30, 34-35, 46, 50-51, 53-54, 90, 111, 114, 129, 131, 139, 144, 168, 239, 259, 265-67, 312, 327, 329, 385, 387, 389, 404, 407, 417-18, 429, 433, 436, 438, 455, 457
Northridge Earthquake, 299, 321
Norton, Ruth A., Prof., 473
Nossoff, Joel L., Asst. Dean & Act. Dean, Undergraduate Studies, 265, 270, 306, 480
Nota, Paul, Lost West Landscape Architecture and Construction, 418
Notables, musical group, 325, 384
Notarangelo, Joe, Outstanding Student, 494
Nova Saxophone Quartet, musical group, 230
Novac, Sjrdan, speaker, 239
Novak, David, storyteller, 207
Novick, Michael, writer, 320
Nowicki, Stephen C., Police Lt., Act. Dir. & Int. Dir., Public Safety, 307, 314, 381, 484
Noyce, Robert, campus booster, 427
Noyes, James, speaker, 398

Nuclear Magnetic Resonance (NMN) spectrometer, 326
Null, David H., Prof., 196, 383
Nummela, Renate M., Prof.—SEE: Caine, Renate M.
Núñez, Jackie, speaker, 414
Nursing, Dept. of, 317, 414, 472
Nursing Laboratory, 464
Nursing Skills Lab Addition, 469
Oak Room, Commons, 212
Oakes, Andrew, graphic designer, 454
Oakland Symphony Youth Orchestra, 74
Oakview Construction Inc., builders, 227, 229
Oberacker, Betty, pianist, 166
Oberhelman, David, SB City Councilman, 306
Oberjuerge, Paul, *SB Sun* columnist, 280-81, 291
Obershaw, Charles D. "Chuck," Hon. Ph.D., PAC Member, auto dealer, 356, 397, 401, 421, 497, 500
Obershaw Scholarship Fund, 397
Obershaw, Shelby, wife of Charles D., Hon. Ph.D., 356, 401, 497
O'Brien, Kathy L., Prof., 287, 295, 501
O'Brien, Robert M., Prof., 15, 156, 490
Occidental College, 202, 226
Ocegueda, Mark, Outstanding Student, 495
Ochoa-Fernández, Elsa M., Dir., International Student Services, Dir., International Institute, 278-79, 371-72, 415, 441, 443
OCLC database, 190
O'Connell, Jack, State Sen., State Superintendent of Public Education, 385-86, 388, 393, 416
O'Connor, Bonnie, Outstanding Student, 493
O'Connor, Lorney, Scenic Artist, 423
The Octopus (play), 159
Oden, Ron, Mayor, Palm Springs, 419
Odiorne, George S., management researcher, 94
O'Doherty, John, speaker, 402
Office of Technology Transfer and Commercialization Building, 14, 18, 404, 412
O'Gara, C. Michael, Chair, Physical Education Dept., 34, 36, 39, 45, 48, 71, 129, 155, 275, 502
Ogike, Ucecukwu C., Prof., 80
Oh, Angela E., attorney, 372, 382
Ohman, Kajsa, singer, 93
Ojanlatva, Ansa T., Act. Dir., Sponsored Programs, 189, 476
Oklahoma Observer (newspaper), 255
Okura, Robert Tadeo, student, 89
Olafson, Frederick, philosopher, 116
Olander, Joseph D., presidential candidate, 169
Old Fire (2003), 16, 395-97, 404
O'Leary, Brian, astronaut, 73
Oliphant Auditorium, PDC, 12
Oliphant, Richard R., Hon. Ph.D., Mayor, Indian Wells, UAB & PAC Member, 284, 358, 389, 497, 499-500
Olive, Gloria, mathematician, 135
Olive Grove, CSUSB, 82, 115
Oliver, J. Corey, speaker, 440
Oliver, JoAnn, Lib. Asst., 467
Oliver, Shari L., Counselor, 423
Oliver, Walter C., Prof., 373, 489
Olivo, Cynthia, Assoc. Dir., Admissions and Student Recruitment, 445
Ollerton, Margaret, UAB Member, 499
Olmedo, Esteban L., speaker, 206
Olmos, Edward James, actor, 323
Olson, Alix, poet, 392
Olson, Maxine, painter, 168
Olvis, William, tenor, 211
Olympians of the Sawdust Circle (Slout), 355
Omar, Ben, actor, 95
Omar, Mahamoud, artist, 191
Ombudsperson position, 405
O'Morrow, Shirley, speaker, 301
Onak, T. P., chemist, 61
Once Upon a Midnight (Astin), 303
Oneill, Maura, speaker, 455
Ongaro, Mary, Dir., Children's Center, 145, 166
Online registration, 409
Ontario Daily Report (newspaper), 31, 33
Ontario Mills Mall, 353
Ontario-Montclair School District, 450
Ontiveros, Ricardo, speaker, 64
Ooms, Terri, speaker, 362
Open College Program, 122

Open House, 159, 196
Operating Engineers' and Plumbers' Union, 59
Operation Bootstrap, 60
Operation Second Chance, 66
Oppenheim, Patsy W., Asst. VP, Student Development, 345, 485
ORACLE, 224
Oracle Corp., 321
Orange County Company, theatre group, 207
Orange Empire Dog Club, 211, 254
Orange Street Band, musical group, 281
Orchestra, 60
The Organizer (play), 148
Orion Saxophone Quartet, musical group, 311
Ornelas, Mary, 126
Orozco, Juan, artist, 106
Orquestra Sinfónica de México, musical group, 322
Orrock, Susan, student, 95
Ortega, Lydia, Dir., Admissions and Records, Int. Assoc. VP, Enrollment Services, Dir., Records, Registration, and Evaluation, Act. Dir., Housing and Residential Services, 278, 364, 374, 391, 486
Ortiz, Alfredo Rolando, harpist, 221
Orton, Randall, speaker, 298
Osborn, Tanya, student, 363
Osher, Bernard, campus booster, 401, 435
Osher Lifelong Learning Institute, 435
Osherow, Jacqueline, poet, 456
Oslund, Maren, Outstanding Student, 494
Ostar, Allan W., Pres., American Assoc. of State Colleges and Universities, 189
Osumi, Kazutaka, Chado specialist, 467
Osumi, Soko, Chado specialist, 467
Other Guys (music group), 42
Otomo-Corgel, Joan, CSU Trustee, 302, 315
Otto, Greg, comedian, 268
Otto, Herbert A., Chair, National Center for the Exploration of Human Potential, 97-98
"Our Constitutional Heritage: Applications in the Classroom," seminar, 243

Our Hospitality (film), 77
"Our Vision: Learning Achieving, Nurturing, Empowering," conference, 254
Outcault, William, sculptor, 225
Outstanding Academic Book (*Choice*), 158, 292
Outstanding Employee Award, 265
Outstanding Professor of the Year Program, 154, 156
Outstanding Reference Source, 293-95
Outstanding Student Award, 206
Overstreet, Penni K., Pres., ASI, 491
Overton, John C., Chief, Custodial Services, 152, 227
Owen, Jim, guitarist, 51
Owens, Patricia, Nursing, 445
Owerkowicz, Tomasz, speaker, 441
Oyarsun, Kemy, speaker, 184
P and A Construction Co., builders, 70
Pace, Charles, actor, 318
Pace, L. Theron, Counselor, Housing Coordinator, Dir., Disabled Student Services, 59, 122, 124, 145, 393
Pacific and Asian Communication Assoc., 403
Pacific Van and Storage, movers, 73
Pacifica Chamber Artists, musical group, 361
Padian, Kevin, speaker, 456
Padilla, Richard, CAB & UAB Member, 198, 499-500
Page, Ann, art critic, 332
Page, E. Philip, Prof., 327, 423
Paige, John C., University Police, 473
Painter, Chuck, speaker, 165
PAL Center (Provisional Accelerated Learning), 216, 268, 289, 291
Palacios, Sarah, speaker, 389
Palancé Productions, musical group, 274
Palestine Liberation Organization, 223
Pallone, David, National League umpire, 292
Palm Desert, Calif., 309-10, 356, 413, 421
Palm Desert Campus of CSUSB, 12, 18, 62, 96, 376, 385, 472
Palm Desert City Council, 331
Palm Desert Health Sciences Building at Palm Desert Campus, 13, 18, 373, 404, 406, 408, 410, 413-14, 416-17,

419, 421-22, 426, 428, 434, 437, 446, 449
Palm Desert National Bank, 390, 417
Palmer, John, speaker, 74
Palmer, Robert, pianist, 261
Palmettes Side Steppers Drill Team, dancers, 306
Palo Alto Cabaret Theatre, 64
Palo Verde College, 397
Palo Verde Trio, musical group, 251, 258, 262
Pamplin, Rick, writer, 277
Pan-Diehl, Lily, pianist, 74, 206, 215
Panagopoulos, Christos, Greek Consul-General, 323
Panchuk, Max, Outstanding Student, 495
Pandemonium Steel Drum Band, musical group, 265, 296, 316, 325
Panetta, Leon E., White House Chief of Staff, 388
Panorama (Alumni Assoc. magazine), 6, 51, 147, 205, 233, 258, 287
Panorama Fire (1980), 15, 155-57, 159-60, 395-96
Panorama Room, Commons, 12, 212
Panter, Gary, artist, 190
Papadopoulos, John K., Assoc. Curator of Antiquities, J. Paul Getty Museum, 350
The Paperback Price Guide No. 2 (Hancer & Burgess), 172
Parenti, Michael, speaker, 268
Parents Night, 68
Parke, Jeff, radio manager, 441
Parker, John Henry, photographer, 273
Parker, Maynard, *Newsweek* correspondent, 202
Parker, Rose Ann, speaker, 386
Parker, Scott, Outstanding Student, 494
Parking and Information Building, 18, 299
Parking fees, 145, 161, 244, 324, 412, 445
Parking Lot A, 14, 329, 436
Parking Lot A, PDC, 14
Parking Lot B, 14, 363, 436
Parking Lot B Annex, 14
Parking Lot B, PDC, 14
Parking Lot C, 14, 363
Parking Lot D, 14, 92, 386

Parking Lot E, 14, 332
Parking Lot F, 14, 329, 334
Parking Lot G, 14, 329, 437
Parking Lot H, 14, 375
Parking Lot M., 14
Parking meters, 437
Parking Services Dept., 325
Parking Structure #1, West, 14, 438
Parking Structure #2, East, 14, 438, 473
Parks, Bernard C., Los Angeles Police Chief and City Councilman, 400
Parkside Elementary School, 163, 204
Parnes, Sidney J., psychologist, 350
Parra, Derek, Olympic skater, 382
Partnership 2000 fundraising campaign, 284, 288
Partridge, Elinore H., Prof., Act. Assoc. Dean, Academic Services, 278, 393, 475
Partridge, Ernest, speaker, 203
Paschel and the Ghetto Scholars, musical group, 315
Pate, Wanda, Secretary, 269
Patel, Tina, co-anchor, KCSB-TV, 396
Patio Playhouse Youtheatre, theatre group, 207
Paton, Karen, Dir., Women's Resource Center and Adult Re-Entry Program, 379
Patterson, Cecil Holden, Distinguished Visiting Prof., 218
Patterson, Daz, singer, 216
Patterson, Kenneth, UAB Member, 500
Patterson, Mary G., Prof., 210, 448, 502
Patterson, Pola N., Libn., 199, 358, 501
Patton State Hospital, 37, 73
Patzer, Gordon L., Prof., Dean, College of Business and Public Administration, 354, 394, 477
Patzert, William, speaker, 437
Paul and Evelyn Magnuson Auditorium, College of Education Building, 451
Paul, Billy, singer, 91
Paul Torrance Award, 453
Paulin, David, speaker, 259
Paull, Susan, student, 173
Pauma Band of Luiseño Indians, 456
Pavano, William, speaker, 149
Pavlo, Walt, MCI executive, 439
Pawprint (student newspaper), 6, 42,

44, 50, 58, 65, 69-70, 81, 149, 191-92
Paxton, Cynthia L., Prof., 432
Paxton, Kent, Alumni Award, 496
Payne, Brian, speaker, 399
Payne, Eileen, Outstanding Student, 493
Paynton, Clifford T., Prof., 67, 71, 286
Paz, Senal, actor, 359
Peace and Freedom Party, 68
Peace Corps, 176, 390
Peace Corps Day, 390
"Peace Symposium," 396
Peacock, Jean, Coordinator, Students with Academic Difficulties, Dir., SAIL and Learning Center, 153, 202, 212
Peake, Lloyd E., Prof., 428, 436, 473, 489-90
Pearson, Jon, speaker, 296
Peck, Edward L., US Ambassador to Iraq, 400
Peck, Michael, co-Dir., L.A. Suicide Center, 68
Pederson, Dennis M., Prof., 473
Pederson, Sally J., Lt. Gov., Iowa, 361
Pederson, Wendy A., Act. Campus Personnel Officer, 198, 203, 210-11, 483
Peigne, Kathy, Administrative Support Coordinator, 446
Peking Acrobats, performers, 330
Los Peldanos Trio, musical group, 252
Pelev, Todor, violinist, 350, 411
Pella-Hartley, Linda, speaker, 454
Pelletier, Dianna, Academic Advisor, 66
Pelletier, Kathie Lynne, Outstanding Student, 493
Pellisier Ranch site, 26-27
Peloza, Susan, Outstanding Student, 493
Pelt, Dean Wilton, student, 165
Peltason, Jack R., speaker, 239
Peltier, Margie, Student Health Center, 432
Peñalosa, Fernando, Prof., 39, 489
Pendleton, Ronald, Prof., 185
Penman, James F., Pres., ASB, Pres., Alumni Assoc., Alumni Award, SB City Attorney, 150, 264, 491-92, 495
Pennario, Leonard, pianist, 130
Pennington, Renona, Elder, Agua Caliente Band of Cahuilla Indians, 407, 456
Penny Dreadfulls, musical group, 284
People of the Pines Pow Wow—SEE: Pow Wow of the San Manuel Band of Mission Indians
People's Fair and Folk Fest, 69
PeopleSoft accounting system, 360
Pepper Linden Dr.—SEE: Campus Pkwy.
Pepsi, 389
Percy, Robert, UAB Member, 500
Pérez, Christopher, Outstanding Student, 495
Pérez, Louis G., speaker, 438
Pérez, Maclovio, TV newscaster, 197, 219
Pérez, Manuel Felipe, filmmaker, 442
Performing Arts Building, 14, 18, 361, 447
Peric, Miroslav, speaker, 440
Perimeter Road, 265-66
Perkins, Neale, Hon. Ph.D., UAB & PAC Member, 433, 497, 500
Perkins, Patricia, campus booster, 433
Perkins, Van L., historian, 41
Perloff, Robert, psychologist, 116
Perris Hill Park (SB), 60
Perry, D. Gaye, Asst. Dean of Students, 88, 485
Perry, Jimmy, student, 73
Perry, John, pianist, 179
Perry, Linda, singer, 332
Perry, Robert, Rev., speaker, 65
Perry, Stephen, writer, 401
Perry, Susan, writer, 401
Persell, Stuart Michael, Prof., 383-84
Persichetti, Vincent, composer, 140
Persona Non Grata, musical group, 283
Personnel Office, 289
Perspectives (Smith), 210
"Perspectives on Gay Rights," seminar, 143
Pesqueira, Ralph R., CSU Trustee, 263, 305, 343
Peters, C. Brooks, writer, 142
Peters, Robin Scott, performer, 341
Peters, Scott, photographer, 230
Peters, Tom, speaker, 369
Petersen, Hal, Building Maintenance, 276

Petersen, Norman V., writer, 62
Petersen, Susan, artist, 74
Peterson, Claudia, student, 45
Peterson, Homer G., UAB Member, 499
Peterson, Janet, speaker, 386
Peterson, Pete, speaker, 238
Peterson, Ralph, speaker, 217
Petherbridge, Mark, student, 185
Pethoud, Geraldine Elizabeth, student, 156
Petit, Leo, Rev., speaker, 65
Petrie Museum, London, 450
Petrie, Ronald G., Prof., Dean, School of Education, 104, 113, 478
Petrucci, Ralph H., Chair, Natural Sciences Div., Dean, Academic Planning, 33, 42, 46, 71, 86-87, 155, 186, 188, 266, 475, 477
Petry, Bonnie L., Libn., 396
Pettigrew, Kathleen "Kay," Clerical Assistant, 307
Pettis, Jerry L., US Rep., 51, 66, 68, 93, 103-05, 108
Pettis, Shirley N., US Rep., 112-13, 147
Pettit, Bryan L., Lect., 345, 501
Pew, Mary Jean, CSUC Trustee, 110
Pezdek, Kathy, Prof., Dir., Faculty Development Center, 122, 147, 156, 304, 330
Pfau Addition Library Support Group, 290
Pfau, Anne, 23
Pfau, Anton, 23
Pfau, Antreen McDonnell, President's Award, wife of John M., 23, 83, 121, 285, 343, 397, 416, 442, 497
Pfau, Ellen, 23, 442
Pfau, John M., President, 9, 15, 21, 171-73, 184, 200, 264, 267-68, 285, 343, 367, 397, 416, 421, 442, 474
  administration, 23-169
  affirmative action, 59, 65, 80, 87-88, 99, 114, 132, 149, 153, 165
  inauguration, 40
  personal background, 24
  President Emeritus, 173
  retirement, 169
  retirement dinner, 168
Pfau, Madelaine, 23, 442
Pfautsch, Lloyd, composer, 274

Pfeiffer, Carl C., pharmacologist, 124, 134
Phat Cat Swingers, musical group, 403, 423, 433
Phelps, Chris, Pres., ASI, 491
Phi Beta Delta, honor society, 319, 372, 472
Phi Beta Sigma, 209
Phi Delta Kappa, education honor society, 263, 268
Phi Delta Phi, French honor society, 65
Phi Kappa Phi, honor society, 139
Phil Salazar Band, musical group, 222, 232, 254
Philibert, Gena, student, 264
Philippe Vieux Quartet, musical group, 321
Phillips, D. Z., philosopher, 149, 195, 218, 218
Phillips, Karen, violinist, 62
Phillips, Kenneth, Exec. Dean, 9, 25-26, 28, 32, 36, 46, 82, 97, 167, 482
Phillips, Kevin, TV newsman, 247
Phillips, Paul, singer, 227
Phillips, Randee, writer, 277
Phillips, Scott, Outstanding Student, 493
Phillips-Thornburgh, Maurita, soprano, 162
Phillipsen, Juanita, soprano, 102
Philosophy Forum, 47
Physical Education (and Recreation) Building, 14, 39, 45, 53, 200-01, 261, 281, 300, 317, 329, 433
Physical Education (and Recreation), Dept. of, 34, 140, 212, 325
Physical Planning and Development, Office of, 247, 366
Physical Plant Building, 14, 17, 34, 42, 51-52, 55-56, 99, 193, 325
Physical Plant, Dept. of, 366
Physical Science(s) Building, 14, 17, 35, 39-41, 46, 49, 51, 63, 171, 234-35, 404, 415, 434, 446, 449
Pi Lambda Theta, education honor society, 49, 263
Pi Iota Chapter of Alpha Kappa Delta, 85
Pia, Ned, *Riverside Press-Enterprise*, 131
Picasso, Pablo, artist, 150

Pickens, William H., Dir., California Postsecondary Education Commission, 231
Picker, Robert D., Dean, Instruction, Dean, Academic Planning, 59, 77, 475
Pick-Up Players, theatre group, 135
Piedmont Dr., 14, 31
Piel, Marion, Accounting Clerk, 188
Pierce, Frederick W. IV, CSU Trustee, 374
Pierce, Pamela, speaker, 396
Pierce, Thomas J., Prof., Assoc. Dean, Undergraduate Programs, Act. Dean, Undergraduate Programs, Act. Dean, Social and Behavioral Sciences, 192, 201, 232, 312, 479-80
Piercy, Richard, student, 165
Pierson, James C., Prof., 126, 412
Pigeon, Renée M., Prof., 341, 490
Pilgrim Award, 295
Pilot Vision (Magness), 453
Pimentel, O. Ricardo, Editor, *San Bernardino Sun*, 330, 350
PIMS personnel and payroll system, 116
Pinch, Tom, artist, 421
Pinckney, Martha, speaker, 354
Pine Room, Commons, 12, 212
Pine, Stanley H., speaker, 263
"Pinecones and Pineapples" fundraising event, 430, 433
Pines, Burt, L.A. City Attorney, 105
Pinkett, Randal, speaker, 449
"Pioneer Alumni" celebration, 397
Pioneer Awards Dinner, 378
Piper, Monica, comedienne, 230
Pipher, Mary, psychologist, 352
Pipkin, Johnny W., student, 117
Pinsky, Robert, poet, 224
Pirelli, Gianna, pianist, 195-96
Pisano, Jane G., speaker, 252
Pisciotta, Eva Mae, Music, 445
Planned Parenthood World Population, 57, 320
Plant/Central Warehouse Building, 14
Plant, W. T., psychologist, 126
Plantinga, Alvin, philosopher, 388
Platske, Lisa Marie, speaker, 438-39
Plaut, Samuel M., Dir., Student Health Center, 36, 117, 438, 486

Players of the Pear Garden, 41
Playing Fields, 152
Plaza, Commons, 212
Plimpton, George, actor, 213
Plotkin, H. M. "Hank," speaker, 145
Plowman, Sharon, speaker, 319
Pocock, John G. A., historian, 40
Podolske, Diane, Dir., CSUSB's Community-University Partnerships and Service Learning Programs, 470
Poetry Society of America, 351
Polek, Fran, 506
Police Explorer Post 308, 454
"The Politics of Change: Becoming a Whole Language Teacher," conference, 271
Pollak, Jenifer, speaker, 156
Pollard, Velma, speaker, 224
Pollin, Robert, speaker, 216
Polmar, Norman, Ed., *Jane's Fighting Ships*, 114
Polyhedra, musical group, 261
Pomona Valley Writers' Assoc., 255
Poncho Sánchez and His Latin Jazz/Soul Ensemble, musical group, 252, 363
Ponder, Bill, speaker, 237
Pontiac Hot Wheels Fest '96, 324
Poole Sisters, musical group, 193
Poolswasdi, Amara, speaker, 452
Pope-Ludlam, Valerie, Housing Coalition Chair, SB City Councilwoman, 96, 309
Popkin, Maggie, attorney, 203
Popular Demand, musical group, 276, 286, 296, 306, 316, 325, 374
Porio, Emma, economist, 406
Porras Campos, Alberto, student, 114
Porras, Jerry, speaker, 252-53
Porras, Ramiro Jr., Dir., Liaison Office for 59 Hispanic-Serving Institutions in Southern Calif., 417
Porter, Cati, poet, 431
Porter, Cheryl, student, 46
Porter, David O., Prof., Dean, School of Business and Public Administration, 221, 294, 477
Porter, Eric, Outstanding Student, 493
Porter, Lee I., Dean, Continuing Education, 161, 200, 324, 345, 479
Portillo, Luis, Pres., ASI, 492

Portland Cement Co., 413
Potter, Ellis, clarinetist, 61
Potter, Kristine L., Outstanding Student, 493
Potter, Vernon F. Jr., CAB Member, 60, 499
Poussaint, Alvin, speaker, 184
Pow Wow of the San Manuel Band of Mission Indians, 376, 386, 395, 405, 415, 425-26, 435, 448, 462
Powell, Beverly, speaker, 254
Powell, Dennis, attorney, 75
Powell, Judith, Kinesiology, 445
Powell, Susan, Outstanding Student, 495
"The Power of Literature: In the Midst of a Revolution," conference, 238
Power Trip, musical group, 271
Pravdo, Steven, speaker, 350
Prenzlow, Alethea J. "Lea," Secretary, 130
Prendergast, Thomas, speaker, 380
Prescott, Bruce, Pres., ASB, 87, 491
Presidential Investment Fund, 404
Presidential Scholars Endowment, 334
Presidential Selection Advisory Committee, 169
President's Academic Excellence Scholarship Program (PAES), 434, 442, 447
President's Dining Room, Commons, 212
President's Distinguished Achievement Awards, 343
President's Higher Education Community Service Honor Roll, 452, 467
"President's Premiere" series, 130
Presley, Robert B., State Sen., 111-12, 123, 130, 132, 154
Press, Gerald A., speaker, 127
Press, Thelma, campus booster, 290
Preston, Kelly C., student, 180
Preston, Michael, Dir., Upward Bound Program, 113, 130
Pretzel, Paul, co-Dir., L.A. Suicide Center, 68
Preucil Family Players, musical group, 226
Preucil, William, violinist, 204
"The Prevention of Crimes Against People," conference, 144

Previti, James, UAB Member, 500
Price, Charles Gower, oboist, 75
Price, Gregory L., Prof., Coach, 207, 473
Price, Helisi, speaker, 241
Price, Reginald L., Prof., Athletic Dir., 192, 250, 412, 488
The Prickly Pear (campus magazine), 58
Prieto, Dora J., campus booster, 407
Prince Frosty and the Bed-Rock Posse, musical group, 286, 315
Prince, Gerald, speaker, 157
Prince, Ralph, SB City Attorney, 100
The Princeton Review (magazine), 424-25, 435, 445, 448, 459
"The Principal's Role in Conflict Management," conference, 69
Pringle, Cynthia E. "Cindi," Dir., Media Relations and Public Information, Dir., Public Relations, Exec. Dir. and Manager, TV station KCSB-TV, Assoc. VP, Development, 220, 384, 473, 487-88
Printing Services, 458
Pritchard, Jerrold E. "Jerry," Assoc. VP, Academic Programs, 188, 221, 361, 403, 475
Pritchett, Anthony, Parking Services, 473
Procida, Richard, speaker, 300
Proctor, Tom, speaker, 99
Profant, Michele, 155
Professional Excellence Award, 265
Professional Firefighters Union Local 891, 460
"Professors for a Day" program, 395
Profeta, Ron, Act. Dir., Parking Services, 471
"Project Cornerstone: Building for the 21st Century" (Strategic Planning Steering Council), 331
Project MAESTRO, 72
Project Upbeat, 202, 293
"The Promise of Women Leaders in Politics," roundtable, 450
Prouty, H. Stephen Jr., Dir. & Assoc. Dean, Admissions & Records, Assoc. Dean, Academic Programs, 33, 36, 57, 188-89, 278, 391, 475, 486
Provenza, Paul, comedian, 219

Provonsha, Jack, Center for Bioethics, 213
Proxmire, William, US Sen., 224
Prudholm, Homer O., Building Maintenance, 473
Prutsman, Deborah, singer, 401, 472
Prutsman, Stephen, pianist, 99, 282, 319
Psalm 150, musical group, 96
Psychedelic Shock—America and the Home Front (musical), 67
Public Administration, Dept. of, 189
Public Affairs, Office of, 220, 405
Public Broadcasting Service, 342
Public Employees Coordinating Council of San Bernardino-Riverside Counties, 112
Public Information Office, 247
Public Policy Institute of California, 460
Public Relations Office, 286
Public Safety Academy, 454
Public Safety Building, 347
Public Safety, Dept. of, 180, 232, 366
Publications Office, 220
Pueblo Eagle Dancers, 294
Pugh, Willard, 272
Purdue University, 132
Purvis, S. E. Claire, Prof., 432
Pytlak, Sheryl, Dir., Accounting, 445, 482
Pyzow, Melvin, speaker, 203
Quanstrom, Patricia A. "Pat," Accounting Manager, Act. Dir., Accounting, 61, 299, 307, 482
Quarter system, 376, 447
Quarton, Barbara A., Libn., 450
Queener-Shaw, Janice, speaker, 196
Quelle, Herbert, German Consul, 193
Quiel, Gordon, UAB Member, SB City Councilman, 180, 200, 221, 499
Quimby, John P., State Assemblyman, 31, 40, 43, 61, 88-89
Quinn, Colin, comedian, 279
Quinn, Noel, printmaker, 93
Quinn, Robert W., speaker, 89
Quinones, Sam, *L.A. Times* reporter, 437
Quinto, Ray, UAB & PAC Member, Assemblyman, 334, 378, 500
R. D. and Joan Dale Hubbard Foundation, 349
R. O. Boyette Co., builders, 45
Rabin, Yitzhak, Israeli Prime Minister, 75
Racina, Thom, writer, 438
"Racism in America," forum, 303
Racobs, William Carroll, student, 115
Racoosin, Charles, SB builder, 26
Radio station, campus, 199—see also: KSSB
Radio Times (magazine), 98
Radomski, James, pianist, 363
Radomski, Teresa, singer, 363
Rael, Jon, musician, 194
Ragan, Zoe, speaker, 194
Rager, Kathleen Williams, Alumni Award, 496
Raghavan, Ramnad, drummer, 158
Rainbow Players, theatre group, 118
"Rainbows to Understanding Children Conference," 468
Raines, Leonard, poet, 360
Raines, Marcia Luna, Prof., 394, 424, 501
The Rainmaker (Nash), 77
Rajabhat Rajanagarindra University, Thailand, 415
Ralph, Johnnie Ann, Libn., Assoc. Library Dir., Library Dir., University Libn., Library Dean, 9, 244, 247, 250, 297, 323, 409, 421, 427, 427, 432-33, 450, 481, 506
Ralphs, John C. Jr., Mayor, SB, 504
Ramage, Jean C., Prof., Dean, School of Education, 276, 310, 478
Ramani, N., flautist, 78
Ramey, Estelle R., endocrinologist, 130
Ramírez, Benjamin Gómez, Lect., 350, 501
Ramírez, Enrique, speaker, 64
Ramírez, Orlando, Food Editor, *Riverside Press-Enterprise*, 350
Ramírez, Romeo, speaker, 399
Ramírez, Sarah, student, 108
Ramírez, Sylvia, Facilities Services, 423
Ramón, Esteban, folksinger, 80
Ramos, Carlos, speaker, 204
Ramos, James, Dir., San Manuel Tribal Unity and Cultural Awareness Program, 405, 414

Rampart Winds, musical group, 279
Rancho Belago Wind Ensemble, musical group, 450
Rancho Mirage, Calif., 373, 410, 416
RAND Corp., 453
Randall, John, biologist, 58
Randisi, Jennifer, Prof., 279
Randles, James, speaker, 79
Randolph, David L., Asst. Dir, EOP, 67
Ranfla González, Arturo, educator, 291, 314
Ranganathan, T., musician, 70
Rangel, Gilbert R., Financial Aid Coordinator, 58
Ransom, Peter L., speaker, 196
Raskoff, Kenneth, NBC TV executive, 214
Rasmussen Construction, builders, 168
Rasmussen, Michael D., Chief Engineer, 163
"Rat Boy" (J. Brown), 293
Ratelle, Jack, City Manager, Fontana, 137
Rather, Dan, TV newsman, 144
Raven, Arlene, artist, 93
Rawles, Dennon, dancer, 240
Rawles, Sayhber, dancer, 240
Ray Briggs and His Jazz Ensemble/Quartet, musical group, 377, 383
Rayburn, Kellie R., Lect., 377, 501
Rayson, theatrical director, 141
Razi, Ali C., Hon. Ph.D., CSU Trustee, 328, 343, 383, 497
R.B. Conclusive Inc., musical group, 181
Reading Conference, 194, 206, 217, 238, 249, 260, 271
"Reading Is Everyone's Concern," conference, 127
Reading Program, 53
"Reading, Rhythms, and Rainbows Conference," 254
Reagan, Ronald W., Gov., CA, & US Pres., 43, 56, 64, 70, 72, 79, 107, 402, 505
Reagon, Bernice Johnson, speaker, 439
REAL, musical group, 253
Reardon, James, speaker, 79
Reay, John R., mathematician, 100
Rebel Pebbles, musical group, 283
"Recent Trends in Education," conference, 97
Recht auf Gewissen (German film), 66
Recycling Center, 99
Red Breams (Stockham), 319
"Reduce, Reuse, and Recycle Conference," 167
"Reading and Writing: The Literature Connection," conference, 166
Reading Conference, 142, 159, 166, 182
"Reading to Unlock the Mysteries of History," conference, 351
Reaves, Michael, Alumni Award, writer, 270, 312, 496
Rebekah Johnson Bobbitt National Prize for Poetry, 411
Rebétez, René, writer, 339
Recchiuti, Michael, conductor, 180
Recital Hall, Performing Arts Building, 12, 14
Re-Creating Your Self (Stone), 266
Recreation Center, 380-81, 396, 418, 420
Recreational Sports Program, 217
Recycling on campus, 344
Red Buffalo, Steven, speaker, 230
Red Hot Skillet Lickers, musical group, 386
Reddy, Laxman "Lex," Alumni Award, 496
Reddy, Prem, campus booster, 424
"Redefining Latin American Identity in the 21st Century," conference, 391
Redevelopment Agency of the City of San Bernardino, 37, 104, 215
Redlands American Institute of Art Award for Architecture, 408
Redlands Daily Facts (newspaper), 38
Redlands New Music Ensemble, musical group, 407
Redlands Public Library, 323
Redlands School District, 141
Redmond, Lee, speaker, 340
Redon, Odilon, artist, 150
Redshaw, Michael, pianist, 206
Reeb, Richard, speaker, 241
Reed, Charles B., Chancellor, CSU, 341, 343, 347-48, 357-58, 364, 369, 380, 383, 407, 421, 505
Reed, James, Groundsworker, 127
Reed, Kenneth C., Instructional Support

Technician, 432
Reed, Patricia D., Lect., 423
Reed, Rhonda, speaker, 218
Reel, Madelyn, 71
Reel to Reel, musical group, 232
"Re-Envisioning Paradise," forum, 421
Reference Guide to Science Fiction, Fantasy, and Horror (Burgess), 292-95
Rega, Elizabeth, anthropologist, 313
Regional Economic Development Council, 37
Regional Educators Symposium, 251
Rego, Manuel, pianist, 363
Rehfeldt, Phillip, clarinetist, 144-45
Reich, Ken, speaker, 266
Reich, Robert, US Secretary of Labor, 293
Reichel, Carmela, speaker, 471
Reid, Suzanne, Outstanding Student, 493
Reider, D. Brian, Alumni Award, UAB & PAC Member, 496, 500
Reilly, Jack, SB City Councilman, 245
Reinecke, Edwin, Lt. Gov., CA, 505
Reingold (Newmannis), 85
Reis, Tim, guitarist, 289
Reisert, Allan, clarinetist, 128
Reisner, Mark, speaker, 363
Reiss, Roland, painter, 330
Rejali, Ali, Outstanding Student, 494
"Relieving African Famine," conference, 217
Renaissance Banquet, 93, 151
The Renaissance Group, 261, 286
"Renaissance Month," 99
Rennick, Dick, speaker, 444
Renolds, Robert, geologist, 50
Renouf, Renée, speaker, 75
Rentfrow, Diane, Dir., SAIL Program, 276
REO Speedwagon, musical group, 352
Repertory Theater of America, 92, 311
Research Career Integration Program, 348
Reseck, John Jr., speaker, 142
Residence Halls, 17, 66, 68, 75, 82, 87; SEE ALSO: Serrano Village
Residential Housing Services, Office of, 327
Reskin, Barbara, speaker, 238
Resnick, Jerome, speaker, 106
Resurrection Mary (film), 446
Return of Disco Korruption Mobil Disc Jockey, musical group, 249
Reveles, Nicolas, Father, pianist, 164
Reverence Singers, campus gospel group, 233, 241, 246
Revolutionary Assoc. of Women of Afghanistan, performers, 377
Rexroth, Kenneth, poet, 51
Reyes, Andrea, speaker, 463
Reyes, Joe, singer, 322
Reynolds, H. Robert, band director, 165
Reynolds, Harry, SB politician, 173
Reynolds, Verna, wife of Harry, 173
Reynolds, W. Ann, Chancellor, CSU, 172, 178, 181-82, 185, 187, 197, 209, 213, 220, 222-23, 227, 239, 243, 253, 261-63, 504
Rheubottom, Harry F., campus booster, 307
Rheubottom/Webster Local History Lecture Series, 287, 307, 323, 332, 344, 352, 362, 373, 382, 392, 401, 411, 453, 464
Rhine, Ramon, psychologist, 134
Rhodes, Anne, speaker, 125, 216
Rhodes, Daniel, artist, 194
Rhodes, Peter, speaker, 251
Rhythm of Life, musical group, 374, 433
Rialto City Unified School District Board, 108-10
Rialto Jaycees, 48
Rialto Record (newspaper), 29, 31
Rialto site, 26
Ribeau, Sidney A., Dean, Undergraduate Studies, 232, 265, 364, 480
Riccards, Michael, speaker, 239
Rice, Thomas, speaker, 270
Rich, Adrienne, poet, 180
Rich, Sharon Turner, schoolteacher, 313
Richard H. Emmons Award for Excellence in College Astronomy Teaching, 424
Richard Moseley Scholarship Fund, 326, 418
Richards, Julie Renée, student, 132
Richards, Margaret, Lib. Asst., 188, 313

Richardson, Bonham, Prof., 72
Richardson, Norma, performer, 306
Richerson, Steve "Trash," magician, 293, 303
Richie, Jeanette, CSUC Trustee, 104
Richter, Charles F., seismologist, 31
Richters, Ken, actor, 173
Rick and the Recuperators, musical group, 286
Rick, Gordon, physician, 123
Rickman, Geraldine, Pres., COPE Foundation, 61
Ricks, Elvin, Rev., 216
Ridder, Herman H., CSC Trustee, 40
Ride, Dale B., CSU Trustee, 209, 220, 238
Ridley, Yvonne, reporter, 422
Riefer, David M. L., Prof., 291, 321, 350, 360, 490
Rigdon, Florence, campus booster, 358, 378
Riggins, Paul L., speaker, 79
"The Rights of Prisoners," panel, 71
Riles, Wilson, State Superintendent of Public Instruction, 68, 102
Riley, Judith Merkle, writer, 277
Riley, Linda Long, Instructor, 222
Riley, Pat, basketball coach, 248
Riley, Richard, US Secretary of Education, 293
Riley, Tim, bagpiper, 441, 454
Rim High School Concert Band, musical group, 305
Rincón, Frank L., VP, Student Services, 9, 308, 485
"Ring Cycle" (Wagner), 118
Rinker-Morris, Donovan, Outstanding Student, 493
Rinne, Dan, Prof., 280, 368
Ríos, Frances, Secretary, 29, 45
Ríos, Francisco, student, 345
Ríos, Reyes E., Groundsworker, 221
Ripston, Ramona, speaker, 392
Ritcheson, Charles R., speaker, 89
Ritchey, Jim, booster, 119
Ritchie, Jim, speaker, 378
Ritchie, Ward, publisher, 50
Rittenburg, Lee, attorney, 380
Rivera, Eloisa, Pres., MEChA, 253
Rivera, Filiberto H., 126
Rivera, John Anthony, student, 178

Rivera, Tom M., Prof., Assoc. Dean, Students, Assoc. Dean, Educational Opportunity Program, Assoc. Dean, Special Services, Assoc. Dean, Educational Support Services, Assoc. Dean, Educational Programs, Int. Dean, Undergraduate Studies, 86, 125, 153, 160-61, 180, 199, 216, 261, 278, 346, 380, 447, 480, 485
Rivera, Tracie, Outstanding Student, 494
Riverside Chamber of Commerce, 27, 186
Riverside City College Wind Ensemble, 137
Riverside Community College, 250, 446, 451, 454
Riverside Community Hospital, 414
Riverside Concert Band, 120, 162, 177
Riverside County, Calif., 377, 422
Riverside County Sheriff's Dept., 471
Riverside Foundation, 56, 63
Riverside Light Opera, 407
Riverside Opera Assoc., 159
Riverside Police Dept., 377
Riverside Press-Enterprise (newspaper), 32, 111, 131, 350
Rivkin, Ellis, speaker, 238
Rizzo, Terry L., Prof., 287, 330, 490
Roach, Fred, Dean, Continuing Education, 59, 103-04, 479
Roadarmel, Norman P., speaker, 81
Robb, Jane, Calif. Teachers' Assoc., 468
The Robber Bridegroom (Uhry & Waldman), 148
Robbin, Alexandra, writer, 190
Robbins, Alan, State Sen., 145
Roberson, Maurice, speaker, 216
Robert H. Carleton Award, 441
Robert Kyle Latin/Brazilian Project, performers, 440
Robert Noyce Scholarship, 427
Robert V. Fullerton Art Museum, 12, 14, 18, 298, 305, 308, 311, 327, 349, 358, 370, 412, 414, 416, 425, 435, 443, 447, 450, 452, 458, 473
Roberts, Donald, singer, 125
Roberts, Jeanne Gordon, Secretary, 439
Roberts, Lauren Elizabeth, student, 426
Roberts, Lee D., Alumni Award, 496

Roberts, Richard, speaker, 97
Roberts, Robert R., Prof., Chair, Social Sciences Div., 29, 33, 35-36, 55, 71, 77, 193, 478, 501
Roberts, Terrence "Little Rock Nine," activist, 386, 398
Robertshaw, Peter T., Prof., 279, 313, 320, 374, 379, 490
Robertson, Cindy, SB Sun writer, 281
Robertson, Phil, speaker, 309
Robertson, R. Joy, Purchasing Officer, Business Services Officer, 40, 137-38, 483
Robinette, Toni L., Alumni Award, 496
Robins, Joan, speaker, 120
Robinson, Barbara, 83
Robinson, Daniel, Music Technician, 460
Robinson, Darryl, performer, 321
Robinson, J. Cordell, VP, Academic Affairs, VP, Academic Personnel, 137, 143, 145, 153, 188, 199, 202, 211, 301, 348, 350, 355, 476, 501
Robinson, James, UAB Member, 499
Robinson, James L., Ethnic Studies Coordinator, 97
Robinson, James M., religious historian, 151
Robinson, John, football coach, 270
Robinson, Randall, writer, 350
Robinson, Robert, speaker, 268
Robinson, Sidney A. "Sid," Dir., Asst. VP, Public Affairs, 9, 384, 417, 488
Robinson-Silas, Dorothy, Custodian, 258
Robles, Ernesto Z., Dir., National Hispanic Scholarship Fund, 283, 333, 343
Robles, Mike, comedian, 393
Robles, Rudolpho, Alumni Award, 495
Robot Olympics, 208, 218
Robotics Technology Workshop, 193
Rocha, Collette, Executive Dir., University Development, 319
Rocha, Jill E., Physician, Act. Dir. & Dir., Student Health Center, 278-79, 296-97, 299, 486
Roche, Joanna, Dir., Alumni Affairs, 211, 243
Rochín, Refugio, speaker, 373
Rockwell International Science Center, 128
Rocky Mountain News, musical group, 71
Roddick, Laird, speaker, 64
Rodelinda (Handel), 180
Rodgers-Gordon, Patricia, Act. Dir., Dir., Career Development Center, 290, 407
Rodman, Joan, psychologist, 398
Rodríguez, Anna María, Alumni Award, 496
Rodríguez, Carolyn B., Prof., 210
Rodríguez, Emerenciano, Mexican Consul, 181, 219, 233
Rodríguez, Frank, speaker, 207
Rodríguez, John H., Asst. Undersecretary, U.S. Dept. of Education, 166
Rodríguez, Julia Chávez, daughter of César Chávez, 429
Rodríguez, Luis J., writer, 401
Rodríguez, Olga, labor activist, 84
Rodríguez, Ramona, Facilities Services, 445
Rodríguez, Robert, magician, 300
Rodríguez, Terri Ann, crime victim, 255
Rodrigo, Joaquín, composer, 74
Rogers, James G., Prof., Dir., Inland Empire Management Center, 115, 373
Rogers, Jim, campus booster, 299
Rogers, John S., campus booster, 315, 328
Rogers, Linda M., Supervisor, Records, Registration, and Evaluation, 423, 468
Rogers, Martha, speaker, 369
Rogers, Mary Stuart, campus booster, 328
Rogers, Patrick, Building Service Engineer, 404
Rohde, Jerry, Pres., ASB, 491
Rohm, C. E. Tapie Jr., Prof., 242, 301, 468, 489-90
Rojas, Armando R., Groundsman, 296
"The Role of Education in the Acculturation of the Black Family," seminar, 146
"The Roles of Women in Science," workshop, 130
Rolfe, Franklin P., Prof., UCLA, 61
Rollings Stars, basketball team, 152
Rollins, Erin, student, 44, 49

Rolston, Dave, member, CVC Advisory Board, 303
Romanovsky, Ron, singer, 227
Rome Prize, 303
Romero, Diego, speaker, 307
Romero, Gloria, State Sen., 468
Romero, Sam, Public Affairs Media Specialist, 9
Romero, Valerie, UAB Member, 500
Romo, Barry, National Chair, Vietnam Veterans Against the War, 91
Romo, Richard, political candidate, 68
Ron McCurdy and His Jazz Quintet/Quartet, musical group, 430, 455
Ronald E. Barnes Theatre, 11, 14, 398
Ronald E. McNair Post Baccalaureate Achievement Program, 318, 353, 378, 435
Rood, Harold W., speaker, 167
Rooney, Andy, TV personality, 159
Roosevelt, Jan, Southern California Edison Co., 282
Roosevelt University, 394
Rosalind (play), 92
Rosas, Olivia, Act. Assoc. VP, Enrollment Services, 467, 486
Roscoe, Will, speaker, 256
Rose Brown Expandable Scholarship Fund, 369
Rose, Lillian Roybal, speaker, 270
Rose, Michael M., Relations-with-Schools Officer, 86, 109, 188-89
Rose, Nancy E., Prof., 473
Rosen, Jim, painter, 125
Rosen, Nathaniel, cellist, 72
Rosenberg, Howard, TV critic, 229
Rosenberg, Richard, speaker, 258
Rosenberg, Stephen, speaker, 97
Rosenthal, Daniel, speaker, 127
Ross, Duane, performer, 306
Ross, Leonard, speaker, 322
Ross, Michael L., Int. Dir. & Dir., Academic Computing and Media, 349, 365, 488
Ross, Robert H., Prof., Chair, Humanities Div., 36, 42, 477
Rossetti Construction Co., builders, 63
Rotaru, Cornelia, Romanian Chamber of Commerce official, 411
Rotary Club (SB), 331
ROTC (Reserve Officer Training Corps) Program, 154, 158, 271, 273, 295
Roth, Howard L., speaker, 300, 329, 340
Roth, Joe, speaker, 241
Roto Rooter Good Time Christmas Band, 111
Rounds, Donald E., biologist, 57
Rousseau, Hector, speaker, 123
Rowe, Jesse C., Stationary Engineer, 52
Rose, Joseph A., campus booster, 362, 364, 437
Rowell, Vernon Frank, student, 133
Rowland, Richard H., Prof., 126, 204, 432, 490
Rowse, A. L., historian, 49
Roy C. Barnett Co., builders, 57, 68, 71, 129
Roybal, Fred, Supervising Electrician, 432
Rozum, Tom, performer, 445
Rubel, Robert J., speaker, 158
Ruben S. Ayala Scholarship, 376
Rubenstein, Moshe, speaker, 120
Rubin, Irv, Dir., Jewish Defense League, 359
Rubinsteen, Jason, speaker, 255
Rubio, Ruby, student, 95
Rucker, Christi, Prof., 411
Ruderman, Naomi, Coach, 196
Rudisill, Amanda Sue, Prof., 160, 334, 436
Ruether, Rosemary, speaker, 311
Ruffino, Kent Devol, student, 383
Ruiz, Eliseo G., CAB Member, 499
Ruiz, Roseanna, Dir., Financial Aid., 423
Rumelhart, Donald, psychologist, 134
"Rumi Conference," 369
Ruml, Beardsley, education planner, 32
Ruml Plan, 16, 32, 35-36, 220, 255
Ruml, Treadwell "Ted," Prof., 354, 489
Rush, Cherlynn A., Outstanding Student, 493
Rush, Harold J. "Skip," Pres., ASB, 491
Russell, Jeffrey Burton, speaker, 250
Rutan, Richard, pilot, 228
Rutherford, Robert D., speaker, 98
Ryan, Beverly A., Libn., 306
Ryan, John, Rev., minister, 40
Ryan, Robin, writer, 342

Rydell, Mireille G. "Mimi," Prof., 243
Ryder, Oliver A., speaker, 369
Ryland, Elisabeth K., Prof., 432
Rymer, Glenn G., Alumni Award, 150, 495
Rymer, Judith M., Prof., Act Exec. Dean & Exec. Dean, University Relations, VP, University Relations, PAC Member, 201, 210-11, 246, 287, 346, 353, 384, 487, 489, 500
Saavedra, Richard, speaker, 274
Sabsevitz, Al, UAB Member, 500
Sachdev, G. S., flautist, 94
Sacks, Karen Brodkin, speaker, 237
Sacksteder, William, philosopher, 128
Sacramento Bee (newspaper), 291
Saenger, Ted J., CSU Trustee, 260
Safford, John, alumnus author, 270
Safirov, Andrei G., speaker, 301
Sahl, Mort, satirist, 83
Saigon Post (newspaper), 48
SAIL Program (Student Assistance in Learning), 161, 181, 211, 221, 249, 276, 295, 334
Sailor, Wayne, speaker, 225
Saiz Huedo, Jesús, guitarist, 392
Saladino, Jean, singer, 285
Salary freeze, 451
Salas, Richard "Dickie," student, 129
Salcedo, Antonio, Outstanding Student, 495
Saleson, Stephen, PAC Member, 500
Salmi, Ralph H., Prof., 359, 432
Salsa Brava, musical group, 119
Salsgiver, Richard, speaker, 294
Saltman, Paul D., Provost, Revelle College, UC San Diego, 85
Saltzman, Alice, healer, 240
Saltzman, Arthur I., Prof., 208, 361
Salus, Peter H., speaker, 234
Salzgiver, Richard, speaker, 304
Salzman, Charles, book dealer, 208
Same Way Again, musical group, 388
San Andreas Fault, 29, 56
San Bernardino Airport, 26
San Bernardino Associated Governments, 471
San Bernardino Bar Assoc., 130
San Bernardino Bicentennial Parade, 471
San Bernardino Board of Education, 245
San Bernardino Business and Professional Women's Club, 137
San Bernardino, Calif., 29, 35, 375, 395, 465
San Bernardino Catholic Diocese, 389, 421
San Bernardino Central Credit Union, 198
San Bernardino Chamber of Commerce, 26, 41, 45, 156, 204, 281, 309, 316, 332
San Bernardino Chamber of Commerce Business Outlook Conference, 256
San Bernardino Chess Club, 114
San Bernardino Cinco de Mayo Parade, 143
San Bernardino City Board of Water Commissioners, 27
San Bernardino City Council, 27-29, 31-34, 40, 200, 387, 417
San Bernardino City Development and Environmental Review Committee, 378
San Bernardino City Hall, 121-22
San Bernardino City Planning Commission, 34, 144, 192, 385
San Bernardino City School District, 32
San Bernardino City Unified School District, 109, 163
San Bernardino City Water Commission, 112
San Bernardino Community Choir, 148, 193
San Bernardino Community Concert Band, 221
San Bernardino Convention Center, 116
San Bernardino County Academic Decathlon, 359
San Bernardino County Board of Supervisors, 27, 29, 31-35, 40, 105, 124, 137
San Bernardino County Children's Fund, 441
San Bernardino County Courthouse, 60
San Bernardino County Fair, 37
San Bernardino County Heart Association, 114, 118
San Bernardino County Job and Employment Dept., 294
San Bernardino County Medical Center,

105
San Bernardino County Museum, 280, 362
San Bernardino County Museum Assoc., 45
San Bernardino County Music Educators Assoc., 108
San Bernardino County Planning Commission, 34
San Bernardino County Probation Dept., 393
San Bernardino County Schools, 367
San Bernardino County Sheriff's Office, 146
San Bernardino County Unified School District, 427
"San Bernardino County Water Conference," 433
San Bernardino Desert Mountain Chapter of Phi Delta Kappa, 268
San Bernardino District 21 Women's Clubs, 39
"San Bernardino Economic Summit," 309
San Bernardino Fine Arts Commission, 214, 375
San Bernardino Fire Dept., 296
San Bernardino High School, 273
San Bernardino Junior Women's Club, 39
San Bernardino Mountains, 249, 344, 395
San Bernardino Municipal Water District, 353
San Bernardino Music Teachers Assoc., 214
San Bernardino Police Dept., 436
San Bernardino Postal Employees Black Heritage Committee, 321
San Bernardino Rape Crisis and Assault Services Program, 146
San Bernardino-Riverside Counties Industry-Education Council, 114
San Bernardino site for state college, 26, 28, 30, 33
San Bernardino Spirit, baseball team, 280
San Bernardino Sun(-Telegram) (newspaper), 6, 9, 28, 35-37, 45, 83, 86, 96, 111, 123, 131, 139, 146, 150, 155, 168, 183-84, 210, 213-14, 226, 231, 264, 280-81, 305, 330, 350, 369, 421, 439, 450
San Bernardino Tennis Championships, 92
San Bernardino Unified School District, 367, 421
San Bernardino Valley Alumnae Chapter, Pi Lambda Theta, 49
San Bernardino Valley College, 27, 32, 62, 91, 98, 106, 394, 406
San Bernardino Valley College MEChA, 159
San Bernardino Valley Municipal Water Dist., 472
San Bernardino Valley Water Conservation Garden, 472
San Bernardino West Side Youths, 67
San Bernardino Youth Symphony Orchestra, 104, 113
San Diego Express, wheelchair basketball team, 319, 329
San Diego Navy Brass Quintet, musical group, 244
San Diego Presidio Brass Quintet, musical group, 467
San Diego State University Balinese Gamelan Ensemble, 157
San Diego State University Faculty Trio, 167
San Francisco Mime Troupe, 55
San Francisco Museum of Modern Art, 227
San Gorgonio High School, 75
San Gorgonio Land Co., 498
San Jose State University, 29
San Manuel Band of Serrano Mission Indians, 367, 376, 386, 391, 393, 395, 405, 409, 415, 425-26, 435, 440, 448, 462
San Manuel Hall, Serrano Village, 14, 17, 87
San Manuel Indian Bingo and Casino, 377
San Timoteo Canyon, 160
San-Val Air Conditioning/Engineering, builders, 160, 195
Sánchez, Adrián, UAB Member, 310, 319, 500
Sánchez, Aurora, 126
Sánchez, Elizabeth, speaker, 389
Sánchez, Francisca, Asst. Superinten-

dent for Curriculum and Instruction, SB County Schools, 383
Sánchez, Georgiana Valoyce, poet, 248
Sánchez, Gilbert, Coordinator, Student Affirmative Action Program, 178
Sánchez, J. M. "Manny," CVC Advisory Board member, 275
Sánchez, Loretta, US Rep., 412
Sánchez, Mary, speaker, 69
Sánchez, Poncho, musician, 252, 363
Sánchez, Rudolph, Outstanding Student, 493
Sánchez, Wallace A., Alumni Award, 495
Sanders, Al, attorney, 80
Sanders, James A., speaker, 282
Sanders, John, speaker, 248
Sanders, Kristen, Lib. Asst., 438
Sando, James F., Exec. Dir., Foundation, 390, 483
Sandos, James, historian, 323
Sandoval, James, speaker, 367
Sandoval, José, pianist, 294
Sandoval, Patricia Márquez, Alumni Award, 496
Santa Cruz Writers' Union Poetry Competition, 195
Santana, Richard, speaker, 349
Santiago, Rowena S., Prof., Dir., Faculty Development Program and Teaching Resource Center, 325-26, 481
Santillán, Richard, speaker, 456
Santimaw, Victoria, Outstanding Student, 494
Santos, Gonzalo, 376
Santos Manuel Student Union, 14, 18, 393, 404-05, 420
Santos Manuel Student Union Courtyard, 12
Santos Manuel Student Union Events Center, 12
Santos Manuel Student Union Multipurpose Room, 12
Santos Manuel Student Union Patio, 12
Santos Manuel Student Union Theater, 12
Santos, Pearl, student, 373
Santos, Sherrod M., Prof. and poet, 182, 186, 220, 252
Saperstein, David, Rabbi, 350
Sapp, Bill, historian, 470
Sapronetti, Donald E., Accounting Officer, 92, 299, 482
Sargent, Anneila, astronomer, 401
Sargent, Lydia, comedienne, 313
Sarmiento, Sam, Police Sergeant, 9
Sarpong, Edmund, speaker, 348
Sartor, Joseph R., Tractor Operator, 144-45
Sartre, Jean-Paul, writer, 41
Sarunay Filipino American Music Ensemble, musical group, 377
Satellite receiving dish, 206
Satie, Erik, composer, 118
Satir, Virginia, psychotherapist, 191
Saturday Night Live (TV show), 333
Saubel, Katherine Siva, playwright, 367
Savage, James R., Dir., Student Health Center, 184, 187, 190, 231, 415, 486
Savage, Karen, speaker, 347
Savage, Phil III, PAC Member, 500
Savala, Lydia, speaker, 164
Save Ferris, musical group, 353, 358, 372
Saylor, Richard S., Prof., 60, 71, 118, 275, 465, 469, 502
Scanlon, James J., Dir., Computing and Information Management Services, 222, 489
Scarborough, Danny, actor, 148, 157
Schaefer, Halmuth H., psychologist, 57
Schafer, Rudolph, speaker, 215
Schaffer, Karl, dancer, 312
Schaffner Players, theater group, 61
Schalow, Christine M., Prof., 432
Schalow, David L., Prof., 432
Scharpf, Fritz W., business analyst, 229
Scharrón, Eladio, guitarist, 442
Schattschneider, Doris, speaker, 281
Scheff, Thomas, sociologist, 126
Schefter, James, speaker, 332
Scheinberg, Seymour, speaker, 94
Scherba, Coral Elise, 171
Scherba, Coral Matthews, 171
Scherba, Gerald M., Prof., VP, Academic Affairs, VP in Charge, Chairman, Natural Sciences Div., Dir., Desert Studies Consortium, 16, 25-26, 28, 36, 42, 45, 52, 127, 169, 177, 189, 199, 201, 205, 275, 370, 474-75, 477, 502

administration as VP in Charge, 170-74
personal background, 171
Scherba, Julia Ann, 171
Scherba, Rachel, 171
Schettino, Macarión, journalist, 454
Schienle, Jan, speaker, 263
Schiff, Gert, art historian, 148
Schille, Carol, painter, 49
Schincke, Ward, speaker, 183
Schindler's List (Keneally), 311
Schisgal Touring Theatre Group, 150
Schlepelern, Peter, speaker, 234
Schlicker pipe organ, 139
Schmidhauser, John R., US Rep., 105
Schmitt, Brandii, student, 240
Schmitz, John G., US Rep., 105
Schnabel, Barbara Ann, student, 403
Schnarre, George H., Arrowhead Award, PAC Member, real estate broker, 419, 498, 500
Schneider, Edward L., speaker, 248
Schneiderhan, Edward J., Counselor, 412
Schnitzer, Mark, UAB Member, 500
Scocozza, Matthew V., speaker, 256
Schofield, Kent M., Prof., Assoc. Dean, Academic Planning, 9, 55, 86, 93, 97, 122, 195, 373, 382, 480
Scholarship Golf Classic, 314
School of Library Science, University of Southern California, 50
Schorr, Lisbeth B., speaker, 346
Schrag, Peter, speaker, 356
Scribner, John A., Prof., 403
Schrock, Thomas S., speaker, 186
Schroeder, Peter R., Prof., 6, 9, 156, 393
Schul, Patrick L., speaker, 196
Schultz, Andrew, Prof., 214
Schumaker, Christopher, sculptor, 249
Schwabe, Robert A., Dir., Institutional Research, 59, 70, 365, 481
Schwandt, Jolene, singer, 146
Schwartz, Gary, Women's Basketball Coach, 281
Schwartz, Howard, speaker, 146
Schwarzenegger, Arnold, actor, Gov., CA, 396, 403-05, 505
Schwegler, Armin, speaker, 471
Schweiger, Heinrich, actor, 66

Schweitzer Auditorium, Visual Arts Center—SEE: Seymour and Mignon Schweitzer Auditorium
Schweitzer, C. R., psychiatrist, 73
Schweitzer, Mignon M., UAB Member, 354, 499
Schweitzer, Seymour, campus booster, 354
Schwennesen Collection of Egyptian Artifacts, 435
Schwichtenberg, Cathy, speaker, 250
Schwitzgebel, Robert, psychologist, 74, 81
Science and Activity-Cafeteria Building, 34
Science Day, 49, 57, 125
Science Education Conference, 247
Science Fiction and Fantasy Literature (Burgess), 158
Science Fiction Research Assoc., 295
Science, Mathematics, and Technical Education, Dept. of, 325
Science Parking Lot, 14, 49, 51, 54, 59, 61, 173, 183, 233-34, 428
Scientific Methods Inc., 116
Sciortino, Victor, Outstanding Student, 494
Sconza, Julie, speaker, 256
Scott, Brian, singer, 442
Scott, Chuck, photojournalist, 94
Scott, Doris, Secretary, 138
Scott, Gerry III, speaker, 282
Scott, Larry B., 272
Scott O'Dell Award, 407
Scott, Samuel C., Alumni Award, 496
Scott, Wayne, CAB & UAB Member, 198, 499-500
Scovel, Helga E.—SEE: Kray, Helga E.
Scribe, Eugène, writer, 132, 152
Scriven, Michael, philosopher, 57
Scrugg Sisters, musical group, 321
Schuiling, Ty, Dir., Policy and Planning, S.B. Associated Governments, 471
Scully, Frank E., music teacher, 113
Schwab, Lynne Scott, student, 224
The Sea Gull (Chekhov), 131
Seaborg, Glenn T., Nobel Peace Prize winner, 242
Seal and mace, University, 183, 324
Searle, John R., philosopher, 66

Seay, Mark, football player, 408
Seccombe, Ormonde W., Mayor, SB, 504
Seccombe, William C., Mayor, SB, 504
SECHABA, musical group, 260
Sechrest, Dale K., Prof., 445
Secondary and Vocational Education, Dept. of, 255
Section 8, musical group, 284
"Secure IT Conference," 392
Security-Storage Facility, 115
Seff, Nancy, speaker, 272
Seff, Philip, speaker, 272
Segesta, James E., Libn., 30, 42, 372
Segura, Vanessa, Outstanding Student, 495
Seidenbaum, Art, Book Editor, *Los Angeles Times*, 140
Seismic Retrofitting Project, 212, 300, 303, 317, 325-26, 328, 355, 415
Seitz, Victoria A., Prof., 382
"Seminar on Criminal Justice and Anti-Terrorism," 397
Semple, Lorenzo Jr., playwright, 129
Sen, Samir K., Indian Air Force Vice Marshall, 369
Senecal, Patty, International Warehouse Logistics Assoc., 472
Senior Citizens Foundation, 360
Senn, Charles, speaker, 228
Senour, Robert A., Prof., Dir., Audio-Visual Services, 67, 121, 310, 366, 488
Sepúlveda, Juan, Dir., White House Initiative on Educational Excellence for Hispanic Americans, 469, 472-73
Sequoia String Quartet, musical group, 161
Sereerojyn, Pichai, student, 112
Serna, Pierrette M., Lect., 501
Serpico, Margaret, speaker, 449
Serrano Village Dr., 14
Serrano Village Residence Halls, 14, 17, 87, 92, 96, 161, 180, 190, 198, 229, 234, 256, 261, 266, 269, 302, 436
Services to Students with Disabilities Office, 319
"Serving the Handicapped of Our Area in Recreation and Education Conference," 193

Sesame Street Live, theatre group, 344
Sessions, Billie P., Prof., 347, 445
Sexual harassment policy, 211, 237
Sexual Harassment Prevention Week, 301
Sexual Harassment Task Group, 211
Seymour and Mignon Schweitzer Auditorium, Robert V. Fullerton Art Museum, 12, 354
Shaagnatty, musical group, 294
Shaanxi University of Science and Technology, China, 419
Shabazz, Attallah, speaker, 259
Shades of Black, theatre group, 148, 180
Shadow Mountain, musical group, 243
Shafer, R. Murray, composer, 263
Shaftel, Fanny R., education researcher, 72
Shake Mouse Band, musical group, 283
Shakespeare, William, playwright, 93, 166
Shakti Dance Company, dancers, 377
Shalchi, Hossein, Prof., 403
Shalom Club, 180
Shanachie, musical group, 254, 275
Shandin Hall, 14, 17, 87
Shandin Hills Golf Course, 210, 289
Shandin Hills Junior High Choir, 91
Shang, comedian, 302, 315
Shangasi, Vusi, speaker, 241
"Shaping Science Education to Meet the Industrial Needs of the 21st Century," conference, 314
Shapiro, Amy, speaker, 249
Shapiro, Peter, VP, Alumni Assoc., 47
Shapiro, Victoria, violist, 94
"Sharing the Waters," conference, 376
Sharp, Larry R., Hon. Ph.D., UAB & PAC Member, Arrowhead Award, Pres. & CEO, Arrowhead Credit Union, 347, 403, 497-98, 500
Shaughnessy, Charles, actor, 238
Shaw, Leila F., wife of Stanford C., 378
Shaw, Stanford C., State Sen., 20-21, 110, 292-93
Shaw, Steven, SB City Fireman, 373, 468
Shawlee, Hal P., Union Oil Co., 89
She Loves Me! She Said So! (Scribe), 152

Sheehan, Maria, Pres., College of the Desert, 383
Sheeran, Edward J., Alumni Award, USAF Col., 333, 495
Sheeran, Pat, newspaper columnist, 111
Sheffield, H. J., Pres., SBVC, 27
Sheffield, Larry, historian, 411
Sheikh Chinna Maulana, musical group, 96
Sheinfeld, Joel, speaker, 119
Sheldon, Vanessa R., harpist, 465
Sheleff, Leon, sociologist, 139
Shelley, Reed, writer, 277
Shelton, Jewel, speaker, 125
Shelton, Margaret, performer, 140
Shepard, Kathryn K. "Kathy"—SEE: Hansen, Kathryn K.
Shepherd, Morris, woodworker, 141
Sheppard, Harry R., US Rep., 35
Shepperd, Wayne, baritone, 209
Sherman, Howard, speaker, 131
Sherman Indian High School Dancers, 72
Sherman Institute, 63
Sherman, Jon, magician, 401
Sherrod, Drury, psychologist, 125, 157
Shervington, Denese, speaker, 283
Sherwin, Gary, Prof., 473
Sherwood, Brad, comedian, 429
Shew, Bobby, trumpeter, 274
Shi, Chuan-Feng, Tibetan monk, 419
Shichor, David, Prof., 334
Shields, Barbara, folksinger, 314
Shiflet, Barbara, Lect., 432
Shimakawa, Ellen, Int. Dir., Research and Sponsored Programs, 467, 476
Shimizu, Ryzoh, educator, 309
Shipping and Receiving Building—see: Warehouse Receiving
Shirfin, Avraham, speaker, 102
Shirinyan, David, UCLA Center for Autism Research and Treatment, 469
Shmueli, Efrain, philosopher, 120
Shockey, Jeffrey S., Alumni Award, 496
Shoesmith, Thomas P., U.S. State Dept., 62
Shorey, Hal, Outstanding Student, 494
Short, Rod, speaker, 233
Shoultz, Mary Jane, writer, 70, 93
Shout for Jesus—Recorded Live at Cal State (Patterson), 216
Show Me (musical), 80
Shriner, Randall Lloyd, student, 89
Shuck, Lenel, speaker, 79
Shukor, Muszaphar, astronaut, 443
Shuler, Dustin, sculptor, 249
Shum, William F. "Bill," Dir., Facility Planning and Policy Coordination, 220
Shusterman, Neal, speaker, 296
Shutt, Ronda, Outstanding Student, 494
Shved, Lyudmila, Outstanding Student, 495
Shyer, Brian, pianist, 231
"Sí Se Puede de Educación," parade float, 143
Siccone, Frank, speaker, 148
Side Street Strutters, musical group, 365, 369
Sidesaddle, musical group, 265, 287
Sierra Club, 419
Sierra Dr., 14, 433
Sierra Hall, 14, 17, 36, 298, 303
Sigma Chi, fraternity, 284-85
Sigma Chi Omicron, 209
Sigma Delta Pi, Spanish Honor Society, 45
Sigma Nu, fraternity, 271
Sigma Phi Epsilon, fraternity, 303
Sigma Xi, National Scientific Research Honor Society, 69, 230
Signer, Michael A., speaker, 282
Silcock, Lawrence, speaker, 420
Silhouette of Slavery (play), 205
Silk, Dick, speaker, 206
Sill, Roma, Extended Education, 150, 218
Sillas, Norman, speaker, 98
Sillias, Herman, Dir., State Dept. of Motor Vehicles, 97
Siporín, Ona, writer, 370
Sisto, Earl, speaker, 328
Sithole, Masipula, political scientist, 330
Silva Hidalgo, Juan Emanuel, pianist, 146
Silva, Silvia, singer, 137
Silva, Simón, artist, 332, 410
Silver C., musical group, 306
Silverston, Randy, speaker, 238
Simard, Rodney J., Prof., 255, 331

Simmons, Leroy, speaker, 74
Simmons, Mara Denise, student, 302
Simmons, Tom, US Ambassador to Pakistan, 400
Simon, Maurya, poet, 257
Simon, Rita J., criminologist, 214, 226
Simonian, Judith, artist, 162
Simpson, Alan, Pres., Vassar Coll., 40
Simpson, Louis, poet, 196
Simpson, Nancy P., Act. Dir & Dir., Athletics, 311, 313, 432, 488
Simpson, Ruth "Dee," archeologist, 76
Simpson, Tony, Int. Dir., Dir. & Sen. Dir., Facilities Services, 360, 404, 484
Sinbad, singer, 324
Singer, Ann, psychologist, 75
Singer, Harry, speaker, 159
Singer, Robert, psychologist, 136
Singh, A. I. Clifford, Prof., 287, 473
Singleton, Charles E. "Chuck," Rev., UAB Member, 333, 499
Sins, musical group, 208
Sirotnik, Barbara, Prof., 206
SIS+ (Student Information System) registration software, 300
Sisley, Christine, speaker, 73
Sista Marmalade, musical group, 285
Siva, Ernest, Hon. Ph.D., Distinguished Guest Artist, flautist, 415, 418, 464, 497
Sixth Finger Funk, musical group, 116
Skeete, John, Pres., Alumni Assoc., 492
Skeletones, musical group, 305, 315
Skillings, Mary Jo, Prof., 473
Skillings, Otis, composer, 98
Skinner Building (San Bernardino), 33
Slackers (film), 366
Slade, Roy, art historian, 50
Slater, Jon, UAB Member, 344, 439, 500
Slatkin, Wendy, speaker, 197
Slaton, Frank T., Manager, Data Processing Services, Dir., Computing Services, 108, 489
The Slaveholding Republic (Fehrenbacher), 383
Sleeping with the Enemy (Cauley), 143
Sleeter, Christine, speaker, 281
Slide Fire (2007), 436
Slosted, Norm, Act. Dir., Housing, 290
Slout, Marte Boyle, actress, wife of William L., 112, 143, 211
Slout, William L., Prof., 112, 143, 160, 211, 248, 259, 286, 292, 355, 409
Slusser, George E., Prof., 109
"Small Business Briefing with NASA," 352
"Small Business Management Strategies for the 1990s," seminar, 259
Small class size, 218
Small, Kevonne, speaker, 322
Small Tribe Band, musical group, 298
Smalley, John, actor, 100
Smith, Alan, Prof., 420
Smith, Allan, speaker, 64
Smith, Andrew, speaker, 79
Smith, Arthur W. Jr., speaker, 114
Smith, Bob, Coach, 358
Smith, Brandon, student, 433
Smith, Cheryl A., Dir., Admissions, Assoc. VP & Act. VP, Enrollment Services, Act. VP, Student Services, 268, 306, 308, 341, 485-86
Smith, Craig, CSU Trustee, 416
Smith, Donald R., speaker, 119
Smith, Edith, CAB Member, 499
Smith, George B. Jr., speaker, 98
Smith, Henry, dancer, 282
Smith, Jack, *Los Angeles Times* columnist, 255, 258
Smith, Julie, Olympic gold medalist, 429
Smith, Lawrence R., speaker, 191
Smith, Lavay, singer, 386
Smith, Lorraine, Serrano Village Adviser, 96
Smith, Lou, Pres., Operation Bootstrap, 60
Smith, Lucinda, Outstanding Student, 493
Smith, Martin A., student, 102
Smith, Mary, Pres., California Organization of Women, 135
Smith, Mary Alyce, wife of Prof. Robert A., 116
Smith, Mary F., Prof., 310, 490
Smith, Nancy E., CAB Member, SB Co. Supervisor, 69, 88, 96-97, 104-05, 110, 137-38, 499
Smith, Patricia A. "Patti," Dir., Student Health and Psychological Center, 413, 486

Smith, Robert A., Prof., 48, 116, 169, 384, 502
Smith, V. Merriline, Alumni Award, mathematician, 44, 219, 496
Smith, Valerie, student, 210
Smithsonian Institution, 126
Smits, Carolyn, Athletics, 432
Smoking on campus, 128, 182, 198, 231, 284
Snell, Barbara J., Accounting Clerk, 52
Snell, M. Jean, Alumni Award, 496
Snook-Bott, Linda, singer, 468
Snortum, John, speaker, 165
Snow, Harry, speaker, 112
Snow on campus, 226, 428
Snyder, Linda L., Graphic Artist, 211
Social and Behavioral Sciences Building, 14, 18, 359, 362, 385, 391, 405, 409
Social and Behavioral Sciences, College of, 457
Social and Behavioral Sciences, School of, 129, 232
Social Lites Club, SB group, 34, 38, 55
Social Science Research and Instructional Council, 381
Social Sciences, Division of, 29, 71, 87
Social Sciences Field Day, 119
Social Sciences Law Day, 246
Social Sciences, School of, 87, 129
Social Work, Dept. of, 266, 450
Social Work, Master of, 286
Social Work, School of, 450
Soderberry, Celeste, alumna, 390
Sodexo Inc., 446
Soffer, Reba, CSU Outstanding Prof., 216
Sohner, Chuck, speaker, 185
Sokoloff, Alexander D., Prof., 39, 47, 59, 70, 78, 96, 115, 119, 123, 266
Sol Azteca International Hispanic Award, 380
Solano, Jim, State Legislative Analyst's Office, 468
Solid Brass, musical group, 158
Solar panels, 161, 433, 470
Sollars, William A. "Andy," pianist, 106
Solo and Ensemble Festival, 141
Solo B of Dab Productions, musical group, 306

Solomon, Charles, *L.A. Times* critic, 305
Solomon, Robert, speaker, 152
Soltek Pacific, builders, 359
Son Cuatro, musical group, 251, 262
Son Real, musical group, 376
Song-Brown Registered Nurse Capitation Grant, 472
Song, Yuan Patricia, Outstanding Student, 493-94
Song, Yufeng, speaker, 241
Songs of the Homeland (film), 362
Sonic Art Show, 165
Sonoma State University, 21, 24, 334, 457
Sonrise, musical group, 106
Sorenson, Don, artist, 166
Soria, Mary, student, 408
Soriano, Esteban, Coordinator, Student Affirmative Action, Chancellor's Off., 184
Soto, Freddy, comedian, 402
Soto, Gary, poet, 261
Soto, Humberto, speaker, 301
Soto, Nell, Assemblywoman, 360
Souez, Ina, opera singer, 131
Soul Force, musical group, 321
Soulliere, Brenda A., Alumni Award, 496
"South Africa," conference, 241
South Asia Colloquium of Southern California, 75
South Coast Air Quality Management District, 264, 298, 367-69
South Coast Repertory Theatre, theatre group, 184, 207, 227
Southern California Academy of Natural Sciences, 219
Southern California Assoc. for the Education of Young Children, 88
Southern California Assoc. of Governments, 472
"Southern California Black Student Union Conference," 150
Southern California Edison Co., 80, 225, 245, 263, 282, 302, 308-09, 345, 376, 433, 452, 469
Southern California Health Fair Expo, 159
Southern California High School Band and Orchestra Festival, 158, 227

Southern California Polynesian (Tongan) Rugby Council, 172
"Southern California Primate Research Forum," 456
Southern, Mara, psychologist, 126
Southern Pacific Railroad, 42
Southern Regional United Black Students Union Conference, 247
Southwest Border Initiative Center, 386
Southwest Society for Eighteenth Century Studies, 89
Southworth, Robert R., student, 124
Spaights, James, pianist, 100
Spanish Club, 137
Spanky D, musical group, 286
Speakers Bureau, 54
Special Collections Department, John M. Pfau Library, 449-50
"Special Education Conference," 148
"Special Education in Crisis," conference, 167
"Special Education: Preparation for Life," conference, 193
Special Programs, Dept. of, 224
Special Services, Dept. of, 153
Special Task Force on Intercollegiate Athletics, 180, 184, 186, 191
Speed bumps, 181, 363
Spelman College Glee Club, 409
Spence, Cynthia, Outstanding Student, 494-95
Spencer, Diane, PDC, 423
Spencer Foundation, 122, 205
Spencer, Neville J., Prof., 131, 501
Sperber, Norman "Skip," forensic scientist, 360
Sperry, Paul, tenor, 180
Sperry, Robert, Testing Office, 423
Spiegel, Hans, speaker, 250
Spiegel, Robert, City Councilman, Mayor, Palm Desert, 317, 358
Spirit of the Entrepreneur Award, 437
Spiritual Awakening, musical group, 322
Spiro T. Agnew Fan Club, 70
Spitz, Elie Kaplan, Rabbi, 371
Spivey-Weber, Frances, speaker, 380
Spoon River Anthology (Aidman), 63
Sprayberry, Sandra, poet, 245
Springer, Kathleen B., Curator, SB County Museum, 352, 362

Squeakin' Wheels, musical group, 355
Squire, David, Prof., 67
St. Anthony's Gospel Choir, musical group, 322
St. Bernard dog mascot, 38, 40, 191, 193
St. Bernardine Medical Center, 309
St. Elmo Village, 165
St. John, Kristoff, 272
St. Paul AME Church Revelations, musical group, 348
St. Valentine's Day Massacre, 55
Stack, Dean, Cafeteria Manager, 90
Stacy, Alan, speaker, 465
Stacy, Lance, speaker, 452
Staff Council, 50, 52, 144
"Staff Morale: The First Victim of Budget Cuts," forum, 322
Staff Recognition Awards, 277
Stafford, Robert, speaker, 152
Stamatis, Alexis, writer, 449
Stanchfield, Jo, speaker, 222
Standard Oil Company of California, 80
Standard Teaching Credential Program, 52
Stanford University, 65
Stanley, Brian, Outstanding Student, 494
Stanley, Charles "Stan," Dir., Sponsored Programs Administration, Foundation, 471
Stansel, Doyle J., Dir. & Assoc. Dean, Placement & Financial Aid, Assoc. Dean, Student Life, Assoc. Dean, Student Development & Dir., Housing, Assoc. Dean, Students, Asst. VP, Student Services & Dir., Housing, 41, 57, 190, 198, 202, 289, 485
Stanton, Gordon E., Prof., 64, 81, 243
Stanton, Helena Villacres, Prof., 265
Stanton, Royal, Dir., De Anza College Chorale, 64
Stark, Susan A., speaker, 79
Starks, Anita, speaker, 395
Stars of the Moscow State Circus, performers, 388, 401, 410
STARTALK, 457
State Accreditation Committee, 45
State Board of Education, 45, 52, 86, 199, 216
State Board of Nursing Education and

Nursing Registration, 98, 102
State Budget Closure Days, 459, 463
"State College Day," festival, 94
State College Faculty Wives—see: Faculty Wives Club
State College Master Plan, 34
State College Pkwy. (SB), 14, 35, 37, 46, 54, 60, 75, 77, 80, 90, 97, 111, 114, 144, 167, 184, 187, 200
State Commission on Teacher Credentialing, 260
State Commission on Teacher Preparation and Licensing, 123, 136, 153
State Coordinating Council for Higher Education, 32, 84
State Debate Competition, 392
State Dept. of Finance, 30
State Dept. of Education, 66, 260
State Highway 30, 285
State Legislative Analyst's Office, 468
State Lottery Commission, 438
State Office of Architecture and Construction, 34
State Office of Statewide Health Planning and Development, 469
State Proposition 1-A (1962), 26-27
State Proposition 3 (1962), 26-27
State Proposition 13 (1978), 136
State Public Works Board, 22, 29-30, 33, 50, 285
State St., 14, 30, 35, 38
State University of New York, Old Westbury, 306
Stater Bros. Markets, 261-62, 297, 326-27, 389, 412, 418, 498
"Statewide Student Research Conference," 381
Stathis-Ochoa, Roberta, Prof., 195, 208
Stauble, Vernon R., Alumni Award, 93, 496
Stavans, Ilán, writer, 419
Staveley, Richard, economist, 125
Steed Woodwind Quintet, 182
Steen, Shandell, student, 294
Steger, Manfred B., speaker, 453
Stein, Andy, violinist, 371
Stein, Gordon, atheist, 226
Stein, Joel A., Prof., 327, 420, 501
Stein, Robert G., Prof., 158, 185, 324, 403
Steinem, Gloria, activist, 429

Steinman, Edna L., Dir., College Publications, Dir., Public Affairs, Dir., Publications, 52-53, 147, 156, 220, 255, 488
Steinman, Lisa, poet, 396
Steinman, Paul, attorney, 107
Stennis, Michael J., CSU Trustee, 343
Step Team Showcase, musical group, 364
Stephens, Cheryl Marie, student, 197
Stephens, Jean M., Alumni Award, 445, 496
Stern, Erik, dancer, 312
Stern, Leo, pianist, 78
Sternberg, Robert J., speaker, 400
Stevens, Carolyn M., Counselor, 466, 473
Stevens, Eileen, speaker, 314
Stevens, Richard, speaker, 177
Stew, Mayfield, performer, 294
Stew Undems Jazz Coalition, musical group, 415
Stewart, Martha, celebrity, 369
Stewart, Pamela, Police Sergeant, 163, 199
Steyer, James, Dir., Children Now, 274
Stiern, Walter W., State Sen., 104, 123
Stimpson, Catherine, speaker, 290
Stine, David O., Prof., 373, 443
Stockham, Linda, alumna playwright, 281, 294, 312, 319, 329
Stockton, Dave, golfer, 321, 326
Stokes, Sheridan, flautist, 363
Stone, Christopher, writer, 266
Stoner, Darleen K., Prof., 214, 221-22, 368-69, 441, 445, 466
Stoops, Gerald W., Chair, Natural Beauty Program, 80
Stoops, Michael, Exec. Dir., National Coalition for the Homeless, 426
"Stop the Violence" memorial bench, 342
Story Line Press, 302
Stout, Cheryl A., Student Services Professional, 365
Stout, Robert, speaker, 69
Strack, Dorothy, Manager, Cafeteria, 47
Strader, Matthew, Outstanding Student, 495
Straight, Susan, writer, 352
Strait, Rayanne, Parking Officer, 365

Straling, Philip F., Bishop, SB Catholic Church Diocese, 153-54, 191
Strand, Mark, poet, 185
Strange, Allen, speaker, 228
Strange, La Tanya, Outstanding Student, 495
Stranges, Frank E., UFO researcher, 82
Strategic Plan, 459
Strategic Planning (Steering) Council/Committee, 316, 318, 326, 330, 461
"Strategies for Personal Growth and Managerial Effectiveness," workshop, 98
"Strategies in Education: Black Is Back," conference, 237
Stratton, Shannon, Pres., ASI, 492
Stravinsky, Igor, composer, 107
Strem, George W., philosopher, 43
Strings of Glass, musical group, 243
Strombotne, James, artist, 53
Stromwall, Frances L. "Fran," Lib. Asst., 211, 354
Strong, Erin, Outstanding Student, 495
Strong Will, musical group, 289, 293-94
The Stronger (play), 92
Strongwill, musical group, 282
Strully, Jeff, speaker, 225
Struzan, Drew, movie illustrator, 261
Stuart, Dorothy, Dir., Children's Center, 140
Stuart, Lila, soprano, 55
Stuart, Val, tenor, 55
Stubblebine, Craig, speaker, 131
Stuckey, Sterling, speaker, 263, 342
Stucki, Larry, anthropologist, 77
Studens, Arturs, student, 165
Student Activities Office, 221
Student Aid Office, 232
Student Assistance in Learning Program—SEE: SAIL
Student Coalition for Peace in the Middle East, 270
Student Emergency Loan Fund, 288
Student evaluation of teaching effectiveness, 73-74, 138
Student fees, 163, 189, 219, 288, 371, 394, 473
Student Health Center, 13, 115, 117, 122, 130, 132, 144, 157, 198, 283, 297, 359, 405, 429, 447, 456-57, 469
Student Housing, Office of, 327
Student Information System registration software—SEE: SIS+
Student Leadership and Development, Office of, 327
Student Life, Office of, 221, 327
Student Organizing Committee (SOC), 37
Student Recreation and Fitness Center, 12, 14, 18, 371, 404, 406, 430, 434, 451, 460
"Student Research Conference," 314
Student Services Building, 14, 17, 76, 87, 90, 103, 115, 132, 140, 168, 186-89, 212-13, 223, 230, 298
Student Services, Division of, 105, 217, 278, 317, 319
Student Services Office, 162
Student Union Board, 421
Student Union Building, 17-18, 44, 54, 63, 74, 121-22, 129, 132-35, 199, 219, 225, 234, 237, 255, 282-83, 301, 304, 308-09, 327, 367, 371, 392
Student Union Courtyard, 12
Student Union Events Center, 12
Student Union Multipurpose Room, 12
Student Union Patio, 12
Student Union Program Board, 392
Students for a Democratic Society, 51
Students United for Furthering Educational Rights (SUFFER), 81
"Students with Disabilities," teleconference, 312
Stull, John, State Sen., 123
Stumpf, Pat I., Head, Payroll Office, 224
Sturnick, Judith A., presidential candidate, 169
Styx, musical group, 388
Suárez, José "Joe," SB City Councilman, 361, 378
Suavé, musical group, 458
Suavecito (Mexican concert), 94
"Successes and Challenges: Strategies to Overcome Historical Barriers," conference, 333
Sue, Stanley, speaker, 321
Suenram, David L., Athletic Dir., 250, 280-81, 291, 305, 311, 313, 488
Sugar Ray, musical group, 351

Sugita de Queiroz, Chizuko Judy, artist, 411
Suitt, Tom, Assemblyman, 123, 130
Sujata, dancer, 111
Suicidal Tendencies, musical group, 358
Sullivan, Arthur, composer, 159
Sullivan, Jack Arthur Jr., Instructor, 98, 501
Sullivan, M. Alayne, Prof., 432
Sullivan, Poppy, Dir., Art Gallery, 142
Sulnick, Robert H., speaker, 152, 159
Sultan, Kenny, singer, 265
Sumar, Eddy, speaker, 452
Sumida, Stuart, Prof., 345, 350, 354, 363, 441, 490
Summer Chautauqua Series, 65
Summer Concert Series, 221
Summer Music 2000 Camp, 365
Summer session, 461, 469
Summer Technology Training Institute, 216
Summer Transition and Enrichment Program, 210
Summers, John D., Groundsman, 319
Summers, Margaret R., Lib. Asst., 375, 384
Summers, Susan E., Act. Dean, CVC, Assoc. Dean & Int. Dean, Extended Education, 261, 264, 346, 385, 413, 431, 438, 479-80
"Summit on the Economic Crisis," conference, 451
Sumney, Kodjoe, Pastor, 357, 378
Sumum, Saeed, speaker, 217
Sun Company, 37
Sun-Telegram 10K Run, 139
"Sunday Afternoon in the Park" celebration, 120
Sundin, Carl, student, 45
SunEdison, 470
Sunshine Generations, musical group, 207
Surado® Distinguished Entrepreneur Lecture Series, 440
Suri, Surendra, speaker, 136
Surindra Rajabhat University, Thailand, 415
Surrealist Exhibition, 119
Sussman, Peter Y., writer, 323
Sutton, Sandy, speaker, 362

Suzuki, David T., environmentalist, 449
Svenson, David, artist, 331
Swan, Howard, choral director, 93
Swanson, Carl Bertram, organist, 217
Swanson, Roland, student, 93
Swartz, Stanley L., Prof., 351, 416
Sweeney, Dwight, Prof., Dir., University Center for Developmental Disabilities, Int. Dir., Athletics, 280, 432, 436, 488
Sweeney, Michael, Rev., Catholic priest, 226
Sweet Adelines of San Bernardino, musical group, 207
Sweet Grass Gathering, 294, 304, 315
Sweezy, Paul, speaker, 283
Swing Sisters, musical group, 316
Switzer, P. Richard, Prof., Chair, Humanities Div., Dean, School of Humanities, 67, 132, 145, 295, 318-19, 477, 502
Swoopes, Sheryl, basketball player, 361
Sycamore Room, Commons, 12, 212
Sykes, Roderick, St. Elmo Village, 165
Sylvester, Austin, speaker, 130
Symphonic Choir, 315
Symphonie Jeunesse Youth Orchestra, 470
"Symposium of Fulbright Scholars," 301
"Symposium on Outdoor Sculpture," 142
"Symposium on the Middle East," 396
"Symposium on the North American Free Trade Agreement," 313
Syria: Between Iraq and a Hard Place (film), 466
Systems Analysis Team, 443
Szczepaniak, Margaret, speaker, 214
T Tauri (yearbook), 6, 41
Tacal, José, speaker, 228
Tacchia, Michael, Alumni Award, pianist, 115, 131-32, 165, 204, 208, 273, 284, 294, 339, 359, 381, 420, 444, 496
Tacchia, Michele—SEE: Brosseau-Tacchia, Michele
Taco Bell franchise, Student Union, 327
Tafolla, Carmen, poet, 229, 240
Tailgators Dixieland Band, musical group, 427

Takahashi, Yoshimoto, speaker, 238
Takeda, Kaori, Outstanding Student, 494
Takehara, William, Assoc. VP, Financial Operations, 307, 450-51, 482
Taking Care of Business (play), 141
"Taking Liberties: A Celebration of America's Constitutional Freedoms," conference, 460
Talley, Marian, Dir., Learning Center, 212, 225
Tallman, Denise, pianist, 113
The Taming of the Shrew (Shakespeare), 166
Tamminen, Terry, Chief, Calif. Environmental Protection Agency, 399
Tamor, Sarah, speaker, 249
Taneman, Steve, attorney, ACLU, 272
Tanno, Dolores V., Prof., 358
Tansey, Dave, speaker, 287
Taraborelli, J. Randy, writer, 277
Target Discount Stores, 261
Tarter, Clemens, student, 45
Task Force on Academic [or Educational] Goals and Programs, 81, 84, 88
Task Force on Campus Safety, 261
Task Force on Early Registration, 220
Task Force on Minority Underrepresentation, 206-07
Tate, James, poet, 146
Tate, John, Prof., 298
Tattersall, Ian, anthropologist, 387
Tatum Foundation and Citizens Volunteer Corps, 406
Tavakoli-Targhi, Mohamed, speaker, 472
Tavser, Clifford, historian, 401
Taylor, Andrew, Chair, Enterprise Rent-a-Car, 454
Taylor, Anita, educator, 242
Taylor, Barbara A., Bookkeeper, 243, 247
Taylor, John, speaker, 314-15
Taylor, Lisa, soprano, 191
Taylor, Natasha, student, 290
Taylor, Phillip A., Int. Dir., Academic Resources, 476
Taylor, Scott Marvin, student, 81
Taylor Woodrow Construction California Ltd., builders, 260

Teacher Corps—see: Bilingual Teacher Corps Project
Teacher Credential Program, 66, 77
Teacher Education, Dept. of, 255
"Teachers Are No. 1" Conference, 211, 222, 232, 243-44, 254-55, 265, 276, 287, 296
Teachers' Bach Festival, 193
"Teachers in Computer Integration in the Classroom," conference, 253
"Teaching About the Holocaust," forum, 400
"Teaching and Learning in Transformation: The Silicon Evolution," conference, 246
Teaching Resource Center, 322, 451
Teal, Sheryl, Outstanding Student, 494
Teasey, Basil, Australian Consul General, 234
Teatro Aztlán, 229
Teatro Aztlán of San Gorgonio High School, 75
Teatro Cultural de Colton, theatre group, 111
El Teatro de la Esperanza de Santa Barbara, theatre group, 151, 159
Teatro de los Puppets, puppet group, 178
Teatro Milagro, theatre group, 377
Teatro Tecato, theatre group, 70
Teatro Urbano, theatre group, 68
Technology Transfer and Commercialization, Office of, 452
"Teddy Bear," radio personality, 315
Teenie, performer, 306
Teer, Michael, Pres., Inland Area Urban League, 148, 165
Tegner, Olaf, Prof., Pepperdine Coll., 61
Telecommunications Office, 288
Telephone 24-hour hotline, 88
Telephone Centrex system, 109
Telephone number prefixes, 69, 249, 411-12, 417
Telephone toll-free number, 85
Televised courses, 107
Television commercial, 150
Television news of campus, 178, 181
Television station, 368, 375, 379-80—SEE ALSO: KCSB-TV
Tell It Like It Is (folk musical), 64

Tempest, musical group, 307
The Tempest (Shakespeare), 166, 223
Tempest in a Teapot: The Falkland Islands War (Burgess), 506
Templeton, Harry, musician, 148
Temporary Academic Modular Buildings, 14
Temporary Classrooms, 14
Temporary Kinesiology Annex, 14
Temporary Offices, 14
Tenorio, Mary, UAB Member, 500
Tenorio-Kerr, Aurora, Alumni Award, 496
Tep, Sotheary, Outstanding Student, 494
Teresa, Eugene, Sister, speaker, 73
Terrazas, Madeline P., Lib. Asst., 411
Terremoto Latin Jazz Band, musical group, 392
Los Terrones, musical group, 127
Terry, Frank, speaker, 149, 152
Terry McAdam Book Award, 359
Terry Tribune (newspaper), 103
Tervalon, Jervey, writer, 357
Tetreau, Danae Linette, pianist, 356
Texas Technological University, 337
Teyber, Edward C., Prof., UAB Member, 154, 500
Thakar, Rosemary, CSU Trustee, 302
Thayer, Christopher, student, 300
Theatre, 17, 131, 246, 398
Theatre Arts, Dept. of, 129, 294, 375
Theatre Festival for Young Audiences, 207, 214, 218, 227
Theatre Project from the Mark Taper Forum, theatre group, 207, 227
Theatre Workshop, 112, 137, 182
Theatrical Arts International, 357
Theodore, Sondra, student, 128
Theriault, Linda Wright, Outstanding Student, 494
Thermo Dr., 14
Theta Psi Omega, 44, 65, 73
Thibeault, Gerald J. "Gerry," speaker, 262, 464
Thiessen, Elizabeth, Manager, Commons, Dir. of Operations, 158, 161
Thomas, Clarence, Justice, US Supreme Court, 240
Thomas, Ed, magician, 300
Thomas Ehrlich Faculty Award for Serving Learning, 399
Thomas, Erene S., CSU Trustee, 386
Thomas, James D., Prof., Dean, Academic Administration, Assoc. VP, Academic Resources, 53, 61, 99, 188, 201, 266, 476
Thomas, Joseph K., Exec. Dean & VP, Administration, 36, 52, 75, 95, 167, 210, 347, 482, 502
Thomas, KaMala, Outstanding Student, 494
Thomas, Nancy, speaker, 282
Thomas, Rich, *Newsweek*, 257
Thomas, Sally, folksinger, 64
Thomason, Ryland M., SB landowner, 28-29
Thomerson, Katherine, speaker, 301, 463-64
Thomlinson, Ralph, speaker, 108
Thompson, Alonza, speaker, 216
Thompson, Barry B., Pres., ASI, 185, 491
Thompson, Carol, speaker, 241
Thompson, Elton N., Prof., 178
Thompson, Eric, singer, 307
Thompson, Jeffrey M., Prof., Assoc. Provost, Research, 387, 414, 445, 476, 491
Thompson, Judi, Exec. Dir., SB Chamber of Commerce, 309
Thompson, Marshall, speaker, 242
Thompson, Suzy, singer, 307
Thompson, Whiting, architect, 39
Thomson, Eric, Outstanding Student, 494
Thomson, Kenneth, student, 95
Thomson, Ralph J., physician, 123
Thorber, Aletha, student, 44
Thornburgh, Maurita, soprano, 174
Thornton, Shirley, speaker, 237
Thorvaldson, Linda, Secretary, 144
Thrush, Gerald R., Prof., 418, 491
Thuot, Pierre, astronaut, 240
Thwing, John B., student, 70
Thygerson, Kenneth J., Prof., 365
Tibbals, John M., Libn., 355
Tibbits, Gretchen M., speaker, 371
Tice, Sandra, Rev., 361
Tillquist, Kristin, speaker, 463
Tim Watson's Group, musical group, 205

Time capsule, 150, 405
"Time for Cooperation! Strategies for Directed Growth in the Inland Empire," conference, 252
Timmreck, Thomas C., Prof., 393-94
Tinsley, Robert, Building Maintenance, 278
Titus, Maria, Secretary, 403
Toad, musical group, 101
Toastmasters Club, 215
"Today's Woman Inside/Out Conference," 395
Together Again (musical revue), 252
Tokay Hall, 14, 17, 87
Tokyo Daze (Coughlin), 330
Tolosa, Gustavo, pianist, 289
Tolosa, María, pianist, 289
Toman, Michael, RAND Corp., 453
Tomlin, Lily, comedienne, 432
Tomlinson, Rebecca, singer, 431
Tompkins, Larisa R., Pres., ASI, 492
Tonight in Samarkand (Deval & Semple), 129
Tonsberg, Rob, speaker, 123
Tools for Education campaign, 434
Tooper, Virginia, speaker, 211
Toote, Gloria E. A., Asst. Secretary, U.S. Dept. of Housing and Urban Development, 96
Topoleski, Chris A., Custodian, 265, 271-72
Tornadoes, musical group, 355, 365, 384, 403, 433
Tornheim, Leonard, mathematician, 72
Toro, Efraín, speaker, 235
Torres, Adam N., Alumni Award, 496
Torres, Cecelia O., Lib. Asst. & Media Services, 161
Torres, Juan, Pres., ASB, 491
Torres, Salvador, speaker, 263
Torres, Sandra, Payroll, 423
Torres-Santos, Raymond, musician, 252
Tórrez, Nena M., Prof., 405
Tortora, Thomas, student, 264
Toshima, Goro, filmmaker, 453
Tosolini, Dino M., student, 288
Toumi, Dhekra, speaker, 464
Touring Theatre Group, 210
Tower of Power, musical group, 141
Townley, Arthur J., Prof., 354
Townsend, Maura Owens, speaker, 411
Toxic Jazz, musical group, 343
Toyota USA Foundation, 356
Tracey, Mike, Inst. Assoc. VP, Development, 389, 408-09
Trader Training Corp. of Denmark, 363
Trailer and modular offices and classrooms, 14, 59, 212, 223, 233, 235, 245, 247, 277, 279, 325, 396-97
Tran, Van Dinh, Vietnamese Ambassador to US, 48
"Transit-Oriented Design," conference, 464
Transportation and Logistics Seminar, 472
Transportation Committee, 340
"Transportation Marketplace Conference," 393
"Transportation Research Conference," 452, 464
Travel policy, 460
Traveler, musical group, 108
Travelers Company of Hollywood, theatre group, 100, 132
Travis Brass Quintet, musical group, 427
Traynum, Elyse, Pres., ASI, Alumni Award, UAB Member, 491, 496, 499
Trefren, Stan, speaker, 194
Treisman, Phillip Uri, speaker, 260
Trelease, Jim, writer, 204, 232
Triangle Construction Co., builders, 46
Tri-City Concrete Co., 37
The Trial of Dr. Jekyll (Slout), 292
Trimble, Virginia, astrophysicist, 362
Trinity Dance Ensemble, dance group, 207
Trio dell'Arte, musical group, 145, 157, 191
Trottier, David, screenwriter, 276
Trujillo, Diane, Dir., Sponsored Programs Administration, Foundation, 471
Troy, Frosty, Editor, *Oklahoma Observer*, 255
Trubnick, Michael E., Prof., 394
Trueblood, Kenneth N., chemist, 57
Truk (island), 94
The Truth of the Matter (play), 341
TRW, 206
Tsai, Loh Seng, psychologist, 69
Tschopp, David E., Pres, First Bank,

275, 284, 317
Tseitlin, Irina, violinist, 153
Tsuchiya, Akiko, speaker, 312
Tucker, Bridget, Counselor, 286
Tucker, Lisa, speaker, 449
Tucker, Tim, Veteran's Affairs Coordinator, 126
Tuckerman, Daniel, Communication Studies, 445
Tuesdays with Morrie (play), 463
Tullis, Garner, printmaker, 213
Tundra, musical group, 69
Tunney, John V., CA Rep. & Sen., 50
Tunno, Dave, businessman, 63
Turadian, Armen, violinist, 94
Ture, Kwame, speaker, 282
Turner, Alice, student, 87
Turner, Ralph, seismologist, 177
Turner, Raymond, Rev., Community Task Force, 315, 317
Turyahikayo-Rugyema, Benoi, speaker, 257
Tusler, Robert L., organist, 140
Tuszynska, Danuta, attorney, 454
Twain, Mark, writer, 92
Twelfth Night Repertory Company, theatre group, 207
Twyman, James, speaker, 396
Typists (play), 150
Tyrannosaurus rex (fossil), 345, 363
Tyrone Anthony Jazz Band, 268, 276
Tyus, Norene, student, 444
Tzeng, Ovid, psychologist, 134
Ubon Ratchathani University, Thailand, 415
UCLATINO, musical group, 252
Ugarte, Marisa, Exec. Dir., Bilateral Safety Corridor Coalition, 470
Uhry, Alfred, composer, 148-49
Ullah, Asif, speaker, 411
Ulmer, Bethany, pianist, 128
Ulrich, Dale A., speaker, 328, 426
Undems, Stew, performer, 415
Under the Volcano (Lawrence & Lee), 229
The Underdog (underground newspaper), 47
"Understanding the Middle East: Perspectives on Politics, Culture, and History," conference, 400
Unforgiven, musical group, 203

Ung, Chinary, composer, 457
Ungar, Tamas, pianist, 136
Ungerleider, J. Thomas, psychiatrist, 47
The Unicorn Horn (student magazine), 58
UniFest '84, open house, 203
Union of Palestine Women's Organizations, 272
Union Oil Co., 89
Union Pacific Foundation, 187
United Black Student Union Southern Regional Conference, 281
United Farmworkers of America, 229, 408, 469
United Parcel Service, 471, 498
United Professors of California—see: UPC
"Unity Forum Town Hall Conference," 376
Universal Studios, 298
Universidad Autónoma de Baja California, 283, 291, 301, 314
Universidad Nacional Autónoma de México (UNAM), 246
University Advancement, Division of, 346, 354
University Advisory Board, 12
University Advisory Committee on Efficiency and Effectiveness, 459
University Center for Developmental Disabilities, 13, 316-17
University College, Dublin, Ireland, 449
University Dance Concert, 310
University Diversity Committee, 397
University Hall, 14, 17, 255, 260, 263, 280, 282, 301, 319
"University Meadows" condominium complex, 144
University of Arizona, 337
University of Botswana, 219
University of California, Berkeley, 47, 52, 136, 176
University of California, Davis, 317, 382
University of California, Irvine Dance Touring Ensemble, 229
University of California, Los Angeles, 319
University of California, Los Angeles Afro-Cuban Omo Ache Ensemble,

musical group, 363
University of California, Los Angeles Anglo-American Ensemble, musical group, 363
University of California, Los Angeles Brain Research Institute, 470
University of California, Los Angeles Cappella Choir, 183
University of California, Los Angeles Center for Autism Research and Treatment, 469
University of California, Los Angeles Chicano Studies Center, 112
University of California, Los Angeles Mariachi Ensemble, musical group, 363
University of California, Los Angeles Wind Ensemble, 160
University of California, Los Angeles Woodwind Quintet, 140
University of California, Riverside, 89, 138, 140, 142, 148, 384, 406
University of California, Riverside Folk Dance Club, 207
University of California, Riverside Guitar Ensemble, 284
University of California, Riverside Madrigal Singers, 74, 83
University of California, San Diego, 85, 225, 235
University of California, Santa Barbara, 306
University of California, Santa Barbara Middle East Ensemble, musical group, 298
University of California System, 412-13
University of Chicago, 24, 171
University of Chicago Press, 337
University of Colorado, 141
University of Fairbanks, 295
University of Florida, 126
University of Hawaii, 176
University of Iași, Romania, 382
University of Illinois, 337
University of Illinois at Urbana, 126
University of Khartoum, Sudan, 151
University of Minnesota Institute of Child Development, 107
University of Nebraska, Kearney, 407
University of Nevada, Los Vegas, 286
University of North Carolina, Greensboro, 235
University of Nottingham, England, 54
University of Paris at Nanterre, 109
University of Redlands, 71, 89, 151, 184, 197, 202, 340
University of Redlands Wind Ensemble, 180
University of Salzburg, Austria, 251
University of Southern California, 50, 55, 141, 508
University of Southern California's American Early Music Consort, 147-48
University of Southampton, England, 229
University of Texas, Austin, 143
University of Wyoming, 337
University Pkwy., 14, 37-38, 200, 205, 239-40, 259, 267, 273, 279, 311, 385
University Police Building, 14, 18, 354, 365, 470
University Police, Dept. of, 366
University Relations, Division of, 254, 346
University status, 190
University Transportation Center, 385, 415, 418, 423
University Village Housing, 14, 18, 385, 387, 404, 407
Unmack, James, speaker, 262
Until Today (Vanzant), 370
Untouchables, musical group, 252
UPC (United Professors of California), 167, 181
Upper Commons, Commons Building, 12
UPS Foundation, 465
Upward Bound Program, 96, 153, 186, 197, 209, 213, 221, 294, 353, 447, 473
Upward Bound Recognition Dinner, 163
Urata, Helen H., wife of James H., campus booster, 427
Urata, James H. "Jimmy," Building Coordinator, Dir., Plant Operations, Act. Exec. Dean, Dir., Administrative Affairs, 9, 31, 105, 108, 112, 140, 168, 180, 188, 199, 218-20, 223, 427, 482-84
Urban Minority Administrators: Poli-

tics, Policy, and Style (Karnig & McClain), 337
Urmann, Michael, Lect., 432
U.S. Air Force Academy, 279
U.S. Air Force Band of the Golden West, musical group, 453
U.S. Army, 413, 418
U.S. Army Field Band and (Soldiers') Chorus, musical group, 322, 348
U.S. Army Jazz Septet, musical group, 441
U.S. Assoc. for Small Business and Entrepreneurship, 466
U.S. Committee in Solidarity with the People of El Salvador, 158
U.S. Dept. of Homeland Security, 444
U.S. Dept. of Transportation, 393
U.S. Environmental Protection Agency, 441
U.S. Highway 395, 38
U.S. Holocaust Memorial Museum, 400
U.S. National Security Agency, 444
U.S. Navy, 366
U.S. News and World Report (magazine), 424, 435, 446
U.S. Office of National Intelligence, 425
U.S. Olympic Women's Volleyball Team, 323
U.S. Rehabilitation Services Administration, 411
"U.S.-Saudi Arabia Relations," conference, 398
U.S. Secret Service, 172
U.S. Small Business Administration, 396
U.S. Strategic Language Initiative, 466-67
USA Cheerleading Competition, 390
USA Collegiate and Pro Dance Camp, 459
Usher, Jon, clarinetist, 398, 417
Usher, Tim, Prof., 280, 382, 449
Utility Tunnel, 58, 67
Vaccination requirement, 225
Valcazar, Jesseca, Outstanding Student, 495
Valdez, Alex, comedian, 359, 371
Valdez, Elsa O., Prof., 340, 432
Valdez, Josh, speaker, 381
Valdez, Luis, film writer and director, 262
Valentine, Jane, speaker, 228
Valerio, Celia Chan, harpist, 422
Valles, Judith, Mayor, SB, 341-43, 345, 354, 356-57, 361, 367-68, 382, 386, 395, 398, 405, 419, 421, 504
Valles, Mike, speaker, 203
Valles, Robin, Alumni Award, 496
Valley Water Dist., 27-28
Van Baron, Judith, Dir., Bronx Museum of the Arts, 119
Van Bibber, April, Outstanding Student, 495
Van Cleave, William R., speaker, 141
Van de Water, John R., attorney, 90, 96
Van Loan, Marta, speaker, 453
Van Marter, Leslie, Prof., 71
Van Mouwerik, James C., student, 147
Van Norman, David, SB County Deputy Coroner, 463
Van Pelt, Peggy, entertainment executive, 383
Vance, Linda S., Administrative Support Coordinator, 365
"Vandalism, Burglary, and Arson," seminar, 140
Vandament, William, CSU Act. Provost, 192
Vanderbilt, Tom, speaker, 463
Vanzant, Iyanla, writer, 370
Vargas, Adriana, Outstanding Student, 495
Varner & Brandt, 498
Varner, Bruce Doyle, Arrowhead Award, UAB & PAC Member, 401, 499-500
Vásquez, Jeremy, Pres., ASI, 492
Vásquez, Raymond Richard "Monie," student, 184
Vaurinek, Trine, Day & Co., 498
Vax, Mike, trumpeter, 148
Vehicular traffic on campus, 264
Velagic, Alen, Outstanding Student, 493
Velamoor, Sesh, speaker, 408
Velásquez, Roberto, CAB Member, 198, 499
Venture in Vain: A Tale of the Deryni (Kurtz), 377
Venus Wrecks, musical group, 299
Verizon, 376, 380, 393

Veruman, Freddie, Dir., Teatro Tecato, 70
Vessey, Ann, Alumni Award, 496
Veterans Club, 116
Veterans Affairs Office, 167
"Vexations" (Satie), 118
Veysey, Victor, State Assemblyman, 64
Vick, Scott, CSU Trustee, 264
Vickers, H. Darwyne, 69
Vicknair, J. Paul, Prof., Act. Dean, School of Natural Sciences, Assoc. Provost, Academic Personnel, 338, 355, 446, 476, 478
La Victima (play), 151
Victor Construction Co., builders, 111
Victor Valley College, 77, 141, 152, 257, 329, 367
Victor Valley College Singers, 163, 177
Victor Valley Community Choir, 159
Vietnam Veterans Against the War, 91
Vietnam War, 51, 60, 65
Vigil, Frederico, speaker, 333
Viking Construction Co., builders, 66, 75
Viksne, Anita, speaker, 81
Vilches, Antonio D. "Tony," Lib. Stock Clerk, 427
Villa, Esteban, artist, 106
Villalobos, Davida G., Natural Sciences, 473
Villanueva, Victor, speaker, 448
Villareal, Elisabeth Joy, Outstanding Student, 494
Villaruel, Fernando, Outstanding Student, 493
Villaseñor, Stephen, Dir., Upward Bound, 473
Villaseñor, Victor, writer, 304, 381
Vincent, Phillip E., speaker, 256
Vint, Sherryl, speaker, 443
Viramontes, Helena María, writer, 318, 352
Virginia Waring International Piano Competition, 430, 455
Vision of Hope Award, 389
Visual Arts Building, 14, 17-18, 153, 158, 195, 198, 201
Visual Arts Center, 14, 18, 269, 305, 325-27, 329, 354, 436
Viswanathan, T., musician, 70
Vitti, Anthony A., CSU Trustee, 257
¡Viva Olympia! (play), 178
Vivarium, 13
Vö, Linda Trinh, speaker, 429
Vogler, Chris, writer, 277
Voices of Inspiration from the Live Church of God in Christ, musical group, 305
Voices of Praise from the Temple Missionary Baptist Church, musical group, 305, 348
Voices of Redemption, musical group, 193
Voices, theatre group, 134
Vollkommer, Harold J., Alumni Award, Pres., Alumni Assoc., UAB Member, 492, 496, 500
"Volunteerism and the American Way of Life," conference, 177
Volz, Nedra, actress, 190
von Blum, Paul, speaker, 431
Von Sydow, Rudolph "Rudy," Equipment Operator, 231
Von Wald, Jo Ann, Admissions Officer, 77, 144, 278
Vons, 240
Voydat, Mitchell L., speaker, 79
W. K. Kellogg Foundation Minority Serving Institutions/National Assoc. for Equal Opportunity in Higher Education Leadership Program, 460
W. M. Keck Foundation, 404
Wada, Frank Y., CSU Trustee, 328
Wagner, Richard, composer, 118
Wagner, Roger, choral director, 102
Wagner, Steven R., Prof., 169, 334
Wagoner, Carl P., Prof., Assoc. Dean, Academic Planning, 78, 86, 92, 334, 480, 489
Wahed, Joseph Sr., speaker, 247
Waifs, musical group, 291, 393
Waites, Althea Mitchell, pianist, 130, 139, 143, 149, 180, 185, 194, 205
Waithe, S. Lamont, musician, 239
Waiting to Exhale (McMillan), 292
Waitley, Denis, speaker, 287
Wakoski, Diane, poet, 120, 194
Walch, Günther, speaker, 237
Walcott, John, *Wall Street Journal* reporter, 239
Wald, George, Nobel Prize winner, 235
Waldman, Robert, composer, 149

Walker, Larry, SB County Supervisor, 232, 245, 305
Walker, Lenore, psychologist, 312
Walker, Phillip E., playwright, 271
Walker, Tina Marie, Outstanding Student, 493
Wall, Richard, alumnus, 300
Wall Street Journal (newspaper), 239
Wallace, Marjorie Sue, Secretary, 26
Wallace, Constance, student, 95
Wallace, Paul, speaker, 75
Waller, Doug, *Newsweek*, 257
Wallerstein, Nina, speaker, 454
Walliser, James, Outstanding Student, 493
Wallock, Joe, speaker, 120
Walter and Lenore Annenberg Foundation, 372
Walters, Dan, political columnist, 240
Walnut Properties Inc., 130
Walsh, Chuck, speaker, 103
Walsh, David, gerontologist, 134
Walsh, Don, oceanographer, 120, 136, 154, 177, 197, 223
Walsh, John, speaker, 472
Walt Disney Feature Animation, 294
Walter E. Dakin Fellowship in Poetry, 317
Walters, Alfred, violinist, 74
Walters, Dan, *Sacramento Bee* writer, 291
Walton, Craig, speaker, 89, 92
Walton, Lana, actress, 341, 350
Wang, Ching-Hua, Prof., 299
Wang Family Excellence Award, 352, 391, 420, 441
Wang, Howard S., Assoc. VP, Student Affairs, 371, 389, 485
Wantz-Sutton, Jacqueline, Outstanding Student, 494
"The War on Homelessness II: Filling the Gaps in the Continuum of Care," conference, 311
Waraksa, Elizabeth, speaker, 451
Ward, Anderson J., speaker, 206
Ward, Doris, Pres. Secretary, 43
Ward Ritchie Press (publisher), 50
Ward, Rosemary T., Libn., 55, 81
Ward, Sharon, Dir., Region XII, Calif. State Employees Assoc., 104
Warehall, William D., Prof., 354

Wareham, Arlan, Mathematics, 423
Warehouse Receiving and Mail Building, 17, 102, 155, 160
Warfield, Marsha, comedienne, 219
Warner, Margaret, *Newsweek*, 257
Warren, David, speaker, 106
Warren, Frank, Chief, Custodial Services, 152
Warren, Lynda W., Prof., 205, 211, 235, 307, 490
Warren, Sandra J., 155
A Warring Absence (Duncan), 279, 284, 288
Wasbauer, Joanne, speaker, 263
Washburn, David, trumpeter, 195
Washburn, Mayor, Lake Elsinore, 299
Washington, Lula, dancer, 389
Wasserman, Lois, City Manager, Rancho Cucamonga, 193
Wasserstrom, Richard, philosopher, 115
Water Conservation Garden, 462
Water Hero Award, WRI, 437, 449, 464
Water polo team, 234
Water Resources Institute, 12, 353, 362, 364, 367-68, 409, 416, 418, 433, 437
"Water Resources Institute Annual Conference," 368, 376, 387, 437
Water Resources Institute Archives, 448
Water Resources Institute Lecture Series, 356, 363
Water Resources Institute Lifetime Achievement Award, 376, 389, 401, 415, 426, 438, 449, 464
Waterman Canyon, 347, 395
Waterman Hall/House, 14, 17, 87, 157-59, 161
Waters, Ethel, singer, 248
Waters, Fred, mathematician, 44
Waters, Maxine, Assemblywoman, US Rep., 257, 292, 354, 378
Waters of the Earth (play), 387
Watkins, J. Patrick, Prof., 334, 339, 501
Watkins, Jack L., US Air Force Major General, 155
Watson, Aaron, Pres., ASI, 492
Watson, Amanda Sue, student, 284
Watson and Associates, 397, 405, 418, 423
Watson, D. J., musician, 299

Watson, Del LaVerne, Prof., 253
Watson, Diane E., State Sen., 267
Watson, Gary, philosopher, 439
Watson, James R., Hon. Ph.D., PAC Member, 421, 425, 497, 500
Watson, Judy, campus booster, 421
Watson Literacy Center, 397, 405, 423
Watson, Paul, speaker, 305
Watson, Sally, Accountant, 140
Watson, Tim, singer, 205
Watts, J. Brian, Prof., 403
Watts, Lynn, harpsichordist, 89
Waybacks, musical group, 365
We Are Still Here (Saubel), 367
We Tell Stories, theatre group, 197, 207, 227
Wearne, Diana Lucille, student, 189
Weather Cocks, musical group, 71
Weather Station, 115, 181-82, 184, 201
"Web-Based Learning Conference," 389
Webb, Hubert, speaker, 449
Weber, LeRoy A., Manager, Bookstore, 146
Website, campus, 438
Webster, Emerson George, campus booster, 287
Webster Junior High Breakdancers, dance group, 207
Weeks, John, *SB Sun* columnist, 369, 450
Weese, Cheryl A., Admissions Officer, 114, 123
Wegman, William, artist, 252
Wehrenberg, William B., appointed Dean, School of Natural Sciences, 322, 478
Weimer, Maryellen, speaker, 313
Weinrich, James D., speaker, 180
Weiny, Arden G., son of George A., 116
Weiny, George A., Prof., 94, 115-16, 235-36, 313, 501
Weir, Alison, Exec. Dir., "If Americans Knew," 416
Weir, James T., Police Officer, 104, 143
Weir-Quiton, Pamela, artist, 109
Weiser, Florence, Asst. Dean, Academic Administration, Dir., Sponsored Programs, 99, 127, 188-89, 476
Weiss, Jerry, speaker, 194
Weisser, Ellen, PAC Member, 500
Weissich, W. O., CSUC Trustee, 110
Weissman, Greg, co-anchor, KCSB-TV, 386, 396
Weitz, Charles H., speaker, 205
Wekre, Froydis Ree, musician, 158
Welch, Gerald, Groundsworker, 286
Welch, Susan, writer, 337
Wells, Carol, speaker, 196
Wells, Harvey, speaker, 72
Welshon, Mary-Alice, historian, 472
Wen, Jia-Rong "Jerome," speaker, 328
Wente, Karl L., CSUC Trustee, 110
Wenzel, Mark, mime, 130
Werness, Hope, speaker, 118
Wessell, Herbert, speaker, 262
West African Ensemble, musical group, 363
West Campus Circle, 14, 438
West Coast Brass Quintet, musical group, 197
West, Dale T., Coll. Personnel Officer, Dir., Human Resources, Asst. VP, Human Resources and Risk Management, 9, 202-03, 211, 306, 427, 483-84
West, Philip, student, 160
West, Richard, speaker, 143
West, Robert L., Prof., Chair & Dean, Education Dept., Dir., Summer Session, Dir., Extension, Dean, School of Education, 38, 44, 59, 104, 152, 381, 478-79, 502
West Valley Material Recovery Facility, 373
Westbrook, L. Curtis Jr., Prof., 403
Westbrook, Phil, Supervising Building Service Engineer, 404
Western Assoc. of College and University Housing Officers, 420
Western Assoc. of Food Chains, 182, 196, 207, 223
Western Assoc. of Schools and Colleges (WASC), 60-62, 198-99, 308, 346, 399-400, 404, 433
Western Ave. (SB), 14, 31, 46
Western Electric Fund, 143
Western Interstate Compact for Higher Education (WICHE), 447
Western Municipal Water Dist., 29

Western Psychology Assoc., 342
"Western Regional Outdoor Leadership Conference," 439
"Western States Communication Assoc. Convention," 419
Weston, Ed, actor, 258
Weston, J. Fred, economist, 195
Westrick, John, Plant Operations, 150
Westside Action Group, SB, 226, 230-31
Westwind Brass, musical group, 265
Westside Latin Band, musical group, 372
Wetterlind, Peter J., Prof., 302, 501
Whale, Cindy-Lea, student, 159
Whaley, W. Paul, speaker, 69
Wheaton, David, student, 93
Wheel of Fortune (TV show), 320
Wheeler, Donald, speaker, 69
Wheeler, Edward, SB City Councilman, 104
Wheeler, Russell, Undergraduate Studies, 445
Whistler, Clare, dancer, 250
Whitaker, Daniel S., Prof., 423
White, Edward M., Prof., 48, 55, 71, 90, 300, 324, 333, 490
White Flag, musical group, 208
White, Hank, Veteran's Affairs Coordinator, 126
White House Initiative on Educational Excellence for Hispanic Americans, 469, 472-73
White, Jack, billiards trick shot artist, 290
White, James, UAB Member, 500
White, Joe, speaker, 264
White, John, writer, 143
White, Louise, speaker, 432
White, Michael, musician, 99
White, Noreen, student, 93
White, Theodore C. "Ted," Engineer, 146
Whitehall, Marianne M., student, 237
Whitehurst, Daniel, Mayor, Fresno, 240
Whitescarver, Katherine, pianist, 141
Whiting, William, Facilities Services, 445
Whitman College, 138
Whittaker, Denise, Pres., San Bernardino Valley College, 406

Whittaker, Tony, speaker, 382
Whittenberger Fellowship in Poetry, 364
"Who's Come a Long Way, Baby?", panel, 69
"Whose Kid Am I, Anyway," conference, 148
"Why Revolution?", forum, 80
"Why Women's Studies?", program, 69
Wichman, Ann, 67
Wichman, Harvey, Prof., 67, 74
Wideman, Natalia, Outstanding Student, 494
Wiese, Katrin, alumna artist, 440
Wiest, Candace Hunter, Arrowhead Award, 410, 498
Wiggins Hill, 65, 97, 289, 418
Wilcox, Amanda, speaker, 406
Wilcox, Don G., conductor, 260
Wilcox, Evlyn, Arrowhead Award, Mayor, SB, 209, 212-13, 216-17, 240, 245, 252, 329, 339, 498, 504
Wilcox, John C., Physician, 158
Wilcox, Willard, 50
Wilcoxen, Jackqueline, Prof., 411
Wilder, Billy, film director, 157
Wildside Press, 419
Wildwood Park (SB), 41
Wiley, D. Linn, UAB & PAC Member, Arrowhead Award, Executive-in-Residence, Pres. & CEO, Citizens Business Bank, 371, 437, 440, 498, 500
Wiley, Dorothy, Clerical Asst., 188
Wilke, LeRoy A., Chief Engineer and Energy Manager, 163, 432
Wilkins, Ron, speaker, 206, 241-42
Wilkinson, Frank, speaker, 379
Wilkinson, Howard, Dir. of Corporate Affairs, California Steel Industries, 207
Wilkman, Dianne L., Alumni Award, 496
Willat, Felice, speaker, 395
William Carlos Williams Award, 351
William E. and Barbara Leonard University Transportation Center, 423, 440, 452, 457, 464, 472
William E. and Barbara Leonard University Transportation Center Forum, 442, 471

William T. Eason Co., builders, 103
Williams, Andy, singer, 454
Williams, Arleigh, Dean of Students, UC Berkeley, 52
Williams, Betty, Nobel Peace Prize winner, 225
Williams, Billy G., Rev., 180
Williams, Chris, speaker, 449
Williams, Danny, comedian, 248
Williams, Elizabeth G., CVC Advisory Board member, 275
Williams, Elva, speaker, 180
Williams, Floyd, speaker, 120
Williams, Franklin P. III, Prof., 339, 366
Williams, Frederick, speaker, 135
Williams, James, speaker, 177
Williams, Janice, Secretary, 144
Williams, Larry O. Jr., 272
Williams, Libby, speaker, 301
Williams, Mary, Secretary, 106, 200, 318
Williams, Peggy, SB County Sheriff's Detective, 146
Williams, Peter, Prof., 368
Williams, Raymond, speaker, 391
Williams, Reginald, Heating & Air Conditioning, 278
Williams, Walter, economist, 357
Williamson, George, speaker, 102
Wilmore, Larry, comedian, 230
Wilson, Alice K., Libn., 168, 189, 502
Wilson, David, Custodial Supervisor, 433
Wilson, Earl "Tiny," CAB Member, 37, 498-99
Wilson, Frank, speaker, 224
Wilson, Gayle, wife of Gov. Pete Wilson, 289
Wilson, Gladys, Switchboard Operator, 220
Wilson, Kate, Activities Advisor, Financial Aid Advisor, 67, 73
Wilson, Kurt, Rialto City Councilman, 389
Wilson, O. Meredith, Dir., Center for Advanced Study in the Behavioral Sciences, Stanford University, 65
Wilson, Pete, Gov., CA, 269, 289, 348, 505
Wilson, Peter A., Dean, Student Services, VP, Student Affairs, Int. Dean & Dean, CVC & PDC, 188, 211, 246, 266, 317, 394, 480, 484
Wilson, Robert, Budget Officer, Assoc. VP, Financial Operations, 450, 482-83
Wilson, Roy, Riverside County Supervisor, 324, 373
Wilson, Ruth C., Prof., 373
Wilson, Talmadge, Alumni Award, 496
Wilson, William H., attorney, 161, 178
Wilson, Woodrow, Supervising Groundsworker, 146
Wind turbines, 473
Winer, Arthur, speaker, 217
Winick, Judd, actor, 311
Winker, Steve, student, 200
Winking, Lawrence, UAB Member, 500
Winnick, Joseph P., speaker, 436
Winser, Joan, Consul General, Canada, 241
Winslade, William J., attorney, 197
Winter Guard International West Power Regional Color Guard Finals, 408
Winterowd, W. Ross, speaker, 101
Winton, Gordon H., speaker, 64
Wisdom in Education Program, 416
Wise, David, speaker, 164
Wise, Tim, speaker, 408
Wissler, Dorothy, Treasurer, Alumni Assoc., 45, 47
"Within Our Reach: Breaking the Cycle of the Disadvantaged," conference, 346
Witkin, Joel-Peter, artist, 229
Wixom, George S., Mayor, SB, 504
Woerner, Janet J., Prof., 279, 432
Wolf, Alvin M., Prof., 185, 384
Wolf, Bob, speaker, 448
Wolff, Geoffrey, writer, 359
Wolfgang, Aurora, Prof., 344
Wolfinbarger, Rachel, Outstanding Student, 495
"Womansong," symposium, 234
"Women in Focus Forum," 395, 406
"Women in Government," conference, 147
"Women in Management," conference, 155
"Women in Science, workshop, 127,

141

"Women to Women Conference," 382
"Women's Activism Conference," 408
Women's Business Center, 396
Women's Center, 386
"Women's Conference," 351, 366, 384, 392, 400, 405, 414, 420
"Women's Day" celebration, 120
Women's Education Equity Grant, 458
"Women's Health Conference," 185
Women's National AAU Cross-Country Championship, 131
Women's Resource (and Adult Re-Entry) Center, 262, 302, 304, 308, 322
"Women's Resource Conference," 361
"Women's Week," festival, 93
Wong, B. D., actor, 305, 421
Wong, Bing Sum, Hon. Ph.D., 497
Wong, Diana Shui-lu, artist, 339
Wong, Eugene H., Prof., 406, 491
Wong, Harry, speaker, 222
Wood, Carl, CA Public Utilities Commissioner, 374
Wood, John P., Alumni Award, 496
Wood, Judith, Outstanding Student, 493
Wood, T. J., Pres., ASI, 492
Woodbridge School, 124
Woodburne, Sylvia, Inland Manpower Assoc., 123
Wooden, John, basketball coach, 236
Woodford, Don, Prof., Dir., Art Gallery, 90, 373-74
Woodpushers Anonymous (chess club), 114, 147, 149
Woodrow Wilson Fellowship, 337
Woodruff, Paul A., Alumni Award, UAB Member, Assemblyman, 246, 251, 253, 258, 264, 275, 299-300, 305, 343, 496, 500
Woods, Donald C., Prof., 243
Woods, Thomas E., Lect., 243
Work Force Development Grant, 428
Work-Study Program, 231
WorkAbility IV Program, 424
World Affairs Council of Inland Southern California, 75, 92, 202
World Championship Wrestling, 339, 357
World Communication Assoc., 403
World Counselors Conference, 149

World Life Research Institute, 74
World Music, musical group, 178
"A World of Fashions" show, 302
"World Trade Conference," 402
World Wrestling Entertainment (WWE), 402, 415, 436
Worth (LaFaye), 407
Worthley, Joanna S., Prof., 473
Wourms, Dennis J., Alumni Award, 496
WrestleMania Revenge, performers, 421
Wright, Charles, poet, 76, 185
Wright, Dean, Manager, Bookstore, 146, 152-53
Wright, Freeman J., Dean, School of Social Sciences, 104, 113
Wright, Letitia, speaker, 395, 406
Writers' Conference, 255
Writers' Workshop, 277
Writing Center, 128
Wroe, Dameon, poet, 395
Wu, Haw-Jan "John," Dir., William and Barbara Leonard University Transportation Center, 440
Wuertenberg, Jacque, speaker, 166, 248
Wulbrecht, Thomas, speaker, 167
Wykoff, Frank, speaker, 228
Wylie, W. P., UAB Member, 499
Wylie's Pub, Commons Building, 12
X, Laura, Dir., National Clearinghouse on Marital and Date Rape, 260
X, Malcolm, 259
Xavier, Mary Ann, speaker, 277
Xipe Totec, dancers, 251, 262
Xlibris Books, 428
X-Mas Fest 5, 358, 388
X-pression, music group, 225
Ya Salaam, Kalamu, poet, 370
Yager, Peter E., speaker, 247
Yale University, 354
Yamamoto, Natsuki, Outstanding Student, 493
Yancey, Antronette "Toni," speaker, 443
Yáñez, René, artist, 106
Yang, Jerry, speaker, 369
Yang, Philip Q., speaker, 342
Yankovic, "Weird Al," comedian, 363
Yao, Leijie, Outstanding Student, 494
Yap, Joselyn, Public Affairs, 9

Yarber, William, speaker, 237
Yasuda Center for Extended Education, 14, 18, 295, 305, 316, 318
Yasuda Institute of Education, Hiroshima, Japan (Yasuda Women's University), 267, 295, 318, 321, 448
Yasuhara, Eri F., Prof., Dean, Arts & Letters, 366, 427, 477
Yates, Alayne, speaker, 117
Yates, Peter, guitarist, 406, 450
Yeager, Jeana, pilot, 228
Yearbook Workshop, 53
Year-round operation of campus, 371
Yedinak, Clyda, violinist, 94
Yee, James, Capt., US Army Chaplain, 415
Yellowfly, Sharon, speaker, 300
The Yeti (CSUSB film), 344
Yetzer, Carl, newspaper writer, 83
Yoakam, Dwight, singer, 378
Yoon, Tae-Hee, speaker, 444
York, John, singer, 354
Yoshino, Masaaki, Pres., Yasuda Women's University, 448
Yothers, Tina, 272
Young, Clifford O. Sr., Prof., Asst. to the President, Executive Asst. to the President for Governmental Relations, SB County Supervisor, 259, 316, 353, 385, 398, 400, 460, 474
Young, Gary, poet, 389
Young, Gregg, performer, 394, 413
Young, Janet, speaker, 271
Young, Laura, Prof., 394
Young, Lyn, Lib. Asst., 52, 275
Young, Paul J., SB Co. Supervisor, 34, 38
Young, Richard, speaker, 339
Young, Robert M., campus booster, 60
Young, Roslyn, violinist, 359
"Young Women's Health Conference," 462-63
Youngbloods, music group, 60
Younglove, Norton, Riverside Co. Supervisor, 120, 241, 262, 299
Younkin, Sharon, Outstanding Student, 493
Youth Soccer and Coaches Clinic, 277
Youth Symphony String Quartet, 104
YWCA, 101, 225
YWCA Conference on Racism, 78

Yunnan University, China, 427
Yurok Brush Dancers, 385
Yuval Ron Ensemble, musical group, 420
Zagazig University, Egypt, 195, 204, 221, 236
Zagha, Rena, pianist, 162
Zakariyya, Abdul Mutakabbir, student, 157
Zaleha, Bernard, VP, Sierra Club, 419
Zall, Paul, writer, 117, 227
Zapata, Carmen, speaker, 210, 227
Zaragossa, Paula, Management, 445
Zarate Macías, Rosa Martha, composer, 251, 332, 387
Zavala, Arturo, speaker, 468
Zdunowki, Gene, speaker, 97
Zecha, Gerhard, speaker, 238
Zeiger, Rich, newspaper writer, 111
Zeigler Construction Co., builders, 54
Zeigler, Lee, speaker, 318
Zein, Cherif, Coach, 196
Zeitlin & VerBrugge Bookstore (Los Angeles), 50
Zeitlin, Jake, bookseller, 50
Zemoudeh, Kay, Prof., 280
Zendik, reggae band, 89
Zenz, Harold, Pres., SB Chamber of Commerce, 28
Zephyr-Voices Unbound, musical group, 399
Zerbe, Anthony, actor, 48
Zero Population Growth, 65
Zeta Phi Beta, sorority, 392
Zeta Pi, CSCSB Chapter of Sigma Delta Pi, 45
Zeugner, Thomas C. M., US Army Major, Officer-in-Charge, CSUSB ROTC Program, 271
Zhang, Meiyun, VP, Shaanxi University of Science and Technology, China, 419
Zhang, Xiwen, Libn., 327
Ziebarth, Donna M., Prof., 306
Ziebarth, Kenneth, SB Judge, 230
Ziegler, Stanley, Equipment Technician, 144
Zimmerman, Gary, speaker, 395
Zimmerman, Roland, physician, 123
Zinn, Howard, historian, 356
Zinn, Jesse, Outstanding Student, 494

Zintgraff, Paul, speaker, 64
Zizzo, Frank, alumnus psychologist, 395
Zmolek, Pam, Police Officer, 118
Zoecklein, Walter, O., Prof., Dir., Center for Professional Development, 107, 112, 501

Zoell, Bob, artist, 190
The Zoo (Gilbert & Sullivan), 159
Zoot Suit (Guerrero), 143
Zorn, Jennifer J. "Jenny," Prof., Assoc. Provost, Academic Programs, 374, 403, 475
Zuniga-Green, Rosa, speaker, 314

www.ingramcontent.com/pod-product-compliance
Lightning Source LLC
Chambersburg PA
CBHW032026150426
43194CB00006B/174